NEW YORK STATE POPULATION

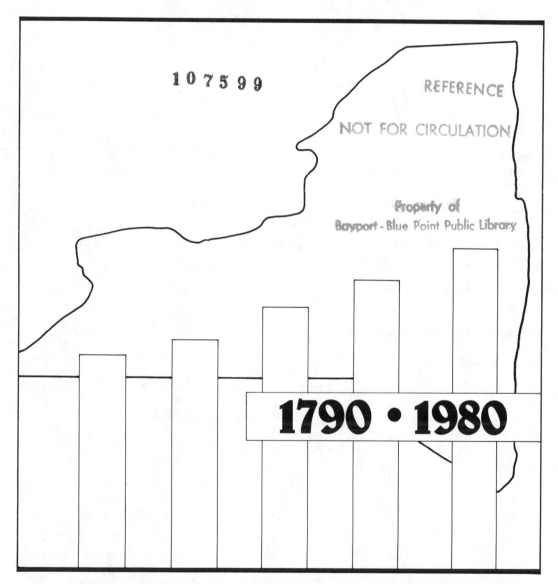

1790 • 1980

A Compilation of Federal Census Data

Barbara Shupe, Janet Steins, Jyoti Pandit

Neal-Schuman Publishers, Inc.
New York • London

Published by Neal-Schuman Publishers, Inc.
23 Leonard Street
New York, NY 10013

Printed and bound in the United States of America.

Library of Congress Cataloging-in-Publication Data
Shupe, Barbara, 1941—
  New York State population, 1790-1980.

  Bibliography: p.
  1. New York (State)—Population—Statistics—
History.   I. Steins, Janet.   II. Pandit, Jyoti.
III. Title.
HA545.S58   1987   304.6'2'09747   86-28487
ISBN 1-55570-009-8

Contents

Preface

New York State Population 1790 to 1980 draws together the population statistics for all places in New York State for the years 1790 to 1980. While population figures for the state and its sixty-two counties and sixty-two cities are readily available, New York State Population 1790 to 1980 is the first publication to include in a single source the population figures for the approximately 3,000 minor civil divisions—towns, villages, and unincorporated communities—together with these city and county figures, both current and historical. Each of the approximately 3,750 entries contains up to twenty figures for population at ten-year intervals and much additional information. Statewide information follows the introduction. It includes a chart of the origin of the state's counties, which provides their establishment dates and indicates whether they are one of the original ten counties established on November 1, 1683 or if they were once a part of one or more other counties; a genealogy of the counties; and two maps of the state—one showing county boundaries in 1790 and one showing the boundaries in 1980.

As a starting point for historical research, New York State Population 1790 to 1980 presents information which will be extremely useful to historians, genealogists, librarians, political scientists, urban planners, environmentalists, teachers, and students. New York State Population 1790 to 1980 makes it possible to determine if and when a place was reported in a federal census without an extensive search through early records, which are seldom readily available to those not living near large libraries. Knowing when a place first appeared in a census indicates that previously it was either unpopulated or was included within a larger political division. Also, inclusion of a place in the census of population alerts the researcher to the existence of other useful information, such as housing units or income data, which may be found in decennial census publications. In addition, since New York State fourth-grade students are now required to study local history, it is expected that they and their teachers will be able to use this work to learn about their communities.

Our research began with an initial list of about 2,000 place names with population, which was obtained from the 1980 U.S. Census of Population. Place names and population figures from each of the nineteen previous decennial censuses were then added, working backward from 1970 to 1790. When a new place name appeared, research was conducted to determine why it was not included in the 1980 list. This occurred for several different reasons. For example, names were officially changed, places (especially villages) were dissolved or merged into other areas, and official political boundaries shifted. Bureau of the Census policies also dictated whether a place was listed or not; size of population or changes in CDP (census designated place) boundaries were determining factors. (The Bureau of the Census currently uses the designation CDP for all unincorporated communities. See the Introduction on Political Geography for further information.) Histories, maps, gazetteers, New York State documents, and many local librarians and historians were consulted in the course of this research.

For each entry we have included:

Place Name. The majority of the names of populated places was obtained from federal censuses. Names of additional communities in Nassau and Suffolk counties, compiled by the Long Island Regional Planning Board from federal census data, were added. Names of villages incorporated since the last federal census in 1980 were obtained from the New York State Legislative Manual, along with their population at incorporation. Previous names, misspelled names, and alternate or early spellings appear as cross references to the most current name in each case.

Designation. Each place is identified as a county, city, town, village, or CDP. The unincorporated communites in Nassau and Suffolk counties, for which population statistics were compiled only by the Long Island Regional Planning Board, are without a designation. A very few of these have received the designation "Unincorporated" to distinguish them from villages of the same name.

Incorporation or Establishment Date. Dates of incorporation for all villages and cities were obtained from various editions of the *New York State Legislative Manual* and from other sources (see Bibliography). In cases where sources disagreed, the *Manual* was used as the final authority. It should be noted that many villages were reported in censuses prior to their official incorporation dates.

Ascertaining establishment dates for some towns was also problematical. For most colonial era towns, the date of official recognition by New York State was used. Although they may have been chartered earlier by various governments, most were only recognized by the state in 1788. In addition, this year was used because in some cases earlier dates are either unknown or in dispute. These and most other establishment dates for towns were obtained from French's 1860 *Gazetteer of New York State.* Local librarians and historians provided dates for both vil-

lages and towns not available in published sources.

Location. For villages and CDP's, appropriate town and county are given. For cities, which are not under the jurisdiction of towns (except for the City of Sherrill), the appropriate county is identified. (See the following section on Political Geography for further information.)

Population Statistics. Population statistics are listed as reported in each of the decennial censuses. Figures subsequently revised by the Bureau of the Census or the Long Island Regional Planning Board are indicated as such. Population for many unincorporated communities in Nassau and Suffolk counties was derived by the LIRPB from data provided by the Bureau of the Census. Figures for recently incorporated villages were taken from the *New York State Legislative Manual.*

Notes. Footnotes to entries explain boundary changes, provide earlier names, indicate alternate or misspellings under which places were reported, and give other information.

An explanation of all abbreviations and symbols used in the entries precedes the population listings.

Acknowledgments _____

The authors were encouraged to undertake this project because of the success of a 1980 publication, *Historical Population of Long Island Communities 1790-1980: Decennial Census Data,* which brought together comparable data for Nassau and Suffolk counties, and which was compiled and published by a group of reference librarians at SUNY Stony Brook and staff at the Long Island Regional Planning Board.

We would like to thank all of our colleagues in the library at the State University of New York at Stony Brook, especially John Brewster Smith, Director, Donald Cook, Irvin Kron, and Nathan Baum, as well as our colleagues at the Nassau Community College Library.

Our thanks go, also, to the staff at the Long Island Regional Planning Board, especially Arthur Kunz, for their assistance with the publication of *Historical Population of Long Island Communities 1790-1980: Decennial Census Data.*

We would like to acknowledge the State University of New York Research Foundation on the Stony Brook campus for a grant used to obtain computer hardware, and the staff of the Computing Center, especially Dominick Seraphin.

William Dollarhide and William Thorndale kindly granted us permission to reprint the 1790 map from their *Map Guide to the U.S. Federal Censuses: New York 1790-1920.* Map sets for all fifty states will appear in their forthcoming book to be published by the Genealogical Publishing Company of Baltimore, Maryland, in 1987.

We are indebted to the helpfulness and interest of many librarians and local historians throughout New York State.

Finally, we are grateful to our families and friends for their patience and encouragement during the past two years.

Introduction _____

POLITICAL GEOGRAPHY OF
NEW YORK STATE

Counties in New York are established by the state legislature as general purpose units of government. They perform state functions at the local level and provide a wide range of services to citizens directly and to the units of local government: the cities, towns and villages. All populated places in New York State are part of a county. Counties are divided into towns and cities, although twenty-one of the counties contain no cities. New York State is divided into sixty-two counties. The five boroughs of New York City are also counties, but do not operate as typical county governments. Outside New York City, counties varied in population in 1980 from Nassau's 1,321,582 to Hamilton's 5,034.

Cities in New York are created by legislative charter. Because there is no general law which provides authority for the incorporation of cities, they differ widely in size of population, geographic area, and governmental structure. In New York there is no concept of progression from village to city status. There are sixty-two cities in the state; only two—New York and Albany—are of colonial origin. There is no minimum population required to incorporate as a city. In fact, in 1980 forty-eight cities had populations smaller than the largest village—Hempstead, with a population of 40,404. New York is the largest city with a 1980 population of 7,071,030 and Sherrill is the smallest with 2,830. Sherrill is also unique in that it remains part of a town.

The state's towns encompass all of the territory within the state except that within the cities or Indian Reservations. Towns were originally established as independent units of government by the English and Dutch during the colonial period. When New York became a state, they were regarded as units to serve state purposes, but are now recognized as primary units of local government, empowered to provide all municipal services. In 1980 there were 1,930 towns in the state, varying in population from 32 (Montague) to 738,517 (Hempstead).

A village is an incorporated municipality, but remains a part of the town where it is located. Villages were formed within towns to provide services for clusters of people, first in rural areas and later in suburban areas near large cities. Village organization is similar to that of cities. Public service responsibilities of villages differ very little from those of cities, towns, and counties. Under the current Village Law, a territory may incorporate as a village if it contains at

TABLE 1   Population of New York State 1790-1980

Census Year	Population	Increase or decrease over preceding census		Percent increase for U.S.
		Number	Percent	
1980	ʳ17,558,072	−683,319	−3.7	11.4
1970	18,241,391	1,459,087	8.0	13.3
1960	16,782,304	1,952,112	13.2	18.5
1950	14,830,192	1,351,050	10.0	14.5
1940	13,479,142	891,076	7.1	7.3
1930	12,588,066	2,202,839	21.2	16.2
1920	10,385,227	1,271,613	14.0	15.0
1910	9,113,614	1,844,720	25.4	21.0
1900	7,268,894	1,265,720	21.1	21.0
1890	6,003,174	920,303	18.1	25.5
1880	5,082,871	700,112	16.0	30.2
1870	4,382,759	502,024	12.9	22.6
1860	3,880,735	783,341	25.3	35.6
1850	3,097,394	668,473	27.5	35.9
1840	2,428,921	510,313	26.6	32.7
1830	1,918,608	545,796	39.8	33.5
1820	1,372,812	413,763	43.1	33.1
1810	959,049	369,998	62.8	36.4
1800	589,051	248,931	73.2	35.1
1790	340,120	. . .	. . .	. . .

ʳ1980 figure revised by U.S. Census Oct.ʹ 23, 1981.
From: New York State Legislative Manual, 1984–85, p. 1003.

least five hundred people and is less than five square miles in size. There were 556 villages in New York in 1983. There are also many populated places in the state which have never been incorporated as villages or cities. In these areas, all services are provided by the towns in which they are located. Many of these places were named in the 1800s when residents requested a post office and were required to send a name to Washington. Some of these communities, like Levittown on Long Island, have thousands of residents. Census publications list these named populated areas as unincorporated communities or census designated places.

As can be seen in Table 1, the state's growth continued unabated from the first census in 1790 through the nineteenth census in 1970. The 1980 Census was the first to report negative growth—the population declined to 17,558,072 from a high of 18,-241,391. The expectation is that the 1990 Census will see a population increase of about a half a million over the 1980 Census.

THE FEDERAL CENSUSES

Since the passage of the First Census Act by the U.S. Congress on March 1, 1790, the federal government has conducted an enumeration of the inhabitants of the United States at ten-year intervals. The tenth was conducted in 1880, the twentieth in 1980, and the twenty-first is not far away. The first, second, third, and fourth censuses required virtually no tabulation, and their reports were produced without employing a clerical force. Summaries were transmitted directly to the printer, which through the Eighth Census of 1860 were private enterprises often designated by the House of Representatives or the Senate.

Responsibility for conducting the Census has rested with various governmental bodies through the years. For example, today the Bureau of the Census is a part of the Department of Commerce; in 1870 the Census Office was a part of the Department of the Interior; in 1800 the enumeration was presented to the Congress by the Department of State. In *New York State Population 1790 to 1980* the general term Census Bureau is used to designate this agency, no matter what the year.

What Places Were Reported and What They Were Called

In 1790 and 1800, the Census Bureau reports the population of New York State as divided into counties and towns. (Note, however, that figures for 1800 are unreliable—see description of the Second Census below.) Only counties are listed in 1810. In 1820, figures are added for the cities of Albany and New York. In 1830, 1840, 1850, and 1860, more cities and some villages are included, but they are not consistently identified as such. For instance, it would be necessary to consult a gazetteer such as this one or a local history to ascertain that the Cohoes reported in 1850 was a village just prior to incorporation, or that the Auburn reported in the same year was a recently incorporated city made up of Auburn Town and Auburn Village.

The Census of 1870 was the first to use the term "minor civil divisions," which are defined as "the principal divisions which were taken to make up the counties in some states, and into which counties in most states have been subdivided for election or magisterial purposes, or for purposes of police or sanitary administration or municipal government." The Ninth Census of 1870 clearly lists villages and unincorporated communities under the towns in which they are a part, and cities which are legally separate from the town or towns in which they are located.

The Tenth Census of 1880 reports a large number of unincorporated communities in a separate list, although this designation is not always correct. The Sixteenth Census of 1940 also lists a large number of unincorporated communities separately. Beginning with the Seventeenth Census of 1950, unincorporated communities are listed in the same tables as counties, towns, cities, and villages. As of the Twentieth Census of 1980, these communities are called census designated places—or "CDPs"—and this terminology will continue in use in 1990. It is important to remember that the population of all unincorporated places was and continues to be estimated, since there are no legal boundaries delineating them.

What Kinds of Information Were Reported

The kind, as well as the amount, of information collected by the Census has grown astronomically during the two-hundred-year history of the United States. The 1790 and 1800 censuses reported population information only in brief pamphlets. By the Third Census of 1810, the Office of the Census was issuing separate reports on such topics as "manufactures" and "agriculture."

Through the Ninth Census of 1870, data on such characteristics as race, sex, age, condition, and nativity are reported inseparably with population figures. (The reader is referred to Schulze's excellent two-volume work on population information available from census publications for guidance in this area.) Beginning with the Tenth Census of 1880, separate tables containing population figures only begin to appear. Of course, the sheer number of census publications produced continues to increase dramatically as each decade passes (U.S. Bureau of the Census catalogs are described in the bibliography), and population figures must be extracted from tables which also characterize inhabitants by sex, age, and other determinants through 1870. Beginning with 1880 they stand alone, but are contained in ever more numerous volumes of census data.

Manuscript Censuses

Otherwise known as census schedules, manuscript censuses are the data collected by enumerators from which the reports are compiled. By law, census schedules are private for seventy years after a census is conducted. After 1990, the National Archives will issue the 1920 Census schedules, in microformat, for use by students of history, genealogy, etc.

The availability of census schedules has fluctuated in recent years. A government-supported microfilm rental program was halted and later resumed. Individual reels continue to be sold to libraries and the public by the National Archives. Arranged alphabetically by county and thereunder by election districts, the 1910 Census schedules for New York State fill 175 reels of microfilm. For further information, see Douglas' *New York State Census Records, 1790-1925* and the catalogs of the U.S. National Archives Trust Fund Board.

The following brief descriptions of the twenty federal censuses attempt to explain what format and context the Census Bureau used in each census to present population figures for New York State. The summaries should give the reader an idea of how the population figures presented in *New York State Population 1790 to 1980* were obtained.

1790

The First Census Act was passed at the second session of the First Congress, and was signed into law by President Washington on March 1, 1790. The enumeration was to be completed within nine months, a time limit which was later extended. A summary of the results of the first Census was subsequently transmitted to Congress by President Washington on October 27, 1791, and this brief, 56-page report was published the same year. Three subsequent editions were published between 1791 and 1802 with some variant spellings for places. The authors have used the edition published by Childs and Swain in Philadelphia in 1791 (Dubester #2) for this work. Revisions to these population counts were made for the 1908 publication described below.

Arranged by state, and thereunder by counties and towns in most instances, counts are given for white males sixteen years of age and above, those under sixteen years, free white females, all other free persons, and slaves. Subtotals are entered for each town and added together for county totals (there were fifteen New York counties in 1790).

In 1907, because of public pressure, the Census Bureau was directed to publish the names of all heads of households counted in the 1790 census, and the opportunity was taken to correct some of the figures for population counts and standardize spellings. Hence, the 1908 publication entitled *Heads of Families at the First Census of the U.S. Taken in the Year 1790: New York* is preceded by a two-page table of New York counties and towns with their population. The authors have included these revised figures in *New York State Population 1790 to 1980* where appropriate.

1800

The Second Census (1800) was published in 1801, and for New York State contains population figures for thirty counties and their towns. Three of these, Dutchess, Ulster, and Orange, are listed separately as a supplement to the main body. In addition, the six towns of Essex and Clinton counties are listed together (Essex had formed from Clinton in March 1799). The authors have not attempted to formulate separate totals for Essex and Clinton Counties for 1800.

Counted in this census are free white males in five age groups, free white females in five age groups, all other free persons except Indians not taxed, and slaves. The category of "Indians not taxed" is defined in the Ninth Census as meaning Indians maintaining their tribal relations and living upon government reservations. Those not living on reservations are included in the enumeration of the bulk of the population. "By the fact of breaking away from their tribal relations, they are regarded as having entered the body of citizens and are subject to taxation," according to the Ninth Census.

The reader will note that all population figures in *New York State Population 1790-1980* for towns in 1800 are followed by asterisks. As a footnote in the 1870 census, the Census Bureau wrote that "the tables for New York, as published in the official census of 1800, are grossly incorrect; they contain typographical and other errors in nearly every county; they duplicate some returns and omit others." Consequently, the Census Bureau conducted recounts from the original schedules and published revised county figures; however, no attempt was made to correct figures for the towns or add missing towns, hence their unreliability today. The revised county figures yielded a total state population of 3,100 more than originally published.

1810

The 1811 publication of the Third Census, entitled *Aggregate Amount of Persons Within the United States in the Year 1810*, is ninety pages long (1814 saw the publication of a second volume comprising the census of arts and manufactures). Categories of people counted are identical to 1800. However, while the population figures for all other states are presented as subdivided into counties and thereunder into towns, New York's population is unfortunately presented in forty-three counties only (plus figures for the cities of Albany, New York, and Schenectady). To go beyond this level of detail would require a researcher to consult the original census schedules (published in microfilm format by the U.S. National Archives), local histories, etc., and literally count every name listed within each county. The authors have done this to derive population counts for the thirteen towns within Nassau (then Queens) and Suffolk counties from the census schedules, hence their inclusion here. Page 90 of the 1810 census contains corrections to the tables for Cortland, Dutchess, and Franklin Counties and for the entire state.

1820

Population for the Fourth Census was reported in the first of two volumes, the second being a digest of accounts of manufacturing establishments. This *Census for 1820,* in eighty pages, once again presents New York's counties (now numbering fifty) as subdivided into towns, plus Albany and New York cities. Thirty-six Northern District counties are presented in the first table and fourteen Southern District counties follow in a second table.

The census counted free white males in six age categories; free white females in five age categories; unnaturalized foreigners; the number of persons engaged in agriculture, commerce, and manufacturing; male and female slaves in four age categories each; free male Blacks and free female Blacks in four age categories each; and all other persons except Indians not taxed.

1830

Two editions of the Fifth Census of population were published in 1832 and bound together into one volume. The second edition, which was corrected at the Department of State for the purpose of congressional reapportionment, adds additional tables for New York State (specifically, recapitulations by county for both the northern and southern districts) and also contains a two-page list of errata at the end. An additional table summarizes total numbers of people in each district by race, age, disability (see below), and whether they are citizens.

Population figures are given for fifty-six New York counties (forty-two in the northern district and fourteen in the southern district); towns, cities, and villages are listed thereunder, but some villages and cities are not clearly identified as such. The census counts free white males and females in thirteen age categories each; male and female slaves in six age categories each; free male and female Blacks in six age categories each; deaf and mute whites; blind whites; aliens; deaf and mute slaves and free Blacks; and blind slaves and free Blacks.

The errata sheets make some minor corrections—to spelling errors and to various figures for categories of people—and two major ones. They add 5,477 people to the total for New York City and the same amount to the total for the Southern District of the State. This inadvertant error is attributed to the Marshall's assistant in the Ninth Ward of New York City, who apparently omitted 5,477 aliens and disabled persons from his totals. The correction was duly transmitted to Congress as House Document 103 of the 22nd Congress, 2nd Session, and reads *"Add aliens, etc. . . . 5,477."*

The entire volume for the Fifth Census is prefixed by a summary of enumerations for all counties in New York State for 1790 to 1820. Finally, it should be noted that two abstracts of the Fifth Census were also published in 1832; both contain discrepancies in population figures when compared with the edition used by the authors.

1840

In 1841 the Sixth Census was published after corrections were made at the Department of State. Subtitled "Enumeration of the Inhabitants of the United States . . . in 1840," its 476 pages are followed by an index and one sheet of corrections, with none for New York.

Tables are headed "Census of the United States, June 1, 1840." Once again, the Northern District of New York State (forty-four counties) is separate from the Southern District (fourteen counties). Under each county is listed its towns, with the incorporated cities or villages of Albany, Buffalo, Rochester, Utica, Troy, Schenectady, New York, Hudson, and Brooklyn also enumerated.

Counted are free white males and females in thirteen age categories each; free Blacks, males and females, in six age categories each; male and female slaves in six age categories each; the number of persons employed in mining, agriculture, commerce, manufactures and trades, navigation of the oceans, navigation of canals, lakes and rivers, and the learned professions and engineering; pensioners for revolutionary or military services; deaf and mute whites and Blacks in three age categories each; blind whites; blind Blacks; and mentally handicapped whites and Blacks divided into those in the charge of public institutions and those at private institutions. In the same table is listed types of schools with numbers of students enrolled and the number of illiterate whites over the age of twenty. Following each district is a recapitulation by county with totals for all categories listed above. Finally, the northern and southern districts are added and state totals given for all categories.

Other volumes published as a result of the Sixth Census include a compendium of the enumeration of inhabitants, a census of pensioners, and a census of mines, agriculture, commerce and manufactures.

1850

The Seventh Census of the United States: 1850, Embracing a Statistical View of Each of the States and Territories, Arranged by Counties, Towns, etc. was published in 1853 in a volume of 1,022 pages. Table I is population by counties, of which fifty-nine are listed for New York State. Counted are male and female whites and male and female free Blacks in fifteen age categories each, with totals for all categories and all counties.

Table II, population by subdivisions of counties, gives counts of male and female whites, and male and female Blacks, with totals for each group and for the subdivision as a whole. The cities of Albany, Hudson, Buffalo, Brooklyn, Rochester, New York, Syracuse, and Troy are enumerated separately from towns. However, other incorporated places are not easily identified in this census. Other tables give nativities of the population; births, marriages, deaths, dwellings, and families; population growth from 1790 to 1850; various categories of disabled persons; colleges, academies, schools, and their enrollments; illiteracy; professions, occupations, and trades of the male population; agriculture; newspapers and periodicals; libraries; and churches. The tables are followed by an appendix which includes seven pages of "Notes on the States," or corrections, but none given for New York State are applicable to *New York State Population 1790 to 1980.*

Other publications from the 1850 Census include digest of manufactures, mortality statistics, a compendium which includes results of previous censuses beginning with 1790, and an abstract with comments and tables relative to the population of the United States and its progress with comparison to experience in other countries. Note that this is the first year that reports designated as "final" are preceded by preliminary reports.

1860

Population of the United States in 1860; Compiled from the Original Returns of the Eighth Census was published in 1864. The volume of 694 pages begins with an analytical introduction, with Table 1 giving population of white males and females, free Blacks and Indians in fifteen age categories each in sixty New York State counties. Table 3 subdivides counties into towns and cities, and gives population counts for whites and free Black males and females in each. The cities reported are Albany, Auburn, Hudson, Poughkeepsie, Buffalo, Brooklyn, Rochester, New York, Utica, Syracuse, Oswego, Troy, and Ogdensburg; no villages are listed. Included is an index and a brief errata sheet with no corrections for New York State.

In addition to this final report, a preliminary report on the Eighth Census, a volume of statistics of the United States covering a wide variety of subjects, and a volume on agriculture and one on manufactures were published between 1862 and 1866.

1870

Final reports, entitled *[Census Reports] Compiled from the Original Returns of the Ninth Census (June 1, 1870)* were published in three volumes in 1872: I. Statistics of the Population; II. Vital Statistics; III. Statistics of Wealth and Industry. Table III of the first volume lists population of "Civil Divisions Less than Counties," and this appears to be the first time the Census Bureau uses this terminology. Population is broken down in the table by nativity (foreign or native born) and race.

Several other publications appeared as a result of the Ninth Census. *The Compendium of the Ninth Census* includes a recapitulation of all county population figures from 1790 to 1870 (Table VIII). Also published was a statistical atlas.

1880

The Tenth Census of 1880 was published in twenty-two volumes between 1883 and 1888, which was a dramatic increase over previous censuses. Volume 1 contains population tables for states, counties, and minor civil divisions. For the first time, data on characteristics of the population (for instance, race, sex, age, occupation) is listed separately from tables giving population counts only.

Tables showing population by counties for each state, from 1860 to 1880, as well as population of minor civil divisions by state and county, were also published in a compendium of 1,171 pages with index, issued in two volumes in 1882. There were two later editions of the compendium.

1890

The final reports of the Eleventh Census were published in fifteen volumes between 1895 and 1897. Part I of Volume I, entitled *Report on Population of the United States at the Eleventh Census: 1890,* begins with a lengthy treatise, "Progress of the Nation," which includes maps and diagrams, followed by 103 tables. Table 4 is of population of states by counties at each census from 1790-1890. Table 5 is of population of states by minor civil divisions, for both 1890 and 1880, arranged alphabetically by county.

Also published as a result of the Eleventh Census were a statistical atlas, an abstract, a compendium and hundreds of census bulletins, many preliminary to the final reports.

1900

The final reports of the Twelfth Census were published in 1901 and 1902 in ten volumes, the first two of which are Parts 1 and 2 of population statistics. Tables are similar to those in the Eleventh Census, with Table 5 giving population of minor civil divisions in 1900 and 1890. Table 8 lists all incorporated villages and cities alphabetically for each state. For the first time, population of Indian Reservations is indicated with figures given separately and as part of the towns in which they are located. (These town population figures were subsequently revised in 1920 to exclude the population of the Indian Reservations.)

Also published were special and miscellaneous reports, an abstract, a statistical atlas, and bulletins.

1910

The final reports of the Thirteenth Census of 1910 were issued in eleven volumes between 1912 and 1914. Volumes I to IV are entitled *Population, 1910,* with the third covering the states of Nebraska through Wyoming, plus territories, and listing statistics of counties, cities, and other civil divisions.

The 1910 census gives population figures for 1890 and 1900 as well as 1910 and, as in 1900, population of Indian Reservations is given separately and as a part of each of the towns in which they are located. These population counts were retroactively subtracted from town totals when the 1920 census was published. Separate tables give population of cities from the earliest census to 1910, and of all incorporated places in 1890, 1900, and 1910.

Also published as a result of the Thirteenth Census were an Abstract of the Census in several editions, a statistical atlas, plus advance, abstract, miscellaneous and special bulletins. The 1913 edition of the Abstract includes individual supplements for each state, which also give population figures.

1920

The final reports of the Fourteenth Census were published in thirteen volumes between 1920 and 1923. Volume I is entitled *Population, 1920. Number and Distribution of Inhabitants.* Table 49 gives population of counties in each state from 1850 through 1920. Table 51 gives population of incorporated villages and cities from 1900 to 1920 and population of wards of incorporated places having 5,000 or more inhabitants. Table 53 gives population of counties by minor civil divisions in 1900, 1910, and 1920. Revised figures for those towns which include parts of Indian Reservations are indicated for 1900 and 1910.

Once again, numerous bulletins, monographs, abstracts, and a statistical atlas complete the documentation of the Fourteenth Census.

1930

Final reports of the Fifteenth Census of 1930 were published in thirty-two volumes from 1931 to 1934, with the first six covering population. Population statistics for New York are contained in Volume I, which is arranged alphabetically by State, and includes the following tables for New York:

1. Population of New York: 1790-1930
2. Population of principal cities and villages from earliest census to 1930 (over 10,000 people)
2a. Population of New York City and its boroughs as now constituted: 1790-1930

3. Area and population of counties: 1890-1930
4. Population of counties by minor civil divisions: 1930, 1920, and 1910
5. Population of incorporated places: 1930 and 1920
6. Population of cities and villages of 5,000 or over by wards: 1930

1940

Final reports of the Sixteenth Census of 1940 were published between 1942 and 1947. Population information encompasses four volumes in seventeen parts, with number of inhabitants presented in Volume I. States are listed alphabetically. Tables for New York, relevant to this work, include:

1. Population of New York, urban and rural: 1790 to 1940
2. Population of incorporated places of 10,000 or more from earliest census to 1940
2a. Population of New York City and its boroughs as now constituted: 1790 to 1940
4. Population of counties by minor civil divisions: 1920 to 1940
5. Population of incorporated and urban places: 1940 and 1930
6. Population of incorporated places of 5,000 or more by wards or assembly districts: 1940

Preceding the tables for each state is a set of maps. The maps for New York (the state is divided into four sections) show all counties, towns, cities, and villages.

Other volumes of the Sixteenth Census are: Volume II (7 parts), *Characteristics of Population;* Volume III (5 parts), *The Labor Force;* and Volume IV (4 parts); *Characteristics by Age.*

For the first time since 1880, a separate and lengthy list of incorporated communities in New York State is available, with population counts presented for 1940 only. This separate publication (Dubester #1007) is subtitled, *Total population of unincorporated communities for which separate figures could be compiled.*

1950

Final reports of the Seventeenth Census of Population for 1950 were issued in December 1952. Volume I, entitled *Number of Inhabitants,* lists states alphabetically. Tables for New York relevant to this work include:

1. Population of New York, urban and rural: 1790-1950

4. Population of urban places of 10,000 or more from earliest census to 1950
6. Population of counties by minor civil divisions: 1930 to 1950
7. Population of all incorporated places and of unincorporated places of 1,000 or more: 1950 and 1940
8. Population of incorporated places of 5,000 or more, by wards or assembly districts: 1950

Volume I also includes maps. One of New York divides the state into four sections and shows all counties, towns, cities, and villages. Another shows counties, places with a population of 25,000 or more, and standard metropolitan areas. Volume II, *Characteristics of the Population* was issued in fifty-seven parts, beginning with a U.S. Summary and including all fifty states plus territories and possessions. New York is Part 32, and it repeats many of the same tables as in Volume I. Volumes I and II originally appeared in the form of three series of state bulletins: Series P-A, Number of Inhabitants; Series P-B, General Characteristics; and Series P-C, Detailed Characteristics.

Statistical data on urban areas designated SMSA's first appear in the reports of the 1950 Census in the tables of general characteristics of the population in Volume II. According to the introduction to Volume II, the concept of a standard metropolitan area—now called standard metropolitan statistical area, or SMSA—was developed during the years prior to the taking of the census. It had become evident that for many types of social and economic analyses it was necessary to consider as a unit the entire population in and around a city whose activities form an integrated social and economic system. Prior to the 1950 Census, areas of this type had been defined in different ways by various agencies; as a result of this lack of comparability, the usefulness of data published was limited.

1960

Final reports of the 1960 Census of Population (the Eighteenth) were published in November 1961, in four volumes plus a joint Population-Housing series of census tract reports. Volume I, *Characteristics of the Population,* contains the major portion of the information compiled from the Census, and consists of Part A and fifty-seven numbered parts. New York is Part 34; all other states as well as Guam, Virgin Islands, American Samoa, and Canal Zone are included.

1960 Census presents tables of population counts for New York State and maps similar to those of the 1950 Census. The detailed tables presented in each numbered part of Volume I were originally published in four separate reports:

PC(1)-A   Number of Inhabitants
PC(1)-B   General Population Characteristics
PC(1)-C   General Social and Economic Characteristics
PC(1)-D   Detailed Characteristics

Part A of Volume I is a compendium of the 57 Series PC(1)-A reports. Volume II (Series PC(2) reports) is Subject Reports. Volume III (Series PC(3) reports) is Selected Area Reports. Volume IV is a Summary and Analytical Report. Series PHC(1) is Census Tract Reports.

The 1960 population census was the first for which the final counts were obtained by machine-processing instead of hand counting. A separate publication, entitled *1960 Censuses of Population and Housing: Procedural History,* appeared in 1966 and describes the innovative data-processing equipment developed and utilized for the project.

1970

The final reports of the 1970 Census of Population (the Nineteenth) were published in May 1972. Tables for New York State can be found in two separate books of Volume I, *Characteristics of the Population: Part A, Number of Inhabitants,* or Part A, Section 1, New York.

Tables 1-5 present population data for the state; 6-8 for places; 9-10 for counties; 11-12 for urbanized areas; 13-14 for metropolitan areas; and 15 for congressional districts. Maps show counties, SMSA's, selected places; country subdivisions (the state is divided into four sections); and selected individual urbanized areas.

The reports giving population information in the 1970 census are identical to 1960. In addition, housing data are presented in the following series of reports:

HC(1)   Housing: Characteristics for States, Cities, and Counties
HC(2)   Metropolitan Housing Characteristics
PHC(1)   Census Tract Reports
PHC(2)   General Demographic Trends for Metropolitan Areas

Each series includes one report for every state and a U.S. Summary Report.

For the first time, a separate series of reports was published which presents data on population and housing of 241 SMSA's in the United States. Computerized census data in the format of summary tapes were made available to the public through the Census Bureau as well as through Summary Tape Processing Centers following the 1970 Census.

1980

Final reports of the 1980 Population Census, the Twentieth, closely follow the 1970 model. Once again, a large portion of the information compiled appears in Volume I, *Characteristics of the Population.* Chapter A presents number of inhabitants; Chapter B, general population characteristics; Chapter C, general social and economic characteristics; and Chapter D, detailed population characteristics. Chapter A was published in fifty-seven numbered parts representing all fifty states plus territories and possessions. New York State is Part 34, which consists of maps, charts and thirteen tables. Tables used for the present work are:

4.   Population of county subdivisions: 1960 to 1980.
5.   Population of places: 1960 to 1980 (incorporated places and CDP's)

Also published were separate reports giving data on 380 SMSA's with accompanying maps for each. Block statistics were published in microfiche format.

Regarding the population of Indian Reservations in the State of New York, the Department of Social Services, Office of Indian Services, has issued revised population figures for these places for 1980. The reader is referred to current *New York State Legislative Manuals* for this information.

ANNOTATED BIBLIOGRAPHY

American Historical Publications, Inc. *New York Gazetteer.* Wilmington, De.: American Historical Publications, 1983.

This historical gazetteer gives detailed information on events that have occurred in New York State and the people who participated in them. It includes a biography index, zip codes of most populated places, and brief histories of major cities. Selected place names include entries such as "Greenwich Village."

Andriot, John L. *Population Abstract of the United States.* 2 vols. McLean, Va.: Andriot Associates, 1983.

Population statistics, a brief history, a map and an index showing names and locations of counties are included for each state, along with historical statistics for counties and cities from 1790 to 1980.

Clint, Florence. *New York Area Key; a Guide to the Genealogical Records of the State of New York including Maps, Histories, Charts, and Other Helpful Materials.* Elizabeth, Co.: Keyline Publishers, 1979.
This unique source is divided into five major sections—history, maps, social and economic influences, official records, and libraries, societies and publications. It includes a list of historical societies and libraries, a bibliography of general materials on New York State, and guides to state and local records.

Collins, Charles W. *New York, an Atlas.* Madison, Wisc.: American Printing and Publishing, 1978.
This atlas contains physical, population, economic, and agriculture maps of New York State. An appendix of statistical data is presented by county.

Douglas, Marilyn and Linda Yates. *New York State Census Records, 1790-1925.* New York State Library Bibliography Bulletin 88. Albany: The State Education Department, 1981.
This bibliography and inventory of all federal and state censuses of New York State is an important information source for historians and genealogists.

Ellis, David Maldwyn et al. *A History of New York State.* Rev. ed. Ithaca, N.Y.: Cornell University Press, 1967.
A revised edition of *A Short History of New York State* (1957), this work is divided into two books: Book I covers 1609 to 1865 and Book II covers 1865 to 1966. It includes maps, tables, a bibliographical essay, and index.

Flick, Alexander C., ed. *History of the State of New York.* 10 vols. New York: Columbia University Press, 1933-1937.
The standard history of New York State; it includes local histories.

French, John Homer. *Gazetteer of the State of New York: Embracing a Comprehensive View of the Geography, Geology and General History of the State, and a Complete History and Description of Every County, City, Town, Village, and Locality.* Syracuse, N.Y.: R. Pearsall Smith, 1860.
French's *Gazetteer* is the standard source for historical information on places in New York State. The research and surveys were performed to support the production of a state map. It is arranged by county and includes statistics, original engravings, and subject and geographic name indexes.

Gordon, Thomas Francis. *Gazetteer of the State of New York: Comprehending Its Colonial History; General Geography, Geology and Internal Improvements; Its Political State; a Minute Description of Its Several Counties, Towns and Villages . . . With a Map of the State, and a Map of Each County, and Plans of the Cities and Principal Villages.* Philadelphia: Printed for the Author, 1836.
A long historical essay on New York State begins this gazetteer, followed by shorter essays on political conditions, the judiciary system, the topography of the state, etc. Place names are arranged by county, with an index at the end of the volume. Maps of the cities and villages show locations of important buildings.

The New York Civil List. Albany: 1855-.
Compilers and printers varied. The authors used the 1865 and 1886 editions, primarily for information on obsolete and existing towns and villages, and accompanying historical notes.

New York State. Department of State. *Local Government Handbook.* 3rd ed. Albany: Department of State, 1982.
This edition provides updated information on the structure of the state and local governments. It also gives 1980 federal census data and explains the relationship between the state and the federal government. Charts, tables, and an index are included.

New York State. Department of State. *Manual for the Use of the Legislature of the State of New York.* Albany: Department of State, 1840-.
Commonly known as the *New York State Legislative Manual,* this annual publication contains information on the political organization of New York and includes lists of counties, cities, towns, villages, unincorporated communities, and post offices, as well as historical notes and population statistics.

New York State. Department of Transportation. *New York State Atlas.* Albany: Department of Transportation, 1983.
This official state atlas contains maps of the sixty-two counties, and an index to the 3,300 place names. It is useful for determining current spellings and identifying places as towns, villages, and communities.

New York State Association of Counties. *New York State Counties: Their Beginnings.* Albany: New York State Association, 1981.

This brief work gives a one-page history of each county in New York.

Proehl, Karl H. and Barbara Shupe. *Long Island Gazetteer: a Guide to Current and Historical Place Names.* Bayside, N.Y.: LDA Publishers, 1984.

This gazetteer consists of approximately 3,700 names of physical features, political divisions, and populated places in Kings, Queens, Nassau, and Suffolk counties. Historical as well as current names are included.

Rabenhorst, Thomas D. and Carville V. Earle, eds. *Historical U.S. County Outline Map Collection 1840-1980.* Baltimore: University of Maryland, Baltimore County. Dept. of Geography, 1984.

This collection is a set of large maps which includes New York State on the Eastern U.S. sheets. The county outline maps do not show much detail and only two changes in boundaries, when Nassau and Bronx counties were formed.

Rayback, Robert J., ed. *Richards Atlas of New York State.* Phoenix, N.Y.: Frank E. Richards, 1959.

Colorful maps and text describe and depict the geography of New York. The historical maps are excellent.

Shupe, Barbara et al. *Historical Population of Long Island Communities 1790-1980: Decennial Census Data.* Hauppauge, N.Y.: Long Island Regional Planning Board, 1982.

Population data for all Nassau County and Suffolk County communities are given. The statistics were originally published by the Census Bureau or derived by the Long Island Regional Planning Board from census data.

Schulze, Suzanne. *Population Information in Nineteenth Century Census Volumes.* Phoenix: Oryx Press, 1983.

This book identifies the population information which can be found in all U.S. Census decennial reports from 1790 to 1890. Based on the work of Henry J. Dubester, chief of the Census Library Project of the Library of Congress in the 1940s, it expands on this earlier work. It is continued by the following volume.

Schulze, Suzanne. *Population Information in Twentieth Century Census Volumes: 1900-1940.* Phoenix: Oryx Press, 1985. See annotation above.

Spafford, Horatio Gates, ed. *A Gazetteer of the State of New York: Embracing an Ample Survey and Description of Its Counties, Towns, Cities, Villages, Canals, Mountains, Lakes, Rivers, Creeks, and Natural Topography. Arranged in One Series, Alphabetically: With an Appendix.* Albany: B. D. Packard and the author, 1824.

One of the earliest and most interesting gazetteers of the state, entries for populated places contain information on geography, history, and give detailed statistics on the people and the economy. Also included is a table of all post offices in existence in January 1824.

Thompson, John Henry, ed. *Geography of New York State.* Syracuse, N.Y.: Syracuse University Press, 1966.

This book contains descriptions covering colonial to modern times. It includes maps, tables, plates, numerous appendixes, and a detailed index. A paperback edition of 1977 was slightly revised.

Thorndale, William and William Dollarhide. *Map Guide to the U.S. Federal Censuses: New York, 1790-1920.* Bountiful, Ut.: American Genealogical Lending Library, 1984.

Actual county boundaries at each decennial census are shown superimposed on a current county boundary map. Seven individual sheets show the boundaries from 1790-1850; two maps cover the periods from 1860-1870 and 1880-1920. The authors are planning a book of similar maps for all fifty states to be published this year.

U.S. Bureau of the Census. *Bureau of the Census Catalog of Publications, 1790-1972.* Washington, D.C.: U.S. Department of Commerce, Bureau of the Census, 1974.

This volume contains two catalogs. *The Catalog of United States Census Publications, 1790-1945,* compiled by Henry J. Dubester, was first published in 1950 and is long out of print. It lists all materials issued by the Bureau of the Census and its predecessor organizations starting with the first census report of 1790. It is followed by the *Bureau of the Census Catalog of Publications, 1946-1972,* which describes an additional 60,000 publications.

U.S. Bureau of the Census. *Bureau of the Census Catalog.* Washington, D.C.: U. S. Government Printing Office, 1963-.

Formerly an annual and now appearing every two years, this publication updates the volume above. The catalog contains a product overview, abstracts of all products released, and a subject index. Frequent title changes have occurred.

U.S. Bureau of the Census. *Historical Statistics of the United States: Colonial Times to 1970.* 3rd ed. 2 vols. Washington, D.C.: U.S. Government Printing Office, 1976.

For this bicentennial edition, several new chapters were added to provide a wide range of statistical data. Data are arranged by broad subjects and into specific detailed subjects in numbered series within each chapter. There is a detailed alphabetical subject index. Statistical tables, charts, and an analysis of subjects makes this a unique reference work.

U.S. Geological Survey. *National Topographic Series.* Scale 1 : 24,000. Reston, Va.: U.S. Geological Survey, 1947–.

Maps in this current topographic series cover almost all of New York State and include names of most populated places.

U.S. Geological Survey. *National Topographic Series.* U.S. Geological Scale 1 : 62,500. Reston, Va.: The U.S. Geological Survey, 1879–.

This was the first national series to cover New York State in detail. Many populated places which are no longer in existence can be located on these historical maps. Most of the maps in this older series are now out of print.

U.S. Geological Survey. National Mapping Division, Office of Geographic Research. *New York Geographic Names.* 2 vols. Reston, Va.: U.S. Geological Survey, 1981.

These volumes are the index to place names on the current USGS *National Topographic Series* maps of New York State. An index to State-County codes (FIPS) is also included.

U.S. National Archives and Records Service. *Federal Population Censuses. 1790-1890: a Catalog of Microfilm Copies of the Schedules.* Washington, D.C.: U.S. National Archives and Records Service, 1975.

This catalog lists the available schedules for 1790 through 1890. The censuses are arranged chronologically, then by state and by county, with microfilm reel numbers. Frequent reprints provide current ordering information. Lists of schedules of the 1900 and 1910 censuses have been published separately, in the publications cited below.

U.S. National Archives and Records Service. *1900 Federal Population Census: a Catalog of Microfilm Copies of the Schedules.* Washington, D.C.: U.S. National Archives and Records Service, 1978.

See annotation above.

U.S. National Archives Trust Fund Board. *The 1910 Federal Population Census: a Catalog of Microfilm Copies of the Schedules.* Washington, D.C.: U.S. National Archives Trust Fund Board, 1982.

See annotation above.

Wolfenden, Hugh Herbert. *Population Statistics and Their Compilation.* Rev. ed. Chicago: University of Chicago Press, 1954.

This book describes the history and development of census taking and some of the primary methods of data collection.

Statewide Information

Origin of New York State Counties

County	Taken From	Established
Albany	Original	November 1, 1683
Allegany	Genesee	April 7, 1806
Bronx	New York	January 1, 1914
Broome	Tioga	March 28, 1806
Cattaraugus	Genesee	March 11, 1808
Cayuga	Onondaga	March 8, 1799
Chautauqua	Genesee	March 11, 1808
Chemung	Tioga	March 20, 1836
Chenango	Tioga and Herkimer	March 15, 1798
Clinton	Washington	March 4, 1788
Columbia	Albany	April 1, 1786
Cortland	Onondaga	April 8, 1808
Delaware	Ulster and Otsego	March 10, 1797
Dutchess	Original	November 1, 1683
Erie	Niagara	April 2, 1821
Essex	Clinton	March 1, 1799
Franklin	Clinton	March 11, 1808
Fulton	Montgomery	April 18, 1838
Genesee	Ontario	March 30, 1802
Greene	Albany and Ulster	March 15, 1800
Hamilton	Montgomery	April 12, 1816
Herkimer	Montgomery	February 16, 1791
Jefferson	Oneida	March 28, 1805
Kings	Original	November 1, 1683
Lewis	Oneida	March 28, 1805
Livingston	Genesee and Ontario	February 23, 1821
Madison	Chenango	March 21, 1806
Monroe	Genesee and Ontario	February 23, 1821
Montgomery	Albany	March 12, 1772
Nassau	Queens	January 1, 1899
New York	Original	November 1, 1683

Origin of New York State Counties, Cont'd.

County	Taken From	Established
Niagara	Genesee	March 11, 1808
Oneida	Herkimer	March 15, 1798
Onondaga	Herkimer and Tioga	March 5, 1794
Ontario	Montgomery	January 27, 1789
Orange	Original	November 1, 1683
Orleans	Genesee	November 12, 1824
Oswego	Oneida and Onondaga	March 1, 1816
Otsego	Montgomery	February 16, 1791
Putnam	Dutchess	June 12, 1812
Queens	Original	November 1, 1683
Rensselaer	Albany	November 7, 1791
Richmond	Original	November 1, 1683
Rockland	Orange	February 23, 1798
St. Lawrence	Clinton	March 3, 1802
Saratoga	Albany	February 7, 1791
Schenectady	Albany	March 27, 1809
Schoharie	Albany and Otsego	April 6, 1795
Schuyler	Chemung, Steuben, and Tompkins	April 17, 1854
Seneca	Cayuga	March 24, 1804
Steuben	Ontario	March 18, 1796
Suffolk	Original	November 1, 1683
Sullivan	Ulster	March 27, 1809
Tioga	Montgomery	February 16, 1791
Tompkins	Cayuga and Seneca	April 7, 1817
Ulster	Original	November 1, 1683
Warren	Washington	March 12, 1813
Washington	Albany	March 12, 1772
Wayne	Ontario and Seneca	April 11, 1823
Westchester	Original	November 1, 1683
Wyoming	Genesee	May 14, 1841
Yates	Ontario	February 5, 1823

From: *New York State Census Records, 1790-1925.*

Genealogy of New York State Counties

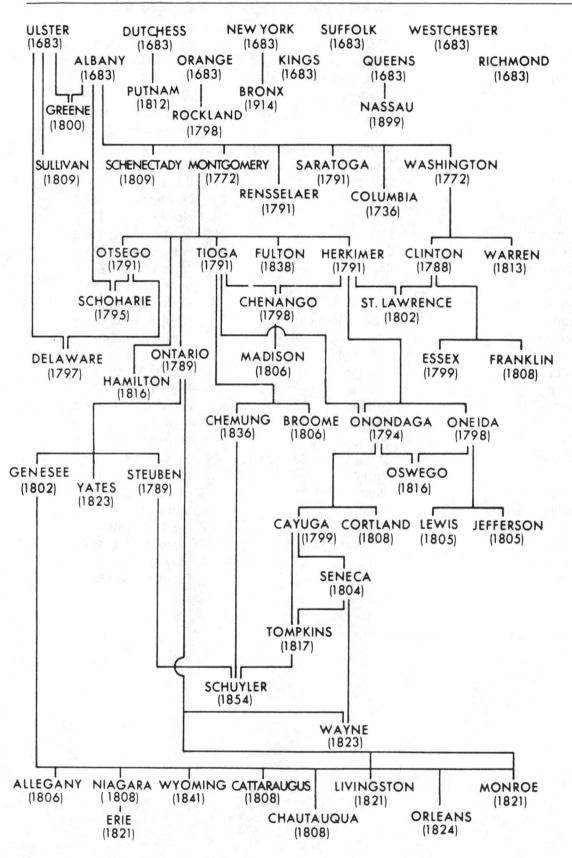

1790 Map of New York State

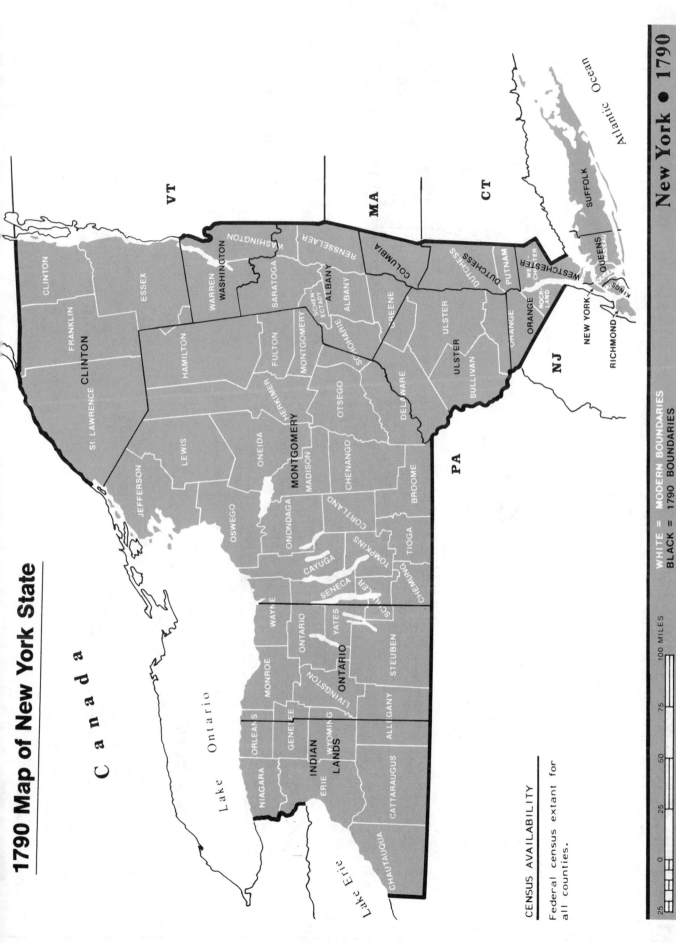

CENSUS AVAILABILITY

Federal census extant for all counties.

New York ● 1790

xxv

1980 Map of New York State

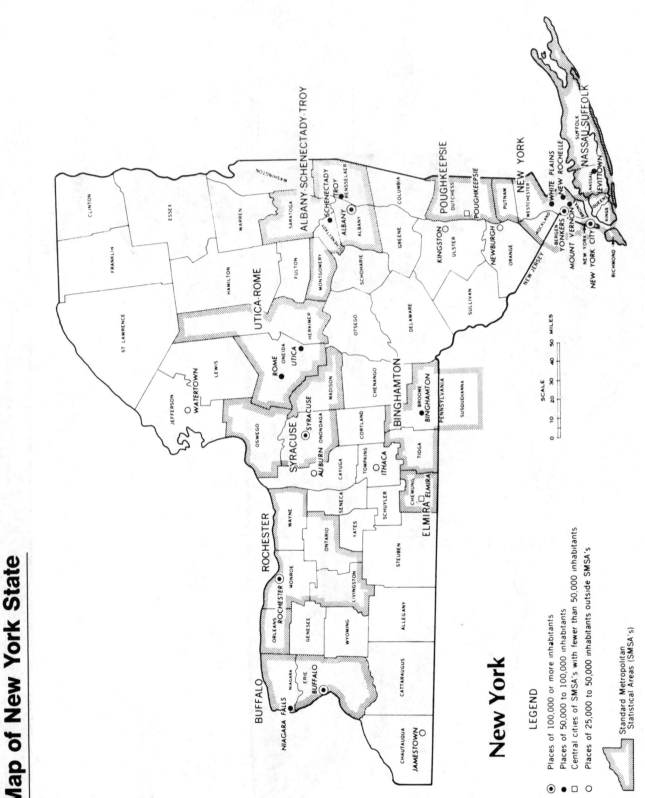

New York

LEGEND

⊙ Places of 100,000 or more inhabitants

● Places of 50,000 to 100,000 inhabitants

□ Central cities of SMSA's with fewer than 50,000 inhabitants

○ Places of 25,000 to 50,000 inhabitants outside SMSA's

Standard Metropolitan Statistical Areas (SMSA's)

U.S. DEPARTMENT OF COMMERCE

BUREAU OF THE CENSUS

Abbreviations & Symbols _____

CDP   Census Designated Place; unincorporated areas without locally designated
political boundaries.

Est.   Established

Inc.   Incorporated

LIRPB   Long Island Regional Planning Board

NA   Not available in printed census reports.

Rev.   Revised by the U.S. Bureau of the
Census.

S.U.N.Y. State University of New York

*   Unreliable figure; see the description of
the 1800 Census in the Introduction.

New York State Population 1790 to 1980

A

ABBOTT'S CORNERS, CDP
  Hamburg Town
    Erie County
      1880   110

ACCORD, CDP
  Rochester Town
    Ulster County
      1940   514

ADAMS, Town (Est. 1802)
    Jefferson County
      1980   4,390
      1970   4,381
      1960   3,964
      1950   3,629
      1940   3,334
      1930   3,284
      1920   3,194
      1910   3,128
      1900   3,081
      1890   3,181
      1880   3,302
      1870   3,348
      1860   3,496
      1850   3,106
      1840   2,966
      1830   2,995
      1820   2,467

ADAMS, Village (Inc. 1851)
  Adams Town
    Jefferson County
      1980   1,701
      1970   1,951
      1960   1,914(a)
      1950   1,762
      1940   1,594
      1930   1,613
      1920   1,557
      1910   1,458
      1900   1,292
      1890   1,360
      1880   1,250
      1870   1,352
(a)Boundary change.

ADAMS BASIN, CDP
  Ogden Town
    Monroe County
      1880   274

ADAMS CENTER, CDP
  Adams Town
    Jefferson County
      1980   1,519
      1950-1970   NA
      1940   714
      1890-1930   NA
      1880   403(a)
(a)Reported as Adams Centre.

ADDISON, Town (Est. 1796)(a)
    Steuben County
      1980   2,734
      1970   2,698
      1960   2,645
      1950   2,368
      1940   2,032
      1930   1,975
      1920   2,122
      1910   2,509
      1900   2,637
      1890   2,908
      1880   2,534
      1870   2,218
      1860   1,715
      1850   3,721
      1840   1,920
      1830   944
      1820   652
      1810   NA
      1800   *174
(a)Established as Middletown in 1796;
   name changed in 1808.

ADDISON, Village (Inc. 1873)
  Addison Town
    Steuben County
      1980   2,028
      1970   2,104
      1960   2,185
      1950   1,920
      1940   1,617
      1930   1,538
      1920   1,699
      1910   2,004
      1900   2,080
      1890   2,166
      1880   1,596

AFTON, Town (Est. 1857)
    Chenango County
      1980   2,728
      1970   2,464
      1960   2,245
      1950   2,047
      1940   1,848
      1930   1,871
      1920   1,840

1910	1,780
1900	1,920
1890	2,083
1880	2,248
1870	1,931
1860	1,770

AFTON, Village (Inc. 1891)
  Afton Town
    Chenango County

1980	982
1970	1,064
1960	956
1950	875
1940	806
1930	812
1920	782
1910	729
1900	722
1890	683
1880	734
1870	457

AKRON, Village (Inc. 1849)
  Newstead Town
    Erie County

1980	2,971(a)
1970	2,863(a)
1960	2,841(a)
1950	2,481
1940	2,263
1930	2,188
1920	1,960
1910	1,677
1900	1,585
1890	1,492
1880	1,036
1870	444

(a)Boundary change.

ALABAMA, CDP
  Alabama Town
    Genesee County

1880	173

ALABAMA, Town (Est. 1826)(a)
  Genesee County

1980	1,926
1970	1,872
1960	1,931
1950	1,766
1940	1,763
1930	1,734
1920	1,530
1910	1,797 Rev.(b)
1900	1,611 Rev.(b)
1890	1,654
1880	1,975
1870	1,805
1860	2,061
1850	2,054
1840	1,798
1830	819

(a)Established as Gerryville in 1826;
   name changed in 1828.
(b)In 1920 the Census Bureau revised the
   1910 figure of 2,231 and the 1900
   figure of 1,957 to exclude the
   TONAWANDA INDIAN RESERVATION.

ALBANY, City (Inc. 1686)
  Albany County

1980	101,727(a)
1970	115,781(a)
1960	129,726
1950	134,995
1940	130,577(a)
1930	127,412(a)
1920	113,344(a)
1910	100,253
1900	94,151
1890	94,923
1880	90,758
1870	76,216 Rev.(b)
1860	62,367
1850	50,763
1840	33,721
1830	24,209
1820	12,630
1810	10,762
1800	5,289 Rev.
1790	*3,498

(a)Boundary change.
(b)The Census Bureau revised the original 1870 figure of 69,622 in a footnote due to a boundary change. Subsequent census publications continue
   to report the unrevised figure.

ALBANY, County (Est. 1683)

1980	285,909
1970	286,742
1960	272,926
1950	239,386
1940	221,315
1930	211,953
1920	186,106
1910	173,666
1900	165,571
1890	164,555
1880	154,890
1870	133,052
1860	113,917
1850	93,279
1840	68,593
1830	53,520
1820	38,116
1810	34,661
1800	34,103
1790	75,736

ALBERTSON, CDP
  North Hempstead Town
    Nassau County

1980	5,561
1970	6,825
1960	6,090(a)
1950	NA
1940	1,238

(a)Derived by LIRPB from U.S. Census
   Data.

ALBION, Town (Est. 1875)
  Orleans County

1980	6,446
1970	6,577
1960	6,416
1950	6,007
1940	5,965

1930	5,994
1920	5,846
1910	6,455
1900	5,749
1890	5,773
1880	5,147

ALBION, Town (Est. 1825)
    Oswego County

1980	1,730
1970	1,452
1960	1,125
1950	1,036
1940	1,094
1930	1,175
1920	1,288
1910	1,472
1900	1,724
1890	2,172
1880	2,569
1870	2,359
1860	2,348
1850	2,010
1840	1,503
1830	669

ALBION, Village
    Albion Town, part in (Inc. 1828)
        Orleans County

1980	4,198
1970	4,765
1960	4,898
1950	4,663
1940	4,506
1930	4,693
1920	4,512
1910	4,901
1900	4,351
1890	4,469
1880	NA
1870	3,322(a)
1860	2,970(a)
1850	2,251(a)

    Gaines Town, part in (Inc. 1951)
        Orleans County

1980	699
1970	357
1960	284
1950	187
1940	154
1930	185
1920	171
1910	115
1900	126
1890	117

    TOTAL

1980	4,897(b)
1970	5,122
1960	5,182
1950	4,850
1940	4,660
1930	4,878
1920	4,683
1910	5,016
1900	4,477
1890	4,586
1880	NA
1850-1870	(c)

(a)Reported in BARRE Town.
(b)Boundary change.
(c)Reported in BARRE Town only.

ALDEN, Town (Est. 1823)
    Erie County

1980	10,093
1970	9,787
1960	7,615
1950	4,899
1940	4,613
1930	4,463
1920	2,433
1910	2,748
1900	2,396
1890	2,304
1880	2,534
1870	2,547
1860	2,442
1850	2,520
1840	1,984
1830	1,258

ALDEN, Village (Inc. 1856)
    Alden Town
        Erie County

1980	2,488
1970	2,651
1960	2,042
1950	1,252
1940	954
1930	846
1920	755
1910	828
1900	607
1890	533
1880	521

ALDEN CENTER, CDP
    Alden Town
        Erie County

1880	116

ALDER CREEK, CDP
    Boonville Town
        Oneida County

1880	28

ALEXANDER, Town (Est. 1812)
    Genesee County

1980	2,367
1970	2,351
1960	1,987
1950	1,591
1940	1,423
1930	1,378
1920	1,287
1910	1,362
1900	1,503
1890	1,587
1880	1,608
1870	1,605
1860	1,801
1850	1,927
1840	2,242
1830	2,331
1820	1,496

ALEXANDER, Village (Inc. 1834)
  Alexander Town
    Genesee County
      1980   483(a)
      1970   474(a)
      1960   335(a)
      1950   304
      1940   265
      1930   212
      1920   194
      1910   212
      1900   230
      1890   NA
      1880   305
(a)Boundary change.

ALEXANDRIA, CDP
  Ticonderoga Town
    Essex County
      1870   680

ALEXANDRIA, Town (Est. 1821)
  Jefferson County
      1980   3,587
      1970   3,515
      1960   3,574
      1950   3,583
      1940   3,533
      1930   3,953
      1920   3,567
      1910   4,259
      1900   3,894
      1890   3,601
      1880   3,135
      1870   3,087
      1860   3,808
      1850   3,178
      1840   3,475
      1830   1,522

ALEXANDRIA BAY, Village (Inc. 1878)
  Alexandria Town
    Jefferson County
      1980   1,265
      1970   1,440
      1960   1,583
      1950   1,688
      1940   1,748
      1930   1,952
      1920   1,649
      1910   1,899
      1900   1,511
      1890   1,123
      1880   587

ALFRED, Town (Est. 1808)
  Allegany County
      1980   6,191
      1970   4,875
      1960   3,730
      1950   2,862
      1940   1,410
      1930   1,404
      1920   1,269
      1910   1,590
      1900   1,615
      1890   1,699
      1880   1,526
      1870   1,555

      1860   1,367
      1850   2,679
      1840   1,630
      1830   1,476
      1820   1,701

ALFRED, Village (Inc. 1881)
  Alfred Town
    Allegany County
      1980   4,967
      1970   3,804(a)
      1960   2,807
      1950   2,053
      1940   694
      1930   639
      1920   598
      1910   759
      1900   756
      1890   786(b)
      1880   513(c)
(a)Boundary change.
(b)Reported as Alfred Center.
(c)This figure was reported in 1890. In
   1880 the Census Bureau reported an
   Alfred, CDP with a population of 135.

ALLEGANY, County (Est. 1806)
      1980   51,742
      1970   46,458
      1960   43,978
      1950   43,784
      1940   39,681
      1930   38,025
      1920   36,842
      1910   41,412
      1900   41,501
      1890   43,240
      1880   41,810
      1870   40,814
      1860   41,881
      1850   37,808(a)
      1840   40,975
      1830   26,276
      1820   9,330
      1810   1,942(b)
(a)Reported as Alleghany.
(b)Reported as Allagany.

ALLEGANY, Town (Est. 1831)(a)
  Cattaraugus County
      1980   8,619
      1970   7,542
      1960   6,483
      1950   5,452
      1940   3,919
      1930   3,731
      1920   3,240
      1910   3,398
      1900   3,692
      1890   3,611
      1880   4,044
      1870   2,485
      1860   2,129
      1850   1,037
      1840   530
(a)Established as Burton in 1831; name
   changed in 1851.

ALLEGANY, Village (Inc. 1906)
  Allegany Town
    Cattaraugus County
      1980   2,078(a)
      1970   2,050(a)
      1960   2,064(a)
      1950   1,738
      1940   1,436
      1930   1,411
      1920   1,350
      1910   1,286
      1890-1900   NA
      1880   1,049
      1870   746
(a)Boundary change.

ALLEGANY INDIAN RESERVATION
  Cattaraugus County
      1980   1,243
      1970   1,113
      1960   1,059
      1950   1,131
      1940   1,151
      1930   972
      1920   934
      1910   1,627
      1900   1,833

ALLEGHANY, County
  see ALLEGANY County

ALLEN, Town (Est. 1823)
  Allegany County
      1980   486
      1970   292
      1960   306
      1950   347
      1940   416
      1930   419
      1920   524
      1910   598
      1900   655
      1890   717
      1880   818
      1870   794
      1860   991
      1850   955
      1840   867
      1830   898

ALMA, Town (Est. 1854)
  Allegany County
      1980   920
      1970   839
      1960   871
      1950   931
      1940   780
      1930   884
      1920   643
      1910   973
      1900   1,182
      1890   1,509
      1880   865
      1870   766
      1860   578

ALMOND, Town (Est. 1821)
  Allegany County
      1980   1,671

      1970   1,524
      1960   1,373
      1950   1,331
      1940   1,234
      1930   1,101
      1920   1,121
      1910   1,297
      1900   1,436
      1890   1,419
      1880   1,567
      1870   1,686
      1860   1,739
      1850   1,914
      1840   1,434
      1830   1,804

ALMOND, Village (Inc. 1921)
  Almond Town, part in
    Allegany County, part in
      1980   529
      1970   627
      1960   665
      1950   636
      1940   511
      1930   428
  Hornellsville Town, part in
    Steuben County, part in
      1980   39
      1970   31
      1960   31
      1950   23
      1940   22
      1930   10
  TOTAL
      1980   568
      1970   658
      1960   696
      1950   659
      1940   533
      1930   438

ALPINE, CDP
  Catharine Town
    Schuyler County
      1880   180

ALPLAUS, CDP
  Glenville Town
    Schenectady County
      1940   505

ALTAMONT, Town (Est. 1890)
  Franklin County
      1980   6,318
      1970   6,698
      1960   6,546
      1950   6,849
      1940   6,537
      1930   6,097
      1920   4,927
      1910   4,691
      1900   3,045

ALTAMONT, Village (Inc. 1890)
  Guilderland Town
    Albany County
      1980   1,292
      1970   1,561
      1960   1,365

1950	1,127
1940	890
1930	858
1920	797
1910	674
1900	689

ALTAY, CDP
Tyrone Town
  Schuyler County

1880	130

ALTMAR, Village (Inc. 1876)(a)
Albion Town
  Oswego County

1980	347
1970	448
1960	277
1950	299
1940	304
1930	378
1920	315
1910	363
1900	416
1890	551
1880	753

(a)Incorporated as Sand Bank in 1876;
name changed in 1896.

ALTONA, Town (Est. 1857)
Clinton County

1980	2,077
1970	1,852
1960	1,750
1950	1,711
1940	2,026
1930	1,834
1920	1,911
1910	2,383
1900	2,465
1890	2,368
1880	3,570
1870	2,759
1860	1,665

AMAGANSETT, CDP
East Hampton Town
  Suffolk County

1980	2,188(a)
1970	709(b)
1960	850 Rev.
1950	NA
1940	974
1890-1930	NA
1880	548

(a)Boundary change.
(b)Derived by LIRPB from U.S. Census
    Data; population of 2,123 is compar-
    able to 1980 boundaries.

AMBER, CDP
Otisco Town
  Onondaga County

1880	156

AMBOY, CDP
Camillus Town
  Onondaga County

1870	128

AMBOY, Town (Est. 1830)
Oswego County

1980	836
1970	557
1960	524
1950	482
1940	493
1930	507
1920	617
1910	736
1900	824
1890	969
1880	1,244
1870	1,431
1860	1,402
1850	1,132
1840	1,070
1830	669

AMBOY CENTER, CDP
Amboy Town
  Oswego County

1880	46

AMENIA, CDP
Amenia Town
  Dutchess County

1980	1,183
1970	1,157
1950-1960	NA
1940	1,052
1890-1930	NA
1880	393

AMENIA, Town (Est. 1788)
Dutchess County

1980	6,299
1970	7,842
1960	7,546
1950	7,481
1940	6,873
1930	1,969
1920	1,831
1910	2,123
1900	2,374
1890	2,362
1880	2,697
1870	2,662
1860	2,288
1850	2,229
1840	2,179
1830	2,389
1820	3,114
1810	NA
1800	*2,978
1790	3,078 Rev.

AMENIA UNION, CDP
Amenia Town
  Dutchess County

1880	54

AMES, Village (Inc. 1924)
Canajoharie Town
  Montgomery County

1980	224
1970	198
1960	162
1950	193

```
              1940                180
              1930                170
              1890-1920            NA
              1880                148
              1870                150
```

AMHERST, Town (Est. 1818)
    Erie County
```
              1980            108,706
              1970             93,929
              1960             62,837
              1950             33,744
              1940         19,356(a)
              1930         13,181(a)
              1920              6,286
              1910              4,629
              1900              4,223
              1890              4,014
              1880              4,519
              1870              4,555
              1860              5,089
              1850              4,153
              1840              2,451
              1830              2,485
              1820              768(b)
```
(a)Boundary change.
(b)Reported in NIAGARA County.

AMITY, CDP
   Warwick Town
      Orange County
```
              1880                131
```

AMITY, Town (Est. 1830)
    Allegany County
```
              1980              2,272
              1970              2,150
              1960              2,006
              1950              1,997
              1940              1,935
              1930              1,867
              1920              1,843
              1910              2,071
              1900              2,216
              1890              1,996
              1880              1,972
              1870              2,087
              1860              2,268
              1850              1,792
              1840              1,354
              1830                872
```

AMITYVILLE, Unincorporated
   Babylon Town
      Suffolk County
```
              1980              43(a)
              1970              33(b)
```
(a)Boundary change; derived by LIRPB
   from U.S. Census Data.
(b)Derived by LIRPB from U.S. Census
   Data; population is comparable to
   1980 boundaries.

AMITYVILLE, Village (Inc. 1894)
   Babylon Town
      Suffolk County
```
              1980              9,076
              1970              9,794
              1960              8,318
```

```
              1950              6,164
              1940              5,058
              1930          4,437(a)
              1920              3,265
              1910              2,517
              1900              2,038
              1890              2,293
              1880              1,063
              1870                500
```
(a)Boundary change.

AMSTERDAM, City (Inc. 1885)(a)
    Montgomery County
```
              1980         21,872(b)
              1970         25,524(b)
              1960             28,772
              1850             32,240
              1940             33,329
              1930             34,817
              1920         33,524(b)
              1910             31,267
              1900             20,929
              1890             17,336
```
(a)AMSTERDAM VILLAGE incorporated as
   AMSTERDAM City and made independent of
   AMSTERDAM and FLORIDA Towns in 1885.
(b)Boundary change.

AMSTERDAM, Town (Est. 1793)
    Montgomery County
```
              1980          5,721(a)
              1970          5,795(a)
              1960              5,400
              1950              4,698
              1940              3,911
              1930              3,818
              1920          3,130(a)
              1910              3,074
              1900              3,202
              1890          2,948(a)
              1880             11,710
              1870              7,706
              1860              4,557
              1850              4,128
              1840              5,333
              1830              3,356
              1820              3,171
              1810                 NA
              1800            *1,064
```
(a)Boundary change.

AMSTERDAM, Village (Inc. 1830)(a)
   Amsterdam Town
      Montgomery County
```
              1880              9,466
              1870          5,426(b)
```
(a)AMSTERDAM Village incorporated as
   AMSTERDAM City and made independent of
   AMSTERDAM and FLORIDA Towns in 1885.
(b)Reported in AMSTERDAM and FLORIDA
   Towns.

ANCRAM, CDP
   Ancram Town
      Columbia County
```
              1880                283
```

ANCRAM, Town (Est. 1803)(a)
  Columbia County
```
        1980            1,332
        1970            1,215
        1960            1,080
        1950              925
        1940            1,005
        1930              850
        1920            1,015
        1910            1,137
        1900            1,238
        1890            1,332
        1880            1,602
        1870            1,793
        1860            1,720
        1850            1,569
        1840            1,770
        1830            1,533(b)
        1820            3,147
```
(a)Established as Gallatin in 1803; name
   changed in 1814.
(b)Boundary change: GALLATIN Town reorganized from part of ANCRAM Town in
   1830.

ANCRAM LEAD MINES, CDP
  Ancram Town
    Columbia County
```
        1880               36
```

ANDES, Town (Est. 1819)
  Delaware County
```
        1980            1,312
        1970            1,193
        1960            1,274
        1950            1,665
        1940            1,687
        1930            1,899
        1920            1,922
        1910            2,007
        1900            1,927
        1890            2,264
        1880            2,639
        1870            2,840
        1860            2,990
        1850            2,672
        1840            2,176
        1830            1,860
        1820            1,378
```

ANDES, Village (Inc. 1861)
  Andes Town
    Delaware County
```
        1980              372
        1970              353
        1960              399
        1950              430
        1940              409
        1930              395
        1920              394
        1910              414
        1900              365
        1890              416
        1880              496
```

ANDOVER, Town (Est. 1824)
  Allegany County
```
        1980            1,956
        1970            1,839
```

```
        1960            1,801
        1950            1,973
        1940            1,996
        1930            1,905
        1920            1,809
        1910            1,990
        1900            1,869
        1890            1,766
        1880            1,988
        1870            1,873
        1860            1,724
        1850            1,476
        1840              848
        1830              598
```

ANDOVER, Village (Inc. 1892)
  Andover Town
    Allegany County
```
        1980            1,120
        1970            1,214
        1960            1,247
        1950            1,351
        1940            1,290
        1930            1,241
        1920            1,132
        1910            1,136
        1900              954
        1890               NA
        1880              794
```

ANGELICA, Town (Est. 1805)
  Allegany County
```
        1980            1,438
        1970            1,306
        1960            1,335
        1950            1,390
        1940            1,410
        1930            1,338
        1920            1,502
        1910            1,668
        1900            1,639
        1890            1,749
        1880            1,620
        1870            1,643
        1860            1,708
        1850            1,592
        1840            1,257
        1830              998
        1820            1,510
```

ANGELICA, Village (Inc. 1835)
  Angelica Town
    Allegany County
```
        1980              982
        1970              948
        1960              898
        1950              928
        1940              928
        1930              838
        1920              972
        1910            1,056
        1900              978
        1890              953
        1880              705
        1870              991
```

ANGOLA, Village (Inc. 1873)
  Evans Town
    Erie County
      1980   2,292
      1970   2,676
      1960   2,499
      1950   1,936
      1940   1,663
      1930   1,543
      1920   1,367
      1910   898
      1900   712
      1890   650
      1880   508
      1870   600

ANGOLA ON THE LAKE, CDP
  Evans Town
    Erie County
      1980   1,907
      1970   1,573

ANNANDALE, CDP
  Red Hook Town
    Dutchess County
      1880   91
      1870   347

ANNANDALE HAMLET, CDP
  Red Hook Town
    Dutchess County
      1880   130

ANNSVILLE, Town (Est. 1823)
  Oneida County
      1980   2,389
      1970   1,917
      1960   1,635
      1950   1,333
      1940   1,217
      1930   1,242
      1920   1,353
      1910   1,449
      1900   1,744
      1890   2,068
      1880   2,554
      1870   2,716
      1860   2,837
      1850   2,686
      1840   1,765
      1830   1,481

ANTWERP, Town (Est. 1810)
  Jefferson County
      1980   1,859
      1970   1,794
      1960   1,905
      1950   1,781
      1940   2,187
      1930   2,292
      1920   2,569
      1910   2,848
      1900   3,008
      1890   3,095
      1880   3,414
      1870   3,310
      1860   3,313
      1850   3,665
      1840   3,109

      1830   2,411
      1820   1,319

ANTWERP, Village (Inc. 1854)
  Antwerp Town
    Jefferson County
      1980   749
      1970   872
      1960   881
      1950   846
      1940   817
      1930   868
      1920   1,012
      1910   974
      1900   929
      1890   912
      1880   731
      1870   773

APALACHIN, CDP
  Owego Town
    Tioga County
      1980   1,227
      1970   1,233
      1890-1960   NA
      1880   223
      1870   300

APULIA, CDP
  Fabius Town
    Onondaga County
      1870   181

AQUEBOGUE, CDP
  Riverhead Town
    Suffolk County
      1980   895(a)
      1970   1,331(b)
      1960   1,277(c)
      1950   NA
      1940   791
      1890-1930   NA
      1880   323
(a)Boundary change; derived by LIRPB from
   U.S. Census Data.
(b)Derived by LIRPB from U.S. Census
   Data; population of 1,241 is comparable to 1980 boundaries.
(c)Derived by LIRPB from U.S. Census
   Data.

ARCADE, Town (Est. 1818)(a)
  Wyoming County
      1980   3,714
      1970   3,048
      1960   2,861
      1950   2,570
      1940   2,387
      1930   2,404
      1920   2,412
      1910   2,131
      1900   1,877
      1890   1,840
      1880   2,000
      1870   1,742
      1860   2,037
      1850   1,961
      1840   1,437(b)
      1830   2,387(b)

```
            1820          780(b)
(a)Established as China in 1818; name
   changed in 1866.
(b)Reported in GENESEE County.
```

ARCADE, Village (Inc. 1871)
  Arcade Town
    Wyoming County

```
            1980        2,052(a)
            1970        1,972(a)
            1960        1,930
            1950        1,818
            1940        1,683
            1930        1,643
            1920        1,609
            1910        1,294
            1900          887
            1880-1890      NA
            1870          573
(a)Boundary change.
```

ARCADIA, Town (Est. 1825)
  Wayne County

```
            1980       14,697 Rev.
            1970       15,245
            1960       15,836
            1950       12,816
            1940       12,108
            1930       10,051
            1920        9,266
            1910        8,672
            1900        7,046
            1890        6,310
            1880        5,702
            1870        5,271
            1860        5,319
            1850        5,145
            1840        4,980
            1830        3,901
```

ARCADIA, Village
  see NEWARK, Village
      Wayne County

ARDSLEY, Village (Inc. 1896)
  Greenburgh Town
    Westchester County

```
            1980        4,183
            1970        4,470
            1960        3,991(a)
            1950        1,744
            1940        1,423(a)
            1930        1,135
            1920          730
            1910          537
            1900          404
(a)Boundary change.
```

ARGUSVILLE, CDP
  Carlisle Town
    Schoharie County

```
            1880          111
```

ARGYLE, Town (Est. 1786)
  Washington County

```
            1980        2,847
            1970        2,415
            1960        1,898
            1950        1,801
```

```
            1940        1,611
            1930        1,452
            1920        1,535
            1910        1,806
            1900        1,995
            1890        2,313
            1880        2,775
            1870        2,850
            1860        3,139
            1850        3,274
            1840        3,111
            1830        3,450
            1820        2,811
            1810           NA
            1800       *4,597
            1790        2,341
```

ARGYLE, Village (Inc. 1838)
  Argyle Town
    Washington County

```
            1980          320
            1970          392
            1960          355
            1950          351
            1940          226
            1930          245
            1920          198
            1910          231
            1900          264
            1890          158
            1880          316
            1870          351
```

ARIETTA, Town (Est. 1836)
  Hamilton County

```
            1980          314
            1970          350
            1960          235
            1950          219
            1940          183
            1930          165(a)
            1920          176
            1910          232
            1900          247
            1890          357
            1880          294
            1870          139
            1860           98
            1850          108(b)
            1840          209
(a)Boundary change.
(b)Reported as Arrietta.
```

ARKPORT, Village (Inc. 1913)
  Hornellsville Town
    Steuben County

```
            1980          811
            1970          984
            1960          837
            1950          701
            1940          618
            1930          575
            1920          463
```

ARKWRIGHT, Town (Est. 1829)
  Chautauqua County

```
            1980          980
            1970          833
            1960          700
```

1950	665
1940	688
1930	746
1920	757
1910	843
1900	918
1890	886
1880	1,076
1870	1,030
1860	1,103
1850	1,283
1840	1,418
1830	926

ARLINGTON, CDP
   Poughkeepsie Town
      Dutchess County

1980	11,305
1970	11,203
1960	8,317
1950	5,374
1940	3,284

ARLINGTON, Town
   see RICHFORD, Town
         Tioga County

ARMONK, CDP
   North Castle Town
      Westchester County

1980	2,238
1890-1970	NA
1880	265

ARRIETTA, Town
   see ARIETTA, Town
         Hamilton County

ARSHAMOMOQUE, CDP
   Southold Town
      Suffolk County

1880	143

ASHAROKEN, Village (Inc. 1925)
   Huntington Town
      Suffolk County

1980	635
1970	540(a)
1960	281 Rev.
1950	116
1940	48
1930	98

(a)Boundary change.

ASHFORD, Town (Est. 1824)
   Cattaraugus County

1980	1,922
1970	1,577
1960	1,490
1950	1,370
1940	1,340
1930	1,214
1920	1,379
1910	1,557
1900	1,645
1890	1,710
1880	1,813
1870	1,801
1860	1,975

1850	1,658
1840	1,469
1830	631

ASHLAND, CDP
   Ashland Town
      Greene County

1880	268

ASHLAND, Town (Est. 1867)
   Chemung County

1980	1,967
1970	1,726
1960	1,273
1950	1,188
1940	951
1930	948
1920	834
1910	769
1900	954
1890	983
1880	1,149
1870	1,558

ASHLAND, Town (Est. 1848)
   Greene County

1980	744
1970	397
1960	548
1950	542
1940	566
1930	482
1920	560
1910	640
1900	692
1890	787
1880	899
1870	992
1860	1,212
1850	1,290

ASHVILLE, CDP
   Harmony Town
      Chautauqua County

1880	214
1870	350

ASSINING, Village
   see OSSINING, Village
         Westchester County

ASTORIA, Village (Inc. 1839)(a)
   Newtown Town
      Queens County

1870	5,204

(a)Merged into QUEENS Borough in NEW
   YORK City in 1898.

ATHENS, Town (Est. 1815)
   Greene County

1980	3,462
1970	3,567
1960	2,804
1950	2,372
1940	2,375
1930	2,254
1920	2,361
1910	2,720
1900	2,891

1890	2,876
1880	3,065
1870	2,942
1860	2,791
1850	2,986
1840	2,387
1830	2,425
1820	2,030

ATHENS, Village (Inc. 1805)
  Athens Town
    Greene County

1980	1,738
1970	1,718
1960	1,754
1950	1,545
1940	1,655
1930	1,618
1920	1,844
1910	1,956
1900	2,171
1890	2,024
1880	2,106
1870	1,793

ATHOL, Town (Est. 1813)(a)
  Warren County

1850	1,590
1840	1,210
1830	909
1820	570

(a)Merged into STONY CREEK and THURMAN
   Towns in 1852.

ATLANTIC BEACH, Unincorporated
  Hempstead Town
    Nassau County

1980	2,008(a)
1970	1,799(a)
1960	1,282(a)

(a)Derived by LIRPB from U.S. Census
   Data.

ATLANTIC BEACH, Village (Inc. 1962)
  Hempstead Town
    Nassau County

1980	1,775
1970	1,640
1960	998(a)
1950	NA
1940	545(b)

(a)Derived by LIRPB from U.S. Census
   Data.
(b)Reported as Atlantic Beach, Uninc.;
   however this area was incorporated in
   1962 and this figure is comparable to
   1960-1980 boundaries.

ATLANTICVILLE, CDP
  see EAST QUOGUE, CDP
        Suffolk County

ATLANTIQUE
  see FIRE ISLAND
        Islip Town
          Suffolk County

ATTICA, Town (Est. 1811)
  Wyoming County

1980	5,693
1970	6,171
1960	5,781
1950	5,722
1940	5,477
1930	2,891
1920	2,743
1910	2,749
1900	2,677
1890	3,002
1880	3,099
1870	2,546
1860	2,544
1850	2,363
1840	2,710(a)
1830	2,492(a)
1820	1,519(a)

(a)Reported in GENESEE County.

ATTICA, Village
  Alexander Town, part in (Inc. 1834)
    Genesee County, part in

1980	16
1970	2
1960	0(a)

  Attica Town, part in (Inc. 1837)
    Wyoming County, part in

1980	2,643
1970	2,909(a)
1960	2,758(a)
1950	2,676
1940	2,379
1930	2,212
1920	2,015
1910	1,869
1900	1,785
1890	1,994
1880	1,935
1870	1,333

  TOTAL

1980	2,659
1970	2,911(a)
1960	2,758(a)
1870-1950	(b)

(a)Boundary change.
(b)Reported in WYOMING County only.

AUBURN, City (Inc. 1848)(a)
  Cayuga County

1980	32,548
1970	34,599
1960	35,249
1950	36,722
1940	35,753
1930	36,652
1920	36,192
1910	34,668
1900	30,345
1890	25,858
1880	21,924
1870	17,225
1860	10,986
1850	9,548

(a)AUBURN Village (Inc. 1815) and AUBURN
   Town consolidated and incorporated as
   AUBURN City in 1848.

AUBURN, Town (Est. 1823)(a)
  Cayuga County
        1840   5,626
        1830   4,486
(a)AUBURN Village (Inc. 1815) and AUBURN
   Town consolidated and incorporated as
   AUBURN City in 1848.

AUBURN, Village
   see AUBURN, City
        Cayuga County

AUGUSTA, Town (Est. 1798)
   Oneida County
        1980   2,080
        1970   2,025
        1960   2,021
        1950   1,933
        1940   1,900
        1930   1,739
        1920   1,911
        1910   1,959
        1900   2,029
        1890   1,984
        1880   2,171
        1870   2,067
        1860   2,213
        1850   2,271
        1840   2,175
        1830   3,058
        1820   2,771
        1810   NA
        1800   *1,598

AUGUSTA, Town
   Ontario County
   see MIDDLESEX, Town
        Yates County

AUGUSTA CENTRE, CDP
   Augusta Town
      Oneida County
        1880   130
        1870   147

AURELIUS, Town (Est. 1789)
   Cayuga County
        1980   2,920
        1970   2,851
        1960   2,600
        1950   2,039
        1940   1,342
        1930   1,430
        1920   1,277
        1910   1,437
        1900   1,563
        1890   1,793
        1880   1,954
        1870   1,952
        1860   2,528
        1850   2,831
        1840   2,645
        1830   2,767
        1820   7,923
        1810   NA
        1800   *3,312

AURIESVILLE, CDP
   Glen Town
      Montgomery County
        1870   96

AURORA, Town (Est. 1804)(a)
   Erie County
        1980   13,872
        1970   14,426
        1960   12,888
        1950   9,271
        1940   7,656
        1930   6,875
        1920   5,312
        1910   4,479
        1900   4,015
        1890   3,266
        1880   2,723
        1870   2,573
        1860   2,580
        1850   3,435
        1840   2,908
        1830   2,423
        1820   1,285(b)
(a)Established as Willink in 1804; name
   changed in 1818.
(b)Reported in NIAGARA County.

AURORA, Village (Inc. 1837)
   Ledyard Town
      Cayuga County
        1980   926(a)
        1970   1,072
        1960   834
        1950   711
        1940   372
        1930   389
        1920   416
        1910   493
        1900   499
        1890   555
        1880   444
        1870   450
(a)Boundary change.

AuSABLE, Town (Est. 1839)
   Clinton County
        1980   2,792
        1970   2,652
        1960   2,605
        1950   1,903
        1940   1,985
        1930   1,868
        1920   1,636
        1910   2,045
        1900   2,195
        1890   2,532
        1880   2,980
        1870   2,863
        1860   3,227
        1850   4,492
        1840   3,222

AUSABLE FORKS, CDP
   Black Brook Town, part in
      Clinton County
        1950   611
        1900-1940   NA
        1890   393

Jay Town, part in
Essex County

1950	1,032
1900-1940	NA
1890	364
1880	532

TOTAL

1950	1,643
1900-1940	NA
1890	757
1880	(a)

(a)Reported in ESSEX County only.

AUSTERLITZ, Town (Est. 1818)
Columbia County

1980	1,314
1970	905
1960	809
1950	753
1940	626
1930	643
1920	666
1910	811
1900	974
1890	1,142
1880	1,341
1870	1,442
1860	1,889
1850	1,873
1840	2,091
1830	2,245
1820	2,355

AVA, Town (Est. 1846)
Oneida County

1980	664
1970	541
1960	518
1950	452
1940	520
1930	588
1920	615
1910	563
1900	706
1890	860
1880	1,039
1870	1,160
1860	1,260
1850	1,037

AVERILL PARK, CDP
Sand Lake Town
Rensselaer County

1980	1,337
1970	1,471
1950-1960	NA
1940	647

AVOCA, Town (Est. 1843)
Steuben County

1980	2,225 Rev.
1970	2,059
1960	2,041
1950	1,755
1940	1,789
1930	1,788
1920	1,888
1910	2,140
1900	2,125
1890	2,242
1880	1,843
1870	1,740
1860	1,885
1850	1,574

AVOCA, Village (Inc. 1883)
Avoca Town
Steuben County

1980	1,144
1970	1,153
1960	1,086(a)
1950	952
1940	1,006
1930	940
1920	1,019
1910	1,057
1900	1,006
1890	953
1880	547
1870	492

(a)Boundary change.

AVON, Town (Est. 1789)(a)
Livingston County

1980	6,185
1970	6,117
1960	4,404
1950	3,725
1940	3,509
1930	3,566
1920	3,350
1910	3,432
1900	3,071
1890	3,179
1880	3,459
1870	3,038
1860	2,910
1850	2,809
1840	2,999
1830	2,372
1820	1,933(b)
1810	NA
1800	*535(b)

(a)Established as Hartford in 1789; name
changed in 1808.
(b)Reported in ONTARIO County.

AVON, Village (Inc. 1867)
Avon Town
Livingston County

1980	3,006(a)
1970	3,260
1960	2,772
1950	2,412
1940	2,339
1930	2,403
1920	2,585
1910	2,053
1900	1,601
1890	1,653
1880	1,617
1870	900

(a)Boundary change.

B

BABYLON, Town (Est. 1872)
    Suffolk County

1980	203,483
1970	204,256 Rev.
1960	142,309
1950	45,556
1940	24,297
1930	19,291
1920	11,315
1910	9,030
1900	7,112
1890	6,035
1880	4,739

BABYLON, Village (Inc. 1893)
    Babylon Town
      Suffolk County

1980	12,388
1970	12,897
1960	11,062
1950	6,015
1940	4,742
1930	4,342
1920	2,523
1910	2,600
1900	2,157
1890	NA
1880	2,142
1870	1,225

BACHELLORSVILLE, CDP
  see BATCHELLERVILLE, CDP
    Saratoga County

BAINBRIDGE, Town (Est. 1791)(a)
    Chenango County

1980	3,331
1970	3,370
1960	3,177
1950	2,706
1940	2,410
1930	2,192
1920	2,009
1910	2,017
1900	1,991
1890	2,117
1880	1,924
1870	1,793
1860	1,588
1850	3,338
1840	3,324
1830	3,038
1820	2,290
1810	NA
1800	*939(b)

(a)Established as Jericho in 1791; name
   changed in 1814.
(b)Reported as Jerichs.

BAINBRIDGE, Village (Inc. 1829)
    Bainbridge Town
      Chenango County

1980	1,603

1970	1,674
1960	1,712
1950	1,505
1940	1,450
1930	1,324
1920	1,259
1910	1,159
1900	1,092
1890	1,049
1880	781
1870	681

BAITING HOLLOW, CDP
    Riverhead Town
      Suffolk County

1880	340

BALDWIN, CDP
    Hempstead Town
      Nassau County

1980	31,630
1970	34,525
1960	30,204
1950	NA
1940	15,507
1890-1930	NA
1880	1,019(a)

(a)Reported as Baldwin's.

BALDWIN, Town (Est. 1856)
    Chemung County

1980	892
1970	889
1960	735
1950	557
1940	457
1930	483
1920	503
1910	476
1900	664
1890	733
1880	968
1870	969
1860	918

BALDWINSVILLE, Village (Inc. 1847)
    Lysander Town, part in
      Onondaga County

1980	3,932
1970	3,943
1960	3,696(a)
1950	2,712
1940	2,243
1930	2,290
1920	2,237
1910	1,865
1900	1,812
1890	1,833
1880	1,375
1870	1,401

    Van Buren Town, part in
      Onondaga County

1980	2,514
1970	2,355
1960	2,289
1950	1,783
1940	1,597
1930	1,555
1920	1,448

1910	1,234
1900	1,180
1890	1,207
1880	746
1870	729

TOTAL

1980	6,446(a)
1970	6,298
1960	5,985(a)
1950	4,495
1940	3,840
1930	3,845
1920	3,685
1910	3,099
1900	2,992
1890	3,040
1880	2,121
1870	2,130

(a)Boundary change.

BALLSTON, Town (Est. 1788)
Saratoga County

1980	7,714
1970	6,720
1960	5,752
1950	3,969
1940	2,630
1930	2,578
1920	2,206
1910	2,091
1900	2,034
1890	2,059
1880	2,035
1870	2,180
1860	2,234
1850	2,269
1840	2,044
1830	2,113
1820	2,407(a)
1810	NA
1800	*2,099(a)
1790	7,333(b)

(a)Reported as Ballstown.
(b)Reported as Balls-Town in ALBANY
County.

BALLSTON SPA, Village (Inc. 1807)
Ballston Town, part in
Saratoga County

1980	995
1970	816
1960	844
1950	803
1940	676
1930	643
1920	558
1910	549
1900	533
1890	508
1880	383
1870	344

Milton Town, part in
Saratoga County

1980	3,716
1970	4,152
1960	4,147
1950	4,134
1940	3,767
1930	3,948

1920	3,545
1910	3,589
1900	3,390
1890	3,019
1880	2,628
1870	2,626

TOTAL

1980	4,711(a)
1970	4,968
1960	4,991
1950	4,937
1940	4,434
1930	4,591(a)
1920	4,103
1910	4,138
1900	3,923
1890	3,527
1880	3,011
1870	2,970

(a)Boundary change.

BALLSTOWN, Town
Albany & Saratoga Counties
see BALLSTON, Town
Saratoga County

BALMVILLE, CDP
Newburgh Town
Orange County

1980	2,919
1970	3,214
1960	1,538
1950	NA
1940	985

BALTIMORE, Town
see NEW BALTIMORE, Town
Greene County

BANGALL, CDP
Stanford Town
Dutchess County

1880	154

BANGOR, CDP
Bangor Town
Franklin County

1880	239

BANGOR, Town (Est. 1812)
Franklin County

1980	1,960
1970	1,909
1960	1,896
1950	1,738
1940	1,734
1930	1,701
1920	1,927
1910	1,946
1900	2,221
1890	2,445
1880	2,440
1870	2,431
1860	2,520
1850	2,159
1840	1,289
1830	1,076
1820	370

BAPTIST HILL, CDP
  Bristol Town
    Ontario County
      1880   150

BARKER, Town (Est. 1831)
    Broome County
      1980   2,244
      1970   2,032
      1960   1,683
      1950   1,456
      1940   1,223
      1930   992
      1920   1,003
      1910   948
      1900   1,072
      1890   1,100
      1880   1,333
      1870   1,396
      1860   1,090
      1850   1,456
      1840   1,259

BARKER, Village (Inc. 1908)
    Somerset Town
      Niagara County
        1980   535
        1970   567(a)
        1960   528(a)
        1950   523
        1940   452
        1930   410
        1920   431
        1910   441
(a)Boundary change.

BARKERSVILLE, CDP
  Providence Town
    Saratoga County
      1880   50

BARNES CORNERS, CDP
  Pinckney Town
    Lewis County
      1880   112(a)
(a)Reported as Barnes' Corners.

BARNEVELD, Village (Inc. 1833)(a)
  Trenton Town
    Oneida County
      1980   396
      1970   423
      1960   363
      1950   331
      1940   296
      1930   313
      1920   269
      1910   289
      1900   298
      1890   284
      1880   289
      1870   204
(a)Established as Oldenbarneveldt in
   1819. Incorporated as Trenton in
   1833; name changed to BARNEVELD in
   1975.

BARRE, Town (Est. 1818)
    Orleans County
      1980   2,164
      1970   2,135
      1960   1,922
      1950   1,623
      1940   1,545
      1930   1,686
      1920   1,622
      1910   1,812
      1900   1,937
      1890   2,154
      1880   2,325
      1870   6,756
      1860   4,258
      1850   4,186
      1840   5,539
      1830   4,768
      1820   1,767(a)
(a)Reported in GENESEE County.

BARREN ISLAND, CDP
  Flatlands Town
    Kings County
      1880   309

BARRINGTON, Town (Est. 1822)
    Yates County
      1980   1,091
      1970   929
      1960   754
      1950   771
      1940   782
      1930   790
      1920   882
      1910   1,044
      1900   1,249
      1890   1,393
      1880   1,478
      1870   1,506
      1860   1,574
      1850   1,550
      1840   1,868
      1830   1,854

BARRYTOWN, CDP
  Red Hook Town
    Dutchess County
      1880   239
      1870   248

BARRYTOWN CORNERS, CDP
  Red Hook Town
    Dutchess County
      1880   75

BARRYVILLE, CDP
  Highland Town
    Sullivan County
      1880   271

BARTON, Town (Est. 1824)
    Tioga County
      1980   8,784
      1970   8,526
      1960   8,365
      1950   8,017
      1940   7,164
      1930   7,219

1920	6,746
1910	6,431
1900	6,381
1890	6,120
1880	5,825
1870	5,087
1860	4,234
1850	3,522
1840	2,324
1830	982

BATAVIA, City (Inc. 1914)(a)
Genesee County

1980	16,703(b)
1970	17,338(b)
1960	18,210(b)
1950	17,799
1940	17,267(b)
1930	17,375
1920	13,541(b)

(a)BATAVIA Village incorporated as
   BATAVIA City and made independent of
   BATAVIA Town in 1914.
(b)Boundary change.

BATAVIA, Town (Est. 1802)
Genesee County

1980	5,565(a)
1970	5,440(a)
1960	4,325(a)
1950	2,824
1940	2,261(a)
1930	2,248
1920	1,752(a)
1910	13,830
1900	11,430
1890	9,341
1880	7,516
1970	6,485
1860	3,316
1850	4,461
1840	4,219
1830	4,264
1820	2,597

(a)Boundary change.

BATAVIA, Village (Inc. 1823)(a)
Batavia Town
  Genesee County

1910	11,613
1900	9,180
1890	7,221
1880	4,845
1870	3,890
1860	2,560

(a)BATAVIA Village incorporated as
   BATAVIA City and made independent of
   BATAVIA Town in 1914.

BATCHELLERVILLE, CDP
Edinburgh Town
  Saratoga County

1880	344
1870	216(a)

(a)Reported as Bachellorsville.

BATH, Town (Est. 1796)
Steuben County

1980	12,268

1970	11,953
1960	11,978
1950	10,926
1940	9,354
1930	7,843
1920	7,317
1910	8,554
1900	8,437
1890	7,881
1880	7,396
1870	6,236(a)
1860	5,129
1850	6,185
1840	4,915
1830	3,387
1820	2,578
1810	NA
1800	*452

(a)Boundary change.

BATH, Village
Rensselaer County
see BATH-ON-HUDSON, Village
    Rensselaer County

BATH, Village (Inc. 1816)
Bath Town
  Steuben County

1980	6,042(a)
1970	6,053(a)
1960	6,166
1950	5,416
1940	4,696
1930	4,015
1920	3,720 Rev.(b)
1910	3,884
1900	4,994
1890	3,261
1880	3,183

(a)Boundary change.
(b)In 1930 the Census Bureau revised the
   1920 figure of 4,795 to exclude the
   State Camp for Veterans (Soldiers and
   Sailors Home).

BATH BEACH, CDP
New Utrecht Town
  Kings County

1890	1,619

BATH-ON-HUDSON, Village (Inc. 1874)(a)
North Greenbush Town
  Rensselaer County

1900	2,504
1890	2,399
1880	2,046(b)
1870	1,465(c)

(a)Dissolved; date unavailable.
(b)Reported as Bath-on-the-Hudson.
(c)Reported as Bath.

BATTENVILLE, CDP
Greenwich Town
  Washington County

1880	142

BAXTER ESTATES, Village (Inc. 1931)
North Hempstead Town
Nassau County
1980   911
1970   1,026 Rev.
1960   932
1950   862
1940   760

BAXTERTOWN, CDP
Wappinger Town
Dutchess County
1880   30

BAYBERRY--LYNELLE MEADOWS, CDP
Clay & Pompey Towns
Onondaga County
1980   14,813

BAY ISLANDS
Hempstead Town
Nassau County
1980   0(a)
1970   13(a)
1960   27(b)
(a)Derived by LIRPB from U.S. Census
Data.
(b)Derived by LIRPB from U.S. Census
Data; reported by LIRPB as Offshore
Islands.

BAY PARK
Hempstead Town
Nassau County
1980   2,353(a)
1970   2,470(a)
1960   2,467(a)
(a)Derived by LIRPB from U.S. Census
Data.

BAYPORT, CDP
Islip Town
Suffolk County
1980   9,282
1970   8,232
1960   5,009(a)
1950   1,463
1940   1,509
1890-1930   NA
1880   481
(a)Derived by LIRPB from U.S. Census
Data.

BAY RIDGE, CDP
New Utrecht Town
Kings County
1890   1,858

BAY SHORE, CDP
Islip Town
Suffolk County
1980   10,784(a)
1970   11,119(a)
1960   9,802(b)
1950   9,665
1940   8,631
1900-1930   NA
1890   2,290(c)
1880   1,615(c)

1870   1,200
(a)Includes crew on vessel.
(b)Derived by LIRPB from U.S. Census
Data.
(c)Reported as Bayshore.

BAYVIEW
see NORTH SOUTHOLD--BAYVIEW
Suffolk County

BAYVILLE, Unincorporated
Oyster Bay Town
Nassau County
1980   487(a)
1970   500(a)
1960   208(a)
(a)Derived by LIRPB from U.S. Census
Data.

BAYVILLE, Village (Inc. 1919)
Oyster Bay Town
Nassau County
1980   7,034
1970   6,147
1960   3,962(a)
1950   1,981
1940   1,516
1930   1,042
(a)Boundary change.

BEACON, City (Inc. 1913)(a)
Dutchess County
1980   12,937
1970   13,255
1960   13,922
1950   14,012
1940   12,572
1930   11,933
1920   10,996
1910   10,629
1900   9,480
(a)FISHKILL LANDING and MATTEAWAN Villages consolidated and incorporated
as BEACON City and made independent
of FISHKILL Town in 1913.

BEAVERDAM LAKE, CDP
Blooming Grove, Cornwall & New Windsor
Towns
Orange County
1980   1,324(a)
(a)Part in BLOOMING GROVE, 13; part in
CORNWALL, 475; part in NEW WINDSOR,
836.

BEAVER FALLS, CDP
Croghan & New Bremen Towns
Lewis County
1940   639

BEAVER MEADOWS, CDP
Otselic Town
Chenango County
1880   105

BEDFORD, CDP
Bedford Town
Westchester County
1980   1,633

```
        1950-1970        NA
        1940             893(a)
        1890-1930        NA
        1880             181
(a)Reported as Bedford Village.

BEDFORD, Town (Est. 1788)
    Westchester County
        1980          15,137(a)
        1970          18,329
        1960          14,656
        1950          10,888
        1940           9,248
        1930           8,653
        1920           5,905
        1910           5,629
        1900           3,497
        1890           3,291
        1880           3,731
        1870           3,697
        1860           3,639
        1850           3,207
        1840           2,822
        1830           2,750
        1820           2,432
        1810             NA
        1800          *2,404
        1790           2,470
(a)Boundary change.

BEDFORD HILLS, CDP
  Bedford Town
    Westchester County
        1940           1,407

BEDFORD STATION, CDP
  Bedford Town
    Westchester County
        1880             209

BEDFORD VILLAGE, CDP
  see BEDFORD, CDP
    Westchester County

BEDLOE ISLAND, CDP
  New York County
        1860               4

BEECHEN HOLLOW, CDP
  Edinburg Town
    Saratoga County
        1880             107

BEEKMAN, CDP
  Beekman Town
    Dutchess County
        1880             105

BEEKMAN, Town (Est. 1788)
    Dutchess County
        1980           7,139
        1970           5,701
        1960           3,326
        1950           1,703
        1940             790
        1930             764
        1920             844
        1910             827
        1900           1,071
```

```
        1890           1,113
        1880           1,578
        1870           1,486
        1860           1,371
        1850           1,386
        1840           1,400
        1830           1,584
        1820           4,257
        1810             NA
        1800          *3,756
        1790           3,597

BEEKMANTOWN, CDP
  Mount Pleasant Town
    Westchester County
        1870           2,206

BEEKMANTOWN, Town (Est. 1820)
    Clinton County
        1980           4,275
        1970           3,189
        1960           2,538
        1950           1,690
        1940           1,704
        1930           1,533
        1920           1,590
        1910           1,866
        1900           2,067
        1890           2,159
        1880           2,644
        1870           2,552
        1860           2,977
        1850           3,384
        1840           2,769
        1830           2,391
        1820           1,343

BELCHER, CDP
  Hebron Town
    Washington County
        1880              57

BELFAST, CDP
  Belfast Town
    Allegany County
        1940             646
        1900-1930        NA
        1890             600
        1880             405

BELFAST, Town (Est. 1824)(a)
    Allegany County
        1980           1,495
        1970           1,339
        1960           1,265
        1950           1,277
        1940           1,213
        1930           1,113
        1920           1,279
        1910           1,773
        1900           1,574
        1890           1,500
        1880           1,470
        1870           1,488
        1860           1,827
        1850           1,679
        1840           1,646
        1830             743
(a)Established as Orrinsburgh in 1824;
```

name changed in 1825.

BELFORT, CDP
  Croghan Town
    Lewis County
      1880   132

BELGIUM, CDP
  Clay Town
    Onondaga County
      1870   166

BELLE ISLE, CDP
  Camillus Town
    Onondaga County
      1870   68

BELLEROSE, Village (Inc. 1924)
  Hempstead Town
    Nassau County
      1980   1,187
      1970   1,136 Rev.
      1960   1,083
      1950   1,134
      1940   1,317
      1930   1,202

BELLEROSE TERRACE
  Hempstead Town
    Nassau County
      1980   1,951(a)
      1970   2,090(a)
      1960   2,314(a)
(a)Derived by LIRPB from U.S. Census
    Data.

BELLE TERRE, Village (Inc. 1931)
  Brookhaven Town
    Suffolk County
      1980   826
      1970   678
      1960   295
      1950   120
      1940   89

BELLEVILLE, Village (Inc. 1860)(a)
  Ellisburg Town
    Jefferson County
      1920   306
      1910   344
      1900   384
      1890   452
      1880   462
(a)Dissolved in 1929.

BELLEVUE--HOMEWOOD PARK, CDP
  Cheektowaga Town
    Erie County
      1940   594

BELLMONT, Town (Est. 1833)
  Franklin County
      1980   1,045
      1970   1,055
      1960   1,088
      1950   1,186
      1940   1,279(a)
      1930   1,303

      1920   1,552(b)
      1910   2,341(b)
      1900   2,414
      1890   2,263(b)
      1880   2,098(b)
      1870   1,619(b)
      1860   1,376(b)
      1850   660(b)
      1840   472
(a)Reported as Bellmar.
(b)Reported as Belmont.

BELLMORE, CDP
  Hempstead Town
    Nassau County
      1980   18,106
      1970   18,431
      1960   12,784
      1950   NA
      1940   6,793

BELLONA, CDP
  Benton Town
    Yates County
      1880   197

BELLONA, Town
  see LE ROY, Town
    Genesee County

BELLPORT, Village (Inc. 1910)
  Brookhaven Town
    Suffolk County
      1980   2,809
      1970   3,046(a)
      1960   2,461
      1950   1,449
      1940   650
      1930   633
      1920   614
      1910   419
      1890-1900   NA
      1880   297
(a)Boundary change.

BELLPORT STATION, CDP
  Brookhaven Town
    Suffolk County
      1880   32

BELLVALE, CDP
  Warwick Town
    Orange County
      1880   197

BELMONT, CDP
  West Farms Town
    Westchester County
      1870   171

BELMONT, Town
  see BELLMONT Town
    Franklin County

BELMONT, Village (Inc. 1871)
  Amity Town
    Allegany County
      1980   1,024
      1970   1,102

1960	1,146
1950	1,211
1940	1,146
1930	1,085
1920	1,021
1910	1,094
1900	1,190
1890	950
1880	804
1870	795

BEMUS POINT, Village (Inc. 1911)
  Ellery Town
    Chautauqua County

1980	444
1970	487
1960	443
1950	424
1940	290
1930	280
1920	227

BENGAL, Town
  see VIENNA, Town
        Oneida County

BENNETTSBURGH, CDP
  Hector Town
    Schuyler County

1880	113

BENNINGTON, Town (Est. 1818)
  Wyoming County

1980	2,889
1970	2,544
1960	1,983
1950	1,558
1940	1,481
1930	1,515
1920	1,557
1910	1,742
1900	1,904
1890	2,029
1880	2,365
1870	2,385
1860	2,618
1850	2,406
1840	2,368(a)
1830	2,224(a)
1820	796(a)

(a)Reported in GENESEE County.

BENNINGTON CENTER, CDP
  Bennington Town
    Wyoming County

1880	102(a)

(a)Reported as Bennington Centre.

BENSON, Town (Est. 1860)
  Hamilton County

1980	156
1970	89
1960	87
1950	85
1940	89
1930	69
1920	119
1910	143
1900	299

1890	322
1880	402
1870	320
1860	380

BENTON, Town (Est. 1803)(a)
  Yates County

1980	1,981
1970	2,159
1960	2,093
1950	1,866
1940	1,879
1930	1,845
1920	1,797
1910	2,032
1900	2,179
1890	2,291
1880	2,413
1870	2,422
1860	2,462
1850	3,456
1840	3,911
1830	3,957
1820	3,357(b)

(a)Established as Vernon in 1803; name
   changed to Snell in 1808 and to BENTON
   in 1810.
(b)Reported in ONTARIO County.

BENTON CENTER, CDP
  Benton Town
    Yates County

1880	144(a)

(a)Reported as Benton Centre.

BERGEN, Town (Est. 1812)
  Genesee County

1980	2,568
1970	2,281
1960	1,996
1950	1,588
1940	1,412
1930	1,512
1920	1,497
1910	1,631
1900	1,699
1890	1,830
1880	2,002
1870	1,997
1860	2,008
1850	1,897
1840	1,832
1830	1,508
1820	2,438

BERGEN, Village (Inc. 1877)
  Bergen Town
    Genesee County

1980	976(a)
1970	1,018(a)
1960	964
1950	786
1940	658
1930	724
1920	576
1910	637
1900	624
1890	623
1880	675

(a)Boundary change.

BERKSHIRE, CDP
  Johnstown Town
    Fulton County
      1980   1,095

BERKSHIRE, Town (Est. 1808)
  Tioga County
      1980   1,335
      1970   1,098
      1960   953
      1950   912
      1940   861
      1930   771
      1920   805
      1910   846
      1900   1,011
      1890   1,160
      1880   1,304
      1870   1,240
      1860   1,151
      1850   1,049
      1840   956
      1830   1,711
      1820   1,502(a)
(a)Reported in BROOME County.

BERLIN, CDP
  Berlin Town
    Rensselaer County
      1880   465

BERLIN, Town (Est. 1806)
  Rensselaer County
      1980   1,696
      1970   1,562
      1960   1,329
      1950   1,409
      1940   1,402
      1930   1,359
      1920   1,305
      1910   1,615
      1900   1,677
      1890   1,704
      1880   2,202
      1870   2,088
      1860   2,223
      1850   2,005
      1840   1,794
      1830   2,019
      1820   1,986

BERNE, Town (Est. 1795)
  Albany County
      1980   2,532
      1970   2,037
      1960   1,542
      1950   1,348
      1940   1,325
      1930   1,210
      1920   1,371
      1910   1,753
      1900   1,947
      1890   2,273
      1880   2,616
      1870   2,562
      1860   3,065
      1850   3,441

      1840   3,740
      1830   3,607(a)
      1820   5,531(a)
      1810   NA
      1800   *3,486(a)
(a)Reported as Bern.

BERNEVILLE, CDP
  Berne Town
    Albany County
      1870   250

BERNHARDS BAY, CDP
  Constantia Town
    Oswego County
      1880   222(a)
(a)Reported as Bernhard's Bay.

BETHANY, Town (Est. 1812)
  Genesee County
      1980   1,876
      1970   1,978
      1960   1,569
      1950   1,410
      1940   1,231
      1930   1,254
      1920   1,196
      1910   1,270
      1900   1,330
      1890   1,517
      1880   1,671
      1870   1,652
      1860   1,897
      1850   1,904
      1840   2,286
      1830   2,374
      1820   1,691

BETHANY CENTER, CDP
  Bethany Town
    Genesee County
      1880   87(a)
(a)Reported as Bethany Centre.

BETHEL, Town (Est. 1809)
  Sullivan County
      1980   3,335
      1970   2,763
      1960   2,366
      1950   2,351
      1940   2,321
      1930   1,799
      1920   1,849
      1910   2,164
      1900   2,248
      1890   2,158
      1880   2,562
      1870   2,736
      1860   2,854
      1850   2,087
      1840   1,483
      1830   1,192
      1820   1,096

BETHLEHEM, Town (Est. 1793)
  Albany County
      1980   24,296(a)
      1970   23,427(a)
      1960   18,936

1950	13,065
1940	9,782(a)
1930	7,160(a)
1920	4,430(a)
1910	4,413
1900	4,226
1890	4,187
1880	3,752
1870	6,950
1860	5,644
1850	4,102
1840	3,238
1830	6,082
1820	5,114
1810	NA
1800	*3,733

(a)Boundary change.

BETHPAGE, CDP
  Oyster Bay Town
    Nassau County

1980	16,840
1970	18,555
1960	15,840(a)
1950	NA
1940	2,590(b)

(a)Derived by LIRPB from U.S. Census
   Data. U.S. Census reported as part of
   BETHPAGE--OLD BETHPAGE with a population of 20,515.
(b)Reported as Central Park, CDP in HEMP-
   STEAD and OYSTER BAY Towns; name
   changed in 1936.

BETHPAGE--OLD BETHPAGE, CDP
  see BETHPAGE & OLD BETHPAGE, CDPs
    Nassau County

BICKNELLVILLE, CDP
  Stockholm Town
    St. Lawrence County

1880	184

BIG FLATS, CDP
  Big Flats Town
    Chemung County

1980	2,892
1970	2,509
1950-1960	NA
1940	523

BIG FLATS, Town (Est. 1822)
  Chemung County

1980	7,649
1970	6,837
1960	3,665
1950	2,460
1940	1,832
1930	1,679
1920	1,454
1910	1,535
1900	1,705
1890	1,687
1880	1,989
1870	1,902
1860	1,853
1850	1,709
1840	1,375
1830	1,149(a)

(a)Reported as Big Flatts in TIOGA
   County.

BILLINGTON HEIGHTS, CDP
  Aurora Town
    Erie County

1980	1,782
1970	1,278

BINGHAM'S MILLS, CDP
  Livingston Town
    Columbia County

1880	123

BINGHAMTON, City (Inc. 1867)(a)
  Broome County

1980	55,860
1970	64,123
1960	75,941(b)
1950	80,674(b)
1940	78,309
1930	76,662
1920	66,800
1910	48,443
1900	39,647
1890	35,005
1880	17,317
1870	12,692

(a)BINGHAMTON Village (Inc. 1813) incorporated as BINGHAMTON City and made
   independent of BINGHAMTON Town in
   1867.
(b)Boundary change.

BINGHAMTON, Town (Est. 1855)
  Broome County

1980	5,007
1970	4,844
1960	3,475
1950	2,073
1940	1,576
1930	1,092
1920	672
1910	675
1900	847(a)
1890	1,519
1880	2,555
1870	2,066(a)
1860	8,325

(a)Boundary change.

BINGHAMTON, Village
  see BINGHAMTON, City
    Broome County

BIRDSALL, Town (Est. 1829)
  Allegany County

1980	257
1970	175
1960	160
1950	249
1940	306
1930	364
1920	464
1910	568
1900	634
1890	883
1880	890
1870	755

1860	909
1850	597
1840	328
1830	543

BIRMINGHAM, CDP
AuSable & Chesterfield Towns
Clinton & Essex Counties

1880	200

BLACK BROOK, Town (Est. 1839)
Clinton County

1980	1,505
1970	1,484
1960	1,595
1950	1,611
1940	1,806
1930	1,692
1920	1,822
1910	1,959
1900	1,933
1890	2,256
1880	3,365
1870	3,561(a)
1860	3,452
1850	2,525
1840	1,064

(a)Reported as Blackbrook.

BLACK CREEK, CDP
New Hudson Town
Allegany County

1880	130

BLACK RIVER, Village (Inc. 1891)
Le Ray Town, part in
Jefferson County

1980	824
1970	720(a)
1960	662
1950	598
1940	535
1930	514
1920	459
1910	485
1900	498
1890	NA
1880	195

Rutland Town, part in
Jefferson County

1980	560
1970	587(a)
1960	575
1950	464
1940	362
1930	409
1920	478
1910	431
1900	451
1880-1890	NA
1870	181

TOTAL

1980	1,384
1970	1,307(a)
1960	1,237
1950	1,062
1940	897
1930	923
1920	937

1910	916
1900	949
1890	NA
1880	(b)
1870	(c)

(a)Boundary change.
(b)Reported in LE RAY Town only.
(c)Reported in RUTLAND Town only.

BLACK ROCK, Town (Est. 1810)(a)
Erie County

1850	7,508
1840	4,625(b)
1830	8,668
1820	2,095(c)
1810	1,508

(a)Established as Buffalo in 1810; name
   changed in 1839. Town merged into
   BUFFALO City in 1853.
(b)Boundary change.
(c)Reported as Buffaloe.

BLACKWELL'S ISLAND, CDP
New York County

1860	4,581

BLASDELL, Village (Inc. 1898)
Hamburg Town
Erie County

1980	3,288
1970	3,910
1960	3,909(a)
1950	3,127
1940	2,322
1930	2,015
1920	1,401
1910	849
1900	415

(a)Boundary change.

BLAUVELT, CDP
Orangetown Town
Rockland County

1970	5,426
1950-1960	NA
1940	716
1890-1930	NA
1880	586(a)

(a)Reported as Blauveltville.

BLEECKER, Town (Est. 1831)
Fulton County

1980	463
1970	294
1960	245
1950	220
1940	190
1930	202
1920	389
1910	500
1900	603
1890	816
1880	1,046
1870	970
1860	1,062(a)
1850	510(a)
1840	346

(a)Reported as Bleeker.

BLENHEIM, CDP
  Blenheim Town
    Schoharie County
      1880   221

BLENHEIM, Town (Est. 1797)
    Schoharie County
      1980   292
      1970   260
      1960   345
      1950   378
      1940   415
      1930   397
      1920   516
      1910   616
      1900   768
      1890   951
      1880   1,191
      1870   1,437
      1860   1,367
      1850   1,314
      1840   2,725
      1830   2,271
      1820   1,826
      1810   NA
      1800   *783

BLOCKVILLE, CDP
  Harmony Town
    Chautauqua County
      1880   107
      1870   200

BLOOD'S, CDP
  Cohocton Town
    Steuben County
      1880   294

BLOODVILLE, CDP
  Milton Town
    Saratoga County   492

BLOOMFIELD, CDP
  Northfield Town
    Richmond County
      1880   149

BLOOMFIELD, Town
  see EAST BLOOMFIELD, Town
    Ontario County

BLOOMINGBURG, Village (Inc. 1924)
  Mamakating Town
    Sullivan County
      1980   338
      1970   323
      1960   303(a)
      1950   263(a)
      1940   197(a)
      1930   215(a)
(a)Reported as Bloomingburgh.

BLOOMINGDALE, Village (Inc. 1905)
  St. Armand Town
    Essex County
      1980   608
      1970   536
      1960   490
      1950   476

      1940   446
      1930   420
      1920   298 Rev.(a)
      1910   382
(a)In 1930 the Census Bureau revised the
   1920 figure of 490 to exclude the
   Trudeau Sanitorium.

BLOOMING GROVE, CDP
  Blooming Grove Town
    Orange County
      1980   1,151

BLOOMING GROVE, Town (Est. 1799)
    Orange County
      1980   12,339
      1970   8,813
      1960   3,777
      1950   2,410
      1940   2,312
      1930   1,922
      1920   1,881
      1910   2,110
      1900   2,188
      1890   2,236
      1880   2,444
      1870   2,502
      1860   2,248
      1850   2,184
      1840   2,396
      1830   2,099
      1820   2,219
      1810   NA
      1800   *1,611(a)
(a)Reported as Bloomingrove.

BLOOMINGTON--HICKORY BUSH, CDP
  Rosendale Town
    Ulster County
      1980   1,002

BLOOMVILLE, CDP
  Kortright Town
    Delaware County
      1880   229

BLOSSOM'S MILLS, CDP
  Elma Town
    Erie County
      1870   99

BLUE POINT, CDP
  Brookhaven Town
    Suffolk County
      1980   4,096(a)
      1970   3,133(b)
      1960   2,358(c)
      1950   1,613(d)
      1940   1,234
      1890-1930   NA
      1880   372
(a)Boundary change; derived by LIRPB from
   U.S. Census Data.
(b)Derived by LIRPB from U.S. Census
   Data; population of 4,738 is comparable to 1980 boundaries.
(c)Derived by LIRPB from U.S. Census
   Data.
(d)Includes 78 people reported in ISLIP

Town.

BLUE STORE, CDP
  Livingston Town
    Columbia County
      1880   49

BOHEMIA, CDP
  Islip Town
    Suffolk County
      1980   9,308(a)
      1970   8,926(b)
      1960   2,860(c)
      1950   NA
      1940   765
      1890-1930   NA
      1880   133
(a)Boundary change.
(b)Population of 7,623 is comparable to
   1980 boundaries.
(c)Derived by LIRPB from U.S. Census
   Data.

BOLIVAR, Town (Est. 1825)
    Allegany County
      1980   2,496
      1970   2,391
      1960   2,441
      1950   2,680
      1940   2,628
      1930   2,813
      1920   1,979
      1910   2,282
      1900   2,035
      1890   2,233
      1880   1,029
      1870   959
      1860   959
      1850   708
      1840   408
      1830   449

BOLIVAR, Village (Inc. 1882)
  Bolivar Town
    Allegany County
      1980   1,345
      1970   1,379
      1960   1,405
      1950   1,490
      1940   1,344
      1930   1,725
      1920   1,146
      1910   1,318
      1900   1,208
      1890   NA
      1880   180

BOLTON, Town (Est. 1799)
    Warren County
      1980   1,793
      1970   1,589
      1960   1,417
      1950   1,184
      1940   1,310
      1930   1,308
      1920   1,184
      1910   1,518
      1900   1,363
      1890   1,387

      1880   1,132
      1870   1,135
      1860   1,289
      1850   1,147
      1840   937
      1830   1,467
      1820   1,087
      1810   NA
      1800   *959(a)
(a)Reported in WASHINGTON County.

BOLTON LANDING, CDP
  Bolton Town
    Warren County
      1940   619

BOMBAY, Town (Est. 1833)
    Franklin County
      1980   1,247
      1970   1,117
      1960   1,103
      1950   1,102
      1940   1,140
      1930   1,216
      1920   1,251
      1910   1,339 Rev.(a)
      1900   1,489 Rev.(a)
      1890   1,496
      1880   1,644
      1870   1,488
      1860   2,440
      1850   1,963
      1840   1,446
(a)In 1920 the Census Bureau revised the
   1910 figure of 2,588 and the 1900
   figure of 2,742 to exclude the ST.
   REGIS INDIAN RESERVATION.

BOONVILLE, Town (Est. 1805)
    Oneida County
      1980   4,094
      1970   3,947
      1960   3,786
      1950   3,593
      1940   3,201
      1930   3,320
      1920   3,147
      1910   3,191
      1900   3,332
      1890   3,509
      1880   3,996
      1870   4,106
      1860   4,212
      1850   3,306(a)
      1840   1,519
      1830   2,746
      1820   1,294
(a)Reported as Booneville.

BOONVILLE, Village (Inc. 1855)
  Boonville Town
    Oneida County
      1980   2,344
      1970   2,488(a)
      1960   2,403
      1950   2,329
      1940   2,076
      1930   2,090
      1920   1,914

1910	1,794
1900	1,745
1890	1,613
1880	1,677
1870	1,418

(a)Boundary change.

BORODINO, CDP
Spafford Town
Onondaga County

1880	160

BOSTON, CDP
Boston Town
Erie County

1880	226

BOSTON, Town (Est. 1817)
Erie County

1980	7,687
1970	7,158
1960	5,106
1950	2,302
1940	1,710
1930	1,368
1920	1,325
1910	1,535
1900	1,398
1890	1,278
1880	1,617
1870	1,633
1860	1,716
1850	1,872
1840	1,745
1830	1,521
1820	686(a)

(a)Reported in NIAGARA County.

BOUCKVILLE, CDP
Madison Town
Madison County

1880	204

BOVINA, Town (Est. 1820)
Delaware County

1980	562
1970	506
1960	594
1950	711
1940	806
1930	771
1920	858
1910	912
1900	932
1890	1,007
1880	1,022
1870	1,022
1860	1,242
1850	1,316
1840	1,403
1830	1,348
1820	1,267

BOWERSVILLE, Town
see CONESUS, Town
Livingston County

BOWMANSVILLE, CDP
Lancaster Town
Erie County

1880	120

BOYLE, Town
see BRIGHTON & PITTSFORD, Towns
Monroe County

BOYLSTON, Town (Est. 1828)
Oswego County

1980	390
1970	276
1960	293
1950	302
1940	365
1930	444
1920	545
1910	667
1900	849
1890	1,081
1880	1,283
1870	1,053
1860	909
1850	661
1840	481
1830	388

BOYSEN BAY, CDP
Cicero Town
Onondaga County

1980	1,160
1970	1,191

BRADFORD, CDP
Bradford Town
Steuben County

1880	207

BRADFORD, Town (Est. 1836)
Steuben County

1980	724
1970	630
1960	558
1950	510
1940	486
1930	507
1920	570
1910	613
1900	771
1890	765
1880	937
1870	1,080
1860	1,211
1850	2,010
1840	1,547

BRAINARD, CDP
Nassau Town
Rensselaer County

1880	83
1870	168

BRAMAN'S CORNERS, CDP
Duanesburg Town
Schenectady County

1880	67

BRANCH, CDP(a)
    Ballston Town
        Saratoga County
            1880   80
(a)Also called SOUTH BALLSTON.

BRANCH, Village
    see VILLAGE OF THE BRANCH, Village
            Suffolk County

BRANCHPORT, Village (Inc. 1867)(a)
    Jerusalem Town
        Yates County
            1890   273
            1880   271
(a)Dissolved a few years later.

BRANDON, CDP
    Santa Clara Town
        Franklin County
            1890   755

BRANDON, Town (Est. 1828)
    Franklin County
            1980   499
            1970   333
            1960   369
            1950   357
            1940   489
            1930   516
            1920   728
            1910   872
            1900   938
            1890   892(a)
            1880   815
            1870   692
            1860   794
            1850   590
            1840   531
            1830   316
(a)Boundary change.

BRANT, Town (Est. 1839)
    Erie County
            1980   2,437
            1970   2,672
            1960   2,290
            1950   1,934
            1940   1,753
            1930   1,693
            1920   1,830
            1910   2,125 Rev.(a)
            1900   1,720 Rev.(a)
            1890   1,396
            1880   1,527(b)
            1870   1,359(b)
            1860   1,097(b)
            1850   1,028(b)
            1840   1,088(b)
(a)In 1920 the Census Bureau revised the
    1910 figure of 2,424 and the 1900
    figure of 2,005 to exclude the
    CATTARAUGUS INDIAN RESERVATION.
(b)Reported as Brandt.

BRANT LAKE, CDP
    Horicon Town
        Warren County
            1940   585

BRANTINGHAM, Town
    see GREIG, Town
            Lewis County

BRASHER, Town (Est. 1825)
    St. Lawrence County
            1980   2,375
            1970   2,410
            1960   2,536
            1950   1,916
            1940   1,892
            1930   1,706
            1920   1,922
            1910   2,179
            1900   2,703
            1890   2,910
            1880   3,578
            1870   3,342
            1860   3,377(a)
            1850   2,582(a)
            1840   2,118
            1830   826
(a)Reported as Brashear.

BRASHER FALLS, CDP
    Brasher Town
        St. Lawrence County
            1940   565
            1900-1930   NA
            1890   570
            1880   513
            1870   450
(a)Reported as BRASHER FALLS--WINTHROP,
    CDP in 1980.

BRASHER FALLS--WINTHROP, CDP
    Brasher, Stockholm & Russell Towns
        St. Lawrence County
            1980   1,454

BRASHER IRON WORKS, CDP
    Brasher Town
        St. Lawrence County
            1870   250

BREESPORT, CDP
    Horseheads Town
        Chemung County
            1880   420
            1870   292

BRENTWOOD, CDP
    Islip Town
        Suffolk County
            1980   44,321(a)
            1970   28,327 Rev.(b)
            1960   15,387
            1950   2,803
            1940   1,704
            1890-1930   NA
            1880   125
(a)Boundary change.
(b)Population of 46,682 is comparable to
    1980 boundaries.

BRESLAU, CDP
    see LINDENHURST, Village
            Suffolk County

BREWERTON, CDP
  Cicero Town, part in
    Onondaga County, part in

1980	1,586
1970	1,201
1950-1960	NA
1940	562
1900-1930	NA
1890	336
1880	305
1870	322
1860	640

  Hastings Town, part in
    Oswego County, part in

1980	384
1880-1970	NA
1870	196

  West Monroe Town, part in
    Oswego County, part in

1980	502

    TOTAL

1980	2,472
1970	1,985
1950-1960	NA
1940	(a)
1900-1930	NA
1880-1890	(a)
1870	518(b)
1860	(a)

(a)Reported in CICERO Town only.
(b)Reported in CICERO and HASTINGS Towns
only.

BREWSTER, Village (Inc. 1894)
  Southeast Town
    Putnam County

1980	1,650
1970	1,638
1960	1,714
1950	1,810
1940	1,863
1930	1,664
1920	859
1910	1,296
1900	1,192

BREWSTER HEIGHTS, CDP
  Southeast Town
    Putnam County

1980	1,054
1970	1,265

BREWSTER HILLS, CDP
  Southeast Town
    Putnam County

1980	2,371(a)
1970	1,745

(a)Reported as Brewster Hill.

BRIARCLIFF MANOR, Village (Inc. 1902)
  Mount Pleasant Town, part in
    Westchester County

1980	795
1970	629
1960	535
1950	407
1940	383
1930	340
1920	5(a)
1910	23

  Ossining Town, part in
    Westchester County

1980	6,320
1970	5,892
1960	4,570(b)
1950	2,087
1940	1,447
1930	1,454
1920	1,022(a)
1910	927

    TOTAL

1980	7,115
1970	6,521
1960	5,105(b)
1950	2,494
1940	1,830
1930	1,794
1920	1,027(a)
1910	950

(a)Boundary change.
(b)Reported as Briar Cliff Manor.

BRIDGEHAMPTON, CDP
  Southampton Town
    Suffolk County

1980	1,941(a)
1970	902(b)
1960	862(c)
1950	NA
1940	1,462
1900-1930	NA
1890	1,394
1880	1,253
1870	1,334

(a)Boundary change.
(b)Derived by LIRPB from U.S. Census
   Data; population of 2,138 is comparable to 1980 boundaries.
(c)Derived by LIRPB from U.S. Census
   Data.

BRIDGEPORT, CDP
  Sullivan Town
    Madison County

1880	212
1870	217

BRIDGEPORT, CDP
  Hempstead Town
    Nassau County

1880	122

BRIDGEWATER, Town (Est. 1797)
  Oneida County

1980	1,455
1970	1,251
1960	966
1950	806
1940	743
1930	730
1920	746
1910	832
1900	931
1890	1,073
1880	1,218
1870	1,258
1860	1,261
1850	1,315

1840	1,418
1830	1,608
1820	1,533
1810	NA
1800	*1,061

BRIDGEWATER, Village (Inc. 1825)
Bridgewater Town
Oneida County

1980	578
1970	601
1960	373
1950	309
1940	238
1930	228
1920	232
1910	245
1900	269
1890	NA
1880	224
1870	230

BRIER HILL, CDP
Morristown Town
St. Lawrence County

1880	185

BRIGHTON, Town (Est. 1859)
Franklin County

1980	1,625
1970	1,473
1960	1,092
1950	962
1940	804
1930	993
1920	684
1910	741
1900	706
1890	480
1880	267
1870	204
1860	208

BRIGHTON, Town (Est. 1814)(a)
Monroe County

1980	35,776(b)
1970	35,065
1960	27,849(b)
1950	18,036(b)
1940	13,132
1930	9,065(b)
1920	3,027 Rev.(c)
1910	3,998
1900	3,815(b)
1890	4,533
1880	3,736
1870	4,304
1860	3,183
1850	3,117
1840	2,336
1830	3,128
1820	1,972(d)

(a)Established as Northfield in ONTARIO County in 1789; name changed to Boyle in 1808 and to Smallwood in 1813. Divided into BRIGHTON and PITTSFORD in 1814.
(b)Boundary change.
(c)Boundary change. In 1930 the Census

Bureau revised the 1920 figure of 2,911 to include the Iola Sanitorium.
(d)Reported in ONTARIO County.

BRIGHTON, Village (Inc. 1885)(a)
Brighton Town
Monroe County

1900	888
1890	705
1880	198

(a)Merged into ROCHESTER City in 1905.

BRIGHTWATERS, Village (Inc. 1916)
Islip Town
Suffolk County

1980	3,286
1970	3,808
1960	3,193
1950	2,336
1940	1,562
1930	1,061
1920	250

BRINCKERHOFF, CDP
Fishkill Town
Dutchess County

1980	3,030
1970	2,094

BRISBEN, CDP
Greene Town
Chenango County

1880	97(a)

(a)Reported as Brisbin.

BRISTOL, Town (Est. 1789)
Ontario County

1980	1,802
1970	1,307
1960	1,002
1950	915
1940	750
1930	743
1920	896
1910	1,247
1900	1,310
1890	1,510
1880	1,650
1870	1,551
1860	1,657
1850	1,733
1840	1,953
1830	2,953
1820	2,429
1810	NA
1800	*751

BRISTOL, Town
Schoharie County
see BROOME, Town
Schoharie County

BROADALBIN, Town (Est. 1793)
Fulton County

1980	4,074
1970	3,542
1960	2,945
1950	2,543
1940	2,300

1930	2,226
1920	1,949
1910	1,845
1900	1,946
1890	2,021
1880	2,175
1870	2,492
1860	2,534
1850	2,476
1840	2,738
1830	2,655(a)
1820	2,428(a)
1810	NA
1800	*1,133(a)

(a)Reported in MONTGOMERY County.

BROADALBIN, Village (Inc. 1924)
  Broadalbin Town, part in
    Fulton County

1980	1,363
1970	1,449
1960	1,422
1950	1,391
1940	1,399
1930	1,341
1900-1920	NA
1890	708

  Mayfield Town, part in
    Fulton County

1980	52
1970	3
1960	16
1950	9

  TOTAL

1980	1,415
1970	1,452
1960	1,438
1950	1,400
1890-1940	(a)

(a)Reported in BROADALBIN Town only.

BROCKPORT, Village (Inc. 1829)
  Clarkson Town, part in
  Monroe County

1980	0
1970	0
1960	0(a)

  Sweden Town, part in
  Monroe County

1980	9,776
1970	7,878(a)
1960	5,256
1950	4,748
1940	3,590
1930	3,511
1920	2,980
1910	3,579
1900	3,398
1890	3,742
1880	4,039
1870	2,817
1850-1860	NA
1840	1,249
1830	791

  TOTAL

1980	9,776
1970	7,878(a)
1960	5,256(a)
1830-1950	(b)

(a)Boundary change.
(b)Reported in SWEDEN Town only.

BROCKWAY, CDP
  Fishkill Town
    Dutchess County

1980	1,301

BROCTON, Village (Inc. 1894)
  Portland Town
    Chautauqua County

1980	1,416
1970	1,370
1960	1,416
1950	1,380
1940	1,293
1930	1,301
1920	1,383
1910	1,181
1900	900
1890	812
1880	288
1870	329

BRONX, Borough
  see NEW YORK City, BRONX Borough

BRONX, County (Est. 1914)(a)

1980	1,168,972 Rev.
1970	1,471,701
1960	1,424,815
1950	1,451,277
1940	1,394,711
1930	1,265,258
1920	732,016

(a)In 1914 BRONX County was established
  with the same boundaries as the
  Borough of the BRONX in NEW YORK
  City.

BRONXVILLE, Village (Inc. 1898)
  Eastchester Town
    Westchester County

1980	6,267
1970	6,674
1960	6,744
1950	6,778
1940	6,888
1930	6,387
1920	3,055
1910	1,863
1900	579
1890	NA
1880	395(a)

(a)Reported in WESTCHESTER Town.

BROOKFIELD, Town (Est. 1795)
  Madison County

1980	2,037
1970	2,064
1960	1,990
1950	1,841
1940	1,703
1930	1,750
1920	2,092
1910	2,403
1900	2,726
1890	3,262
1880	3,685

1870	3,565
1860	3,729
1850	3,585
1840	3,695
1830	4,367
1820	4,240
1810	NA
1800	*1,973(a)

(a)Reported in CHENANGO County.

BROOKFIELD, Village (Inc. 1887)(a)
Brookfield Town
Madison County

1920	317
1910	395
1900	485
1890	561

(a)Dissolved in 1922.

BROOKHAVEN, CDP
Brookhaven Town
Suffolk County

1980	3,050(a)
1970	2,268(b)
1960	1,312(c)
1950	NA
1940	518
1890-1930	NA
1880	182

(a)Boundary change; derived by LIRPB from U.S. Census Data.
(b)Derived by LIRPB from U.S. Census Data; population of 2,327 is comparable to 1980 boundaries.
(c)Derived by LIRPB from U.S. Census Data.

BROOKHAVEN, Town (Est. 1788)
Suffolk County

1980	364,812
1970	245,135 Rev.
1960	109,900
1950	44,522
1940	32,117
1930	28,291
1920	21,847
1910	16,737
1900	14,592
1890	12,772
1880	11,544
1870	10,159
1860	9,923
1850	8,595
1840	7,050
1830	6,095
1820	5,218
1810	4,176
1800	*4,022(a)
1790	3,224

(a)Reported as Brook Haven.

BROOKHAVEN NATIONAL LABORATORIES
Brookhaven Town
Suffolk County

1980	295(a)
1970	343(b)

(a)Boundary change; derived by LIRPB from U.S. Census Data.
(b)Derived by LIRPB from U.S. Census

Data; population is comparable to 1980 boundaries.

BROOKLYN, Borough
see NEW YORK City, BROOKLYN Borough

BROOKLYN, City (Inc. 1834)(a)
Kings County

1890	806,343(b)
1880	566,663
1870	396,099
1860	266,661
1850	96,838
1840	36,233
1830	12,406

(a)BROOKLYN Town and BROOKLYN Village (Inc. 1816) consolidated and incorporated as BROOKLYN City in 1834. Merged into BROOKLYN Borough, NEW YORK City in 1898.
(b)Boundary change.

BROOKLYN, Town (Est. 1788)(a)
Kings County

1830	2,988
1820	7,175
1810	NA
1800	*2,378(b)
1790	1,603

(a)BROOKLYN Town and BROOKLYN Village (Inc. 1816) consolidated and incorporated as BROOKLYN City in 1834.
(b)Reported as Brooklynn.

BROOKLYN, Village
see BROOKLYN, City
Kings County

BROOKLYNN, Town
see BROOKLYN, Town
Kings County

BROOKVILLE, Village (Inc. 1931)
Oyster Bay Town
Nassau County

1980	3,290
1970	3,212
1960	1,468(a)
1950	337
1940	204

(a)Boundary change.

BROOME, County (Est. 1806)

1980	213,648
1970	221,815
1960	212,661
1950	184,698
1940	165,749
1930	147,022
1920	113,610
1910	78,809
1900	69,149
1890	62,973
1880	49,483
1870	44,103
1860	35,906
1850	30,660
1840	22,338
1830	17,579

1820	14,343
1810	8,130

BROOME, Town (Est. 1797)(a)
    Schoharie County

1980	761
1970	551
1960	517
1950	635
1940	768
1930	650
1920	743
1910	933
1900	1,153
1890	1,367
1880	1,636
1870	1,834
1860	2,182
1850	2,268
1840	2,404
1830	3,133
1820	2,680
1810	NA
1800	*1,078

(a)Established as Bristol in 1797; name
    changed in 1908.

BROWNVILLE, Town (Est. 1802)
    Jefferson County

1980	5,113
1970	4,321
1960	3,985
1950	3,806
1940	3,671
1930	3,489
1920	3,856
1910	3,615
1900	3,698
1890	3,110
1880	2,624
1870	3,219
1860	3,966(a)
1850	4,282(a)
1840	3,968
1830	2,928
1820	3,990

(a)Reported as Brownsville.

BROWNVILLE, Village (Inc. 1828)
  Brownville Town
    Jefferson County

1980	1,099
1970	1,187
1960	1,082
1950	1,013
1940	907
1930	842
1920	976
1910	854
1900	767
1890	666
1880	409
1870	450

BROWNSVILLE, Town
  see BROWNVILLE, Town
    Jefferson County

BRUNSWICK, Town (Est. 1807)
    Rensselaer County

1980	10,974
1970	11,193
1960	9,004
1950	5,967
1940	4,917
1930	3,949
1920	2,812
1910	2,832(a)
1900	3,513
1890	3,654
1880	3,402
1870	3,128
1860	3,110
1850	3,146
1840	3,051
1830	2,575
1820	2,318

(a)Boundary change.

BRUSHLAND, CDP
  Bovina Town
    Delaware County

1880	140

BRUSHTON, Village (Inc. 1925)
  Moira Town
    Franklin County

1980	577
1970	547
1960	553
1950	516
1940	487
1930	470
1900-1920	NA
1890	598
1880	328

BRUTUS, Town (Est. 1802)
    Cayuga County

1980	4,212
1970	3,530
1960	2,804
1950	2,348
1940	2,188
1930	2,109
1920	2,186
1910	2,221
1900	2,582
1890	2,871
1880	2,736
1870	2,621
1860	2,598
1850	3,046
1840	2,044
1830	1,827
1820	3,579

BUCHANAN, Village (Inc. 1928)
  Cortlandt Town
    Westchester County

1980	2,041
1970	2,110
1960	2,019
1950	1,820
1940	1,600(a)
1930	1,346

(a)Boundary change.

BUCK MOUNTAIN, CDP
  Crown Point Town
    Essex County
      1880   76

BUCKTOOTH, Town
  see SALAMANCA, Town
      Cattaraugus County

BUFFALO, City (Inc. 1832)(a)
  Erie County
      1980   357,870
      1970   462,768
      1960   532,759
      1950   580,132
      1940   575,901
      1930   573,076
      1920   506,775
      1910   423,715
      1900   352,387
      1890   255,664
      1880   155,134
      1870   117,714
      1860   81,129(b)
      1850   42,261
      1840   18,213
(a)Buffalo Village (Inc. 1813) incorporated as BUFFALO City and made independent of BLACK ROCK Town in 1832.
(b)Boundary change.

BUFFALO, Town
  see BLACK ROCK, Town
      Erie County

BUFFALO, Village
  see BUFFALO, City
      Erie County

BURDETT, Village (Inc. 1898)
  Hector Town
    Schuyler County
      1980   410(a)
      1970   454
      1960   420
      1950   432
      1940   408
      1930   310
      1920   380
      1910   382
      1900   409
      1890   NA
      1880   292
(a)Boundary change.

BURKE, Town (Est. 1844)
  Franklin County
      1980   1,237
      1970   1,257
      1960   1,475
      1950   1,348
      1940   1,414
      1930   1,512
      1920   1,578
      1910   1,772
      1900   1,936
      1890   2,072
      1880   2,161
      1870   2,141

      1860   2,240
      1850   2,477

BURKE, Village (Inc. 1922)
  Burke Town
    Franklin County
      1980   226
      1970   237
      1960   273(a)
      1950   316
      1940   344
      1930   325
      1890-1920   NA
      1880   96
(a)Boundary change.

BURLINGTON, Town (Est. 1792)
  Otsego County
      1980   1,045
      1970   803
      1960   809
      1950   959
      1940   956
      1930   913
      1920   999
      1910   1,108
      1900   1,263
      1890   1,334
      1880   1,599
      1870   1,476
      1860   1,818
      1850   1,836
      1840   2,154
      1830   2,459
      1820   2,457
      1810   NA
      1800   *2,380

BURLINGTON FLATS, CDP
  Burlington Town
    Otsego County
      1880   124

BURLINGTON GREEN, CDP
  Burlington Town
    Otsego County
      1880   90

BURNS, CDP
  Dansville Town
    Steuben County
      1880   81

BURNS, Town (Est. 1826)
  Allegany County
      1980   1,211
      1970   1,256
      1960   1,238
      1950   1,185
      1940   1,187
      1930   1,152
      1920   1,214
      1910   1,524
      1900   1,424
      1890   1,506
      1880   1,671
      1870   1,340
      1860   1,064
      1850   943

1840	867
1830	702

BURNT HILLS, CDP
Ballston Town
Saratoga County

1880	180

BURT, Town
see MANCHESTER, Town
Ontario County

BURTON, Town
see ALLEGANY, Town
Cattaraugus County

BURTONVILLE, CDP
Charleston Town
Montgomery County

1880	138
1870	160

BUSHNELL'S BASIN, CDP
Perinton Town
Monroe County

1880	171

BUSHWICK, Town (Est. 1788)(a)
Kings County

1850	3,739
1840	1,295
1830	1,620(b)
1820	930
1810	NA
1800	*656
1790	540

(a)Merged into BROOKLYN City in 1854.
(b)Reported with WILLIAMSBURG Town.

BUSKIRK'S BRIDGE, CDP
White Creek Town
Washington County

1880	36

BUSTI, Town (Est. 1823)
Chautauqua County

1980	8,728
1970	8,367
1960	7,766
1950	5,806
1940	4,336
1930	3,508
1920	1,995
1910	2,136
1900	2,192
1890	2,089
1880	1,901
1870	1,844
1860	2,011
1850	1,990
1840	1,894
1830	1,680

BUSTI CORNERS, CDP
Busti Town
Chautauqua County

1870	278

BUTCHERVILLE, CDP
Northfield Town
Richmond County

1880	75

BUTLER, Town (Est. 1826)
Wayne County

1980	1,720
1970	1,593
1960	1,441
1950	1,429
1940	1,411
1930	1,384
1920	1,452
1910	1,610
1900	1,786
1890	1,836
1880	2,161
1870	2,023
1860	2,338
1850	2,272
1840	2,271
1830	1,764

BUTTERNUTS, CDP
Butternuts Town
Otsego County

1870	675

BUTTERNUTS, Town (Est. 1796)
Otsego County

1980	1,486
1970	1,433
1960	1,352
1950	1,315
1940	1,369
1930	1,260
1920	1,383
1910	1,453
1900	1,698
1890	1,813
1880	2,036
1870	2,174
1860	2,365
1850	1,928
1840	4,057
1830	3,991
1820	3,601(a)
1810	NA
1800	*1,388(a)

(a)Reported as Butternutts.

BUTTERVILLE, CDP
New Paltz Town
Ulster County

1880	35

BYRNESVILLE, CDP
Fishkill Town
Dutchess County

1880	217

BYRON, Town (Est. 1820)
Genesee County

1980	2,242
1970	2,020
1960	1,589
1950	1,381
1940	1,374

1930	1,347
1920	1,273
1910	1,520
1900	1,512
1890	1,578
1880	1,754
1870	1,734
1860	1,864
1850	1,566
1840	1,907
1830	1,936

BYRON CENTRE, CDP
Byron Town
Genesee County

1880	201

C

CADOSIA, CDP
Hancock Town
Delaware County

1940	641

CADYVILLE, CDP
Plattsburgh & Schuyler Falls Towns
Clinton County

1940	745

CAIRO, CDP
Cairo Town
Greene County

1980	1,281
1900-1970	NA
1890	573

CAIRO, Town (Est. 1803)(a)
Greene County

1980	4,729
1970	3,546
1960	2,825
1950	1,944
1940	1,905
1930	1,772
1920	1,487
1910	1,841
1900	2,176
1890	2,191
1880	2,287
1870	2,283
1860	2,479
1850	2,831
1840	2,862
1830	2,912
1820	2,353

(a)Established as Canton in 1803; name
changed in 1808.

CALDWELL, CDP
Caldwell Town
Warren County

1880	319

CALDWELL, Town
see LAKE GEORGE, Town
Warren County

CALEDONIA, Town (Est. 1802)(a)
Livingston County

1980	4,034
1970	3,832
1960	3,067
1950	2,529
1940	2,009
1930	2,305
1920	1,988
1910	2,248
1900	2,072
1890	2,188
1880	1,927
1870	1,813
1860	2,014
1850	1,804
1840	1,987
1830	1,618
1820	2,645(b)

(a)Established as Southampton in 1802;
name changed in 1806.
(b)Reported in GENESEE County.

CALEDONIA, Village (Inc. 1891)
Caledonia Town
Livingston County

1980	2,188(a)
1970	2,327(a)
1960	1,917(a)
1950	1,683
1940	1,226
1930	1,487
1920	1,170
1910	1,290
1900	1,073
1890	NA
1880	777
1870	597

(a)Boundary change

CALHOUN, Town
see MOUNT HOPE, Town
Orange County

CALLICOON, CDP
Delaware Town
Sullivan County

1940	602
1890-1930	NA
1880	310(a)

(a)Reported as Callicoon Depot.

CALLICOON, Town (Est. 1842)
Sullivan County

1980	2,998
1970	2,398
1960	2,176
1950	2,134
1940	2,092
1930	1,996

1920	1,739
1910	2,059
1900	2,054
1890	2,083
1880	2,180
1870	2,763
1860	2,771
1850	1,981

CALLICOON CENTER, CDP
Callicoon Town
    Sullivan County

1880	94(a)

(a)Reported as Callicoon Centre.

CALLICOON DEPOT, CDP
see CALLICOON, CDP
        Sullivan County

CALVERTON, CDP(a)
Riverhead Town
    Suffolk County

1970	2,303(b)
1960	1,327(b)
1950	NA
1940	590
1890-1930	NA
1880	210

(a)Included in CALVERTON--ROANOKE, CDP in 1980.
(b)Derived by LIRPB from U.S. Census Data.

CALVERTON--ROANOKE, CDP(a)
Riverhead Town
    Suffolk County

1980	4,952(b)
1970	3,832(c)

(a)Formerly included, in part, in CALVERTON and ROANOKE, CDPs.
(b)Boundary change.
(c)Derived by LIRPB from U.S. Census Data; population is comparable to 1980 boundaries.

CAMBDEN, Town
see CAMDEN, Town
        Oneida County

CAMBRIA, Town (Est. 1808)
Niagara County

1980	4,419
1970	4,193
1960	3,661
1950	2,346
1940	1,925
1930	1,786
1920	1,596
1910	1,749
1900	1,880
1890	2,007
1880	2,267
1870	2,145
1860	2,308
1850	2,366
1840	2,099
1830	1,712
1820	1,134

CAMBRIDGE, Town (Est. 1788)
Washington County

1980	1,848
1970	1,702
1960	1,610
1950	1,567
1940	1,434
1930	1,677
1920	1,620
1910	1,694
1900	1,878
1890	2,162
1880	2,324
1870	2,589
1860	2,419
1850	2,593
1840	2,005
1830	2,325
1820	2,491
1810	NA
1800	*6,187
1790	4,996(a)

(a)Reported in ALBANY County.

CAMBRIDGE, Village (Inc. 1866)
Cambridge Town, part in
Washington County

1980	550
1970	493
1960	519
1950	546
1940	511(a)
1930	593
1920	456
1910	472
1900	486
1890	445
1880	489
1870	563

White Creek Town, part in
Washington County

1980	1,270
1970	1,276
1960	1,229
1950	1,146
1940	1,061
1930	1,169
1920	1,103
1910	1,056
1900	1,092
1890	1,153
1880	993
1870	967

TOTAL

1980	1,820
1970	1,769
1960	1,748
1950	1,692
1940	1,572
1930	1,762
1920	1,559
1910	1,528
1900	1,578
1890	1,598
1880	1,482
1870	1,530

(a)Reported as 1,511 in 1950 Census.

CAMDEN, Town (Est. 1799)
  Oneida County
```
        1980        4,925
        1970        4,942
        1960        4,318
        1950        3,655
        1940        3,096
        1930        2,977
        1920        3,054
        1910        3,426
        1900        3,745
        1890        3,391
        1880        3,392
        1870        3,687
        1860        3,187
        1850        2,820
        1840        2,331
        1830        1,945
        1820        1,772
        1810          NA
        1800       *384(a)
```
(a)Reported as Cambden.

CAMDEN, Village (Inc. 1834)
  Camden Town
    Oneida County
```
        1980        2,667
        1970        2,936
        1960        2,694
        1950        2,407
        1940        2,021
        1930        1,912
        1920        1,941
        1910        2,170
        1900        2,370
        1890        1,902
        1880        1,589
        1870        1,703
```

CAMERON, CDP
  Cameron Town
    Steuben County
```
        1880          262
        1870          161
```

CAMERON, Town (Est. 1822)
  Steuben County
```
        1980          917
        1970          741
        1960          587
        1950          688
        1940          664
        1930          704
        1920          779
        1910        1,066
        1900        1,353
        1890        1,564
        1880        1,611
        1870        1,334
        1860        1,569
        1850        1,701
        1840        1,359
        1830          924
```

CAMERON MILLS, CDP
  Rathbone Town
    Steuben County
```
        1880           77
```

CAMILLUS, Town (Est. 1799)
  Onondaga County
```
        1980       24,333
        1970       26,841
        1960       18,328
        1950        6,735
        1940        4,394
        1930        4,066
        1920        2,905
        1910        2,642
        1900        2,453
        1890        2,678
        1880        2,416
        1870        2,423
        1860        2,940
        1850        3,105
        1840        3,957
        1830        2,518
        1820        5,791
        1810          NA
        1800       *336
```

CAMILLUS, Village (Inc. 1852)
  Camillus Town
    Onondaga County
```
        1980        1,298
        1970        1,534
        1960        1,416(a)
        1950        1,225
        1940        1,133
        1930        1,036
        1920          808
        1910          763
        1900          567
        1890          487
        1880          477
        1870          598
```
(a)Boundary change.

CAMPBELL, Town (Est. 1831)
  Steuben County
```
        1980        3,801
        1970        3,180
        1960        2,471
        1950        1,814
        1940        1,472
        1930        1,263
        1920        1,032
        1910        1,204
        1900        1,467
        1890        1,533
        1880        1,881
        1870        1,989
        1860        1,622
        1850        1,175
        1840          852
```

CAMPVILLE, CDP
  Owego Town
    Tioga County
```
        1880           94
```

CANAAN, Town (Est. 1788)
  Columbia County
```
        1980        1,654
        1970        1,472
        1960        1,272
        1950        1,284
        1940        1,042
```

1930	979
1920	1,085
1910	1,167
1900	1,307
1890	1,561
1880	1,654
1870	1,877
1860	2,197
1850	1,941
1840	1,957
1830	2,063
1820	2,078
1810	NA
1800	*5,195
1790	6,692(a)

(a)Reported as Canan-Town.

CANAAN FOUR CORNERS, CDP
  Canaan Town
    Columbia County

1880	315

CANADA, CDP
  Bethany Town
    Genesee County

1880	80

CANADEA, Town
  see CANEADEA, Town
    Allegany County

CANADICE, Town (Est. 1829)
  Ontario County

1980	1,467
1970	971
1960	558
1950	303
1940	324
1930	317
1920	457
1910	559
1900	674
1890	730
1880	895
1870	905
1860	1,026
1850	1,075
1840	1,341
1830	1,379(a)

(a)Reported as Candice.

CANAJOHARIE, Town (Est. 1788)
  Montgomery County

1980	4,140
1970	4,319
1960	4,233
1950	4,294
1940	4,062
1930	4,023
1920	3,784
1910	3,889
1900	3,888
1890	4,267
1880	4,294
1870	4,256
1860	4,134
1850	4,097
1840	5,146
1830	4,347

1820	4,677
1810	NA
1800	*2,266(a)
1790	6,156(b)

(a)Reported as Canajohary.
(b)Reported as Connasoxharrie.

CANAJOHARIE, Village (Inc. 1829)
  Canajoharie Town
    Montgomery County

1980	2,412(a)
1970	2,686
1960	2,681(a)
1950	2,761(a)
1940	2,577
1930	2,519
1920	2,415
1910	2,273
1900	2,101
1890	2,089
1880	2,013
1870	1,822

(a)Boundary change.

CANAJOHARY, Town
  see CANAJOHARIE, Town
    Montgomery County

CANANDAIGUA, City (Inc. 1913)(a)
  Ontario County

1980	10,419
1970	10,488
1960	9,370
1950	8,332
1940	8,321
1930	7,541
1920	7,299 Rev.(b)

(a)CANANDAIGUA Village incorporated as
   CANANDAIGUA City and made independent
   of CANANDAIGUA Town in 1913.
(b)In 1930 the Census Bureau revised the
   1920 figure of 7,356 to exclude the
   Ontario County Orphan Asylum.

CANANDAIGUA, Town (Est. 1789)
  Ontario County

1980	6,060
1970	5,419
1960	4,894
1950	4,218
1940	3,083
1930	1,938
1920	1,915 Rev.(a)
1910	9,405
1900	8,284
1890	8,229
1880	8,363
1870	7,274
1860	7,075
1850	6,143
1840	5,652
1830	5,162
1820	4,680
1810	NA
1800	*1,153
1790	464

(a)Boundary change. In 1930 the Census
   Bureau revised the 1920 figure of
   1,972 to exclude the Ontario County

Orphan Asylum.

CANANDAIGUA, Village (Inc.1815)(a)
  Canandaigua Town
    Ontario County

1910	7,217
1900	6,151
1890	5,868
1880	5,726
1870	4,862

(a)CANANDAIGUA Village incorporated as
CANANDAIGUA City and made independent
of CANANDAIGUA Town in 1913.

CANARSIE, CDP
  Flatlands Town
    Kings County

1890	2,452
1880	1,760

CANASERAGA, CDP
  Sullivan Town
    Madison County

1880	144

CANASERAGA, Village (Inc. 1892)
  Burns Town
    Allegany County

1980	700
1970	750
1960	730
1950	693
1940	698
1930	620
1920	651
1910	754
1900	685
1890	659
1880	701

CANASTOTA, Village (Inc. 1835)
  Lenox Town
    Madison County

1980	4,773(a)
1970	5,033
1960	4,896(a)
1950	4,458(a)
1940	4,150
1930	4,235(a)
1920	3,995
1910	3,247
1900	3,030
1890	2,774
1880	1,569
1870	1,492

(a)Boundary change.

CANDICE, Town
  see CANADICE, Town
      Ontario County

CANDOR, Town (Est. 1811)
  Tioga County

1980	4,919
1970	4,190
1960	3,488
1950	2,879
1940	2,601
1930	2,564
1920	2,639
1910	2,911
1900	3,330
1890	3,674
1880	4,323
1870	4,250
1860	3,840
1850	3,433
1840	3,370
1830	2,656
1820	1,655

CANDOR, Village (Inc. 1900)
  Candor Town
    Tioga County

1980	917
1970	939
1960	956
1950	802
1940	661
1930	669
1920	699
1910	737
1890-1900	NA
1880	965

CANEADEA, CDP
  Caneadea Town
    Allegany County

1880	192
1870	236

CANEADEA, Town (Est. 1808)
  Allegany County

1980	2,421
1970	2,364
1960	1,911
1950	1,845
1940	1,089
1930	1,066
1920	1,183
1910	1,354
1900	1,310
1890	1,639
1880	1,764
1870	1,869
1860	2,125
1850	1,477
1840	1,633
1830	780
1820	696(a)

(a)Reported as Canadea.

CANISTEO, Town (Est. 1796)
  Steuben County

1980	3,991
1970	3,777
1960	3,652
1950	3,568
1940	3,381
1930	3,391
1920	2,901
1910	3,441
1900	3,432
1890	3,629
1880	3,694
1870	2,435
1860	2,337
1850	2,030

1840	941
1830	619
1820	891
1810	NA
1800	*510(a)

(a)Reported as Canistia.

CANISTEO, Village (Inc. 1873)
  Canisteo Town
    Steuben County

1980	2,679
1970	2,772
1960	2,731
1950	2,625
1940	2,550
1930	2,548
1920	2,201
1910	2,259
1900	2,077
1890	2,071
1880	1,907

CANISTIA, Town
  see CANISTEO, Town
        Steuben County

CANNONSVILLE, CDP
  Tompkins Town
    Delaware County

1880	258
1870	319

CANOGA, CDP
  Fayette Town
    Seneca County   177

CANTON, Town
    Greene County
  see CAIRO, Town
        Greene County

CANTON, Town (Est. 1805)(a)
    St. Lawrence County

1980	11,568
1970	10,348
1960	8,935
1950	7,652
1940	6,130
1930	6,795
1920	6,497
1910	6,151
1900	6,387
1890	6,096
1880	6,275
1870	6,014
1860	6,379
1850	4,685
1840	3,456
1830	2,439
1820	1,337

(a)In 1800 the Census Bureau reported
   a Canton Town in ONEIDA County, population of 24.

CANTON, Village (Inc. 1845)
  Canton Town
    St. Lawrence County

1980	7,055(a)
1970	6,398(a)

1960	5,046
1950	4,379
1940	3,018
1930	2,822
1920	2,522 Rev.(b)
1910	2,701
1900	2,757
1890	2,580
1880	2,049
1870	1,681

(a)Boundary change.
(b)In 1930 the Census Bureau revised the
   1920 figure of 2,631 to exclude the
   St. Lawrence County Almshouse.

CAPE VINCENT, Town (Est. 1849)
    Jefferson County

1980	1,823
1970	1,748
1960	1,756
1950	1,842
1940	1,954
1930	1,958
1920	2,111
1910	2,575
1900	2,882
1890	3,014
1880	3,143
1870	3,342
1860	3,585
1850	3,044

CAPE VINCENT, Village (Inc. 1853)
  Cape Vincent Town
    Jefferson County

1980	785
1970	820
1960	770
1950	812
1940	931
1930	898
1920	913
1910	1,155
1900	1,310
1890	1,324
1880	1,361
1870	1,269

CAPTREE ISLAND
  Babylon Town
    Suffolk County

1980	37(a)
1970	23(b)

(a)Boundary change; derived by LIRPB from
   U.S. Census Data.
(b)Derived by LIRPB from U.S. Census
   Data; population is comparable to 1980
   boundaries.

CARDIFF, CDP
  Lafayette Town
    Onondaga County
      1870   147

CARLE PLACE, CDP
  North Hempstead Town
    Nassau County

1980	5,470
1970	6,326

1960	5,625(a)
1950	NA
1940	991

(a)Derived by LIRPB from U.S. Census
Data.

CARLISLE, CDP
  Carlisle Town
    Schoharie County

1880	128

CARLISLE, Town (Est. 1807)
    Schoharie County

1980	1,417
1970	1,040
1960	900
1950	1,010
1940	917
1930	796
1920	861
1910	1,024
1900	1,225
1890	1,349
1880	1,720
1870	1,730
1860	1,760
1850	1,817
1840	1,850
1830	1,748
1820	1,583

CARLTON, Town (Est. 1822)(a)
    Orleans County

1980	2,818
1970	2,540
1960	2,600
1950	1,775
1940	1,540
1930	1,699
1920	1,832
1910	2,259
1900	2,338
1890	2,374
1880	2,477
1870	2,327
1860	2,447
1850	2,809
1840	2,275
1830	1,222

(a)Established as Oak Orchard in 1822;
   name changed in 1825.

CARMEL, CDP
  Carmel Town, part in
    Putnam County

1970	2,453
1960	NA
1950	1,336
1940	1,315
1890-1930	NA
1880	571
1870	590

  Kent Town, part in
    Putnam County

1970	942
1960	NA
1950	190

  TOTAL

1970	3,395

1960	NA
1950	1,526
1870-1940	(a)

(a)Reported in CARMEL Town only.

CARMEL, Town (Est. 1795)
    Putnam County

1980	27,948
1970	21,639
1960	9,113
1950	5,458
1940	4,195
1930	3,434
1920	2,299
1910	2,610
1900	2,598
1890	2,912
1880	2,811
1870	2,797
1860	2,559
1850	2,442
1840	2,263
1830	2,371
1820	2,247
1810	NA
1800	*1,797(a)

(a)Reported as Cormell in DUTCHESS
   County.

CAROGA, CDP
  Ephratah Town
    Fulton County

1880	59(a)

(a)Reported as Garoga.

CAROGA, Town (Est. 1842)
    Fulton County

1980	1,177
1970	822
1960	568(a)
1950	462
1940	408
1930	306
1920	332
1910	441
1900	470
1890	624
1880	855
1870	828
1860	629(b)
1850	589(b)

(a)Reported as Varoga.
(b)Reported as Garoga.

CAROLINE, Town (Est. 1811)
    Tompkins County

1980	2,754
1970	2,536
1960	2,118
1950	1,900
1940	1,737
1930	1,617
1920	1,542
1910	1,646
1900	1,938
1890	2,092(a)
1880	2,171
1870	2,175
1860	2,345

```
          1850            2,537
          1840            2,457
          1830            2,633
          1820            1,608(b)
(a)Boundary change.
(b)Reported in TIOGA County.

CAROLINE CENTRE, CDP
   Caroline Town
      Tompkins County
         1880               9

CARROLL, Town (Est. 1825)
   Chautauqua County
      1980            3,579
      1970            3,115
      1960            2,661
      1950            2,286
      1940            2,086
      1930            1,972
      1920            1,761
      1910            1,564
      1900            1,684
      1890            1,787
      1880            1,718
      1870            1,548
      1860            1,525
      1850            1,833
      1840            1,649
      1830            1,015

CARROLLTON, Town (Est. 1842)
   Cattaraugus County
      1980            1,566
      1970            1,507
      1960            1,399
      1950            1,332
      1940            1,235
      1930            1,026
      1920            1,013
      1910            1,179 Rev.(a)
      1900            1,385 Rev.(a)
      1890            1,884(b)
      1880            2,171(b)
      1870            1,142(b)
      1860              779(b)
      1850              515
(a)In 1920 the Census Bureau revised the
   1910 figure of 1,516 and the 1900
   figure of 2,035 to exclude the
   ALLEGANY INDIAN RESERVATION.
(b)Reported as Carrolton.

CARTHAGE, Village (Inc. 1841)
   Wilna Town
      Jefferson County
         1980            3,643
         1970            3,889
         1960            4,216
         1950            4,420
         1940            4,207
         1930            4,460
         1920            4,320
         1910            3,563
         1900            2,895
         1890            2,278
         1880            1,912
```

```
CARTHAGE LANDING, CDP
   Wappinger Town
      Dutchess County
         1880              251

CARY, CDP
   Oakfield Town
      Genesee County
         1880              439

CASENOVIA, Town
   Chenango County
   see CAZENOVIA, Town
      Madison County

CASSADAGA, Village (Inc. 1921)
   Stockton Town
      Chautauqua County
         1980              821
         1970              905
         1960              820
         1950              676(a)
         1940              514
         1930              480
         1880-1920          NA
         1870              225
(a)Boundary change.

CASSVILLE, CDP
   Paris Town
      Oneida County
         1880              226
         1870              152

CASTILE, Town (Est. 1821)
   Wyoming County
      1980            2,865
      1970            3,156
      1960            2,609
      1950            2,361
      1940            2,172
      1930            1,996
      1920            2,290
      1910            2,406
      1900            2,539
      1890            2,451
      1880            2,315
      1870            2,186
      1860            2,323
      1850            2,446
      1840            2,833
      1830            2,269

CASTILE, Village (Inc. 1877)
   Castile Town
      Wyoming County
         1980            1,135
         1970            1,330
         1960            1,146
         1950            1,072
         1940              902
         1930              900
         1920            1,013
         1910            1,040
         1900            1,088
         1890            1,146
         1880              965
         1870              712
```

CASTLE CREEK, CDP
  Chenango Town
    Broome County
      1880   110

CASTLETON, Town (Est. 1788)(a)
  Richmond County
      1890   16,423(b)
      1880   12,679(b)
      1870   9,504
      1860   6,778
      1850   5,389
      1840   4,275
      1830   2,216
      1820   1,527
      1810   NA
      1800   *1,056(c)
      1790   805(c)
(a)Merged into STATEN ISLAND Borough in
   NEW YORK CITY in 1898.
(b)CASTLETON Town and NEW BRIGHTON Village shared the same boundaries.
(c)Reported as Castle-Town.

CASTLETON-ON-HUDSON, Village (Inc. 1827)
  Schodack Town
    Rensselaer County
      1980   1,627(a)
      1970   1,730
      1960   1,752
      1950   1,751
      1940   1,515
      1930   1,506
      1920   1,595(b)
      1910   1,396
      1900   1,214(b)
      1890   1,127(b)
      1880   912(b)
      1870   580(b)
(a)Boundary change.
(b)Reported as Castleton.

CASTORLAND, Village (Inc. 1929)
  Denmark Town
    Lewis County
      1980   277
      1970   327
      1960   321
      1950   308
      1940   309
      1930   315

CATEN, Town
  see CATON, Town
    Steuben County

CATHARINE, Town (Est. 1798)
  Schuyler County
      1980   1,932
      1970   1,886
      1960   1,605
      1950   1,399
      1940   1,284
      1930   1,177
      1920   1,178
      1910   1,222
      1900   1,386
      1890   1,398
      1880   1,617

      1870   1,629
      1860   3,688
      1850   3,096(a)
      1840   2,424(b)
      1830   2,062(c)
      1820   2,478(d)
      1810   NA
      1800   *266(d)
(a)Reported in CHEMUNG County.
(b)Reported as Catharine's in CHEMUNG
   County.
(c)Reported as Catharines in TIOGA
   County.
(d)Reported in TIOGA County.

CATLIN, Town (Est. 1823)
  Chemung County
      1980   2,719
      1970   2,461
      1960   1,831
      1950   690
      1940   715
      1930   670
      1920   737
      1910   870
      1900   1,109
      1890   1,180
      1880   1,450
      1870   1,346
      1860   1,308
      1850   1,474
      1840   1,119
      1830   2,015(a)
(a)Reported in TIOGA County.

CATO, Town (Est 1802)
  Cayuga County
      1980   2,139
      1970   1,975
      1960   1,815
      1950   1,513
      1940   1,458
      1930   1,286
      1920   1,394
      1910   1,569
      1900   1,624
      1890   1,996
      1880   2,059
      1870   2,091
      1860   2,350
      1850   2,247
      1840   2,380
      1830   1,782
      1820   4,021

CATO, Village (Inc. 1880)
  Cato Town, part in
    Cayuga County
      1980   144
      1970   196
      1960   138
      1950   119
      1940   127
      1930   113
      1920   106
      1910   112
  Ira Town, part in
    Cayuga County
      1980   331

1970	405
1960	338
1950	312
1940	285
1930	290
1920	298
1910	262
1900	350
1890	NA
1880	313

TOTAL

1980	475
1970	601
1960	476
1950	431
1940	412
1930	403
1920	404
1910	374
1880-1900	(a)

(a)Reported in IRA Town only.

CATON, Town (Est. 1839)(a)
  Steuben County

1980	1,847
1970	1,747
1960	1,359
1950	1,199
1940	976
1930	915
1920	688
1910	1,078
1900	1,345
1890	1,445
1880	1,642
1870	1,544
1860	1,550
1850	1,214
1840	797(b)

(a)Established as Wormly in 1839; name
  changed in 1840.
(b)Reported as Caten.

CATSKILL, Town (Est. 1788)
  Greene County

1980	11,453
1970	10,432
1960	9,906
1950	8,575
1940	8,630
1930	8,200
1920	7,670
1910	9,066
1900	8,566
1890	8,263
1880	8,311
1870	7,677
1860	6,275
1850	5,454
1840	5,339(a)
1830	4,861(a)
1820	3,510
1810	NA
1800	*2,408
1790	1,780(b)

(a)Reported as Cattskill.
(b)Reported as Katts-Kill in ALBANY
  County.

CATSKILL, Village (Inc. 1806)
  Catskill Town
    Greene County

1980	4,718(a)
1970	5,317
1960	5,825
1950	5,392
1940	5,429
1930	5,082
1920	4,728
1910	5,296
1900	5,484
1890	4,920
1880	4,320
1870	3,791

(a)Boundary change.

CATTARAUGUS, County (Inc. 1808)

1980	85,697
1970	81,666
1960	80,187
1950	77,901
1940	72,652
1930	72,398
1920	71,323
1910	65,919
1900	65,643
1890	60,866
1880	55,806
1870	43,909
1860	43,886
1850	38,950
1840	28,872
1830	16,724
1820	4,090

CATTARAUGUS, Village (Inc. 1882)
  New Albion Town
    Cattaraugus County

1980	1,200
1970	1,200
1960	1,258
1950	1,190
1940	1,145
1930	1,236
1920	1,347
1910	1,165
1900	1,382
1890	878
1880	705

CATTARAUGUS INDIAN RESERVATION
  Cattaraugus County, part in

1980	352
1970	277
1960	262
1950	215
1940	205
1930	174
1920	92
1910	180
1900	149

  Chautauqua County, part in

1980	14
1970	0
1960	19
1950	13
1940	27
1930	22

1920	39
1910	69
1900	31
Erie County, part in	
1980	1,628
1970	1,107
1960	1,426
1950	1,421
1940	1,411
1930	1,196
1920	1,067
1910	1,125
1900	1,163
TOTAL	
1980	1,994
1970	1,384
1960	1,707
1950	1,649
1940	1,643
1930	1,392
1920	1,198
1910	1,374
1900	1,343

CATTSKILL, Town
  see CATSKILL, Town
    Greene County

CAUGHDENOY, CDP
  Hastings Town
    Oswego County

1880	215
1870	220

CAUGHNEWAGA, Town (Est. 1788)(a)
    Montgomery County

1790	4,261

(a)Divided into BROADALBIN, JOHNSTOWN,
  AMSTERDAM AND MANSFIELD Towns in
  1793.

CAYUGA, County (Est. 1799)

1980	79,894
1970	77,439
1960	73,942
1950	70,136
1940	65,508
1930	64,751
1920	65,221
1910	67,106
1900	66,234
1890	65,302
1880	65,081
1870	59,550
1860	55,767
1850	55,458
1840	50,338
1830	47,948
1820	38,897
1810	29,843
1800	15,907

CAYUGA, Village (Inc. 1857)
  Aurelius Town
    Cayuga County

1980	604
1970	693
1960	621
1950	534

1940	472
1930	344
1920	300
1910	348
1900	390
1890	511
1880	484
1870	435

CAYUGA HEIGHTS, Village (Inc. 1915)
  Ithaca Town
    Tompkins County

1980	3,170
1970	3,130
1960	2,788(a)
1950	1,131
1940	651
1930	507
1920	179

(a)Boundary change.

CAYUTA, CDP
  Cayuta Town
    Schuyler County

1880	53

CAYUTA, Town (Est. 1824)
    Schuyler County

1980	566
1970	557
1960	538
1950	459
1940	311
1930	258
1920	282
1910	345
1900	459
1890	560
1880	601
1870	641
1860	708
1850	1,035(a)
1840	835(a)
1830	641(b)

(a)Reported in CHEMUNG County.
(b)Reported in TIOGA County.

CAYUTA, Town
    Tioga County
  see NEWFIELD, Town
    Tompkins County

CAZENOVIA, Town (Est. 1795)
    Madison County

1980	5,880
1970	6,092
1960	4,968
1950	3,969
1940	3,424
1930	3,504
1920	3,343
1910	3,687
1900	3,830
1890	4,182
1880	4,363
1870	4,265
1860	2,711
1850	4,812
1840	4,153

1830	4,344
1820	3,909
1810	NA
1800	*3,080(a)

(a)Reported as Casenovia in CHENANGO
County.

CAZENOVIA, Village (Inc. 1810)
Cazenovia Town
Madison County

1980	2,599(a)
1970	3,031
1960	2,584
1950	1,946
1940	1,689
1930	1,788
1920	1,683
1910	1,861
1900	1,819
1890	1,987
1880	1,918
1870	1,718

(a)Boundary change.

CECILIUS, Town
see MANSFIELD, Town
Cattaraugus County

CEDARHURST, Village (Inc. 1910)
Hempstead Town
Nassau County

1980	6,162
1970	6,941
1960	6,954(a)
1950	6,051
1940	5,463
1930	5,065
1920	2,838

(a)Boundary change.

CELORON, Village (Inc. 1896)
Ellicott Town
Chautauqua County

1980	1,405
1970	1,456
1960	1,507
1950	1,555
1940	1,349
1930	1,182
1920	757
1910	619
1900	506(a)

(a)Reported as Celeron.

CENTEREACH, CDP
Brookhaven Town
Suffolk County

1980	30,136(a)
1970	9,427(b)
1960	6,676 Rev.
1950	NA
1940	628

(a)Boundary change.
(b)Population of 24,302 is comparable
to 1980 boundaries.

CENTER MORICHES, CDP
Brookhaven Town
Suffolk County

1980	5,703(a)
1970	3,802(b)
1960	2,562 Rev.
1950	1,761
1940	1,469
1890-1930	NA
1880	396

(a)Boundary change.
(b)Population of 4,930 is comparable to
1980 boundaries.

CENTERPORT, CDP
Huntington Town
Suffolk County

1980	6,576(a)
1970	3,065(b)
1960	2,602 Rev.
1950	NA
1940	554
1890-1930	NA
1880	425(c)

(a)Boundary change.
(b)Derived by LIRPB from U.S. Census
Data; population of 5,558 is comparable to 1980 boundaries.
(c)Reported as Centreport.

CENTERVILLE, CDP
Onondaga County
see CENTREVILLE, CDP
Onondaga County

CENTERVILLE, CDP
Corning Town
Steuben County

1880	298

CENTERVILLE, Town (Est. 1819)
Allegany County

1980	696
1970	526
1960	491
1950	545
1940	559
1930	553
1920	668
1910	781
1900	833
1890	911
1880	956(a)
1870	1,043(a)
1860	1,323
1850	1,441(a)
1840	1,513(a)
1830	1,195(a)
1820	421(a)

(a)Reported as Centreville.

CENTERVILLE STATION, Village
see WOODRIDGE, Village
Sullivan County

CENTRAL BRIDGE, CDP
Schoharie Town
Schoharie County

1880	195

CENTRAL ISLIP, CDP
Islip Town
Suffolk County
1980	19,734(a)
1970	36,391(b)
1960	16,607(c)
1950	3,067
1940	2,447
1890-1930	NA
1880	110
(a)Boundary change.
(b)Population of 17,408 is comparable to 1980 boundaries.
(c)Derived by LIRPB from U.S. Census Data.

CENTRAL ISLIP PSYCHIATRIC CENTER
Islip Town
Suffolk County
1980	2,194(a)
1970	6,550(a)
1960	10,461(a)
(a)Derived by LIRPB from U.S. Census Data.

CENTRAL MOUNT VERNON, CDP(a)
Eastchester Town
Westchester County
1870	450
(a)CENTRAL MOUNT VERNON, CDP and West Mount Vernon incorporated as WEST MOUNT VERNON Village in 1869.

CENTRAL NYACK, CDP
Clarkstown Town
Rockland County
1940	769(a)
(a)Reported as Central Wyack.

CENTRAL PARK, CDP
see BETHPAGE, CDP
Nassau County

CENTRAL SQUARE, Village (Inc. 1889)
Hastings Town
Oswego County
1980	1,418(a)
1970	1,298(a)
1960	935
1950	665
1940	568
1930	542
1920	448
1910	429
1900	364
1890	NA
1880	309
1870	359
(a)Boundary change.

CENTRAL VALLEY, CDP
Woodbury Town
Orange County
1980	1,705
1950-1970	NA
1940	1,015

CENTRAL WYACK, CDP
see CENTRAL NYACK, CDP
Rockland County

CENTRE, CDP
Colesville Town
Broome County
1870	146

CENTRE ISLAND, Village (Inc. 1926)
Oyster Bay Town
Nassau County
1980	378
1970	374
1960	270
1950	199
1940	134
1930	139

CENTREPORT, CDP
See CENTERPORT, CDP
Suffolk County

CENTRE POST, CDP
Mentz Town
Cayuga County
1880	95

CENTREVILLE, CDP
Centerville Town
Allegany County
1870	167

CENTREVILLE, CDP
Portland Town
Chautauqua County
1880	125
1870	141

CENTREVILLE, CDP
Cicero Town, part in
Onondaga County
1870	46(a)
Clay Town
Onondaga County
1880	200
1870	242(a)
TOTAL
1880	(b)
1870	288(c)
(a)Reported as Centerville.
(b)Reported in CLAY Town only.
(c)Census Bureau reported as 289.

CENTREVILLE, Town
see CENTERVILLE, Town
Allegany County

CERES, CDP
Genesee Town
Allegany County
1880	100

CHADWICKS, CDP
New Hartford Town
Oneida County
1940	654

CHAMPION, Town (Est. 1800)
    Jefferson County
        1980   4,056
        1970   4,371
        1960   3,878
        1950   3,499
        1940   3,103
        1930   3,001
        1920   2,854
        1910   2,704
        1900   2,525
        1890   2,191
        1880   2,259
        1870   2,156
        1860   2,132
        1850   2,085
        1840   2,206
        1830   2,342
        1820   2,080
        1810   NA
        1800   *143(a)
(a)Reported in ONEIDA County.

CHAMPLAIN, Town (Est. 1788)
    Clinton County
        1980   5,889
        1970   5,633
        1960   5,544
        1950   5,118
        1940   4,938
        1930   4,848
        1920   4,535
        1910   4,637
        1900   4,748
        1890   5,207
        1880   5,407
        1870   5,080
        1860   5,857
        1850   5,067
        1840   3,632
        1830   2,456
        1820   1,618
        1810   NA
        1800   *1,169
        1790   578

CHAMPLAIN, Village (Inc. 1873)
    Champlain Town
    Clinton County
        1980   1,410(a)
        1970   1,426
        1960   1,549
        1950   1,505
        1940   1,354
        1930   1,197
        1920   1,140
        1910   1,280
        1900   1,311
        1890   1,275
        1880   1,509
        1870   1,850
(a)Boundary change.

CHAMPLAIN PARK, CDP
    Plattsburgh Town
    Clinton County
        1980   1,051
        1970   1,207

CHANNINGVILLE, CDP
    Poughkeepsie Town
    Dutchess County
        1870   1,350

CHAPPAQUA, CDP
    New Castle Town
    Westchester County
        1940   2,286
        1900-1930   NA
        1890   733
        1880   330

CHARLESTON, CDP
    Charleston Town
    Montgomery County
        1880   51

CHARLESTON, Town (Est. 1793)
    Montgomery County
        1980   1,013
        1970   658
        1960   546
        1950   575
        1940   609
        1930   594
        1920   785
        1910   900
        1900   1,052
        1890   1,174
        1880   1,334
        1870   1,601
        1860   1,837
        1850   2,216
        1840   2,103
        1830   2,148(a)
        1820   5,365(a)
        1810   NA
        1800   *2,001(a)
(a)Reported as Charlestown.

CHARLESTON, Town
    Ontario County
    see LIMA, Town
            Livingston County

CHARLESTON FOUR CORNERS, CDP
    Charleston Town
    Montgomery County
        1880   106

CHARLESTOWN, Town
    see CHARLESTON, Town
            Montgomery County

CHARLOTTE, CDP
    Newfane Town
    Niagara County
        1880   260

CHARLOTTE, County
    see WASHINGTON, County

CHARLOTTE, Town (Est. 1829)
    Chautauqua County
        1980   1,494
        1970   1,400
        1960   1,323
        1950   1,195

1940	1,146
1930	1,208
1920	1,173
1910	1,258
1900	1,406
1890	1,441
1880	1,667
1870	1,682
1860	1,711
1850	1,718
1840	1,428
1830	886

CHARLOTTE, Village (Inc. 1869)(a)
  Greece Town
    Monroe County

1910	1,938
1900	1,400
1890	930
1880	962

(a)Merged into ROCHESTER City in 1915.

CHARLOTTEVILLE, CDP
  Summit Town
    Schoharie County

1880	126

CHARLTON, CDP
  Charlton Town
    Saratoga County

1880	175

CHARLTON, Town (Est. 1792)
  Saratoga County

1980	4,019
1970	3,772
1960	3,024
1950	1,298
1940	1,063
1930	978
1920	914
1910	1,030
1900	1,109
1890	1,175
1880	1,474
1870	1,607
1860	1,752
1850	1,902
1840	1,933
1830	2,023
1820	1,953
1810	NA
1800	*1,746

CHASE'S MILLS, CDP
  Louisville Town
    St. Lawrence County

1880	114

CHATAUQUE, County & Town
  see CHAUTAUQUA, County & Town

CHATEAUGAY, Town (Est. 1799)
  Franklin County

1980	1,863
1970	1,948
1960	2,176
1950	2,407
1940	2,602

1930	2,687
1920	2,856
1910	2,840
1900	2,723
1890	2,965
1880	2,828
1870	2,971
1860	3,183
1850	3,728
1840	2,824
1830	2,016
1820	828(a)
1810	NA
1800	*443(b)

(a)Reported as Chateaguay.
(b)Reported as Chattangay in CLINTON
   County.

CHATEAUGAY, Village (Inc. 1869)
  Chateaugay Town
    Franklin County

1980	869
1970	976
1960	1,097
1950	1,234
1940	1,183
1930	1,169
1920	1,291
1910	1,045
1900	973
1890	1,172
1880	680

CHATHAM, Town (Est. 1795)
  Columbia County

1980	4,294
1970	3,770
1960	3,402
1950	3,188
1940	2,873
1930	2,908
1920	2,705
1910	3,396
1900	3,537
1890	4,019
1880	4,574
1870	4,372
1860	4,163
1850	3,839
1840	3,662
1830	3,538
1820	3,372
1810	NA
1800	*3,716

CHATHAM, Village (Inc. 1869)
  Chatham Town, part in
    Columbia County

1980	889
1970	952
1960	998
1950	968
1940	956
1930	1,118
1920	1,573
1910	1,114
1900	1,065
1890	1,082
1880	1,062

1870	818

Ghent Town, part in
  Columbia County

1980	1,112
1970	1,287
1960	1,428
1950	1,336
1940	1,298(a)
1930	1,306
1920	1,137
1910	1,137
1900	953
1890	830
1880	703
1870	569

TOTAL

1980	2,001
1970	2,239
1960	2,426
1950	2,304
1940	2,254(a)
1930	2,424
1920	2,710
1910	2,251
1900	2,018
1890	1,912
1880	1,765
1870	1,387

(a)Boundary change.

CHATHAM CENTER, CDP
  Chatham Town
    Columbia County

1880	223(a)

(a)Reported as Chatham Centre.

CHATTANGAY, Town
  see CHATEAUGAY, Town
      Franklin County

CHAUMONT, Village (Inc. 1874)
  Lyme Town
    Jefferson County

1980	620
1970	567(a)
1960	523
1950	513
1940	534
1930	596
1920	595
1910	708
1900	738
1890	623
1880	479
1870	370

(a)Boundary change.

CHAUTAUQUA, County (Est. 1808)

1980	146,925
1970	147,305
1960	145,377
1950	135,189
1940	123,580
1930	126,457
1920	115,348
1910	105,126
1900	88,314
1890	75,202
1880	65,342
1870	59,327
1860	58,422
1850	50,493(a)
1840	47,975(a)
1830	34,671(a)
1820	12,568(b)

(a)Reported as Chautauque; spelling
    changed by County Supervisors in
    1859.
(b)Reported as Chatauque.

CHAUTAUQUA, Town (Est. 1804)
  Chautauqua County

1980	4,728
1970	4,341
1960	4,376
1950	4,222
1940	3,819
1930	3,802
1920	3,533
1910	3,515
1900	3,590
1890	3,259
1880	3,576
1870	3,064
1860	2,837
1850	2,622(a)
1840	2,980(a)
1830	2,442(a)
1820	2,518(b)

(a)Reported as Chautauque; spelling
    changed in 1859.
(b)Reported as Chatauque.

CHAUTAUQUE, County & Town
  see CHAUTAUQUA, County & Town

CHAZEY, Town
  see CHAZY, Town
      Clinton County

CHAZY, CDP
  Chazy Town
    Clinton County

1880	262

CHAZY, Town (Est. 1804)
  Clinton County

1980	3,766
1970	3,393
1960	3,386
1950	2,741
1940	2,813
1930	2,916
1920	2,607
1910	2,973
1900	2,796
1890	2,867
1880	3,147
1870	3,206
1860	3,399
1850	4,324
1840	3,584(a)
1830	3,097
1820	2,313

(a)Reported as Chazey.

CHECOTOWAGO, Town
  see CHEEKTOWAGA, Town
        Erie County

CHEEKTOWAGA, CDP
  Cheektowaga Town
    Erie County
        1980   92,145
        1950-1970   NA
        1940   11,105

CHEEKTOWAGA, Town (Est. 1839)
    Erie County
        1980   109,442(a)
        1970   113,844
        1960   84,056
        1950   45,354
        1940   25,006
        1930   20,849
        1920   11,923
        1910   7,650
        1900   5,156
        1890   2,974
        1880   2,327
        1870   2,465(b)
        1860   2,743
        1850   3,042
        1840   1,137(c)
(a)Boundary change.
(b)Reported as Chictawauga.
(c)Reported as Checotowago.

CHEESECOCKS, Town
  see MONROE, Town
        Orange County

CHELSEA, CDP
  Northfield Town
    Richmond County
        1880   66

CHEMING, Town
    Tioga County
  see CHEMUNG, Town
        Chemung County

CHEMUNG, County (Est. 1836)
        1980   97,656
        1970   101,537
        1960   98,706
        1950   86,827
        1940   73,718
        1930   74,680
        1920   65,872
        1910   54,662
        1900   54,063
        1890   48,265
        1880   43,065
        1870   35,281
        1860   26,917(a)
        1850   28,821
        1840   20,732
(a)Boundary change.

CHEMUNG, Town (Est. 1789)
    Chemung County
        1980   2,436
        1970   2,156
        1960   1,842

        1950   1,553
        1940   1,363
        1930   1,285
        1920   1,147
        1910   1,328
        1900   1,500
        1890   1,610
        1880   2,098
        1870   1,907
        1860   2,128
        1850   2,673
        1840   2,377
        1830   1,461(a)
        1820   1,327(a)
        1810   NA
        1800   *515(b)
        1790   2,391(c)
(a)Reported in TIOGA County.
(b)Reported as Cheming in TIOGA County.
(c)Reported in MONTGOMERY County.

CHENANGO, County (Est. 1798)
        1980   49,344
        1970   46,368
        1960   43,243
        1950   39,138
        1940   36,454
        1930   34,665
        1920   34,969
        1910   35,575
        1900   36,568
        1890   37,776
        1880   39,891
        1870   40,564
        1860   40,934
        1850   40,311
        1840   40,785
        1830   37,238
        1820   31,215
        1810   21,704
        1800   16,087

CHENANGO, Town (Est. 1791)
    Broome County
        1980   12,233
        1970   12,267
        1960   9,858
        1950   5,747
        1940   3,265
        1930   2,074
        1920   1,183
        1910   1,237
        1900   1,372
        1890   1,448
        1880   1,590
        1870   1,680
        1860   1,841
        1850   8,734
        1840   5,465
        1830   3,730
        1820   2,626
        1810   NA
        1800   *1,149(a)
        1790   45(b)
(a)Reported in TIOGA County.
(b)Reported in MONTGOMERY County.

CHENANGO BRIDGE, CDP(a)
  Chenango Town
    Broome County
      1940   735
(a)Included in NIMMONSBURG--CHENANGO
    BRIDGE, CDP in 1970.

CHENANGO FORKS, CDP
  Barker Town
    Broome County
      1880   153

CHERRY CREEK, Town (Est. 1829)
  Chautauqua County
      1980   1,227
      1970   1,140
      1960   1,206
      1950   1,132
      1940   1,088
      1930   1,114
      1920   1,204
      1910   1,380
      1900   1,745
      1890   1,481
      1880   1,354
      1870   1,359
      1860   1,359
      1850   1,311
      1840   1,141
      1830   574

CHERRY CREEK, Village (Inc. 1893)
  Cherry Creek Town
    Chautauqua County
      1980   677
      1970   658
      1960   649
      1950   631
      1940   529
      1930   539
      1920   527
      1910   606
      1900   701
      1890   676
      1880   448
      1870   271

CHERRY GROVE
  see FIRE ISLAND
        Brookhaven Town
          Suffolk County

CHERRY VALLEY, Town (Est. 1791)
  Otsego County
      1980   1,205
      1970   1,122
      1960   1,156
      1950   1,330
      1940   1,274
      1930   1,326
      1920   1,400
      1910   1,706
      1900   1,802
      1890   1,803
      1880   2,260
      1870   2,337
      1860   2,552
      1850   4,186
      1840   3,923

      1830   4,098
      1820   3,684
      1810   NA
      1800   *1,550

CHERRY VALLEY, Village (Inc. 1812)
  Cherry Valley Town
    Otsego County
      1980   684
      1970   661
      1960   668
      1950   760
      1940   704
      1930   707
      1920   728
      1910   792
      1900   772
      1890   685
      1880   856
      1870   930

CHERUBUSCO, CDP
  Clinton Town
    Clinton County
      1880   111

CHESHIRE, CDP
  Canandaigua Town
    Ontario County
      1880   204

CHESTER, CDP
  Chester Town
    Warren County
      1880   349

CHESTER, Town (Est. 1845)
  Orange County
      1980   6,850
      1970   4,767
      1960   3,494
      1950   2,878
      1940   2,776
      1930   2,164
      1920   1,803
      1910   2,061
      1900   2,186
      1890   2,112
      1880   2,229
      1870   2,113
      1860   1,849
      1850   1,641

CHESTER, Town (Est. 1799)
  Warren County
      1980   2,909
      1970   2,330
      1960   1,974
      1950   1,927
      1940   1,825
      1930   1,610
      1920   1,572
      1910   1,721
      1900   2,052
      1890   2,173
      1880   2,247
      1870   2,329
      1860   2,412
      1850   1,850

1840	1,633
1830	1,284
1820	1,013
1810	NA
1800	*508(a)

(a)Reported in WASHINGTON County.

CHESTER, Village (Inc. 1892)
Chester Town
Orange County

1980	1,910
1970	1,627(a)
1960	1,492(a)
1950	1,215
1940	1,140
1930	1,154
1920	1,049
1910	1,210
1900	1,250
1880-1890	NA
1870	666

(a)Boundary change.

CHESTERFIELD, Town (Est. 1802)
Essex County

1980	2,398
1970	2,010
1960	2,003
1950	1,903
1940	1,694
1930	1,599
1920	1,538
1910	1,829
1900	2,362
1890	2,548
1880	2,752
1870	2,795
1860	3,179
1850	4,171
1840	1,716
1830	1,671
1820	667

CHESTERVILLE, CDP
Westerlo Town
Albany County

1880	167
1870	247

CHICTAWAUGA, Town
See CHEEKTOWAGA, Town
Erie County

CHILI, Town (Est. 1822)
Monroe County

1980	23,676
1970	19,609
1960	11,237(a)
1950	5,283(a)
1940	3,392
1930	2,493
1920	1,780
1910	2,071
1900	2,099
1890	2,109
1880	2,274
1870	2,367
1860	2,205
1850	2,247

1840	2,174
1830	2,010

(a)Boundary change.

CHINA, Town
Genesee & Wyoming Counties
see ARCADE, Town
Wyoming County

CHITTENANGO, Village (Inc. 1842)
Sullivan Town
Madison County

1980	4,290(a)
1970	3,605(a)
1960	3,180(a)
1950	1,307
1940	885
1930	815
1920	650
1910	678
1900	787
1890	792
1880	954
1870	968

(a)Boundary change.

CHITTENANGO STATION, CDP
Sullivan Town
Madison County

1880	97(a)
1870	92

(a)Reported as Chittenango Depot.

CHURCH TRACT, Town
See GROVE, Town
Allegany County

CHURCHVILLE, Village (Inc. 1867)
Riga Town
Monroe County

1980	1,399
1970	1,065(a)
1960	1,003(a)
1950	755
1940	601
1930	652
1920	513
1910	565
1900	505
1890	493
1880	513

(a)Boundary change.

CICERO, CDP
Cicero Town
Onondaga County

1880	275

CICERO, Town (Est. 1807)
Onondaga County

1980	23,689
1970	22,539
1960	14,725
1950	5,956
1940	4,346
1930	3,684
1920	2,536
1910	2,475
1900	2,611

1890	2,636
1880	2,934
1870	2,902
1860	2,637
1850	2,980
1840	2,464
1830	1,808
1820	1,303

CICERO CORNERS, CDP
  Cicero Town
    Onondaga County

1870	212

CINCINNATUS, CDP
  Cincinnatus Town
    Cortland County

1940	668
1890-1930	NA
1880	429
1870	350

CINCINNATUS, Town (Est. 1804)
    Cortland County

1980	1,151
1970	1,080
1960	960
1950	977
1940	957
1930	901
1920	941
1910	965
1900	912
1890	956
1880	1,093
1870	1,155
1860	1,213
1850	1,206
1840	1,301
1830	1,308
1820	885

CITY ISLAND, CDP(a)
  Pelham Town
    Westchester County

1890	1,206
1880	989

(a)Merged into NEW YORK City in 1895.

CLAIRMONT, CDP
  West Farms Town
    Westchester County

1870	158

CLARE, Town (Est. 1880)
    St. Lawrence County

1980	121
1970	97
1960	87
1950	107
1940	139
1930	227
1920	152
1910	420
1900	330
1890	281

CLARENCE, CDP
  Clarence Town
    Erie County

1950	1,018
1940	655

CLARENCE, Town (Est. 1808)
    Erie County

1980	18,146
1970	18,168
1960	13,267
1950	6,331
1940	4,426
1930	3,208
1920	2,660
1910	2,991
1900	2,948
1890	3,195
1880	3,495
1870	3,147
1860	3,356
1850	2,727
1840	2,271
1830	3,360
1820	3,278(a)

(a)Reported in NIAGARA County.

CLARENCE CENTER, CDP
  Clarence Town
    Erie County

1980	1,300
1970	1,332

CLARENCE COMPACT, CDP
  Clarence Town
    Erie County

1970	2,014
1960	1,456

CLARENDON, Town (Est. 1821)
    Orleans County

1980	2,148
1970	1,969
1960	1,659
1950	1,287
1940	1,176
1930	1,224
1920	1,139
1910	1,335
1900	1,518
1890	1,731
1880	1,797
1870	1,668
1860	1,831
1850	1,809
1840	2,251
1830	1,893

CLARK MILLS, CDP
  Kirkland Town
    Oneida County

1980	1,412
1970	1,206
1960	1,148
1950	NA
1940	929(a)
1890-1930	NA
1880	393(b)

(a)Reported in KIRKLAND, WESTMORELAND and

WHITESTOWN Towns.
(b)Reported as Clark's Mills.

CLARKSON, CDP
  Clarkson Town
    Monroe County
      1880   319

CLARKSON, Town (Est. 1819)
  Monroe County
    1980   4,016
    1970   3,642
    1960   2,339
    1950   1,912
    1940   1,449
    1930   1,456
    1920   1,403
    1910   1,549
    1900   1,581
    1890   1,741
    1880   2,100
    1870   1,884
    1860   2,093
    1850   4,555
    1840   3,486
    1830   3,249
    1820   1,612(a)
(a)Reported in GENESEE County.

CLARKSTOWN, Town (Est. 1791)
  Rockland County
    1980   77,091
    1970   61,653
    1960   33,196
    1950   15,674(a)
    1940   12,251
    1930   10,188
    1920   7,317
    1910   7,980
    1900   6,305
    1890   5,216
    1880   4,378
    1870   4,137
    1860   3,874
    1850   3,111
    1840   2,533
    1830   2,298
    1820   1,808
    1810   NA
    1800   *1,806(b)
(a)Boundary change.
(b)Reported as Clarks Town.

CLARKSVILLE, CDP
  New Scotland Town
    Albany County
      1880   260
      1870   236

CLARKSVILLE, CDP
  Clarksville Town
    Allegany County
      1880   93

CLARKSVILLE, CDP
  Niagara Town
    Niagara County
      1880   189

CLARKSVILLE, CDP
  Middlefield Town
    Otsego County
      1880   185

CLARKSVILLE, Town (Est. 1835)
  Allegany County
    1980   938
    1970   874
    1960   840
    1950   828
    1940   766
    1930   768
    1920   770
    1910   794
    1900   836
    1890   891
    1880   852
    1870   784
    1860   865
    1850   668
    1840   326

CLARKVILLE, Village (Inc. 1834)(a)
  Brookfield Town
    Madison County
      1880   581
      1870   322
(a)Dissolved; date unavailable.

CLAVERACK, CDP(a)
  Claverack Town
    Columbia County
      1880   311
(a)Reported, in part, in CLAVERACK--RED
    MILLS, CDP in 1980.

CLAVERACK, Town (Est. 1788)
  Columbia County
    1980   6,061
    1970   5,711
    1960   4,989
    1950   4,406
    1940   4,071
    1930   4,168
    1920   3,747
    1910   4,114
    1900   4,416
    1890   4,518
    1880   4,347
    1870   3,671
    1860   3,477
    1850   3,208
    1840   3,056
    1830   3,000
    1820   2,813
    1810   NA
    1800   *4,414
    1790   3,262

CLAVERACK--RED MILLS, CDP
  Claverack Town
    Columbia County
      1980   1,217

CLAY, Town (Est. 1827)
  Onondaga County
    1980   52,838
    1970   36,274

1960	17,760
1950	7,001
1940	4,050
1930	3,560
1920	2,488
1910	2,431
1900	2,578
1890	2,630
1880	2,910
1870	3,156
1860	3,583
1850	3,402
1840	2,852
1830	2,095

CLAYSBURGH, CDP
  Black Brook Town
    Clinton County

1880	299

CLAYTON, Town (Est. 1833)
  Jefferson County

1980	4,028
1970	4,021
1960	3,753
1950	3,758
1940	3,768
1930	3,698
1920	3,618
1910	4,028
1900	4,313
1890	4,411
1880	4,214
1870	4,082
1860	4,696
1850	4,191
1840	3,990

CLAYTON, Village (Inc. 1872)
  Clayton Town
    Jefferson County

1980	1,816
1970	1,970(a)
1960	1,996
1950	1,981
1940	1,999
1930	1,940
1920	1,849
1910	1,941
1900	1,913
1890	1,748
1880	1,621
1870	1,020

(a)Boundary change.

CLAYVILLE, Village (Inc. 1887)
  Paris Town
    Oneida County

1980	478(a)
1970	535
1960	686
1950	719
1940	711
1930	801
1920	999
1910	649
1900	568
1890	843
1880	847

1870	944

(a)Boundary change.

CLERMONT, CDP
  Clermont Town
    Columbia County

1880	109

CLERMONT, Town (Est. 1787)
  Columbia County

1980	1,269
1970	1,120
1960	980
1950	898
1940	806
1930	805
1920	667
1910	800
1900	812
1890	798
1880	918
1870	1,021
1860	968
1850	1,130
1840	1,231
1830	1,203
1820	1,164
1810	NA
1800	*1,142
1790	867

CLEVELAND, Village (Inc. 1857)
  Constantia Town
    Oswego County

1980	855
1970	821
1960	732
1950	555
1940	440
1930	416
1920	541
1910	687
1900	689
1890	839
1880	724
1870	895
1860	902

CLIFTON, CDP
  Chili Town
    Monroe County

1880	150

CLIFTON, Town (Est. 1868)
  St. Lawrence County

1980	1,005
1970	1,207
1960	1,306
1950	1,382
1940	1,005
1930	1,291
1920	1,573
1910	1,674
1900	1,382
1890	342
1880	71
1870	221

CLIFTON, Town
   Saratoga County
  see CLIFTON PARK, Town
       Saratoga County

CLIFTONDALE, CDP
  see CLINTONDALE, CDP
       Ulster County

CLIFTON KNOLLS, CDP
  Clifton Park Town
    Saratoga County
      1980   5,636
      1970   5,771

CLIFTON PARK, CDP
  Halfmoon Town
    Saratoga County
      1880   49

CLIFTON PARK, Town (Est. 1828)(a)
  Saratoga County
      1980   23,989(b)
      1970   14,867
      1960   4,512
      1950   3,281
      1940   2,253
      1930   2,222
      1920   1,983
      1910   2,225
      1900   2,140
      1890   2,228
      1880   2,454
      1870   2,657
      1860   2,804
      1850   2,868
      1840   2,719
      1830   2,494
(a)Established as Clifton in 1828; name
   changed in 1829.
(b)Boundary change.

CLIFTON SPRINGS, Village (Inc. 1859)
  Manchester Town, part in
    Ontario County
      1980   1,533
      1970   1,556
      1960   1,498
      1950   1,463
      1940   1,093
      1930   1,455
      1920   1,293
      1910   1,189
      1900   1,277
      1890   1,046
      1880   790
      1870   641
  Phelps Town, part in
    Ontario County
      1980   506
      1970   502
      1960   455
      1950   375
      1940   320
      1930   364
      1920   335
      1910   411
      1900   340
      1890   251

      1880   112
      1870   105
  TOTAL
      1980   2,039
      1970   2,058
      1960   1,953
      1950   1,838
      1940   1,413
      1930   1,819
      1920   1,628
      1910   1,600
      1900   1,617
      1890   1,297
      1880   902
      1870   746

CLINTON, County (Est. 1788)
      1980   80,750
      1970   72,934
      1960   72,722
      1950   53,622
      1940   54,006
      1930   46,687
      1920   43,898
      1910   48,230
      1900   47,430
      1890   46,437
      1880   50,897
      1870   47,947
      1860   45,735
      1850   40,047
      1840   28,157
      1830   19,344
      1820   12,070
      1810   8,002
      1800   8,516(a)
      1790   1,614
(a)Includes population of ESSEX County.

CLINTON, Town (Est. 1845)
  Clinton County
      1980   685
      1970   712
      1960   796
      1950   844
      1940   1,157
      1930   1,191
      1920   1,395
      1910   1,598
      1900   1,574
      1890   1,750
      1880   2,194
      1870   2,206
      1860   1,924
      1850   1,436

CLINTON, Town (Est. 1786)
  Dutchess County
      1980   3,394
      1970   2,604
      1960   1,639
      1950   1,233
      1940   1,070
      1930   1,041
      1920   1,198
      1910   1,278
      1900   1,370
      1890   1,426
      1880   1,640

1870	1,708
1860	1,922
1850	1,795
1840	1,830
1830	2,130
1820	6,611
1810	NA
1800	*5,208
1790	4,607

CLINTON, Town
   Rensselaer County
   see EAST GREENBUSH, Town
      Rensselaer County

CLINTON, Village (Inc. 1843)
   Kirkland Town
      Oneida County

1980	2,107
1970	2,271
1960	1,855
1950	1,630
1940	1,478
1930	1,475
1920	1,270
1910	1,236
1900	1,340
1890	1,269
1880	1,236
1870	1,640

CLINTONDALE, CDP
   Plattekill Town
      Ulster County

1980	1,193
1950-1970	NA
1940	548(a)
1890-1930	NA
1880	371(b)

(a)Reported in LLOYD and PLATTEKILL
   Towns.
(b)Reported as Cliftondale.

CLINTON PRISON, CDP
   Dannemora Town
      Clinton County

1880	525

CLINTONVILLE, Village (Inc. 1825)(a)
   AuSable Town & Chesterfield Towns
      Clinton & Essex Counties

1890	306(b)
1880	205

(a)Dissolved; date unavailable.
(a)Part in CLINTON County, 290; part in
   ESSEX County, 16.

CLOCKVILLE, CDP
   Lenox Town
      Madison County

1880	182

CLYDE, Village (Inc. 1835)
   Galen Town
      Wayne County

1980	2,491
1970	2,828
1960	2,693
1950	2,492

1940	2,356
1930	2,374
1920	2,528
1910	2,695
1900	2,507
1890	2,638
1880	2,826
1870	2,735

CLYMER, CDP
   Clymer Town
      Chautauqua County

1870	400

CLYMER, Town (Est. 1821)
   Chautauqua County

1980	1,484
1970	1,352
1960	1,377
1950	1,421
1940	1,244
1930	1,181
1920	1,205
1910	1,164
1900	1,229
1890	1,363
1880	1,455
1870	1,486
1860	1,330
1850	1,127
1840	909
1830	567

COBLESKILL, Town (Est. 1797)
   Schoharie County

1980	7,048
1970	6,017
1960	4,964
1950	4,709
1940	4,005
1930	3,980
1920	3,798
1910	3,579
1900	3,973
1890	3,443
1880	3,370
1870	2,847
1860	2,357(a)
1850	2,229
1840	3,583
1830	2,988
1820	2,440
1810	NA
1800	*1,765(b)

(a)Reported as Cobbleskill.
(b)Reported as Cobuskill.

COBLESKILL, Village (Inc. 1868)
   Cobleskill Town
      Schoharie County

1980	5,272
1970	4,368
1960	3,471
1950	3,208
1940	2,617
1930	2,594
1920	2,410
1910	2,088
1900	2,327

1890	1,822
1880	1,222
1870	1,030

COBUSKILL, Town
  See COBLESKILL, Town
      Schoharie County

COCHECTON, CDP
  Cochecton Town
    Sullivan County

1880	188

COCHECTON, Town (Est. 1828)
  Sullivan County

1980	1,330
1970	1,181
1960	1,070
1950	1,136
1940	1,189
1930	1,154
1920	1,112
1910	1,142
1900	1,117
1890	1,174
1880	1,328
1870	1,490
1860	3,174
1850	1,671
1840	622
1830	438

COEYMANS, CDP
  Coeymans Town
    Albany County

1940	1,055
1890-1930	NA
1880	654

COEYMANS, Town (Est. 1791)
  Albany County

1980	7,896
1970	6,715
1960	5,622
1950	4,713
1940	4,536
1930	4,542
1920	4,147
1910	4,252
1900	3,952(a)
1890	3,669
1880	2,912
1870	3,077
1860	3,117
1850	3,050
1840	3,170
1830	2,723
1820	2,872
1810	NA
1800	*3,095(b)

(a)Reported as Coeyman.
(b)Reported as Coyemans.

COHOCTON, Town (Est. 1812)
  Steuben County

1980	2,466
1970	2,379
1960	2,451
1950	2,418
1940	2,474
1930	2,516
1920	2,585
1910	2,926
1900	3,197
1890	3,444
1880	3,346
1870	2,710
1860	2,535
1850	1,993
1840	2,965
1830	2,544
1820	1,560(a)

(a)Reported as Conhocton.

COHOCTON, Village (Inc. 1891)
  Cohocton Town
    Steuben County

1980	902
1970	897
1960	929
1950	943
1940	931
1930	860
1920	843
1910	838
1900	879

COHOES, City (Inc. 1869)(a)
  Albany County

1980	18,144
1970	18,653
1960	20,129
1950	21,272
1940	21,955
1930	23,226
1920	22,987
1910	24,709
1900	23,910
1890	22,509
1880	19,416
1870	15,357

(a)COHOES Village incorporated as COHOES
City and made independent of WATER-
VLIET Town in 1869.

COHOES, Village (Inc. 1855)(a)
  Watervliet Town
    Albany County

1860	8,800
1850	4,229

(a)COHOES Village incorporated as COHOES
City and made independent of WATER-
VLIET Town in 1869.

COLCHESTER, Town (Est. 1792)
  Delaware County

1980	1,848
1970	1,665
1960	1,920
1950	2,340
1940	2,092
1930	2,489
1920	2,849
1910	3,193
1900	3,156
1890	2,973
1880	2,941
1870	2,652

1860	2,480
1850	2,184
1840	1,567
1830	1,424
1820	1,064
1810	NA
1800	*1,207

COLD BROOK, CDP
    Black Brook and Saranac Towns
        Clinton County

1880	366

COLD BROOK, Village (Inc. 1903)
    Russia Town
        Herkimer County

1980	402
1970	413
1960	372
1950	342
1940	271
1930	288
1920	261
1910	358
1890-1900	NA
1880	117
1870	170

COLDEN, Town (Est. 1827)
    Erie County

1980	3,128
1970	3,020
1960	2,384
1950	1,720
1940	1,528
1930	1,217
1920	1,259
1910	1,303
1900	1,260
1890	1,378
1880	1,464
1870	1,472
1860	1,568
1850	1,344
1840	1,088
1830	464

COLDENHAM, CDP
    Montgomery Town
        Orange County

1980	1,064

COLDEN HILL, CDP
    Montgomery & Newburgh Towns
        Orange County

1980	1,741(a)
1970	1,688(b)

(a)Part in MONTGOMERY Town, 268; part in
    NEWBURGH Town, 1,473.
(b)Reported in NEWBURGH Town only.

COLD SPRING, CDP
    Huntington Town
        Suffolk County

1880	857
1870	730(a)

(a)Reported as Cold Springs.

COLD SPRING, Town (Est. 1823)
    Cattaraugus County
    see NAPOLI, Town
            Cattaraugus County

COLD SPRING, Town (Est. 1837)
    Cattaraugus County

1980	708(a)
1970	638(b)
1960	580
1950	619
1940	596
1930	541
1920	567
1910	685 Rev.(c)
1900	790 Rev.(c)
1890	901
1880	984
1870	835
1860	667
1850	591
1840	673

(a)Reported as Coldspring.
(b)Boundary change.
(c)In 1920 the Census Bureau revised the
    1910 figure of 898 and the 1900 figure
    of 1,030 to exclude the ALLEGANY
    INDIAN RESERVATION.

COLD SPRING, Village (Inc. 1846)
    Philipstown Town
        Putnam County

1980	2,161
1970	2,083
1960	2,083
1950	1,788
1940	1,897
1930	1,784
1920	1,433
1910	2,549
1900	2,067
1890	NA
1880	2,111
1870	3,086
1860	2,770

COLD SPRING HARBOR, CDP
    Huntington Town
        Suffolk County

1980	5,336
1970	5,450 Rev.
1960	3,976 Rev.

COLD SPRINGS, CDP
    see COLD SPRING, CDP
            Suffolk County

COLESVILLE, Town (Est. 1821)
    Broome County

1980	4,965
1970	4,420
1960	3,773
1950	3,084
1940	2,652
1930	2,394
1920	2,311
1910	2,415
1900	2,773
1890	3,126

1880	3,208
1870	3,400
1860	3,250
1850	3,061
1840	2,528
1830	2,387

COLLEGE POINT, Village (Inc. 1867)(a)
  Flushing Town
    Queens County

1890	6,127
1880	4,192
1870	3,652

(a)Merged into QUEENS Borough in NEW YORK
   City in 1898.

COLLINS, CDP
  Collins Town
    Erie County

1940	894

COLLINS, Town (Est. 1821)
  Erie County

1980	5,037
1970	6,400
1960	6,984
1950	6,862
1940	5,819
1930	4,424
1920	4,061
1910	3,742 Rev.(a)
1900	2,875 Rev.(a)
1890	2,362
1880	2,371
1870	2,100
1860	2,119
1850	4,001
1840	4,257
1830	2,123

(a)In 1920 the Census Bureau revised the
   1910 figure of 4,568 and the 1900
   figure of 3,753 to exclude the
   CATTARAUGUS INDIAN RESERVATION.

COLLINS CENTER, CDP
  Collins Town
    Erie County

1880	345(a)

(a)Reported as Collins Centre.

COLONIE, Town (Est. 1895)(a)
  Albany County

1980	74,593(b)
1970	69,147
1960	52,760
1950	29,522
1940	20,631
1930	17,468
1920	10,196(b)
1910	8,385
1900	7,035

(a)An earlier Colonie Town was established in ALBANY County in 1808; it
   merged into ALBANY City and WATER-
   VLIET Town in 1815.
(b)Boundary change.

COLONIE, Village (Inc. 1921)(a)
  Colonie Town
    Albany County

1980	8,869
1970	8,701
1960	6,992(b)
1950	2,068
1940	1,407
1930	1,176

(a)An earlier Colonie Village was incorporated as Watervliet Village in
   WATERVLIET Town in 1801. It's name
   was changed to Colonie in 1804 and it
   merged into ALBANY City in 1815.
(b)Boundary change.

COLTON, CDP
  Colton Town
    St. Lawrence County

1890	635
1880	606
1870	633

COLTON, Town (Est. 1843)
  St. Lawrence County

1980	1,292
1970	1,249
1960	1,195
1950	960
1940	1,096
1930	986
1920	1,299
1910	1,499
1900	1,678
1890	1,843
1880	1,974
1870	1,719
1860	1,400
1850	506

COLUMBIA, County (Est. 1786)

1980	59,487
1970	51,519
1960	47,322
1950	43,182
1940	41,464
1930	41,617
1920	38,930
1910	43,658
1900	43,211
1890	46,172
1880	47,928
1870	47,044
1860	47,172
1850	43,073
1840	43,252
1830	39,907
1820	38,330
1810	32,390
1800	35,472
1790	27,732

COLUMBIA, Town (Est. 1812)
  Herkimer County

1980	1,537
1970	1,387
1960	1,327
1950	1,132

1940	931
1930	915
1920	911
1910	1,071
1900	1,268
1890	1,380
1880	1,616
1870	1,637
1860	1,893
1850	2,000
1840	2,129
1830	2,181
1820	2,051

COLUMBIA CENTRE, CDP
  Columbia Town
    Herkimer County

1880	99

COLUMBIAVILLE, CDP(a)
  Stockport Town
    Columbia County

1860	234

(a)Incorporated as a village in 1812 and
   dissolved in 1833.

COLUMBUS, Town (Est. 1805)
  Chenango County

1980	802
1970	723
1960	706
1950	655
1940	711
1930	724
1920	683
1910	838
1900	997
1890	1,109
1880	1,177
1870	1,197
1860	1,407
1850	1,381
1840	1,561
1830	1,661
1820	1,805

COLUMBUS CENTER, CDP
  Columbus Town
    Chenango County

1880	124

COLUMBUSVILLE, CDP
  Newtown Town
    Queens County

1870	1,251

COMMACK, CDP
  Huntington Town, part in
    Suffolk County

1980	13,687
1970	16,232 Rev.
1960	6,247

  Smithtown Town, part in
    Suffolk County

1980	21,032(a)
1970	7,906(b)
1960	3,366

  TOTAL

1980	34,719(a)

1970	24,138 Rev.(c)
1960	9,613

(a)Boundary change.
(b)Population of 24,920 is comparable to
   1980 boundaries.
(c)Population of 41,152 is comparable to
   1980 boundaries.

CONCORD, Town (Est. 1812)
  Erie County

1980	8,171
1970	7,573
1960	6,452
1950	5,291
1940	4,524
1930	4,453
1920	4,223
1910	4,391
1900	4,086
1890	3,881
1880	3,400
1870	3,171
1860	3,183
1850	3,242
1840	3,021
1830	1,895
1820	2,786(a)

(a)Reported in NIAGARA County.

CONCORD, Town
  Saratoga County
  see DAY, Town
        Saratoga County

CONESUS, CDP
  Conesus Town
    Livingston County

1880	190
1870	231(a)

(a)Reported as Conesus Centre.

CONESUS, Town (Est. 1819)(a)
  Livingston County

1980	1,970
1970	1,533
1960	1,221
1950	809
1940	809
1930	832
1920	814
1910	937
1900	1,149
1890	1,196
1880	1,397
1870	1,362
1860	1,443
1850	1,418
1840	1,654
1830	1,690
1820	1,288(b)

(a)Established as Freeport in 1819; name
   changed to Bowersville in Mar., 1825,
   and to CONESUS in Apr., 1825.
(b)Reported in ONTARIO County.

CONESUS CENTRE, CDP
  see CONESUS, CDP
        Livingston County

CONESVILLE, Town (Est. 1836)
   Schoharie County
      1980   681
      1970   489
      1960   593
      1950   626
      1940   673
      1930   569
      1920   652
      1910   708
      1900   793
      1890   929
      1880   1,127
      1870   1,314
      1860   1,478
      1850   1,582
      1840   1,621

CONEWANGO, Town (Est. 1823)
   Cattaraugus County
      1980   1,578
      1970   1,393
      1960   1,162
      1950   1,045
      1940   952
      1930   1,011
      1920   931
      1910   1,098
      1900   1,224
      1890   1,273
      1880   1,299
      1870   1,281
      1860   1,359
      1850   1,408
      1840   1,317
      1830   1,712

CONEY ISLAND, CDP(a)
   Gravesend Town
      Kings County
      1890   3,313
      1880   1,184
(a)Merged into BROOKLYN City in 1894.

CONGERS, CDP
   Clarkstown Town
      Rockland County
      1980   7,123
      1970   5,928
      1960   NA
      1950   1,949
      1940   1,673

CONHOCTON, Town
   see COHOCTON, Town
         Steuben County

CONKLIN, Town (Est. 1824)
   Broome County
      1980   6,204
      1970   5,399
      1960   4,347
      1950   2,872
      1940   2,156
      1930   1,332
      1920   796
      1910   850
      1900   946
      1890   1,033

      1880   1,420
      1870   1,440
      1860   1,146
      1850   2,232
      1840   1,475
      1830   906

CONKLINGVILLE, CDP
   Hadley Town
      Saratoga County
      1880   326

CONNASOXHARRIE, Town
   see CANAJOHARIE, Town
         Montgomery County

CONNERSVILLE, CDP(a)
   Rensselaerville Town
      Albany County
      1880   22
(a)Also called WILLIAMSBURG.

CONQUEST, CDP
   Conquest Town
      Cayuga County
      1880   101

CONQUEST, Town (Est. 1821)
   Cayuga County
      1980   1,628
      1970   1,362
      1960   1,170
      1950   1,103
      1940   890
      1930   906
      1920   1,044
      1910   1,103
      1900   1,360
      1890   1,549
      1880   1,661
      1870   1,821
      1860   1,892
      1850   1,863
      1840   1,911
      1830   1,507

CONSTABLE, Town (Est. 1807)
   Franklin County
      1980   1,218
      1970   1,149
      1960   1,153
      1950   983
      1940   919
      1930   1,016
      1920   1,100
      1910   1,323
      1900   1,266
      1890   1,439
      1880   1,532
      1870   1,546
      1860   1,680
      1850   1,447
      1840   1,122
      1830   693
      1820   637

CONSTABLEVILLE, Village (Inc. 1877)
  West Turin Town
    Lewis County

1980	330
1970	347
1960	439
1950	378
1940	340
1930	348
1920	380
1910	407
1900	450
1890	NA
1880	593
1870	712

CONSTANTIA, CDP(a)
  Constantia Town
    Oswego County

1980	1,254
1950-1970	NA
1940	647
1900-1930	NA
1890	241
1880	355
1870	587

(a)Incorporated as a village in 1836;
   dissolved, date unavailable.

CONSTANTIA, Town (Est. 1808)
  Oswego County

1980	4,312
1970	3,547
1960	2,730
1950	1,947
1940	1,538
1930	1,405
1920	1,789
1910	2,023
1900	2,259
1890	2,691
1880	3,124
1870	3,437
1860	2,511
1850	2,495
1840	1,476
1830	1,193
1820	767

COOKSBURG, CDP
  Rensselaerville Town
    Albany County

1880	82
1870	67

COOPERSTOWN, Village (Inc. 1807)(a)
  Middlefield Town, part in
    Otsego County

1980	238
1970	172
1960	97
1950	63
1940	73
1930	61
1920	58
1910	48
1900	42

  Otsego Town, part in
    Otsego County

1980	2,104
1970	2,231
1960	2,456
1950	2,664
1940	2,526
1930	2,848
1920	2,667
1910	2,436
1900	2,326
1890	2,657(b)
1880	2,199

TOTAL

1980	2,342
1970	2,403
1960	2,553
1950	2,727
1940	2,599
1930	2,909
1920	2,725
1910	2,484
1900	2,368
1880-1890	(c)
1870	NA
1860	1,597

(a)Incorporated as Otsego in 1807; name
   changed in 1812.
(b)Boundary change.
(c)Reported in OTSEGO Town only.

COOPERSVILLE, CDP
  Champlain Town
    Clinton County

1880	113
1870	205

COPAKE, CDP
  Copake Town
    Columbia County

1940	557
1890-1930	NA
1880	190

COPAKE, Town (Est. 1824)
  Columbia County

1980	2,854
1970	2,209
1960	1,630
1950	1,478
1940	1,498
1930	1,165
1920	1,114
1910	1,283
1900	1,277
1890	1,515
1880	1,905
1870	1,847
1860	1,839
1850	1,652
1840	1,505
1830	1,676

COPAKE IRON WORKS, CDP
  Copake Town
    Columbia County

1880	337

COPENHAGEN, Village (Inc. 1870)
  Denmark Town
    Lewis County
        1980   656
        1970   734
        1960   673
        1950   690
        1940   608
        1930   539
        1920   554
        1910   585
        1900   587
        1890   777
        1880   702
        1870   575

COPIAGUE, CDP
  Babylon Town
    Suffolk County
        1980   20,132
        1970   19,632
        1960   14,081
        1950   NA
        1940   1,584(a)
(a)Reported as Copiague Station.

CORAM, CDP
  Brookhaven Town
    Suffolk County
        1980   24,752(a)
        1970   6,717(b)
        1960   2,942(c)
        1890-1950   NA
        1880   158
(a)Boundary change.
(b)Derived by LIRPB from U.S. Census
   Data; population of 6,875 is comparable to 1980 boundaries.
(c)Derived by LIRPB from U.S. Census
   Data.

CORBETTSVILLE, CDP
  Conklin Town
    Broome County
        1880   239

CORFU, Village (Inc. 1868)
  Pembroke Town
    Genesee County
        1980   689
        1970   722
        1960   616
        1950   542
        1940   462
        1930   418
        1920   458
        1910   413
        1900   401
        1890   398
        1880   353

CORINTH, Town (Est. 1818)
  Saratoga County
        1980   5,216
        1970   5,442 Rev.
        1960   5,167
        1950   4,879
        1940   4,478
        1930   3,760

        1920   3,696
        1910   3,102
        1900   3,104
        1890   2,124
        1880   1,737
        1870   1,500
        1860   1,558
        1850   1,501
        1840   1,365
        1830   1,412
        1820   1,490

CORINTH, Village (Inc. 1886)
  Corinth Town
    Saratoga County
        1980   2,702
        1970   3,267
        1960   3,193
        1950   3,161
        1940   3,054
        1930   2,613
        1920   2,576
        1910   2,166
        1900   2,039
        1890   1,222
        1880   510

CORMELL, Town
  Dutchess County
  see CARMEL, Town
        Putnam County

CORNERS, CDP
  New Paltz Town
    Ulster County
        1880   39

CORNING, City (Inc. 1890)(a)
  Steuben County
        1980   12,953
        1970   15,792
        1960   17,085(b)
        1950   17,684
        1940   16,212
        1930   15,777
        1920   15,820
        1910   13,730
        1900   11,061
        1890   8,550
(a)CORNING Village incorporated as COR-
   NING City and made independent of
   CORNING Town in 1890.
(b)Boundary change.

CORNING, Town (Est. 1796)(a)
  Steuben County
        1980   6,846
        1970   7,523
        1960   6,732(b)
        1950   4,275
        1940   3,152
        1930   2,997
        1920   2,857
        1910   2,391
        1900   1,937
        1890   1,638(b)
        1880   7,402
        1870   6,502
        1860   6,003

1850	4,372
1840	1,674
1830	794
1820	2,088
1810	NA
1800	*262

(a)Established as PAINTED POST in 1796;
   name changed in 1852.
(b)Boundary change.

CORNING, Village (Inc. 1848)(a)
   Corning Town
      Steuben County

1880	4,802
1870	4,018

(a)CORNING Village incorporated as COR-
   NING City and made independent of
   CORNING Town in 1890.

CORNWALL, Town (Est. 1788)(a)
   Orange County

1980	10,774
1970	9,672
1960	8,094
1950	6,154
1940	5,299
1930	5,067
1920	4,259
1910	5,690
1900	4,258
1890	3,766
1880	3,833
1870	5,989
1860	4,800
1850	4,471
1840	3,925
1830	3,486
1820	3,020
1810	NA
1800	*1,648(b)
1790	4,225

(a)Established as New Cornwall in 1788;
   name changed in 1797.
(b)Reported as New Cornwall.

CORNWALL, Village
   see CORNWALL-ON-HUDSON, Village
      Orange County

CORNWALL LANDING, CDP
   Cornwall Town
      Orange County

1870	200

CORNWALL-ON-HUDSON, Village
   (Inc. 1884)(a)
   Cornwall Town
      Orange County

1980	3,164
1970	3,131(b)
1960	2,785
1950	2,211
1940	1,978
1930	1,910
1920	1,755
1910	2,658
1900	1,966
1890	760(c)

(a)Incorporated as CORNWALL in 1884;

   name changed in 1978.
(b)Boundary change.
(c)Reported as Cornwall-on-Hudson.

CORONA, CDP
   Newtown Town
      Queens County

1890	2,362
1880	750

CORTLAND, City (Inc. 1900)(a)
   Cortland County

1980	20,138(b)
1970	19,621
1960	19,181
1950	18,152
1940	15,881
1930	15,043
1920	13,294
1910	11,504
1900	9,014

(a)CORTLAND Village incorporated as
   CORTLAND City and made independent of
   CORTLANDVILLE Town in 1900.
(b)Boundary change.

CORTLAND, Village (Inc. 1864)(a)
   Cortlandville Town
      Cortland County

1890	8,590
1880	4,050
1870	3,066

(a)CORTLAND Village incorporated as
   CORTLAND City and made independent of
   CORTLANDVILLE Town in 1900.

CORTLAND, County (Inc. 1808)

1980	48,820
1970	45,894
1960	41,113
1950	37,158
1940	33,668
1930	31,709
1920	29,625
1910	29,249
1900	27,576
1890	28,657
1880	25,825
1870	25,173
1860	26,294
1850	25,140(a)
1840	24,607(a)
1830	23,791(b)
1820	16,507(c)
1810	8,869 Rev.(a)

(a)Reported as Cortlandt.
(b)Reported as Courtlandt.
(c)Reported as Courtland.

CORTLANDT, Town (Est. 1788)
   Westchester County

1980	35,705
1970	34,393
1960	26,336
1950	14,146
1940	11,016(a)
1930	26,492
1920	21,023
1910	22,255

1900	18,703
1890	15,139
1880	12,664
1870	11,694
1860	10,074(b)
1850	7,758
1840	5,592
1830	3,840(c)
1820	3,421(c)
1810	NA
1800	*2,752
1790	1,932

(a)Boundary change.
(b)Reported as Cortland.
(c)Reported as Courtlandt.

CORTLANDVILLE, Town (Est. 1829)
    Cortland County

1980	8,299(a)
1970	7,469
1960	5,660
1950	4,058
1940	3,823
1930	3,520
1920	3,237
1910	3,155
1900	2,907(a)
1890	11,451
1880	7,114
1870	6,082
1860	4,817
1850	4,203(b)
1840	3,799
1830	3,673(c)

(a)Boundary change.
(b)Reported as Cortlandtville.
(c)Reported as Courtlandtville.

CORTLAND WEST, CDP
    Cortlandville Town
    Cortland County

1980	1,149

COTTAM HILL, CDP
    Poughkeepsie Town
    Dutchess County

1980	1,380

COUNTRY KNOLLS, CDP
    Clifton Park Town
    Saratoga County

1980	2,497
1970	2,082

COVE NECK, Village (Inc. 1927)
    Oyster Bay Town
    Nassau County

1980	331
1970	344
1960	299
1950	200
1940	130
1930	276

COVENTRY, CDP
    Coventry Town
    Chenango County

1880	151

COVENTRY, Town (Est. 1806)
    Chenango County

1980	1,271
1970	974
1960	859
1950	796
1940	722
1930	780
1920	733
1910	764
1900	987
1890	1,166
1880	1,317
1870	1,490
1860	1,671
1850	1,677
1840	1,681
1830	1,576
1820	1,431

COVERT, Town (Est. 1817)
    Seneca County

1980	2,188
1970	2,097
1960	1,965
1950	1,843
1940	1,633
1930	1,578
1920	1,661
1910	1,947
1900	1,897
1890	1,963
1880	2,166
1870	2,238
1860	2,410
1850	2,253
1840	1,563
1830	1,791
1820	3,439

COVEVILLE, CDP
    Day Town
    Saratoga County

1880	53

COVINGTON, Town (Est. 1817)
    Wyoming County

1980	1,075
1970	953
1960	827
1950	789
1940	698
1930	696
1920	788
1910	923
1900	930
1890	1,151
1880	1,176
1870	1,189
1860	1,286
1850	1,385
1840	2,438(a)
1830	2,716(a)
1820	2,144(a)

(a)Reported in GENESEE County.

COVINGTON CENTRE, CDP
  Covington Town
    Wyoming County
      1880   78

COXSACKIE, Town
  Greene County
    1980   6,018
    1970   4,236
    1960   4,794
    1950   4,703
    1940   4,146
    1930   3,139
    1920   2,994
    1910   3,620
    1900   4,102
    1890   3,773
    1880   4,009
    1870   3,829
    1860   3,661
    1850   3,741
    1840   3,539
    1830   3,373
    1820   2,355(a)
    1810   NA
    1800   *4,676
    1790   3,406(b)
(a)Reported as Coxackie.
(b)Reported as Coxackie in ALBANY
   County.

COXSACKIE, Village (Inc. 1867)
  Coxsackie Town
    Greene County
      1980   2,786
      1970   2,399
      1960   2,849
      1950   2,722
      1940   2,352
      1930   2,195
      1920   1,121
      1910   2,494
      1900   2,735
      1890   1,611
      1880   1,661

COYEMANS, Town
  see COEYMANS, Town
        Albany County

CRANE'S, CDP
  Amsterdam Town
    Montgomery County
      1880   76

CRAWFORD, Town (Est. 1823)
  Orange County
    1980   4,910
    1970   3,896
    1960   2,574
    1950   2,410
    1940   1,786
    1930   1,800
    1920   1,507
    1910   1,659
    1900   1,778
    1890   1,876
    1880   1,951
    1870   2,024

    1860   2,003
    1850   1,912
    1840   2,075
    1830   2,019

CRESCENT, CDP
  Halfmoon Town
    Saratoga County
      1880   287

CREW ON VESSEL
  Brookhaven Town
    Suffolk County
      1970   108(a)
(a)Derived by LIRPB from U.S. Census
   Data.

CRITTENDEN, CDP
  Alden Town
    Erie County
      1880   124

CROGHAN, Town (Est. 1841)
  Lewis County
    1980   2,824
    1970   2,559
    1960   2,697
    1950   2,544
    1940   2,557
    1930   2,392
    1920   2,551
    1910   2,807
    1900   3,159
    1890   3,527
    1880   3,374
    1870   2,433
    1860   2,035
    1850   1,135

CROGHAN, Village (Inc. 1906)
  Croghan Town, part in
    Lewis County
      1980   383
      1970   396
      1960   453
      1950   432
      1940   476
      1930   449
      1920   412
      1910   434
      1890-1900   NA
      1880   445
  New Bremen Town, part in
    Lewis County
      1980   320
      1970   369
      1960   368
      1950   340
      1940   325
      1930   283
      1920   234
      1910   187
  TOTAL
      1980   703
      1970   765
      1960   821
      1950   772
      1940   801
      1930   732

1920	646
1910	621
1890-1900	NA
1880	(a)

(a)Reported in CROGHAN Town only.

CROTON, CDP
  Franklin Town
    Delaware County

1880	223

CROTON FALLS, CDP
  North Salem Town
    Westchester County

1880	403

CROTON LANDING, CDP
  Cortlandt Town
    Westchester County

1880	865

CROTON-ON-HUDSON, Village (Inc. 1898)
  Cortlandt Town
    Westchester County

1980	6,889
1970	7,523
1960	6,812
1950	4,837
1940	3,843(a)
1930	2,447
1920	2,286
1910	1,806
1900	1,533

(a)Boundary change.

CROWN HEIGHTS, CDP
  Poughkeepsie Town
    Dutchess County

1980	3,225
1970	3,292

CROWN POINT, Town (Est. 1786)
  Essex County

1980	1,837
1970	1,857
1960	1,685
1950	1,707
1940	1,661
1930	1,468
1920	1,413
1910	1,690
1900	2,112
1890	3,135
1880	4,287
1870	2,449
1860	2,252
1850	2,378
1840	2,212
1830	2,041
1820	1,522(a)
1810	NA
1800	*941
1790	203(b)

(a)Reported as Crownpoint.
(b)Reported in Crown-Point in CLINTON County.

CRUGER'S, CDP
  Cortlandt Town
    Westchester County

1880	145

CRYSTAL SPRINGS, CDP
  Barrington Town
    Yates County

1880	150

CUBA, Town (Est. 1822)
  Allegany County

1980	3,428
1970	3,165
1960	3,116
1950	2,784
1940	2,507
1930	2,256
1920	2,395
1910	2,431
1900	2,369
1890	2,328
1880	2,203
1870	2,397
1860	2,187
1850	2,243
1840	1,768
1830	1,059

CUBA, Village (Inc. 1850)
  Cuba Town
    Allegany County

1980	1,739
1970	1,735
1960	1,949
1950	1,783
1940	1,699
1930	1,422
1920	1,611
1910	1,556
1900	1,502
1890	1,386
1880	1,251

CUMBERLAND, County (Est. 1786)(a)
(a)Became Windham and Windsor Counties in Vermont State in 1790.

CUMMINGSVILLE, CDP
  North Dansville Town
    Livingston County

1880	126

CUTCHOGUE, CDP(a)
  Southold Town
    Suffolk County

1970	2,540(b)
1960	1,418(b)
1950	NA
1940	1,050
1890-1930	NA
1880	825

(a)Included in CUTCHOGUE--NEW SUFFOLK, CDP in 1980.
(b)Derived by LIRPB from U.S. Census Data.

CUTCHOGUE--NEW SUFFOLK, CDP
  Southold Town
    Suffolk County
        1980   2,788(a)
        1970   2,713(b)
(a)Boundary change.
(b)Derived by LIRPB from U.S. Census
    Data; population is comparable to 1980
    boundaries.

CUYLER, CDP
  Cuyler Town
    Cortland County
        1880   131
        1870   90

CUYLER, Town (Est. 1858)
    Cortland County
        1980   846
        1970   836
        1960   753
        1950   704
        1940   708
        1930   748
        1920   813
        1910   881
        1900   991
        1890   1,095
        1880   1,382
        1870   1,357
        1860   1,658

CUYLERVILLE, CDP(a)
  Leicester Town
    Livingston County
        1880   254
(a)Reported as Cuylersville.

D

DANBY, CDP
  Danby Town
    Tompkins County
        1880   137

DANBY, Town (Est. 1811)
    Tompkins County
        1980   2,449
        1970   2,141
        1960   2,059
        1950   1,555
        1940   1,253
        1930   1,407
        1920   1,143
        1910   1,235
        1900   1,449
        1890   1,707
        1880   2,065
        1870   2,126
        1860   2,261

        1850   2,411
        1840   2,570
        1830   2,481
        1820   2,001(a)
(a)Reported in TIOGA County.

DANFORTH, CDP(a)
  Onondaga Town
    Onondaga County
        1880   802
(a)Merged into SYRACUSE City in 1886.

DANNEMORA, Town (Est. 1854)
    Clinton County
        1980   4,717
        1970   4,719
        1960   6,141
        1950   5,614
        1940   6,362
        1930   4,720
        1920   4,061
        1910   4,203
        1900   3,720
        1890   3,977
        1880   2,962
        1870   1,512
        1860   1,271

DANNEMORA, Village (Inc. 1881)
  Dannemora Town, part in
    Clinton County
        1980   3,327
        1970   3,260
        1960   4,421
        1950   3,848
        1940   4,569
        1930   3,185
        1920   2,291
        1910   2,541 Rev.(a)
        1890-1900   NA
        1880   557
  Saranac Town, part in
    Clinton County
        1980   443
        1970   475
        1960   414
        1950   274
        1940   261
        1930   163
        1920   332
        1910   96
  TOTAL
        1980   3,770
        1970   3,735
        1960   4,835
        1950   4,122
        1940   4,830
        1930   3,348
        1920   2,623
        1910   2,637 Rev.(a)
        1890-1900   NA
        1880   (b)
(a)In 1930 the Census Bureau revised the
    1910 figure of 1,050 for that part of
    village in DANNEMORA Town and the 1910
    figure of 1,146 for the total of
    DANNEMORA Village.
(b)Reported in DANNEMORA Town only.

DANSVILLE, Town
    Essex County
  see WILMINGTON, Town
      Essex County

DANSVILLE, Town (Est. 1796)
    Steuben County

Year	Population
1980	1,455
1970	1,453
1960	1,125
1950	1,113
1940	794
1930	995
1920	1,031
1910	1,303
1900	1,417
1890	1,559
1880	1,788
1870	1,981
1860	2,187
1850	2,545
1840	2,725(a)
1830	1,726
1820	1,565

(a)Reported as Demsville.

DANSVILLE, Village (Inc. 1845)
  North Dansville Town
    Livingston County

Year	Population
1980	4,979
1970	5,436
1960	5,460(a)
1950	5,253
1940	4,976
1930	4,928
1920	4,631
1910	3,938
1900	3,633
1890	3,758
1880	3,625
1870	3,387

(a)Boundary change.

DANUBE, Town (Est. 1817)
    Herkimer County

Year	Population
1980	1,081
1970	1,015
1960	911
1950	847
1940	849
1930	790
1920	746
1910	941
1900	1,043
1890	1,116
1880	1,235
1870	1,324
1860	1,711
1850	1,730
1840	1,960
1830	1,724
1820	3,187

DARIEN, CDP
  Darien Town
    Genesee County

Year	Population
1880	106

DARIEN, Town (Est. 1832)
    Genesse County

Year	Population
1980	2,950
1970	2,745
1960	2,357
1950	1,899
1940	1,667
1930	1,740
1920	1,617
1910	1,779
1900	1,887
1890	1,964
1880	2,046
1870	2,054
1860	2,143
1850	2,084
1840	2,406

DARIEN CENTER, CDP
  Darien Town
    Genesee County

Year	Population
1880	197(a)

(a)Reported as Darien Centre.

DAVENPORT, Town (Est. 1817)
    Delaware County

Year	Population
1980	1,971
1970	1,617
1960	1,261
1950	1,233
1940	1,240
1930	1,197
1920	1,313
1910	1,427
1900	1,620
1890	1,789
1880	1,939
1870	2,187
1860	2,362
1850	2,305
1840	2,052(a)
1830	1,778
1820	1,384

(a)Reported as Devonport.

DAVID'S ISLAND, CDP
  New Rochelle Town
    Westchester County

Year	Population
1880	290

DAVIS PARK(a)
  Brookhaven Town
    Suffolk County

Year	Population
1970	18(b)

(a)Included in FIRE ISLAND, BROOKHAVEN
    Town in 1980.
(b)Derived by LIRPB from U.S. Census
    Data.

DAY, Town (Est. 1819)(a)
    Saratoga County

Year	Population
1980	656
1970	615
1960	466
1950	436
1940	475
1930	328
1920	473
1910	628

1900	719
1890	852
1880	1,238
1870	1,127
1860	1,209
1850	1,045
1840	942
1830	758
1820	571

(a)Established as Concord in 1819; name
   changed in 1827.

DAYTON, CDP
   Dayton Town
      Cattaraugus County

1880	367

DAYTON, Town (Est. 1835)
   Cattaraugus County

1980	1,981
1970	2,004
1960	1,931
1950	1,873
1940	1,725
1930	1,602
1920	1,712
1910	1,710
1900	1,691
1890	1,735
1880	1,705
1870	1,267
1860	1,294
1850	1,448
1840	946

DEAN'S CORNERS, CDP
   Middletown Town
      Delaware County

1880	47

DEANSVILLE, CDP
   Marshall Town
      Oneida County

1880	200

DECATUR, Town (Est. 1808)
   Otsego County

1980	312
1970	281
1960	254
1950	279
1940	324
1930	336
1920	422
1910	476
1900	559
1890	597
1880	779
1870	802
1860	902
1850	927
1840	1,071
1830	1,110
1820	908

DEERFIELD, CDP
   Deerfield Town
      Oneida County

1890	691

1880	716(a)

(a)Reported as Deerfield Corners.

DEERFIELD, Town (Est. 1798)
   Oneida County

1980	3,934
1970	4,104
1960	3,554
1950	1,621
1940	1,147
1930	983
1920	706(a)
1910	1,660
1900	1,756
1890	1,954
1880	2,082
1870	2,045
1860	2,249
1850	2,287(b)
1840	3,120
1830	4,182
1820	2,346

(a)Boundary change.
(b)Reported as Deersfield.

DEERFIELD CORNERS, CDP
   see DEERFIELD, CDP
         Oneida County

DEER PARK, CDP
   Babylon Town
      Suffolk County

1980	30,394(a)
1970	32,274 Rev.(b)
1960	17,914 Rev.

(a)Boundary change.
(b)Population of 33,668 is comparable to
   1980 boundaries.

DEERPARK, Town (Est. 1798)
   Orange County

1980	5,633
1970	4,370
1960	2,777
1950	2,519(a)
1940	2,227
1930	1,779
1920	1,615
1910	1,696(a)
1900	11,317(b)
1890	11,483
1880	11,420
1870	9,387
1860	5,186(b)
1850	4,032
1840	1,607
1830	1,167(b)
1820	1,340(b)
1810	NA
1800	*955(b)

(a)Boundary change.
(b)Reported as Deer Park.

DEERSFIELD, Town
   see DEERFIELD, Town
         Oneida County

DEFERIET, Village (Inc. 1921)
  Wilna Town
    Jefferson County
      1980   326
      1970   347
      1960   470
      1950   616
      1940   620
      1930   739

DE FREESTVILLE, CDP
  North Greenbush Town
    Rensselaer County
      1880   90

DE KALB, Town (Est. 1806)
  St. Lawrence County
      1980   2,130
      1970   2,062
      1960   2,137
      1950   2,063
      1940   2,116
      1930   2,346
      1920   2,419(a)
      1910   2,516(a)
      1900   2,723
      1890   2,840(a)
      1880   3,027
      1870   3,116
      1860   3,182
      1850   2,389
      1840   1,531
      1830   1,268(a)
      1820   709(a)
(a)Reported as Dekalb.

DE LANCEY, CDP
  Hamden Town
    Delaware County
      1880   112(a)
(a)Reported as De Lancy.

DELANSON, Village (Inc. 1921)
  Duanesburg Town
    Schenectady County
      1980   448
      1970   508
      1960   398
      1950   430
      1940   326
      1930   372

DE LANTI, CDP
  Stockton Town
    Chautauqua County
      1880   326
      1870   245(a)
(a)Reported as Delanti.

DELAWARE, County (Est. 1797)
      1980   46,824 Rev.
      1970   44,718
      1960   43,540
      1950   44,420
      1940   40,989
      1930   41,163
      1920   42,774
      1910   45,575
      1900   46,413

      1890   45,496
      1880   42,721
      1870   42,972
      1860   42,465
      1850   39,834
      1840   35,396
      1830   33,024
      1820   26,587
      1810   20,303
      1800   10,228

DELAWARE, Town (Est. 1869)
  Sullivan County
      1980   2,783
      1970   2,260
      1960   2,141
      1950   2,089
      1940   1,934
      1930   1,777
      1920   1,740
      1910   1,842
      1900   1,541
      1890   1,734
      1880   1,830
      1870   1,998

DELEVAN, Village (Inc. 1915)(a)
  Yorkshire Town
    Cattaraugus County
      1980   1,113
      1970   994
      1960   777(b)
      1950   611
      1940   554
      1930   558
      1920   547
      1900-1910   NA
      1890   511
      1880   430
(a)Reported as Yorkshire Center, CDP in
   1880-1890; name changed to DELEVAN in
   1892 and incorporated as Village in
   1915.
(b)Boundary change.

DELHI, Town (Est. 1798)
  Delaware County
      1980   5,295
      1970   4,617
      1960   3,398
      1950   3,311
      1940   2,950
      1930   2,853
      1920   2,721
      1910   2,815
      1900   3,243
      1890   2,908
      1880   2,941
      1870   2,920
      1860   2,900
      1850   2,909
      1840   2,554
      1830   1,679
      1820   2,285
      1810   NA
      1800   *820

DELHI, Village (Inc. 1821)
  Delhi Town
    Delaware County
        1980   3,374(a)
        1970   3,017(a)
        1960   2,307
        1950   2,223
        1940   1,841
        1930   1,840
        1920   1,669
        1910   1,736
        1900   2,078
        1890   1,564
        1880   1,384
        1870   1,223
        1840-1860   NA
        1830   435
(a)Boundary change.

DELMAR, CDP
  Bethlehem Town
    Albany County
        1980   8,423
        1950-1970   NA
        1940   2,992

DELPHI, CDP
  Pompey Town
    Onondaga County
        1880   230

DELTA, CDP
  Lee Town
    Oneida County
        1880   186

DEMSVILLE, Town
  see DANSVILLE, Town
        Steuben County

DENEITER, Town
    Chenango County
  see DE RUYTER, Town
        Madison County

DENMARK, Town (Est. 1807)
    Lewis County
        1980   2,448
        1970   2,359
        1960   2,214
        1950   2,154
        1940   1,992
        1930   1,987
        1920   1,905
        1910   1,889
        1900   2,193
        1890   2,275
        1880   2,204
        1870   2,109
        1860   2,559
        1850   2,824
        1840   2,388
        1830   2,370
        1820   1,745

DENNING, Town (Est. 1849)
    Ulster County
        1980   474
        1970   297

        1960   215
        1950   233
        1940   300
        1930   292
        1920   419
        1910   615
        1900   783
        1890   897
        1880   1,036
        1870   1,044
        1860   1,073
        1850   447

DENTON, CDP
  see NEW HAMPTON--DENTON, CDP
        Orange County

DEPAUVILLE, CDP
  Clayton Town
    Jefferson County
        1880   216
        1870   225

DEPEAU, Town
  see HERMON, Town
        St. Lawrence County

DEPEW, Village (Inc. 1894)
  Cheektowaga Town, part in
    Erie County
        1980   12,768(a)
        1970   14,392(a)
        1960   7,359
        1950   2,058
        1940   1,399
        1930   1,235
        1920   902
        1910   750
        1900   659
  Lancaster Town, part in
    Erie County
        1980   7,051
        1970   7,766(a)
        1960   6,221
        1950   5,159
        1940   4,685
        1930   5,301
        1920   4,948
        1910   3,171
        1900   2,720
  TOTAL
        1980   19,819(a)
        1970   22,158(a)
        1960   13,580
        1950   7,217
        1940   6,084
        1930   6,536
        1920   5,850
        1910   3,921
        1900   3,379
(a)Boundary change.

DE PEYSTER, Town (Est. 1825)
    St. Lawrence County
        1980   917
        1970   769
        1960   759
        1950   642
        1940   768

1930	805
1920	806(a)
1910	907(a)
1900	936
1890	947
1880	1,194
1870	1,138
1860	1,249
1850	906
1840	1,074
1830	804

(a)Reported as Depeyster.

DEPOSIT, Town (Est. 1880)
    Delaware County

1980	1,810
1970	1,656
1960	1,560
1950	1,570
1940	1,443
1930	1,469
1920	1,415
1910	1,641
1900	1,747
1890	1,664
1880	1,714

DEPOSIT, Village (Inc. 1811)
  Sanford Town, part in
  Broome County, part in

1980	1,017
1970	1,119
1960	1,187
1950	1,134
1940	1,252
1930	1,127
1920	1,202
1910	1,144
1900	1,298
1890	964
1880	875
1870	790

  Deposit Town, part in
  Delaware County, part in

1980	880
1970	942
1960	838
1950	882
1940	776
1930	760
1920	741
1910	720
1900	753
1890	566
1880	544
1870	496(a)

  TOTAL

1980	1,897
1970	2,061
1960	2,025
1950	2,016
1940	2,028
1930	1,887
1920	1,943
1910	1,864
1900	2,051
1890	1,530
1880	1,419
1870	1,286

(a)Reported in TOMPKINS Town.

DERBY, CDP
  Evans Town
    Erie County

1940	714

DERING HARBOR, Village (Inc. 1916)
  Shelter Island Town
    Suffolk County

1980	16
1970	24
1960	19
1950	4
1940	34
1930	39
1920	3

DE RUYTER, Town (Est. 1798)
  Madison County

1980	1,349
1970	1,366
1960	1,290
1950	1,165
1940	1,069
1930	1,047
1920	1,141
1910	1,196
1900	1,410
1890	1,500
1880	1,584
1870	2,009
1860	1,817
1850	1,931
1840	1,799
1830	1,447
1820	1,214
1810	NA
1800	*310(a)

(a)Reported as Deneiter in CHENANGO
County.

DE RUYTER, Village (Inc. 1833)
  De Ruyter Town
    Madison County

1980	542
1970	643
1960	627
1950	561
1940	526
1930	466
1920	519
1910	538
1900	623
1890	667
1880	586
1870	605

DEVONPORT, Town
  see DAVENPORT, Town
            Delaware County

DE WITT, CDP
  De Witt Town
    Onondaga County

1980	9,024
1970	10,032

DE WITT, Town (Est. 1835)
    Onondaga County
        1980   26,868
        1970   29,198
        1960   22,740
        1950   15,329
        1940   10,836
        1930   9,536(a)
        1920   10,279
        1910   7,422
        1900   5,435
        1890   4,560(b)
        1880   3,975
        1870   3,105
        1860   3,043
        1850   3,302
        1840   2,802
(a)Boundary change.
(b)Reported as Dewitt.

DEWITTVILLE, CDP
    Chautauqua Town
        Chautauqua County
        1880   198
        1870   262(a)
        1860   358(b)
(a)Reported as De Wittville.
(b)Reported as Dexterville.

DEXTER, Village (Inc. 1855)
    Brownville Town
        Jefferson County
        1980   1,053
        1970   1,061
        1960   1,009
        1950   1,038
        1940   1,109
        1930   1,020
        1920   1,164
        1910   1,005
        1900   945
        1890   737
        1880   487

DEXTERVILLE, CDP
    see DEWITTVILLE, CDP
        Chautauqua County

DIAL CITY, CDP
    Waterford Town
        Saratoga County
        1880   365

DIANA, Town (Est. 1830)
    Lewis County
        1980   1,709
        1970   1,649
        1960   1,641
        1950   1,717
        1940   1,871
        1930   2,080
        1920   2,181
        1910   2,279
        1900   2,083
        1890   2,395
        1880   2,026
        1870   1,778
        1860   1,483
        1850   970

        1840   883
        1830   309

DICKINSON, Town (Est. 1890)
    Broome County
        1980   5,594
        1970   5,687
        1960   6,591(a)
        1950   5,450(a)
        1940   5,060
        1930   4,255
        1920   1,975
        1910   832
        1900   728
(a)Boundary change.

DICKINSON, Town (Est. 1808)
    Franklin County
        1980   786
        1970   832
        1960   857
        1950   834
        1940   934
        1930   1,061
        1920   1,312
        1910   1,609
        1900   1,691
        1890   1,664(a)
        1880   2,329
        1870   1,990
        1860   1,917
        1850   1,119
        1840   1,005
        1830   446
        1820   495
(a)Boundary change.

DIVISION, Town
    see GROTON, Town
            Tompkins County

DIX, Town (Est. 1825)
    Schuyler County
        1980   4,138
        1970   4,201
        1960   3,916
        1950   3,871
        1940   3,739
        1930   3,583
        1920   3,486
        1910   3,625
        1900   3,894
        1890   3,700(a)
        1880   4,168
        1870   4,282
        1860   2,908
        1850   2,953(b)
        1840   1,990(b)
(a)Boundary change.
(b)Reported in CHEMUNG County.

DIX HILLS, CDP
    Huntington Town
        Suffolk County
        1980   26,693(a)
        1970   10,050(b)
        1960   4,464(c)
(a)Boundary change.
(b)Population of 22,569 is comparable to

1980 boundaries.
(c)Derived by LIRPB from U.S. Census
   Data.

DOBBS FERRY, Village (Inc. 1873)
   Greenburgh Town
      Westchester County
         1980   10,053
         1970   10,353
         1960   9,260
         1950   6,268
         1940   5,883
         1930   5,741
         1920   4,401
         1910   3,455
         1900   2,888
         1890   2,083

DOLGEVILLE, Village (Inc. 1891)
   Oppenheim Town, part in
      Fulton County
         1980   162
         1970   175
         1960   185
         1950   166
         1940   158
         1930   184
         1920   218
         1910   175
         1900   108
   Manheim Town, part in
      Herkimer County
         1980   2,440
         1970   2,697
         1960   2,873
         1950   3,038
         1940   3,037
         1930   3,125
         1920   3,230
         1910   2,510
         1900   1,807
   TOTAL
         1980   2,602
         1970   2,872
         1960   3,058
         1950   3,204
         1940   3,195
         1930   3,309
         1920   3,448
         1910   2,685
         1900   1,915

DORLACH, Town
   see SHARON, Town
         Schoharie County

DOSORIS, CDP
   Oyster Bay Town
      Nassau County
         1880   150(a)
(a)Reported in QUEENS County.

DOVER, Town (Est. 1807)
   Dutchess County
         1980   7,261
         1970   8,475
         1960   8,776
         1950   7,460
         1940   7,385

         1930   3,775
         1920   1,710
         1910   2,016
         1900   1,959
         1890   1,863
         1880   2,281
         1870   2,279
         1860   2,305
         1850   2,146
         1840   2,000
         1830   2,198
         1820   2,193

DOVER PLAINS, CDP
   Amenia, Dover & Washington Towns
      Dutchess County
         1980   1,753
         1950-1970   NA
         1940   730(a)
         1900-1930   NA
         1890   662(a)
         1880   721(a)
(a)Reported in DOVER Town only.

DOWNSVILLE, Village (Inc. 1921)(a)
   Colchester Town
      Delaware County
         1950   720
         1940   582
         1930   532
(a)Dissolved in 1950.

DOYLE, CDP
   Cheektowaga Town
      Erie County
         1940   998

DRESDEN, Town (Est. 1822)(a)
   Washington County
         1980   559
         1970   480
         1960   426
         1950   433
         1940   508
         1930   470
         1920   495
         1910   582
         1900   545
         1890   636
         1880   730
         1870   684
         1860   779
         1850   674
         1840   679
         1830   495
(a)Established as South Bay in Mar.,
   1822; name changed in Apr., 1822.

DRESDEN, Village (Inc. 1867)
   Torrey Town
      Yates County
         1980   378
         1970   450
         1960   437
         1950   373
         1940   257
         1930   276
         1920   295
         1910   345

1900	306
1890	348
1880	366

DRESSERVILLE, CDP
Sempronius Town
Cayuga County

1880	103

DRYDEN, Town (Est. 1803)
Tompkins County

1980	12,156
1970	9,770
1960	7,353
1950	5,006
1940	3,947
1930	3,534
1920	3,186
1910	3,590
1900	3,785
1890	4,043(a)
1880	4,805
1870	4,818
1860	4,962
1850	5,122
1840	5,446
1830	5,206
1820	3,951

(a)Boundary change.

DRYDEN, Village (Inc. 1857)
Dryden Town
Tompkins County

1980	1,761
1970	1,490(a)
1960	1,263
1950	976
1940	747
1930	666
1920	707
1910	709
1900	699
1890	663
1880	779
1870	672

(a)Boundary change.

DUANE, Town (Est. 1828)
Franklin County

1980	184
1970	111
1960	95
1950	117
1940	121
1930	177
1920	209
1910	300
1900	312
1890	421
1880	285
1870	234
1860	279
1850	222
1840	324
1830	247

DUANESBURG, CDP(a)
Duanesburg Town
Schenectady County

1880	91

(a)Reported as Duanesburgh.

DUANESBURG, Town (Est. 1788)
Schenectady County

1980	4,729
1970	3,800
1960	3,070
1950	2,822
1940	2,141
1930	1,937
1920	2,115
1910	2,211
1900	2,428
1890	2,557
1880	2,995(a)
1870	3,042(a)
1860	3,222
1850	3,464
1840	3,357
1830	2,837(a)
1820	3,510(a)
1810	NA
1800	*2,787(b)
1790	1,470(c)

(a)Reported as Duanesburgh.
(b)Reported in ALBANY County.
(c)Reported as Duanesburgh in ALBANY
   County.

DUBLIN, CDP
Junius Town
Seneca County

1880	80

DUCHESS, County
see DUTCHESS, County

DUGWAY, CDP
Albion Town
Oswego County

1880	87

DUNDEE, Village (Inc. 1847)
Starkey Town
Yates County

1980	1,556(a)
1970	1,539(a)
1960	1,468
1950	1,165
1940	1,168
1930	1,086
1920	1,143
1910	1,228
1900	1,291
1890	1,200
1880	1,025
1870	730
1860	733

(a)Boundary change.

DUNKIRK, City (Inc. 1880)(a)
Chautauqua County

1980	15,310
1970	16,855
1960	18,205(b)

1950	18,007
1940	17,713
1930	17,802
1920	19,336
1910	17,221
1900	11,616
1890	9,416(c)
1880	7,248

(a)Incorporated and made independent of
   DUNKIRK Town in 1880.
(b)Boundary change.
(c)Includes DUNKIRK Town.

DUNKIRK, Town (Est. 1859)
   Chautauqua County

1980	1,584
1970	1,646
1960	1,541(a)
1950	887
1940	672
1930	726
1920	512
1910	429
1900	454
1890	9,416(b)
1880	NA(a)
1870	6,912
1860	5,616

(a)Boundary change.
(b)Includes DUNKIRK City.

DUNKIRK, Village (Inc. 1837)(a)
   Dunkirk Town
   Chautauqua County

1870	5,231

(a)Merged into DUNKIRK City in 1885.

DUNNSVILLE, CDP
   Guilderland Town
   Albany County

1880	46

DURHAM, Town (Est. 1790)(a)
   Greene County

1980	2,283
1970	1,651
1960	1,313
1950	1,223
1940	1,233
1930	1,104
1920	1,211
1910	1,475
1900	1,636
1890	1,925
1880	2,173
1870	2,257
1860	2,558
1850	2,600
1840	2,813
1830	3,039
1820	2,979
1810	NA
1800	*3,812
1790	1,822(b)

(a)Established as Freehold in 1790; name
   changed in 1805.
(b)Reported as Free Hold in ALBANY
   County.

DURHAMVILLE, Village (Inc. 1869)(a)
   Verona Town
   Oneida County

1940	544
1900-1930	NA
1890	730
1880	NA
1870	859(b)

(a)Dissolved; date unavailable.
(b)Includes 148 reported in LENOX Town,
   MADISON County.

DUTCHESS, County (Est. 1683)

1980	245,055
1970	222,295
1960	176,008
1950	136,781
1940	120,542
1930	105,462
1920	91,747
1910	87,661
1900	81,670
1890	77,879
1880	79,184(a)
1870	74,041
1860	64,941
1850	58,992
1840	52,398
1830	50,926
1820	46,615
1810	51,363 Rev.
1800	47,775
1790	45,266

(a)Reported as Duchess.

E

EAGLE, Town (Est.1823)
   Wyoming County

1980	1,216
1970	996
1960	896
1950	868
1940	922
1930	960
1920	1,059
1910	1,141
1900	1,114
1890	1,131
1880	1,203
1870	1,040
1860	1,312
1850	1,381
1840	1,187(a)
1830	892(a)

(a)Reported in ALLEGANY County.

EAGLE, CDP
  Eagle Town
    Wyoming County
      1880   183
      1870   110

EAGLE, Town (Est.1823)
  Wyoming County
      1980   1,216
      1970   996
      1960   896
      1950   868
      1940   922
      1930   960
      1920   1,059
      1910   1,141
      1900   1,114
      1890   1,131
      1880   1,203
      1870   1,040
      1860   1,312
      1850   1,381
      1840   1,187(a)
      1830   892(a)
(a)Reported in ALLEGANY County.

EAGLE BRIDGE, CDP
  White Creek Town
    Washington County
      1880   96

EAGLE HARBOR, CDP
  Gaines Town
    Orleans County
      1870   315

EARLVILLE, Village (Inc. 1887)
  Sherburne Town, part in
  Chenango County, part in
      1980   363
      1970   377
      1960   370
      1950   274
      1940   270
      1930   255
      1920   243
      1910   262
      1900   223
      1890   187
      1880   NA
      1870   183
  Hamilton Town, part in
  Madison County, part in
      1980   622
      1970   673
      1960   634
      1950   671
      1940   594
      1930   613
      1920   549
      1910   612
      1900   488
      1890   349
      1880   NA
      1870   216
    TOTAL
      1980   985
      1970   1,050
      1960   1,004

      1950   945
      1940   864
      1930   868
      1920   792
      1910   874
      1900   711
      1890   536
      1880   293
      1870   399

EAST AURORA, Village (Inc. 1874)
  Aurora Town
    Erie County
      1980   6,803(a)
      1970   7,033
      1960   6,791
      1950   5,962(a)
      1940   5,253
      1930   4,815
      1920   3,703
      1910   2,781
      1910   2,366
      1900   2,366
      1890   1,582
      1880   1,109
(a)Boundary change.

EAST BERNE, CDP
  Berne Town
    Albany County
      1880   490

EAST BETHANY, CDP
  Bethany Town
    Genesee County
      1880   92

EAST BLOOMFIELD, Town (Est. 1789)(a)
  Ontario County
      1980   3,327
      1970   3,151
      1960   2,297
      1950   1,848
      1940   1,700
      1930   1,631
      1920   1,715
      1910   1,892
      1900   1,940
      1890   2,039
      1880   2,527
      1870   2,250
      1860   2,163
      1850   2,262
      1840   1,986
      1830   3,861
      1820   3,621
      1810   NA
      1800   *1,940
(a)Established as BLOOMFIELD in 1789;
  name changed in 1833.

EAST BLOOMFIELD, Village (Inc. 1916)
  East Bloomfield Town
    Ontario County
      1980   587
      1970   643
      1960   488(a)
      1950   425
      1940   565

```
        1930              531
        1920              556
        1890-1910         NA
        1880              474
        1870              320
(a)Boundary change.
```

EAST BLOOMFIELD STATION, CDP
   East Bloomfield Town
      Ontario County
         1880   198

EAST CASSADAGA, CDP
   Stockton Town
      Chautauqua County
         1880   253

EAST CAYUGA HEIGHTS, CDP
   Ithaca Town
      Tompkins County
         1980   2,630
         1970   2,611

EAST CHATHAM, CDP
   Chatham Town
      Columbia County
         1880   224

EASTCHESTER, CDP
   Eastchester Town
      Westchester County
         1980   20,305
         1970   23,750

EASTCHESTER, Town (Est. 1788)
   Westchester County
         1980   32,648
         1970   36,660
         1960   33,613
         1950   27,174
         1940   23,492
         1930   20,340
         1920   9,372
         1910   6,422
         1900   3,040(a)
         1890   15,442
         1880   8,737(b)
         1870   7,491(b)
         1860   5,582(b)
         1850   1,679(b)
         1840   1,502(b)
         1830   1,030(b)
         1820   1,021(b)
         1810   NA
         1800   *738(b)
         1790   740(b)
(a)Boundary change.
(b)Reported as East Chester.

EAST COMMACK(a)
   Smithtown Town
      Suffolk County
         1970   20,595(b)
         1960   5,903(b)
(a)Included in COMMACK and HAUPPAUGE,
   CDPs in 1980.
(b)Derived by LIRPB from U.S. Census
   Data.

EAST DAY, CDP
   Day Town
      Saratoga County
         1880   124

EAST ELMA, CDP
   Elma Town
      Erie County
         1880   78
         1870   112

EASTERN, Town
   see GUILFORD, Town
      Chenango County

EAST EVANS, CDP
   Evans Town
      Erie County
         1870   100

EAST FARMINGDALE, CDP
   Babylon Town
      Suffolk County
         1980   5,522(a)
         1970   2,803(b)
         1960   3,962(c)
(a)Boundary change.
(b)Derived by LIRPB from U.S. Census
   Data; population of 4,522 is
   comparable to 1980 boundaries which
   include S.U.N.Y. at Farmingdale.
(c)Derived by LIRPB from U.S. Census
   Data.

EAST FISHKILL, Town (Est. 1849)
   Dutchess County
         1980   18,091
         1970   11,092
         1960   4,778
         1950   2,565
         1940   2,024
         1930   1,845
         1920   1,944
         1910   2,226
         1900   1,970
         1890   2,175
         1880   2,574
         1870   2,306
         1860   2,544
         1850   2,610

EAST GAINESVILLE, CDP
   Gainesville Town
      Wyoming County
         1880   247

EAST GARDEN CITY
   Hempstead Town
      Nassau County
         1980   2,781(a)
         1970   2,157(a)
         1960   2,999(a)
(a)Derived by LIRPB from U.S. Census
   Data.

EAST GLENVILLE, CDP
   Glenville Town
      Schenectady County
         1980   6,537

```
        1970            5,898
```

EAST GREENBUSH, CDP
  East Greenbush Town
    Rensselaer County
```
        1980            1,325
        1950-1970         NA
        1940              837
```

EAST GREENBUSH, Town (Est. 1855)(a)
  Rensselaer County
```
        1980           12,913
        1970           10,679
        1960            9,107
        1950            6,338
        1940            4,550
        1930            3,267
        1920            1,558
        1910            1,350
        1900            2,036
        1890            2,171
        1880            2,127
        1870            1,845
        1860            1,607
```
(a)Established as Clinton in 1855; name
   changed in 1858.

EAST GREENLAWN(a)
  Huntington Town
    Suffolk County
```
        1970            1,112(b)
        1960              912(b)
```
(a)Included in CENTERPORT, CDP in 1980.
(b)Derived by LIRPB from U.S. Census
   Data.

EAST HALF HOLLOW HILLS, CDP(a)
  Huntington Town
    Suffolk County
```
        1970            9,691
        1960              990(b)
```
(a)Included in DIX HILLS, CDP in 1980.
(b)Derived by LIRPB from U.S. Census
   Data.

EAST HAMBURG, Town
  see ORCHARD PARK, Town
    Erie County

EAST HAMILTON, CDP
  Hamilton Town
    Madison County
```
        1870               53
```

EAST HAMPTON, Town (Est.1788)
  Suffolk County
```
        1980           14,029
        1970           10,980
        1960            8,827
        1950            6,325
        1940            6,529
        1930            6,569(a)
        1920            4,852(a)
        1910            4,722(a)
        1900            3,746(a)
        1890            2,431(a)
        1880            2,515
        1870            2,372
        1860            2,267
```

```
        1850            2,122
        1840            2,076
        1830            1,668
        1820            1,646
        1810            1,484
        1800           *1,549
        1790            1,497
```
(a)Reported as Easthampton.

EAST HAMPTON, Village (Inc. 1920)
  East Hampton Town
    Suffolk County
```
        1980            1,886
        1970            1,753
        1960            1,772
        1950            1,737(a)
        1940            1,756
        1930            1,934(b)
        1890-1920         NA
        1880              807
```
(a)Boundary change.
(b)Reported as Easthampton.

EAST HEMPSTEAD, CDP
  Hempstead Town
    Nassau County
```
        1940            2,881
```

EAST HENRIETTA, CDP
  Henrietta Town
    Monroe County
```
        1880              152
```

EAST HERKIMER, CDP
  Herkimer Town
    Herkimer County
```
        1960            1,068
        1950              NA
        1940              683
```

EAST HILLS, Village (Inc. 1931)
  North Hempstead Town, part in
    Nassau County
```
        1980            7,146
        1970            8,605 Rev.
        1960            7,184
        1950            2,547
        1940              343(a)
```
  Oyster Bay Town, part in
    Nassau County
```
        1980               14
        1970               19(a)
```
  TOTAL
```
        1980            7,160
        1970            8,624 Rev.(a)
        1940-1960        (b)
```
(a)Boundary change.
(b)Reported in NORTH HEMPSTEAD Town
   only.

EAST HOLBROOK(a)
  Islip Town
    Suffolk County
```
        1970            1,404(b)
        1960              124(b)
```
(a)Included in HOLBROOK, CDP in 1980.
(b)Derived by LIRPB from U.S. Census
   Data.

EAST HOMER, CDP
  Homer Town
    Cortland County
      1880   76

EAST HUNTINGTON, CDP(a)
  Huntington Town
    Suffolk County
      1970   4,853(b)
      1960   3,232(b)
(a)Included in HUNTINGTON, CDP in 1980.
(b)Derived by LIRPB from U.S. Census
   Data.

EAST ISLIP, CDP
  Islip Town
    Suffolk County
      1980   13,852(a)
      1970   6,861(b)
      1960   4,946(c)
      1950   2,834
      1940   2,203
(a)Boundary change.
(b)Population of 13,882 is comparable
   to 1980 boundaries.
(c)Derived by LIRPB from U.S. Census
   Data.

EAST KINGSTON, CDP
  Ulster Town
    Ulster County
      1940   756
      1890-1930   NA
      1880   484

EAST LAKE RONONKOMA(a)
  Brookhaven Town
    Suffolk County
      1970   2,110(b)
      1960   1,298(b)
(a)Included in LAKE RONKONKOMA, CDP
   in 1980.
(b)Derived by LIRPB from U.S. Census
   Data.

EAST MARION
  Southold Town
    Suffolk County
      1980   656(a)
      1970   832(b)
      1960   720(c)
      1890-1950   NA
      1880   340
(a)Boundary change; derived by LIRPB
   from U.S. Census Data.
(b)Derived by LIRPB from U.S. Census
   Data; population of 531 is comparable
   to 1980 boundaries.
(c)Derived by LIRPB from U.S. Census
   Data.

EAST MASSAPEQUA, CDP
  Oyster Bay Town
    Nassau County
      1980   13,987
      1970   15,926
      1960   14,779

EAST MATTITUCK
  see LAUREL--EAST MATTITUCK
    Suffolk County

EAST MEADOW, CDP
  Hempstead Town
    Nassau County
      1980   39,317
      1970   46,290
      1960   46,036
      1950   NA
      1940   3,145

EAST MEREDITH, CDP
  Meredith Town
    Delaware County
      1880   50

EAST MIDDLETOWN, CDP
  Wallkill Town
    Orange County
      1980   4,330
      1970   2,640
      1960   1,752
      1950   1,485

EAST MORICHES, CDP
  Brookhaven Town
    Suffolk County
      1980   3,613(a)
      1970   1,702(b)
      1960   1,169 Rev.
      1950   NA
      1940   943
      1890-1930   NA
      1880   388
(a)Boundary change; derived by LIRPB
   from U.S. Census Data.
(b)Population of 2,461 is comparable
   to 1980 boundaries.

EAST MOUNT VERNON, CDP
  Eastchester Town
    Westchester County
      1870   500

EAST NASSAU, CDP
  Nassau Town
    Rensselaer County
      1880   88
      1870   192

EAST NECK, CDP(a)
  Huntington Town
    Suffolk County
      1970   5,221
      1960   3,789
(a)Included in CENTERPORT, CDP in 1980.

EAST NORTHPORT, CDP
  Huntington Town
    Suffolk County
      1980   20,187(a)
      1970   12,392(b)
      1960   8,647 Rev.
      1950   3,842
      1940   2,418
(a)Boundary change.
(b)Boundary change; population of 20,317

is comparable to 1980 boundaries.

EAST NORWICH
Oyster Bay Town
Nassau County

1980	2,841(a)
1970	3,610(a)
1960	2,778(a)

(a)Derived by LIRPB from U.S. Census
    Data.

EASTON, Town
Albany County
see GORHAM, Town
        Ontario County

EASTON, Town
Ontario County
see GORHAM, Town
        Ontario County

EASTON, Town (Est. 1789)
Washington County

1980	2,020
1970	1,956
1960	1,681
1950	1,659
1940	1,691
1930	1,726
1920	1,851
1910	2,133
1900	2,247
1890	2,500
1880	2,740
1870	3,072
1860	3,083
1850	3,225
1840	2,988
1830	3,758
1820	3,051
1810	NA
1800	*3,069

EAST OTTO, Town (Est. 1854)
Cattaraugus County

1980	942
1970	910
1960	701
1950	743
1940	732
1930	751
1920	915
1910	1,093
1900	1,138
1890	1,288
1880	1,251
1870	1,164
1860	1,300

EAST PATCHOGUE, CDP
Brookhaven Town
Suffolk County

1980	18,139(a)
1970	8,092(b)
1960	6,284(c)
1950	4,124
1940	2,143

(a)Boundary change.
(b)Boundary change; population of 14,200

is comparable to 1980 boundaries.
(c)Derived by LIRPB from U.S. Census
    Data.

EAST PEMBROKE, CDP
Pembroke Town
Genesee County

1880	97
1870	156

EAST PHARSALIA, CDP
Pharsalia Town
Chenango County

1880	129

EAST PIKE, CDP
Pike Town
Wyoming County

1880	223

EASTPORT, CDP
Brookhaven Town, part in
Suffolk County

1980	425(a)
1970	429
1960	335(a)
1950	444(b)

Southampton Town, part in
Suffolk County

1980	852(a)
1970	879
1960	376(a)
1950	598(b)

TOTAL

1980	1,277(a)
1970	1,308
1960	711(a)
1950	1,042(b)
1940	870
1890-1930	NA
1880	359
1870	135

(a)Derived by LIRPB from U.S. Census
    Data.
(b)Reported as EASTPORT--SPEONK, CDP.

EASTPORT--SPEONK, CDP(a)
Brookhaven & Southampton Towns
Suffolk County

1950	1,042(b)

(a)Included, in part, in EASTPORT, CDP in
    1960-1980; in SPEONK, CDP in 1870; in
    REMSENBURG--SPEONK, CDP in 1960-1980.
(b)Part in BROOKHAVEN Town, 444; part
    in SOUTHAMPTON Town, 598.

EAST QUOGUE, CDP
Southampton Town
Suffolk County

1980	3,668(a)
1970	1,143(b)
1960	437(c)
1890-1950	NA
1880	267(d)
1870	179(d)

(a)Boundary change.
(b)Population of 2,469 is comparable
    to 1980 boundaries.
(c)Derived by LIRPB from U.S. Census

Data.
(d)Reported as Atlanticville; name
   changed in 1891.

EAST RANDOLPH, Village (Inc. 1881)
   Conewango Town, part in
      Cattaraugus County
         1980   248
         1970   257
         1960   201
         1950   215 Rev.
         1940   174
         1930   169
         1920   144
         1910   185
         1900   198
   Randolph Town, part in
      Cattaraugus County
         1980   407
         1970   379
         1960   393
         1950   413
         1940   322
         1930   333
         1920   400
         1910   408
         1900   446
         1890   NA
         1880   286
      TOTAL
         1980   655
         1970   636
         1960   594
         1950   628 Rev.
         1940   496
         1930   502
         1920   544
         1910   593
         1900   644
         1890   NA
         1880   (a)
(a)Reported in RANDOLPH Town only.

EAST ROCHESTER, Town (Est. 1981)
   see EAST ROCHESTER, Village
   Monroe County

EAST ROCHESTER, Village (Inc. 1906)(a)
   Perinton Town, part in
      Monroe County
         1980   3,473(b)
         1970   3,485
         1960   3,214(b)
         1950   2,864
         1940   2,790(b)
         1930   2,914
         1920   1,968
         1910   1,473
   Pittsford Town, part in
      Monroe County
         1980   4,123(b)
         1970   4,862
         1960   4,938(b)
         1950   4,258
         1940   3,901(b)
         1930   3,713
         1920   1,933
         1910   935

      TOTAL
         1980   7,596(b)
         1970   8,347
         1960   8,152(b)
         1950   7,122
         1940   6,691(b)
         1930   6,627
         1920   3,901
         1910   2,398
(a)Established town and village of
   EAST ROCHESTER, with identical
   boundaries, in 1981; made independent of PERINTON and PITTSFORD Towns.
(b)Boundary change.

EAST ROCKAWAY, Village (Inc. 1900)
   Hempstead Town
      Nassau County
         1980   10,917(a)
         1970   11,795 Rev.
         1960   10,721(a)
         1950   7,970(a)
         1940   5,610
         1930   4,340
         1920   2,005
         1910   1,200
         1900   739
         1890   NA
         1880   509(b)
(a)Boundary change.
(b)Reported in QUEENS County.

EAST SETAUKET, CDP(a)
   Brookhaven Town
      Suffolk County
         1970   1,389(b)
         1960   1,127
         1950   NA
         1940   704
(a)Included in SETAUKET--EAST SETAUKET,
   CDP in 1980.
(b)Derived by LIRPB from U.S. Census
   Data.

EAST SHOREHAM, CDP
   Brookhaven Town
      Suffolk County
         1980   3,817(a)
         1970   2,141(b)
         1960   257(c)
(a)Boundary change; derived by LIRPB
   from U.S. Census Data.
(b)Derived by LIRPB from U.S. Census
   Data; population of 2,046 is
   comparable to 1980 boundaries.
(c)Derived by LIRPB from U.S. Census
   Data.

EAST SPRINGFIELD, CDP
   Springfield Town
      Otsego County
         1880   82

EAST STEAMBURGH, CDP
   Hector Town
      Schuyler County
         1880   82

EAST STOCKHOLM, CDP
Stockholm Town
St. Lawrence County
1880   86

EAST SYRACUSE, Village (Inc. 1881)
De Witt Town
Onondaga County
1980   3,412
1970   4,333
1960   4,708
1950   4,766
1940   4,520
1930   4,646
1920   4,106
1910   3,274
1900   2,509
1890   2,231
1880   1,099

EAST TARRYTOWN, CDP
Greenburgh Town
Westchester County
1880   61

EAST VARICK, CDP
Varick Town
Seneca County
1880   62

EAST VESTAL, CDP
Vestal Town
Broome County
1970   10,472

EAST VICTOR, CDP
Victor Town
Ontario County
1880   106

EAST WAVERLY, CDP
Barton Town
Tioga County
1880   191

EAST WHITE PLAINS
Harrison Town
Westchester County
1940   2,447

EAST WILLIAMSON, CDP
Williamson Town
Wayne County
1880   96

EAST WILLISTON, Village (Inc. 1926)
North Hempstead Town
Nassau County
1980   2,708
1970   2,808
1960   2,940
1950   1,734
1940   1,152(a)
1930   493
(a)Boundary change.

EASTWOOD, Village (Inc. 1894)(a)
De Witt Town
Onondaga County
1920   2,194
1910   810
1900   341
(a)Merged into SYRACUSE City in 1926.

EATON, Town (Est. 1807)
Madison County
1980   5,182
1970   4,458
1960   3,196
1950   2,854
1940   2,245
1930   2,168
1920   2,223
1910   2,417
1900   2,705
1890   3,799
1880   3,799
1870   3,690
1860   2,871
1850   3,944
1840   3,409
1830   3,559
1820   3,021

EATONS NECK, CDP
Huntington Town
Suffolk County
1980   1,574(a)
1970   1,569(b)
1960   214(c)
(a)Boundary change.
(b)Derived by LIRPB from U.S. Census
   Data; population of 1,472 is
   comparable to 1980 boundaries.
(c)Derived by LIRPB from U.S. Census
   Data.

EATONS NECK COAST GUARD STATION
Huntington Town
Suffolk County
1980   58(a)
1970   97(b)
(a)Boundary change; derived by LIRPB
   from U.S. Census Data.
(b)Derived by LIRPB from U.S. Census
   Data; population is comparable to
   1980 boundaries.

EBENEZER, CDP
West Seneca Town
Erie County
1940   1,818

EDDYTOWN, CDP
Starkey Town
Yates County
1880   148

EDDYVILLE, CDP
Ulster Town
Ulster County
1880   617

EDDYVILLE, CDP
   Easton Town
      Washington County
         1880   320

EDEN, CDP
   Eden Town
      Erie County
         1980   3,000
         1970   2,962
         1960   2,366
         1950   1,394
         1940   615
         1890-1930   NA
         1880   272
         1870   2,270

EDEN, Town (Est. 1812)
   Erie County
         1980   7,327
         1970   7,644
         1960   6,630
         1950   4,201
         1940   3,295
         1930   2,773
         1920   2,352
         1910   2,526
         1900   2,638
         1890   2,288
         1880   2,363
         1870   2,439
         1860   NA
         1850   2,494
         1840   2,174
         1830   1,066
         1820   1,065(a)
(a)Reported in NIAGARA County.

EDENVILLE, CDP
   Warwick Town
      Orange County
         1880   130

EDGEWOOD(a)
   Islip Town
      Suffolk County
         1970   4,142(b)
         1960   2,739(b)
(a)Included in BRENTWOOD, CDP in 1980.
(b)Derived by LIRPB from U.S. Census
   Data.

EDINBURG, Town (Est.1801)(a)
   Saratoga County
         1980   1,126
         1970   844
         1960   602
         1950   530
         1940   534
         1930   512
         1920   595
         1910   793
         1900   1,032
         1890   1,203
         1880   1,523
         1870   1,405
         1860   1,479
         1850   1,336
         1840   1,458(b)

         1830   1,571
         1820   1,469
(a)Established as Northfield in 1801;
   name changed in 1808.
(b)Reported as Edinburgh.

EDMASTON, Town
   see EDMESTON, Town
      Otsego County

EDMESTON, CDP
   Edmeston Town
      Otsego County
         1940   573
         1890-1930   NA
         1880   361

EDMESTON, Town (Est. 1808)
   Otsego County
         1980   1,732
         1970   1,709
         1960   1,721
         1950   1,563
         1940   1,580
         1930   1,556
         1920   1,553
         1910   1,567
         1900   1,767
         1890   1,703
         1880   1,794
         1870   1,744
         1860   1,804
         1850   1,885
         1840   1,907(a)
         1830   2,087
         1820   1,841
(a)Reported as Edmaston.

EDWARDS, Town (Est. 1827)
   St. Lawrence County
         1980   1,208
         1970   1,219
         1960   1,366
         1950   1,426
         1940   1,410
         1930   1,399
         1920   1,497
         1910   1,387
         1900   1,340
         1890   1,267
         1880   1,082
         1870   1,076
         1860   1,287
         1850   1,023
         1840   956
         1830   633

EDWARDS, Village (Inc. 1893)
   Edwards Town
      St. Lawrence County
         1980   561
         1970   576
         1960   658
         1950   584
         1940   624
         1930   562
         1920   577
         1910   476
         1900   373

1890	NA
1880	379

EGGERTSVILLE, CDP
  Amherst Town
    Erie County

1960	44,807
1950	NA
1940	5,708

EGYPT, CDP
  Perinton Town
    Monroe County

1880	151

ELBA, Town (Est. 1820)
  Genesee County

1980	2,487
1970	2,312
1960	2,260
1950	1,920
1940	1,855
1930	1,695
1920	1,394
1910	1,384
1900	1,526
1890	1,746
1880	1,968
1870	1,905
1860	2,040
1850	1,772
1840	3,161
1830	2,678
1820	1,333

ELBA, Village (Inc. 1884)
  Elba Town
    Genesee County

1980	750
1970	752
1960	739
1950	569
1940	614
1930	492
1920	386
1910	351
1900	395
1890	428

ELBRIDGE, Town (Est. 1829)
  Onondaga County

1980	5,885
1970	5,503
1960	4,644
1950	3,338
1940	2,975
1930	2,814
1920	2,736
1910	2,980
1900	3,327
1890	3,560
1880	4,087
1870	3,796
1860	4,509
1850	3,924
1840	4,647
1830	3,357

ELBRIDGE, Village (Inc. 1848)
  Elbridge Town
    Onondaga County

1980	1,099
1970	1,040(a)
1960	828
1950	586
1940	497
1930	452
1920	382
1910	462
1900	549
1890	693
1880	516
1870	468

(a)Boundary change.

ELGIN, Town
  see LYNDON, Town
        Cattaraugus County

ELIZABETHTOWN, Town (Est. 1798)
  Essex County

1980	1,267
1970	1,284
1960	1,328
1950	1,208
1940	1,181
1930	1,113
1920	1,042
1910	1,108
1900	1,131
1890	1,399
1880	1,363
1870	1,488
1860	1,343
1850	1,635
1840	1,061
1830	1,015
1820	889
1810	NA
1800	*899(a)

(a)Reported as Elizabeth.

ELIZABETHTOWN, Village (Inc. 1875)(a)
  Elizabethtown Town
    Essex County

1980	659
1970	607
1960	779
1950	665
1940	640
1930	656
1920	518
1910	505
1900	491
1890	573

(a)Dissolved in 1980.

ELKO, Town (Est. 1890)(a)
  Cattaraugus County

1960	73
1950	95
1940	125
1930	160
1920	220
1910	246 Rev.(b)
1900	364 Rev.(b)

(a)Merged into COLD SPRING Town in 1965.

(b)In 1920 the Census Bureau revised
   the 1910 figure of 475 and the 1900
   figure of 571 to exclude the ALLEGANY
   INDIAN RESERVATION.

ELLENBURG, Town (Est. 1830)
    Clinton County
        1980   1,751
        1970   1,775
        1960   1,945
        1950   2,098
        1940   2,428
        1930   2,243
        1920   2,475
        1910   3,079
        1900   3,248
        1890   3,046
        1880   3,162
        1870   3,042
        1860   2,348
        1850   1,504(a)
        1840   1,171
(a)Reported as Ellenburgh.

ELLENVILLE, Village (Inc. 1856)
    Wawarsing Town
      Ulster County
        1980   4,405
        1970   4,482(a)
        1960   5,003
        1950   4,225(a)
        1940   4,000
        1930   3,280
        1920   3,116
        1910   3,114
        1900   2,879
        1890   2,881
        1880   2,750
(a)Boundary change.

ELLERY, Town (Est.1821)
    Chautauqua County
        1980   4,617
        1970   4,594
        1960   3,953
        1950   2,852
        1940   2,088
        1930   1,919
        1920   1,496
        1910   1,695
        1900   1,628
        1890   1,789
        1880   1,555
        1870   1,616
        1860   1,751
        1850   2,104
        1840   2,242
        1830   2,002

ELLICOTT, Town (Est. 1812)
    Chautauqua County
        1980   9,979
        1970   10,233
        1960   10,451
        1950   9,265
        1940   8,041
        1930   8,237
        1920   5,463
        1910   4,371

        1900   3,118
        1890   1,746(a)
        1880   10,842
        1870   6,679
        1860   1,599(a)
        1850   3,523
        1840   2,571
        1830   2,101
        1820   1,462
(a)Boundary change.

ELLICOTT, Town
    Erie County
    see ORCHARD PARK, Town
        Erie County

ELLICOTTVILLE, Town (Est. 1820)
    Cattaraugus County
        1980   1,677
        1970   1,779
        1960   1,968
        1950   1,830
        1940   1,790
        1930   1,793
        1920   1,766
        1910   2,067
        1900   2,038
        1890   1,931
        1880   1,949
        1870   1,833
        1860   1,881
        1850   1,725
        1840   1,084
        1830   626

ELLICOTTVILLE, Village (Inc. 1837)
    Ellicottville Town
      Cattaraugus County
        1980   713(a)
        1970   955
        1960   1,150
        1950   1,073
        1940   1,024
        1930   978
        1920   950
        1910   985
        1900   896
        1890   852
        1880   748
        1870   579
(a)Boundary change.

ELLINGTON, CDP
    Ellington Town
      Chautauqua County
        1870   314

ELLINGTON, Town (Est. 1829)
    Chautauqua County
        1980   1,690
        1970   1,384
        1960   1,314
        1950   1,142
        1940   1,073
        1930   1,079
        1920   1,061

1910	1,235
1900	1,330
1890	1,430
1880	1,602
1870	1,556
1860	1,937
1850	2,001
1840	1,725
1830	1,279

ELLISBURG, Town (Est. 1803)
  Jefferson County

1980	3,312
1970	3,385
1960	3,285
1950	3,116
1940	3,183
1930	3,026
1920	3,192
1910	3,634
1900	3,888
1890	4,145
1880	4,810(a)
1870	4,822
1860	5,614
1850	5,524
1840	5,349(a)
1830	5,292
1820	3,531

(a)Reported as Ellisburgh.

ELLISBURG, Village (Inc. 1895)
  Ellisburg Town
    Jefferson County

1980	307
1970	337
1960	328
1950	285
1940	253
1930	253
1920	275
1910	702
1900	292
1890	336
1880	222(a)

(a)Reported as Ellisburgh.

ELLIS ISLAND, CDP
  New York County

1860	5

ELLSWORTH, CDP
  Pierrepont Town
    St. Lawrence County

1870	179

ELMA, CDP
  Elma Town
    Erie County

1880	108
1870	165

ELMA, Town (Est.1857)
  Erie County

1980	10,574
1970	10,011
1960	7,468
1950	4,020
1940	2,801

1930	2,320
1920	1,966
1910	2,130
1900	2,202
1890	2,163
1880	2,555
1870	2,827
1860	2,091

ELMA CENTER, CDP
  Elma Town
    Erie County

1980	2,459
1970	2,784

ELMIRA, City (Inc. 1864)(a)
  Chemung County

1980	35,327
1970	39,945(b)
1960	46,517
1950	49,716
1940	45,106
1930	47,397
1920	45,393(b)
1910	37,176
1900	35,672
1890	30,893
1880	20,541
1870	15,863(c)

(a)Incorporated as Newtown Village in
   1815; name changed to Elmira Village
   in 1828. Elmira Village incorporated
   as ELMIRA City and made independent
   of ELMIRA Town in 1864.
(b)Boundary change.
(c)Reported as Elmira Village.

ELMIRA, Town (Est. 1792)(a)
  Chemung County

1980	7,635
1970	8,408
1960	8,413
1950	6,346
1940	5,290
1930	5,084
1920	2,651
1910	1,605
1900	1,260
1890	890(b)
1880	1,986
1870	1,190(b)
1860	8,082
1850	8,166
1840	4,791
1830	2,892(c)
1820	2,945(c)
1810	NA
1800	*1,333(d)

(a)Established as Newtown in 1792; name
   changed in 1808.
(b)Boundary change.
(c)Reported in TIOGA County.
(d)Reported as New-town in TIOGA County.

ELMIRA, Village
  see ELMIRA, City
    Chemung County

ELMIRA HEIGHTS, Village (Inc. 1896)
  Elmira Town, part in
    Chemung County
        1980   1,009
        1970   1,318
        1960   1,734
        1950   1,263
        1940   1,269
        1930   1,354
        1920   1,004
        1910   492
        1900   518
  Horseheads Town, part in
    Chemung County
        1980   3,270
        1970   3,588
        1960   3,783
        1950   3,746
        1940   3,560
        1930   3,707
        1920   3,184
        1910   2,240
        1900   1,445
  TOTAL
        1980   4,279
        1970   4,906
        1960   5,157
        1950   5,009
        1940   4,829
        1930   5,061
        1920   4,188
        1910   2,732
        1900   1,763

ELMIRA HEIGHTS NORTH, CDP
  Horseheads Town
    Chemung County
        1980   2,659
        1970   2,906
        1960   2,528

ELMIRA SOUTHEAST, CDP
  Southport Town
    Chemung County
        1960   6,698

ELMONT, CDP
  Hempstead Town
    Nassau County
        1980   27,592
        1970   29,363
        1960   30,138
        1950   NA
        1940   8,957
        1930   492

ELMSFORD, Village (Inc. 1910)
  Greenburgh Town
    Westchester County
        1980   3,361
        1970   3,911
        1960   3,795
        1950   3,147
        1940   3,078
        1930   2,955
        1920   1,535
        1910   411

ELSMERE, CDP
  Bethlehem Town
    Albany County
        1940   1,941

ELWOOD, CDP
  Huntington Town
    Suffolk County
        1980   11,847(a)
        1970   15,031(b)
        1960   7,080(c)
(a)Boundary change.
(b)Population of 11,848 is comparable
   to 1980 boundaries.
(c)Derived by LIRPB from U.S. Census
   Data.

EMMONSBURG, CDP
  Stratford Town
    Fulton County
        1880   50

ENDICOTT, Village (Inc. 1906)
  Union Town
    Broome County
        1980   14,457
        1970   16,556(a)
        1960   18,775
        1950   20,050(a)
        1940   17,702
        1930   16,231(a)
        1920   9,500
        1910   2,408
(a)Boundary change.

ENDWELL, CDP
  Union Town
    Broome County
        1980   13,745
        1970   15,999
        1950-1960   NA
        1940   3,436

ENFIELD, Town (Est. 1821)
    Tompkins County
        1980   2,375
        1970   2,028
        1960   1,573
        1950   1,316
        1940   1,082
        1930   939
        1920   867
        1910   1,000
        1900   1,214
        1890   1,393
        1880   1,690
        1870   1,693
        1860   1,919
        1850   2,117
        1840   2,340
        1830   2,332

EPHRATAH, CDP
  Ephratah Town
    Fulton County
        1880   309

EPHRATAH, Town (Est. 1827)
    Fulton County
        1980   1,564
        1970   1,297
        1960   1,237
        1950   1,063
        1940   1,045
        1930   949(a)
        1920   1,038
        1910   1,312
        1900   1,566
        1890   1,864
        1880   2,157
        1870   2,207
        1860   2,202
        1850   2,079
        1840   2,009
        1830   1,818(b)
(a)Boundary change.
(b)Reported in MONTGOMERY County.

ERIE, County (Est. 1821)
        1980   1,015,472
        1970   1,113,491
        1960   1,064,688
        1950   899,238
        1940   798,377
        1930   762,408
        1920   634,688
        1910   528,925
        1900   433,686
        1890   322,981
        1880   218,884
        1870   178,699
        1860   141,971
        1850   100,993
        1840   62,465
        1830   35,719

ERIE, Town
    see NEWSTEAD, Town
            Erie County

ERIEVILLE, CDP
    Nelson Town
        Madison County
            1880   190

ERIN, Town (Est. 1822)
    Chemung County
        1980   2,037
        1970   1,669
        1960   1,175
        1950   930
        1940   789
        1930   774
        1920   761
        1910   889
        1900   996
        1890   1,289
        1880   1,562
        1870   1,392
        1860   1,339
        1850   1,833
        1840   1,441
        1830   975(a)
(a)Reported in TIOGA County.

ERWIN, Town
    Ontario County
    see ERWIN, Town
            Steuben County

ERWIN, Town (Est. 1826)(a)
    Steuben County
        1980   6,445
        1970   6,275
        1960   5,829
        1950   4,393
        1940   3,716
        1930   3,518
        1920   3,086
        1910   1,224
        1900   1,851
        1890   1,884
        1880   2,095
        1870   1,977
        1860   1,839
        1850   1,435
        1840   785
        1830   795
(a)In 1790 the Census Bureau reported
    an ERWIN Town in ONTARIO County,
    population of 168.

ESOPUS, Town (Inc. 1811)
    Ulster County
        1980   7,605
        1970   6,974
        1960   6,597
        1950   4,738
        1940   4,220
        1930   4,167
        1920   3,913
        1910   4,732
        1900   4,907
        1890   4,659
        1880   4,736
        1870   4,557
        1860   4,734
        1850   2,900
        1840   1,939
        1830   1,770
        1820   1,513

ESPERANCE, Town (Est. 1846)
    Schoharie County
        1980   1,951
        1970   1,567
        1960   1,232
        1950   1,128
        1940   887
        1930   881
        1920   890
        1910   977
        1900   1,096
        1890   1,232
        1880   1,378
        1870   1,276
        1860   1,409
        1850   1,428

ESPERANCE, Village (Inc. 1818)
    Esperance Town
        Schoharie County
            1980   374(a)
            1970   408

1960	314
1950	322
1940	219
1930	233
1920	219
1910	263
1900	290
1890	274
1880	341

(a)Boundary change.

ESSEX, County (Est. 1799)

1980	36,176
1970	34,631
1960	35,300
1950	35,086
1940	34,178
1930	33,959
1920	31,871
1910	33,458
1900	30,707
1890	33,052
1880	34,515
1870	29,042
1860	28,214
1850	31,148
1840	23,634
1830	19,287
1820	12,811
1810	9,477
1800	8,516(a)

(a)Includes the population of CLINTON
County.

ESSEX, Town (Est.1805)
  Essex County

1980	880
1970	837
1960	880
1950	1,012
1940	1,002
1930	1,116
1920	1,025
1910	1,276
1900	1,333
1890	1,437
1880	1,462
1870	1,600
1860	1,633
1850	2,351
1840	1,681
1830	1,543
1820	1,225

ETNA, CDP
  Dryden Town
    Tompkins County

1870	230

EUCLID, CDP
  Clay Town
    Onondaga County

1870	138

EVANS, Town (Est. 1821)
  Erie County

1980	17,961
1970	14,570
1960	12,078
1950	7,663
1940	5,047
1930	3,827
1920	3,468
1910	3,124
1900	2,795
1890	2,692
1880	2,610
1870	2,593
1860	2,510
1850	2,182
1840	1,807
1830	1,185

EVANS CENTER, CDP
  Evans Town
    Erie County

1870	150

EVANS MILLS, Village (Inc. 1922)
  Le Ray Town
    Jefferson County

1980	651
1970	714
1960	618(a)
1950	518
1940	523
1930	514
1890-1920	NA
1880	578(b)
1870	500(b)

(a)Boundary change.
(b)Reported as Evan's Mill.

EXETER, Town (Est. 1799)
  Otsego County

1980	968
1970	996
1960	923
1950	924
1940	760
1930	691
1920	814
1910	1,067
1900	1,087
1890	1,245
1880	1,353
1870	1,256
1860	1,570
1850	1,526
1840	1,423
1830	1,690
1820	1,430
1810	NA
1800	*712

EXETER CENTER, CDP
  Exeter Town
    Otsego County

1880	58

EZRAVILLE, Town
  see MALONE, Town
    Franklin County

F

FABIUS, Town (Est. 1798)
Onondaga County
1980	1,811
1970	1,607
1960	1,565
1950	1,432
1940	1,348
1930	1,252
1920	1,285
1910	1,557
1900	1,686
1890	1,717
1880	2,069
1870	2,047
1860	2,305
1850	2,410
1840	2,562
1830	3,070
1820	2,494
1810	NA
1800	*844

FABIUS, Village (Inc. 1880)
Fabius Town
Onondaga County
1980	367
1970	374
1960	378
1950	369
1940	308
1930	267
1920	240
1910	344
1900	387
1890	312
1880	405
1870	378

FAIRFIELD, CDP
Fairfield Town
Herkimer County
1880	150
1870	281

FAIRFIELD, Town (Est. 1796)
Herkimer County
1980	1,455
1970	1,446
1960	1,282
1950	1,204
1940	1,095
1930	1,248
1920	1,337
1910	1,305
1900	1,390
1890	1,553
1880	1,656
1870	1,653
1860	1,712
1850	1,646
1840	1,836
1830	2,266
1820	2,610
1810	NA
1800	*2,065

FAIRFIELD, Town
Washington County
see LAKE LUZERNE, Town
Warren County

FAIR HARBOR, CDP
see FIRE ISLAND, Islip Town
Suffolk County

FAIR HAVEN, Village (Inc. 1880)
Sterling Town
Cayuga County
1980	976
1970	859(a)
1960	764
1950	628
1940	471
1930	562
1920	552
1910	571
1900	610
1890	738
1880	621
1870	532(b)

(a)Boundary change.
(b)Reported as Fairhaven.

FAIRMOUNT, CDP
Camillus & Geddes Towns
Onondaga County
1980	13,415
1970	15,317
1950-1960	NA
1940	1,127

FAIRMOUNT, CDP
West Farms Town
Westchester County
1870	508

FAIRPORT, Village
Chemung County
see HORSEHEADS, Village
Chemung County

FAIRPORT, Village (Inc. 1867)
Perinton Town
Monroe County
1980	5,970
1970	6,474(a)
1960	5,507(a)
1950	5,287
1940	4,644(a)
1930	4,604
1920	4,626
1910	3,112
1900	2,489
1890	2,552
1880	1,920

(a)Boundary change.

FAIRVIEW, CDP
Hyde Park & Poughkeepsie Towns
Dutchess County
1980	5,852
1970	8,517

1960	8,626
1950	1,721

FAIRVILLE, CDP
  Arcadia Town
    Wayne County

1880	124

FALCONER, Village (Inc. 1891)
  Ellicott Town
    Chautauqua County

1980	2,778(a)
1970	2,983
1960	3,343(a)
1950	3,292
1940	3,222
1930	3,579
1920	2,742
1910	2,141
1900	1,136
1890	574

(a)Boundary change.

FALLSBURG, Town (Est. 1826)
    Sullivan County

1980	9,862
1970	7,959
1960	6,748
1950	6,321
1940	5,622
1930	4,716
1920	4,769
1910	3,782
1900	2,974
1890	3,041
1880	2,945
1870	3,206
1860	3,333
1850	2,626(a)
1840	1,782
1830	1,173

(a)Reported as Fallsburgh Town.

FARMER, CDP
  Covert Town
    Seneca County

1880	544

FARMERSVILLE, CDP
  Farmersville Town
    Cattaraugus County

1880	116

FARMERSVILLE, Town (Est. 1821)
    Cattaraugus County

1980	978
1970	754
1960	721
1950	733
1940	778
1930	719
1920	999
1910	948
1900	1,043
1890	1,082
1880	1,128
1870	1,114
1860	1,389
1850	1,554

1840	1,294
1830	1,005

FARMINGDALE, Village (Inc. 1904)
  Oyster Bay Town
    Nassau County

1980	7,946
1970	9,297
1960	6,128
1950	4,492(a)
1940	3,524
1930	3,373
1920	2,091
1910	1,567
1890-1900	NA
1880	524(b)

(a)Boundary change.
(b)Reported in QUEENS County.

FARMINGTON, Town (Est. 1789)
    Ontario County

1980	8,933
1970	3,565
1960	2,114
1950	1,399
1940	1,453
1930	1,477
1920	1,465
1910	1,568
1900	1,607
1890	1,703
1880	1,978
1870	1,896
1860	1,858
1850	1,876
1840	2,122
1830	1,773
1820	4,214
1810	NA
1800	*633

FARMINGVILLE, CDP
  Brookhaven Town
    Suffolk County

1980	13,398(a)
1970	9,131(b)
1960	2,134

(a)Boundary change.
(b)Derived by LIRPB from U.S. Census
   Data; population of 9,131 is
   comparable to 1980 boundaries.

FARNHAM, Village (Inc. 1892)
  Brant Town
    Erie County

1980	404
1970	546
1960	422
1950	396
1940	388
1930	453
1920	516
1910	540
1900	262

FAR ROCKAWAY, Village (Inc. 1888)(a)
  Hempstead Town
    Queens County

1890	2,288

(a) Merged into QUEENS Borough in
    NEW YORK City in 1898.

FAYETTE, Town (Est. 1800)(a)
  Seneca County

1980	3,561
1970	2,997
1960	2,825
1950	2,557
1940	2,383
1930	2,396
1920	2,215
1910	2,593
1900	2,711
1890	2,912
1880	3,316
1870	3,364
1860	3,742
1850	3,786
1840	3,731
1830	1,890
1820	2,869
1810	NA
1800	*863(b)

(a) Established as Washington in 1800;
    name changed in 1808.
(b) Reported in CAYUGA County.

FAYETTEVILLE, Village (Inc. 1844)
  Manlius Town
    Onondaga County

1980	4,709(a)
1970	4,996(a)
1960	4,311
1950	2,624
1940	2,172(a)
1930	2,008
1920	1,584
1910	1,481
1900	1,304
1890	1,410
1880	1,556
1870	1,402

(a) Boundary change.

FAYVILLE, CDP
  Providence Town
    Saratoga County

1880	67

FEEDER DAM, CDP
  Moreau Town
    Saratoga County

1880	220

FELTS MILLS, CDP
  Rutland Town
    Jefferson County

1880	436
1870	235

FENNER, Town (Est. 1823)
  Madison County

1980	1,580
1970	1,321
1960	900
1950	852
1940	794
1930	795

1920	780
1910	807
1900	911
1890	1,040
1880	1,272
1870	1,381
1860	1,649
1850	1,690
1840	1,997
1830	2,017

FENTON, Town (Est. 1855)(a)
  Broome County

1980	7,400
1970	6,719
1960	5,920
1950	4,168
1940	2,732
1930	2,003
1920	1,111
1910	1,050
1900	1,171
1890	1,280
1880	1,555
1870	1,499
1860	1,345

(a) Established as Port Crane in 1855;
    name changed in 1867.

FENTONVILLE, CDP
  Carroll Town
    Chautauqua County

1870	82

FERNWOOD, CDP
  Moreau Town
    Saratoga County

1980	3,640
1970	3,659
1960	2,108

FILLMORE, Village (Inc. 1924)
  Hume Town
    Allegany County

1980	563
1970	537
1960	522
1950	527
1940	518
1930	488
1890-1920	NA
1880	215

FINE, CDP
  Fine Town
    St. Lawrence County

1880	207

FINE, Town (Est. 1844)
  St. Lawrence County

1980	2,243
1970	2,302 Rev.
1960	2,391
1950	1,875
1940	1,208
1930	1,053
1920	1,459
1910	2,234
1900	1,694

1890	1,207
1880	893
1870	603
1860	519
1850	293

FIRE ISLAND(a)
  Brookhaven Town
    Suffolk County

1980	83(b)
1970	42(c)

(a)Includes Cherry Grove, Davis Park,
   Fire Island Pines, Ocean Bay Park
   and Point O'Woods.
(b)Boundary change; derived by LIRPB
   from U.S. Census Data.
(c)Derived by LIRPB from U.S. Census
   Data; population is comparable to
   1980 boundaries.

FIRE ISLAND(a)
  Islip Town
    Suffolk County

1980	236(b)
1970	36(c)
1960	72(c)
1890-1950	NA
1880	77

(a)Includes Atlantique, Fair Harbor,
   Kismet and Seaview.
(b)Boundary change; derived by LIRPB
   from U.S. Census Data.
(b)Derived by LIRPB from U.S. Census
   Data.

FIRE ISLAND PINES
  see FIRE ISLAND
        Brookhaven Town
          Suffolk County

FIRTHCLIFFE, CDP
  Cornwall & New Windsor Towns
    Orange County

1980	4,430
1970	4,025
1960	2,824
1950	NA
1940	644

FISHERS, CDP
  Victor Town
    Ontario County

1880	98

FISHERS ISLAND, CDP
  Southold Town
    Suffolk County

1980	318(a)
1970	462(a)
1960	508(a)
1950	NA
1940	572
1890-1930	NA
1880	134

(a)Derived by LIRPB from U.S. Census
   Data.

FISH HOUSE, CDP
  Northampton Town
    Fulton County

1880	163

FISHKILL, Town (Est. 1788)
  Dutchess County

1980	15,506
1970	11,935
1960	7,083
1950	3,863
1940	3,615
1930	2,890
1920	2,095(a)
1910	13,858
1900	13,016
1890	11,840
1880	10,732
1870	11,732
1860	2,546
1850	9,240
1840	10,437
1830	8,292
1820	8,203
1810	NA
1800	*6,168
1790	5,941

(a)Boundary change.

FISHKILL, Village (Inc. 1889)
  Fishkill Town
    Dutchess County

1980	1,555
1970	913(a)
1960	1,033
1950	841
1940	720
1930	553
1920	479
1910	516
1900	589
1890	745
1880	682
1870	737

(a)Boundary change.

FISHKILL LANDING, Village (Inc. 1864)(a)
  Fishkill Town
    Dutchess County

1910	3,902
1900	3,673
1890	3,617
1880	2,503(b)
1870	2,992

(a)FISHKILL LANDING and MATTEAWAN
   Villages consolidated and
   incorporated as BEACON City and made
   independent of FISHKILL Town in 1913.
(b)Reported as Fishkill-on-Hudson.

FIVE CORNERS, CDP
  Genoa Town
    Cayuga County

1880	123

FLANDERS, CDP(a)
  Southampton Town
    Suffolk County

1970	1,905(b)

```
        1960            1,494 Rev.
        1890-1950         NA
        1880             126
        1870             160
(a)Included in RIVERSIDE--FLANDERS, CDP
   in 1980.
(b)Boundary change.
```

FLACKVILLE, CDP
   Lisbon Town
      St. Lawrence County
```
        1880              30
```

FLATBUSH, CDP
   Saugerties Town
      Ulster County
```
        1880             155
```

FLATBUSH, Town (Est. 1788)(a)
   Kings County
```
        1890          12,338
        1880           7,634
        1870           6,309
        1860           3,471
        1850           3,177
        1840           2,099
        1830           1,143
        1820           1,027
        1810             NA
        1800            *946
        1790             941
```
(a)Merged into BROOKLYN City in 1894.

FLATLANDS, CDP
   Flatlands Town
      Kings County
```
        1880             881
```

FLATLANDS, Town (Est. 1788)(a)
   Kings County
```
        1890           4,075
        1880           3,127
        1870           2,286
        1860           1,632
        1850           1,155
        1840             810
        1830             596
        1820             512
        1810             NA
        1800            *493
        1790             423
```
(a)Merged into BROOKLYN City in 1896.

FLATLANDS NECK, CDP
   Flatlands Town
      Kings County
```
        1880             163
```

FLEISCHMANNS, Village (Inc. 1913)
   Middletown Town
      Delaware County
```
        1980             346
        1970             434
        1960             450
        1950             469
        1940             546
        1930             495
        1920             525
```

FLEMING, CDP
   Fleming Town
      Cayuga County
```
        1880             123
```

FLEMING, Town (Est. 1821)
   Cayuga County
```
        1980           2,394
        1970           2,242
        1960           2,071
        1950           1,502
        1940           1,259
        1930             987
        1920             886
        1910           1,017
        1900           1,076
        1890           1,055
        1880             893
        1870           1,207
        1860           1,231
        1850           1,193
        1840           1,317
        1830           1,461
```

FLEMINGVILLE, CDP
   Owego Town
      Tioga County
```
        1880              37
        1870              91
```

FLINT CREEK, CDP
   Seneca Town
      Ontario County
```
        1880              92
```

FLORAL PARK, Village (Inc. 1908)
   Hempstead Town, part in
      Nassau County
```
        1980          14,478
        1970          16,527
        1960          15,121(a)
        1950          12,183
        1940          10,769(a)
        1930           8,003(a)
        1920           1,551
        1910             928
```
   North Hempstead Town, part in
      Nassau County
```
        1980           2,327
        1970           1,939
        1960           2,378(a)
        1950           2,399
        1940           2,181(a)
        1930           2,013(a)
        1920             546
        1910             297
```
   TOTAL
```
        1980          16,805
        1970          18,466
        1960          17,499(a)
        1950          14,582
        1940          12,950(a)
        1930          10,016(a)
        1920           2,097
        1910           1,225
```
(a)Boundary change.

FLORENCE, CDP
  Florence Town
    Oneida County
      1880   282

FLORENCE, Town (Est. 1805)
    Oneida County
      1980   688
      1970   610
      1960   583
      1950   510
      1940   620
      1930   641
      1920   701
      1910   936
      1900   1,207
      1890   1,489
      1880   2,073
      1870   2,299
      1860   2,802
      1850   2,575
      1840   1,259
      1830   964
      1820   640

FLORIDA, Town (Est. 1793)
    Montgomery County
      1980   2,578
      1970   2,283
      1960   2,168
      1950   2,032
      1940   1,848
      1930   1,805
      1920   1,651
      1910   1,904
      1900   1,988
      1890   2,296
      1880   3,249
      1870   3,002
      1860   2,991
      1850   3,571
      1840   5,214
      1830   2,851
      1820   2,743
      1810   NA
      1800   *1,238

FLORIDA, Village (Inc. 1946)
    Warwick Town
      Orange County
      1980   1,947(a)
      1970   1,674(a)
      1960   1,550
      1950   1,576
      1940   1,140
      1890-1930   NA
      1880   555
      1870   459
(a)Boundary change.

FLOWERFIELD(a)
    Smithtown Town
      Suffolk County
      1970   1,227(b)
      1960   1,064(b)

(a)Included in ST. JAMES, CDP in 1980.
(b)Derived by LIRPB from U.S. Census
   Data.

FLOWER HILL, Village (Inc. 1931)
    North Hempstead Town
      Nassau County
      1980   4,558
      1970   4,486
      1960   4,594
      1950   1,948
      1940   666

FLOYD, Town (Est. 1796)
    Oneida County
      1980   3,863
      1970   3,620
      1960   2,234
      1950   1,014
      1940   828
      1930   752
      1920   663
      1910   697
      1900   785
      1890   920
      1880   1,115
      1870   1,209
      1860   1,440
      1850   1,495
      1840   1,742
      1830   1,699
      1820   1,498
      1810   NA
      1800   *767

FLOYD CORNERS, CDP
    Floyd Town
      Oneida County
      1870   95

FLUSHING, Town (Est. 1788)(a)
    Queens County
      1890   19,803
      1880   15,906
      1870   14,650
      1860   10,189
      1850   5,376
      1840   4,124
      1830   2,820
      1810-1820   NA
      1800   *1,818
      1790   1,607
(a)Merged into QUEENS Borough in
   NEW YORK City in 1898.

FLUSHING, Village (Inc. 1813)(a)
    Flushing Town
      Queens County
      1890   8,436
      1880   6,683
      1870   6,223
(a)Merged into QUEENS Borough in
   NEW YORK City in 1898.

FLY CREEK, CDP
    Otsego Town
      Otsego County
      1880   236

FONDA, Village (Inc. 1850)
  Mohawk Town
    Montgomery County
        1980   1,006(a)
        1970   1,120
        1960   1,004
        1950   1,026
        1940   1,123
        1930   1,170
        1920   1,208
        1910   1,100
        1900   1,145
        1890   1,190
        1880   944
        1870   1,092
(a)Boundary change.

FONDA'S BUSH, CDP
  Broadalbin Town
    Fulton County
        1880   656

FORDHAM, CDP(a)
  West Farms Town
    Westchester County
        1870   2,151
(a)In 1800 the Census Bureau reported a
   Fordham in WESTCHESTER County,
   population of 122.

FORESTBURG, Town (Est. 1837)
  Sullivan County
        1980   796(a)
        1970   474(a)
        1960   356
        1950   364
        1940   389
        1930   415
        1920   405
        1910   545
        1900   625
        1890   714
        1880   1,058(a)
        1870   915(a)
        1860   911
        1850   715(b)
        1840   433(c)
(a)Reported as Forestburgh.
(b)Reported as Forrestburgh.
(c)Reported as Forrestburg.

FORDSBUSH, CDP
  Minden Town
    Montgomery County
        1880   99

FOREST HOME, CDP
  Ithaca Town
    Tompkins County
        1880   114

FORESTPORT, Town (Est. 1870)
  Oneida County
        1980   1,380
        1970   1,173
        1960   821
        1950   723
        1940   730
        1930   796

        1920   862
        1910   1,100
        1900   1,562
        1890   1,519
        1880   1,358
        1870   1,276

FORESTVILLE, Village (Inc. 1848)
  Hanover Town
    Chautauqua County
        1980   804
        1970   908(a)
        1960   905
        1950   786
        1940   692
        1930   677
        1920   620
        1910   721
        1900   623
        1890   788
        1880   724
        1870   722
        1860   574(b)
(a)Boundary change.
(b)Reported as Forrestville.

FORGE HOLLOW, CDP
  Marshall Town
    Oneida County
        1880   99

FORKS, CDP
  Cheektowaga Town
    Erie County
        1940   558

FORREST, CDP
  Altona Town
    Clinton County
        1880   170

FORRESTBURGH, Town
  see FORESTBURG, Town
        Sullivan County

FORRESTVILLE, Village
  see FORESTVILLE, Village
        Chautauqua County

FORT ANN, Town (Est. 1786)(a)
  Washington County
        1980   4,425
        1970   3,749
        1960   3,124
        1950   3,122
        1940   3,653
        1930   2,977
        1920   2,357
        1910   2,236
        1900   2,263
        1890   2,696
        1880   3,263
        1870   3,329
        1860   3,127
        1850   3,383
        1840   3,559
        1830   3,200

```
            1820        2,911
            1810          NA
            1800       *2,103
(a)Established as Westfield in 1786;
   name changed in 1808.
```

FORT ANN, Village (Inc. 1820)
  Fort Ann Town
    Washington County
```
            1980         509
            1970         562
            1960         453
            1950         463
            1940         439
            1930         589
            1920         538
            1910         436
            1900         431
            1880-1890     NA
            1870         639
```

FORT COVINGTON, Town (Est. 1817)
  Franklin County
```
            1980       1,804
            1970       1,963
            1960       1,905
            1950       1,764
            1940       1,767
            1930       1,728
            1920       1,966
            1910       2,028
            1900       2,043
            1890       2,207
            1880       2,424
            1870       2,436
            1860       2,757
            1850       2,641
            1840       2,094
            1830       2,901
            1820         979
```

FORT COVINGTON, Village (Inc. 1889)(a)
  Fort Covington Town
    Franklin County
```
            1970         983
            1960         976
            1950         891
            1940         813
            1930         764
            1920         836
            1910         877
            1900         822
            1890         870
            1880         931
            1870         953
(a)Dissolved in 1975.
```

FORT EDWARD, Town (Est. 1818)
  Washington County
```
            1980       6,479
            1970       6,719
            1960       6,523
            1950       6,213
            1940       5,716
            1930       5,841 Rev.
            1920       5,845
            1910       5,740
```

```
            1900       5,216
            1890       4,424
            1880       4,680
            1870       5,125
            1860       3,544
            1850       2,328
            1840       1,726
            1830       1,816
            1820       1,631
```

FORT EDWARD, Village (Inc. 1849)
  Fort Edward Town
    Washington County
```
            1980       3,561(a)
            1970       3,733
            1960       3,737
            1950       3,797
            1940       3,620
            1930       3,850
            1920       3,871
            1910       3,762
            1900       3,521
            1890         NA
            1880       2,988
            1870       3,492
(a)Boundary change.
```

FORT HUNTER, CDP
  Florida Town
    Montgomery County
```
            1880         212
            1870         200
```

FORT JACKSON, CDP
  Hopkinton Town
    St. Lawrence County
```
            1880         153
```

FORT JOHNSON, Village (Inc. 1909)
  Amsterdam Town
    Montgomery County
```
            1980         646
            1970         711
            1960         876
            1950         930
            1940         868
            1930         833
            1920         680
```

FORT MILLER, CDP
  Fort Edward Town
    Washington County
```
            1880         124
```

FORT MONTGOMERY, CDP
  Highlands Town
    Orange County
```
            1980       1,396
            1950-1970     NA
            1940         651
```

FORT PLAIN, Village (Inc. 1832)
  Canajoharie Town, part in
    Montgomery County
```
            1980           7
            1970           6
            1960           0
            1950           9
            1940           7
```

Minden Town, part in
Montgomery County

1980	2,548
1970	2,809
1960	2,809
1950	2,926
1940	2,763
1930	2,725(a)
1920	2,747(a)
1910	2,762
1900	2,444
1890	2,864
1880	2,443
1870	1,797

TOTAL

1980	2,555
1970	2,809
1960	2,809
1950	2,935
1940	2,770
1870-1930	(a)

(a)Reported in MINDEN Town only.

FORT SALONGA, CDP
   Huntington & Smithtown Towns
   Suffolk County

1980	9,550

FOSTERS MEADOW, CDP
   Hempstead Town
   Nassau County

1880	477(a)

(a)Reported in QUEENS County.

FOSTERVILLE, CDP
   Aurelius Town
   Cayuga County

1880	77

FOSTERVILLE, CDP
   Moreau Town
   Saratoga County

1880	50

FOWLER, Town (Est. 1816)
   St. Lawrence County

1980	1,721
1970	1,576
1960	1,722
1950	1,602
1940	1,772
1930	1,608
1920	1,310
1910	1,655
1900	1,716
1890	1,592
1880	1,590
1870	1,785
1860	1,808
1850	1,813
1840	1,752
1830	1,447
1820	605

FOWLERVILLE, CDP
   York Town
   Livingston County

1880	386

FRANKFORT, Town (Est. 1796)
   Herkimer County

1980	7,686
1970	7,805
1960	7,550
1950	6,598
1940	6,247
1930	6,918
1920	6,483
1910	5,105
1900	4,472
1890	3,988
1880	3,025
1870	3,065
1860	3,247
1850	3,023
1840	3,096
1830	2,620
1820	1,860
1810	NA
1800	*946

FRANKFORT, Village (Inc. 1863)
   Frankfort Town
   Herkimer County

1980	2,995
1970	3,305
1960	3,872
1950	3,844
1940	3,859
1930	4,203
1920	4,198
1910	3,303
1900	2,664
1890	2,291
1880	1,085
1870	1,083

FRANKLIN, CDP
   Kirkland Town
   Oneida County

1870	379

FRANKLIN, County (Est. 1808)

1980	44,929
1970	43,931
1960	44,742
1950	44,830
1940	44,286
1930	45,694
1920	43,541
1910	45,717
1900	42,853
1890	38,110
1880	32,390
1870	30,271
1860	30,837
1850	25,102
1840	16,318
1830	11,312
1820	4,439
1810	2,717 Rev.

FRANKLIN, Town (Est. 1792)
   Delaware County

1980	2,431
1970	2,202
1960	2,133
1950	2,156

1940	2,019
1930	2,037
1920	2,132
1910	2,403
1900	2,529
1890	2,897
1880	2,907
1870	3,283
1860	3,308
1850	3,087
1840	3,025
1830	2,786
1820	2,481
1810	NA
1800	*1,390

FRANKLIN, Town
    Dutchess County
  see PATTERSON, Town
        Putnam County

FRANKLIN, Town (Est. 1836)
    Franklin County

1980	926
1970	550
1960	695
1950	872
1940	1,002
1930	1,242
1920	1,280
1910	1,447
1900	1,501
1890	1,345
1880	1,184
1870	1,195
1860	1,105
1850	724
1840	192

FRANKLIN, Village (Inc. 1874)
    Franklin Town
    Delaware County

1980	440
1970	552
1960	525
1950	558
1940	481
1930	451
1920	476
1910	473
1900	473
1890	581
1880	660
1870	681

FRANKLIN IRON WORKS, CDP
    Kirkland Town
    Oneida County

1880	352

FRANKLIN SQUARE, CDP
    Hempstead Town
    Nassau County

1980	29,051
1970	32,156
1960	32,483
1950	NA
1940	5,765
1890-1930	NA

1880	267(a)

(a)Reported in QUEENS County.

FRANKLINTON, CDP
    Broome Town
    Schoharie County

1880	77

FRANKLINVILLE, CDP
    Southold Town
    Suffolk County

1880	128

FRANKLINVILLE, Town (Est. 1812)(a)
    Cattaraugus County

1980	3,102
1970	2,847
1960	3,090
1950	3,055
1940	2,762
1930	2,963
1920	3,003
1910	2,663
1900	2,514
1890	2,224
1880	1,982
1870	1,559
1860	1,819
1850	1,706
1840	1,293
1830	903
1820	1,453

(a)Established as Hebe in 1812; name
    changed to Ischua in 1816 and to
    FRANKLINVILLE in 1824.

FRANKLINVILLE, Village (Inc. 1874)
    Franklinville Town
    Cattaraugus County

1980	1,887
1970	1,948
1960	2,124
1950	2,092
1940	1,884
1930	2,021
1920	2,015
1910	1,568
1900	1,360
1890	1,021

FREDERICK, Town
    Dutchess County
  see KENT, Town
        Putnam County

FREDERICKSTOWN, Town
    Dutchess County
  see KENT, Town
        Putnam County

FREDONIA, Village (Inc. 1829)
    Pomfret Town
    Chautauqua County

1980	11,126(a)
1970	10,326
1960	8,477
1950	7,095
1940	5,738
1930	5,814

1920	6,051
1910	5,285
1900	4,127
1890	3,399
1880	NA
1870	2,546

(a)Boundary change.

FREDRICK, Town
  see WAYNE, Town
      Steuben County

FREDRICKSBURGH, Town
  see VOLNEY, Town
      Oswego County

FREDRICKSTOWN, Town
  Steuben County
  see WAYNE, Town
      Steuben County

FREEDOM, Town (Est. 1820)
  Cattaraugus County

1980	1,840
1970	1,355
1960	1,059
1950	1,031
1940	947
1930	863
1920	1,016
1910	1,159
1900	1,209
1890	1,251
1880	1,312
1870	1,371
1860	1,424
1850	1,652
1840	1,831
1830	1,505

FREEDOM, Town
  Dutchess County
  see LA GRANGE, Town
      Dutchess County

FREEHOLD, CDP
  Greenville Town
    Greene County

1880	140

FREE HOLD, Town
  see DURHAM & GREENVILLE, Towns
      Greene County

FREEPORT, Town
  see CONESUS, Town
      Livingston County

FREEPORT, Village (Inc. 1892)
  Hempstead Town
    Nassau County

1980	38,272
1970	40,374
1960	34,419(a)
1950	24,680
1940	20,410(a)
1930	15,467(a)

1920	8,599
1910	4,836
1900	2,612
1890	NA
1880	1,217(b)

(a)Boundary change.
(b)Reported in QUEENS County.

FREETOWN, CDP
  Freetown Town
    Cortland County

1880	79

FREETOWN, CDP(a)
  East Hampton Town
    Suffolk County

1970	1,543(b)
1960	1,269 Rev.

(a)Included in AMAGANSETT and NORTHWEST
  HARBOR, CDPs in 1980.
(b)Boundary change; derived by LIRPB
  from U.S. Census Data.

FREETOWN, Town (Est. 1818)
  Cortland County

1980	572
1970	522
1960	542
1950	534
1940	510
1930	418
1920	485
1910	551
1900	610
1890	677
1880	844
1870	906
1860	981
1850	1,035
1840	950
1830	1,051
1820	663

FREETOWN, Town
  Wayne County
  see ONTARIO, Town
      Wayne County

FREEVILLE, Village (Inc. 1887)
  Dryden Town
    Tompkins County

1980	449
1970	664
1960	471
1950	373
1940	379
1930	374
1920	303
1910	318
1900	440
1890	312

FREMONT, Town (Est. 1854)
  Steuben County

1980	865
1970	884
1960	779
1950	782
1940	739

1930	697
1920	645
1910	860
1900	1,033
1890	1,047
1880	1,277
1870	1,119
1860	1,117

FREMONT, Town (Est. 1851)
Sullivan County

1980	1,346
1970	1,047
1960	1,047
1950	1,170
1940	1,251
1930	1,386
1920	1,435
1910	1,931
1900	2,184
1890	2,168
1880	2,025
1870	2,218
1860	1,728

FRENCH CREEK, Town (Est. 1829)
Chautauqua County

1980	878
1970	848
1960	906
1950	817
1940	694
1930	768
1920	806
1910	882
1900	1,014
1890	1,033
1880	1,042
1870	973
1860	968
1850	725
1840	621
1830	420

FRESH POND, CDP
Oyster Bay Town
Nassau County

1880	50(a)

(a)Reported in QUEENS County.

FREWSBURG, CDP
Carroll Town
Chautauqua County

1980	1,908
1970	1,772
1960	1,623
1950	1,585
1940	1,275
1890-1930	NA
1880	538
1870	379

FRIENDSHIP, CDP(a)
Friendship Town
Allegany County

1980	1,461
1970	1,285

1960	1,231
1950	1,344
1940	1,148
1930	1,154
1920	1,026
1910	1,218
1900	1,214
1890	1,369
1880	1,134
1870	474

(a)Incorporated as a village in 1898;
village dissolved in 1977.

FRIENDSHIP, Town (Est. 1815)
Allegany County

1980	2,164
1970	2,106
1960	2,020
1950	2,162
1940	1,932
1930	1,868
1920	1,788
1910	2,100
1900	2,136
1890	2,216
1880	2,127
1870	1,528
1860	1,889
1850	1,675
1840	1,244
1830	1,502
1820	662

FULLERVILLE, CDP
Fowler Town
St. Lawrence County

1880	117
1870	149

FULTON, City (Inc. 1902)(a)
Oswego County

1980	13,312
1970	14,003
1960	14,261(b)
1950	13,922
1940	13,362
1930	12,462
1920	13,043
1910	10,480(b)
1900	5,281(c)
1890	4,214(c)
1880	3,941(c)
1870	3,507(c)

(a)FULTON and OSWEGO FALLS Villages
consolidated and incorporated as
FULTON City and made independent of
GRANBY, SANDY CREEK and VOLNEY Towns
in 1902.
(b)Boundary change.
(c)Reported as FULTON Village.

FULTON, County (Est. 1838)

1980	55,153
1970	52,637
1960	51,304
1950	51,021
1940	48,597
1930	46,560
1920	44,927

1910	44,534
1900	42,842
1890	37,650
1880	30,985
1870	27,064
1860	24,162
1850	20,171
1840	18,049

FULTON, Town (Est. 1828)
Schoharie County

1980	1,394
1970	1,060
1960	1,008
1950	1,050
1940	1,010
1930	1,010
1920	1,227
1910	1,450
1900	1,998
1890	2,316
1880	2,683
1870	2,700
1860	2,944
1850	2,566
1840	2,147
1830	1,604

FULTON, Village (Inc. 1835)(a)
Volney & Sandy Creek Towns
Oswego County

1900	5,281
1890	4,214
1880	3,941
1870	3,507(b)

(a)FULTON and OSWEGO FALLS Villages
consolidated and incorporated as
FULTON City and made independent of
GRANBY, SANDY CREEK and VOLNEY Towns
in 1902.
(b)Reported in VOLNEY Town only.

FULTONVILLE, Village (Inc. 1848)
Glen Town
Montgomery County

1980	777
1970	812
1960	815
1950	840
1940	806
1930	831
1920	869
1910	812
1900	977
1890	1,122
1880	NA
1870	1,117

FURNACEVILLE, CDP
Ontario Town
Wayne County

1880	177

G

GAINES, CDP
Gaines Town
Orleans County

1880	185
1870	250

GAINES, Town (Est. 1816)
Orleans County

1980	2,692
1970	2,385
1960	2,090
1950	1,812
1940	1,667
1930	1,702
1920	1,669
1910	1,946
1900	1,889
1890	2,070
1880	2,338
1870	2,196
1860	2,542
1850	2,722
1840	2,268
1830	1,833
1820	1,134(a)

(a)Reported in GENESEE County.

GAINESVILLE, Town (Est. 1814)(a)
Wyoming County

1980	2,133
1970	2,177
1960	2,032
1950	2,121
1940	1,923
1930	2,074
1920	2,276
1910	2,690
1900	2,325
1890	2,166
1880	1,787
1870	1,612
1860	1,732
1850	1,760
1840	2,367(b)
1830	1,934(b)
1820	1,088(b)

(a)Established as Hebe in 1814; name
changed in 1816.
(b)Reported in GENESEE County.

GAINESVILLE, Village (Inc. 1902)
Gainesville Town
Wyoming County

1980	334
1970	385
1960	369
1950	314
1940	283
1930	270
1920	341

1910	327
1880-1900	NA
1870	114

GALEN, Town (Est. 1812)
  Wayne County

1980	4,480
1970	4,619
1960	4,419
1950	4,036
1940	3,858
1930	3,901
1920	4,172
1910	4,630
1900	4,606
1890	4,922
1880	5,461
1870	5,706
1860	5,340
1850	4,609
1840	4,234
1830	3,631
1820	2,979

GALLATIN, Town (Est. 1803)
    Columbia County
  see ANCRAM, Town
    Columbia County

GALLATIN, Town (Est. 1830)(a)
  Columbia County

1980	1,292
1970	737
1960	621
1950	613
1940	554
1930	511
1920	633
1910	720
1900	823
1890	1,016
1880	1,252
1870	1,416
1860	1,533
1850	1,586
1840	1,644
1830	1,588

(a)GALLATIN Town reorganized from part
  of ANCRAM Town in 1830.

GALLUPVILLE, CDP
  Wright Town
    Schoharie County

1880	258

GALWAY, Town (Est. 1792)
  Saratoga County

1980	3,018
1970	2,506
1960	1,746
1950	1,408
1940	1,244
1930	1,137
1920	1,101
1910	1,205
1900	1,350
1890	1,635
1880	1,902
1870	2,174

1860	2,427
1850	2,158
1840	2,412
1830	2,710
1820	2,579
1810	NA
1800	*2,310

GALWAY, Village (Inc. 1838)
  Galway Town
    Saratoga County

1980	245
1970	270
1960	309
1950	188
1940	161
1930	119
1920	94
1910	112
1900	177
1890	177
1880	187

GANG MILLS, CDP
  Trenton Town
    Oneida County

1870	104

GANG MILLS, CDP
  Erwin Town
    Steuben County

1980	2,300
1970	1,258
1890-1960	NA
1880	372

GANSEVOORT, CDP
  Northumberland Town
    Saratoga County

1880	159

GARBUTTSVILLE, CDP
  Wheatland Town
    Monroe County

1880	172

GARDEN CITY, Village (Inc. 1919)
  Hempstead Town
    Nassau County

1980	22,927
1970	25,373
1960	23,948(a)
1950	14,486(b)
1940	11,223
1930	7,180
1920	2,420
1890-1910	NA
1880	574(c)

(a)Boundary change; population of 2 reported in NORTH HEMPSTEAD Town.
(b)Boundary change; part in HEMPSTEAD
   Town, 14,368; part in NORTH HEMPSTEAD
   Town, 118.
(c)Reported in QUEENS County.

GARDEN CITY PARK, CDP
  North Hempstead Town
    Nassau County

1980	7,712

```
              1970        7,488
              1960        8,302(a)
(a)Derived by LIRPB from U.S. Census
   Data.  U.S. Census reported as part of
   GARDEN CITY PARK--HERRICKS, CDP with
   a population of 15,364.
```

GARDEN CITY PARK--HERRICKS, CDP
    see GARDEN CITY PARK & HERRICKS, CDPs
        Nassau County

GARDEN CITY SOUTH
    Hempstead Town
    Nassau County
```
              1980        4,273(a)
              1970        4,788(a)
              1960        5,133(a)
(a)Derived by LIRPB from U.S. Census
   Data.
```

GARDENVILLE, CDP
    West Seneca Town
    Erie County
```
              1940          951
              1890-1930      NA
              1880          294
```

GARDINER, CDP
    Gardiner Town
    Ulster County
```
              1880          130
```

GARDINER, Town (Est. 1853)
    Ulster County
```
              1980        3,552
              1970        2,598
              1960        1,660
              1950        1,289
              1940        1,317
              1930          988
              1920        1,088
              1910        2,779
              1900        1,509
              1890        1,703
              1880        1,794
              1870        1,991
              1860        2,096
```

GARDINER'S ISLAND
    East Hampton Town
    Suffolk County
```
              1980            4(a)
              1970            2(b)
(a)Boundary change; derived by LIRPB
   from U.S. Census Data.
(b)Derived by LIRPB from U.S. Census
   Data; population is comparable to
   1980 boundaries.
```

GARDNER'S ISLAND, CDP
    Clayton Town
    Jefferson County
```
              1870            7
```

GARDNERTOWN, CDP
    Newburgh Town
    Orange County
```
              1980        4,238
```

```
              1970        4,614
              1950-1960      NA
              1940          783
```

GARLIC FALLS, CDP
    Black Brook Town
    Clinton County
```
              1880           67
```

GAROGA, CDP & Town
    see CAROGA, CDP & Town
        Fulton County

GARRISON, CDP
    Philipstown Town
    Putnam County
```
              1880          127
```

GASPORT, CDP
    Royalton Town
    Niagara County
```
              1980        1,339
              1950-1970      NA
              1940          788
```

GATES, Town (Est. 1802)(a)
    Monroe County
```
              1980       29,756(b)
              1970       26,442
              1960       13,755(b)
              1950        7,925(b)
              1940        4,965
              1930        3,634
              1920        1,419
              1910        4,862
              1900        3,468
              1890        2,910
              1880        1,988
              1870        3,541
              1860        2,710
              1850        2,005
              1840        1,728
              1830        1,441
              1820        2,643(c)
              1810          NA
              1800        *778(d)
(a)Established as Northampton in 1802;
   name changed in 1812.
(b)Boundary change.
(c)Reported in GENESEE County.
(d)Reported in ONTARIO County.
```

GATES CENTER, CDP
    Gates Town
    Monroe County
```
              1940          799
```

GATES--NORTH GATES, CDP
    Gates Town
    Monroe County
```
              1980       15,244
```

GEDDES, CDP
    Geddes Town
    Onondaga County
```
              1870        3,629
```

GEDDES, Town (Est. 1848)
    Onondaga County

1980	18,528
1970	21,032
1960	19,679
1950	13,284
1940	11,237
1930	10,210
1920	7,995
1910	5,959
1900	4,387
1890	1,571
1880	7,088
1870	4,505
1860	2,528
1850	2,011

GENESE, Town
    Ontario County
  see GENESEO, Town
      Livingston County

GENESSE, Town
    Ontario County
  see GENESEO, Town
      Livingston County

GENESEE, County (Est. 1802)

1980	59,400
1970	58,722
1960	53,994
1950	47,584
1940	44,481
1930	44,468
1920	37,976
1910	37,615
1900	34,561
1890	33,265
1880	32,806
1870	31,606
1860	32,189
1850	28,488
1840	59,587
1830	52,147
1820	58,093(a)
1810	12,588

(a)Reported as Genessee.

GENESEE, Town (Est. 1830)
    Allegany County

1980	1,787
1970	1,187
1960	1,193
1950	1,134
1940	1,188
1930	1,119
1920	911
1910	1,105
1900	1,052
1890	1,076
1880	974
1870	888
1860	963
1850	672
1840	578
1830	219

GENESEE, Village
  see WELLSVILLE, Village
    Allegany County

GENESEE FALLS, Town (Est. 1846)
    Wyoming County

1980	553
1970	397
1960	397
1950	436
1940	413
1930	509
1920	542
1910	615
1900	650
1890	740
1880	860
1870	979
1860	1,020
1850	1,322

GENESEO, Town (Est. 1789)
    Livingston County

1980	8,673
1970	7,278
1960	4,337
1950	3,782
1940	3,133
1930	3,135
1920	3,007
1910	3,188
1900	3,613
1890	3,534
1880	3,340
1870	3,032
1860	3,002
1850	2,958
1840	2,892
1830	2,675
1820	1,598(a)
1810	NA
1800	*348(b)
1790	168(c)

(a)Reported in ONTARIO County.
(b)Reported as Genesse in ONTARIO County.
(c)Reported as Genese in ONTARIO County.

GENESEO, Village (Inc. 1832)
    Geneseo Town
      Livingston County

1980	6,746(a)
1970	5,714(a)
1960	3,284
1950	2,638
1940	2,144
1930	2,261
1920	2,157
1910	2,067
1900	2,400
1890	2,286
1880	1,925

(a)Boundary change.

GENESSEE, County
  see GENESEE, County

GENEVA, City (Inc. 1898)(a)
    Ontario & Seneca Counties
        1980   15,133(b)
        1970   16,793(c)
        1960   17,286(b)
        1950   17,144(b)
        1940   15,555(d)
        1930   16,053(d)
        1920   14,648(d)
        1910   12,446(d)
        1900   10,433(d)
(a)GENEVA Village incorporated as GENEVA
   City and made independent of GENEVA
   Town in 1898.
(b)Boundary change.
(c)Boundary change; no population
   reported in that part in SENECA
   County.
(d)Reported in ONTARIO County only.

GENEVA, Town (Est. 1872)
    Ontario County
        1980   3,077(a)
        1970   2,781(a)
        1960   2,603(a)
        1950   1,771(a)
        1940   1,436
        1930   1,327
        1920   1,251
        1910   1,086
        1900   1,091(a)
        1890   8,877(b)
        1880   7,412
        1870   5,521(c)
(a)Boundary change.
(b)In 1900 the Census Bureau reported an
   1890 figure of 1,320 which excludes
   GENEVA Village.
(c)Reported in SENECA County.

GENEVA, Village (Inc. 1806)(a)
   Geneva Town
     Ontario County
        1890   7,557
        1880   5,878
        1870   5,521(b)
(a)GENEVA Village incorporated as GENEVA
   City and made independent of GENEVA
   Town in 1898.
(b)Reported in SENECA County.

GENOA, CDP
   Genoa Town
     Cayuga County
        1880   397

GENOA, Town (Est. 1789)(a)
     Cayuga County
        1980   1,921
        1970   1,744
        1960   1,794
        1950   1,672
        1940   1,425
        1930   1,407
        1920   1,483
        1910   1,866
        1900   2,075
        1890   2,320

        1880   2,517
        1870   2,205
        1860   2,429
        1850   2,503
        1840   2,593
        1830   2,768
        1820   2,585
        1810   NA
        1800   *3,553
(a)Established as Milton in 1789; name
   changed in 1808.

GEORGETOWN, CDP
   Georgetown Town
     Madison County
        1880   270

GEORGETOWN, Town (Est. 1815)
     Madison County
        1980   779
        1970   816
        1960   633
        1950   616
        1940   734
        1930   684
        1920   854
        1910   925
        1900   998
        1890   1,172
        1880   1,490
        1870   1,423
        1860   1,476
        1850   1,411
        1840   1,130
        1830   1,094
        1820   824

GERMAN, Town (Est. 1806)
     Chenango County
        1980   250
        1970   188
        1960   253
        1950   245
        1940   234
        1930   303
        1920   365
        1910   371
        1900   423
        1890   542
        1880   664
        1870   712
        1860   781
        1850   903
        1840   965
        1830   884
        1820   2,675

GERMAN CORNERS, CDP
   German Town
     Chenango County
        1880   38

GERMAN FLATTS, Town (Est. 1788)
     Herkimer County
        1980   14,981
        1970   15,430
        1960   15,742
        1950   14,106
        1940   13,053

1930	13,923
1920	14,089
1910	10,160
1900	8,663
1890	7,255
1880	6,746
1870	5,718
1860	3,940
1850	3,578
1840	3,245(a)
1830	2,466
1820	2,665
1810	NA
1800	*1,637
1790	1,307(b)

(a)Reported as German Flat.
(b)Reported in MONTGOMERY County.

GERMANTOWN, Town (Est. 1788)
    Columbia County

1980	1,922
1970	1,782
1960	1,504
1950	1,418
1940	1,427
1930	1,462
1920	1,424
1910	1,649
1900	1,686
1890	1,683
1880	1,608
1870	1,393
1860	1,353
1850	1,023
1840	969
1830	967(a)
1820	891
1810	NA
1800	*736
1790	516

(a)Reported as German-Town.

GERRY, Town (Est. 1812)
    Chautauqua County

1980	2,022
1970	1,636
1960	1,468
1950	1,347
1940	1,073
1930	1,112
1920	993
1910	1,155
1900	1,198
1890	1,088
1880	1,174
1870	1,096
1860	1,315
1850	1,332
1840	1,288
1830	1,110
1820	947

GERRYVILLE, Town
    see ALABAMA, Town
        Genesee County

GHENT, Town (Est. 1818)
    Columbia County

1980	4,636

1970	3,729
1960	3,485
1950	3,173
1940	2,948
1930	2,818
1920	2,451
1910	2,819
1900	2,698
1890	2,903
1880	2,953
1870	2,886
1860	2,803
1850	2,293
1840	2,558
1830	2,783
1820	2,379

GIBSON, CDP
    Corning Town
        Steuben County

1880	278
1870	372
1860	278

GILBERTSVILLE, Village (Inc. 1896)
    Butternuts Town
        Otsego County

1980	455(a)
1970	552
1960	522
1950	456
1940	377
1930	362
1920	419
1910	455
1900	476

(a)Boundary change.

GILBOA, CDP
    Gilboa Town
        Schoharie County

1880	293

GILBOA, Town (Est. 1848)
    Schoharie County

1980	1,078
1970	854
1960	782
1950	943
1940	1,061
1930	978
1920	1,541
1910	1,467
1900	1,448
1890	1,718
1880	2,040
1870	2,227
1860	2,541
1850	3,024

GILGO--OAK BEACH
    Babylon Town
        Suffolk County

1980	381(a)
1970	181(b)
1960	175(b)

(a)Boundary change; derived by LIRPB
    from U.S. Census Data.
(b)Derived by LIRPB from U.S. Census

Data.

GILMAN, Town (Est. 1839)(a)
    Hamilton County
        1850   101
        1840   98(b)
(a)Dissolved in 1860.
(b)Reported as Gillman.

GLASCO, CDP
    Saugerties Town
      Ulster County
        1980   1,179
        1970   1,169
        1890-1960   NA
        1880   900

GLEN, CDP
    Glen Town
      Montgomery County
        1870   145(a)
(a)Reported as Glenn.

GLEN, Town (Est. 1823)
    Montgomery County
        1980   1,893
        1970   1,797
        1960   1,734
        1950   1,742
        1940   1,754
        1930   1,749
        1920   1,782
        1910   2,002
        1900   2,281
        1890   2,648
        1880   2,622
        1870   2,782(a)
        1860   2,884
        1850   3,043
        1840   3,678
        1830   2,451
(a)Reported as Glenn.

GLEN AUBRY, CDP
    Nanticoke Town
      Broome County
        1880   97

GLENCEE MILLS, CDP
    Livingston Town
      Columbia County
        1880   100

GLEN COVE, City (Inc. 1918)
    Nassau County
        1980   24,618
        1970   25,770
        1960   23,817
        1950   15,130
        1940   12,415(a)
        1930   11,430(a)
        1920   8,664
(a)Boundary change.

GLENDALE, CDP
    Martinsburg Town
      Lewis County
        1880   111

GLENERIC, CDP
    Saugerties Town
      Ulster County
        1880   124

GLENHAM, CDP
    Fishkill Town
      Dutchess County
        1980   2,832
        1970   2,720
        1950-1960   NA
        1940   552
        1890-1930   NA
        1880   1,353
        1870   924

GLEN HEAD, CDP
    Oyster Bay Town
      Nassau County
        1980   4,513(a)
        1970   4,274(a)
        1960   4,235(a)
        1950   NA
        1940   1,262
(a)Derived by LIRPB from U.S. Census
Data.

GLENMORE, CDP
    Annsville Town
      Oneida County
        1880   50

GLENN, CDP & Town
    see GLEN, CDP & Town
           Montgomery County

GLEN PARK, Village (Inc. 1893)
    Brownville Town, part in
      Jefferson County
        1980   470
        1970   540
        1960   476
        1950   503
        1940   518
        1930   537
        1920   618
        1910   522
        1900   494
    Pamelia Town, part in
      Jefferson County
        1980   34
        1970   47
        1960   83
        1950   13
        1940   4
        1930   22
        1920   43
    TOTAL
        1980   504
        1970   587
        1960   561
        1950   516
        1940   523
        1930   559
        1920   661
        1900-1910   (a)
(a)Reported in BROWNVILLE Town only.

GLENS FALLS, City (Inc. 1908)(a)
     Warren County
          1980   15,897
          1970   17,222
          1960   18,580
          1950   19,610
          1940   18,636
          1930   18,531
          1920   16,638
          1910   15,243
(a)GLENS FALLS Village incorporated as
   GLENS FALLS City and made independent
   of QUEENSBURY Town in 1908.

GLENS FALLS, Village (Inc. 1839)(a)
     Queensbury Town
        Warren County
          1900   12,613
          1890   9,509
          1880   4,900
          1870   4,500
          1860   3,780(b)
(a)GLENS FALLS Village incorporated as
   GLENS FALLS City and made independent
   of QUEENSBURY Town in 1908.
(b)Estimated.

GLENS FALLS NORTH, CDP
     Queensbury Town
        Warren County
          1980   6,956

GLENVILLE, CDP
     Greenburgh Town
        Westchester County
          1880   183

GLENVILLE, Town (Est. 1820)
     Schenectady County
          1980   28,519
          1970   28,969
          1960   25,707
          1950   17,912
          1940   13,343
          1930   12,069
          1920   7,036
          1910   5,201
          1900   3,010
          1890   2,468
          1880   2,746
          1870   2,973
          1860   3,192
          1850   3,409
          1840   3,068
          1830   2,497
          1820   2,514

GLENWOOD, CDP
     Oyster Bay Town
        Nassau County
          1880   150(a)
(a)Reported in QUEENS County.

GLENWOOD LANDING, CDP
     North Hempsted Town, part in
        Nassau County
          1980   220(a)

          1970   255(a)
          1960   214(a)
     Oyster Bay Town, part in
        Nassau County
          1980   3,335(a)
          1970   3,458(a)
          1960   3,693(a)
          1950   NA
          1940   1,343
     TOTAL
          1980   3,555(a)
          1970   3,713(a)
          1960   3,907(a)
          1950   NA
          1940   (b)
(a)Derived by LIRPB from U.S. Census
   Data.
(b)Reported in OYSTER BAY Town only.

GLENWOOD PARK, CDP
     Newburgh Town
        Orange County
          1960   1,317

GLOUCESTER, County (Est. 1770)(a)
(a)Became Caledonia, Essex, New Orange,
   Orleans and Washington Counties in
   Vermont State in 1790.

GLOVERSVILLE, City (Inc. 1890)
     Fulton County
          1980   17,836(a)
          1970   19,677(a)
          1960   21,741(a)
          1950   23,634(a)
          1940   23,329
          1930   23,099
          1920   22,075(a)
          1910   20,642
          1900   18,349
          1890   13,864
          1880   7,133(b)
          1870   4,518(b)
(a)Boundary change.
(b)Reported as a CDP in JOHNSONTOWN Town.

GOLDENS BRIDGE, CDP
     Lewisboro Town
        Westchester County
          1980   1,367
          1970   1,101
          1950-1960   NA
          1940   509

GOOD GROUND, CDP
     see HAMPTON BAYS, CDP
          Suffolk County

GORDON HEIGHTS
     Brookhaven Town
        Suffolk County
          1980   1,590(a)
          1970   1,307(b)
(a)Boundary change; derived by LIRPB
   from U.S. Census Data.
(b)Derived by LIRPB from U.S. Census

Data; population is comparable
to 1980 boundaries.

GORHAM, CDP
  Gorham Town
    Ontario County
      1880   286

GORHAM, Town (Est. 1789)(a)
  Ontario County
      1980   3,598
      1970   3,033
      1960   2,664
      1950   2,354
      1940   2,027
      1930   1,843
      1920   1,936
      1910   2,134
      1900   2,131
      1890   2,203
      1880   2,521
      1870   2,389
      1860   2,537
      1850   2,645
      1840   2,779
      1830   2,981
      1820   3,991
      1810   NA
      1800   *476
      1790   2,539(b)
(a)Established as Easton in 1789; name
   changed to Lincoln in 1806 and to
   GORHAM in 1807.
(b)Reported in ALBANY County.

GOSHEN, Town (Est. 1788)
  Orange County
      1980   10,463
      1970   8,393
      1960   6,835
      1950   5,832
      1940   5,697
      1930   5,182
      1920   5,016
      1910   5,149
      1900   4,564
      1890   5,021
      1880   4,387
      1870   3,903
      1860   3,480
      1850   3,149
      1840   3,889
      1830   3,361
      1820   3,441
      1810   NA
      1800   *2,563
      1790   2,448

GOSHEN, Village (Inc. 1809)
  Goshen Town
    Orange County
      1980   4,874(a)
      1970   4,342(a)
      1960   3,906(a)
      1950   3,311
      1940   3,073
      1930   2,891
      1920   2,813
      1910   3,081

      1900   2,826
      1890   2,907
      1880   2,557
      1870   2,205
(a)Boundary change.

GOUVERNEUR, Town (Est. 1810)
  St. Lawrence County
      1980   6,629(a)
      1970   6,710(a)
      1960   6,757(a)
      1950   6,506
      1940   5,900
      1930   5,512
      1920   5,762
      1910   6,020
      1910   5,915
      1890   5,851
      1880   4,165
      1870   3,539
      1860   3,201
      1850   2,783
      1840   2,538
      1830   1,430
      1820   765
(a)Boundary change.

GOUVERNEUR, Village (Inc. 1850)
  Gouverneur Town
    St. Lawrence County
      1980   4,285(a)
      1970   4,574(a)
      1960   4,946(a)
      1950   4,916
      1930   4,015
      1920   4,143
      1910   4,128
      1900   3,689
      1890   3,458
      1880   2,071
      1870   1,627
(a)Boundary change.

GOVERNOR'S ISLAND, CDP
  New York County
      1860   696

GOWANDA, Village (Inc. 1848)
  Persia Town, part in
    Cattaraugus County, part in
      1980   1,864
      1970   2,098
      1960   2,273
      1950   2,221
      1940   2,206
      1930   2,087
      1920   1,833
      1910   1,549
      1900   1,475
      1880-1890   NA
      1870   581
  Collins Town, part in
    Erie County, part in
      1980   849
      1970   1,012
      1960   1,079
      1950   1,068
      1940   950
      1930   955

1920	840
1910	663
1900	668
1880-1890	NA
1870	413

TOTAL

1980	2,713
1970	3,110
1960	3,352
1950	3,289
1940	3,156
1930	3,042
1920	2,673
1910	2,012
1900	2,143
1880-1890	NA
1870	994

GRAFTON, Town (Est. 1807)
    Rensselaer County

1980	1,665
1970	1,307
1960	1,009
1950	964
1940	836
1930	633
1920	733
1910	1,019
1900	1,136
1890	1,457
1880	1,676
1870	1,599
1860	3,930
1850	2,033
1840	2,019
1830	1,681
1820	1,611

GRANBY, Town (Est. 1818)
    Oswego County

1980	6,341
1970	4,718
1960	3,704
1950	2,775
1940	2,220
1930	2,130
1920	1,913
1910	2,022(a)
1900	2,195
1890	2,317
1880	4,514
1870	3,972
1860	4,057
1850	3,368
1840	2,385
1830	1,423
1820	555

(a)Boundary change.

GRAND ISLAND, Town (Est. 1852)
    Erie County

1980	16,770
1970	13,977
1960	9,607
1950	3,090
1940	1,055
1930	626
1920	728
1910	914

1900	1,036
1890	1,048
1880	1,156
1870	1,126
1860	954

GRAND VIEW-ON-HUDSON, Village (Inc. 1918)
    Orangetown Town
    Rockland County

1980	312
1970	325
1960	330(a)
1950	302
1940	588
1930	252
1920	175
1910	368

(a)Boundary change.

GRANGER, Town (Est. 1838)(a)
    Allegany County

1980	508
1970	450
1960	429
1950	455
1940	484
1930	477
1920	590
1910	708
1900	800
1890	954
1880	1,086
1870	1,050
1860	1,257
1850	1,309
1840	1,064

(a)Established as West Grove in 1838;
name changed in 1839.

GRANT, CDP
    Harmony Town
        Chautauqua County

1880	108

GRANT, CDP
    Russia Town
        Herkimer County

1880	117
1870	71

GRANVILLE, CDP
    North Hempstead Town
        Nassau County

1880	78(a)

(a)Reported in QUEENS County.

GRANVILLE, Town (Est. 1786)
    Washington County

1980	5,566
1970	5,412
1960	5,015
1950	5,116
1940	5,508
1930	5,806
1920	4,965
1910	6,434
1900	5,217
1890	4,716
1880	4,149

1870	4,003
1860	3,474
1850	3,434
1840	3,846
1830	3,881
1820	3,727
1810	NA
1800	*3,175
1790	2,240

GRANVILLE, Village (Inc. 1885)
Granville Town
Washington County

1980	2,696
1970	2,784
1960	2,715
1950	2,826
1940	3,173
1930	3,483
1920	3,024
1910	3,920
1900	2,700

GRAVESEND, Town (Est. 1788)(a)
Kings County

1890	6,937
1880	3,631
1870	2,131
1860	1,286
1850	1,064
1840	799
1830	565(b)
1820	534
1810	NA
1800	*489
1790	426

(a)Merged into BROOKLYN City in 1896.
(b)Reported as Graves End.

GRAVESVILLE, CDP
Russia Town
Herkimer County

1880	79
1870	67

GREAT BEND, CDP
Champion Town
Jefferson County

1880	181

GREAT NECK, Unincoporated
North Hempstead Town
Nassau County

1980	7,033(a)
1970	8,337(a)
1960	7,971(a)
1890-1950	NA
1880	1,112(b)

(a)Derived by LIRPB from U.S. Census
Data.
(b)Reported in QUEENS County.

GREAT NECK, Village (Inc. 1921)
North Hempstead Town
Nassau County

1980	9,168
1970	10,798 Rev.
1960	10,171(a)
1950	7,759

1940	6,167(a)
1930	4,010

(a)Boundary change.

GREAT NECK ESTATES, Village (Inc. 1911)
North Hempstead Town
Nassau County

1980	2,936
1970	3,131
1960	3,262
1950	2,464
1940	1,969
1930	1,738
1920	339

GREAT NECK PLAZA, Village (Inc. 1930)
North Hempstead Town
Nassau County

1980	5,604
1970	6,043 Rev.
1960	4,948
1950	4,246
1940	2,031

GREAT RIVER
Islip Town
Suffolk County

1980	1,631(a)
1970	8,742(b)
1960	6,554(c)

(a)Boundary change; derived by LIRPB
from U.S. Census Data.
(b)Derived by LIRPB from U.S. Census
Data; population of 1,721 is
comparable to 1980 boundaries.
(c)Derived by LIRPB from U.S. Census
Data.

GREAT VALLEY, Town (Est. 1818)
Cattaraugus County

1980	2,014
1970	1,745
1960	1,408
1950	1,375
1940	1,215
1930	1,366
1920	1,336
1910	1,775 Rev.(a)
1900	1,497 Rev.(a)
1890	1,705
1880	1,859
1870	1,641
1860	1,525
1850	1,638
1840	852
1830	647
1820	271

(a)In 1920 the Census Bureau revised
the 1910 figure of 2,236 and the 1900
figure of 1,697 to exclude the
ALLEGANY INDIAN RESERVATION.

GREECE, CDP
Greece Town
Monroe County

1980	16,177
1880-1970	NA
1870	737

GREECE, Town (Est. 1822)
Monroe County

1980	81,367
1970	75,136
1960	48,670(a)
1950	25,508
1940	14,925
1930	12,113
1920	3,350(a)
1910	7,777
1900	5,579
1890	5,145
1880	4,848
1870	4,314
1860	4,149
1850	4,219
1840	3,669
1830	2,571

(a)Boundary change.

GREEN, County & Town
  see GREENE, County & Town

GREENBURGH, Town (Est. 1788)
Westchester County

1980	82,881
1970	85,827 Rev.
1960	76,213
1950	47,527
1940	40,145
1930	35,821
1920	28,881
1910	23,193
1900	15,564
1890	11,613
1880	8,934
1870	10,790
1860	8,929(a)
1850	4,291
1840	3,369
1830	2,195
1820	2,064
1810	NA
1800	*1,581
1790	1,400

(a)Reported as Greenburg.

GREENBUSH, Town (Est. 1792)(a)
Rensselaer County

1890	7,301
1880	6,743
1870	6,202
1860	3,992
1850	4,945
1840	3,701
1830	3,216
1820	2,764
1810	NA
1800	*3,472

(a)GREENBUSH Village and GREENBUSH Town
  consolidated and incorporated as
  RENSSELAER City in 1897.

GREENBUSH, Village (Inc. 1815)(a)
  Greenbush Town
  Rensselaer County

1890	7,301
1880	3,295
1870	NA

(a)GREENBUSH Village and GREENBUSH Town
  consolidated and incorporated as
  RENSSELAER City in 1897.

GREENE, County (Est. 1800)

1980	40,861
1970	33,136
1960	31,372
1950	28,745
1940	27,926
1930	25,808
1920	25,796
1910	30,214
1900	31,478
1890	31,598
1880	32,695
1870	31,832
1860	31,930
1850	33,126
1840	30,446
1830	29,525
1820	22,996
1810	19,536
1800	13,074(a)

(a)Reported as Green.

GREENE, Town (Est. 1798)
Chenango County

1980	5,729
1970	5,347
1960	4,624
1950	3,712
1940	3,188
1930	3,048
1920	2,917
1910	2,992
1900	3,152
1890	3,164
1880	3,378
1870	3,537
1860	3,809
1850	3,763
1840	3,462
1830	2,962
1820	2,590
1810	NA
1800	*655(a)

(a)Reported as Green.

GREENE, Village (Inc. 1842)
  Greene Town
  Chenango County

1980	1,747
1970	1,874
1960	2,051
1950	1,628
1940	1,431
1930	1,379
1920	1,297
1910	1,275
1900	1,236
1890	1,067
1880	935
1870	1,025

GREENFIELD, CDP
  Wawarsing Town
  Ulster County

1880	971

GREENFIELD, Town
    Greene County
  see GREENVILLE, Town
      Greene County

GREENFIELD, Town (Est. 1793)
    Saratoga County

Year	Pop.
1980	5,104(a)
1970	4,378 Rev.
1960	2,548
1950	1,961
1940	1,696
1930	1,544
1920	1,481
1910	1,552
1900	1,837
1890	2,169
1880	2,448
1870	2,698
1860	2,970
1850	2,890
1840	2,803
1830	3,144
1820	3,024
1810	NA
1800	*3,073

(a)Boundary change.

GREEN ISLAND, Town (Est. 1890)
  see GREEN ISLAND, Village
    Albany County

GREEN ISLAND, Village (Inc. 1869)(a)
    Green Island Town
      Albany County

Year	Pop.
1980	2,696
1970	3,297
1960	3,533
1950	4,016
1940	3,988
1930	4,331
1920	4,411
1910	4,737
1900	4,770
1890	4,463(b)
1880	4,160(b)
1870	3,135(b)
1860	1,600

(a)Established town and village of GREEN ISLAND, with identical boundaries, in 1890.
(b)Reported in WATERVLIET Town.

GREENLAND, Town
  see HUNTER, Town
    Greene County

GREENLAWN, CDP
    Huntington Town
      Suffolk County

Year	Pop.
1980	13,869(a)
1970	8,493 Rev.(b)
1960	5,422
1950	1,000
1940	1,450
1890-1930	NA
1880	127

(a)Boundary change.
(b)Derived by LIRPB from U.S. Census Data; population of 13,533 is comparable to 1980 boundaries.

GREENPORT, Town (Est. 1837)
    Columbia County

Year	Pop.
1980	4,029
1970	3,686
1960	3,299
1950	2,055
1940	1,864
1930	1,800
1920	1,103
1910	1,639
1900	1,191
1890	1,247
1880	1,275
1870	1,325
1860	1,431
1850	1,300
1840	1,161

GREENPORT, Village (Inc. 1838)
    Southold Town
      Suffolk County

Year	Pop.
1980	2,273
1970	2,481(a)
1960	2,608
1950	3,028
1940	3,259
1930	3,062
1920	3,122
1910	3,089
1900	2,366
1890	NA
1880	2,370
1870	1,819

(a)Boundary change.

GREENPORT WEST, CDP
    Southold Town
      Suffolk County

Year	Pop.
1980	1,571(a)
1970	1,303(b)
1960	1,142(c)

(a)Boundary change.
(b)Derived by LIRPB from U.S. Census Data; population of 1,682 is comparable to 1980 boundaries.
(c)Derived by LIRPB from U.S. Census Data.

GREENVALE, CDP
    North Hempstead Town, part in
      Nassau County

Year	Pop.
1980	766(a)
1970	841(a)
1960	931(a)
1950	NA
1940	1,006

    Oyster Bay Town, part in
      Nassau County

Year	Pop.
1980	232(a)
1970	210(a)
1960	276(a)
1890-1950	NA
1880	498(c)

TOTAL
1980	998(a)
1970	1,051(a)
1960	1,207(a)
1950	NA
1940	(b)
1890-1930	NA
1880	(c)

(a)Derived by LIRPB from U.S. Census
   Data.
(b)Reported in NORTH HEMPSTEAD Town only.
(c)Reported in OYSTER BAY Town in QUEENS
   County.

GREENVILLE, CDP
   Greenville Town
      Greene County
| 1880 | 365 |

GREENVILLE, CDP
   Greenburgh Town
      Westchester County
1980	8,706
1950-1970	NA
1940	2,645

GREENVILLE, Town (Est. 1803)(a)
   Greene County
1980	2,849
1970	2,279
1960	1,879
1950	1,613
1940	1,477
1930	1,276
1920	1,362
1910	1,556
1900	1,651
1890	1,951
1880	2,043
1870	2,084
1860	2,268
1850	2,242
1840	2,338
1830	2,588(b)
1820	2,374

(a)Established as Greenfield in 1803;
   name changed to Freehold in 1808 and
   to GREENVILLE in 1809.
(b)Reported as Grenville.

GREENVILLE, Town (Est. 1853)
   Orange County
1980	2,085
1970	1,379
1960	890
1950	737
1940	732
1930	674
1920	618
1910	644
1900	800
1890	862
1880	1,002
1870	1,123
1860	1,198

GREENWICH, Town (Est. 1803)
   Washington County
1980	4,276
1970	4,177
1960	3,969
1950	3,611
1940	3,766
1930	3,872
1920	4,030
1910	4,227
1900	4,172
1890	4,196
1880	3,860
1870	4,030
1860	3,941
1850	3,803
1840	3,382
1830	3,847
1820	3,197

GREENWICH, Village (Inc. 1809)
   Easton Town, part in
      Washington County
1980	282
1970	334
1960	322
1950	334
1940	309
1930	337
1920	331
1910	361
Greenwich Town, part in
Washington County
1980	1,673
1970	1,758
1960	1,941
1950	1,878
1940	1,961
1930	1,953
1920	2,053
1910	1,953
1900	1,869
1890	1,663
1880	1,231
TOTAL
1980	1,955
1970	2,092
1960	2,263
1950	2,212
1940	2,270
1930	2,290
1920	2,384
1910	2,314
1880-1900	(a)

(a)Reported in GREENWICH Town only.

GREENWOOD, CDP
   Greenwood Town
      Steuben County
| 1880 | 263 |

GREENWOOD, Town (Est. 1827)
   Steuben County
1980	883
1970	845
1960	839
1950	872
1940	914
1930	968
1920	941
1910	1,111
1900	1,129

1890	1,312
1880	1,386
1870	1,394
1860	1,306
1850	1,185
1840	1,138
1830	899

GREENWOOD CENTER, CDP
  Greenwood Town
    Steuben County

1870	100

GREENWOOD LAKE, Village (Inc. 1924)
  Warwick Town
    Orange County

1980	2,809
1970	2,262
1960	1,236
1950	819
1940	483
1930	332

GREIG, CDP
  Greig Town
    Lewis County

1880	236

GREIG, Town (Est. 1828)(a)
  Lewis County

1980	1,115
1970	774
1960	693
1950	642
1940	747
1930	821
1920	635
1910	807
1900	1,100
1890	1,481
1880	1,570
1870	2,638
1860	1,733
1850	1,074
1840	592

(a)Established as Brantingham in 1828;
name changed in 1832.

GRENVILLE, Town
    Greene County
  see GREENVILLE, Town
      Greene County

GRENVILLE, Town
    Washington County
  see GRANVILLE, Town
      Washington County

GRIFFINS CORNERS, CDP
  Middletown Town
    Delaware County

1880	192

GRINDSTONE ISLAND, CDP
  Clayton Town
    Jefferson County

1870	770

GRINNEL'S ISLAND, CDP
  Clayton Town
    Jefferson County

1870	3

GROTON, Town (Est. 1817)(a)
  Tompkins County

1980	5,213
1970	4,881
1960	4,469
1950	4,246
1940	3,879
1930	3,789
1920	4,122
1910	3,289
1900	3,564
1890	3,572
1880	3,450
1870	3,512
1860	3,544
1850	3,342
1840	3,618
1830	3,597
1820	2,742

(a)Established as Division in 1817; name
changed in 1818.

GROTON, Village (Inc. 1860)
  Groton Town
    Tompkins County

1980	2,313(a)
1970	2,112
1960	2,123
1950	2,150
1940	2,087
1930	2,004
1920	2,235
1910	1,260
1900	1,344
1890	1,280
1880	913
1870	863

(a)Boundary change.

GROTON CITY, CDP
  Groton Town
    Tompkins County

1880	71

GROVE, Town (Est. 1827)(a)
  Allegany County

1980	497
1970	415
1960	469
1950	566
1940	568
1930	534
1920	602
1910	740
1900	812
1890	956
1880	1,125
1870	1,056
1860	1,139
1850	1,154
1840	623
1830	1,388

(a)Established as Church Tract in 1827;
name changed in 1828.

GROVELAND, Town (Est. 1812)
    Livingston County
        1980   2,140
        1970   3,004
        1960   3,373
        1950   3,381
        1940   4,135
        1930   3,295
        1920   2,920
        1910   2,820
        1900   1,949
        1890   1,307
        1880   1,342
        1870   1,455
        1860   1,063
        1850   1,724
        1840   2,000
        1830   1,703
        1820   1,273(a)
(a)Reported in ONTARIO County.

GROVENOR'S CORNERS, CDP
    Carlisle Town
        Schoharie County
        1880   60

GROVEVILLE, CDP
    Fishkill Town
        Dutchess County
        1880   379

GUILDERLAND, Town (Est. 1803)
    Albany County
        1980   26,515
        1970   21,208
        1960   16,710
        1950   7,284
        1940   5,522
        1930   4,394
        1920   3,117
        1910   3,333
        1900   3,530
        1890   3,606
        1880   3,459
        1870   3,132
        1860   3,246
        1850   3,279
        1840   2,790
        1830   2,740
        1820   2,270

GUILDERLAND CENTER, CDP
    Guilderland Town
        Albany County
        1880   222

GUILFORD, CDP
    Guilford Town
        Chenango County
        1880   294
        1870   331

GUILFORD, Town (Est. 1813)(a)
    Chenango County
        1980   2,442
        1970   2,358
        1960   2,368
        1950   2,283
        1940   1,884

        1930   1,719
        1920   1,818
        1910   2,013
        1900   2,208
        1890   2,236
        1880   2,441
        1870   2,806
        1860   2,743
        1850   2,600
        1840   2,827
        1830   2,636
        1820   2,175
(a)Established as Eastern in 1813; name
    changed in 1817.

GUILFORD CENTER, CDP
    Guilford Town
        Chenango County
        1880   54

GULL ISLAND, CDP
    Southold Town
        Suffolk County
        1880   7

H

HADLEY, CDP
    see LAKE LUZERNE--HADLEY, CDP
        Saratoga County

HADLEY, Town (Est. 1801)
    Saratoga County
        1980   1,351
        1970   1,128
        1960   982
        1950   801
        1940   679
        1930   841
        1920   581
        1910   672
        1900   914
        1890   1,103
        1880   1,095
        1870   1,039
        1860   1,017
        1850   1,003
        1840   865
        1830   829
        1820   798

HAGAMAN, Village (Inc. 1892)
    Amsterdam Town
        Montgomery County
        1980   1,331
        1970   1,410
        1960   1,292
        1950   1,114
        1940   933

1930	867
1920	855
1910	875
1900	646
1890	596

HAGEDORNS MILLS, CDP
Providence Town
Saratoga County

1880	61

HAGEMAN'S MILL
Amsterdam Town
Montgomery County

1870	250

HAGERMAN--NORTH BELLPORT, CDP(a)
Brookhaven Town
Suffolk County

1950	1,605

(a)Included, in part, in NORTH BELLPORT,
CDP in 1960-1980.

HAGUE, CDP
Hague Town
Warren County

1940	632

HAGUE, Town
St. Lawrence County
see MORRISTOWN, Town
St. Lawrence County

HAGUE, Town (Est. 1807)(a)
Warren County

1980	766
1970	910
1960	771
1950	761
1940	739
1930	741
1920	1,028
1910	1,043
1900	1,042
1890	682
1880	807
1870	637
1860	708
1850	717
1840	610
1830	721
1820	514

(a)Established as Rochester in 1807;
name changed in 1808.

HAIGHT, Town
see NEW HUDSON, Town
Allegany County

HAILSBORO, CDP
Fowler Town
St. Lawrence County

1880	243
1870	177

HALCOTT, Town (Est. 1851)
Greene County

1980	150
1970	199

1960	193
1950	244
1940	273
1930	223
1920	272
1910	331
1900	350
1890	357
1880	396
1870	426
1860	504

HALCOTT CENTER, CDP
Halcott Town
Greene County

1880	50

HALCOTTVILLE, CDP
Middletown Town
Delaware County

1880	45

HALESITE, CDP(a)
Huntington Town
Suffolk County

1970	2,820(b)
1960	2,857
1950	NA
1940	553

(a)Included in HUNTINGTON, CDP in 1980.
(b)Derived by LIRPB from U.S. Census
Data.

HALF HOLLOW HILLS, CDP(a)
Huntington Town
Suffolk County

1970	12,081(b)
1960	2,171(b)

(a)Included in DIX HILLS, CDP in 1980.
(b)Derived by LIRPB from U.S. Census
Data.

HALFMOON, Town (Est. 1788)(a)
Saratoga County

1980	11,860
1970	9,287
1960	4,120
1950	2,836
1940	1,969
1930	1,739
1920	1,534(b)
1910	5,980
1900	5,101
1890	3,732
1880	3,102
1870	3,093
1860	3,130
1850	2,788
1840	2,631
1830	2,042
1820	4,024
1810	NA
1800	*3,851
1790	3,602(c)

(a)Name changed to Orange in 1816;
original name restored in 1820.
(b)Boundary change.
(c)Reported as Half-Moon.

HALFMOON JUNCTION, CDP
  Halfmoon Town
    Saratoga County
      1970   1,915

HALLS CORNERS, CDP
  Seneca Town
    Ontario County
      1880   87

HALSEY, CDP
  Tioga Town
    Tioga County
      1870   376

HAMBURG, Town (Est.1812)
  Erie County
    1980   53,270
    1970   47,644
    1960   41,288
    1950   25,067
    1940   17,190
    1930   13,058
    1920   8,656
    1910   6,059
    1900   4,673
    1890   3,802
    1880   3,234
    1870   2,934
    1860   2,991
    1850   5,219
    1840   3,727
    1830   3,351(a)
    1820   2,034(b)
(a)Reported as Hamburgh.
(b)Reported in NIAGARA County.

HAMBURG, Village (Inc. 1874)
  Hamburg Town
    Erie County
      1980   10,582(a)
      1970   10,215(a)
      1960   9,145
      1950   6,938(a)
      1940   5,467(a)
      1930   4,731
      1920   3,185
      1910   2,134
      1900   1,683
      1890   1,331
      1880   758
(a)Boundary change.

HAMBURGH, Town
  see HAMBURG, Town
        Erie County

HAMBURG--LAKE SHORE, CDP
  Hamburg Town
    Erie County
      1960   11,527

HAMDEN, CDP
  Hamden Town
    Delaware County
      1880   178
      1870   133

HAMDEN, Town (Est. 1825)(a)
  Delaware County
    1980   1,276
    1970   1,169
    1960   1,108
    1950   1,114
    1940   1,177
    1930   1,171
    1920   1,248
    1910   1,373
    1900   1,378
    1890   1,507
    1880   1,496
    1870   1,762
    1860   1,851
    1850   1,919
    1840   1,469
    1830   1,230
(a)Established as Hampden in 1825;
  spelling corrected in 1826.

HAMILTON, County (Est. 1816)
    1980   5,034
    1970   4,714
    1960   4,267
    1950   4,105
    1940   4,188
    1930   3,929
    1920   3,970
    1910   4,373
    1900   4,947
    1890   4,762
    1880   3,923
    1870   2,960
    1860   3,024
    1850   2,188
    1840   1,907
    1830   1,325
    1820   1,251

HAMILTON, Town (Est. 1795)
  Madison County
    1980   6,027
    1970   5,906
    1960   5,438
    1950   5,455
    1940   3,618
    1930   3,687
    1920   3,354
    1910   3,825
    1900   3,744
    1890   3,923
    1880   3,912
    1870   3,687
    1860   2,295
    1850   3,599
    1840   3,738
    1830   3,220
    1820   2,681
    1810   NA
    1800   *2,673(a)
(a)Reported in CHENANGO County.

HAMILTON, Village (Inc. 1816)
  Hamilton Town
    Madison County
      1980   3,725(a)
      1970   3,636(a)
      1960   3,348(a)

1950	3,507
1940	1,790
1930	1,700
1920	1,505
1910	1,689
1900	1,627
1890	1,744
1880	NA
1870	1,529

(a)Boundary change.

HAMILTON STATION, CDP
  Livonia Town
    Livingston County

1880	57

HAMLET, CDP
  Villenova Town
    Chautauqua County

1880	232
1870	155
1860	240

HAMLIN, Town (Est. 1852)(a)
  Monroe County

1980	7,675
1970	4,167
1960	2,755
1950	2,321
1940	2,080
1930	2,079
1920	1,999
1910	2,184
1900	2,188
1890	2,338
1880	2,556
1870	2,304
1860	2,460

(a)Established as Union in 1852; name
  changed in 1861.

HAMMOND, Town (Est. 1827)
  St. Lawrence County

1980	1,090
1970	1,015
1960	1,076
1950	1,251
1940	1,260
1930	1,338
1920	1,507
1910	1,745
1900	1,764
1890	1,774
1880	1,860
1870	1,757
1860	1,968
1850	1,819
1840	1,845
1830	767

HAMMOND, Village (Inc. 1901)
  Hammond Town
    St. Lawrence County

1980	271
1970	273
1960	314
1950	329
1940	323
1930	364

1920	409
1910	404

HAMMONDSPORT, Village (Inc. 1871)
  Urbana Town
    Steuben County

1980	1,065
1970	1,066
1960	1,176(a)
1950	1,190
1940	1,112
1930	1,063(a)
1920	1,060
1910	1,254
1900	1,169
1890	934
1880	755
1870	602

(a)Boundary change.

HAMPDEN, Town
  see HAMDEN, Town
        Delaware County

HAMPSTEAD, Town
  see RAMAPO, Town
        Rockland County

HAMPTON, CDP
  Westmoreland Town
    Oneida County

1870	444

HAMPTON, CDP
  East Greenbush Town
    Rensselaer County

1940	870

HAMPTON, Town (Est. 1786)
  Washington County

1980	559
1970	464
1960	469
1950	576
1940	594
1930	673
1920	552
1910	645
1900	689
1890	791
1880	833
1870	955
1860	876
1850	899
1840	972
1830	1,069
1820	963
1810	NA
1800	*700
1790	463

HAMPTON BAYS, CDP
  Southampton Town
    Suffolk County

1980	7,256(a)
1970	1,862(b)
1960	930 Rev.
1950	1,269
1940	997

```
        1900-1930           NA
        1890              825(c)
        1880              553(c)
        1870              504(c)
(a)Boundary change.
(b)Population of 4,923 is comparable to
   1980 boundaries.
(c)Reported as Good Ground; name changed
   to HAMPTON BAYS in 1922.

HAMPTON BAYS BEACH(a)
   Southampton Town
     Suffolk County
        1970               27(b)
        1960               33(b)
(a)Included in HAMPTON BAYS, CDP in
   1980.
(b)Derived by LIRPB from U.S. Census
   Data.

HAMPTONBURGH, Town (Est. 1830)
     Orange County
        1980             2,945
        1970             2,204
        1960             1,695
        1950             1,272
        1940             1,086
        1930             1,130
        1920             1,104
        1910             1,168
        1900             1,072
        1890             1,129
        1880             1,143
        1870             1,224
        1860             1,295
        1850             1,343
        1840             1,379
        1830             1,363

HAMPTON PARK, CDP
   Southampton Town
     Suffolk County
        1980             1,331
        1970             1,156(a)
        1960               796(a)
(a)Derived by LIRPB from U.S. Census
   Data.

HANCOCK, Town (Est. 1806)
     Delaware County
        1980             3,497
        1970             3,604
        1960             3,907
        1950             3,517
        1940             3,813
        1930             3,953
        1920             4,122
        1910             5,191
        1900             5,308
        1890             4,745
        1880             3,238
        1870             3,069
        1860             2,862
        1850             1,798
        1840             1,026
        1830               766
        1820               525
```

```
HANCOCK, Village (Inc. 1888)
   Hancock Town
     Delaware County
        1980             1,526
        1970             1,688
        1960             1,830
        1950             1,560
        1940             1,581
        1930             1,427
        1920             1,326
        1910             1,329
        1900             1,283
        1890             1,279
        1880               686

HANNIBAL, Town (Est. 1806)
     Oswego County
        1980             4,027
        1970             3,165
        1960             2,673
        1950             2,230
        1940             2,010
        1930             1,855
        1920             1,834
        1910             2,148
        1900             2,473
        1890             2,688
        1880             3,173
        1870             3,234
        1860             3,246
        1850             2,857
        1840             2,269
        1830             1,794
        1820               935

HANNIBAL, Village (Inc. 1876)
   Hannibal Town
     Oswego County
        1980               680
        1970               686
        1960               611
        1950               501
        1940               437
        1930               410
        1920               400
        1910               330
        1900               410
        1890               452
        1880               490
        1870               454

HANNIBAL CENTER, CDP
   Hannibal Town
     Oswego County
        1880               148

HANOVER, Town (Est. 1812)
     Chautauqua County
        1980             7,876
        1970             7,829
        1960             7,301
        1950             6,375
        1940             5,846
        1930             5,993
        1920             5,977
        1910             5,601
        1900             4,747 Rev.(a)
        1890             4,616 Rev.(a)
        1880             4,221
```

1870	4,037
1860	2,310
1850	5,144
1840	3,998
1830	2,614
1820	2,217

(a)In 1920 the Census Bureau revised the
   1910 figure of 5,670 and the 1900
   figure of 4,778 to exclude the
   CATTARAUGUS INDIAN RESERVATION.

HARDENBERGH, Town (Est. 1859)
   Ulster County

1980	280
1970	239(a)
1960	252
1950	284
1940	326
1930	313
1920	420
1910	598
1900	772
1890	784
1880	801
1870	628(b)
1860	505(c)

(a)Boundary change.
(b)Reported as Hardenburgh.
(c)Reported as Hardenburg.

HARFORD, Town (Est. 1845)
   Cortland County

1980	855
1970	748
1960	635
1950	584
1940	572
1930	554
1920	553
1910	623
1900	753
1890	861
1880	1,034
1870	997
1860	946
1850	949

HARFORD MILLS, CDP
   Harford Town
   Cortland County

1880	107

HARLEMVILLE, CDP
   Hillsdale Town
   Columbia County

1880	60

HARMONY, Town (Est.1816)
   Chautauqua County

1980	2,121
1970	1,922
1960	1,797
1950	1,736
1940	1,473
1930	1,425
1920	1,443
1910	2,847
1900	2,988
1890	3,174

1880	3,455
1870	3,416
1860	3,606
1850	3,749
1840	3,340
1830	1,989
1820	845

HARPERSFIELD, CDP
   Harpersfield Town
   Delaware County

1880	99

HARPERSFIELD, Town (Est. 1788)
   Delaware County

1980	1,495
1970	1,423
1960	1,193
1950	1,263
1940	1,200
1930	1,265
1920	1,184
1910	1,244
1900	1,221
1890	1,386
1880	1,420
1870	1,485
1860	1,468
1850	1,613
1840	1,708
1830	1,976(a)
1820	1,884
1810	NA
1800	*1,007
1790	1,726(b)

(a)Reported as Harper Field.
(b)Reported in MONTGOMERY County.

HARPERSVILLE, CDP
   Colesville Town
   Broome County

1870	218

HARRIETSTOWN, Town (Est. 1841)
   Franklin County

1980	5,604
1970	5,643
1960	5,664
1950	6,014
1940	6,117
1930	6,856
1920	4,797
1910	4,753
1900	3,390
1890	1,582
1880	533
1870	416
1860	340
1850	181

HARRIMAN, Village (Inc. 1914)
   Monroe Town, part in
   Orange County

1980	781
1970	934
1960	718
1950	658
1940	678
1930	657

1920	680

Woodbury Town, part in
Orange County

1980	15
1970	21
1960	34
1950	16
1940	25

TOTAL

1980	796
1970	955
1960	752
1950	674
1940	703
1920-1930	(a)

(a)Reported in MONROE Town only.

HARRIMAN SOUTH, CDP
   Monroe Town
      Orange County

1980	1,254

HARRISBURG, Town (Est. 1803)
   Lewis County

1980	418
1970	431
1960	423
1950	480
1940	537
1930	589
1920	619
1910	686
1900	770
1890	816
1880	1,089(a)
1870	1,090(a)
1860	1,388
1850	1,367(a)
1840	850(a)
1830	712(a)
1820	520(a)

(a)Reported as Harrisburgh.

HARRIS HILL, CDP
   Clarence Town
      Erie County

1980	5,087
1970	NA
1960	3,944

HARRISON, CDP
   Harrison Town
      Westchester County

1940	6,307

HARRISON, Town
   Cortland County
   see MARATHON, Town
         Cortland County

HARRISON, Town
   Franklin County
   see MALONE, Town
         Franklin County

HARRISON, Town
   Jefferson County
   see RODMAN, Town
         Jefferson County

HARRISON, Town (Est. 1788)(a)
   Westchester County

1980	23,046
1970	21,544
1960	19,201
1950	13,577
1940	11,783
1930	10,195
1920	5,006
1910	4,226
1900	2,048
1890	1,485
1880	1,494
1870	787
1860	1,413
1850	1,262
1840	1,139
1830	1,085
1820	994
1810	NA
1800	*855
1790	1,004

(a)Established town and village of
   HARRISON, with identical boundaries,
   in 1975.

HARRISON, Village (Inc. 1975)
   see HARRISON, Town
         Westchester County

HARRISVILLE, Village (Inc. 1892)
   Diana Town
      Lewis County

1980	937
1970	836
1960	842
1950	868
1940	832
1930	896
1920	900
1910	920
1900	639
1890	617
1880	353

HARTFORD, CDP
   Hartford Town
      Washington County

1880	392

HARTFORD, Town
   Ontario County
   see AVON, Town
         Livingston County

HARTFORD, Town (Est.1793)
   Washington County

1980	1,742
1970	1,398
1960	1,058
1950	1,271
1940	1,088
1930	1,102
1920	1,102
1910	1,216
1900	1,290
1890	1,470
1880	1,760

1870	1,989
1860	2,046
1850	2,051
1840	2,164
1830	2,420
1820	2,493
1810	NA
1800	*2,108

HARTLAND, Town (Est. 1812)
Niagara County

1980	4,105
1970	4,223
1960	3,577
1950	2,849
1940	2,527
1930	2,500
1920	1,987
1910	2,638
1900	2,728
1890	2,843
1880	3,340
1870	3,226
1860	3,256
1850	3,028
1840	2,350
1830	1,584
1820	1,448

HARTSDALE, CDP
Greenburgh Town
Westchester County

1980	10,216
1970	12,226
1950-1960	NA
1940	2,664

HART'S FALLS, CDP
Schaghticoke Town
Rensselaer County

1870	1,111

HART'S ISLAND, CDP
Pelham Town
Westchester County

1880	756

HARTSVILLE, Town (Est. 1844)
Steuben County

1980	509
1970	467
1960	479
1950	518
1940	498
1930	470
1920	545
1910	651
1900	787
1890	757
1880	1,015
1870	993
1860	1,154
1850	854

HARTWICK, Town (Est. 1802)
Otsego County

1980	1,796
1970	1,631
1960	1,400

1950	1,473
1940	1,438
1930	1,487
1920	1,648
1910	1,813
1900	1,800
1890	1,894
1880	2,340
1870	2,339
1860	2,496
1850	2,352
1840	2,490
1830	2,772
1820	2,579

HASTINGS, Town (Est. 1825)
Oswego County

1980	7,095
1970	6,042
1960	4,457
1950	3,063
1940	2,361
1930	2,149
1920	2,153
1910	2,315
1900	2,303
1890	2,364
1880	3,866
1870	3,058
1860	3,345
1850	2,920
1840	1,983
1830	1,494

HASTINGS-ON-HUDSON, Village (Inc. 1879)
Greenburgh Town
Westchester County

1980	8,573
1970	9,479
1960	8,979
1950	7,565
1940	7,057
1930	7,097
1920	5,526
1910	4,552
1900	2,002
1890	1,466
1880	1,290

HAUPPAUGE, CDP
Islip Town, part in
Suffolk County

1980	10,196(a)
1970	0(b)
1890-1960	NA
1880	91

Smithtown Town, part in
Suffolk County

1980	10,764(a)
1970	13,957(c)

TOTAL

1980	20,960(a)
1970	13,957(d)
1950-1960	NA
1940	804
1890-1930	NA
1880	(e)

(a) Boundary change.
(b) Population of 7,931 is comparable to

1980 boundaries.
(c)Population of 10,842 is comparable to
1980 boundaries.
(d)Population of 18,773 is comparable to
1980 boundaries.
(e)Reported in ISLIP Town only.

HAVANA, Village
    see MONTOUR FALLS, Village
        Schuyler County

HAVERSTRAW, Town (Est. 1788)
    Rockland County
        1980   31,929
        1970   25,311
        1960   16,632
        1950   12,979
        1940   12,443
        1930   11,603
        1920   9,027
        1910   9,335
        1900   9,874
        1890   9,079
        1880   6,973
        1870   6,412
        1860   5,400
        1850   3,306
        1840   3,449
        1830   2,306
        1820   2,700
        1810   NA
        1800   *1,229(a)
        1790   4,826
(a)Reported as Haverstan.

HAVERSTRAW, Village (Inc. 1854)(a)
    Haverstraw Town
    Rockland County
        1980   8,800
        1970   8,198(b)
        1960   5,771
        1950   5,818
        1940   5,909
        1930   5,621
        1920   5,226
        1910   5,669
        1900   5,935
        1890   5,070
        1880   NA
        1870   3,469
        1860   2,723
(a)Incorporated as Warren in 1854; name
    changed in 1874.
(b)Boundary change.

HAVILAND, CDP
    Hyde Park Town
    Dutchess County
        1980   3,578
        1970   3,447

HAWKINSVILLE, CDP
    Boonville Town
    Oneida County
        1870   150
        1880   239

HAWTHORNE, CDP
    Mamaroneck Town
    Westchester County
        1980   5,010

HAWTHORNE, CDP
    Mount Pleasant Town
    Westchester County
        1940   2,062

HEAD OF THE HARBOR, Village (Inc. 1928)
    Smithtown Town
    Suffolk County
        1980   1,023
        1970   943
        1960   524
        1950   334
        1940   255
        1930   244

HEBE, Town
    Cattaraugus County
    see FRANKLINVILLE, Town
        Cattaraugus County

HEBE, Town
    Wyoming County
    see GAINESVILLE, Town
        Wyoming County

HEBRON, Town (Est. 1786)
    Washington County
        1980   1,288
        1970   1,212
        1960   1,026
        1950   1,134
        1940   1,228
        1930   1,191
        1920   1,184
        1910   1,505
        1900   1,679
        1890   2,044
        1880   2,393
        1870   2,399
        1860   2,543
        1850   2,548
        1840   2,498
        1830   2,686
        1820   2,754
        1810   NA
        1800   *2,528
        1790   1,703

HECTOR, Town (Est. 1802)
    Schuyler County
        1980   3,793
        1970   3,671
        1960   3,209
        1950   3,129
        1940   2,949
        1930   2,904
        1920   3,030
        1910   3,514
        1900   4,137
        1890   4,443
        1880   5,025
        1870   4,905
        1860   5,623
        1850   6,052(a)

1840	5,652(a)
1830	5,212(a)
1820	4,012(a)

(a)Reported in TOMPKINS County.

HEETA, CDP
Westmoreland Town
Oneida County

1870	125

HELENA, CDP
Brasher Town
St. Lawrence County

1880	129

HEMLOCK LAKE, CDP
Livonia Town
Livingston County

1880	259

HEMPSTEAD, Town (Est. 1788)(a)
Nassau County

1980	738,517
1970	801,592 Rev.
1960	740,738
1950	432,506(b)
1940	259,318
1930	186,735(b)
1920	70,790
1910	44,297
1900	27,066
1890	23,756(c)
1880	18,164(c)
1870	13,999(c)
1860	12,376(c)
1850	8,811(c)
1840	7,609(c)
1830	6,215(d)
1820	NA
1810	5,084(c)
1800	*4,141(d)
1790	3,828(d)

(a)Established by patent in 1644; name
   changed to South Hempstead in 1784.
   Recognized by the State in 1788
   and original name restored in 1796.
(b)Boundary change.
(c)Reported in QUEENS County.
(d)Reported in QUEENS County as South
   Hempstead.

HEMPSTEAD, Town
see RAMAPO, Town
Rockland County

HEMPSTEAD, Village (Inc. 1853)
Hempstead Town
Nassau County

1980	40,404(a)
1970	39,411
1960	34,641(a)
1950	29,135(a)
1940	20,856(a)
1930	12,650(a)
1920	6,382
1910	4,964
1900	3,582
1890	4,831(b)
1880	2,521(b)

1870	2,316(b)

(a)Boundary change.
(b)Reported in QUEENS County.

HEMPSTEAD GARDENS, CDP(a)
Hempstead Town
Nassau County

1940	1,568

(a)Included in WEST HEMPSTEAD, CDP
   in 1960-1980.

HENDERSON, Town (Est. 1806)
Jefferson County

1980	1,330
1970	1,364
1960	1,207
1950	1,171
1940	1,163
1930	1,165
1920	1,229
1910	1,485
1900	1,615
1890	1,688
1880	1,842
1870	1,926
1860	2,419
1850	2,239
1840	2,480
1830	2,428
1820	1,919

HENDERSON, Village (Inc. 1886)(a)
Henderson Town
Jefferson County

1930	262
1920	299
1910	340
1900	374
1890	358
1880	407
1870	339

(a)Dissolved in 1932.

HENDERSON HARBOR, CDP
Henderson Town
Jefferson County

1880	89

HENRIETTA, Town (Est. 1791)(a)
Monroe County

1980	36,134
1970	33,017
1960	11,598
1950	3,385
1940	2,728
1930	2,142
1920	1,794 Rev.(a)
1910	1,972
1900	2,062
1890	2,135
1880	2,243
1870	2,280
1860	2,249
1850	2,513
1840	2,085
1830	2,322
1820	2,182(b)

(a)In 1930 the Census Bureau revised the
   1920 figure to exclude the Iola

Sanitorium.
(b)Reported in ONTARIO County.

HENRIETTA NORTHEAST, CDP
  Henrietta Town
    Monroe County
      1960   6,403

HENSONVILLE, CDP
  Windham Town
    Greene County
      1880   129

HENVELTON, CDP
  see HEUVELTON, Village
        St. Lawrence County

HERKIMER, County (Est. 1791)
      1980   66,714
      1970   67,407 Rev.
      1960   66,370
      1950   61,407
      1940   59,527
      1930   64,006
      1920   64,962
      1910   56,356
      1900   51,049
      1890   45,608
      1880   42,669
      1870   39,929
      1860   40,561
      1850   38,244
      1840   37,477
      1830   35,870
      1820   30,945
      1810   22,046
      1800   14,503

HERKIMER, Town (Est. 1788)
    Herkimer County
      1980   11,027
      1970   11,451
      1960   11,568
      1950   11,235
      1940   11,345
      1930   12,327
      1920   11,982
      1910   8,797
      1900   6,748
      1890   4,666
      1880   3,593
      1870   2,949
      1860   2,804
      1850   2,601
      1840   2,369
      1830   2,486
      1820   3,055
      1810   NA
      1800   *2,534
      1790   1,525(a)
(a)Reported in MONTGOMERY County.

HERKIMER, Village (Inc. 1807)
  Herkimer Town
    Herkimer County
      1980   8,383(a)
      1970   8,960(a)
      1960   9,396
      1950   9,400

      1940   9,617
      1930   10,446
      1920   10,453
      1910   7,520
      1900   5,555
      1890   NA
      1880   2,359
      1870   1,220
(a)Boundary change.

HERMON, Town (Est. 1830)(a)
    St. Lawrence County
      1980   1,083
      1970   1,087
      1960   1,255
      1950   1,350
      1940   1,147
      1930   1,356
      1920   1,505
      1910   1,526
      1900   1,542
      1890   1,521
      1880   1,634
      1870   1,792
      1860   1,690
      1850   1,690
      1840   1,271
      1830   668
(a)Established as Depeau in 1830; name
   changed in 1834.

HERMON, Village (Inc. 1877)
  Hermon Town
    St. Lawrence County
      1980   490
      1970   521
      1960   612
      1950   547
      1940   487
      1930   527
      1920   622
      1910   587
      1900   503
      1890   473
      1880   522
      1870   557

HERRICKS, CDP
  North Hempstead Town
    Nassau County
      1980   8,123
      1970   9,112
      1960   7,062(a)
(a)Derived by LIRPB from U.S. Census
   Data. U.S. Census reported as part of
   GARDEN CITY PARK--HERRICKS, CDP with a
   population of 15,364.

HERRINGS, Village (Inc. 1921)
  Wilna Town
    Jefferson County
      1980   170
      1970   137
      1960   171
      1950   192
      1940   232
      1930   274

HEUVELTON, Village (Inc. 1912)
    Oswegatchie Town
        St. Lawrence County
            1980   777
            1970   770
            1960   810
            1950   712
            1940   620
            1930   578
            1920   559
            1890-1910   NA
            1880   513(a)
(a)Reported as Henvelton.

HEWLETT, CDP
    Hempstead Town
        Nassau County
            1980   6,986
            1970   6,796
            1960   7,398(a)
            1950   NA
            1940   3,485
(a)Derived by LIRPB from U.S. Census
Data.

HEWLETT BAY PARK, Village (Inc. 1928)
    Hempstead Town
        Nassau County
            1980   489
            1970   586
            1960   520
            1950   466
            1940   438
            1930   407

HEWLETT HARBOR, Village (Inc. 1925)
    Hempstead Town
        Nassau County
            1980   1,331(a)
            1970   1,512 Rev.
            1960   1,610(a)
            1950   411
            1940   228
            1930   240
(a)Boundary change.

HEWLETT NECK, Village (Inc. 1927)
    Hempstead Town
        Nassau County
            1980   472
            1970   529
            1960   507
            1950   369(a)
            1940   252
            1930   253
(a)Boundary change.

HICKORY BUSH, CDP
    see BLOOMINGTON--HICKORY BUSH, CDP
        Ulster County

HICKSVILLE, CDP
    Oyster Bay Town
        Nassau County
            1980   43,245
            1970   49,820 Rev.
            1960   50,405
            1950   NA
            1940   6,835

            1890-1930   NA
            1880   1,621(a)
(a)Reported in QUEENS County.

HIGGINSVILLE, CDP
    Verona Town
        Oneida County
            1870   3,189

HIGH FALLS, CDP
    Marbletown Town
        Ulster County
            1880   571

HIGHLAND, CDP
    Lloyd Town
        Ulster County
            1980   3,967
            1970   2,184
            1960   2,931
            1950   3,035
            1940   1,832

HIGHLAND, Town
    Orange County
    see HIGHLANDS, Town
        Orange County

HIGHLAND, Town (Est. 1853)
    Sullivan County
            1980   1,878
            1970   1,377
            1960   1,138
            1950   1,140
            1940   1,036
            1930   880
            1920   875
            1910   1,031
            1900   964
            1890   979
            1880   1,013
            1870   958

HIGHLAND FALLS, Village (Inc. 1906)
    Highlands Town
        Orange County
            1980   4,187(a)
            1970   4,638(a)
            1960   4,469(a)
            1950   3,930
            1940   3,711
            1930   2,910
            1920   2,588
            1910   2,470
            1890-1900   NA
            1880   1,976
(a)Boundary change.

HIGHLAND MILLS, CDP
    Woodbury Town
        Orange County
            1980   2,034
            1950-1970   NA
            1940   764
            1890-1930   NA
            1880   490

HIGHLANDS, Town (Est. 1872)
    Orange County
        1980   14,004
        1970   14,661
        1960   11,990
        1950   10,467
        1940   9,307
        1930   7,057
        1920   6,136
        1910   6,133
        1900   4,519
        1890   4,099
        1880   3,404(a)
(a)Reported as Highland.

HIGH MARKET, Town (Est. 1852)(a)
    Lewis County
        1970   89
        1960   95
        1950   121
        1940   190
        1930   222
        1920   316
        1910   409
        1900   593
        1890   723
        1880   941
        1870   1,051
        1860   1,170
(a)Merged into WEST TURIN Town in 1973.

HILLBURN, Village (Inc. 1893)
    Ramapo Town
        Rockland County
        1980   926
        1970   1,058
        1960   1,114(a)
        1950   1,212
        1940   1,161
        1930   1,502
        1920   1,112
        1910   1,090
        1900   824
(a)Boundary change.

HILLCREST, CDP
    Ramapo Town
        Rockland County
        1980   5,733
        1970   5,357
        1950-1960   NA
        1940   1,245

HILLIS, CDP
    Poughkeepsie Town
        Dutchess County
        1980   2,591
        1970   2,750

HILLSDALE, CDP
    Hillsdale Town
        Columbia County
        1880   236

HILLSDALE, Town (Est. 1788)
    Columbia County
        1980   1,648
        1970   1,447
        1960   1,299

        1950   1,183
        1940   1,050
        1930   968
        1920   1,052
        1910   1,504
        1900   1,390
        1890   1,554
        1880   1,939
        1870   2,083
        1860   2,552
        1850   2,123
        1840   2,470
        1830   2,446
        1820   2,511
        1810   NA
        1800   *4,702
        1790   4,556(a)
(a)Reported as Hills-Dale.

HILLSIDE LAKE, CDP
    East Fishkill Town
        Dutchess County
        1980   1,382

HILTON, Village (Inc. 1885)(a)
    Parma Town
        Monroe County
        1980   4,151(b)
        1970   2,440(b)
        1960   1,334
        1950   1,036
        1940   895
        1930   923
        1920   827
        1910   627
        1900   486
        1890   487
        1880   376
(a)Incorporated as North Parma in 1885;
    name changed in 1894.
(b)Boundary change.

HIMRODS CORNERS, CDP
    Milo Town
        Yates County
        1880   310

HINDERHOOK, Town
    see KINDERHOOK, Town
            Columbia County

HINKLEYVILLE, CDP
    Parma Town
        Monroe County
        1880   96

HINMANVILLE, CDP
    Schroeppel Town
        Oswego County
        1880   152
        1870   154

HINSDALE, CDP
    Hinsdale Town
        Cattaraugus County
        1880   300
        1870   321

HINSDALE, CDP
    Hempstead Town
        Nassau County
            1880   110(a)
(a)Reported in QUEENS County.

HINSDALE, Town (Est. 1820)
    Cattaraugus County
            1980   2,182
            1970   1,781
            1960   1,538
            1950   1,240
            1940   1,079
            1930   969
            1920   972
            1910   1,125
            1900   1,218
            1890   1,312
            1880   1,594
            1870   1,491
            1860   1,708
            1850   1,302
            1840   1,937
            1830   919

HITHER HILLS
        Suffolk County
    see NAPEAGUE--HITHER HILLS
        Suffolk County

HOBART, Village (Inc. 1888)
    Stamford Town
        Delaware County
            1980   473
            1970   531
            1960   585
            1950   618
            1940   638
            1930   580
            1920   587
            1910   544
            1900   550
            1890   561
            1880   290

HOGANSBURGH, CDP
    Bombay Town
        Franklin County
            1880   333

HOLBROOK, CDP
    Brookhaven Town, part in
        Suffolk County
            1980   4,899(a)
            1970   4,311(b)
    Islip Town, part in
        Suffolk County
            1980   19,483(a)
            1970   7,946(b)
    TOTAL
            1980   24,382(a)
            1970   12,257(b)
            1950-1960   NA
            1940   719
            1890-1930   NA
            1880   201
(a)Boundary change.
(b)Derived by LIRPB from U.S. Census
    Data; population is comparable to

1980 boundaries. Included, in part,
in HOLBROOK--HOLTSVILLE, CDP.

HOLBROOK--HOLTSVILLE, CDP(a)
    Brookhaven Town
        Suffolk County
            1970   12,103
            1960   4,583(b)
(a)Included in HOLBROOK and HOLTSVILLE,
    CDPs in 1980.
(b)Derived by LIRPB from U.S. Census
    Data.

HOLCOMB, Village (Inc. 1916)
    East Bloomfield Town
        Ontario County
            1980   952
            1970   778(a)
            1960   460
            1950   313
            1940   304
            1930   294
            1920   488
(a)Boundary change.

HOLLAND, CDP
    Holland Town
        Erie County
            1980   1,347
            1950-1970   NA
            1940   642

HOLLAND, Town (Est. 1818)
    Erie County
            1980   3,446
            1970   3,140
            1960   2,304
            1950   1,728
            1940   1,496
            1930   1,473
            1920   1,410
            1910   1,468
            1900   1,434
            1890   1,595
            1880   1,720
            1870   1,451
            1860   1,538
            1850   1,315
            1840   1,242
            1830   1,071
            1820   768(a)
(a)Reported in NIAGARA County.

HOLLAND PATENT, Village (Inc. 1885)
    Trenton Town
        Oneida County
            1980   534
            1970   556
            1960   538
            1950   400
            1940   388
            1930   337
            1920   328
            1910   337
            1900   352
            1890   406
            1880   401
            1870   320

HOLLEY, Village (Inc. 1867)
  Murray Town
    Orleans County
      1980   1,882(a)
      1970   1,868
      1960   1,788
      1950   1,551
      1940   1,230
      1930   1,558
      1920   1,625
      1910   1,679
      1900   1,380
      1890   1,381
(a)Boundary change.

HOLLOWVILLE, CDP
  Claverack Town
    Columbia County
      1880   132

HOLMAN CITY, CDP
  Paris Town
    Oneida County
      1870   73

HOLTSVILLE, CDP
  Brookhaven Town, part in
    Suffolk County
      1980   11,073(a)
      1970   6,537(b)
      1890-1960   NA
      1880   128
  Islip Town
    Suffolk County
      1980   2,442(a)
      1970   1,461(b)
  TOTAL
      1980   13,515(a)
      1970   7,998(b)
      1890-1960   NA
      1880   (c)
(a)Boundary change.
(b)Derived by LIRPB from U.S. Census
   Data; population is comparable to
   1980 boundaries. Included, in part,
   in HOLBROOK--HOLTSVILLE, CDP.
(c)Reported in BROOKHAVEN Town only.

HOMER, Town (Est. 1794)
  Cortland County
      1980   6,599
      1970   6,480
      1960   5,751
      1950   5,055
      1940   4,233
      1930   3,991
      1920   3,554
      1910   3,891
      1900   3,864
      1890   4,206
      1880   3,691
      1870   3,813
      1860   4,356
      1850   3,836
      1840   3,572
      1830   3,307
      1820   5,504
      1810   NA
      1800   *612(a)

(a)Reported in ONONDAGA County.

HOMER, Village (Inc. 1835)
  Cortlandville Town, part in
    Cortland County
      1980   21(a)
      1970   80(a)
      1960   53
      1950   67
      1940   67
      1930   611
      1920   68
      1910   59
      1900   39
  Homer Town, part in
    Cortland County
      1980   3,614(a)
      1970   4,063(a)
      1960   3,569
      1950   3,177
      1940   2,861
      1930   2,584
      1920   2,288
      1910   2,695
      1900   2,342
      1890   2,566
      1880   2,331
      1870   2,008
  TOTAL
      1980   3,635(a)
      1970   4,143(a)
      1960   3,622
      1950   3,244
      1940   2,928
      1930   3,195
      1920   2,356
      1910   2,695
      1900   2,381
      1870-1890   (b)
(a)Boundary change.
(b)Reported in HOMER Town only.

HOMEWOOD PARK, CDP
  see BELLEVUE--HOMEWOOD PARK, CDP
         Erie County

HOMOWACK, CDP
  Mamakating Town
    Sullivan County
      1880   209

HONEOYE, CDP
  Richmond Town
    Ontario County
      1880   321

HONEOYE, Town
  see RICHMOND, Town
        Ontario County

HONEOYE FALLS, Village (Inc. 1838)
  Mendon Town
    Monroe County
      1980   2,410(a)
      1970   2,248(a)
      1960   2,143
      1950   1,416
      1940   1,274
      1930   1,187

1920	1,107
1910	1,169
1900	1,175
1890	1,128
1880	1,098
1870	921

(a)Boundary change.

HOOK, CDP
  see THE HOOK, CDP
        Washington County

HOOSICK, Town (Est. 1788)
  Rensselaer County

1980	6,732
1970	6,651
1960	6,490
1950	6,520
1940	6,549
1930	7,026
1920	6,858
1910	8,315
1900	8,631
1890	10,471
1880	7,914
1870	5,728
1860	4,446
1850	3,724
1840	3,539
1830	3,584
1820	3,373
1810	NA
1800	*3,141
1790	3,035(a)

(a)Reported as Hosack in ALBANY County.

HOOSICK FALLS, Village (Inc. 1827)
  Hoosick Town
    Rensselaer County

1980	3,609
1970	3,897
1960	4,023
1950	4,297
1940	4,279
1930	4,755
1920	4,894
1910	5,532
1900	5,671
1890	7,014
1880	4,530

HOPE, Town (Est. 1818)
  Hamilton County

1980	311
1970	269
1960	234
1950	180
1940	164
1930	134
1920	203
1910	258
1900	463
1890	560
1880	651
1870	698
1860	745
1850	789
1840	711
1830	719

1820	608

HOPEWELL, Town (Est. 1822)
  Ontario County

1980	2,509
1970	2,347
1960	1,822
1950	1,506
1940	1,456
1930	1,365
1920	1,339
1910	1,493
1900	1,550
1890	1,655
1880	1,894
1870	1,863
1860	1,950
1850	1,923
1840	1,976
1830	2,198

HOPEWELL JUNCTION, CDP
  East Fishkill Town
    Dutchess County

1980	1,754
1970	2,055

HOPKINTON, CDP
  Hopkinton Town
    St. Lawrence County

1880	195
1870	200

HOPKINTON, Town (Est. 1805)
  St. Lawrence County

1980	1,064
1970	884
1960	1,032
1950	935
1940	1,044
1930	1,046
1920	1,244
1910	1,469
1900	2,521
1890	1,832
1880	1,922
1870	1,907
1860	1,990
1850	1,476
1840	1,147
1830	827
1820	581

HORICON, Town (Est. 1838)
  Warren County

1980	1,082
1970	890
1960	833
1950	791
1940	850
1930	800
1920	754
1910	1,001
1900	1,136
1890	1,582
1880	1,633
1870	1,500
1860	1,542
1850	1,152

1840	659

HORNBY, Town (Est. 1826)
Steuben County

1980	1,786
1970	1,377
1960	1,383
1950	1,014
1940	837
1930	683
1920	700
1910	870
1900	959
1890	1,011
1880	1,209
1870	1,202
1860	1,291
1850	1,314
1840	1,048
1830	1,572

HORNBY FORKS, CDP
Hornby Town
Steuben County

1880	60

HORNELL, City (Inc. 1888)(a)
Steuben County

1980	10,234
1970	12,144(b)
1960	13,907(b)
1950	15,049
1940	15,649
1930	16,250
1920	15,025
1910	13,617
1900	11,918
1890	10,996
1880	8,195
1870	4,552

(a)Hornellsville Village (Inc. 1867) incorporated as HORNELL City and made
independent of HORNELLSVILLE Town in
1888.
(b)Boundary change.

HORNELLSVILLE, Town (Est. 1820)
Steuben County

1980	4,066
1970	3,993(a)
1960	3,413(a)
1950	2,912
1940	2,761
1930	2,505
1920	1,829
1910	2,047
1900	1,833
1890	1,939(a)
1880	9,852
1870	5,837
1860	4,230
1850	2,637
1840	2,121
1830	657(b)

(a)Boundary change.
(b)Reported as Hornsville.

HORNELLSVILLE, Village
see HORNELL, City
Steuben County

HORNSVILLE, Town
see HORNELLSVILLE, Town
Steuben County

HORSEHEADS, Town (Est. 1854)
Chemung County

1980	20,238
1970	20,552
1960	17,808
1950	11,118
1940	8,804
1930	8,420
1920	6,809
1910	5,376
1900	4,944
1890	3,482
1880	3,449
1870	2,361
1860	2,277

HORSEHEADS, Village (Inc. 1837)(a)
Horseheads Town
Chemung County

1980	7,348
1970	7,989
1960	7,207(b)
1950	3,606(b)
1940	2,570
1930	2,430
1920	2,078
1910	1,778
1900	1,901
1890	1,716
1880	1,684
1870	1,410

(a)Incorporated as Fairport in 1837;
name changed to North Elmira in 1885
and to HORSEHEADS in 1886.
(b)Boundary change.

HORSEHEADS NORTH, CDP
Horseheads Town
Chemung County

1980	3,081
1970	2,753

HOSACK, Town
Albany County
see HOOSICK, Town
Rensselaer County

HOUGHTON, CDP
Caneadea Town
Allegany County

1980	1,604
1970	1,620

HOUNSFIELD, Town (Est. 1806)
Jefferson County

1980	2,645
1970	2,771
1960	2,722
1950	2,630
1940	3,137
1930	2,926

1920	2,297
1910	2,217
1900	2,772
1890	2,651
1880	2,770
1870	2,636
1860	3,339
1850	4,136
1840	4,146
1830	3,415
1820	3,429

HOWARD, CDP
  Howard Town
    Steuben County

1880	80
1870	167

HOWARD, Town (Est. 1812)
  Steuben County

1980	1,236
1970	1,029
1960	929
1950	902
1940	893
1930	1,032
1920	1,127
1910	1,461
1900	1,704
1890	1,938
1880	2,131
1870	2,122
1860	2,746
1850	3,244
1840	3,247
1830	1,365
1820	1,140

HOWELLS DEPOT, CDP
  Wallkill Town
    Orange County

1880	156

HUBBARDSVILLE, CDP
  Hamilton Town
    Madison County

1880	129
1870	117

HUDSON, City (Inc. 1785)
  Columbia County

1980	7,986
1970	8,940
1960	11,075
1950	11,629
1940	11,517
1930	12,337(a)
1920	11,745
1910	11,417
1900	9,528(a)
1890	9,970
1880	8,670
1870	8,615
1860	7,187
1850	6,286
1840	5,672
1830	5,392
1820	5,310
1810	4,048

1800	3,664
1790	2,584

(a)Boundary change.

HUDSON FALLS, Village (Inc. 1810)(a)
  Kingsbury Town
    Washington County

1980	7,419
1970	7,917
1960	7,752
1950	7,236
1940	6,654
1930	6,449(b)
1920	5,761
1910	5,189
1900	4,473
1890	2,895
1880	2,487
1870	2,347

(a)Incorporated as Sandy Hill in 1810;
  name changed in 1910.
(b)Boundary change.

HUGHSONVILLE, CDP
  Wappingers Town
    Dutchess County

1880	682

HUGUENOT, CDP
  Deerpark Town
    Orange County

1940	740

HUME, CDP
  Hume Town
    Allegany County

1870	254

HUME, Town (Est. 1821)
  Allegany County

1980	2,040
1970	1,838
1960	1,729
1950	1,660
1940	1,577
1930	1,574
1920	1,701
1910	1,736
1900	1,749
1890	1,913
1880	1,905
1870	1,920
1860	2,142
1850	2,159
1840	2,303
1830	951

HUMPHREY, Town (Est. 1830)
  Cattaraugus County

1980	529	
1970	405	
1960	415	
1950	367	
1940	424	Rev.
1930	526	
1920	531	
1910	626	
1900	794	
1890	866	

1880	997
1870	1,065
1860	963
1850	824
1840	444

HUNTER, Town (Est. 1813)(a)
Greene County

1980	2,252
1970	1,742
1960	1,799
1950	2,028
1940	2,166
1930	2,299
1920	2,309
1910	2,699
1900	2,788
1890	2,436
1880	1,882
1870	1,524
1860	1,098
1850	1,849
1840	2,019
1830	1,960
1820	1,025

(a)Established as Greenland in 1813;
name changed in 1814.

HUNTER, Village (Inc. 1894)
Hunter Town
Greene County

1980	511
1970	238
1960	457
1950	526
1940	626
1930	624
1920	683
1910	408
1900	431
1890	699
1880	481

HUNTERS LAND, CDP
Middleburg Town
Schoharie County

1880	172

HUNTER'S POINT, CDP
Newtown Town
Queens County

1870	1,596

HUNTINGTON, CDP
Huntington Town
Suffolk County

1980	21,727(a)
1970	12,601 Rev.(b)
1960	11,255
1950	9,324
1940	6,373(c)
1900-1930	NA
1890	3,028
1880	2,952
1870	2,433

(a)Boundary change.
(b)Population of 24,121 is comparable
to 1980 boundaries.
(c)Reported as Huntington Village, CDP.

HUNTINGTON, Town (Est. 1788)
Suffolk County

1980	201,512
1970	200,172 Rev.
1960	126,221
1950	47,506
1940	31,768
1930	25,582
1920	13,893
1910	12,004
1900	9,483
1890	8,277
1880	8,098(a)
1870	10,704
1860	8,924
1850	7,481
1840	6,562
1830	5,582
1820	4,935
1810	4,424
1800	3,894
1790	3,260

(a)Boundary change.

HUNTINGTON BAY, Village (Inc. 1924)
Huntington Town
Suffolk County

1980	1,783
1970	1,789
1960	1,267
1950	585
1940	408
1930	357

HUNTINGTON STATION, CDP
Huntington Town
Suffolk County

1980	28,769
1970	28,817
1960	23,438
1950	9,924
1940	9,370

HUNTSVILLE, Town
see OTEGO, Town
Otsego County

HURLEY, CDP
Hurley & Ulster Towns
Ulster County

1980	4,892
1970	4,081

HURLEY, Town (Est. 1788)
Ulster County

1980	6,992
1970	6,496
1960	4,526
1950	1,980
1940	1,531
1930	1,168
1920	846
1910	1,734
1900	1,903
1890	2,135
1880	2,521
1870	2,987
1860	2,364
1850	2,003

1840	2,201
1830	1,408
1820	1,352
1810	NA
1800	*1,159
1790	847

HURLEYVILLE, CDP
  Fallsburg Town
    Sullivan County

1940	661

HURON, Town (Est. 1826)(a)
  Wayne County

1980	1,820
1970	1,739
1960	1,356
1950	1,409
1940	1,412
1930	1,313
1920	1,416
1910	1,531
1900	1,667
1890	1,793
1880	2,036
1870	2,000
1860	1,966
1850	1,966
1840	1,943
1830	1,082

(a)Established as Port Bay in 1826; name
changed in 1834.

HYDE PARK, CDP
  Hyde Park Town
    Dutchess County

1980	2,550
1970	2,805
1960	1,979
1950	1,059
1940	949
1890-1930	NA
1880	715
1870	600

HYDE PARK, CDP
  Hempstead Town
    Nassau County

1880	82(a)

(a)Reported in QUEENS County.

HYDE PARK, Town (Est. 1821)
  Dutchess County

1980	20,768
1970	16,910 Rev.
1960	12,681
1950	6,138
1940	4,058
1930	3,388
1920	2,880
1910	3,019
1900	2,806
1890	2,821
1880	2,873
1870	2,695
1860	2,749
1850	2,425
1840	2,364
1830	2,554

HYNDSVILLE, CDP
  Chazy Town
    Clinton County

1880	82

ILION, Village (Inc. 1852)
  German Flatts Town
    Herkimer County

1980	9,450 Rev.(a)
1970	9,808
1960	10,199
1950	9,363
1940	8,927
1930	9,890
1920	10,169
1910	6,588
1900	5,138
1890	4,057
1880	3,711
1870	2,876

(a)Boundary change.

INDEPENDENCE, Town (Est. 1821)
  Allegany County

1980	1,138
1970	1,031
1960	1,004
1950	1,053
1940	1,110
1930	1,056
1920	1,028
1910	1,202
1900	1,280
1890	1,249
1880	1,186
1870	1,175
1860	1,199
1850	1,701
1840	1,440
1830	877

INDIAN LAKE, Town (Est. 1858)
  Hamilton County

1980	1,410
1970	1,290
1960	1,186
1950	1,099
1940	1,257
1930	1,120
1920	1,031
1910	1,045
1900	1,219
1890	1,047
1880	615
1870	202
1860	256

INDIAN LAKE SETTLEMENT, CDP
   Indian Lake Town
      Hamilton County
         1850   46

INGRAHAM, CDP
   Chazy Town
      Clinton County
         1880   82

INLET, Town (Est. 1901)
   Hamilton County
      1980   320
      1970   287
      1960   307
      1950   319
      1940   310
      1930   251
      1920   171
      1910   197

INTERLAKEN, Village (Inc. 1904)
   Covert Town
      Seneca County
      1980   685(a)
      1970   733(a)
      1960   780
      1950   770
      1940   661
      1930   660
      1920   633
      1910   693
(a)Boundary change.

INVERNESS, Town
   see WHEATLAND, Town
      Monroe County

INWOOD, CDP(a)
   Hempstead Town
      Nassau County
      1980   8,228
      1970   8,433
      1960   10,362
      1950   NA
      1940   8,022
      1900-1930   NA
      1890   1,277
(a)Includes NORTH LAWRENCE, CDP in
   1960-1980.

IONIA, CDP
   Van Buren Town
      Onondaga County
      1880   76

IRA, Town (Est. 1821)
   Cayuga County
      1980   1,869
      1970   1,720
      1960   1,448
      1950   1,473
      1940   1,336
      1930   1,342
      1920   1,361
      1910   1,451
      1900   1,668
      1890   1,873
      1880   2,113

      1870   2,014
      1860   2,238
      1850   2,110
      1840   2,283
      1830   2,199

IRONDEQUOIT, CDP
   Irondequoit Town
      Monroe County
      1980   57,648

IRONDEQUOIT, Town (Est. 1839)
   Monroe County
      1980   57,648
      1970   64,897 Rev.
      1960   55,337
      1950   34,417
      1940   23,376
      1930   18,024
      1920   5,123
      1910   3,526
      1900   2,863
      1890   2,415
      1880   1,986
      1870   3,990
      1860   3,547
      1850   2,397
      1840   1,252

IRVING, CDP
   Hanover Town
      Chautauqua County
      1870   355
      1860   510

IRVINGTON, Village (Inc. 1872)
   Greenburgh Town
      Westchester County
      1980   5,774
      1970   5,878
      1960   5,494
      1950   3,657
      1940   3,272
      1930   3,067
      1920   2,701
      1910   2,319
      1900   2,231
      1890   2,299
      1880   1,904

ISCHUA, CDP
   Ischua Town
      Cattaraugus County
      1880   163

ISCHUA, Town (Est. 1812)
   Cattaraugus County
   see FRANKLINVILLE, Town
      Cattaraugus County

ISCHUA, Town (Est. 1846)(a)
   Cattaraugus County
      1980   775
      1970   655
      1960   562(b)
      1950   622
      1940   503
      1930   566
      1920   656

1910	803
1900	832
1890	853
1880	935
1870	872
1860	986
1850	906

(a)Established as Rice in 1846; name
   changed in 1855.
(b)Includes part of OIL SPRING INDIAN
   RESERVATION, which was not reported
   separately.

ISLANDIA, Village (Inc. 1985)(a)
   Islip Town
      Suffolk County
(a)Population of 2,349 at incorporation.

ISLAND PARK
   Hempstead Town
      Nassau County

1980	4,108(a)
1970	3,734(a)
1960	2,555(a)

(a)Derived by LIRPB from U.S. Census
   Data.

ISLAND PARK, Village (Inc. 1926)
   Hempstead Town
      Nassau County

1980	4,847
1970	5,396
1960	3,846
1950	2,031
1940	1,531
1930	1,002

ISLIP, CDP
   Islip Town
      Suffolk County

1980	13,438(a)
1970	7,692(b)
1960	6,362(c)
1950	5,254
1940	3,499
1890-1930	NA
1880	1,127

(a)Boundary change.
(b)Population of 10,574 is comparable
   to 1980 boundaries.
(c)Derived by LIRPB from U.S. Census
   Data.

ISLIP, Town (Est. 1788)
   Suffolk County

1980	298,897
1970	278,880 Rev.
1960	172,959
1950	71,465
1940	51,182
1930	33,194
1920	20,709
1910	18,346
1900	12,545
1890	8,783
1880	6,453
1870	4,597
1860	3,845
1850	2,602

1840	1,909
1830	1,653
1820	1,156
1810	885
1800	*958
1790	609

ISLIP TERRACE, CDP
   Islip Town
      Suffolk County

1980	5,588
1970	4,944(a)
1960	2,532(a)
1950	1,579
1940	1,338

(a)Derived by LIRPB from U.S. Census
   Data.

ITALY, Town (Est. 1815)
   Yates County

1980	953
1970	532
1960	428
1950	455
1940	457
1930	510
1920	731
1910	861
1900	1,094
1890	1,206
1880	1,444
1870	1,341
1860	1,605
1850	1,627
1840	1,634
1830	1,092
1820	728(a)

(a)Reported in ONTARIO County.

ITHACA, City (Inc. 1888)(a)
   Tompkins County

1980	28,732
1970	26,226(b)
1960	28,799(b)
1950	29,257
1940	19,730
1930	20,708(b)
1920	17,004
1910	14,802
1900	13,136
1890	11,079

(a)ITHACA Village incorporated as ITHACA
   City and made independent of ITHACA
   Town in 1888.
(b)Boundary change.

ITHACA, Town (Est. 1821)
   Tompkins County

1980	16,022
1970	15,620
1960	9,072
1950	7,282
1940	3,821
1930	2,943
1920	1,480
1910	1,288
1900	1,516
1890	1,364(a)
1880	11,198

1870	10,107
1860	6,843
1850	6,909
1840	5,650
1830	5,270

(a)Boundary change.

ITHACA, Village (Inc. 1821)(a)
   Ithaca Town
      Tompkins County

1880	9,105
1870	8,462

(a)ITHACA Village incorporated as ITHACA City and made independent of ITHACA Town in 1888.

J

JACKSON, Town (Est. 1815)
   Washington County

1980	1,228
1970	941
1960	795
1950	857
1940	798
1930	822
1920	836
1910	985
1900	1,059
1890	1,278
1880	1,562
1870	1,662
1860	1,863
1850	2,129
1840	1,730
1830	2,057
1820	2,004

JACKSONVILLE, CDP
   Ulysses Town
      Tompkins County

1880	193

JAMAICA, Town (Est. 1788)(a)
   Queens County

1890	14,441
1880	10,088
1870	7,745
1860	6,515
1850	4,247
1840	3,781
1830	2,376
1810-1820	NA
1800	*1,661
1790	1,675

(a)Merged into QUEENS Borough in NEW YORK City in 1898.

JAMAICA, Village (Inc. 1814)(a)
   Jamaica Town
      Queens County

1890	5,361
1880	3,922
1870	3,791

(a)Merged into QUEENS Borough in NEW YORK City in 1898.

JAMAICA SQUARE, Village
   see SOUTH FLORAL PARK, Village
      Nassau County

JAMESPORT, CDP
   Riverhead Town
      Suffolk County

1980	1,069(a)
1970	890(b)
1960	673(c)
1950	NA
1940	510
1890-1930	NA
1880	453
1870	323

(a)Boundary change.
(b)Derived by LIRPB from U.S. Census Data; population of 933 is comparable to 1980 boundaries.
(c)Derived by LIRPB from U.S. Census Data.

JAMESTOWN, City (Inc. 1886)(a)
   Chautauqua County

1980	35,775
1970	39,795
1960	41,818
1950	43,354
1940	42,638
1930	45,155
1920	38,917(b)
1910	31,297
1900	22,692
1890	16,038

(a)Jamestown Village incorporated as JAMESTOWN City and made independent of ELLICOTT Town in 1886.
(b)Boundary change.

JAMESTOWN, Village (Inc. 1827)(a)
   Ellicott Town
      Chautauqua County

1880	9,357
1870	5,336
1860	3,155

(a)JAMESTOWN Village incorporated as JAMESTOWN City and made independent of ELLICOTT Town in 1886.

JAMESTOWN WEST, CDP
   Ellicott Town
      Chautauqua County

1980	2,680
1970	2,491

JAMESVILLE, CDP
   De Witt Town
      Onondaga County

1940	933
1890-1930	NA

1880	353		1860	2,514
1870	402		1850	2,688
			1840	2,258

JASPER, CDP
  Jasper Town
    Steuben County

1880	283		1830	1,629
			1820	1,647
			1810	NA
			1800	*601

JASPER, Town (Est. 1827)
  Steuben County

JEDDO, CDP
  Ridgeway Town
    Orleans County

1980	1,128
1970	1,042
1960	1,008
1950	983
1940	967
1930	986
1920	943
1910	1,264
1900	1,430
1890	1,690
1880	1,806
1870	1,683
1860	1,850
1850	1,749
1840	1,187
1830	2,402

1880	125

JEFFERSON, County (Est. 1805)

1980	88,151
1970	88,508
1960	87,835
1950	85,521
1940	84,003
1930	83,574
1920	82,250
1910	80,382
1900	76,743
1890	68,806
1880	66,103
1870	65,415
1860	69,825
1850	68,153
1840	60,984
1830	48,493
1820	32,952
1810	15,140

JASPER FOUR CORNERS, CDP
  Jasper Town
    Steuben County

1870	200

JAVA, CDP
  Java Town
    Wyoming County

JEFFERSON, Town
  Cayuga County
  see MENTZ, Town
    Cayuga County

1880	239

JAVA, Town (Est. 1832)
  Wyoming County

JEFFERSON, Town (Est. 1803)
  Schoharie County

1980	2,273
1970	1,949
1960	1,757
1950	1,455
1940	1,364
1930	1,403
1920	1,469
1910	1,633
1900	1,770
1890	1,824
1880	1,953
1870	1,956
1860	2,358
1850	2,245
1840	2,331

1980	1,108
1970	840
1960	800
1950	819
1940	845
1930	916
1920	1,065
1910	1,280
1900	1,409
1890	1,469
1880	1,636
1870	1,712
1860	1,716
1850	1,748
1840	2,033
1830	1,743
1820	1,573

JAY, Town (Est. 1798)
  Essex County

1980	2,221
1970	2,132
1960	2,257
1950	2,181
1940	2,226
1930	2,153
1920	2,226
1910	2,231
1900	1,744
1890	1,933
1880	2,443
1870	2,496

JEFFERSON, Village
  see WATKINS GLEN, Village
    Schuyler County

JEFFERSON HEIGHTS, CDP
  Catskill Town
    Greene County

1980	1,610

JEFFERSON VALLEY--YORKTOWN, CDP(a)
Yorktown Town
Westchester County
1980 13,380
1970 9,008
(a)Reported, in part, in YORKTOWN, CDP
in 1960.

JEFFERSONVILLE, Village (Inc. 1924)
Callicoon Town
Sullivan County
1980 554
1970 421
1960 434
1950 450
1940 403
1930 448
1890-1920 NA
1880 324(a)
(a)Reported in CALLICOON and DELAWARE
Towns.

JERICHO, CDP
Oyster Bay Town
Nassau County
1980 12,739
1970 14,010
1960 10,795
1950 NA
1940 551

JERICHO, Town
see BAINBRIDGE, Town
Chenango County

JERSEY, Town
Steuben County
see ORANGE, Town
Schuyler County

JERUSALEM, Town (Est. 1789)
Yates County
1980 3,908
1970 3,581
1960 2,847
1950 2,732
1940 2,043
1930 2,072
1920 2,025
1910 2,444
1900 2,775
1890 2,957
1880 2,626
1870 2,612
1860 2,873
1850 2,912
1840 2,935
1830 2,783
1820 1,610(a)
1810 NA
1800 *1,219(a)
1790 99(a)
(a)Reported in ONTARIO County.

JEWETT, Town (Est.1849)
Greene County
1980 723
1970 442

1960 562
1950 692
1940 732
1930 835
1920 883
1910 1,057
1900 1,028
1890 976
1880 1,075
1870 1,105
1860 1,145
1850 1,452

JOHNSBURG, Town (Est. 1805)
Warren County
1980 2,173
1970 2,377
1960 2,250
1950 2,076
1940 2,000
1930 1,887
1920 2,242
1910 2,315
1900 2,374
1890 2,894
1880 2,742
1870 2,599
1860 2,188
1850 1,503
1840 1,139
1830 985(a)
1820 727
(a)Reported as Johnsburgh.

JOHNSON CITY, Village (Inc. 1892)(a)
Union Town
Broome County
1980 17,126
1970 18,025(b)
1960 19,118
1950 19,249
1940 18,039(b)
1930 13,567
1920 8,587
1910 3,775
1900 3,111
(a)Incorporated as Lestershire in 1892;
name changed in 1916.
(b)Boundary change.

JOHNSONVILLE, CDP
Pittstown Town
Rensselaer County
1880 397
1870 500

JOHNSTON, CDP
Livingston Town
Columbia County
1880 150

JOHNSTOWN, City (Inc. 1895)(a)
Fulton County
1980 9,360(b)
1970 10,045(b)
1960 10,390
1950 10,923
1940 10,666
1930 10,801

1920	10,908
1910	10,447
1900	10,130

(a)JOHNSTOWN Village incorporated as
JOHNSTOWN City and made independent
of JOHNSTOWN Town in 1895.
(b)Boundary change.

JOHNSTOWN, Town (Est. 1793)
Fulton County

1980	6,719(a)
1970	5,750
1960	5,120
1950	4,153
1940	3,561
1930	2,612
1920	1,948
1910	2,511
1900	2,661(a)
1890	10,959(b)
1880	16,603
1870	12,273
1860	8,811
1850	6,131
1840	5,409
1830	7,700(c)
1820	6,527(c)
1810	NA
1800	*3,932(c)

(a)Boundary change.
(b)In 1900 the Census Bureau reported an
1890 figure of 3,191 which excludes
JOHNSTOWN Village.
(c)Reported in MONTGOMERY County.

JOHNSTOWN, Village (Inc. 1808)(a)
Johnstown Town
Fulton County

1890	7,768
1880	5,013
1870	3,282

(a)JOHNSTOWN Village incorporated as
JOHNSTOWN City and made independent
of JOHNSTOWN Town in 1895.

JORDAN, Village (Inc. 1835)
Elbridge Town
Onondaga County

1980	1,371
1970	1,493
1960	1,390
1950	1,295
1940	1,115
1930	1,145
1920	1,012
1910	978
1900	1,118
1890	1,271
1880	1,344
1870	1,263

JOY, CDP
Sodus Town
Wayne County

1880	90
1870	122

JUNIUS, Town (Est. 1803)
Seneca County

1980	1,354
1970	1,111
1960	871
1950	846
1940	738
1930	775
1920	829
1910	957
1900	1,053
1890	1,134
1880	1,356
1870	1,420
1860	1,316
1850	1,516
1840	1,594
1830	1,581
1820	5,113

K

KANONA, CDP
Bath Town
Steuben County

1870	190

KATONAH, CDP
Bedford Town
Westchester County

1940	1,764

KATTS-KILL, Town
Albany County
see CATSKILL, Town
Greene County

KEENE, CDP
Keene Town
Essex County

1940	538
1890-1930	NA
1880	131

KEENE, Town (Est. 1808)
Essex County

1980	919
1970	763
1960	726
1950	938
1940	1,060
1930	1,001
1920	1,032
1910	1,227
1900	1,394
1890	1,258
1880	910
1870	720
1860	784
1850	756

1840	730
1830	787
1820	605

KEESEVILLE, Village (Inc. 1878)
  AuSable Town, part in
    Clinton County, part in

1980	1,055
1970	1,210
1960	1,239
1950	1,092
1940	1,090
1930	1,025
1920	813
1910	1,046
1900	1,118
1890	1,125
1880	1,128

  Chesterfield Town, part in
    Essex County, part in

1980	970
1970	912
1960	974
1950	885
1940	831
1930	769
1920	711
1910	789
1900	992
1890	978
1880	1,053

  TOTAL

1980	2,025
1970	2,122
1960	2,213
1950	1,977
1940	1,921
1930	1,794
1920	1,524
1910	1,835
1900	2,110
1890	2,103
1880	2,181

KENDALL, Town (Est. 1837)
  Orleans County

1980	2,388
1970	2,183
1960	1,680
1950	1,343
1940	1,341
1930	1,311
1920	1,275
1910	1,585
1900	1,616
1890	1,775
1880	1,893
1870	1,744
1860	1,920
1850	2,289
1840	1,692

KENDIA, CDP
  Romulus Town
    Seneca County

1880	99

KENMORE, Village (Inc. 1899)
  Tonawanda Town
    Erie County

1980	18,474
1970	20,980
1960	21,261
1950	20,066
1940	18,612
1930	16,482
1920	3,160
1910	1,020
1900	318

KENNEDY, CDP
  Poland Town
    Chautauqua County

1940	526
1890-1930	NA
1880	417

KENSICO, CDP
  North Castle Town
    Westchester County

1880	115

KENSINGTON, Village (Inc. 1921)
  North Hempstead Town
    Nassau County

1980	1,132
1970	1,402 Rev.
1960	1,166(a)
1950	978
1940	933
1930	824

(a)Boundary change.

KENT, Town (Est. 1788)(a)
  Putnam County

1980	12,433
1970	8,106
1960	3,924
1950	2,146
1940	1,546
1930	770
1920	696
1910	968
1900	1,026
1890	1,147
1880	1,361
1870	1,547
1860	1,479
1850	1,557
1840	1,830
1830	1,931
1820	1,801
1810	NA
1800	*1,661(b)
1790	5,932(c)

(a)Established as Frederickstown in 1788;
  name changed in 1817.
(b)Reported as Frederick in DUTCHESS
  County.
(c)Reported in DUTCHESS County.

KERHONKSON, CDP
  Rochester & Wawarsing Towns
    Ulster County

1980	1,646
1970	1,243

1950-1960	NA
1940	690

KEUKA PARK, CDP
Jerusalem Town
  Yates County

1980	1,153

KIANTONE, CDP
Kiantone Town
  Chautauqua County

1870	62

KIANTONE, Town (Est. 1853)
Chautauqua County

1980	1,443
1970	1,340
1960	1,254
1950	976
1940	849
1930	706
1920	623
1910	520
1900	491
1890	496
1880	513
1870	539
1860	552

KILLAWOG, CDP
Lisle Town
  Broome County

1880	155

KINDERHOOK, Town (Est. 1788)
Columbia County

1980	7,674
1970	5,688
1960	4,185
1950	3,284
1940	3,094
1930	3,104
1920	2,935
1910	2,947
1900	3,333
1890	3,709
1880	4,200
1870	4,055
1860	4,331
1850	3,970
1840	3,512
1830	2,706
1820	3,963
1810	NA
1800	*4,348(a)
1790	4,661

(a)Reported as Hinderhook.

KINDERHOOK, Village (Inc. 1838)
Kinderhook Town
  Columbia County

1980	1,377
1970	1,233
1960	1,078
1950	853
1940	745
1930	822
1920	722
1910	698

1900	913
1890	963

KINGS, County (Est. 1683)(a)

1980	2,231,028 Rev.
1970	2,602,012
1960	2,627,319
1950	2,738,175
1940	2,698,285(b)
1930	2,560,401(b)
1920	2,018,356(b)
1910	1,634,351
1900	1,166,582
1890	838,547
1880	599,495
1870	419,921
1860	279,122
1850	138,882
1840	47,613
1830	20,535
1820	11,187
1810	8,303
1800	5,740
1790	4,495

(a)In 1898 the Borough of BROOKLYN in NEW YORK City was established with the same boundaries as KINGS County.
(b)Boundary change.

KINGSBERRY, Town
see KINGSBURY, Town
  Washington County

KINGSBORO, CDP
Johnstown Town
  Fulton County

1880	747

KINGSBURY, Town (Est. 1786)
Washington County

1980	11,660
1970	11,737
1960	11,012
1950	9,503
1940	8,697
1930	8,094
1920	7,228
1910	7,080
1900	6,100
1890	4,677
1880	4,614
1870	4,277
1860	3,471
1850	3,032
1840	2,773
1830	2,606
1820	2,203
1810	NA
1800	*1,651
1790	1,120(a)

(a)Reported as Kingsberry.

KINGS PARK, CDP
Smithtown Town
  Suffolk County

1980	16,131(a)
1970	5,555(b)
1960	4,949(a)
1950	10,960

```
        1940              2,464
(a)Boundary change.
(b)Population of 13,558 is comparable
   to 1980 boundaries.
```

KINGS PARK PSYCHIATRIC CENTER
   Smithtown Town
      Suffolk County
```
        1980              2,681(a)
        1970              6,385(a)
        1960              8,836(a)
```
(a)Derived by LIRPB from U.S. Census
   Data.

KINGS POINT, Village (Inc. 1924)
   North Hempstead Town
      Nassau County
```
        1980              5,234
        1970              5,614 Rev.
        1960              5,410(a)
        1950              2,445
        1940              1,247
        1930              1,294
```
(a)Boundary change.

KINGSTON, City (Inc. 1872)(a)
   Ulster County
```
        1980             24,481
        1970             25,544
        1960             29,260
        1950             28,817
        1940             28,589
        1930             28,088
        1920             26,688
        1910             25,908
        1900             24,535
        1890             21,261
        1880             18,344
```
(a)KINGSTON Village incorporated as
   KINGSTON City and made independent of
   KINGSTON Town in 1872.

KINGSTON, Town (Est. 1702)
   Ulster County
```
        1980                924
        1970                748
        1960                490
        1950                227
        1940                196
        1930                194
        1920                166
        1910                343
        1900                524
        1890                651
        1880              1,093(a)
        1870             21,943
        1860             16,640
        1850             10,232
        1840              5,824
        1830              4,170
        1820              2,956
        1810                 NA
        1800             *4,615
        1790              3,929
```
(a)Boundary change.

KINGSTON, Village (Inc. 1805)(a)
   Kingston, Town
      Ulster County
```
        1870              6,315
```
(a)KINGSTON Village incorporated as
   KINGSTON City and made independent of
   KINGSTON Town in 1872.

KIRKLAND, CDP
   Kirkland Town
      Oneida County
```
        1880                132
```

KIRKLAND, Town (Est. 1827)
   Oneida County
```
        1980             10,334
        1970              9,688
        1960              7,978
        1950              6,164
        1940              5,211
        1930              5,059
        1920              4,744
        1910              4,333
        1900              4,545
        1890              4,852
        1880              4,984
        1870              4,912
        1860              4,185
        1850              3,421
        1840              2,984
        1830              2,505
```

KIRKVILLE, CDP
   Manlius Town
      Onondaga County
```
        1880                926
        1870                150
```

KIRKWOOD, Town (Est. 1859)
   Broome County
```
        1980              5,834
        1970              5,687
        1960              4,651
        1950              2,997
        1940              2,150
        1930              1,237
        1920                899
        1910                852
        1900                918
        1890              1,119
        1880              1,344
        1870              1,402
        1860              1,399
```

KIRYAS JOEL, Village (Inc. 1977)
   Monroe Town
      Orange County
```
        1980              2,088
```

KISMET
   see FIRE ISLAND
      Islip Town
         Suffolk County

KNAPPS CREEK, CDP
   Allegany Town
      Cattaraugus County
```
        1880                390
```

KNOWERSVILLE, CDP
  Guilderland Town
    Albany County
      1880   329

KNOWLESVILLE, CDP
  Ridgeway Town
    Orleans County
      1880   321

KNOX, CDP
  Knox Town
    Albany County
      1880   182

KNOX, Town (Est. 1822)
  Albany County
      1980   2,471
      1970   1,819
      1960   1,320
      1950   1,172
      1940   960
      1930   863
      1920   975
      1910   1,007
      1900   1,244
      1890   1,411
      1880   1,694
      1870   1,656
      1860   2,025
      1850   2,021
      1840   2,143
      1830   2,189

      1860   2,023
      1850   2,181
      1840   2,441
      1830   2,870
      1820   2,548
      1810   NA
      1800   *1,513

KNOXBORO, CDP
  Augusta Town
    Oneida County
      1880   262

KNOX CORNERS, CDP
  Augusta Town
    Oneida County
      1870   208

KNOXVILLE, CDP
  Stockbridge Town
    Madison County
      1870   241

KNOXVILLE, CDP
  Corning Town
    Steuben County
      1880   858
      1870   785

KORTRIGHT, Town (Est. 1793)
  Delaware County
      1980   1,250
      1970   1,236
      1960   1,073
      1950   1,239
      1940   1,288
      1930   1,340
      1920   1,559
      1910   1,481
      1900   1,475
      1890   1,588
      1880   1,730
      1870   1,812

L

LACKAWANNA, City (Inc. 1909)(a)
  Erie County
      1980   22,701
      1970   28,657
      1960   29,564
      1950   27,658(b)
      1940   24,058(b)
      1930   23,948
      1920   17,918
      1910   14,549
(a)Incorporated and made independent of
   WEST SENECA Town in 1909.
(b)Boundary change.

LACKAWAREN, CDP
  Highland Town
    Sullivan County
      1880   81

LACONA, Village (Inc. 1878)
  Sandy Creek Town
    Oswego County
      1980   582
      1970   556
      1960   556
      1950   540
      1940   413
      1930   546
      1920   451
      1910   443
      1900   388
      1890   333
      1880   378

LA FARGEVILLE, CDP
  Orleans Town
    Jefferson County
      1940   616
      1890-1930   NA
      1880   307

LAFAYETTE, CDP
  Lafayette Town
    Onondaga County
      1880   146
      1870   135

LAFAYETTE, CDP
  Groton Town
    Tompkins County
      1880   29

LAFAYETTE, Town (Est.1825)
  Onondaga County
      1980   4,488
      1970   4,401
      1960   3,379
      1950   2,083
      1940   1,550
      1930   1,438
      1920   1,132
      1910   1,293 Rev.(a)
      1900   1,413 Rev.(a)
      1890   1,874
      1880   2,160
      1870   2,233(b)
      1860   2,537
      1850   2,533
      1840   2,600
      1830   2,560(b)
(a)In 1920 the Census Bureau revised the
   1910 figure of 1,601 and the 1900
   figure of 1,892 to exclude the
   ONONDAGA INDIAN RESERVATION.
(b)Reported as La Fayette.

LA FAYETTEVILLE, CDP
  Milan Town
    Dutchess County
      1880   79

LA GRANGE, CDP
  Covington Town
    Wyoming County
      1880   57

LA GRANGE, Town (Est. 1821)(a)
  Dutchess County
      1980   12,375
      1970   10,902
      1960   6,079
      1950   2,280
      1940   1,638
      1930   1,210
      1920   1,132
      1910   1,350
      1900   1,304
      1890   1,463
      1880   1,745
      1870   1,774
      1860   1,850
      1850   1,941
      1840   1,851
      1830   2,044
(a)Established as Freedom in 1821; name
   changed in 1828.

LA GRANGEVILLE, CDP
  La Grange Town
    Dutchess County
      1880   324

LAKE, CDP
  Warwick Town
    Orange County
      1980   1,210

      1970   1,352

LAKE CARMEL, CDP
  Kent & Patterson Towns
    Putnam County
      1980   7,295
      1970   4,796
      1960   2,735
      1950   1,055(a)
(a)Part in KENT Town, 1,001; part in
   PATTERSON Town, 54.

LAKE ERIE BEACH, CDP
  Evans Town
    Erie County
      1980   4,625
      1970   3,467
      1960   2,117

LAKE GEORGE, Town (Est. 1810)(a)
  Warren County
      1980   3,394
      1970   2,806
      1960   2,429
      1950   1,621
      1940   1,467
      1930   1,730
      1920   1,297
      1910   1,482
      1900   1,465
      1890   1,377
      1880   1,223
      1870   1,041
      1860   1,073
      1850   752
      1840   NA
      1830   797
      1820   723
(a)Established as Caldwell in 1810; name
   changed in 1962.

LAKE GEORGE, Village (Inc. 1903)
  Lake George Town
    Warren County
      1980   1,047
      1970   1,046
      1960   1,026
      1950   1,005
      1940   803
      1930   848
      1920   630
      1910   632

LAKE GROVE, Village (Inc. 1968)
  Brookhaven Town
    Suffolk County
      1980   9,692
      1970   8,133
      1960   2,253(a)
      1890-1950   NA
      1880   398
(a)Derived by LIRPB from U.S. Census
   Data.

LAKE KATRINE, CDP
  Ulster Town
    Ulster County
      1980   2,011
      1970   1,092

1960	1,149

LAKELAND
Islip Town
Suffolk County

1970	3,707(a)
1960	912(a)

(a)Derived by LIRPB from U.S. Census
Data.

LAKE LUZERNE, CDP
Lake Luzerne Town
Warren County

1940	505

LAKE LUZERNE, Town (Est. 1792)(a)
Warren County

1980	2,672
1970	2,174
1960	1,830
1950	1,426
1940	1,251
1930	1,150
1920	1,018
1910	1,185
1900	1,341
1890	1,679
1880	1,438
1870	1,174
1860	1,328
1850	1,300
1840	NA
1830	1,362
1820	1,430
1810	NA
1800	*591(b)

(a)Established as Fairfield in 1792;
name changed to Luzerne in 1808 and
to LAKE LUZERNE in 1963.
(b)Reported in WASHINGTON County.

LAKE LUZERNE--HADLEY, CDP
Hadley & Lake Luzerne Towns
Saratoga & Warren Counties

1980	1,988(a)

(a)Part in SARATOGA County, 825; part in
WARREN COUNTY, 1,163.

LAKE PLACID, Village (Inc. 1900)
North Elba Town
Essex County

1980	2,490
1970	2,731(a)
1960	2,998
1950	2,999
1940	3,136(a)
1930	2,950
1920	2,099
1910	1,682

(a)Boundary change.

LAKE PLEASANT, Town (Est. 1812)
Hamilton County

1980	859
1970	812
1960	718
1950	696
1940	584
1930	540

1920	393
1910	458
1900	469
1890	416
1880	343
1870	318
1860	356
1850	305
1840	296
1830	266
1820	312

LAKEPORT, CDP
Sullivan Town
Madison County

1880	91
1870	134

LAKE RIDGE, CDP
Lansing Town
Tompkins County

1880	84

LAKE RONKONKOMA, CDP
Brookhaven Town, part in
Suffolk County

1980	14,305(a)
1970	11,187(b)
1960	2,158
1950	NA
1940	770

Islip Town, part in
Suffolk County

1980	19,692(a)
1970	12,042(c)
1960	1,577

Smithtown Town, part in
Suffolk County

1980	4,339(a)
1970	2,770(b)
1960	1,106

TOTAL

1980	38,336(a)
1970	25,999 Rev.(b)
1960	4,841
1950	NA
1940	(d)

(a)Boundary change.
(b)Derived by LIRPB from U.S. Census
Data; population is comparable to
1980 boundaries.
(c)Derived by LIRPB from U.S. Census
Data. Population of 12,042 is
comparable to 1980 boundaries.
Population of 3,646 is comparable to
1960 boundaries.
(d)Reported in BROOKHAVEN Town only.

LAKE SHENOROCK, CDP
Somers Town
Westchester County

1960	1,402

LAKE SHORE, CDP
see HAMBURG--LAKE SHORE, CDP
Erie County

LAKE SUCCESS, Village (Inc. 1927)(a)
  North Hempstead Town
    Nassau County
        1980   2,396
        1970   3,254
        1960   2,954(b)
        1950   1,264
        1940   203
        1930   295
(a)Incorporated as Success in 1927;
   name changed in 1928.
(b)Boundary change.

LAKEVIEW, CDP
  Hempstead Town
    Nassau County
        1980   5,276
        1970   5,471
        1960   4,829(a)
        1950   NA
        1940   3,271
(a)Derived by LIRPB from U.S. Census
   Data. U.S. Census reported as WEST
   HEMPSTEAD--LAKEVIEW, CDP with a
   population of 24,783.

LAKEVILLE, CDP
  Livonia Town
    Livingston County
        1880   151

LAKEWOOD, Village (Inc. 1893)
  Busti Town
    Chautauqua County
        1980   3,941
        1970   3,864
        1960   3,933
        1950   3,013
        1940   2,314
        1930   1,837
        1920   714
        1910   564
        1900   574

LAMB'S CORNERS, CDP
  Nanticoke Town
    Broome County
        1880   83

LANCASTER, Town
    Chenango County
  see NEW BERLIN, Town
      Chenango County

LANCASTER, Town (Est. 1833)
  Erie County
        1980   30,144
        1970   30,634(a)
        1960   25,605
        1950   18,471
        1940   15,299
        1930   15,260
        1920   13,172
        1910   9,663
        1900   8,757
        1890   3,962
        1880   3,944
        1870   4,336
        1860   2,933

        1850   3,794
        1840   2,083
(a)Boundary change.

LANCASTER, Village (Inc. 1849)
  Lancaster Town
    Erie County
        1980   13,056
        1970   13,365
        1960   12,254
        1950   8,665
        1940   7,236
        1930   7,040
        1920   6,059
        1910   4,364
        1900   3,750
        1890   1,692
        1880   1,602
        1870   1,697
        1860   1,706

LANDING, Village
  see VILLAGE OF THE LANDING, Village
      Suffolk County

LANSING, Town (Est. 1817)
    Tompkins County
        1980   8,317
        1970   5,972
        1960   4,221
        1950   3,195
        1940   2,786
        1930   2,720
        1920   2,380
        1910   2,676
        1900   2,550
        1890   2,505
        1880   3,000
        1870   2,874
        1860   3,222
        1850   3,318
        1840   3,672
        1830   4,020
        1820   3,631

LANSING, Village (Inc. 1974)
  Lansing Town
    Tompkins County
        1980   3,039(a)
(a)Boundary change.

LANSINGBURGH, Town (Est. 1807)(a)
    Rensselaer County
        1900   12,939
        1890   10,871
        1880   7,759
        1870   6,804
        1860   5,577
        1850   5,752
        1840   3,330
        1830   2,663
        1820   2,035
(a)Merged into TROY City in 1901.

LANSINGBURGH, Village (Inc. 1790)(a)
  Lansingburgh Town
    Rensselaer County
        1900   12,595
        1890   10,550

```
                    1880         7,432
                    1870         6,372
(a)Merged into TROY City in 1901.
```

LANSINGVILLE, CDP
    Hamden Town
        Delaware County
            1870   110

LANSINGVILLE, CDP
    Lansing Town
        Tompkins County
            1880   133
            1870   67

LAONA, CDP
    Pomfret Town
        Chautauqua County
            1870   218

LAPATA, CDP
    Marbletown Town
        Ulster County
            1880   128

LAPEER, Town (Est. 1845)
    Cortland County
            1980   592
            1970   507
            1960   459
            1950   432
            1940   450
            1930   393
            1920   423
            1910   475
            1900   538
            1890   585
            1880   757
            1870   735
            1860   803
            1850   822

LARCHMONT, Village (Inc. 1891)
    Mamaroneck Town
        Westchester County
            1980   6,308
            1970   7,203
            1960   6,789
            1950   6,330
            1940   5,970
            1930   5,282
            1920   2,468
            1910   1,958
            1900   945

LA SALLE, Village (Inc. 1897)(a)
    Niagara Town
        Niagara County
            1920   3,813
            1910   1,299
            1900   661
            1890   NA
            1880   197(b)
(a)Merged into NIAGARA FALLS City in
    1927.
(b)Reported as Lasalle.

LASELLVILLE, CDP
    Ephratah Town
        Fulton County
            1880   142

LATHAM, CDP
    Colonie Town
        Albany County
            1980   11,182
            1970   9,661

LATTINGTOWN, Village (Inc. 1931)
    Oyster Bay Town
        Nassau County
            1980   1,749
            1970   1,773
            1960   1,461
            1950   745
            1940   613(a)
            1890-1930   NA
            1880   200(b)
(a)Boundary change.
(b)Reported in QUEENS County.

LAUREL(a)
    Southold Town
        Suffolk County
            1980   962(b)
            1970   598 Rev.(c)
(a)Included, in part, in LAUREL--EAST
    MATTITUCK in 1960.
(b)Boundary change; derived by LIRPB
    from U.S. Census Data.
(c)Derived by LIRPB from U.S. Census
    Data; population is comparable
    to 1980 boundaries.

LAUREL--EAST MATTITUCK(a)
    Southold Town
        Suffolk County
            1970   1,712(b)
            1960   1,231(b)
(a)Included in LAUREL in 1980.
(b)Derived by LIRPB from U.S. Census
    Data.

LAUREL HOLLOW, Village (Inc. 1926)(a)
    Oyster Bay Town
        Nassau County
            1980   1,527
            1970   1,401
            1960   834(b)
            1950   169
            1940   110
            1930   161(c)
(a)Incorporated as Laurelton in 1926;
    name changed in 1935.
(b)Boundary change.
(c)Reported as Laurelton Village.

LAURELTON, Village
    see LAUREL HOLLOW, Village
        Nassau County

LAURENS, Town (Est. 1810)
    Otsego County
            1980   2,101
            1970   1,730
            1960   1,498
```
```

1950	1,447
1940	1,395
1930	1,423
1920	1,335
1910	1,453
1900	1,483
1890	1,659
1880	1,827
1870	1,919
1860	1,936
1850	2,168
1840	2,173
1830	2,231
1820	2,074

LAURENS, Village (Inc. 1834)
  Laurens Town
    Otsego County

1980	276
1970	320
1960	291
1950	261
1940	203
1930	246
1920	228
1910	242
1900	233
1890	255
1880	252

LAWRENCE, Town (Est. 1828)
  St. Lawrence County

1980	1,658
1970	1,632
1960	1,785
1950	1,625
1940	1,431
1930	1,526
1920	1,588
1910	1,676
1900	1,963
1890	2,037
1880	2,483
1870	2,577
1860	2,828
1850	2,214(a)
1840	1,845
1830	1,097

(a)Reported as Lawrenceville.

LAWRENCE, Village (Inc. 1897)
  Hempstead Town
    Nassau County

1980	6,175
1970	6,566
1960	5,907
1950	4,681(a)
1940	3,649
1930	3,041(a)
1920	2,861
1910	1,189
1900	558
1890	626

(a)Boundary change.

LAWRENCEVILLE, CDP
  Lawrence Town
    St. Lawrence County

1880	118

LAWRENCEVILLE, Town
  see LAWRENCE, Town
        St. Lawrence County

LEANDER, Town
  see PAMELIA, Town
        Jefferson County

LEBANON, CDP
  Lebanon Town
    Madison County

1880	157

LEBANON, Town
  Columbia County
  see NEW LEBANON, Town
          Columbia County

LEBANON, Town (Est. 1807)
  Madison County

1980	1,117
1970	969
1960	880
1950	890
1940	914
1930	895
1920	940
1910	1,079
1900	1,243
1890	1,277
1880	1,586
1870	1,559
1860	1,678
1850	1,709
1840	1,794
1830	2,249
1820	1,940

LEDYARD, Town (Est. 1823)
  Cayuga County

1980	1,869
1970	1,886
1960	1,646
1950	1,577
1940	1,322
1930	1,236
1920	1,475
1910	1,719
1900	1,909
1890	2,185
1880	2,199
1870	2,221
1860	2,219
1850	2,043
1840	2,143
1830	2,427

LEE, Town (Est. 1811)
  Oneida County

1980	6,892
1970	6,095
1960	4,302
1950	1,856
1940	1,482
1930	1,300
1920	1,134
1910	1,379
1900	1,571
1890	1,845

1880	2,360
1870	2,656
1860	2,796
1850	3,033
1840	2,936
1830	2,514
1820	2,186

LEE CENTER, CDP
  Lee Town
    Oneida County

1880	320(a)
1870	355

(a)Reported as Lee Centre.

LEICESTER, Town (Est. 1802)(a)
  Livingston County

1980	1,888
1970	1,799
1960	1,392
1950	1,350
1940	1,371
1930	1,565
1920	1,656
1910	1,702
1900	1,415
1890	1,647
1880	1,679
1870	1,744
1860	2,008
1850	2,142
1840	2,415
1830	2,042
1820	1,331(b)

(a)Established as Leister in 1802; name
  changed in 1805.
(b)Reported in GENESEE County.

LEICESTER, Village (Inc. 1907)(a)
  Leicester Town
    Livingston County

1980	462
1970	368(b)
1960	365
1950	364
1940	327
1930	285
1920	279
1910	304
1890-1900	NA
1880	262
1870	245

(a)Incorporated as Moscow in 1907; name
  changed in 1917.
(b)Boundary change.

LEISTER, Town
  see LEICESTER, Town
    Livingston County

LENOX, Town (Est. 1809)
  Madison County

1980	8,539
1970	8,871
1960	7,729
1950	6,515
1940	5,770
1930	5,887
1920	5,536

1910	4,851
1900	4,679
1890	6,732
1880	10,246
1870	9,816
1860	8,024
1850	7,507
1840	5,440
1830	5,039
1820	3,360

LEON, CDP
  Leon Town
    Cattaraugus County

1880	193

LEON, Town (Est. 1832)
  Cattaraugus County

1980	1,055
1970	878
1960	808
1950	738
1940	755
1930	720
1920	729
1910	859
1900	1,003
1890	1,194
1880	1,192
1870	1,204
1860	1,399
1850	1,340
1840	1,326

LEONARDSVILLE, CDP
  Brookfield Town
    Madison County

1880	236

LE RAY, Town (Est. 1806)
  Jefferson County

1980	5,039
1970	3,973
1960	3,627
1950	2,821
1940	2,551
1930	2,422
1920	2,366
1910	2,555
1900	2,576
1890	2,565
1880	2,660
1870	2,862
1860	3,159
1850	3,654
1840	3,721(a)
1830	3,419
1820	2,944

(a)Reported as Leray.

LE RAYSVILLE, CDP
  Le Ray Town
    Jefferson County

1880	84

LE ROY, Town (Est. 1812)(a)
  Genesee County

1980	8,019
1970	7,991

1960	6,779
1950	6,275
1940	5,838
1930	6,007
1920	5,510
1910	5,442
1900	4,823
1890	4,722
1880	4,469
1870	4,627
1860	4,247
1850	3,473
1840	4,323
1830	3,902
1820	2,611

(a)Established as Bellona in 1812; name
   changed in 1813.

LE ROY, Village (Inc. 1834)
   Le Roy Town
      Genesee County

1980	4,900
1970	5,118(a)
1960	4,662
1950	4,721
1940	4,413
1930	4,474
1920	4,203
1910	3,771
1900	3,144
1890	2,743
1880	NA
1870	2,634

(a)Boundary change.

LESTERSHIRE, Village
   see JOHNSON CITY, Village
      Broome County

LEVITTOWN, CDP
   Hempstead Town
      Nassau County

1980	57,045
1970	65,440
1960	65,276

LEWIS, CDP
   Lewis Town
      Essex County

1880	68

LEWIS, County (Est. 1805)

1980	25,035
1970	23,644
1960	23,249
1950	22,521
1940	22,815
1930	23,447
1920	23,704
1910	24,849
1900	27,427
1890	29,806
1880	31,416
1870	28,699
1860	28,580
1850	24,564
1840	17,830
1830	15,239
1820	9,227

1810	6,433

LEWIS, Town (Est. 1805)
   Essex County

1980	922
1970	763
1960	803
1950	782
1940	791
1930	667
1920	753
1910	937
1900	1,123
1890	1,323
1880	1,774
1870	1,724
1860	1,807
1850	2,058
1840	1,505
1830	1,305
1820	779

LEWIS, Town (Est. 1852)
   Lewis County

1980	720
1970	649
1960	587
1950	584
1940	413
1930	677
1920	753
1910	801
1900	917
1890	999
1880	1,161
1870	1,252
1860	1,407

LEWISBORO, Town (Est. 1788)(a)
   Westchester County

1980	8,871
1970	6,610
1960	4,165
1950	2,352
1940	1,929
1930	1,427
1920	1,069
1910	1,127
1900	1,311
1890	1,417
1880	1,612
1870	1,601(b)
1860	1,875(c)
1850	1,608
1840	1,619
1830	1,537
1820	1,429
1810	NA
1800	*1,696
1790	1,453

(a)Established as Salem in 1788, name
   changed to South Salem in 1806 and to
   LEWISBORO in 1844.
(b)Reported as Lewisborough.
(c)Reported as Lewiston.

LEWISTON, Town (Est. 1818)
   Niagara County

1980	16,219

1970	15,888
1960	13,686
1950	6,921
1940	4,448
1930	3,420
1920	2,750 Rev.(a)
1910	2,846 Rev.(a)
1900	3,221
1890	2,577
1880	2,768
1870	2,959
1860	3,379
1850	2,924
1840	2,533
1830	1,528
1820	869

(a)In 1920 the Census Bureau revised the
   1910 figure of 3,263 and the 1900
   figure of 3,221 to exclude the
   TUSCARORA INDIAN RESERVATION.

LEWISTON, Town
      Westchester County
   see LEWISBORO, Town
         Westchester County

LEWISTON, Village (Inc. 1822)
   Lewiston Town
      Niagara County

1980	3,326
1970	3,292
1960	3,320
1950	1,626
1940	1,280
1930	1,013
1920	723
1910	713
1900	697
1890	633
1880	680
1870	770

LEXINGTON, Town (Est. 1813)(a)
   Greene County

1980	819
1970	666
1960	698
1950	833
1940	827
1930	815
1920	1,075
1910	1,054
1900	1,153
1890	1,229
1880	1,356
1870	1,371
1860	1,657
1850	2,263
1840	2,813
1830	2,548
1820	1,798

(a)Established as New Goshen in Jan.,
   1813; name changed in Mar., 1813.

LEYDEN, Town (Est. 1797)
   Lewis County

1980	1,660
1970	1,677
1960	1,715

1950	1,622
1940	1,519
1930	1,482
1920	1,515
1910	1,613
1900	1,629
1890	1,624
1880	1,933
1870	2,048
1860	1,859
1850	2,253
1840	2,438
1830	1,502
1820	1,203
1810	NA
1800	*622(a)

(a)Reported in ONEIDA County.

LIBERTY, CDP
   Cohocton Town
      Steuben County

1880	683

LIBERTY, Town (Est. 1807)
   Sullivan County

1980	9,879
1970	9,329
1960	8,676
1950	7,979
1940	7,235
1930	6,967
1920	6,030
1910	5,402
1900	4,568
1890	3,357
1880	3,209
1870	3,389
1860	3,016
1850	2,612
1840	1,569
1830	1,277
1820	851

LIBERTY, Village (Inc. 1870)
   Liberty Town
      Sullivan County

1980	4,293(a)
1970	4,514 Rev.
1960	4,704(a)
1950	4,658(a)
1940	3,788(a)
1930	3,427
1920	2,459
1910	2,072
1900	1,700
1890	734
1880	478

(a)Boundary change.

LIBERTYVILLE, CDP
   Gardiner Town
      Ulster County

1880	61

LIDO--POINT LOOKOUT
   Hempstead Town
      Nassau County

1980	4,504(a)
1970	4,397(a)

```
            1960              2,358(a)
(a)Derived by LIRPB from U.S. Census
   Data.

LIMA, Town (Est. 1789)(a)
    Livingston County
            1980              3,859
            1970              3,445
            1960              2,716
            1950              2,336
            1940              1,986
            1930              1,900
            1920              1,890
            1910              2,068
            1900              2,279
            1890              2,438
            1880              2,782
            1870              2,912
            1860              2,782
            1850              2,433
            1840              2,176
            1830              1,764
            1820              1,963(b)
            1810              NA
            1800              *1,060(b)
(a)Established as Charleston in 1789;
   name changed in 1808.
(b)Reported in ONTARIO County.

LIMA, Village (Inc. 1867)
    Lima Town
    Livingston County
            1980              2,025
            1970              1,686(a)
            1960              1,366(a)
            1950              1,147
            1940              942
            1930              897
            1920              843
            1910              866
            1900              949
            1890              1,003
            1880              1,878
            1870              1,257
(a)Boundary change.

LIME LAKE--MACHIAS, CDP
    Mansfield Town
    Cattaraugus County
            1980              1,191

LIMERICK, CDP
    Brownville Town
    Jefferson County
            1880              122

LIMESTONE, Village (Inc. 1877)
    Carrollton Town
    Cattaraugus County
            1980              466
            1970              535
            1960              539
            1950              601
            1940              558
            1930              599
            1920              454
            1910              684
            1900              732
            1890              NA
```

```
            1880              923

LINCKLAEN, Town (Est. 1823)
    Chenango County
            1980              473
            1970              414
            1960              364
            1950              341
            1940              397
            1930              447
            1920              532
            1910              570
            1900              646
            1890              726
            1880              901
            1870              926
            1860              1,094
            1850              1,196
            1840              1,249
            1830              1,425(a)
(a)Reported as Linklean.

LINCOLN, Town (Est. 1896)
    Madison County
            1980              1,722
            1970              1,168
            1960              1,102
            1950              924
            1940              853
            1930              869
            1920              821
            1910              985
            1900              1,052

LINCOLN, Town
    Ontario County
    see GORHAM, Town
            Ontario County

LINCOLN PARK, CDP
    Ulster Town
    Ulster County
            1980              2,664
            1970              2,851
            1960              2,707
            1950              1,527

LINDEN, CDP
    Bethany Town
    Genesee County
            1880              163

LINDEN, Town
    see LYNDON, Town
            Cattaraugus County

LINDENHURST, Village (Inc. 1923)
    Babylon Town
    Suffolk County
            1980              26,919
            1970              28,359
            1960              20,905
            1950              8,644
            1940              4,756
            1930              4,040
            1900-1920         NA
            1890              974
            1880              606(a)
(a)Reported as Breslau.
```

LINDLEY, Town (Est. 1837)(a)
Steuben County

1980	1,831
1970	1,414
1960	1,313
1950	1,043
1940	961
1930	945
1920	1,024
1910	1,153
1900	1,306
1890	1,537
1880	1,563
1870	1,251
1860	886
1850	686
1840	638

(a)In 1800 the Census Bureau reported a
    Lindsley Town in STEUBEN County,
    population of 132.

LINDSLEY, Town
    see LINDLEY, Town
            Steuben County

LINKLEAN, Town
    see LINCKLAEN, Town
            Chenango County

LINOLEUMVILLE, CDP
    Northfield Town
        Richmond County

1880	134

LISBON, Town
    Otsego County
    see NEW LISBON, Town
            Otsego County

LISBON, Town (Est. 1801)
    St. Lawrence County

1980	3,548
1970	3,271
1960	3,040
1950	2,557
1940	2,633
1930	2,642
1920	2,673
1910	2,981(a)
1900	5,255
1890	3,809
1880	4,297
1870	4,475
1860	5,640
1850	5,295
1840	3,508
1830	1,891
1820	930

(a)Boundary change.

LISBON CENTER, CDP
    Lisbon Town
        St. Lawrence County

1880	125

LISLE, Town (Est. 1801)
    Broome County

1980	2,039
1970	1,917
1960	1,587
1950	1,534
1940	1,397
1930	1,299
1920	1,219
1910	1,429
1900	1,710
1890	1,962
1880	2,399
1870	2,525
1860	1,791
1850	1,680
1840	1,560
1830	4,378
1820	3,083
1810	NA
1800	*660(a)

(a)Reported in TIOGA County.

LISLE, Village (Inc. 1866)
    Lisle Town
        Broome County

1980	357
1970	336
1960	335
1950	306
1940	342
1930	325
1920	294
1910	329
1900	392
1890	421
1880	429

LITCHFIELD, Town (Est. 1796)
    Herkimer County

1980	1,187
1970	961
1960	963
1950	776
1940	779
1930	712
1920	747
1910	803
1900	931
1890	1,055
1880	1,218
1870	1,384
1860	1,520
1850	1,676
1840	1,672
1830	1,750
1820	1,729
1810	NA
1800	*1,976

LITTLE FALLS, City (Inc. 1895)(a)
    Herkimer County

1980	6,156(b)
1970	7,629
1960	8,935(b)
1950	9,541
1940	10,163(b)
1930	11,105
1920	13,029
1910	12,273(b)
1900	10,381

(a)LITTLE FALLS Village incorporated as
    LITTLE FALLS City and made indepen-

dent of LITTLE FALLS Town in 1895.
(b)Boundary change.

LITTLE FALLS, Town (Est. 1829)
    Herkimer County
        1980   1,434(a)
        1970   1,411
        1960   1,188(a)
        1950   874
        1940   777
        1930   741
        1920   684
        1910   638
        1900   718(a)
        1890   7,512
        1880   6,913
        1870   5,612
        1860   5,989
        1850   4,855
        1840   3,881
        1830   2,539
(a)Boundary change.

LITTLE FALLS, Village (Inc. 1811)(a)
    Little Falls Town
        Herkimer County
        1890   8,783
        1880   5,979
        1870   5,387
(a)Name changed to Rocton in 1850; ori-
ginal name restored in 1852. LITTLE
FALLS Village incorporated as LITTLE
FALLS City and made independent of
LITTLE FALLS Town in 1895.

LITTLE GENESEE, CDP
    Genesee Town
        Allegany County
        1880   89

LITTLE UTICA, CDP
    Lysander Town
        Onondaga County
        1880   58

LITTLE VALLEY, Town (Est. 1818)
    Cattaraugus County
        1980   1,830
        1970   1,838
        1960   1,737
        1950   1,724
        1940   1,601
        1930   1,542
        1920   1,683
        1910   1,905
        1900   1,616
        1890   1,326
        1880   1,196
        1870   1,108
        1860   1,206
        1850   1,383
        1840   700
        1830   336
        1820   484

LITTLE VALLEY, Village (Inc. 1876)
    Little Valley Town
        Cattaraugus County
        1980   1,203

        1970   1,340
        1960   1,244
        1950   1,287
        1940   1,234
        1930   1,196
        1920   1,253
        1910   1,368
        1900   1,085
        1890   698
        1880   566

LITTLE YORK, CDP
    Fowler Town
        St. Lawrence County
        1880   87
        1870   117

LIVERPOOL, Village (Inc. 1830)
    Salina Town
        Onondaga County
        1980   2,849
        1970   3,307
        1960   3,487(a)
        1950   2,933
        1940   2,500(a)
        1930   2,244
        1920   1,831
        1910   1,388
        1900   1,133
        1890   1,284
        1880   1,330
        1870   1,555
(a)Boundary change.

LIVINGSTON, County (Est. 1821)
        1980   57,006
        1970   54,041
        1960   44,053
        1950   40,257
        1940   38,510
        1930   37,560(a)
        1920   36,830
        1910   38,037
        1900   37,059
        1890   37,801
        1880   39,562
        1870   38,309
        1860   39,546
        1850   40,875
        1840   35,140
        1830   27,729
(a)Boundary change.

LIVINGSTON, Town (Est. 1788)
    Columbia County
        1980   3,087
        1970   2,280
        1960   1,770
        1950   1,457
        1940   1,564
        1930   1,473
        1920   1,339
        1910   1,620
        1900   1,707
        1890   2,080
        1880   2,060
        1870   1,938
        1860   2,014
        1850   2,020

1840	2,190
1830	2,087
1820	1,938
1810	NA
1800	*7,405
1790	4,594

LIVINGSTON MANOR, CDP
  Rockland Town
    Sullivan County

1980	1,436
1970	1,522
1960	2,080
1950	NA
1940	1,373

LIVINGSTONVILLE, CDP
  Broome Town
    Schoharie County

1880	97

LIVONIA, Town (Est. 1808)
  Livingston County

1980	5,742
1970	5,304
1960	3,526
1950	2,896
1940	2,596
1930	2,644
1920	2,600
1910	2,819
1900	2,788
1890	2,859
1880	3,119
1870	2,705
1860	2,593
1850	2,627
1840	2,719
1830	2,665
1820	2,427(a)

(a)Reported in ONTARIO County.

LIVONIA, Village (Inc. 1882)
  Livonia Town
    Livingston County

1980	1,238
1970	1,278
1960	946(a)
1950	837
1940	751
1930	774
1920	743
1910	823(b)
1900	865(b)
1890	738(b)
1880	NA
1870	399(b)

(a)Boundary change.
(b)Reported as Livonia Station.

LIVONIA CENTER, CDP
  Livonia Town
    Livingston County

1880	293(a)
1870	193(a)

(a)Reported as Livonia Centre.

LIVONIA STATION, Village
  see LIVONIA, Village
    Livingston County

LLOYD, Town (Est. 1845)
  Ulster County

1980	7,875
1970	7,032
1960	5,842
1950	4,503
1940	3,795
1930	3,709
1920	3,079
1910	2,803
1900	2,608
1890	2,516
1880	2,713
1870	2,658
1860	2,499
1850	2,035

LLOYD HARBOR, Village (Inc. 1926)
  Huntington Town
    Suffolk County

1980	3,405
1970	3,371
1960	2,521
1950	945
1940	603
1930	480

LOCK BERLIN, CDP
  Galen Town
    Wayne County

1880	110

LOCKE, Town (Est. 1802)
  Cayuga County

1980	1,751
1970	1,152
1960	982
1950	811
1940	748
1930	714
1920	770
1910	864
1900	1,079
1890	1,001
1880	1,141
1870	1,077
1860	1,325
1850	1,478
1840	1,654
1830	3,310
1820	2,559

LOCKPORT, City (Inc. 1865)(a)
  Niagara County

1980	24,844
1970	25,399(b)
1960	26,443(b)
1950	25,133(b)
1940	24,379
1930	23,160
1920	21,308
1910	17,970
1900	16,581
1890	16,038
1880	13,522

```
          1870              12,426
          1860              10,671(c)
(a)LOCKPORT Village incorporated as
   LOCKPORT City and made independent
   of LOCKPORT Town in 1865.
(b)Boundary change.
(c)Estimated.

LOCKPORT, Town (Est. 1824)
     Niagara County
          1980              12,942
          1970               8,177
          1960               6,492
          1950               3,945
          1940               3,160
          1930               2,720
          1920               1,833
          1910               2,399
          1900               2,585
          1890               2,773
          1880               2,847
          1870               3,032(a)
          1860              13,523
          1850              12,323
          1840               9,125
          1830               1,801
(a)Boundary change.

LOCKPORT, Village (Inc. 1829)(a)
   Lockport Town
     Niagara County
          1830               2,022
(a)LOCKPORT Village incorporated as
   LOCKPORT City and made independent
   of LOCKPORT Town in 1865.

LOCUST GROVE, CDP
   Oyster Bay Town
     Nassau County
          1980               9,670
          1970              11,626
          1960              11,558

LOCUST VALLEY, CDP
   Oyster Bay Town
     Nassau County
          1980               3,576(a)
          1970               3,932(a)
          1960               3,321(a)
          1950                 NA
          1940               2,534
          1890-1930            NA
          1880               1,309(b)
(a)Derived by LIRPB from U.S. Census
   Data.
(b)Reported in QUEENS County.

LODI, Town (Est. 1826)
     Seneca County
          1980               1,184
          1970               1,287
          1960               1,267
          1950               1,118
          1940               1,051
          1930               1,044
          1920               1,137
          1910               1,408
```

```
          1900               1,636
          1890               1,694
          1880               1,947
          1870               1,825
          1860               2,067
          1850               2,269
          1840               2,236
          1830               1,786

LODI, Village (Inc. 1926)
   Lodi Town
     Seneca County
          1980                334
          1970                353
          1960                396
          1950                362
          1940                366
          1930                322
          1890-1920            NA
          1880                433

LONG BEACH, City (Inc. 1922)(a)
     Nassau County
          1980              34,073
          1970              33,127
          1960              26,473
          1950              15,586
          1940               9,036
          1930               5,817(b)
          1920                282
(a)LONG BEACH Village (Inc. 1913) incor-
   porated as LONG BEACH City and made
   independent of HEMPSTEAD Town in
   1922.
(b)Boundary change.

LONG BEACH, Village
   see LONG BEACH, City
     Nassau County

LONG EDDY, CDP
   Fremont Town
     Sullivan County
          1880                237

LONG ISLAND CITY, City (Inc. 1870)(a)
   Newtown Town
     Queens County
          1890              30,506
          1880              17,129
          1870               3,867
(a)Long Island City, Village (Inc. 1839)
   incorporated as LONG ISLAND CITY, City
   and made independent of NEWTOWN Town
   in 1870. LONG ISLAND CITY, City merged
   into QUEENS Borough in NEW YORK City
   in 1898.

LONG ISLAND CITY, Village
   see LONG ISLAND CITY, City
     Queens County

LONG LAKE, Town (Est. 1837)
     Hamilton County
          1980                935
          1970                900
          1960                896
          1950                896
```

1940	943
1930	1,038
1920	1,116
1910	1,149
1900	1,023
1890	580
1880	324
1870	280
1860	223
1850	111
1840	59

LORAINE, Town
see LORRAINE, Town
        Jefferson County

LORENZ PARK, CDP
  Greenport Town
    Columbia County

1980	1,720
1970	1,995

LORRAINE, Town (Est. 1804)(a)
  Jefferson County

1980	720
1970	628
1960	609
1950	681
1940	782
1930	848
1920	790
1910	940
1900	1,019
1890	1,174
1880	1,435
1870	1,377
1860	1,687(b)
1850	1,511
1840	1,699
1830	1,727
1820	112

(a)Established as Malta in 1804; name
   changed in 1808.
(b)Reported as Loraine.

LOUDONVILLE, CDP
  Colonie Town
    Albany County

1980	11,480
1970	9,299
1950-1960	NA
1940	732

LOUISVILLE, CDP
  Louisville Town
    St. Lawrence County

1880	207

LOUISVILLE, Town
  Oneida County
see LOUISVILLE, Town
        St. Lawrence County

LOUISVILLE, Town (Est. 1810)(a)
  St. Lawrence County

1980	2,946
1970	2,727
1960	2,520
1950	1,825

1940	1,589
1930	1,355
1920	1,364
1910	1,492
1900	1,621
1890	1,676
1880	2,019
1870	2,132
1860	2,310
1850	2,054
1840	1,693
1830	1,076
1820	831

(a)In 1800 the Census Bureau reported a
   Louisville Town in ONEIDA County,
   population of 13.

LOUISVILLE LANDING, CDP
  Louisville Town
    St. Lawrence County

1880	40

LOWELL, CDP
  Westmoreland Town
    Oneida County

1870	171

LOWER EBENEZER, CDP
  West Seneca Town
    Erie County

1880	287

LOWER JAY, CDP
  Jay Town
    Essex County

1880	381

LOWER NEW YORK MILLS, CDP
  Whitestown Town
    Oneida County

1880	373

LOWVILLE, CDP
  Manlius Town
    Onondaga County

1880	84

LOWVILLE, Town (Est. 1800)
  Lewis County

1980	4,575
1970	4,754
1960	4,635
1950	4,623
1940	4,586
1930	4,336
1920	3,915
1910	3,875
1900	3,746
1890	3,624
1880	3,188
1870	2,805
1860	2,373
1850	2,377
1840	2,047
1830	2,334
1820	1,943
1810	NA
1800	*300(a)

(a)Reported in ONEIDA County.

LOWVILLE, Village (Inc. 1871)
  Lowville Town
    Lewis County
      1980   3,364
      1970   3,671
      1960   3,616(a)
      1950   3,671(a)
      1940   3,578
      1930   3,424
      1920   3,127
      1910   2,940
      1900   2,352
      1890   2,511
(a)Boundary change.

LUDLOWVILLE, CDP
  Lansing Town
    Tompkins Town
      1880   262
      1870   376

LUMBERLAND, Town (Est. 1798)
    Sullivan County
      1980   1,210
      1970   857
      1960   538
      1950   494
      1940   490
      1930   499
      1920   480
      1910   716
      1900   809
      1890   875
      1880   1,050
      1870   1,065
      1860   970
      1850   2,635
      1840   1,205
      1830   953
      1820   569
      1810   NA
      1800   *733(a)
(a)Reported in ULSTER County.

LUMBERVILLE, CDP
  Middletown Town
    Delaware County
      1880   66

LUZERNE, CDP
  Lake Luzerne Town
    Warren County
      1880   488

LUZERNE, Town
  see LAKE LUZERNE, Town
        Warren County

LYME, Town (Est. 1818)
    Jefferson County
      1980   1,695
      1970   1,550
      1960   1,448
      1950   1,458
      1940   1,462
      1930   1,585
      1920   1,642
      1910   1,955
      1900   2,200

      1890   2,175
      1880   2,277
      1870   2,465
      1860   2,702
      1850   2,919
      1840   5,472
      1830   2,873
      1820   1,724

LYNBROOK, Village (Inc. 1911)
  Hempstead Town
    Nassau County
      1980   20,424 Rev.
      1970   23,151 Rev.
      1960   19,881
      1950   17,314
      1940   14,557(a)
      1930   11,993(a)
      1920   4,371
(a)Boundary change.

LYNCOURT, CDP
  De Witt & Salina Towns
    Onondaga County
      1980   5,129

LYNDON, Town (Est. 1829)(a)
    Cattaraugus County
      1980   610
      1970   339
      1960   406
      1950   409
      1940   391
      1930   463
      1920   587
      1910   603
      1900   690
      1890   677
      1880   831
      1870   894
      1860   1,161(b)
      1850   1,090
      1840   628
      1830   271
(a)Name changed to Elgin in 1857; original name restored in 1858.
(b)Reported as Linden.

LYNDONVILLE, Village (Inc. 1903)
  Yates Town
    Orleans County
      1980   916(a)
      1970   888(a)
      1960   755
      1950   777
      1940   745
      1930   708
      1920   738
      1910   647
      1890-1900   NA
      1880   419
      1870   400
(a)Boundary change.

LYNELLE MEADOWS, CDP
  see BAYBERRY--LYNELLE MEADOWS, CDP
        Onondaga County

LYON MOUNTAIN, CDP
  Dannemora Town
    Clinton County

1950	1,053
1940	1,091

LYONS, Town (Est. 1811)
  Wayne County

1980	6,073
1970	6,015
1960	6,147
1950	5,379
1940	5,076
1930	5,072
1920	5,559
1910	5,913
1900	5,824
1890	6,228
1880	5,762
1870	5,115
1860	5,076
1850	4,925
1840	4,302
1830	3,608
1820	3,972(a)

(a)Reported in ONTARIO County.

LYONS, Village (Inc. 1831)
  Lyons Town
    Wayne County

1980	4,160(a)
1970	4,496(a)
1960	4,673
1950	4,217
1940	3,863
1930	3,956
1920	4,253
1910	4,460
1900	4,300
1890	4,475
1880	3,820
1870	3,350

(a)Boundary change.

LYONSDALE, Town (Est. 1873)
  Lewis County

1980	1,135
1970	1,013
1960	942
1950	873
1940	909
1930	762
1920	918
1910	1,007
1900	1,371
1890	1,451
1880	1,475

LYONS FALLS, Village (Inc. 1899)
  Lyonsdale Town, part in
    Lewis County

1980	84
1970	101
1960	71
1950	70
1940	47
1930	43(a)
1920	32
1910	37

1900	3

West Turin Town, part in
  Lewis County

1980	671
1970	751
1960	816
1950	794
1940	771
1930	839(a)
1920	786
1910	722
1900	467

TOTAL

1980	755
1970	852
1960	887
1950	864
1940	818
1930	882(a)
1920	818
1910	759
1900	470

(a)Boundary change.

LYSANDER, CDP
  Lysander Town
    Onondaga County

1880	240
1870	268

LYSANDER, Town (Est. 1794)
  Onondaga County

1980	13,897
1970	11,968
1960	10,225
1950	6,798
1940	5,207
1930	4,849
1920	4,725
1910	4,509
1900	4,838
1890	5,163
1880	4,903
1870	4,944
1860	4,741
1850	5,833
1840	4,306
1830	3,228
1820	1,723
1810	NA
1800	*121

M

MACEDON, Town (Est. 1823)
  Wayne County

1980	6,508
1970	5,488
1960	3,617

1950	2,560
1940	2,277
1930	2,330
1920	2,202
1910	2,355
1900	2,488
1890	2,564
1880	2,871
1870	2,636
1860	2,523
1850	2,384
1840	2,396
1830	1,989

MACEDON, Village (Inc. 1857)
  Macedon Town
    Wayne County

1980	1,400(a)
1970	1,168(a)
1960	645
1950	614
1940	557
1930	566
1920	526
1910	536
1900	592
1890	533
1880	538
1870	451

(a)Boundary change.

MACEDON CENTER, CDP
  Macedon Town
    Wayne County

1880	158

MACHIAS, CDP(a)
  Machias Town
    Cattaraugus County

1880	333

(a)Reported, in part, in LIME LAKE--
    MACHIAS, CDP in 1980.

MACHIAS, Town (Est. 1827)
  Cattaraugus County

1980	2,058
1970	1,749
1960	1,390
1950	1,341
1940	1,362
1930	1,255
1920	1,431
1910	1,529
1900	1,557
1890	1,536
1880	1,545
1870	1,170
1860	1,161
1850	1,342
1840	1,085
1830	735

MACOMB, Town (Est. 1841)
  St. Lawrence County

1980	816
1970	813
1960	881

1950	848
1940	891
1930	953
1920	1,055
1910	1,168
1900	1,374
1890	1,415
1880	1,731
1870	1,673
1860	1,816
1850	1,197

MADALIN, CDP
  Red Hook Town
    Dutchess County

1870	629

MADISON, County (Est. 1806)

1980	65,150
1970	62,864
1960	54,635
1950	46,214
1940	39,598
1930	39,790
1920	39,535
1910	39,289
1900	40,545
1890	42,892
1880	44,112
1870	43,522
1860	43,545
1850	43,072
1840	40,008
1830	39,038
1820	32,208
1810	25,144

MADISON, Town (Est. 1807)
  Madison County

1980	2,314
1970	2,221
1960	1,915
1950	1,615
1940	1,592
1930	1,515
1920	1,629
1910	1,926
1900	2,024
1890	2,316
1880	2,474
1870	2,402
1860	2,457
1850	2,405
1840	2,344
1830	2,544
1820	2,420

MADISON, Village (Inc. 1816)
  Madison Town
    Madison County

1980	396
1970	386
1960	327
1950	335
1940	300
1930	287
1920	265
1910	309
1900	321

1890	390
1880	320

MADRID, CDP
  Madrid Town
    St. Lawrence County

1940	504
1890-1930	NA
1880	761
1870	670

MADRID, Town (Est. 1802)
  St. Lawrence County

1980	1,852
1970	1,635
1960	1,623
1950	1,551
1940	1,383
1930	1,388
1920	1,390
1910	1,457
1900	1,668
1890	1,969
1880	2,145
1870	2,071
1860	1,978
1850	4,846
1840	4,511
1830	3,469
1820	1,930
1810	NA
1800	*13(a)

(a)Reported in ONEIDA County.

MAHOPAC, CDP
  Carmel Town
    Putnam County

1980	7,681
1970	5,265
1960	1,337
1950	NA
1940	1,109

MAINE, CDP
  Maine Town
    Broome County

1880	331
1870	303

MAINE, Town (Est.1848)
  Broome County

1980	5,262
1970	5,842
1960	3,931
1950	2,315
1940	2,076
1930	1,628
1920	1,360
1910	1,363
1900	1,534
1890	1,692
1880	2,129
1870	2,035
1860	1,609
1850	1,843

MALDEN, CDP
  Chatham Town
    Columbia County

1880	244

MALONE, Town (Est. 1805)(a)
  Franklin County

1980	11,276
1970	11,400
1960	11,997
1950	12,644
1940	11,987
1930	11,798
1920	10,830
1910	10,154
1900	10,009
1890	8,991
1880	7,909
1870	7,186
1860	6,466
1850	4,550
1840	3,229
1830	2,207
1820	1,130

(a)Established as Harrison in 1805; name
changed to Ezraville in 1808 and to
MALONE in 1812.

MALONE, Village (Inc. 1833)
  Malone Town
    Franklin County

1980	7,668
1970	8,048
1960	8,737(a)
1950	9,501
1940	8,743
1930	8,657
1920	7,556
1910	6,467
1900	5,935
1890	4,986
1880	7,909
1870	4,193

(a)Boundary change.

MALOREYVILLE, CDP
  Dryden Town
    Tompkins County

1880	61

MALTA, Town
  Jefferson County
  see LORRAINE, Town
      Jefferson County

MALTA, Town (Est. 1802)
  Saratoga County

1980	6,968(a)
1970	3,813
1960	2,223
1950	1,882
1940	1,354
1930	1,277
1920	1,152
1910	1,285
1900	1,322
1890	1,285
1880	1,234
1870	1,212

1860	1,240
1850	1,349
1840	1,457
1830	1,517
1820	1,518

(a)Boundary change.

MALVERNE, Unincorporated
Hempstead Town
  Nassau County

1980	1,183(a)
1970	829(a)
1960	1,317(a)

(a)Derived by LIRPB from U.S. Census
  Data.

MALVERNE, Village (Inc. 1921)
Hempstead Town
  Nassau County

1980	9,262
1970	10,036
1960	9,968(a)
1950	8,086
1940	5,153
1930	2,256

(a)Boundary change.

MAMAKATING, Town (Est. 1788)
  Sullivan County

1980	7,717
1970	4,319
1960	3,356
1950	2,632
1940	2,407
1930	2,277
1920	2,395
1910	2,922
1900	3,128
1890	3,401
1880	3,845
1870	4,866
1860	3,828
1850	4,107
1840	3,418
1830	3,070
1820	2,702
1810	NA
1800	*1,631(a)
1790	1,728(b)

(a)Reported in ULSTER County.
(b)Reported as Mama-cating in ULSTER
  County.

MAMARONECK, Town (Est. 1788)
  Westchester County

1980	29,017
1970	31,243
1960	29,107
1950	25,103
1940	22,260
1930	19,040
1920	7,801
1910	5,602
1900	3,849
1890	2,385
1880	1,863
1870	1,483
1860	1,351
1850	928

1840	1,416
1830	838
1820	878
1810	NA
1800	*503
1790	452

MAMARONECK, Village (Inc. 1895)
Mamaroneck Town, part in
  Westchester County

1980	10,281
1970	11,038
1960	10,555(a)
1950	8,851
1940	7,822
1930	7,110
1920	3,536
1910	3,414

Rye Town, part in
  Westchester County

1980	7,335
1970	7,871
1960	7,118(a)
1950	6,165
1940	5,212
1930	4,656
1920	3,035
1910	2,285
1900	1,818

TOTAL

1980	17,616
1970	18,909
1960	17,673(a)
1950	15,016
1940	13,034
1930	11,766
1920	6,571
1910	5,699
1900	(b)

(a)Boundary change.
(b)Reported in RYE Town only.

MANCHESTER, CDP
Kirkland Town
  Oneida County

1870	158

MANCHESTER, Town (Est. 1821)(a)
  Ontario County

1980	9,002
1970	7,840
1960	6,242
1950	5,755
1940	5,252
1930	5,882
1920	5,567
1910	4,889
1900	4,733
1890	4,439
1880	3,920
1870	3,546
1860	3,280
1850	2,940
1840	2,912
1830	2,811

(a)Established as Burt in 1821; name
  changed in 1822.

MANCHESTER, Village (Inc. 1892)
  Manchester Town
    Ontario County
```
        1980        1,698(a)
        1970        1,305
        1960        1,344
        1950        1,262
        1940        1,330
        1930        1,429
        1920        1,418
        1910          881
        1900          711
        1890           NA
        1880          320
```
(a)Boundary change.

MANDANA, CDP
  Skaneateles Town
    Onondaga County
```
        1880           91
```

MANHASSET, CDP
  North Hempstead Town
    Nassau County
```
        1980        8,485
        1970        8,541
        1960        8,914(a)
        1950           NA
        1940        5,099
        1890-1930      NA
        1880          507(b)
```
(a)Derived by LIRPB from U.S. Census
   Data.
(b)Reported in QUEENS County.

MANHATTAN, Borough
  see NEW YORK City, MANHATTAN Borough

MANHEIM, Town (Est. 1817)(a)
  Herkimer County
```
        1980        3,634
        1970        3,752
        1960        3,872
        1950        3,897
        1940        3,748
        1930        3,831
        1920        3,886
        1910        3,355
        1900        2,648
        1890        2,078
        1880        2,421
        1870        2,000
        1860        1,868
        1850        1,902
        1840        2,095
        1830        1,937
        1820        1,777
```
(a)In 1800 the Census Bureau reported a
   Manheim Town in HERKIMER County,
   population of 1,037.

MANLIUS, Town (Est. 1794)
  Onondaga County
```
        1980       28,489
        1970       26,071
        1960       19,351
        1950       10,221
        1940        7,845
        1930        7,620
```

```
        1920        6,509
        1910        6,016
        1900        5,374
        1890        5,453
        1880        5,954
        1870        5,833
        1860        6,028
        1850        6,298
        1840        5,509
        1830        7,375
        1820        5,372
        1810           NA
        1800         *989
```

MANLIUS, Village (Inc. 1842)
  Manlius Town
    Onondaga County
```
        1980        5,241(a)
        1970        4,295(a)
        1960        1,997
        1950        1,742
        1940        1,520
        1930        1,538
        1920        1,296
        1910        1,314
        1900        1,219
        1890          942
        1880          834
        1870          879
```
(a)Boundary change.

MANLIUS CENTER
  Manlius Town
    Onondaga County
```
        1870          100
```

MANLIUS STATION
  Manlius Town
    Onondaga County
```
        1870          200
```

MANNSVILLE, Village (Inc. 1879)
  Ellisburg Town
    Jefferson County
```
        1980          431
        1970          494
        1960          446
        1950          378
        1940          348
        1930          313
        1920          265
        1910          330
        1900          352
        1890          389
        1880          473
```

MANORHAVEN, Village (Inc. 1930)
  North Hempstead Town
    Nassau County
```
        1980        5,384
        1970        5,488 Rev.
        1960        3,566
        1950        1,819
        1940          484(a)
```
(a)Boundary change.

MANORVILLE, CDP
    Brookhaven Town
        Suffolk County
            1980   6,548(a)
            1970   3,272(b)
            1960   2,371(c)
            1890-1950   NA
            1880   318
(a)Boundary change; derived by LIRPB
    from U.S. Census Data.
(b)Derived by LIRPB from U.S. Census
    Data; population of 1,602 is
    comparable to 1980 boundaries.
(c)Derived by LIRPB from U.S. Census
    Data.

MANSFIELD, Town (Est. 1830)(a)
    Cattaraugus County
            1980   784
            1970   605
            1960   632
            1950   672
            1940   620
            1930   661
            1920   717
            1910   912
            1900   968
            1890   1,022
            1880   1,126
            1870   1,135
            1860   1,265
            1850   1,057
            1840   942
            1830   378
(a)Established as Cecilius in 1830; name
    changed in 1831.

MAPLE TOWN, CDP
    Canajoharie Town
        Montgomery County
            1880   81

MAPLEWOOD, CDP
    Colonie Town
        Albany County
            1940   1,528

MARATHON, Town (Est. 1818)(a)
    Cortland County
            1980   1,804
            1970   1,777
            1960   1,696
            1950   1,577
            1940   1,417
            1930   1,322
            1920   1,296
            1910   1,589
            1900   1,664
            1890   1,806
            1880   1,700
            1870   1,611
            1860   1,502
            1850   1,149
            1840   1,063
            1830   895
            1820   807
(a)Established as Harrison in 1818; name
    changed in 1827.

MARATHON, Village (Inc. 1861)
    Marathon Town
        Cortland County
            1980   1,046
            1970   1,053
            1960   1,079
            1950   1,057
            1940   955
            1930   860
            1920   800
            1910   1,079
            1900   1,092
            1890   1,198
            1880   1,006
            1870   871

MARBLETOWN, Town (Est. 1788)
    Ulster County
            1980   4,956
            1970   4,146
            1960   3,191
            1950   2,364
            1940   2,543
            1930   2,276
            1920   2,017
            1910   4,713
            1900   3,511
            1890   3,639
            1880   3,970
            1870   4,223
            1860   4,120
            1850   3,836
            1840   3,813
            1830   3,223
            1820   3,809
            1810   NA
            1800   *2,847(a)
            1790   2,190
(a)Reported as Marble Town.

MARCELLUS, Town (Est. 1794)
    Onondaga County
            1980   6,180
            1970   5,744
            1960   4,527
            1950   3,607
            1940   3,046
            1930   2,993
            1920   2,854
            1910   2,826
            1900   2,581
            1890   2,739
            1880   2,678
            1870   2,337
            1860   2,908
            1850   2,759
            1840   2,726
            1830   2,626
            1820   6,503
            1810   NA
            1800   *909

MARCELLUS, Village (Inc. 1846)
    Marcellus Town
        Onondaga County
            1980   1,870(a)
            1970   2,017(a)
            1960   1,697
            1950   1,382

1940	1,112
1930	1,083
1920	989
1910	917
1900	589
1890	563
1880	480
1870	428

(a)Boundary change.

MARCY, Town (Est. 1832)
Oneida County

1980	6,456
1970	7,877 Rev.
1960	7,024
1950	5,210
1940	4,528
1930	2,604
1920	1,191
1910	1,301
1900	1,398
1890	1,213
1880	1,413
1870	1,451
1860	1,687
1850	1,857
1840	1,799

MARENGO, CDP
Galen Town
Wayne County

1880	82

MARGARETVILLE, Village (Inc. 1875)
Middletown Town
Delaware County

1980	755
1970	816
1960	833
1950	905
1940	812
1930	771
1920	650
1910	669
1900	640
1890	616
1880	418

MARIAVILLE, CDP
Duanesburg Town
Schenectady County

1880	116

MARIETTA, CDP
Marcellus Town
Onondaga County

1880	147

MARILLA, CDP
Marilla Town
Erie County

1870	250

MARILLA, Town (Est. 1853)
Erie County

1980	4,861
1970	3,250
1960	2,252

1950	1,482
1940	1,364
1930	1,282
1920	1,237
1910	1,382
1900	1,441
1890	1,599
1880	1,825
1870	1,804
1860	1,596

MARINER'S HARBOR, CDP
Northfield Town
Richmond County

1880	434

MARION, CDP
Marion Town
Wayne County

1980	1,080
1950-1970	NA
1940	771
1890-1930	NA
1880	412
1870	432

MARION, Town (Est. 1825)(a)
Wayne County

1980	4,456
1970	3,784
1960	2,785
1950	2,412
1940	2,240
1930	2,172
1920	2,158
1910	2,102
1900	2,015
1890	2,144
1880	2,100
1870	1,967
1860	2,033
1850	1,839
1840	1,903
1830	1,967

(a)Established as Winchester in 1825;
name changed in 1826.

MARLBORO, CDP
Marlborough Town
Ulster County

1980	2,275
1970	1,580
1960	1,733
1950	1,709
1940	1,863(a)
1920-1930	NA
1910	920(a)

(a)Reported as Marlborough.

MARLBOROUGH, Town (Est. 1788)
Ulster County

1980	7,055
1970	5,657
1960	4,863
1950	4,003
1940	3,794
1930	3,627

1920	3,274
1910	3,841
1900	3,978(a)
1890	3,598(a)
1880	3,472
1870	2,975
1860	2,776
1850	2,406
1840	2,523
1830	2,273
1820	2,248
1810	NA
1800	*1,656
1790	2,241(b)

(a)Reported as Marlboro.
(b)Reported as New Marlboro.

MARSHALL, Town (Est. 1829)
    Oneida County

1980	2,131
1970	2,072
1960	1,902
1950	1,616
1940	1,541
1930	1,431
1920	1,490
1910	1,744
1900	1,804
1890	2,145
1880	2,276
1870	2,145
1860	2,134
1850	2,115
1840	2,251
1830	1,908

MARTINDALE, CDP
    Claverack Town
    Columbia County

| 1880 | 50 |

MARTINSBURG, CDP
    Martinsburg Town
    Lewis County

| 1880 | 285 |

MARTINSBURG, Town (Est. 1803)
    Lewis County

1980	1,494
1970	1,516
1960	1,469
1950	1,387
1940	1,363
1930	1,860
1920	1,566
1910	1,546
1900	1,845
1890	1,982
1880	2,386(a)
1870	2,282
1860	2,855
1850	2,677
1840	2,272
1830	2,382
1820	1,497

(a)Reported as Martinsburgh.

MARTVILLE, CDP
    Sterling Town
    Cayuga County

| 1880 | 38 |
| 1870 | 126 |

MARYLAND, Town (Est. 1808)
    Otsego County

1980	1,690
1970	1,465
1960	1,386
1950	1,556
1940	1,460
1930	1,530
1920	1,529
1910	1,852
1900	1,998
1890	2,199
1880	2,324
1870	2,402
1860	2,228
1850	2,152
1840	2,085
1830	1,834
1820	1,439

MASENA, Town
    Oneida County
    see MASSENA, Town
        St. Lawrence County

MASONVILLE, CDP
    Masonville Town
    Delaware County

| 1880 | 255 |

MASONVILLE, Town (Est. 1811)
    Delaware County

1980	1,156
1970	1,140
1960	1,030
1950	1,010
1940	931
1930	854
1920	878
1910	1,053
1900	1,245
1890	1,397
1880	1,673
1870	1,738
1860	1,684
1850	1,550
1840	1,420
1830	1,145
1820	719

MASSAPEQUA, CDP
    Oyster Bay Town
    Nassau County

1980	24,454
1970	26,821(a)
1960	32,900(b)
1950	NA
1940	2,676

(a)Boundary change.
(b)Included part of NORTH MASSAPEQUA;
    population of 21,405 is comparable
    to 1970 boundaries.

MASSAPEQUA PARK, Village (Inc. 1931)
  Oyster Bay Town
    Nassau County
        1980   19,779
        1970   22,112
        1960   19,904
        1950   2,334
        1940   488

MASSENA, Town (Est. 1802)(a)
  St. Lawrence County
        1980   14,856
        1970   16,021
        1960   17,730
        1950   14,862
        1940   12,979
        1930   12,029
        1920   8,975
        1910   4,806
        1900   3,904
        1890   2,740
        1880   2,739
        1870   2,560
        1860   2,925
        1850   2,870
        1840   2,726
        1830   2,068
        1820   944
(a)In 1800 the Census Bureau reported a
   Masena Town in ONEIDA County,
   population of 102.

MASSENA, Village (Inc. 1886)
  Louisville Town, part in
    St. Lawrence County
        1980   217(a)
        1970   160
        1960   92(a)
  Massena Town, part in
    St. Lawrence County
        1980   12,634(a)
        1970   13,882
        1960   15,386(a)
        1950   13,137
        1940   11,328
        1930   10,637(a)
        1920   5,993
        1910   2,951
        1900   2,032
        1890   1,049
        1880   NA
        1870   483
    TOTAL
        1980   12,851(a)
        1970   14,042
        1960   15,478(a)
      1870-1950   (b)
(a)Boundary change.
(b)Reported in MASSENA Town only.

MASTIC, CDP
  Brookhaven Town
    Suffolk County
        1980   10,413(a)
        1970   4,676(b)
        1960   2,931

      1890-1950   NA
        1880   63
(a)Boundary change.
(b)Boundary change; derived by LIRPB
   from U.S. Census Data; population of
   4,118 is comparable to 1980
   boundaries.

MASTIC BEACH, CDP
  Brookhaven Town
    Suffolk County
        1980   8,318
        1970   4,870
        1960   3,035
        1950   1,079

MASTIC--SHIRLEY, CDP(a)
  Brookhaven Town
    Suffolk County
        1960   3,397
(a)Included in MASTIC and SHIRLEY, CDPs
   in 1970-1980.

MATINECOCK, Village (Inc. 1928)
  Oyster Bay Town
    Nassau County
        1980   985
        1970   841
        1960   824
        1950   507
        1940   428
        1930   484

MATTEAWAN, Village (Inc. 1886)(a)
  Fishkill Town
    Dutchess County
        1910   6,727
        1900   5,807
        1890   4,278
        1880   4,411
(a)FISHKILL LANDING and MATTEAWAN
   Villages consolidated and incorporated
   as BEACON City and made independent of
   FISHKILL Town in 1913.

MATTITUCK, CDP
  Southold Town
    Suffolk County
        1980   3,923(a)
        1970   1,995(b)
        1960   1,485 Rev.
        1950   1,089
        1940   1,578
      1890-1930   NA
        1880   843
(a)Boundary change.
(b)Population of 3,039 is comparable to
   1980 boundaries.

MATTYDALE, CDP
  Salina Town
    Onondaga County
        1980   7,511
        1970   8,292

MAYBROOK, Village (Inc. 1925)
  Hamptonburgh Town, part in
    Orange County
        1980   13

1970	36
1960	18

Montgomery Town, part in
Orange County

1980	1,994
1970	1,500(a)
1960	1,330
1950	1,316
1940	1,189
1930	1,159

TOTAL

1980	2,007
1970	1,536(a)
1960	1,348
1930-1950	(b)

(a)Boundary change.
(b)Reported in MONTGOMERY Town only.

MAYFIELD, Town (Est. 1793)
Fulton County

1980	5,439
1970	4,522
1960	3,613
1950	3,145
1940	2,734
1930	2,077
1920	1,866
1910	2,065
1900	2,136
1890	2,181
1880	2,231
1870	2,241
1860	2,367
1850	2,429
1840	2,615
1830	2,609(a)
1820	2,025(a)
1810	NA(a)
1800	*876(b)

(a)Reported in MONTGOMERY County.
(b)Reported as Wayfield in MONTGOMERY
   County.

MAYFIELD, Village (Inc. 1896)
Mayfield Town
Fulton County

1980	944
1970	981
1960	818
1950	761
1940	759
1930	722
1920	592
1910	590
1900	589
1890	NA
1880	219

MAYVILLE, Village (Inc. 1830)
Chautauqua Town
Chautauqua County

1980	1,626
1970	1,567
1960	1,619(a)
1950	1,492
1940	1,354
1930	1,273
1920	1,207

1910	1,122
1900	943
1890	1,164
1880	1,051(b)
1870	701

(a)Boundary change.
(b)Estimated.

MAYWOOD, CDP
Colonie Town
Albany County

1940	1,226

McCONNELLSVILLE, CDP
Vienna Town
Oneida County

1870	118

McDONOUGH, CDP
McDonough Town
Chenango County

1880	284
1870	256

McDONOUGH, Town (Est. 1816)
Chenango County

1980	796
1970	703
1960	639
1950	709
1940	675
1930	598
1920	765
1910	813
1900	907
1890	1,025
1880	1,298
1870	1,280
1860	1,483
1850	1,522
1840	1,369
1830	1,232
1820	789

McGRAW, Village (Inc. 1869)
Cortlandville Town
Cortland County

1980	1,188
1970	1,319
1960	1,276
1950	1,197
1940	1,201
1930	1,082
1920	1,032
1910	931(a)
1890	750(a)
1880	733(a)
1870	517(a)

(a)Reported as McGrawville.

McKOWNVILLE, CDP
Guilderland Town
Albany County

1940	873

McLEAN, CDP
Groton Town
Tompkins County

1880	320

MECHANICVILLE, City (Inc. 1915)(a)
Saratoga County

1980	5,500
1970	6,247
1960	6,831
1950	7,385
1940	7,449
1930	7,924
1920	8,166

(a)MECHANICVILLE Village incorporated as
   MECHANICVILLE City and made independent of HALFMOON and STILLWATER Towns
   in 1915.

MECHANICVILLE, Village (Inc. 1859)(a)
Halfmoon Town, part in
   Saratoga County

1910	4,238
1900	3,195
1890	1,890
1880	750(b)
1870	581(b)

Stillwater Town, part in
   Saratoga County

1910	3,396
1900	1,500
1890	789
1880	515(b)
1870	494(b)

TOTAL

1910	7,634
1900	4,695
1890	2,679
1880	1,265(b)
1870	1,075(b)

(a)MECHANICVILLE Village incorporated as
   MECHANICVILLE City and made independent of HALFMOON and STILLWATER Towns
   in 1915.
(b)Reported as Mechanicsville.

MECKLENBURG, CDP
Hector Town
   Schuyler County

1880	260

MEDFORD, CDP
Brookhaven Town
   Suffolk County

1980	20,418(a)
1970	10,235(b)
1950-1960	NA
1940	806
1890-1930	NA
1880	7

(a)Boundary change.
(b)Derived by LIRPB from U.S. Census
   Data; population is comparable to
   1980 boundaries.

MEDINA, Village (Inc. 1832)
Ridgeway Town, part in
   Orleans County

1980	3,766(a)
1970	3,831
1960	4,010(a)
1950	3,798
1940	3,555
1930	3,760

1920	3,822
1910	3,741
1900	3,145
1890	2,888
1880	2,370
1870	1,968

Shelby Town, part in
Orleans County

1980	2,626(a)
1970	2,584
1960	2,671(a)
1950	2,381
1940	2,316
1930	2,311
1920	2,189
1910	1,942
1900	1,571
1890	1,604
1880	1,262
1870	853

TOTAL

1980	6,392(a)
1970	6,415
1960	6,681(a)
1950	6,179
1940	5,871
1930	4,627
1920	6,011
1910	5,683
1900	4,716
1890	4,492
1880	3,632
1870	2,821

(a)Boundary change.

MEDUSA, CDP
Rensselaerville Town
   Albany County

1880	141
1870	94

MELLENVILLE, CDP
Claverack Town
   Columbia County

1880	360

MELROSE PARK, CDP
Owasco Town
   Cayuga County

1980	2,171
1970	2,189
1960	2,058
1950	1,497
1940	998

MELVILLE, CDP
Huntington Town
   Suffolk County

1980	8,139(a)
1970	6,641(b)
1960	5,400(c)

(a)Boundary change.
(b)Population of 6,756 is comparable to
   1980 boundaries.
(c)Derived by LIRPB from U.S. Census
   Data.

MEMPHIS, CDP
   Van Buren Town
      Onondaga County
         1880   152

MENANDS, Village (Inc. 1924)
   Colonie Town
      Albany County
         1980   4,012
         1970   3,449(a)
         1960   2,314(a)
         1950   2,453
         1940   1,764
         1930   1,522
(a)Boundary change.

MENDON, Town (Est. 1812)
   Monroe County
         1980   5,434
         1970   4,541
         1960   3,902
         1950   2,903
         1940   2,700
         1930   2,636
         1920   2,509
         1910   2,754
         1900   2,760
         1890   2,991
         1880   3,193
         1870   2,900
         1860   2,936
         1850   3,353
         1840   3,435
         1830   3,029
         1820   2,012(a)
(a)Reported in ONTARIO County.

MENDON CENTER, CDP
   Mendon Town
      Monroe County
         1880   80(a)
(a)Reported as Mendon Centre.

MENTZ, Town (Est. 1802)(a)
   Cayuga County
         1980   2,441
         1970   2,338
         1960   2,105
         1950   1,783
         1940   1,677
         1930   1,553
         1920   1,758
         1910   1,909
         1900   1,914
         1890   1,952
         1880   2,288
         1870   2,278
         1860   2,232
         1850   5,239
         1840   4,215
         1830   4,143
         1820   3,010
(a)Established as Jefferson in 1802;
   name changed in 1808.

MERCHANTVILLE, CDP
   Thurston Town
      Steuben County
         1880   131

MEREDITH, CDP
   Meredith Town
      Delaware County
         1880   73

MEREDITH, Town (Est. 1800)
   Delaware County
         1980   1,374
         1970   1,129
         1960   1,112
         1950   1,133
         1940   1,182
         1930   1,295
         1920   1,394
         1910   1,393
         1900   1,508
         1890   1,555
         1880   1,563
         1870   1,462
         1860   1,630
         1850   1,634
         1840   1,640
         1830   1,666
         1820   1,375
         1810   NA
         1800   *213

MEREDITH HOLLOW, CDP
   Meredith Town
      Delaware County
         1880   86

MERIDIAN, Village (Inc. 1854)
   Cato Town
      Cayuga County
         1980   344
         1970   369
         1960   379
         1950   334
         1940   307
         1930   264
         1920   274
         1910   326
         1900   335
         1880-1890   NA
         1870   249

MERRICK, CDP
   Hempstead Town
      Nassau County
         1980   24,478
         1970   25,904
         1960   18,789
         1950   NA
         1940   2,935

MERRIEWOLD LAKE, CDP
   Blooming Grove Town
      Orange County
         1980   3,661
         1970   2,564

MEXICO, Town (Est. 1792)
   Oswego County
         1980   4,790
         1970   4,174
         1960   3,435
         1950   3,035
         1940   2,710

1930	2,720
1920	2,824
1910	2,982
1900	3,091
1890	3,404
1880	3,687
1870	3,802
1860	4,074
1850	4,221
1840	3,729
1830	2,681
1820	1,590
1810	NA
1800	*241(a)

(a)Reported in ONEIDA county.

MEXICO, Village (Inc. 1851)
  Mexico Town
    Oswego County

1980	1,621
1970	1,555
1960	1,465
1950	1,398
1940	1,348
1930	1,297
1920	1,336
1910	1,233
1900	1,249
1890	1,315
1880	1,273
1870	1,204

MIDDLE, CDP
  Springfield Town
    Otsego County

1880	64

MIDDLE BRUSH, CDP
  Wappinger Town
    Dutchess County

1880	61

MIDDLEBURG, Town
    Genesee County
  see MIDDLEBURY, Town
    Wyoming County

MIDDLEBURG, Town (Est. 1797)(a)
    Schoharie County

1980	2,980(b)
1970	2,486
1960	2,437
1950	2,460
1940	2,113
1930	1,927
1920	2,109
1910	2,553
1900	2,738
1890	3,007
1880	3,376
1870	3,180(b)
1860	3,259
1850	2,967(b)
1840	3,843
1830	3,278(b)
1820	3,782(b)
1810	NA
1800	*1,834

(a)Established as Middletown in 1797;

name changed in 1801.
(b)Reported as Middleburgh.

MIDDLEBURG, Village (Inc. 1881)
  Middleburg Town
    Schoharie County

1980	1,358(a)
1970	1,410
1960	1,317
1950	1,298
1940	1,074
1930	948
1920	986
1910	1,114
1900	1,135
1890	1,139
1880	1,123
1870	863(b)

(a)Boundary change. Reported as
  Middleburgh.
(b)Reported as Middleburgh.

MIDDLEBURY, Town (Est. 1812)
    Wyoming County

1980	1,561
1970	1,503
1960	1,416
1950	1,248
1940	1,123
1930	1,091
1920	1,204
1910	1,395
1900	1,406
1890	1,781
1880	1,822
1870	1,620
1860	1,708
1850	1,799
1840	2,445(a)
1830	2,416(a)
1820	1,782(b)

(a)Reported in GENESEE County.
(b)Reported as Middleburg in GENESEE
  County.

MIDDLEFIELD, Town (Est. 1797)
    Otsego County

1980	1,870
1970	1,457
1960	1,376
1950	1,481
1940	1,592
1930	1,504
1920	1,547
1910	1,949
1900	2,100
1890	2,200
1880	2,726
1870	2,868
1860	2,825
1850	3,131
1840	3,319
1830	3,323
1820	2,579
1810	NA
1800	*1,044

MIDDLEFIELD CENTER, CDP
Middlefield Town
  Otsego County
    1880   89

MIDDLE GRANVILLE, CDP
Granville Town
  Washington County
    1940   869

MIDDLE GROVE, CDP
Greenfield Town
  Saratoga County
    1880   144

MIDDLEHOPE, CDP
Newburgh Town
  Orange County
    1980   3,229(a)
    1970   2,327
    1950-1960 NA
    1940   598
(a)Reported as Middle Hope.

MIDDLE ISLAND, CDP(a)
Brookhaven Town
  Suffolk County
    1980   5,703(a)
    1970   2,620(b)
    1890-1960 NA
    1880   283
(a)Boundary change.
(b)Reported, in part, in MIDDLE ISLAND--
  RIDGE in 1960. Derived by LIRPB from
  U.S. Census Data.

MIDDLE ISLAND--RIDGE, CDP(a)
Brookhaven Town
  Suffolk County
    1970   4,433(b)
    1960   2,788(b)
(a)Included in MIDDLE ISLAND and RIDGE,
  CDPs in 1980.
(b)Derived by LIRPB from U.S. Census
  Data.

MIDDLEPORT, Village (Inc. 1859)
Hartland Town, part in
  Niagara County
    1980   163
    1970   383(a)
    1960   142(a)
    1950   125
    1940   129
    1930   120
    1920   134
    1910   121
    1900   141
Royalton Town, part in
  Niagara County
    1980   1,832
    1970   1,749(a)
    1960   1,740(a)
    1950   1,516
    1940   1,446
    1930   1,476
    1920   1,282
    1910   1,409
    1900   1,290

TOTAL
    1980   1,995
    1970   2,132(a)
    1960   1,882(a)
    1950   1,631
    1940   1,575
    1930   1,596
    1920   1,416
    1910   1,530
    1900   1,431
    1890   1,217
    1880   771
    1870   731
(a)Boundary change.

MIDDLE ROAD, CDP
Riverhead Town
  Suffolk County
    1880   106

MIDDLESEX, Town (Est. 1789)(a)
Yates County
    1980   1,127
    1970   925
    1960   817
    1950   765
    1940   764
    1930   839
    1920   951
    1910   1,122
    1900   1,282
    1890   1,387
    1880   1,457
    1870   1,314
    1860   1,303
    1850   1,385
    1840   1,439
    1830   3,428
    1820   2,718(b)
    1810   NA(b)
    1800   *483(b)
(a)Established as Augusta in 1789; name
  changed in 1808.
(b)Reported in ONTARIO County.

MIDDLETOWN, CDP
Halfmoon Town
  Saratoga County
    1880   147

MIDDLETOWN, City (Inc. 1888)(a)
Orange County
    1980   21,454(b)
    1970   22,607(b)
    1960   23,475(b)
    1950   22,586(b)
    1940   21,908(b)
    1930   21,276
    1920   18,420
    1910   15,313
    1900   14,522
    1890   11,971
(a)MIDDLETOWN Village incorporated as
  MIDDLETOWN City and made independent
  of WALLKILL Town in 1888.
(b)Boundary change.

MIDDLETOWN, Town (Est. 1789)
   Delaware County

1980	3,555
1970	3,466
1960	3,310
1950	3,737
1940	3,520
1930	3,532
1920	3,522
1910	3,802
1900	3,619
1890	3,313
1880	2,977
1870	3,035
1860	3,201
1850	3,005
1840	2,608
1830	2,383
1820	1,949
1810	NA
1800	*1,064
1790	1,019(a)

(a)Reported in ULSTER County.

MIDDLETOWN, Town
   Ontario County
  see NAPLES, Town
      Ontario County

MIDDLETOWN, Town (Est. 1860)(a)
   Richmond County

1890	10,557
1880	9,029
1870	7,589

(a)Merged into STATEN ISLAND Borough in
NEW YORK City in 1898.

MIDDLETOWN, Town
   Schoharie County
  see MIDDLEBURG, Town
      Schoharie County

MIDDLETOWN, Town
   Steuben County
  see ADDISON, Town
      Steuben County

MIDDLETOWN, Village (Inc. 1848)(a)
  Wallkill Town
   Orange County

1880	8,494
1870	6,049

(a)MIDDLETOWN Village incorporated as
MIDDLETOWN City and made independent
of WALLKILL Town in 1888.

MIDDLE VILLAGE, CDP
  Newtown Town
   Queens County

1890	503

MIDDLEVILLE, Village (Inc. 1890)
  Fairfield Town, part in
   Herkimer County

1980	454
1970	562
1960	412
1950	431
1940	399

1930	446
1920	442
1910	357
1900	361
1880-1890	NA
1870	152

Newport Town, part in
  Herkimer County

1980	193
1970	163
1960	236
1950	216
1940	213
1930	314
1920	348
1910	268
1900	306
1880-1890	NA
1870	254

TOTAL

1980	647
1970	725
1960	648
1950	647
1940	612
1930	760
1920	790
1910	625
1900	667
1890	NA
1880	533
1870	406

MILAN, Town (Est. 1818)
  Dutchess County

1980	1,668
1970	1,322
1960	944
1950	806
1940	695
1930	622
1920	704
1910	893
1900	950
1890	1,026
1880	1,275
1870	1,474
1860	1,522
1850	1,764
1840	1,725
1830	1,885
1820	1,797

MILFORD, Town (Est. 1796)(a)
  Otsego County

1980	2,685
1970	2,485
1960	2,055
1950	1,913
1940	1,666
1930	1,635
1920	1,616
1910	1,825
1900	2,007
1890	2,051
1880	2,319
1870	2,301
1860	2,210
1850	2,227

1840	2,095
1830	3,025
1820	2,505
1810	NA
1800	*711

(a)Established as Suffrage in 1796; name changed in 1800.

MILFORD, Village (Inc. 1890)
Milford Town
Otsego County

1980	514
1970	527
1960	548
1950	502
1940	460
1930	491
1920	506
1910	511
1900	533
1890	NA
1880	567

MILLBROOK, Village (Inc. 1896)
Washington Town
Dutchess County

1980	1,343
1970	1,735
1960	1,717
1950	1,568
1940	1,340
1930	1,296
1920	1,096
1910	1,136
1900	1,027
1890	693

MILLBURN, CDP
Conklin Town
Broome County

1880	122

MILLER PLACE, CDP
Brookhaven Town
Suffolk County

1980	7,877(a)
1970	4,622(b)
1960	1,744(c)
1890-1950	NA
1880	134(d)

(a)Boundary change.
(b)Derived by LIRPB from U.S. Census Data; population of 4,413 is comparable to 1980 boundaries.
(c)Derived by LIRPB from U.S. Census Data.
(d)Reported as Miller's Place.

MILLER'S CORNERS, CDP
West Bloomfield Town
Ontario County

1880	200

MILLER'S MILLS, CDP
Columbia Town
Herkimer County

1880	166

MILLER'S PLACE, CDP
see MILLER PLACE, CDP
Suffolk County

MILLERTON, Village (Inc. 1875)
Northeast Town
Dutchess County

1980	1,013
1970	1,042
1960	1,027(a)
1950	1,048
1940	953
1930	829
1920	829
1910	858
1900	802
1890	638

(a)Boundary change.

MILLGROVE, CDP
Alden Town
Erie County

1880	58

MILL NECK, Village (Inc. 1925)
Oyster Bay Town
Nassau County

1980	959
1970	982
1960	701
1950	505
1940	101(a)
1930	516

(a)Boundary change.

MILLPORT, Village (Inc. 1923)
Veteran Town
Chemung County

1980	440
1970	480
1960	425
1950	362
1940	340
1930	389
1890-1920	NA
1880	500
1870	741

MILO, Town (Est. 1818)
Yates County

1980	6,732
1970	6,654
1960	6,965
1950	6,576
1940	6,377
1930	6,561
1920	5,817
1910	6,088
1900	6,318
1890	6,028
1880	5,755
1870	4,779
1860	2,028
1850	4,791
1840	3,986
1830	3,610
1820	2,612(a)

(a)Reported in ONTARIO County.

MILO CENTER, CDP
Milo Town
Yates County
1880   120

MILTON, CDP
Milton Town
Saratoga County
1980   2,063
1970   1,861

MILTON, CDP
Marlborough Town
Ulster County
1980   1,253
1950-1970   NA
1940   1,144

MILTON, Town
Cayuga County
see GENOA, Town
Cayuga County

MILTON, Town (Est. 1792)
Saratoga County
1980   12,876
1970   10,450
1960   7,114
1950   6,294
1940   5,768
1930   5,672
1920   5,294
1910   5,724
1900   5,926
1890   5,820
1880   5,565
1870   4,946
1860   5,254
1850   4,220
1840   3,166
1830   3,079
1820   2,796
1810   NA
1800   *2,146

MINA, Town (Est. 1824)
Chautauqua County
1980   1,245
1970   1,129
1960   1,188
1950   1,012
1940   818
1930   944
1920   903
1910   1,033
1900   1,038
1890   1,125
1880   1,102
1870   1,092
1860   1,200
1850   996
1840   871
1830   1,388

MINAVILLE, CDP
Florida Town
Montgomery County
1880   166

MINDEN, Town (Est. 1798)
Montgomery County
1980   4,743
1970   4,691
1960   4,560
1950   4,656
1940   4,376
1930   4,232
1920   4,366
1910   4,645
1900   4,541
1890   5,198
1880   5,100
1870   4,600
1860   4,412
1850   4,623
1840   3,507
1830   2,619
1820   1,954
1810   NA
1800   *2,929

MINDENVILLE, CDP
Minden Town
Montgomery County
1880   140

MINEOLA, Village (Inc. 1906)
Hempstead Town, part in
Nassau County
1980   52
1970   101
1960   68
1950   27(a)
North Hempstead Town, part in
Nassau County
1980   20,705
1970   21,744
1960   20,451
1950   14,804(a)
1940   10,064
1930   8,155(a)
1920   3,016
1910   1,981
1890-1900   NA
1880   313(b)
TOTAL
1980   20,757
1970   21,845
1960   20,587
1950   14,831(a)
1880-1940   (c)
(a)Boundary change.
(b)Reported in QUEENS County.
(c)Reported in NORTH HEMPSTEAD Town only.

MINERVA, Town (Est. 1817)
Essex County
1980   781
1970   733
1960   700
1950   681
1940   505
1930   567
1920   610
1910   840
1900   1,052
1890   979
1880   1,162

1870	908
1860	903
1850	586
1840	455
1830	358
1820	271

MINETTO, CDP
  Minetto Town
    Oswego County

1980	1,629
1950-1970	NA
1940	600

MINETTO, Town (Est. 1915)
    Oswego County

1980	1,905
1970	1,688
1960	1,290(a)
1950	1,025
1940	1,052
1930	856
1920	913

(a)Reported as Minnetto.

MINEVILLE, CDP(a)
  Moriah Town
    Essex County

1960	1,181
1950	NA
1940	938
1890-1930	NA
1880	2,561

(a)Included, in part, in MINEVILLE--
  WITHERBEE, CDP in 1950 and 1980.

MINEVILLE--WITHERBEE, CDP(a)
  Moriah Town
    Essex County

1980	1,925
1960-1970	NA
1950	2,384(b)

(a)Included in MINEVILLE and WITHERBEE,
  CDPs in 1880-1960.
(b)Reported as WITHERBEE--MINEVILLE.

MINISINK, Town (Est. 1788)
    Orange County

1980	2,488
1970	1,942
1960	1,433
1950	1,367
1940	1,343
1930	1,360
1920	1,250
1910	1,304
1900	1,505
1890	1,269
1880	1,360
1870	1,443
1860	1,266
1850	4,972
1840	5,093
1830	4,979
1820	5,053
1810	NA
1800	*3,584
1790	2,215

MINNETTO, Town
  see MINETTO, Town
      Oswego County

MINOA, Village (Inc. 1913)
  Manlius Town
    Onondaga County

1980	3,640(a)
1970	2,245
1960	1,838
1950	1,008
1940	902
1930	899
1920	867

(a)Boundary change.

MINTZESKILL, CDP
  Schodack Town
    Rensselaer County

1880	62

MOERS, Village
  see MOOERS, Village
      Clinton County

MOHAWK, Town (Est. 1837)(a)
    Montgomery County

1980	3,795
1970	3,677
1960	3,070
1950	2,680
1940	2,753
1930	2,730
1920	2,353
1910	2,488
1900	2,711
1890	2,839
1880	2,943
1870	3,015
1860	3,136
1850	3,095
1840	3,112

(a)In 1790 the Census Bureau reported
  a Mowhawk Town in MONTGOMERY County,
  population of 4,440.

MOHAWK, Village (Inc. 1844)
  German Flatts Town
    Herkimer County

1980	2,956
1970	3,301
1960	3,533
1950	3,196(a)
1940	2,882
1930	2,835
1920	2,919
1910	2,079
1900	2,028
1890	1,806
1880	1,441
1870	1,404

(a)Boundary change.

MOIRA, Town (Est. 1828)
  Franklin County

1980	2,624
1970	2,468
1960	2,362
1950	2,137

1940	2,072
1930	2,101
1920	2,264
1910	2,346
1900	2,484
1890	2,512
1880	2,254
1870	2,064
1860	1,798
1850	1,340
1840	962
1830	791

MONGAUP, CDP
  Bethel Town
    Sullivan County

1880	270

MONROE, County (Est. 1821)

1980	702,238
1970	711,917
1960	586,387
1950	487,632
1940	438,230
1930	423,881
1920	352,034
1910	283,212
1900	217,854
1890	189,586
1880	144,903
1870	117,868
1860	100,648
1850	87,650
1840	64,902
1830	49,855

MONROE, Town (Est. 1799)(a)
  Orange County

1980	14,948
1970	9,169
1960	5,965
1950	3,714
1940	3,302
1930	3,000
1920	2,630
1910	2,285
1900	1,784
1890	1,694
1880	5,096
1870	4,666
1860	3,975
1850	4,280
1840	3,914
1830	3,671
1820	2,969
1810	NA
1800	*2,116

(a)Established as Cheesecocks in 1799;
name changed to Southfield in 1801
and to MONROE in 1808.

MONROE, Village (Inc. 1894)
  Monroe Town
    Orange County

1980	5,996(a)
1970	4,439(a)
1960	3,323(a)
1950	1,753
1940	1,616

1930	1,621
1920	1,527
1910	1,195
1900	796
1890	630
1880	459

(a)Boundary change.

MONROE SOUTHWEST, CDP
  Monroe Town
    Orange County

1980	1,267

MONSEY, CDP
  Ramapo Town
    Rockland County

1980	12,380
1970	8,797
1950-1960	NA
1940	667
1890-1930	NA
1880	237

MONTAGUE, Town (Est. 1850)
  Lewis County

1980	32
1970	58
1960	73
1950	139
1940	329
1930	366
1920	450
1910	531
1900	766
1890	905
1880	975
1870	718
1860	707

MONTAUK, CDP
  East Hampton Town
    Suffolk County

1980	2,828(a)
1970	503(b)
1960	472(c)

(a)Boundary change.
(b)Derived by LIRPB from U.S. Census
    Data; population of 1,728 is compar-
    able to 1980 boundaries.
(c)Derived by LIRPB from U.S. Census
    Data.

MONTAUK POINT(a)
  East Hampton Town
    Suffolk County

1970	1,225(b)
1960	814(b)

(a)Included in MONTAUK, CDP in 1980.
(b)Derived by LIRPB from U.S. Census
    Data.

MONTEREY, CDP
  Orange Town
    Schuyler County

1880	276

MONTEREY, CDP
  West Farms Town
    Westchester County
      1870   118

MONTEZUMA, CDP
  Montezuma Town
    Cayuga County
      1870   473

MONTEZUMA, Town (Est. 1859)
  Cayuga County
      1980   1,125
      1970   857
      1960   743
      1950   769
      1940   746
      1930   690
      1920   669
      1910   941
      1900   991
      1890   1,047
      1880   1,294
      1870   1,292
      1860   1,439

MONTGOMERY, County (Est. 1772)(a)
      1980   53,439
      1970   55,883
      1960   57,240
      1950   59,594
      1940   59,142
      1930   60,076
      1920   57,928
      1910   57,567
      1900   47,488
      1890   45,699
      1880   38,315
      1870   34,457
      1860   30,866
      1850   31,992
      1840   35,818
      1830   43,715
      1820   37,561
      1810   41,214
      1800   22,051
      1790   28,848
(a)Established as Tryon in 1772; name
   changed in 1784.

MONTGOMERY, Town (Est. 1788)
  Orange County
      1980   16,576
      1970   13,995
      1960   11,672
      1950   9,868
      1940   8,418
      1930   8,082
      1920   8,351
      1910   7,439
      1900   5,939
      1890   5,061
      1880   4,795
      1870   4,536
      1860   3,973
      1850   3,933
      1840   4,100
      1830   3,885
      1820   5,541

      1810   NA
      1800   *4,106
      1790   3,563

MONTGOMERY, Village (Inc. 1810)
  Montgomery Town
    Orange County
      1980   2,316(a)
      1970   1,533
      1960   1,312
      1950   1,063(a)
      1940   844
      1930   884
      1920   906
      1910   941
      1900   973
      1890   1,024
      1880   935
      1870   960
(a)Boundary change.

MONTICELLO, Village (Inc. 1830)
  Thompson Town
    Sullivan County
      1980   6,306(a)
      1970   5,991(a)
      1960   5,222(a)
      1950   4,223
      1940   3,737
      1930   3,450
      1920   2,330
      1910   1,941
      1900   1,160
      1890   1,016
      1880   941
      1870   912
(a)Boundary change.

MONTOUR, Town (Est. 1860)
  Schuyler County
      1980   2,607
      1970   2,324
      1960   2,182
      1950   1,985
      1940   1,774
      1930   1,868
      1920   1,967
      1910   1,608
      1900   1,623
      1890   1,987(a)
      1880   1,771
      1870   1,828
(a)Boundary change.

MONTOUR FALLS, Village (Inc. 1836)(a)
  Dix Town, part in
    Schuyler County
      1980   94
      1970   25(b)
      1960   0
      1950   5
      1940   0
      1930   7
      1890-1920   NA
      1880   66
      1870   100
  Montour Town, part in
    Schuyler Coounty
      1980   1,697

1970	1,509(b)
1960	1,533
1950	1,452
1940	1,345
1930	1,489
1920	1,560
1910	1,208
1900	1,193
1890	1,751
1880	1,208
1870	1,273
TOTAL	
1980	1,791
1970	1,534(b)
1960	(c)
1950	1,457
1940	(c)
1930	1,496
1890-1920	(c)
1880	1,274
1870	1,373

(a)Established as Havana in 1836; name changed in 1895.
(b)Boundary change.
(c)Reported in MONTOUR Town only.

MOOERS, Town (Est. 1804)
Clinton County

1980	2,927
1970	2,606
1960	2,587
1950	2,509
1940	2,686
1930	2,655
1920	2,788
1910	3,163
1900	3,572
1890	3,467
1880	4,381
1870	4,634
1860	3,926
1850	3,365
1840	1,703
1830	1,222
1820	562(a)

(a)Reported as Moers.

MOOERS, Village (Inc. 1899)
Mooers Town
Clinton County

1980	549
1970	536
1960	543
1950	496
1940	477
1930	465
1920	512
1910	560
1900	527
1890	NA
1880	345

MOOERS FORKS, CDP
Mooers Town
Clinton County

1880	194

MORAVIA, Town (Est. 1833)
Cayuga County

1980	2,640
1970	2,668
1960	2,406
1950	2,279
1940	1,910
1930	1,913
1920	2,066
1910	2,160
1900	2,373
1890	2,498
1880	2,269
1870	2,169
1860	1,917
1850	1,876
1840	2,010

MORAVIA, Village (Inc. 1837)
Moravia Town
Cayuga County

1980	1,582
1970	1,642
1960	1,575
1950	1,480
1940	1,331
1930	1,295
1920	1,331
1910	1,324
1900	1,442
1890	1,486
1880	1,540
1870	2,169

MOREAU, Town (Est. 1805)
Saratoga County

1980	11,188
1970	10,411 Rev.
1960	8,406
1950	6,065
1940	4,930
1930	4,471
1920	3,222
1910	3,340
1900	2,999
1890	2,698
1880	2,555
1870	2,256
1860	2,210
1850	1,834
1840	1,576
1830	1,690
1820	1,549

MOREHOUSE, Town (Est. 1835)
Hamilton County

1980	102
1970	113
1960	65
1950	104
1940	91
1930	85
1920	109
1910	149
1900	319
1890	182
1880	181
1870	186
1860	228

1850	242
1840	169

MORIAH, CDP
  Moriah Town
    Essex County

1940	667

MORIAH, Town (Est. 1808)
  Essex County

1980	5,139
1970	5,244
1960	5,837
1950	5,796
1940	5,952
1930	6,191
1920	6,626
1910	6,754
1900	4,447
1890	6,787
1880	7,379
1870	4,683
1860	3,466
1850	3,065
1840	2,595
1830	1,742
1820	842

MORIAH CENTER, CDP
  Moriah Town
    Essex County

1880	179

MORIAH CORNERS, CDP
  Moriah Town
    Essex County

1880	208

MORICHES, CDP
  Brookhaven Town
    Suffolk County

1880	259

MORISENA, Town
  see MORRISANIA, Town
        Westchester County

MORRIS, Town (Est. 1849)
  Otsego County

1980	1,780
1970	1,630
1960	1,525
1950	1,440
1940	1,376
1930	1,355
1920	1,207
1910	1,434
1900	1,689
1890	1,920
1880	2,404
1870	2,253
1860	2,320
1850	2,155

MORRIS, Village (Inc. 1870)
  Morris Town
    Otsego County

1980	681
1970	675

1960	677
1950	641
1940	599
1930	554
1920	420
1910	535
1900	553
1890	601
1880	768

MORRISANIA, Town (Est. 1855)(a)
  Westchester County

1870	19,609
1860	9,245

(a)Merged into NEW YORK City in 1873.
  In 1790 the Census Bureau reported a
  Morrisina Town in WESTCHESTER County,
  population of 133. In 1800 the Census
  Bureau reported a Morisena Town in
  WESTCHESTER County, population of 258.

MORRISONVILLE, CDP
  Plattsburgh & Schuyler Falls Towns
    Clinton County

1980	1,721
1970	1,276
1950-1960	NA
1940	725

MORRISTOWN, Town (Est. 1821)
  St. Lawrence County

1980	1,921
1970	1,823
1960	1,776
1950	1,569
1940	1,635
1930	1,658
1920	1,719
1910	1,888
1900	1,798
1890	1,966
1880	2,186
1870	1,954
1860	2,284
1850	2,274
1840	2,809
1830	1,600
1820	827(a)

(a)Reported as Hague.

MORRISTOWN, Village (Inc. 1884)
  Morristown Town
    St. Lawrence County

1980	461
1970	532
1960	541
1950	546
1940	540
1930	505
1920	489
1910	540
1900	485
1890	472
1880	397

MORRISVILLE, Village (Inc. 1819)
  Eaton Town
    Madison County

1980	2,707

1970	2,296
1960	1,304
1950	1,250
1940	666
1930	583
1920	497
1910	500
1900	624
1890	726
1880	741
1870	570

MOSCOW, Village
   see LEICESTER, Village
      Livingston County

MOTTVILLE, CDP
   Skaneateles Town
    Onondaga County

1940	538
1890-1930	NA
1880	533
1870	276

MOUNTAIN LODGE, CDP
   Blooming Grove Town
    Orange County

1980	1,230

MOUNT EDEN, CDP
   West Farms Town
    Westchester County

1870	116

MOUNT HOPE, CDP
   West Farms Town
    Westchester County

1870	487

MOUNT HOPE, Town (Est. 1825)(a)
   Orange County

1980	4,398
1970	2,966
1960	2,291
1950	2,296
1940	1,817
1930	1,847
1920	1,708
1910	1,786
1900	1,236
1890	1,437
1880	1,549
1870	1,842
1860	1,575
1850	1,512
1840	1,565
1830	1,535

(a)Established as Calhoun in 1825; name
   changed in 1833.

MOUNT KISCO, Town (Est. 1977)
   see MOUNT KISCO, Village
      Westchester County

MOUNT KISCO, Village (Inc. 1874)(a)
   Bedford Town, part in
    Westchester County

1970	3,020
1960	2,580
1950	2,417
1940	2,441
1930	1,938(b)
1920	1,335

New Castle Town, part in
   Westchester County

1970	5,152
1960	4,225
1950	3,490
1940	3,500
1930	3,189(b)
1920	2,059

TOTAL

1980	8,025
1970	8,172(b)
1960	6,805
1950	5,907
1940	5,941
1930	5,127(b)
1920	3,394
1910	2,802
1900	1,346
1890	1,095
1880	728(c)

(a)Established town and village of MOUNT
   KISCO, with identical boundaries, in
   1977. MOUNT KISCO Village made
   independent of BEDFORD and NEW CASTLE
   Towns. Separate figures for each Town
   are available for 1890-1910.
(b)Boundary change.
(c)Reported in BEDFORD Town only.

MOUNT MORRIS, Town (Est. 1818)
   Livingston County

1980	4,478
1970	4,579
1960	4,567
1950	4,836
1940	4,904
1930	4,234
1920	4,470
1910	4,004
1900	3,715
1890	3,761
1880	3,931
1870	3,877
1860	3,963
1850	4,531
1840	4,576
1830	2,534
1820	1,002(a)

(a)Reported in GENESEE County.

MOUNT MORRIS, Village (Inc. 1835)
   Mount Morris Town
    Livingston County

1980	3,039
1970	3,417
1960	3,250
1950	3,450
1940	3,530
1930	3,238
1920	3,312
1910	2,782
1900	2,410
1890	2,286
1880	1,899
1870	1,930

MOUNT PLEASANT, Town (Est. 1788)
  Westchester County

1980	39,298
1970	38,535
1960	34,955
1950	26,022
1940	24,138
1930	20,944
1920	14,004
1910	11,863
1900	8,698
1890	5,844
1880	5,450
1870	5,210
1860	4,517
1850	3,323
1840	7,307
1830	4,932
1820	3,684
1810	NA
1800	*2,744
1790	1,924

MOUNT SINAI, CDP
  Brookhaven Town
    Suffolk County

1980	6,591(a)
1970	5,998(b)
1960	1,239(c)
1890-1950	NA
1880	276

(a)Boundary change.
(b)Derived by LIRPB From U.S. Census
    Data; population of 2,157 is compar-
    able to 1980 boundaries.
(c)Derived by LIRPB from U.S. Census
    Data.

MOUNT VERNON, City (Inc. 1892)(a)
  Westchester County

1980	66,713
1970	72,778
1960	76,010
1950	71,899(b)
1940	67,362
1930	61,499
1920	42,726
1910	30,919
1900	21,228

(a)MOUNT VERNON Village incorporated as
    MOUNT VERNON City and made independent
    of EASTCHESTER Town in 1892.
(b)Boundary change.

MOUNT VERNON, Village (Inc. 1853)(a)
  Eastchester Town
    Westchester County

1890	10,830
1880	4,586
1870	2,700

(a)MOUNT VERNON Village incorporated as
    MOUNT VERNON City and made independent
    of EASTCHESTER Town in 1892.

MOUNT VISION, CDP
  Laurens Town
    Otsego County

1880	191

MOWHAWK, Town
  see MOHAWK, Town
    Montgomery County

MUMFORD, CDP
  Wheatland Town
    Monroe County

1940	530
1890-1930	NA
1880	455

MUNNSVILLE, Village (Inc. 1915)
  Stockbridge Town
    Madison County

1980	499
1970	435
1960	391
1950	412
1940	357
1930	345
1920	377
1890-1910	NA
1880	329
1870	313

MUNSEY PARK, Village (Inc. 1930)
  North Hempstead Town
    Nassau County

1980	2,806
1970	2,980
1960	2,847
1950	2,048
1940	1,456
1930	411

MUNSON, CDP(a)
  Hempstead Town
    Nassau County

1940	1,373

(a)Included in FRANKLIN SQUARE, CDP in
  1980.

MUNSONS CORNERS, CDP
  Cortlandville Town
    Cortland County

1980	2,478
1970	2,076

MURRAY, Town (Est. 1820)
  Orleans County

1980	4,754
1970	4,638
1960	3,767
1950	3,200
1940	2,764
1930	3,251
1920	3,390
1910	3,959
1900	3,656
1890	3,465
1880	2,812
1870	2,522
1860	2,612
1850	2,520
1840	2,675
1830	2,790
1820	1,562(a)

(a)Reported in GENESEE County.

MUTTONTOWN, Village (Inc. 1931)
   Oyster Bay Town
      Nassau County
         1980   2,725(a)
         1970   2,081
         1960   1,265(a)
         1950   382
         1940   335
(a)Boundary change.

MYERS CORNERS, CDP
   Wappinger Town
      Dutchess County
         1980   5,180
         1970   2,826

N

NANTICOKE, Town (Est. 1831)
   Broome County
         1980   1,425
         1970   1,020
         1960   794
         1950   627
         1940   546
         1930   454
         1920   444
         1910   536
         1900   666
         1890   723
         1880   999
         1870   1,058
         1860   797
         1850   576
         1840   400

NANUET, CDP
   Clarkstown Town
      Rockland County
         1980   12,578
         1970   10,447
         1950-1960   NA
         1940   2,057

NAPANOCH, CDP
   Wawarsing Town
      Ulster County
         1980   1,260
         1960-1970   NA
         1950   1,094
         1940   1,014

NAPEAUGE--HITHER HILLS
   East Hampton Town
      Suffolk County
         1980   151(a)
         1970   72(a)
         1960   90(a)
(a)Derived by LIRPB from U.S. Census
   Data.

NAPLES, Town (Est. 1789)(a)
   Ontario County
         1980   2,338
         1970   2,236
         1960   1,955
         1950   1,906
         1940   1,972
         1930   1,933
         1920   2,122
         1910   2,349
         1900   2,370
         1890   2,455
         1880   2,699
         1870   2,188
         1860   2,067
         1850   2,376
         1840   2,345
         1830   1,941
         1820   1,038
         1810   NA
         1800   *259
(a)Established as Middletown in 1789;
   name changed in 1808.

NAPLES, Village (Inc. 1894)
   Naples Town
      Ontario County
         1980   1,225
         1970   1,324
         1960   1,237
         1950   1,141
         1940   1,152
         1930   1,070
         1920   1,148
         1910   1,093
         1900   1,048
         1890   1,266
         1880   1,360
         1870   902

NAPOLI, Town (Est. 1823)(a)
   Cattaraugus County
         1980   886
         1970   778
         1960   670
         1950   619
         1940   570
         1930   578
         1920   636
         1910   741
         1900   967
         1890   962
         1880   1,126
         1870   1,174
         1860   1,238
         1850   1,233
         1840   1,145
         1830   852
(a)Established as Cold Spring in 1823;
   name changed in 1828.

NARROWSBURG, CDP
   Tusten Town
      Sullivan County
         1880   313

NASHVILLE, CDP
  Hanover Town
    Chautauqua County
       1860   40

NASSAU, County (Est. 1899)(a)
       1980   1,321,582
       1970   1,428,838 Rev.
       1960   1,300,171
       1950   672,765(b)
       1940   406,748
       1930   303,053(b)
       1920   126,120
       1910   83,930
       1900   55,448
       1890   45,760
       1880   37,647
       1870   31,134
       1860   26,963
       1850   20,002
       1840   17,365
       1830   14,470
       1820   NA(c)
       1810   12,509
       1800   11,102
       1790   10,621
(a)Prior to 1900, population derived by
   totaling HEMPSTEAD, NORTH HEMPSTEAD
   and OYSTER BAY Towns which separated
   from QUEENS County in 1899 to form
   NASSAU County.
(b)Boundary change.
(c)In 1820 the Census Bureau did not
   report towns separately in QUEENS
   County.

NASSAU, Town (Est. 1806)(a)
    Rensselaer County
       1980   4,479
       1970   4,043
       1960   3,721
       1950   3,122
       1940   2,405
       1930   2,020
       1920   2,015
       1910   2,115
       1900   2,073
       1890   2,273
       1880   2,629
       1870   2,705
       1860   3,039
       1850   3,261
       1840   3,236
       1830   3,255
       1820   2,873
(a)Established as Philipstown in 1806;
   name changed in 1808.

NASSAU, Village (Inc. 1819)
  Nassau Town, part in
    Rensselaer County
       1980   1,206
       1970   1,363(a)
       1960   1,248
       1950   952
       1940   698
       1930   670
       1920   655
       1910   529

       1900   418
       1890   356
       1880   449
       1870   348
  Schodack Town, part in
    Rensselaer County
       1980   79
       1970   103
    TOTAL
       1980   1,285
       1970   1,466(a)
       1870-1960   (b)
(a)Boundary change.
(b)Reported in NASSAU Town only.

NASSAU LAKE, CDP
  Nassau & Schodack Towns
    Rensselaer County
       1980   1,304

NATURAL DAM, CDP
  Gouverneur Town
    St. Lawrence County
       1880   222

NAVARINO, CDP
  Onondaga Town
    Onondaga County
       1870   83

NAVESINK, Town
  Ulster County
  see NEVERSINK, Town
          Sullivan County

NEALVILLE, CDP
  Hunter Town
    Greene County
       1880   97

NEDROW, CDP
  Onondaga Town
    Onondaga County
       1940   1,704

NELLISTON, Village (Inc. 1878)
  Palatine Town
    Montgomery County
       1980   691
       1970   716
       1960   729
       1950   693
       1940   638
       1930   553
       1920   664
       1910   737
       1900   634
       1890   721
       1880   558

NELSON, CDP
  Nelson Town
    Madison County
       1880   103

NELSON, Town (Est. 1807)
    Madison County
       1980   1,495
       1970   1,410

1960	1,170
1950	993
1940	928
1930	1,026
1920	1,099
1910	1,139
1900	1,296
1890	1,350
1880	1,649
1870	1,730
1860	1,797
1850	1,965
1840	2,100
1830	2,445
1820	2,329

NELSONVILLE, Village (Inc. 1855)
  Philipstown Town
    Putnam County

1980	567
1970	583
1960	555
1950	522
1940	457
1930	470
1920	412
1910	765
1900	624
1890	NA
1880	541

NESCONSET, CDP
  Smithtown Town
    Suffolk County

1980	10,706(a)
1970	10,048(b)
1960	3,070 Rev.

(a)Boundary change.
(b)Population of 7,278 is comparable to
   1980 boundaries.

NEVERSINK, Town (Est. 1798)
  Sullivan County

1980	2,840
1970	2,055
1960	1,565
1950	1,465
1940	1,494
1930	1,256
1920	1,609
1910	1,743
1900	2,039
1890	2,013
1880	2,152
1870	2,458
1860	2,486
1850	2,281
1840	1,681
1830	1,257
1820	1,380
1810	NA
1800	*858(a)

(a)Reported as Navesink in ULSTER County.

NEW ALBION, CDP
  New Albion Town
    Cattaraugus County

1880	104

NEW ALBION, Town (Est. 1830)
  Cattaraugus County

1980	2,156
1970	1,988
1960	1,981
1950	1,894
1940	1,747
1930	2,004
1920	2,053
1910	1,989
1900	2,372
1890	1,858
1880	1,732
1870	1,487
1860	1,579
1850	1,633
1840	1,016
1830	380

NEWARK, Town
  see NEWARK VALLEY, Town
    Tioga County

NEWARK, Village (Inc. 1853)(a)
  Arcadia Town
    Wayne County

1980	10,017(b)
1970	11,644(b)
1960	12,868(b)
1950	10,295
1940	9,646
1930	7,649
1920	6,964
1910	6,227
1900	4,578
1890	3,698
1880	2,450
1870	2,248

(a)Established as Arcadia; incorporated
   as NEWARK in 1853.
(b)Boundary change.

NEWARK VALLEY, Town (Est. 1823)(a)
  Tioga County

1980	3,765
1970	3,323
1960	2,880
1950	2,384
1940	2,210
1930	1,843
1920	1,889
1910	2,102
1900	2,164
1890	2,339
1880	2,577
1870	2,321
1860	2,169
1850	1,983
1840	1,616
1830	1,027

(a)Established as Westville in 1823;
   name changed to Newark in 1824, and
   to NEWARK VALLEY in 1862.

NEWARK VALLEY, Village (Inc. 1894)
  Newark Valley Town
    Tioga County

1980	1,190(a)
1970	1,286

1960	1,234
1950	1,027
1940	949
1930	795
1920	821
1910	925
1900	818
1890	875

(a)Boundary change.

NEW BALTIMORE, CDP
  New Baltimore Town
    Greene County

1890	734

NEW BALTIMORE, Town (Est. 1811)
  Greene County

1980	3,050
1970	2,068
1960	1,972
1950	1,781
1940	1,489
1930	1,434
1920	1,536
1910	1,936
1900	2,283
1890	2,455
1880	2,620
1870	2,617
1860	2,512
1850	2,381
1840	2,306
1830	2,370(a)
1820	2,036

(a)Reported as Baltimore.

NEW BERLIN, Town (Est. 1807)(a)
  Chenango County

1980	3,025
1970	2,823
1960	2,633
1950	2,359
1940	2,112
1930	2,123
1920	2,104
1910	2,328
1900	2,525
1890	2,427
1880	2,572
1870	2,460
1860	2,617
1850	2,562
1840	3,086
1830	2,680
1820	2,366

(a)Name changed to Lancaster in 1821;
  original name restored in 1822.

NEW BERLIN, Village (Inc. 1816)
  New Berlin Town
    Chenango County

1980	1,392
1970	1,369
1960	1,262
1950	1,178
1940	999
1930	1,076
1920	1,070
1910	1,114

1900	1,156
1890	979
1880	937

NEW BREMEN, Town (Est. 1848)
  Lewis County

1980	2,316
1970	2,040
1960	1,963
1950	1,729
1940	1,707
1930	1,597
1920	1,609
1910	1,609
1900	1,775
1890	1,974
1880	2,414
1870	1,908
1860	1,786
1850	1,510

NEW BRIGHTON, Village (Inc. 1866)(a)
  Castleton Town
    Richmond County

1890	16,423(b)
1880	12,679(b)
1870	7,495

(a)Merged into STATEN ISLAND Borough in
  NEW YORK City in 1898.
(b)NEW BRIGHTON Village and CASTLETON
  Town shared the same boundaries.

NEWBURGH, City (Inc. 1865)(a)
  Orange County

1980	23,438
1970	26,219
1960	30,979
1950	31,956
1940	31,883
1930	31,275(b)
1920	30,366(b)
1910	27,805
1900	24,943(c)
1890	23,087(c)
1880	18,049(c)
1870	17,014
1860	12,578(d)

(a)Newburgh Village (Inc. 1800) incorporated as NEWBURGH City and made independent of NEWBURGH Town in 1865.
(b)Boundary change.
(c)Reported as Newburg.
(d)Estimated.

NEWBURGH, Town (Est. 1788)
  Orange County

1980	22,747
1970	21,593
1960	15,547
1950	8,686
1940	6,092
1930	5,072(a)
1920	4,034(a)
1910	5,132
1900	4,246(b)
1890	4,543(b)
1880	3,918(b)
1870	3,541(a)
1860	15,196

1850	11,415(b)
1840	8,933(b)
1830	6,424
1820	5,812
1810	NA
1800	*3,258(b)
1790	2,365

(a)Boundary change.
(b)Reported as Newburg.

NEWBURGH, Village
    see NEWBURGH, City
        Orange County

NEWBURGH WEST, CDP
    Newburgh Town
    Orange County

1980	1,381

NEW CARTHAGE, CDP
    Fishkill Town
    Dutchess County

1870	241

NEW CASSEL, CDP
    North Hempstead Town
    Nassau County

1980	9,635
1970	8,721
1960	7,555(a)

(a)Derived by LIRPB from U.S. Census
Data.

NEW CASTLE, Town (Est. 1791)
    Westchester County

1980	15,425(a)
1970	19,837
1960	14,388
1950	8,802
1940	7,903
1930	6,792(b)
1920	3,639
1910	3,573
1900	2,401(b)
1890	2,110
1880	2,297
1870	2,152
1860	1,817(b)
1850	1,800
1840	1,529
1830	1,336
1820	1,368
1810	NA
1800	*1,468

(a)Boundary change.
(b)Reported as Newcastle.

NEW CITY, CDP
    Clarkstown Town
    Rockland County

1980	35,859
1970	27,344
1950-1960	NA
1940	992
1890-1930	NA
1880	270

NEWCOMB, Town (Est. 1828)
    Essex County

1980	681
1970	957
1960	1,187
1950	1,212
1940	460
1930	437
1920	313
1910	509
1900	507
1890	283
1880	237
1870	178
1860	157
1850	277(a)
1840	74
1830	62

(a)Reported as Newcombe.

NEW CORNWALL, Town
    see CORNWALL, Town
        Orange County

NEW DANSVILLE, CDP
    see NORTH DANSVILLE, CDP
        Livingston County

NEWFANE, CDP
    Newfane Town
    Niagara County

1980	3,120
1970	2,588
1960	1,423
1950	1,578
1940	1,134

NEWFANE, Town (Est. 1824)
    Niagara County

1980	9,268
1970	9,459
1960	8,523
1950	5,801
1940	4,635
1930	4,225
1920	3,515
1910	4,060
1900	3,248
1890	3,170
1880	3,462
1870	3,097
1860	3,363
1850	3,271
1840	2,372(a)
1830	1,450(a)

(a)Reported as New Fane.

NEWFIELD, Town (Est. 1811)(a)
    Tompkins County

1980	4,401
1970	3,390
1960	2,193
1950	1,891
1940	1,521
1930	1,451
1920	1,456
1910	1,509
1900	1,902
1890	2,214

1880	2,608
1870	2,602
1860	2,984
1850	3,816
1840	3,567
1830	2,664
1820	1,889(b)

(a)Established as Cayuta in 1811; name
   changed in 1822.
(b)Reported in TIOGA County.

NEWFIELD, Village (Inc. 1895)(a)
   Newfield Town
      Tompkins County

1920	302
1910	354
1900	378
1890	NA
1880	419

(a)Dissolved in 1926.

NEW GOSHEN, Town
   see LEXINGTON, Town
         Greene County

NEW HACKENSACK, CDP
   Wappinger Town
      Dutchess County

1980	1,532
1970	1,111

NEW HAMBURG, CDP
   Poughkeepsie Town
      Dutchess County

1970	1,064
1890-1960	NA
1880	501(a)
1870	400

(a)Reported as New Hamburgh.

NEW HAMPSTEAD, Town
   see RAMAPO, Town
         Rockland County

NEW HAMPTON--DENTON, CDP
   Goshen & Wawayanda Towns
      Orange County

1980	1,385

NEW HARTFORD, Town (Est. 1827)
   Oneida County

1980	21,286
1970	21,430(a)
1960	18,444(a)
1950	11,071
1940	8,109
1930	7,121(a)
1920	8,646(a)
1910	5,947
1900	5,230
1890	5,005
1880	4,394
1870	4,037
1860	4,395
1850	4,847
1840	3,819
1830	3,599

(a)Boundary change.

NEW HARTFORD, Village (Inc. 1870)
   New Hartford Town
      Oneida County

1980	2,313
1970	2,433(a)
1960	2,468(a)
1950	1,947
1940	1,914
1930	1,885
1920	1,621
1910	1,195
1900	1,007
1890	912
1880	710
1870	743

(a)Boundary change.

NEW HAVEN, Town (Est. 1813)
   Oswego County

1980	2,421
1970	1,845
1960	1,478
1950	1,259
1940	1,194
1930	1,116
1920	1,256
1910	1,461
1900	1,408
1890	1,557
1880	1,713
1870	1,764
1860	2,073
1850	2,015
1840	1,738
1830	1,426
1820	899

NEW HEMPSTEAD, Village (Inc. 1983)(a)
   Ramapo Town
      Rockland County
(a)Population of 4,172 at incorporation.

NEW HUDSON, Town (Est. 1825)(a)
   Allegany County

1980	669
1970	579
1960	612
1950	618
1940	601
1930	565
1920	663
1910	852
1900	926
1890	978
1880	1,034
1870	1,142
1860	1,316
1850	1,433
1840	1,502
1830	655

(a)Established as Haight in 1825; name
   changed in 1837.

NEW HYDE PARK, Village (Inc. 1927)
   Hempstead Town, part in
      Nassau County

1980	4,047
1970	4,304
1960	4,429

1950	2,747
1940	2,171
1930	1,607

North Hempstead Town, part in
Nassau County

1980	5,754
1970	5,812
1960	6,379
1950	4,602
1940	2,520
1930	1,707

TOTAL

1980	9,801
1970	10,116
1960	10,808
1950	7,349
1940	4,691
1930	3,314

NEW LEBANON, Town (Est. 1818)
Columbia County

1980	2,271
1970	2,035
1960	1,674
1950	1,415
1940	1,259
1930	1,081
1920	1,133
1910	1,378
1900	1,556
1890	1,765
1880	2,245
1870	2,124
1860	2,187
1850	2,300
1840	2,536
1830	2,695
1820	2,808(a)

(a)Reported as Lebanon.

NEW LISBON, Town (Est. 1806)(a)
Otsego County

1980	948
1970	823
1960	812
1950	877
1940	801
1930	781
1920	912
1910	1,039
1900	1,225
1890	1,323
1880	1,569
1870	1,545
1860	1,733
1850	1,773
1840	1,909
1830	2,232
1820	2,221(b)

(a)Established as Lisbon in 1806; name
changed in 1808.
(b)Reported as New-Lisbon.

NEW LONDON, Village (Inc. 1848)(a)
Verona Town
Oneida County

1920	90
1910	108
1900	177

1890	NA
1880	391
1870	453

(a)Dissolved, date unavailable.

NEW LOTS, Town (Est. 1852)(a)
Kings County

1880	13,655
1870	9,800
1860	3,271

(a)Merged into BROOKLYN City in 1886.

NEW MARLBORO, Town
see MARLBORO, Town
Ulster County

NEW MILFORD, CDP
Warwick Town
Orange County

1880	98

NEW PALTZ, Town (Est. 1788)
Ulster County

1980	10,183
1970	10,415
1960	5,841
1950	3,749
1940	2,815
1930	2,550
1920	2,163
1910	3,025
1900	2,264(a)
1890	2,242(a)
1880	1,958
1870	2,040
1860	2,023
1850	2,729
1840	5,408
1830	4,973
1820	4,612
1810	NA
1800	*3,255(b)
1790	2,309

(a)Reported as Newpaltz.
(b)Reported as New-Palk.

NEW PALTZ, Village (Inc. 1887)
New Paltz Town
Ulster County

1980	4,938 Rev.(a)
1970	6,058(a)
1960	3,041(a)
1950	2,285
1940	1,492
1930	1,362
1920	1,056
1910	1,230
1900	1,022(b)
1890	935(b)
1880	493
1870	425

(a)Boundary change.
(b)Reported as Newpaltz

NEWPORT, Town (Est. 1806)
Herkimer County

1980	2,206
1970	1,992
1960	1,907

1950	1,626
1940	1,481
1930	1,768
1920	1,700
1910	1,490
1900	1,613
1890	1,835
1880	1,953
1870	1,954
1860	2,113
1850	2,125
1840	2,020
1830	1,863
1820	1,746

NEWPORT, Village (Inc. 1857)
Newport Town
Herkimer County

1980	746
1970	908
1960	827
1950	752
1940	627
1930	696
1920	703
1910	583
1900	610
1890	659
1880	713
1870	651

NEW ROCHELLE, City (Inc. 1899)(a)
Westchester County

1980	70,794
1970	75,385
1960	76,812
1950	59,725
1940	58,408
1930	54,000
1920	36,213
1910	28,867
1900	14,720

(a)NEW ROCHELLE Town and NEW ROCHELLE
Village consolidated and incorporated
as NEW ROCHELLE City in 1899.

NEW ROCHELLE, Town (Est. 1788)(a)
Westchester County

1890	9,057
1880	5,276
1870	3,915
1860	3,519
1850	2,458
1840	1,816
1830	1,274
1820	1,135
1800-1810	NA
1790	692

(a)NEW ROCHELLE Town and NEW ROCHELLE
Village consolidated and incorporated
as NEW ROCHELLE City in 1899.

NEW ROCHELLE, Village (Inc. 1857)(a)
Westchester County

1890	8,217
1880	NA
1870	279

(a)NEW ROCHELLE Town and NEW ROCHELLE
Village consolidated and incorporated

as NEW ROCHELLE City in 1899.

NEW SALEM, CDP
New Scotland Town
Albany County

1880	175
1870	219

NEW SALEM, CDP
Farmington Town
Ontario County

1880	141

NEW SCOTLAND, CDP
New Scotland Town
Albany County

1870	103

NEW SCOTLAND, Town (Est. 1832)
Albany County

1980	8,976
1970	8,481
1960	5,818
1950	3,956
1940	3,302
1930	2,841
1920	2,470
1910	2,834
1900	3,058
1890	3,207
1880	3,251
1870	3,411
1860	3,304
1850	3,459
1840	2,912

NEW SPRINGVILLE, CDP
Northfield Town
Richmond County

1880	380

NEW SQUARE, Village (Inc. 1961)
Ramapo Town
Rockland County

1980	1,750
1970	1,156

NEWSTEAD, Town (Est. 1804)(a)
Erie County

1980	7,231
1970	6,322
1960	5,825
1950	4,653
1940	4,268
1930	4,334
1920	4,043
1910	3,697
1900	3,742
1890	3,721
1880	3,570
1870	3,380
1860	3,162
1850	2,899
1840	2,653
1830	1,926

(a)Established as Erie in GENESEE County
in 1804; name changed in 1831.

NEW SUFFOLK, CDP
    see CUTCHOGUE--NEW SUFFOLK, CDP
        Suffolk County

NEWTON, CDP
    see NEWTOWN, CDP
        Queens County

NEWTON FALLS, CDP
    Clifton Town
        St. Lawrence County
            1940   657

NEWTOWN, CDP
    Newtown Town
        Queens County
            1880   133(a)
(a)Reported as Newton.

NEWTOWN, Town
        Chemung County
        see ELMIRA, Town
            Chemung County

NEWTOWN, Town (Est. 1788)(a)
    Queens County
            1890   17,549
            1880   9,804(b)
            1870   20,274
            1860   13,725
            1850   7,208
            1840   5,054
            1830   2,610
            1810-1820   NA
            1800   *2,312
            1790   2,111(c)
(a)Merged into QUEENS Borough in NEW
    YORK City in 1898.
(b)Boundary change.
(c)Reported as New-Town.

NEWTOWN, Village
    see ELMIRA, City
        Chemung County

NEWTOWNVILLE, CDP
    Newtown Town
        Queens County
            1870   2,108

NEW UTRECHT, Town (Est. 1788)(a)
    Kings County
            1890   8,854
            1880   4,742
            1870   3,296
            1860   2,781
            1850   2,129
            1840   1,283
            1830   1,217
            1820   1,009
            1810   NA
            1800   *778
            1790   562
(a)Merged into BROOKLYN City in 1894.

NEW VERNON, CDP
    Mount Hope Town
        Orange County
            1880   55

NEWVILLE, CDP
    Danube Town
        Herkimer County
            1870   112

NEW WINDSOR, CDP
    New Windsor Town
        Orange County
            1980   7,812
            1970   8,803
            1960   4,041
            1950   2,754
            1940   1,932
            1900-1930   NA
            1890   614

NEW WINDSOR, Town (Est. 1788)
    Orange County
            1980   19,534
            1970   16,650
            1960   11,908
            1950   5,100
            1940   3,765
            1930   3,126
            1920   2,984
            1910   2,667
            1900   2,392
            1890   2,621
            1880   2,576
            1870   2,482
            1860   2,452
            1850   2,457
            1840   2,482
            1830   2,310
            1820   2,425
            1810   NA
            1800   *2,001
            1790   1,819(a)
(a)Reported in ULSTER County.

NEW WINDSOR WEST, CDP
    Newburgh Town
        Orange County
            1980   2,120

NEW WOODSTOCK, CDP
    Cazenovia Town
        Madison County
            1880   334

NEW YORK, City (Inc. 1653)(a)
    TOTAL
            1980   7,071,639 Rev.
            1970   7,895,563 Rev.
            1960   7,781,984
            1950   7,891,957
            1940   7,454,995
            1930   6,930,446
            1920   5,620,048
            1910   4,766,883
            1900   3,437,202(b)
            1890   1,515,301
            1880   1,206,299
            1870   942,292
            1860   813,669
            1850   515,547
            1840   312,710
            1830   202,589 Rev.
            1820   123,706

1810	96,373
1800	60,515
1790	32,305 Rev.

BRONX, Borough (Inc. 1898)
  Bronx County

1980	1,168,972 Rev.
1970	1,471,701
1960	1,424,815
1950	1,451,277
1940	1,394,711
1930	1,265,258
1920	732,016
1910	430,980
1900	200,507(b)
1890	88,908(c)
1880	51,980(c)
1870	37,393(c)
1860	23,593(c)
1850	8,032(c)
1840	5,346(c)
1830	3,023(c)
1820	2,782(c)
1810	2,267(c)
1800	1,755(c)
1790	1,781(c)

BROOKLYN, Borough (Inc. 1898)
  Kings County

1980	2,231,028 Rev.
1970	2,602,012
1960	2,627,319
1950	2,738,175
1940	2,698,285
1930	2,560,401
1920	2,018,356(b)
1910	1,634,351
1900	1,166,582(b)
1890	838,547(c)
1880	599,495(c)
1870	419,921(c)
1860	279,122(c)
1850	138,882(c)
1840	47,613(c)
1830	20,535(c)
1820	11,187(c)
1810	8,303(c)
1800	5,740(c)
1790	4,495(c)

MANHATTAN, Borough (Inc. 1898)
  New York County

1980	1,428,285 Rev.
1970	1,539,233
1960	1,698,281
1950	1,960,101
1940	1,889,924
1930	1,867,312
1920	2,284,103
1910	2,331,542
1900	1,850,093(b)
1890	1,441,216(c)
1880	1,164,673(c)
1870	942,292(c)
1860	813,669(c)
1850	515,547(c)
1840	312,710(c)
1830	202,589(c)
1820	123,706(c)
1810	96,373(c)
1800	60,515(c)
1790	33,131(c)

QUEENS, Borough (Inc. 1898)
  Queens County

1980	1,891,325
1970	1,987,174 Rev.
1960	1,809,578
1950	1,550,849
1940	1,297,634
1930	1,079,129
1920	469,042(b)
1910	284,041
1900	152,999(b)
1890	87,050(c)
1880	56,559(c)
1870	45,468(c)
1860	32,903(c)
1850	18,593(c)
1840	14,480(c)
1830	9,049(c)
1820	8,246(c)
1810	7,444(c)
1800	6,642(c)
1790	6,159(c)

STATEN ISLAND, Borough (Inc. 1898)(d)
  Richmond County

1980	352,029 Rev.
1970	295,443
1960	221,991
1950	191,555
1940	174,441
1930	158,346
1920	116,531
1910	85,969
1900	67,021(b)
1890	51,693(c)
1880	38,991(c)
1870	33,029(c)
1860	25,492(c)
1850	15,061(c)
1840	10,965(c)
1830	7,082(c)
1820	6,135(c)
1810	5,347(c)
1800	4,564(c)
1790	3,835(c)

(a)Greater NEW YORK City, consisting of five boroughs, was established in 1898. Since establishment, BROOKLYN, QUEENS and STATEN ISLAND Boroughs have shared boundaries with the Counties in which they are located. MANHATTAN and BRONX Boroughs were located in NEW YORK County until BRONX County and Borough were separated in 1914. The following table shows the total population of NEW YORK City from 1790 to 1890, comparable to present boundaries:

1890	2,507,414
1880	1,911,698
1870	1,478,103
1860	1,174,779
1850	696,115
1840	391,114
1830	242,278
1820	152,056
1810	119,734
1800	79,216
1790	49,401

(b)Boundary change.

(c)Population is comparable to 1980
   boundaries.
(d)Established as Richmond Borough in
   1898; name changed in 1975.

NEW YORK, County (Est. 1683)(a)

1980	1,428,285 Rev.
1970	1,539,233
1960	1,698,281
1950	1,960,101
1940	1,889,924
1930	1,867,312
1920	2,284,103(b)
1910	2,762,522
1900	2,050,600(b)
1890	1,515,301
1880	1,206,299
1870	942,292
1860	813,669
1850	515,547
1840	312,710
1830	202,589 Rev.
1820	123,706
1810	96,373
1800	60,515 Rev.
1790	33,131

(a)In 1898 the Boroughs of MANHATTAN
   and the BRONX in NEW YORK City were
   established and together formed NEW
   YORK County. BRONX County and
   Borough were separated from NEW YORK
   County in 1914.
(b)Boundary change.

NEW YORK MILLS, Village (Inc. 1922)
   New Hartford Town, part in
     Oneida County

1980	1,930
1970	1,868(a)
1960	1,605(a)
1950	1,380
1940	1,352
1930	1,404
1900-1920	NA
1890	1,196
1880	931(b)

   Whitestown Town, part in
     Oneida County

1980	1,619
1970	1,937
1960	2,183
1950	1,986(a)
1940	2,276
1930	2,602
1900-1920	NA
1890	1,356
1880	902(c)
1870	1,264

   TOTAL

1980	3,549
1970	3,805(a)
1960	3,788(a)
1950	3,366(a)
1940	3,628
1930	4,906
1900-1920	NA
1890	2,552
1880	1,833
1870	(d)

(a)Boundary change.
(b)Reported as New York Upper Mills.
(c)Reported as New York Mills Proper.
(d)Reported in WHITESTOWN Town only.

NIAGARA, County (Est. 1808)

1980	227,354 Rev.
1970	235,720
1960	242,269
1950	189,992
1940	160,110
1930	149,329
1920	118,705
1910	92,036
1900	74,961
1890	62,491
1880	54,173
1870	50,437
1860	50,399
1850	42,276
1840	31,132
1830	18,482
1820	22,990
1810	8,971

NIAGARA, Town (Est. 1812)(a)
   Niagara County

1980	9,648
1970	8,368
1960	7,503(b)
1950	4,729
1940	2,618
1930	865(b)
1920	4,173
1910	1,648
1900	1,066(b)
1890	10,979
1880	7,432
1870	6,832
1860	6,603
1850	1,951
1840	1,277
1830	1,401
1820	484

(a)Established as Schlosser in 1812;
   name changed in 1816.
(b)Boundary change.

NIAGARA CITY, Village
   see SUSPENSION BRIDGE, Village
      Niagara County

NIAGARA FALLS, City (Inc. 1892)(a)
   Niagara County

1980	71,384
1970	85,615
1960	102,394(b)
1950	90,872
1940	78,029
1930	75,460(b)
1920	50,760
1910	30,445
1900	19,457

(a)NIAGARA FALLS and SUSPENSION BRIDGE
   Villages consolidated and incorporated
   as NIAGARA FALLS City and made independent of NIAGARA Town in 1892.
(b)Boundary change.

NIAGARA FALLS, Village (Inc. 1848)(a)
    Niagara Town
        Niagara County
            1890   5,502
            1880   3,320
            1870   3,006
(a)NIAGARA FALLS and SUSPENSION BRIDGE
    Villages consolidated and incorporated
    as NIAGARA FALLS City and made inde-
    pendent of NIAGARA Town in 1892.

NICHOLS, Town (Est. 1824)
    Tioga County
            1980   2,567
            1970   2,271
            1960   1,998
            1950   1,685
            1940   1,481
            1930   1,407
            1920   1,392
            1910   1,466
            1900   1,564
            1890   1,701
            1880   1,709
            1870   1,663
            1860   1,932
            1850   1,905
            1840   1,986
            1830   1,284

NICHOLS, Village (Inc. 1903)
    Nichols Town
        Tioga County
            1980   613
            1970   638
            1960   663
            1950   578
            1940   541
            1930   533
            1920   554
            1910   533
            1880-1900   NA
            1870   281

NICHOLVILLE, CDP
    Lawrence Town
        St. Lawrence County
            1880   280
            1870   300

NILES, Town (Est. 1833)
    Cayuga County
            1980   1,115
            1970   965
            1960   943
            1950   941
            1940   834
            1930   903
            1920   1,076
            1910   1,209
            1900   1,402
            1890   1,579
            1880   1,875
            1870   1,912
            1860   2,013
            1850   2,053
            1840   2,234

NIMMONSBURG--CHENANGO BRIDGE, CDP(a)
    Chenango Town
        Broome County
            1970   5,059
(a)Included, in part, in CHENANGO BRIDGE,
    CDP in 1940.

NINEVEH, CDP
    Colesville & Afton Towns
        Broome & Chenango Counties
            1870   127(a)
(a)Part in BROOME County, 93; part in
    CHENANGO County, 34.

NISKAYUNA, CDP
    Niskayuna Town
        Schenectady County
            1980   5,223
            1970   6,186
            1890-1960   NA
            1880   73

NISKAYUNA, Town (Est. 1809)
    Schenectady County
            1980   17,471
            1970   17,879
            1960   14,032
            1950   9,442(a)
            1940   6,348(a)
            1930   4,931(a)
            1920   3,149(a)
            1910   1,907
            1900   1,327
            1890   1,040
            1880   990
            1870   1,105
            1860   789
            1850   783
            1840   693
            1830   452
            1820   516
(a)Boundary change.

NISSEQUOGUE, Village (Inc. 1926)
    Smithtown Town
        Suffolk County
            1980   1,462
            1970   1,120
            1960   332
            1950   219
            1940   188
            1930   174

NIVERVILLE, CDP
    Chatham & Kinderhook Towns
        Columbia County
            1980   1,856
            1890-1970   NA
            1880   219

NORFOLK, CDP
    Norfolk Town
        St. Lawrence County
            1980   1,599
            1970   1,379(a)
            1960   1,353

1950	1,252
1940	1,288
1880-1930	NA
1870	540

(a)Reported as Norfolk Center.

NORFOLK, Town (Est. 1823)
   St. Lawrence County

1980	4,992
1970	4,701
1960	4,590
1950	3,481
1940	3,427
1930	3,047
1920	3,066
1910	2,938
1900	1,911
1890	2,024
1880	2,471
1870	2,441
1860	2,329
1850	1,753
1840	1,728
1830	1,039

NORFOLK CENTER, CDP
  see NORFOLK, CDP
    St. Lawrence County

NORTH AMITYVILLE, CDP
  Babylon Town
   Suffolk County

1980	13,140(a)
1970	11,936(b)
1960	8,369(c)

(a)Boundary change.
(b)Population of 10,847 is comparable to 1980 boundaries.
(c)Derived by LIRPB from U.S. Census Data.

NORTHAMPTON, Town (Est. 1799)
  Fulton County

1980	2,829
1970	2,379
1960	2,033
1950	1,925
1940	1,761
1930	1,919
1920	2,191
1910	2,228
1900	2,226
1890	1,992
1880	2,069
1870	1,927
1860	1,937
1850	1,701
1840	1,526
1830	1,380(a)
1820	1,291(a)
1810	NA
1800	*990(a)

(a)Reported in MONTGOMERY County.

NORTHAMPTON, Town
  Ontario County
  see GATES, Town
    Monroe County

NORTH ARGYLE, CDP
  Argyle Town
   Washington County

1880	95

NORTH BABYLON, CDP
  Babylon Town
   Suffolk County

1980	19,019(a)
1970	39,526 Rev.(b)
1960	29,257(c)

(a)Boundary change.
(b)Population of 20,955 is comparable to 1980 boundaries.
(c)Derived by LIRPB from U.S. Census Data.

NORTH BALLSTON SPA, CDP
  Milton Town
   Saratoga County

1980	1,350
1970	1,296

NORTH BANGOR, Village (Inc. 1914)(a)
  Bangor Town
   Franklin County

1930	319
1920	362

(a)Dissolved in 1937.

NORTH BAY, CDP
  Vienna Town
   Oneida County

1870	348

NORTH BAY SHORE, CDP
  Islip Town
   Suffolk County

1980	35,020(a)
1970	15,840(b)
1960	7,160(c)

(a)Boundary change.
(b)Derived by LIRPB from U.S. Census Data; population of 33,614 is comparable to 1980 boundaries.
(c)Derived by LIRPB from U.S. Census Data.

NORTH BELLMORE, CDP
  Hempstead Town
   Nassau County

1980	20,630
1970	22,893
1960	19,639
1950	NA
1940	3,519

NORTH BELLPORT, CDP(a)
  Brookhaven Town
   Suffolk County

1980	7,432(b)
1970	5,903(c)
1960	4,419(d)

(a)Included, in part, in HAGERMAN--NORTH BELLPORT, CDP in 1950.
(b)Boundary change.
(c)Population of 5,720 is comparable to 1980 boundaries.
(d)Derived by LIRPB from U.S. Census

Data.

NORTH BERGEN, CDP
  Bergen Town
    Genesee County
      1880   139

NORTH BLOOMFIELD, CDP
  West Bloomfield Town
    Ontario County
      1880   142

NORTH BOSTON, CDP
  Boston Town
    Erie County
      1980   2,743
      1970   1,635

NORTH BRANCH, CDP
  Callicoon Town
    Sullivan County
      1880   97

NORTH BRIDGEWATER, CDP
  Bridgewater Town
    Oneida County
      1880   52

NORTH BROOKFIELD, CDP
  Brookfield Town
    Madison County
      1880   180
      1870   226

NORTH CASTLE, Town (Est. 1788)
  Westchester County
      1980   9,467
      1970   9,591
      1960   6,797
      1950   3,855
      1940   3,306
      1930   2,540
      1920   1,705(a)
      1910   1,522
      1900   1,471
      1890   1,475
      1880   1,818
      1870   1,996
      1860   2,487
      1850   2,189
      1840   2,058
      1830   1,653
      1820   1,480
      1810   NA
      1800   *1,168
      1790   2,478
(a)Boundary change.

NORTH CENTEREACH(a)
  Brookhaven Town
    Suffolk County
      1970   10,843(b)
      1960   552(b)
(a)Included in SELDEN, CDP in 1980.
(b)Derived by LIRPB from U.S. Census
   Data.

NORTH CHATHAM, CDP
  Chatham Town
    Columbia County
      1880   163

NORTH CHILI, CDP
  Chili Town
    Monroe County
      1970   3,163
      1880-1960   NA
      1870   104

NORTH COHOCTON, CDP
  Cohocton Town
    Steuben County
      1880   268

NORTH COLLINS, CDP
  North Collins Town
    Erie County
      1880   421

NORTH COLLINS, Town (Est. 1852)(a)
  Erie County
      1980   3,791
      1970   4,090
      1960   3,805
      1950   2,943
      1940   2,550
      1930   2,522
      1920   2,271
      1910   2,424
      1900   2,362
      1890   2,016
      1880   1,856
      1870   1,617
      1860   1,948
(a)Established as Shirley in 1852; name
   changed in 1853.

NORTH COLLINS, Village (Inc. 1911)
  North Collins Town
    Erie County
      1980   1,496
      1970   1,675
      1960   1,574
      1950   1,325
      1940   1,182
      1930   1,165
      1920   1,158
      1900-1910   NA
      1890   636
      1880   421

NORTH CREEK, CDP
  Johnsburg Town
    Warren County
      1940   703

NORTH CUBA, CDP
  Cuba Town
    Allegany County
      1880   50

NORTH DANSVILLE, Town (Est. 1846)
  Livingston County
      1980   5,994
      1970   6,358
      1960   6,095

1950	5,755
1940	5,332
1930	5,310
1920	4,793
1910	4,328
1900	3,961
1890	4,099
1880	4,178
1870	4,015
1860	3,738
1850	4,377(a)

(a)Reported as New Dansville.

NORTHEAST, Town (Est. 1788)
   Dutchess County

1980	2,877(a)
1970	2,730
1960	2,489
1950	2,308
1940	2,201
1930	2,119
1920	1,922
1910	2,110
1900	2,047
1890	2,026
1880	2,181(a)
1870	2,179
1860	1,735(a)
1850	1,555(a)
1840	1,385
1830	1,689(a)
1820	2,037(a)
1810	NA
1800	*3,252(a)
1790	3,401

(a)Reported as North East.

NORTH EAST MORICHES(a)
   Brookhaven Town
      Suffolk County

1970	217(b)
1960	100(b)

(a)Included in EAST MORICHES, CDP in
   1980.
(b)Derived by LIRPB from U.S. Census
   Data.

NORTH ELBA, Town (Est. 1849)
   Essex County

1980	6,597
1970	5,776
1960	6,005
1950	6,069
1940	6,092
1930	6,472
1920	4,343
1910	3,896
1900	1,986
1890	1,117
1880	480
1870	349
1860	366
1850	210

NORTH ELMIRA, Town
   see HORSEHEADS, Town
      Chemung County

NORTH EVANS, CDP
   Evans Town
      Erie County

1880	149
1870	150

NORTHFIELD, CDP
   Northfield Town
      Richmond County

1880	136

NORTHFIELD, Town (Est. 1789)(a)
   Ontario County

1800	*414

(a)Established as NORTHFIELD in 1789;
   name changed to Boyle in 1808 and
   to Smallwood in 1813. Divided into
   BRIGHTON and PITTSFORD Towns in
   MONROE County in 1814.

NORTHFIELD, Town (Est. 1788)(a)
   Richmond County

1890	9,811
1880	7,014
1870	5,949
1860	4,841
1850	4,020
1840	2,745
1830	2,162
1820	1,980
1810	NA
1800	*1,377
1790	1,021

(a)Merged into STATEN ISLAND Borough in
   NEW YORK City in 1898.

NORTHFIELD, Town
   Saratoga County
   see EDINBURG, Town
      Saratoga County

NORTH GATES, CDP
   see GATES--NORTH GATES, CDP
      Monroe County

NORTH GREAT RIVER, CDP
   Islip Town
      Suffolk County

1980	11,416(a)
1970	12,080(b)
1960	6,280(c)

(a)Boundary change.
(b)Population of 12,211 is comparable
   to 1980 boundaries.
(c)Derived by LIRPB from U.S. Census
   Data.

NORTH GREENBUSH, Town (Est. 1855)
   Rensselaer County

1980	10,396
1970	10,513
1960	8,161
1950	4,913
1940	3,223
1930	2,215
1920	1,425 Rev.
1910	1,293(a)
1900	4,719
1890	4,768

1880	4,131
1870	3,058
1860	2,170

(a)Boundary change.

NORTH HAMPSTEAD, Town
Queens County
see NORTH HEMPSTEAD, Town
Nassau County

NORTH HARMONY, Town (Est. 1918)
Chautauqua County

1980	2,263
1970	2,264
1960	2,132
1950	1,675
1940	1,453
1930	1,462
1920	1,235

NORTH HARPERSFIELD, CDP
Harpersfield Town
Delaware County

1880	57

NORTH HAVEN, Village (Inc. 1931)
Southampton Town
Suffolk County

1980	738
1970	694
1960	450
1950	153
1940	131
1890-1930	NA
1880	100
1870	112

NORTH HEBRON, CDP
Hebron Town
Washington County

1880	66

NORTH HECTOR, CDP
Hector Town
Schuyler County

1880	211

NORTH HEMPSTEAD, Town (Est. 1784)
Nassau County

1980	218,624
1970	235,007 Rev.
1960	219,088
1950	142,613
1940	83,385
1930	62,202
1920	26,370
1910	17,831
1900	12,048
1890	8,134(a)
1880	7,560
1870	6,540
1860	5,419
1850	4,291
1840	3,891
1830	3,062(b)
1820	NA
1810	2,700
1800	2,413(c)
1790	2,696(b)

(a)Reported in QUEENS County prior to
1900.
(b)Reported as North Hampstead.
(c)Reported as North Hemstead.

NORTH HILLS, Village (Inc. 1929)
North Hempstead Town
Nassau County

1980	1,587
1970	295
1960	359(a)
1950	330(a)
1940	295(a)
1930	339

(a)Boundary change.

NORTH HOOSICK, CDP
Hoosick Town
Rensselaer County

1880	239

NORTH HORNELL, Village (Inc. 1924)
Hornellsville Town
Steuben County

1980	813
1970	919
1960	917
1950	605
1940	589
1930	452

NORTH HUDSON, Town (Est. 1848)
Essex County

1980	179
1970	212
1960	220
1950	258
1940	244
1930	235
1920	397
1910	434
1900	544
1890	656
1880	693
1870	738
1860	297
1850	561

NORTH HUDSON FALLS, CDP
Kingsbury Town
Washington County

1980	2,309

NORTH ISLIP(a)
Islip Town
Suffolk County

1970	21,594(b)
1960	13,161(b)

(a)Included in NORTH BAY SHORE and WEST
ISLIP, CDPs in 1980.
(b)Derived by LIRPB from U.S. Census
Data.

NORTH JAVA, CDP
Java Town
Wyoming County

1880	205

NORTH LAWRENCE, CDP(a)
    Hempstead Town
        Nassau County
            1940   1,114
(a)Included in INWOOD, CDP after 1940.

NORTH LAWRENCE, CDP
    Lawrence Town
        St. Lawrence County
            1880   466
            1870   550

NORTH LINDENHURST, CDP
    Babylon Town
        Suffolk County
            1980   11,511
            1970   11,117
            1960   9,111(a)
(a)Derived by LIRPB from U.S. Census
    Data.

NORTH MASSAPEQUA, CDP
    Oyster Bay Town
        Nassau County
            1980   21,385
            1970   23,123
            1960   22,396(a)
(a)Derived by LIRPB from U.S. Census
    Data.

NORTH MERRICK, CDP
    Hempstead Town
        Nassau County
            1980   12,848
            1970   13,650
            1960   12,976
            1950   NA
            1940   2,072

NORTH NEW HYDE PARK, CDP
    North Hempstead Town
        Nassau County
            1980   15,114
            1970   18,154
            1960   17,929

NORTH NORWICH, CDP
    North Norwich Town
        Chenango County
            1880   164

NORTH NORWICH, Town (Est. 1849)
    Chenango County
            1980   1,687
            1970   1,579
            1960   1,096
            1950   875
            1940   770
            1930   689
            1920   619
            1910   691
            1900   801
            1890   858
            1880   964
            1870   1,075
            1860   1,171
            1850   1,172

NORTH OLEAN, Village (Inc. 1894)(a)
    Olean Town
        Cattaraugus County
            1900   1,549
(a)Merged into OLEAN City in 1906.

NORTH OWEGO, CDP
    Owego Town
        Tioga County
            1880   45

NORTH PARMA, Village
    see HILTON, Village
        Monroe County

NORTH PATCHOGUE, CDP
    Brookhaven Town
        Suffolk County
            1980   7,126(a)
            1970   7,178 Rev.(b)
            1960   4,847(c)
(a)Boundary change.
(b)Population of 4,711 is comparable to
    1980 boundaries.
(c)Derived by LIRPB from U.S. Census
    Data.

NORTH PELHAM, Village (Inc. 1896)(a)
    Pelham Town
        Westchester County
            1970   5,184
            1960   5,326
            1950   5,046
            1940   5,052
            1930   4,890
            1920   2,385
            1910   1,311
            1900   684
(a)Merged into PELHAM Village in 1975.

NORTH PEMBROKE, CDP
    Pembroke Town
        Genesee County
            1880   92

NORTH PETERSBURG, CDP
    Petersburg Town
        Rensselaer Town
            1880   149

NORTH PHARSALIA, CDP
    Pharsalia Town
        Chenango County
            1880   83

NORTH PITCHER, CDP
    Pitcher Town
        Chenango County
            1880   131

NORTHPORT, Village (Inc. 1894)
    Huntington Town
        Suffolk County
            1980   7,651
            1970   7,494 Rev.
            1960   5,972
            1950   3,859
            1940   3,093
            1930   2,528

1920	1,977
1910	2,096
1900	1,794
1890	NA
1880	1,381
1870	1,060

NORTHPORT VETERANS ADMINISTRATION HOSPITAL
Huntington Town
  Suffolk County

1980	650(a)
1970	1,828(a)
1960	2,795(a)

(a)Derived by LIRPB from U.S. Census Data.

NORTH ROSE, CDP
Rose Town
  Wayne County

1940	584
1890-1930	NA
1880	120

NORTH SALEM, Town (Est. 1788)
Westchester County

1980	4,569
1970	3,828
1960	2,345
1950	1,622
1940	1,194
1930	1,128
1920	934
1910	1,258
1900	1,133
1890	1,730
1880	1,693
1870	1,754
1860	1,497
1850	1,335
1840	1,161
1830	1,276
1820	1,165
1810	NA
1800	*1,155
1790	1,058

NORTH SEA, CDP
Southampton Town
  Suffolk County

1980	1,171
1970	669(a)
1960	389(b)

(a)Boundary change; derived by LIRPB from U.S. Census Data.
(b)Derived by LIRPB from U.S. Census Data.

NORTH SELDEN(a)
Brookhaven Town
  Suffolk County

1970	10,199(b)
1960	2,120(b)

(a)Included in SELDEN, CDP in 1980.
(b)Derived by LIRPB from U.S. Census Data.

NORTH SIDE, CDP
Waterford Town
  Saratoga County

1880	757

NORTH SOUTHOLD--BAYVIEW(a)
Southold Town
  Suffolk County

1970	1,719(b)
1960	1,339(b)

(a)Included in SOUTHOLD, CDP in 1980.
(b)Derived by LIRPB from U.S. Census Data.

NORTH SMITHTOWN(a)
Smithtown Town
  Suffolk County

1970	4,991(b)
1960	1,940(b)

(a)Included in SMITHTOWN, CDP in 1980.
(b)Derived by LIRPB from U.S. Census Data.

NORTH SYRACUSE, Village (Inc. 1925)
Cicero Town, part in
  Onondaga County

1980	2,095
1970	2,528
1960	2,261
1950	1,233
1940	928
1930	797

Clay Town, part in
  Onondaga County

1980	5,875
1970	6,159
1960	5,151(a)
1950	2,123(a)
1940	1,115(a)
1930	969

TOTAL

1980	7,970
1970	8,687
1960	7,412(a)
1950	3,356(a)
1940	2,083(a)
1930	1,766

(a)Boundary change.

NORTH TARRYTOWN, Village (Inc. 1875)
Mount Pleasant Town
  Westchester County

1980	7,994
1970	8,334
1960	8,818(a)
1950	8,740
1940	8,804
1930	7,417
1920	5,927
1910	5,421
1900	4,241
1890	3,179
1880	2,684

(a)Boundary change.

NORTHTON, Town
see YATES, Town
  Orleans County

NORTH TONAWANDA, City (Inc. 1897)(a)
  Niagara County
    1980   35,760
    1970   36,012
    1960   34,757
    1950   24,731
    1940   20,254
    1930   19,019
    1920   15,482
    1910   11,955
    1900   9,069
(a)NORTH TONAWANDA Village incorporated
   as NORTH TONAWANDA City and made independent of WHEATFIELD Town in 1897.

NORTH TONAWANDA, Village (Inc. 1865)(a)
  Wheatfield Town
    Niagara County
    1890   4,793
    1880   1,492
(a)NORTH TONAWANDA Village incorporated
   as NORTH TONAWANDA City and made independent of WHEATFIELD Town in 1897.

NORTHUMBERLAND, Town (Est. 1798)
  Saratoga County
    1980   2,732
    1970   1,779
    1960   1,353
    1950   1,263
    1940   1,109
    1930   1,059
    1920   1,048
    1910   1,127
    1900   1,227
    1890   1,410
    1880   1,583
    1870   1,655
    1860   1,666
    1850   1,775
    1840   1,672
    1830   1,606
    1820   1,279
    1810   NA
    1800   *2,007

NORTH VALLEY STREAM, CDP
  Hempstead Town
    Nassau County
    1980   14,530
    1970   14,881
    1960   17,239
    1950   NA
    1940   1,090

NORTH VICTORY, CDP
  Victory Town
    Cayuga County
    1880   35

NORTHVILLE, CDP
  Genoa Town
    Cayuga County
    1880   304

NORTHVILLE, CDP(a)
  Riverhead Town
    Suffolk County
    1980   2,583(b)

    1970   2,503(c)
    1960   2,022(c)
    1940-1950   NA
    1930   618
    1890-1920   NA
    1880   469
(a)Incorporated as Sound Avenue Village
   in 1921; name changed in 1927.
   Village dissolved in 1930.
(b)Boundary change.
(c)Derived by LIRPB from U.S. Census
   Data.

NORTHVILLE, Village (Inc. 1873)
  Northampton Town
    Fulton County
    1980   1,304
    1970   1,192
    1960   1,156
    1950   1,114
    1940   1,111
    1930   1,250
    1920   1,190
    1910   1,130
    1900   1,046
    1890   792
    1880   763

NORTH WANTAGH, CDP
  Hempstead Town
    Nassau County
    1980   12,677
    1970   15,053
    1960   15,278(a)
(a)Derived by LIRPB from U.S. Census
   Data. Census Bureau reported as part
   of WANTAGH, CDP with a population of
   34,172.

NORTHWEST, CDP
  East Hampton Town
    Suffolk County
    1880   78

NORTH WESTERN, CDP
  Western Town
    Oneida County
    1880   183

NORTHWEST HARBOR, CDP
  East Hampton Town
    Suffolk County
    1980   2,459(a)
    1970   1,022(b)
    1960   701(c)
(a)Boundary change.
(b)Derived by LIRPB from U.S. Census
   Data; population of 2,050 is
   comparable to 1980 boundaries.
(c)Derived by LIRPB from U.S. Census
   Data.

NORTON HILL, CDP
  Greenville Town
    Greene County
    1880   85

NORWAY, CDP
  Norway Town
    Herkimer County
      1880   140

NORWAY, Town (Est. 1792)
    Herkimer County
      1980   662
      1970   605
      1960   427
      1950   447
      1940   386
      1930   482
      1920   488
      1910   642
      1900   680
      1890   818
      1880   1,045
      1870   1,117
      1860   1,105
      1850   1,052
      1840   1,046
      1830   1,151
      1820   1,612
      1810   NA
      1800   *1,913

NORWICH, City (Inc. 1915)(a)
    Chenango County
      1980   8,082(b)
      1970   8,843
      1960   9,175
      1950   8,816
      1940   8,694
      1930   8,378
      1920   8,268
(a)NORWICH Village incorporated as NOR-
   WICH City and made independent of
   NORWICH Town in 1915.
(b)Boundary change.

NORWICH, Town (Est. 1793)
    Chenango County
      1980   4,042(a)
      1970   3,221
      1960   2,587
      1950   1,738
      1940   1,296
      1930   1,131
      1920   1,063(a)
      1910   8,560
      1900   7,004
      1890   6,524
      1880   5,756
      1870   5,601
      1860   4,356
      1850   3,615
      1840   4,145
      1830   3,619
      1820   3,257
      1810   NA
      1800   *2,219
(a)Boundary change.

NORWICH, Village (Inc. 1816)(a)
  Norwich Town
    Chenango County
      1910   7,422
      1900   5,766

      1890   5,212
      1880   NA
      1870   4,279
(a)NORWICH Village incorporated as NOR-
   WICH City and made independent of
   NORWICH Town in 1915.

NORWOOD, CDP
  Hempstead Town
    Nassau County
      1880   47(a)
(a)Reported in QUEENS County.

NORWOOD, Village (Inc. 1871)(a)
  Norfolk Town, part in
    St. Lawrence County
      1980   70
      1970   67
      1960   44
      1950   79
      1940   83
      1930   32
      1920   59
      1910   61
      1900   58
  Potsdam Town, part in
    St. Lawrence County
      1980   1,832
      1970   2,031
      1960   2,156(b)
      1950   1,916
      1940   1,822
      1930   1,848
      1920   1,749
      1910   1,932
      1900   1,656
      1890   1,463
      1880   1,221
    TOTAL
      1980   1,902
      1970   2,098
      1960   2,200(b)
      1950   1,995
      1940   1,905
      1930   1,880
      1920   1,808
      1910   1,993
      1900   1,714
      1880-1890   (c)
(a)Census Bureau reported a part of
   NORWOOD Village in STOCKHOLM Town
   in 1950-1970 with no population.
(b)Boundary change.
(c)Reported in POTSDAM Town only.

NOYACK, CDP
  Southampton Town
    Suffolk County
      1980   2,657(a)
      1970   1,759(b)
      1960   1,504(c)
      1890-1950   NA
      1880   227
(a)Boundary change.
(b)Derived by LIRPB from U.S. Census
   Data; population of 1,567 is
   comparable to 1980 boundaries.
(c)Derived by LIRPB from U.S. Census
   Data.

NUNDA, Town (Est. 1808)
  Livingston County

1980	2,692
1970	2,574
1960	2,309
1950	2,272
1940	2,113
1930	2,100
1920	2,272
1910	2,361
1900	2,397
1890	2,426
1880	2,790
1870	2,686
1860	2,849
1850	3,128
1840	2,637(a)
1830	1,291(a)
1820	1,188(a)

(a)Reported in ALLEGANY County.

NUNDA, Village (Inc. 1839)
  Nunda Town
    Livingston County

1980	1,169(a)
1970	1,254
1960	1,224
1950	1,224
1940	1,077
1930	1,085
1920	1,152
1910	1,043
1900	1,018
1890	1,010
1880	1,037
1870	1,189

(a)Boundary change.

NUNDA STATION, CDP
  Nunda Town
    Livingston County

1880	419

NYACK, Village (Inc. 1883)
  Clarkstown Town, part in
    Rockland County

1980	696
1970	715
1960	52(a)
1880-1950	NA
1870	432

  Orangetown Town, part in
    Rockland County

1980	5,732
1970	5,944
1960	6,010
1950	5,889
1940	5,206
1930	5,392
1920	4,444
1910	4,619
1900	4,275
1890	4,111
1880	3,881
1870	3,006

  TOTAL

1980	6,428
1970	6,659
1960	6,062(a)

1880-1950	(b)
1870	3,438

(a)Boundary change.
(b)Reported in ORANGETOWN Town only.

O

OAK BEACH, CDP
  see GILGO--OAK BEACH, CDP
    Suffolk County

OAKDALE, CDP
  Islip Town
    Suffolk County

1980	8,090
1970	7,334
1960	2,774(a)
1890-1950	NA
1880	187

(a)Derived by LIRPB from U.S. Census
  Data.

OAKFIELD, Town (Est. 1842)
  Genesee County

1980	3,213
1970	3,364
1960	3,388
1950	3,041
1940	2,896
1930	3,115
1920	2,438
1910	2,115
1900	1,589
1890	1,441
1880	1,495
1870	1,471
1860	1,597
1850	1,457

OAKFIELD, Village (Inc. 1858)
  Oakfield Town
    Genesee County

1980	1,791
1970	1,964
1960	2,070(a)
1950	1,781
1940	1,876
1930	1,919
1920	1,422
1910	1,236
1900	714
1890	578

(a)Boundary change

OAK HILL, CDP
  Durham Town
    Greene County

1880	151

OAK ORCHARD, CDP
  Ridgeway Town
    Orleans County
      1880   52

OAK ORCHARD, Town
  see CARLTON, Town
        Orleans County

OAK RIDGE, CDP
  Charleston Town
    Montgomery County
      1880   34

OAKSVILLE, CDP
  Otsego Town
    Otsego County
      1880   141

OCEAN BAY PARK
  see FIRE ISLAND
        Brookhaven Town
          Suffolk County

OCEAN BEACH, Village (Inc. 1921)
  Islip Town
    Suffolk County
      1980   155
      1970   109
      1960   111
      1950   73
      1940   81
      1930   205

OCEAN POINT, CDP
  Hempstead Town
    Nassau County
      1880   282(a)
(a)Reported in QUEENS County.

OCEANSIDE, CDP
  Hempstead Town
    Nassau County
      1980   33,639
      1970   35,372
      1960   30,488
      1950   NA
      1940   9,744

ODESSA, Village (Inc. 1903)
  Catharine Town, part in
    Schuyler County
      1980   529
      1970   568
      1960   530(a)
      1950   526
      1940   424
      1930   379
      1920   366
      1910   330
      1890-1900   NA
      1880   230
  Montour Town, part in
    Schuyler County
      1980   84
      1970   38
      1960   43(a)
    TOTAL
      1980   613

      1970   606
      1960   573(a)
      1880-1950   (b)
(a)Boundary change.
(b)Reported in CATHARINE Town only.

OFFSHORE ISLANDS
  see BAY ISLANDS
        Nassau County

OGDEN, Town (Est. 1817)
  Monroe County
      1980   14,693
      1970   11,736
      1960   7,262
      1950   3,970
      1940   3,435
      1930   3,159
      1920   2,681
      1910   3,143
      1900   2,616
      1890   2,571
      1880   2,967
      1870   2,874
      1860   2,712
      1850   2,598
      1840   2,404
      1830   2,399
      1820   1,435(a)
(a)Reported in GENESEE County.

OGDENSBURG, City (Inc. 1868)(a)
  St. Lawrence County
      1980   12,375(b)
      1970   14,554
      1960   16,122(b)
      1950   16,166
      1940   16,346
      1930   16,915
      1920   14,609(b)
      1910   15,933
      1900   12,633
      1890   11,662
      1880   10,341
      1870   10,076
(a)OGDENSBURG Village incorporated as
   OGDENSBURG City and made independent
   of OSWEGATCHIE Town in 1868.
(b)Boundary change.

OGDENSBURG, Village (Inc. 1817)(a)
  Oswegatchie Town
    St. Lawrence County
      1860   7,409(b)
      1850   NA
      1840   2,526
(a)OGDENSBURG Village incorporated as
   OGDENSBURG City and made independent
   of OSWEGATCHIE Town in 1868.
(b)Reported as Ogdensburg City.

OHIO, Town (Est. 1823)(a)
  Herkimer County
      1980   788
      1970   468
      1960   480
      1950   547
      1940   460
      1930   457

1920	583(b)
1910	527
1900	660
1890	832
1880	961
1870	1,009
1860	1,135
1850	1,051
1840	692
1830	713

(a)Established as West Brunswick in 1823;
   name changed in 1836.
(b)Boundary change.

OHIOVILLE, CDP
   New Paltz Town
      Ulster County

1880	44

OIL SPRING INDIAN RESERVATION
   Allegany County, part in

1980	2
1970	0 Rev.

   Cattaraugus County, part in

1980	4
1970	5

   TOTAL

1980	6
1970	5

OLCOTT, CDP
   Newfane Town
      Niagara County

1980	1,571
1970	1,592
1960	1,215
1950	NA
1940	772
1890-1930	NA
1880	260

OLD BETHPAGE, CDP
   Oyster Bay Town
      Nassau County

1980	6,215
1970	7,084
1960	5,273(a)

(a)Derived by LIRPB from U.S. Census
   Data. U.S. Census reported as part
   of BETHPAGE--OLD BETHPAGE, CDP with
   a population of 20,515.

OLD BROOKVILLE, Village (Inc. 1929)
   Oyster Bay Town
      Nassau County

1980	1,574
1970	1,785 Rev.
1960	1,126
1950	644
1940	356
1930	423

OLD CHATHAM, CDP
   Chatham Town
      Columbia County

1880	242

OLDENBARNEVELDT
   see BARNEVELD, Village
      Oneida County

OLD FIELD, Village (Inc. 1927)
   Brookhaven Town
      Suffolk County

1980	829
1970	812
1960	373
1950	238
1940	123
1930	202

OLD FORGE, CDP(a)
   Webb Town
      Herkimer County

1980	1,061
1950-1970	NA
1940	780
1930	840
1920	565
1910	465

(a)Incorporated as Old Forge Village in
   1906; Village dissolved in 1933.

OLD PLACE, CDP
   Northfield Town
      Richmond County

1880	187

OLD WESTBURY, Unincorporated
   North Hempstead Town
      Nassau County

1980	96(a)
1970	124(a)
1960	131(a)

(a)Derived by LIRPB from U.S. Census
   Data.

OLD WESTBURY, Village (Inc. 1924)
   North Hempstead Town, part in
      Nassau County

1980	2,175
1970	2,186
1960	1,756
1950	940(a)
1940	817(a)
1930	1,264

   Oyster Bay Town, part in
      Nassau County

1980	1,102
1970	481
1960	308
1950	220(a)
1940	200(a)

   TOTAL

1980	3,277
1970	2,667
1960	2,064
1950	1,160(a)
1940	1,017(a)
1930	(b)

(a)Boundary change.
(b)Reported in NORTH HEMPSTEAD Town only.

OLEAN, City (Inc. 1893)(a)
   Cattaraugus County

1980	18,207

1970	19,169
1960	21,868
1950	22,884
1940	21,506
1930	21,790(b)
1920	20,506
1910	14,743(b)
1900	9,462

(a)OLEAN Village incorporated as OLEAN City and made independent of OLEAN Town in 1893.
(b)Boundary change.

OLEAN, Town (Est. 1808)
    Cattaraugus County

1980	2,130
1970	2,211
1960	2,268
1950	1,800
1940	1,432
1930	1,162(a)
1920	1,316
1910	885(a)
1900	4,854(a)
1890	11,507
1880	6,575
1870	2,668
1860	2,706
1850	899
1840	638
1830	561
1820	1,047

(a)Boundary change.

OLEAN, Village (Inc. 1854)(a)
    Olean Town
    Cattaraugus County

1890	7,358
1880	3,036
1870	1,327

(a)OLEAN Village incorporated as OLEAN City and made independent of OLEAN Town in 1893.

OLINVILLE, CDP
    Westchester Town
    Westchester County

1880	476

OLIVE, Town (Est. 1823)
    Ulster County

1980	3,924
1970	2,857
1960	1,999
1950	1,463
1940	1,320
1930	1,196
1920	1,237
1910	4,497
1900	2,465
1890	2,649
1880	2,927
1870	3,083
1860	3,262
1850	2,710
1840	2,023(a)
1830	1,636

(a)Reported as Oliver.

OLMSTEADVILLE, CDP
    Minerva Town
    Essex County

1880	173

OMAR, CDP
    Orleans Town
    Jefferson County

1880	105

ONEIDA, City (Inc. 1901)(a)
    Madison County

1980	10,810
1970	11,658
1960	11,677
1950	11,325
1940	10,291
1930	10,558
1920	10,541
1910	8,317

(a)ONEIDA Village and ONEIDA Town consolidated and incorporated as ONEIDA City in 1901.

ONEIDA, County (Est. 1798)

1980	253,466
1970	273,070 Rev.
1960	264,401
1950	222,855
1940	203,636
1930	198,763
1920	182,833
1910	154,157
1900	132,800
1890	122,922
1880	115,475
1870	110,008(a)
1860	105,202
1850	99,566
1840	85,310
1830	71,326
1820	50,997
1810	33,792
1800	22,258 Rev.

(a)Boundary change.

ONEIDA, Town (Est. 1896)(a)
    Madison County

1900	7,538

(a)ONEIDA Village and ONEIDA Town consolidated and incorporated as ONEIDA City in 1901.

ONEIDA, Village (Inc. 1848)(a)
    Lenox Town
    Madison County

1900	6,364
1890	6,083
1880	3,934(b)
1870	3,262

(a)ONEIDA Village and ONEIDA Town consolidated and incorporated as ONEIDA City in 1901.
(b)Estimated.

ONEIDA CASTLE, Village (Inc. 1841)
    Vernon Town
    Oneida County

1980	751

1970	788
1960	754
1950	596
1940	556
1930	490
1920	466
1910	393
1900	291
1890	317
1880	239
1870	262

ONEIDA COMMUNITY, CDP
Lenox Town
  Madison County

1880	248

ONEIDA VALLEY, CDP
Lenox Town
  Madison County

1870	273

ONEONTA, City (Inc. 1909)(a)
Otsego County

1980	14,933(b)
1970	16,030(b)
1960	13,412
1950	13,564(b)
1940	11,731(b)
1930	12,536
1920	11,582(b)
1910	9,491

(a)ONEONTA Village incorporated as
   ONEONTA City and made independent of
   ONEONTA Town in 1909.
(b)Boundary change.

ONEONTA, Town (Est. 1796)(a)
Otsego County

1980	4,655(b)
1970	4,185(b)
1960	4,068
1950	3,508(b)
1940	2,673(b)
1930	2,314
1920	1,601(b)
1910	1,307(b)
1900	8,910
1890	8,018
1880	4,461
1870	2,568
1860	2,158
1850	1,902
1840	1,936
1830	1,757
1820	1,416
1810	NA
1800	*1,362(c)

(a)Established as Otego in 1796; name
   changed in 1830.
(b)Boundary change.
(c)Otego Town was not reported in 1800,
   but Otego Town appeared twice with
   different figures. The figure above
   is most likely the one for Otego,
   now ONEONTA Town.

ONEONTA, Village (Inc. 1870)(a)
Oneonta Town
  Otsego County

1900	7,147
1890	6,272
1880	3,002
1870	1,061

(a)ONEONTA Village incorporated as
   ONEONTA City and made independent of
   ONEONTA Town in 1909.

ONIAD LAKE, CDP
Wappinger Town
  Dutchess County

1970	1,587

ONONDAGA, County (Est. 1794)

1980	463,920 Rev.
1970	472,835 Rev.
1960	423,028
1950	341,719
1940	295,108
1930	291,606
1920	241,465
1910	200,298
1900	168,735
1890	146,247
1880	117,893
1870	104,183
1860	90,686
1850	85,890
1840	67,911
1830	58,973
1820	41,467
1810	25,987
1800	7,698 Rev.(a)

(a)Reported as Onondago.

ONONDAGA, CDP
Onondaga Town
  Onondaga County

1870	176

ONONDAGA, Town (Est. 1798)
Onondaga County

1980	17,824(a)
1970	16,555(a)
1960	13,429(a)
1950	9,351
1940	6,905
1930	5,826(a)
1920	6,620(a)
1910	5,963 Rev.(b)
1900	5,264 Rev.(b)
1890	5,135(a)
1880	6,358
1870	5,530
1860	5,113
1850	5,694
1840	5,657 Rev.
1830	5,668
1820	5,552
1810	NA
1800	*893(c)

(a)Boundary change.
(b)Boundary change. In 1920 the Census
   Bureau revised the 1910 figure
   of 6,340 and the 1900 figure of 5,580
   to exclude the ONONDAGA INDIAN

RESERVATION.
(c)Reported as Onondago.

ONONDAGA HILL, CDP
Onondaga Town
Onondaga County
1880   210

ONONDAGA INDIAN RESERVATION
Onondaga County
1980   596 Rev.
1970   785
1960   941
1950   894
1940   762
1930   611
1920   475
1910   565
1900   530

ONONDAGA VALLEY, CDP
Onondaga Town
Onondaga County
1880   194
1870   571

ONONDAGO, County & Town
see ONONDAGA, County & Town

ONTARIO, CDP
Ontario Town
Wayne County
1940   654
1890-1930   NA
1880   429

ONTARIO, County (Est. 1789)
1980   88,909
1970   78,849
1960   68,070
1950   60,172
1940   55,307
1930   54,276(a)
1920   52,652
1910   52,286
1900   49,605
1890   48,453
1880   49,541
1870   45,108
1860   44,563
1850   43,929
1840   43,501
1830   40,288
1820   88,267
1810   42,032
1800   15,218 Rev.
1790   1,075
(a)Boundary change.

ONTARIO, Town (Est. 1807)(a)
Wayne County
1980   7,480
1970   6,014
1960   4,259
1950   3,297
1940   2,851
1930   2,713
1920   2,620
1910   2,672

1900   2,550
1890   2,611
1880   2,962
1870   2,295
1860   2,320
1850   2,246
1840   1,889
1830   1,585
1820   2,233(b)
(a)Established as Freetown in 1807;
name changed in 1808.
(b)Reported in ONTARIO County.

ONTARIO CENTER, CDP
Ontario Town
Wayne County
1880   127(a)
(a)Reported as Ontario Centre.

OPPENHEIM, Town (Est. 1808)
Fulton County
1980   1,806
1970   1,431
1960   1,223
1950   1,190
1940   1,202
1930   1,147
1920   1,182
1910   1,241
1900   1,258
1890   1,563
1880   1,845
1870   1,950
1860   2,363
1850   2,315
1840   2,169(a)
1830   3,654(b)
1820   3,045(b)
(a)Reported as Openheim.
(b)Reported in MONTGOMERY County.

ORAMEL, Village (Inc. 1856)(a)
Caneadea Town
Allegany County
1920   123
1910   131
1890-1900   NA
1880   215
1870   289
(a)Dissolved in 1925.

ORANGE, County (Est. 1683)
1980   259,603
1970   221,657
1960   183,734
1950   152,255
1940   140,113
1930   130,383
1920   119,844
1910   116,001
1900   103,859
1890   97,859
1880   88,220
1870   80,902
1860   63,812
1850   57,145
1840   50,739
1830   45,366
1820   41,213

1810	34,347
1800	29,355 Rev.
1790	18,492

ORANGE, Town
  Oneida County
  see VIENNA, Town
      Oneida County

ORANGE, Town
  Rockland County
  see ORANGETOWN, Town
      Rockland County

ORANGE, Town
  Saratoga County
  see HALFMOON, Town
      Saratoga County

ORANGE, Town (Est. 1813)(a)
  Schuyler County

1980	1,358
1970	1,076
1960	1,047
1950	890
1940	693
1930	812
1920	889
1910	1,087
1900	1,391
1890	1,557
1880	2,020
1870	1,960
1860	2,364
1850	2,055(b)
1840	1,824(b)
1830	2,391(b)
1820	912(b)

(a)Established as Jersey in 1813; name
   changed in 1836.
(b)Reported in STEUBEN County.

ORANGEBURG, CDP
  Orangetown Town
  Rockland County

1940	582

ORANGE LAKE, CDP
  Newburgh Town
  Orange County

1980	5,120
1970	4,348

ORANGETOWN, Town (Est. 1788)
  Rockland County

1980	48,612
1970	53,533
1960	43,172
1950	34,554(a)
1940	26,662
1930	18,029
1920	14,284
1910	14,370
1900	10,456
1890	10,343
1880	8,077
1870	6,810
1860	7,060
1850	4,769(b)

1840	2,771
1830	1,947
1820	2,257
1810	NA
1800	*1,337(b)
1790	1,175(c)

(a)Boundary change.
(b)Reported as Orange.
(c)Reported as Orange-Town in ORANGE
   County.

ORANGEVILLE, Town (Est. 1816)
  Wyoming County

1980	1,103
1970	820
1960	633
1950	648
1940	699
1930	679
1920	838
1910	952
1900	1,005
1890	1,148
1880	1,164
1870	1,217
1860	1,419
1850	1,438
1840	1,949(a)
1830	1,525(a)
1820	1,556(a)

(a)Reported in GENESEE County.

ORCHARD PARK, Town (Est. 1850)(a)
  Erie County

1980	24,359
1970	19,978
1960	15,876
1950	8,491
1940	5,453
1930	4,234
1920	3,120
1910	2,636
1900	2,350
1890	2,304
1880	2,409
1870	2,270
1860	2,136

(a)Established as Ellicott in 1850; name
   changed to East Hamburg in 1852, and
   to ORCHARD PARK in 1934.

ORCHARD PARK, Village (Inc. 1921)
  Orchard Park Town
  Erie County

1980	3,671(a)
1970	3,732(a)
1960	3,278(a)
1950	2,054(a)
1940	1,304
1930	1,144(b)

(a)Boundary change.
(b)Reported in East Hamburg Town.

ORIENT, CDP
  Southold Town
  Suffolk County

1980	855(a)
1970	787(b)
1960	697(c)

1950	NA
1940	572
1900-1930	NA
1890	808
1880	786

(a)Boundary change; derived by LIRPB
  from U.S. Census Data.
(b)Derived by LIRPB from U.S. Census
  Data; population of 709 is
  comparable to 1980 boundaries.
(c)Derived by LIRPB from U.S. Census
  Data.

ORISKANY, Village (Inc. 1914)
  Whitestown Town
    Oneida County

1980	1,680
1970	1,627
1960	1,580
1950	1,346
1940	1,115
1930	1,142
1920	1,101
1900-1910	NA
1890	860
1880	597
1870	584

ORISKANY FALLS, Village (Inc. 1890)
  Augusta Town
    Oneida County

1980	802
1970	927
1960	972
1950	893
1940	930
1930	853
1920	1,014
1910	892
1900	811
1890	625
1880	598
1870	628(a)

(a)Part in AUGUSTA Town, 599; part in
  MARSHALL Town, 29.

ORLEANS, CDP
  Phelps Town
    Ontario County

1880	194

ORLEANS, County (Est. 1824)

1980	38,496
1970	37,305
1960	34,159
1950	29,832
1940	27,760
1930	28,795
1920	28,619
1910	32,000
1900	30,164
1890	30,803
1880	30,128
1870	27,689
1860	28,717
1850	28,501
1840	25,127
1830	17,732

ORLEANS, Town (Est. 1821)
  Jefferson County

1980	2,007
1970	1,927
1960	1,982
1950	1,807
1940	1,664
1930	1,790
1920	1,869
1910	2,160
1900	2,367
1890	2,196
1880	2,318
1870	2,445
1860	2,934
1850	3,265
1840	3,001
1830	3,091

ORRINSBURGH, Town
  see BELFAST, Town
    Allegany County

ORVILLE, CDP
  De Witt Town
    Onondaga County

1870	157

ORWELL, Town (Est. 1817)
  Oswego County

1980	1,031
1970	836
1960	663
1950	752
1940	806
1930	826
1920	890
1910	929
1900	1,149
1890	1,370
1880	1,550
1870	1,215
1860	1,435
1850	1,106
1840	808
1830	501
1820	488

OSCEOLA, CDP
  Osceola Town
    Lewis County

1880	92

OSCEOLA, Town (Est. 1844)
  Lewis County

1980	321
1970	167
1960	181
1950	244
1940	281
1930	319
1920	431
1910	456
1900	629
1890	587
1880	666
1870	688
1860	595
1850	412

OSSIAN, Town (Est. 1808)
    Livingston County

1980	667
1970	551
1960	489
1950	507
1940	532
1930	510
1920	596
1910	730
1900	780
1890	940
1880	1,204
1870	1,168
1860	1,269
1850	1,283
1840	938(a)
1830	812(a)
1820	921(a)

(a)Reported in ALLEGANY County.

OSSINING, Town (Est. 1845)(a)
    Westchester County

1980	30,680
1970	32,397
1960	26,199
1950	20,137
1940	18,911
1930	17,724
1920	12,358
1910	12,828
1900	10,895
1890	10,058
1880	8,769
1870	7,798
1860	5,345
1850	4,939

(a)Established as Ossingsing in 1845;
name changed in 1846.

OSSINING, Village (Inc. 1813)(a)
    Ossining Town
    Westchester County

1980	20,196
1970	21,659
1960	18,662(b)
1950	16,098
1940	15,996
1930	15,241(b)
1920	10,739
1910	11,480
1900	7,939
1890	9,352
1880	6,578
1870	4,696
1860	1,421(c)

(a)Incorporated as Sing Sing in 1813;
name changed in 1901.
(b)Boundary change.
(c)Reported as Assining.

OSWEGATCHIE, Town (Est. 1802)(a)
    St. Lawrence County

1980	3,846(b)
1970	3,162
1960	2,836(b)
1950	2,363
1940	2,193
1930	2,269(b)

1920	2,156
1910	2,235
1900	2,368
1890	2,346
1880	2,881
1870	3,018(b)
1860	3,412
1850	7,756
1840	3,193
1830	3,993
1820	1,661

(a)In 1800 the Census Bureau reported
an Oswegotchie Town in ONEIDA County
with a population of 159.
(b)Boundary change.

OSWEGO, City (Inc. 1848)(a)
    Oswego County

1980	19,793
1970	20,913 Rev.
1960	22,155
1950	22,647
1940	22,062
1930	22,652
1920	23,626
1910	23,368
1900	22,199
1890	21,842
1880	21,116
1870	20,910
1860	16,816
1850	12,205

(a)Oswego Village (Inc. 1828) incorporated as OSWEGO City and made independent of OSWEGO Town in 1848.

OSWEGO, County (Est. 1816)

1980	113,901
1970	100,897
1960	86,118
1950	77,181
1940	71,275
1930	69,645
1920	71,045
1910	71,664
1900	70,881
1890	71,883
1880	77,911
1870	77,941
1860	75,958
1850	62,198
1840	43,619
1830	27,119
1820	12,374

OSWEGO, Town (Est. 1818)
    Oswego County

1980	7,865
1970	6,514 Rev.
1960	2,796
1950	2,106
1940	1,972
1930	1,830
1920	1,662(a)
1910	2,671
1900	2,737
1890	2,772
1880	3,022
1870	3,043

1860	3,181
1850	2,445(a)
1840	4,665
1830	2,703
1820	992

(a)Boundary change.

OSWEGO, Town
    Tioga County
  see OWEGO, Town
        Tioga County

OSWEGO, Village
  see OSWEGO, City
        Oswego County

OSWEGO FALLS, Village (Inc. 1853)(a)
  Granby Town
    Oswego County

1900	2,925
1890	1,821
1880	1,831
1870	1,119

(a)FULTON and OSWEGO FALLS Villages
   consolidated and incorporated as
   FULTON City and made independent of
   VOLNEY, SANDY CREEK and GRANBY Towns
   in 1902.

OSWEGOTCHIE, Town
    Oneida County
  see OSWEGATCHIE, Town
        St. Lawrence County

OTEGO, Town (Est. 1796)
    Otsego County
  see ONEONTA, Town
        Otsego County

OTEGO, Town (Est. 1822)(a)
    Otsego County

1980	2,801
1970	2,249
1960	2,008
1950	1,769
1940	1,508
1930	1,373
1920	1,366
1910	1,699
1900	1,817
1890	1,840
1880	1,918
1870	2,052
1860	1,957
1850	1,792
1840	1,919
1830	1,149

(a)Established as Huntsville in 1822;
   name changed in 1830.

OTEGO, Village (Inc. 1892)
  Otego Town
    Otsego County

1980	1,089(a)
1970	956
1960	875
1950	699
1940	580
1930	555

1920	540
1910	676
1900	658
1890	NA
1880	749

(a)Boundary change.

OTESGO, Town
    Montgomery County
  see OTSEGO, Town
        Otsego County

OTISCO, Town (Est. 1806)
  Onondaga County

1980	2,112
1970	1,470
1960	1,188
1950	975
1940	873
1930	871
1920	914
1910	1,066
1900	1,202
1890	1,326
1880	1,558
1870	1,602
1860	1,848
1850	1,804
1840	1,906
1830	1,938
1820	1,726

OTISCO CENTRE, CDP
  Otisco Town
    Onondaga County

1880	159

OTISVILLE, Village (Inc. 1921)
  Mount Hope Town
    Orange County

1980	953
1970	933(a)
1960	896
1950	911
1940	889
1930	809
1890-1930	NA
1880	471

(a)Boundary change.

OTSEGO, County (Est. 1791)

1980	59,075
1970	56,181
1960	51,942
1950	50,763
1940	46,082
1930	46,710
1920	46,200
1910	47,216
1900	48,939
1890	50,861
1880	51,397
1870	48,967
1860	50,157
1850	48,638
1840	49,628
1830	51,372
1820	44,856
1810	38,802

1800	21,343 Rev.

OTSEGO, Town (Est. 1788)
Otsego County

1980	4,012
1970	3,998
1960	4,121
1950	4,304
1940	4,074
1930	4,345
1920	4,223
1910	4,287
1900	4,497
1890	4,917(a)
1880	4,690
1870	4,590
1860	2,706
1850	3,901
1840	4,120
1830	4,363
1820	4,186
1810	NA
1800	*4,224(b)
1790	1,702(c)

(a)Boundary change.
(b)Otsego Town appeared twice; the other
   reported figure was most likely for
   Otego Town, now ONEONTA.
(c)Reported as Otesgo in MONTGOMERY
   County.

OTSEGO, Village
see COOPERSTOWN, Village
   Otsego County

OTSELIC, CDP
Otselic Town
   Chenango County

1880	83

OTSELIC, Town (Est. 1817)
Chenango County

1980	955
1970	925
1960	854
1950	896
1940	905
1930	880
1920	996
1910	1,104
1900	1,234
1890	1,284
1880	1,512
1870	1,733
1860	1,752
1850	1,800
1840	1,621
1830	1,236
1820	526

OTTO, Town (Est. 1823)
Cattaraugus County

1980	828
1970	731
1960	715
1950	685
1940	642
1930	704
1920	773

1910	922
1900	1,105
1890	1,042
1880	1,111
1870	1,028
1860	1,075
1850	2,267
1840	2,133
1830	1,224

OVID, Town (Est. 1794)
Seneca County

1980	2,530
1970	3,107
1960	3,097
1950	3,442
1940	3,200
1930	2,843
1920	2,855
1910	3,355
1900	3,734
1890	3,651
1880	3,569
1870	2,403
1860	2,538
1850	2,248
1840	2,721
1830	2,756
1820	2,654
1810	NA
1800	*2,169(a)

(a)Reported in CAYUGA County.

OVID, Village (Inc. 1852)
Ovid Town, part in
   Seneca County

1980	642
1970	748
1960	762(a)
1950	646
1940	578
1930	537
1920	438
1910	548
1900	624
1890	641
1880	705
1870	724

Romulus Town, part in
   Seneca County

1980	24
1970	31
1960	27(a)

TOTAL

1980	666
1970	779
1960	789(a)
1870-1950	(b)

(a)Boundary change.
(b)Reported in OVID Town only.

OWASCO, CDP
Owasco Town
   Cayuga County

1880	240

OWASCO, Town (Est. 1802)
Cayuga County

1980	3,612

1970	3,619
1960	3,409
1950	2,543
1940	2,100
1930	1,754
1920	1,458
1910	1,393
1900	1,331
1890	1,162
1880	1,297
1870	1,261
1860	1,351
1850	1,254
1840	1,319
1830	1,350
1820	1,290

OWEGO, Town (Est. 1791)
  Tioga County

1980	20,471
1970	20,336
1960	14,710
1950	9,941
1940	8,717
1930	7,804
1920	6,707
1910	7,474
1900	8,378
1890	9,008
1880	9,884
1870	9,442
1860	8,935
1850	7,159
1840	5,340
1830	3,076
1820	1,741
1810	NA
1800	*1,284(a)

(a)Reported as Oswego.

OWEGO, Village (Inc. 1827)
  Owego Town
    Tioga County

1980	4,364
1970	5,152
1960	5,417
1950	5,350
1940	5,068
1930	4,742
1920	4,147
1910	4,633
1900	5,039
1890	NA
1880	5,525
1870	4,756

OXBOW, CDP
  Antwerp Town
    Jefferson County

1880	212

OXFORD, Town (Est. 1793)
  Chenango County

1980	3,961
1970	3,761
1960	3,457
1950	3,423
1940	3,121
1930	2,904

1920	2,871
1910	3,014
1900	3,545
1890	3,138
1880	3,035
1870	3,278
1860	3,290
1850	3,227
1840	3,179
1830	2,947
1820	2,317
1810	NA
1800	*1,405

OXFORD, Village (Inc. 1808)
  Oxford Town
    Chenango County

1980	1,765
1970	1,944
1960	1,871
1950	1,811
1940	1,713
1930	1,601
1920	1,590
1910	1,654
1900	1,931
1890	1,477
1880	1,209
1870	1,278

OYSTER BAY, CDP
  Oyster Bay Town
    Nassau County

1980	6,497
1970	6,822
1960	6,096(a)
1950	5,215
1940	4,981
1890-1930	NA
1880	1,255(b)
1870	889(b)

(a)Derived by LIRPB from U.S. Census
    Data.
(b)Reported in QUEENS County.

OYSTER BAY, Town (Est. 1788)
  Nassau County

1980	305,750
1970	333,342 Rev.
1960	290,055
1950	66,930
1940	42,594
1930	36,869
1920	20,296(a)
1910	21,802
1900	16,334
1890	13,870(b)
1880	11,923
1870	10,595
1860	9,168
1850	6,900
1840	5,865
1830	5,348
1820	NA
1810	4,725
1800	*4,548
1790	4,097

(a)Boundary change.
(b)Reported in QUEENS County prior to

1900.

OYSTER BAY COVE, Village (Inc. 1931)
  Oyster Bay Town
    Nassau County
         1980   1,799(a)
         1970   1,320
         1960   988
         1950   561
         1940   466
(a)Boundary change.

OZONE PARK, CDP
  Jamaica Town
    Queens County
         1890   539

P

PAINTED POST, Town
  see CORNING, Town
         Steuben County

PAINTED POST, Village (Inc. 1893)
  Erwin Town
    Steuben County
         1980   2,196
         1970   2,496(a)
         1960   2,570(a)
         1950   2,405
         1940   2,337
         1930   2,328
         1920   2,170
         1910   1,224
         1900   775
         1890   688
         1880   701
(a)Boundary change.

PALATINE, Town (Est. 1788)
  Montgomery County
         1980   2,819
         1970   2,711
         1960   2,556
         1950   2,529
         1940   2,420
         1930   2,287
         1920   2,232
         1910   2,517
         1900   2,569
         1890   2,871
         1880   2,786
         1870   2,814
         1860   2,605
         1850   2,856
         1840   2,823
         1830   2,742
         1820   3,936
         1810   NA
         1800   *3,517

         1790   3,404

PALATINE BRIDGE, Village (Inc. 1867)
  Palatine Town
    Montgomery County
         1980   604
         1970   601
         1960   578
         1950   592
         1940   585
         1930   503
         1920   443
         1910   392
         1900   360
         1890   NA
         1880   332
         1870   493

PALENVILLE, CDP
  Catskill Town
    Greene County
         1890   558

PALERMO, Town (Est. 1832)
  Oswego County
         1980   3,253
         1970   2,321
         1960   1,663
         1950   1,397
         1940   1,148
         1930   1,012
         1920   1,046
         1910   1,255
         1900   1,407
         1890   1,607
         1880   1,996
         1870   2,052
         1860   2,088
         1850   2,053
         1840   1,928

PALMYRA, Town (Est. 1789)
  Wayne County
         1980   7,652
         1970   7,417
         1960   6,179
         1950   4,934
         1940   4,337
         1930   4,223
         1920   4,040
         1910   4,169
         1900   3,758
         1890   4,188
         1880   4,435
         1870   4,188
         1860   4,232
         1850   3,893
         1840   3,549
         1830   3,427
         1820   3,724(a)
         1810   NA
         1800   *994(a)
(a)Reported in ONTARIO County.

PALMYRA, Village (Inc. 1819)
  Palmyra Town
    Wayne County
         1980   3,729(a)
         1970   3,776(a)

1960	3,476
1950	3,034
1940	2,709
1930	2,592
1920	2,480
1910	2,268
1900	1,937
1890	2,131
1880	2,308
1870	2,152

(a)Boundary change.

PAMELIA, Town (Est. 1819)(a)
   Jefferson County

1980	2,417
1970	1,894
1960	1,414
1950	992
1940	855
1930	979
1920	988
1910	976
1900	1,031
1890	1,104
1880	1,143
1870	1,292
1860	2,789
1850	2,528
1840	2,104
1830	2,273(b)
1820	1,342(c)

(a)Name changed to Leander in 1824;
   original name restored in 1825.
(b)Reported as Pamela.
(c)Reported as Parmelia.

PANAMA, Village (Inc. 1861)
   Harmony Town
      Chautauqua County

1980	511
1970	489
1960	450
1950	456
1940	374
1930	320
1920	298
1910	337
1900	359
1890	379
1880	473
1870	650

PARIS, Town (Est. 1792)
   Oneida County

1980	4,456
1970	4,579
1960	4,219
1950	3,459
1940	3,073
1930	2,994
1920	3,004
1910	2,659
1900	2,626
1890	3,211
1880	3,573
1870	3,575
1860	3,762
1850	4,283
1840	2,844

1830	2,765
1820	6,707
1810	NA
1800	*4,721

PARISH, Town (Est. 1828)
   Oswego County

1980	2,172
1970	1,782
1960	1,439
1950	1,264
1940	1,199
1930	1,249
1920	1,265
1910	1,311
1900	1,530
1890	1,770
1880	1,817
1870	1,929
1860	2,027
1850	1,799
1840	1,543
1830	968

PARISH, Village (Inc. 1883)
   Parish Town
      Oswego County

1980	535
1970	634
1960	567
1950	574
1940	521
1930	508
1920	476
1910	490
1900	548
1890	541
1880	402

PARISHVILLE, CDP
   Parishville Town
      St. Lawrence County

1890	578
1880	496
1870	312

PARISHVILLE, Town (Est. 1818)
   St. Lawrence County

1980	1,951
1970	1,631
1960	1,473
1950	1,245
1940	1,309
1930	1,284
1920	1,453
1910	1,785
1900	2,086
1890	2,272
1880	2,384
1870	2,241
1860	2,296
1850	2,132(a)
1840	2,250
1830	1,477
1820	594

(a)Reported as Parrishville.

PARK VIEW, CDP
  Allegany Town
    Cattaraugus County
       1880   193

PARKVILLE, CDP
  Flatbush Town
    Kings County
       1890   831

PARMA, CDP
  Parma Town
    Monroe County
       1880   146

PARMA, Town (Est. 1808)
  Monroe County
       1980   12,585
       1970   10,748
       1960   6,277
       1950   4,049
       1940   3,387
       1930   3,222
       1920   2,923
       1910   2,954
       1900   2,814
       1890   2,912
       1880   3,180
       1870   2,864
       1860   2,902
       1850   2,947
       1840   2,652
       1830   2,639
       1820   1,342(a)
(a)Reported in GENESEE County.

PARMELIA, Town
  see PAMELIA, Town
       Jefferson County

PARRISHVILLE, Town
  see PARISHVILLE, Town
       St. Lawrence County

PATCHOGUE, Village (Inc. 1893)
  Brookhaven Town
    Suffolk County
       1980   11,291
       1970   11,582
       1960   8,838(a)
       1950   7,361
       1940   7,181(a)
       1930   6,860(a)
       1920   4,031
       1910   3,824
       1900   2,926
       1890   NA
       1880   2,503
(a)Boundary change.

PATCHOGUE HIGHLANDS, CDP
  Brookhaven Town
    Suffolk County
       1950   1,159

PATTERSON, CDP
  Patterson Town
    Putnam County
       1940   538

       1890-1930   NA
       1880   315

PATTERSON, Town (Est. 1795)(a)
  Putnam County
       1980   7,247
       1970   4,124
       1960   2,853
       1950   2,075
       1940   1,328
       1930   1,196
       1920   1,231
       1910   1,536
       1900   1,644
       1890   1,402
       1880   1,579
       1870   1,418
       1860   1,501
       1850   1,371
       1840   1,349
       1830   1,529
       1820   1,578
       1810   NA
       1800   *1,546(b)
(a)Established as Franklin in 1795;
   name changed in 1808.
(b)Reported in DUTCHESS County.

PAVILION, CDP
  Pavilion Town
    Genesee County
       1940   538
       1890-1930   NA
       1880   264

PAVILION, Town (Est. 1841)
  Genesee County
       1980   2,375
       1970   2,122
       1960   1,721
       1950   1,459
       1940   1,361
       1930   1,236
       1920   1,337
       1910   1,462
       1900   1,542
       1890   1,581
       1880   1,649
       1870   1,614
       1860   1,723
       1850   1,640

PAWLING, Town (Est. 1788)
  Dutchess County
       1980   5,795
       1970   4,764
       1960   3,938
       1950   2,891
       1940   2,752
       1930   2,391
       1920   1,955
       1910   1,927
       1900   1,921
       1890   1,949
       1880   2,006
       1870   1,760
       1860   1,743
       1850   1,720
       1840   1,571(a)

1830	1,705(a)
1820	1,804(a)
1810	NA
1800	*4,269
1790	4,330

(a)Reported as Pawlings.

PAWLING, Village (Inc. 1893)
    Pawling Town
        Dutchess County

1980	1,996
1970	1,914
1960	1,734
1950	1,430
1940	1,446
1930	1,204
1920	1,032
1910	848
1900	781
1890	630
1880	580

PAWLINGS, Town
    see PAWLING, Town
        Dutchess County

PEACH LAKE, CDP
    Southeast & New Rochelle Towns
    Putnam & Westchester Counties

1980	1,464(a)

(a)Part in PUTNAM County, 998; part in
WESTCHESTER County, 466.

PEARL CREEK, CDP
    Covington Town
        Wyoming County

1880	73

PEARL RIVER, CDP
    Orangetown Town
        Rockland County

1980	15,893
1970	17,146
1950-1960	NA
1940	3,416

PEARSALL'S, CDP
    Hempstead Town
        Nassau County

1880	965(a)

(a)Reported in QUEENS County.

PEASLEYVILLE, CDP
    Peru Town
        Clinton County

1880	48

PECONIC, CDP
    Southold Town
        Suffolk County

1980	1,056(a)
1970	943(b)
1960	862(c)
1950	NA
1940	608
1890-1930	NA
1880	455

(a)Boundary change.
(b)Derived by LIRPB from U.S. Census

Data; population of 835 is
comparable to 1980 boundaries.
(c)Derived by LIRPB from U.S. Census
Data.

PEEKSKILL, City (Inc. 1940)(a)
    Westchester County

1980	18,236
1970	19,283
1960	18,737
1950	17,731
1940	17,311

(a)PEEKSKILL Village incorporated as
PEEKSKILL City and made independent
of CORTLANDT Town in 1940.

PEEKSKILL, Village (Inc. 1816)(a)
    Cortlandt Town
        Westchester County

1930	17,125
1920	15,868
1910	15,245
1900	10,358
1890	9,676
1880	6,893
1870	6,560

(a)PEEKSKILL Village incorporated as
PEEKSKILL City and made independent
of CORTLANDT Town in 1940.

PEKIN, CDP
    Cambria & Lewiston Towns
        Niagara County

1880	218

PELHAM, Town (Est. 1788)
    Westchester County

1980	12,978
1970	13,933
1960	13,404
1950	12,195(a)
1940	12,272
1930	11,851
1920	5,195
1910	2,998
1900	1,571(a)
1890	3,941
1880	2,540
1870	1,790
1860	1,025
1850	577
1840	789
1830	334
1820	283
1810	NA
1800	*943
1790	199

(a)Boundary change.

PELHAM, Village (Inc. 1896)
    Pelham Town
        Westchester County

1980	6,848(a)
1970	2,076
1960	1,964
1950	1,843
1940	1,918
1930	2,053
1920	1,056

1910	681
1900	303

(a)Boundary change.

PELHAM MANOR, Village (Inc. 1891)
Pelham Town
Westchester County

1980	6,130
1970	6,673
1960	6,114
1950	5,306(a)
1940	5,302
1930	4,908
1920	1,754
1910	852

(a)Boundary change.

PELHAMVILLE, CDP
Pelham Town
Westchester County

1880	218

PEMBROKE, Town (Est. 1812)
Genesee County

1980	4,146
1970	3,959
1960	3,451
1950	2,866
1940	2,391
1930	2,209
1920	2,202
1910	2,301
1900	2,425
1890	2,679
1880	2,845
1870	2,810
1860	2,855
1850	2,279
1840	1,970
1830	3,828
1820	2,576

PENDLETON, CDP
Pendleton Town
Niagara County

1880	136
1870	214

PENDLETON, Town (Est. 1827)
Niagara County

1980	4,726
1970	4,733
1960	3,589
1950	1,815
1940	1,516
1930	1,253
1920	1,175
1910	1,267
1900	1,364
1890	1,514
1880	1,730
1870	1,772
1860	1,833
1850	2,166
1840	1,098
1830	572

PENFIELD, CDP
Penfield & Perinton Towns
Monroe County

1950	1,113(a)
1940	807
1890-1930	NA
1880	394(b)

(a)Part in PENFIELD Town, 963; part in
   PERINTON Town, 50.
(b)Reported in PENFIELD Town only.

PENFIELD, Town (Est. 1810)
Monroe County

1980	27,201
1970	23,782
1960	12,601
1950	4,847
1940	3,774
1930	3,306
1920	2,087
1910	2,977
1900	2,857
1890	2,845
1880	2,955
1870	2,928
1860	3,210
1850	3,185
1840	2,842
1830	4,474
1820	3,244

PENN YAN, Village (Inc. 1833)
Benton Town, part in
Yates County

1980	410
1970	335
1960	351
1950	384
1940	279
1930	295
1920	202
1910	211
1900	209
1890	222
1880	165
1870	485

Jerusalem Town, part in
Yates County

1980	53
1970	17
1960	87
1950	7
1940	0

Milo Town, part in
Yates County

1980	4,779
1970	4,941
1960	5,332(a)
1950	5,090
1940	5,029
1930	5,034
1920	4,315
1910	4,386
1900	4,441
1890	4,032
1880	3,310
1870	3,003

TOTAL

1980	5,242(a)

1970	5,293 Rev.
1960	5,770(a)
1950	5,481
1940	5,308(a)
1930	5,329
1920	4,517
1910	4,597
1900	4,650
1890	4,254
1880	3,475
1870	3,488
1860	2,388

(a)Boundary change.

PEORIA, CDP
  Covington Town
    Wyoming County

1880	75

PERINTON, Town (Est. 1812)
  Monroe County

1980	41,802
1970	31,568
1960	16,314
1950	11,559
1940	10,170
1930	9,854
1920	7,799
1910	6,566
1900	4,703
1890	4,450
1880	4,030
1870	3,261
1860	3,015(a)
1850	2,891
1840	2,513(b)
1830	2,183(b)
1820	1,664(c)

(a)Reported as Perrinton.
(b)Reported as Perrington.
(c)Reported in ONTARIO County.

PERKINSVILLE, CDP
  Wayland Town
    Steuben county

1880	170

PERRINGTON, Town
  see PERINTON, Town
    Monroe County

PERRINTON, Town
  see PERINTON, Town
    Monroe County

PERRY, Town
    Cattaraugus County
  see PERRYSBURG, Town
    Cattaraugus County

PERRY, Town (Est. 1814)
  Wyoming County

1980	5,437
1970	5,367
1960	5,372
1950	5,342
1940	5,251
1930	5,086
1920	5,400

1910	5,360
1900	3,862
1890	2,928
1880	2,571
1870	2,342
1860	2,452
1850	2,832
1840	3,082(a)
1830	2,792(a)
1820	2,317(a)

(a)Reported in GENESEE County.

PERRY, Village (Inc. 1830)
  Castile Town, part in
    Wyoming County

1980	317
1970	475
1960	424
1950	348
1940	304
1930	227
1920	267
1910	264
1900	251

  Perry Town, part in
    Wyoming County

1980	3,881
1970	4,063
1960	4,205
1950	4,185
1940	4,164
1930	4,004
1920	4,450
1910	4,124
1900	2,512
1890	1,528
1880	1,115
1870	867

  TOTAL

1980	4,198
1970	4,538
1960	4,629
1950	4,533
1940	4,468
1930	4,231
1920	4,717
1910	4,388
1900	2,763
1870-1890	(a)

(a)Reported in PERRY Town only.

PERRY CENTER, CDP
  Perry Town
    Wyoming County

1880	159(a)
1870	183(a)

(a)Reported as Perry Centre.

PERRY CITY, CDP
  Hector town
    Schuyler County

1880	142

PERRYSBURG, Town (Est. 1814)(a)
    Cattaraugus County

1980	2,180
1970	2,236
1960	1,857
1950	1,507

1940	1,805
1930	1,358
1920	1,150
1910	1,004 Rev.(b)
1900	1,067 Rev.(b)
1890	1,123
1880	1,376
1870	1,313
1860	1,439
1850	1,861
1840	1,660(c)
1830	2,440(c)
1820	835(c)

(a)Established as Perry in 1814; name
   changed in 1818.
(b)In 1920 the Census Bureau revised the
   1910 figure of 1,184 and the 1900
   figure of 1,216 to exclude the
   CATTARAUGUS INDIAN RESERVATION.
(c)Reported as Perrysburgh.

PERRYSBURG, Village (Inc. 1916)
   Perrysburg Town
      Cattaraugus County

1980	405
1970	433
1960	434
1950	361
1940	375
1930	317
1920	271
1890-1910	NA
1880	371

PERRYSBURGH, Town
   see PERRYSBURG, Town
          Cattaraugus County

PERRY'S MILLS, CDP
   Champlain Town
      Clinton County

1880	283
1870	276

PERRYVILLE, CDP
   Sullivan Town
      Madison County

1880	119

PERSIA, Town (Est. 1835)
   Cattaraugus County

1980	2,442
1970	2,587
1960	2,756
1950	2,615
1940	2,671
1930	2,510
1920	2,194
1910	1,730
1900	1,940
1890	1,506
1880	1,370
1870	1,220
1860	1,304
1850	1,955
1840	892

PERTH, Town (Est. 1831)
   Fulton County

1980	3,261
1970	2,383
1960	1,768
1950	1,299
1940	1,000
1930	838
1920	596
1910	695
1900	667
1890	769
1880	915
1870	1,013
1860	1,085
1850	1,140
1840	737

PERU, CDP
   Peru Town
      Clinton County

1980	1,716
1970	1,261
1950-1960	NA
1940	737
1890-1930	NA
1880	343

PERU, Town (Est. 1792)
   Clinton County

1980	5,352
1970	4,312
1960	3,848 Rev.
1950	2,348
1940	2,287
1930	1,989
1920	2,000
1910	2,236
1900	2,372
1890	2,356
1880	2,610
1870	2,632
1860	3,389
1850	3,640
1840	3,134
1830	4,949
1820	2,710
1810	NA
1800	*1,347

PERU, Town (Est. 1792)(a)
   Onondaga County
(a)Divided into AURELIUS, MILTON, OVID,
   ROMULUS and SCIPIO Towns in 1794.

PERUVILLE, CDP
   Groton Town
      Tompkins County

1880	141

PETERBORO, CDP
   Smithfield Town
      Madison County

1880	330
1870	368

PETERSBURG, CDP
  Petersburg Town
    Rensselaer County
      1880   315

PETERSBURG, Town (Est. 1791)
    Rensselaer County
      1980   1,369
      1970   1,187
      1960   989
      1950   1,010
      1940   955
      1930   976
      1920   1,066
      1910   1,238
      1900   1,449
      1890   1,461
      1880   1,785
      1870   1,732(a)
      1860   3,807
      1850   1,908(a)
      1840   1,901
      1830   2,011(a)
      1820   2,248(a)
      1810   NA
      1800   *4,412
(a)Reported as Petersburgh.

PHARSALIA, Town (Est. 1806)(a)
    Chenango County
      1980   606
      1970   520
      1960   515
      1950   480
      1940   676
      1930   464
      1920   553
      1910   657
      1900   780
      1890   915
      1880   1,147
      1870   1,141
      1860   1,261
      1850   1,185
      1840   1,213
      1830   1,011
      1820   873
(a)Established as Stonington in 1806;
   name changed in 1808.

PHELPS, Town (Est. 1796)
    Ontario County
      1980   6,522
      1970   6,330(a)
      1960   5,825
      1950   4,890
      1940   4,425
      1930   4,590
      1920   4,205
      1910   4,733
      1900   4,788
      1890   5,086
      1880   5,189
      1870   5,130
      1860   5,586
      1850   5,542
      1840   5,563
      1830   4,876
      1820   5,688

      1810   NA
      1800   *1,097
(a)Boundary change.

PHELPS, Village (Inc. 1855)
    Phelps Town
    Ontario County
      1980   2,004
      1970   1,989
      1960   1,887
      1950   1,650
      1940   1,499
      1930   1,397
      1920   1,200
      1910   1,354
      1900   1,306
      1890   1,336
      1880   1,369
      1870   1,355

PHENIX, Village
    see PHOENIX, Village
        Oswego County

PHILADELPHIA, Town (Est. 1821)
    Jefferson County
      1980   1,417
      1970   1,355
      1960   1,297
      1950   1,222
      1940   1,372
      1930   1,562
      1920   1,549
      1910   1,640
      1900   1,750
      1890   1,662
      1880   1,750
      1870   1,679
      1860   1,785
      1850   1,915
      1840   1,888
      1830   1,167

PHILADELPHIA, Village (Inc. 1872)
    Philadelphia Town
    Jefferson County
      1980   855
      1970   858
      1960   868
      1950   870
      1940   722
      1930   817
      1920   794
      1910   842
      1900   873
      1890   783
      1880   NA
      1870   384

PHILIPSTOWN, Town (Est. 1788)
    Putnam County
      1980   9,155
      1970   7,717
      1960   5,918
      1950   4,332
      1940   4,246
      1930   3,982
      1920   3,272
      1910   5,345

1900	4,642
1890	4,113
1880	4,375
1870	5,117
1860	1,760(a)
1850	5,063
1840	3,814
1830	4,761(b)
1820	3,733(b)
1810	NA
1800	*2,754(c)
1790	2,079(d)

(a)Reported as Phillipstown.
(b)Reported as Phillips.
(c)Reported as Philips.
(d)Reported as Phillipstown in DUTCHESS
   County.

PHILIPSTOWN, Town
     Rensselaer County
   see NASSAU, Town
        Rensselaer County

PHILLIPS, Town
   see PHILIPSTOWN, Town
        Putnam County

PHILLIP'S CREEK, CDP
   Ward Town
     Allegany County

1880	48

PHILLIPSPORT, CDP
   Mamakating Town
     Sullivan County

1880	661

PHILLIPSTOWN, Town
   see PHILIPSTOWN, Town
        Putnam County

PHILMONT, Village (Inc. 1892)
   Claverack Town
     Columbia County

1980	1,539(a)
1970	1,674
1960	1,750
1950	1,792
1940	1,679
1930	1,868
1920	1,919
1910	1,813
1900	1,964
1890	1,818
1880	1,343
1870	699

(a)Boundary change.

PHOENIX, Village (Inc. 1849)
   Schroeppel Town
     Oswego County

1980	2,357(a)
1970	2,617
1960	2,408
1950	1,917
1940	1,757
1930	1,758
1920	1,747
1910	1,642

1900	1,532
1890	1,466(b)
1880	1,312
1870	1,418
1860	NA
1850	872

(a)Boundary change.
(b)Reported as Phenix.

PIERCEFIELD, Town (Est. 1900)
   St. Lawrence County

1980	365
1970	422
1960	420
1950	554
1940	667
1930	1,330
1920	1,454
1910	770

PIERMONT, Village (Inc. 1847)
   Orangetown Town
     Rockland County

1980	2,269
1970	2,386
1960	1,906
1950	1,897
1940	1,876
1930	1,765
1920	1,600
1910	1,380
1900	1,153
1890	1,219
1880	1,369
1870	1,703

PIERREPONT, Town (Est. 1818)
   St. Lawrence County

1980	2,207
1970	1,726
1960	1,523
1950	1,192
1940	1,312
1930	1,379
1920	1,425
1910	1,628
1900	1,885
1890	1,954
1880	2,494
1870	2,391
1860	2,267(a)
1850	1,459(a)
1840	1,430(a)
1830	749(a)
1820	235(b)

(a)Reported as Pierpont.
(b)Reported as Pierpoint.

PIFFARD, CDP
   York Town
     Livingston County

1880	134(a)

(a)Reported as Piffardina.

PIKE, Town (Est. 1818)
   Wyoming County

1980	991
1970	916
1960	878

1950	885
1940	838
1930	913
1920	1,003
1910	1,194
1900	1,277
1890	1,443
1880	1,797
1870	1,730
1860	1,824
1850	2,003
1840	2,176(a)
1830	2,016(a)
1820	1,622(a)

(a)Reported in ALLEGANY County.

PIKE, Village (Inc. 1848)
  Pike Town
    Wyoming County

1980	367
1970	373
1960	345
1950	286
1940	307
1930	321
1920	304
1910	422
1900	458
1890	483
1880	644
1870	551

PIKE POND, CDP
  Delaware Town
    Sullivan County

1880	120

PILGRIM PSYCHIATRIC CENTER
  Islip Town
    Suffolk County

1980	3,865(a)
1970	8,199(a)
1960	12,112(a)

(a)Derived by LIRPB from U.S. Census
   Data.

PINCKNEY, Town (Est. 1808)
  Lewis County

1980	305
1970	319
1960	357
1950	439
1940	613
1930	646
1920	688
1910	806
1900	934
1890	1,004
1880	1,152
1870	1,149
1860	1,393
1850	1,208
1840	907
1830	763
1820	507

PINE BUSH, CDP
  Crawford Town
    Orange County

1980	1,255
1970	1,183
1960	1,016
1950	NA
1940	687

PINEFIELD, Town
  see TOMPKINS, Town
       Delaware County

PINE HILL, Village (Inc. 1895)
  Shandaken Town
    Ulster County

1980	216
1970	247
1960	180
1950	233
1940	242
1930	289
1920	248
1910	417
1900	425

PINE ISLAND, CDP
  Warwick Town
    Orange County

1880	65

PINELAWN(a)
  Babylon Town
    Suffolk County

1970	6,442(b)
1960	4,174(b)

(a)Included in WYANDANCH, CDP in 1980.
(b)Derived by LIRPB from U.S. Census
   Data.

PINE NECK--WEST TIANA, CDP(a)
  Southampton Town
    Suffolk County

1970	1,326
1960	848(b)

(a)Included in EAST QUOGUE, CDP in
   1980.
(b)Derived by LIRPB from U.S. Census
   Data.

PINE PLAINS, CDP
  Pine Plains Town
    Dutchess County

1980	1,303
1950-1970	NA
1940	665
1890-1930	NA
1880	529
1870	401

PINE PLAINS, Town (Est. 1823)
  Dutchess County

1980	2,199
1970	1,792
1960	1,608
1950	1,360
1940	1,301
1930	1,209
1920	1,252

1910	1,420
1900	1,263
1890	1,308
1880	1,352
1870	1,503
1860	1,412
1850	1,416
1840	1,334
1830	1,503

PINE VALLEY, CDP
  Catlin & Veteran Towns
    Chemung County

1880	276
1870	260

PITCAIRN, Town (Est. 1836)
  St. Lawrence County

1980	792
1970	676 Rev.
1960	647
1950	569
1940	521
1930	570
1920	646
1910	816
1900	902
1890	1,103
1880	790
1870	667
1860	577
1850	503
1840	396(a)

(a)Reported as Pitkin.

PITCHER, CDP
  Pitcher Town
    Chenango County

1880	144
1870	148

PITCHER, Town (Est. 1827)
  Chenango County

1980	735
1970	627
1960	650
1950	636
1940	643
1930	598
1920	609
1910	664
1900	751
1890	983
1880	1,075
1870	1,124
1860	1,276
1850	1,403
1840	1,562
1830	1,214

PITCHER HILL, CDP
  Clay & Salina Towns
    Onondaga County

1980	6,063

PITKIN, Town
  see PITCAIRN, Town
    St. Lawrence County

PITTSFIELD, Town (Est. 1797)
  Otsego County

1980	1,067
1970	968
1960	880
1950	850
1940	796
1930	727
1920	813
1910	917
1900	1,101
1890	1,218
1880	1,450
1870	1,469
1860	1,480
1850	1,591
1840	1,395
1830	1,006
1820	830
1810	NA
1800	*1,206

PITTSFORD, Town (Est. 1814)(a)
  Monroe County

1980	26,743
1970	25,058
1960	15,156
1950	9,413
1940	7,741
1930	7,192
1920	4,614
1910	3,634
1900	2,373
1890	2,129
1880	2,236
1870	1,974
1860	2,028
1850	2,061
1840	1,983
1830	1,831
1820	1,582(b)

(a)Established as Northfield in ONTARIO
   County in 1789; name changed to Boyle
   in 1808 and to Smallwood in 1813.
   Divided into BRIGHTON and PITTSFORD
   Towns in 1814.
(b)Reported in ONTARIO County.

PITTSFORD, Village (Inc. 1827)
  Pittsford Town
    Monroe County

1980	1,568
1970	1,755
1960	1,749
1950	1,668
1940	1,544
1930	1,460
1920	1,328
1910	1,205
1900	1,000
1890	852
1880	756
1870	505

PITTSTOWN, Town
  Ontario County
  see RICHMOND, Town
    Ontario County

PITTSTOWN, Town (Est. 1788)
Rensselaer County
1980	4,901
1970	3,905
1960	2,973
1950	2,666
1940	2,491
1930	2,426
1920	2,342
1910	2,920
1900	3,236
1890	4,056
1880	4,095
1870	4,093
1860	1,717
1850	3,732
1840	3,784
1830	3,702
1820	3,772
1810	NA
1800	*3,483
1790	2,447(a)

(a)Reported as Pitts-Town in ALBANY
County.

PLAINEDGE, CDP
Oyster Bay Town
Nassau County
1980	9,629
1970	10,759(a)
1960	11,072(b)

(a)Boundary change.
(b)Derived by LIRPB from U.S. Census
Data; population is comparable to
1970-1980 boundaries. U.S. Census
included part of NORTH MASSAPEQUA,
CDP with a population of 21,973.

PLAINFIELD, CDP
Hempstead Town
Nassau County
1880	107(a)

(a)Reported in QUEENS County.

PLAINFIELD, Town (Est. 1799)
Otsego County
1980	847
1970	742
1960	764
1950	729
1940	670
1930	707
1920	791
1910	844
1900	897
1890	1,025
1880	1,195
1870	1,248
1860	1,354
1850	1,450
1840	1,450
1830	1,626
1820	1,611
1810	NA
1800	*1,005

PLAINVIEW, CDP
Oyster Bay Town
Nassau County
1980	28,037
1970	31,695 Rev.
1960	27,941 Rev.
1950	NA
1940	527

PLAINVILLE, CDP
Lysander Town
Onondaga County
1880	138
1870	161

PLANDOME, Village (Inc. 1911)
North Hempstead Town
Nassau County
1980	1,503
1970	1,593
1960	1,379
1950	1,102
1940	897
1930	769(a)
1920	319

(a)Boundary change.

PLANDOME HEIGHTS, Village (Inc. 1929)
North Hempstead Town
Nassau County
1980	986 Rev.
1970	1,032
1960	1,025
1950	882(a)
1940	317
1930	265

(a)Boundary change.

PLANDOME MANOR, Village (Inc. 1931)
North Hempstead Town
Nassau County
1980	883
1970	835
1960	705
1950	323
1940	262

PLATKILL, Town
see PLATTEKILL, Town
Ulster County

PLATO, Town
see SUMMERHILL, Town
Cayuga County

PLATTEKILL, CDP
Saugerties Town
Ulster County
1880	574

PLATTEKILL, Town (Est. 1800)
Ulster County
1980	7,409
1970	4,458
1960	3,009
1950	2,215
1940	2,082
1930	1,713
1920	1,798

1910	1,879
1900	1,866
1890	2,038
1880	2,205
1870	2,031
1860	1,918
1850	1,998
1840	2,125
1830	2,044
1820	2,139
1810	NA
1800	*1,625(a)

(a)Reported as Platkill.

PLATTSBOROUGH, Town
    see PLATTSBURGH, Town
        Clinton County

PLATTSBURG, Town
    see PLATTSBURGH, Town
        Clinton County

PLATTSBURGH, City (Inc. 1902)(a)
    Clinton County

1980	21,057(b)
1970	18,715
1960	20,172
1950	17,738
1940	16,351(b)
1930	13,349
1920	10,909
1910	11,138(b)

(a)PLATTSBURGH Village incorporated as
    PLATTSBURGH City and made independ-
    ent of PLATTSBURGH Town in 1902.
(b)Boundary change.

PLATTSBURGH, Town (Est. 1785)
    Clinton County

1980	16,384(a)
1970	15,881
1960	14,515 Rev.
1950	3,713
1940	3,163(a)
1930	2,132
1920	2,085
1910	2,362(a)
1900	11,612
1890	9,500
1880	8,283
1870	8,414
1860	3,648(b)
1850	5,618
1840	6,416
1830	4,913
1820	3,519
1810	NA
1800	*1,400(c)
1790	458

(a)Boundary change.
(b)Reported as Plattsburg.
(c)Reported as Plattsborough.

PLATTSBURGH, Village (Inc. 1815)(a)
    Plattsburgh Town
        Clinton County

1900	8,434
1890	7,010
1880	5,245

1870	5,139
1860	3,032

(a)PLATTSBURGH Village incorporated as
    PLATTSBURGH City and made indepen-
    dent of PLATTSBURGH Town in 1902.

PLATTSBURGH AIR FORCE BASE, CDP
    Plattsburgh Town
        Clinton County

1980	5,905
1970	7,078

PLATTSBURGH WEST, CDP
    Plattsburgh Town
        Clinton County

1980	1,210

PLEASANT BROOK, CDP
    Roseboom Town
        Otsego County

1880	94

PLEASANT PLAINS, CDP
    Westfield Town
        Richmond County

1880	489

PLEASANT VALLEY, CDP(a)
    Pleasant Valley Town
        Dutchess County

1980	1,255
1970	1,372
1930-1960	NA
1920	384
1910	427
1900	NA
1890	438
1880	429

(a)Incorporated as Pleasant Valley
    Village in 1903; Village dissolved
    in 1926.

PLEASANT VALLEY, CDP
    Whitestown Town
        Oneida County

1870	87

PLEASANT VALLEY, Town (Est. 1821)
    Dutchess County

1980	6,892
1970	6,021
1960	4,046
1950	2,751
1940	2,061
1930	1,520
1920	1,160
1910	1,358
1900	1,483
1890	1,531
1880	1,785
1870	1,963
1860	2,343
1850	2,226
1840	2,219
1830	2,419

PLEASANTVILLE, Village (Inc. 1897)
  Mount Pleasant Town
    Westchester County
      1980   6,749
      1970   7,110
      1960   5,877(a)
      1950   4,861(a)
      1940   4,454(a)
      1930   4,540
      1920   3,590
      1910   2,207
      1900   1,204
(a)Boundary change.

PLESSIS, CDP
  Alexandria Town
    Jefferson County
      1880   214

PLUM ISLAND, CDP
  Southold Town
    Suffolk County
      1880   15

PLYMOUTH, CDP
  Plymouth Town
    Chenango County
      1880   144
      1870   179

PLYMOUTH, Town (Est. 1806)
  Chenango County
      1980   1,515
      1970   1,174
      1960   1,004
      1950   858
      1940   792
      1930   767
      1920   885
      1910   913
      1900   1,026
      1890   1,156
      1880   1,302
      1870   1,523
      1860   1,668
      1850   1,551
      1840   1,625
      1830   1,609
      1820   1,496

POESTENKILL, CDP
  Poestenkill Town
    Rensselaer County
      1980   1,031
      1890-1970   NA
      1880   250

POESTENKILL, Town (Est. 1848)
  Rensselaer County
      1980   3,664
      1970   3,426
      1960   2,493
      1950   1,799
      1940   1,438
      1930   1,164
      1920   1,002
      1910   1,078
      1900   1,362
      1890   1,602

      1880   1,672
      1870   1,769
      1860   1,833
      1850   2,092

POINT LOOKOUT
  see LIDO--POINT LOOKOUT
    Suffolk County

POINT O' WOODS--CHERRY GROVE--FIRE
ISLAND PINES(a)
  Brookhaven Town
    Suffolk County
      1970   24(b)
(a)Included in FIRE ISLAND, BROOKHAVEN
   Town, in 1980.
(b)Derived by LIRPB from U.S. Census
   Data.

POINT PLEASANT, CDP
  Irondequoit Town
    Monroe County
      1940   1,122

POLAND, Town (Est. 1832)
  Chautauqua County
      1980   2,639
      1970   2,318
      1960   2,036
      1950   1,949
      1940   1,625
      1930   1,598
      1920   1,308
      1910   1,447
      1900   1,613
      1890   1,608
      1880   1,539
      1870   1,418
      1860   1,794
      1850   1,174
      1840   1,087

POLAND, Village (Inc. 1890)
  Newport Town, part in
    Herkimer County
      1980   149
      1970   154
      1960   160
      1950   112
      1940   102
      1930   109
      1920   79
      1910   79
      1900   100
  Russia Town, part in
    Herkimer County
      1980   404
      1970   475
      1960   404
      1950   399
      1940   376
      1930   353
      1920   270
      1910   253
      1900   270
  TOTAL
      1980   553
      1970   629
      1960   564

1950	511
1940	478
1930	462
1920	349
1910	332
1900	370
1890	NA
1880	282

POLKVILLE, CDP
Lysander Town
Onondaga County

1880	34

POMFRET, Town (Est. 1808)
Chautauqua County

1980	14,992
1970	13,890
1960	11,459
1950	9,596
1940	7,782
1930	8,062
1920	7,973
1910	7,309
1900	6,313
1890	5,479
1880	4,551
1870	4,306
1860	4,293
1850	4,483
1840	4,566
1830	3,386
1820	2,306

POMONA, Village (Inc. 1967)
Haverstraw Town, part in
Rockland County

1980	1,170
1970	762

Ramapo Town, part in
Rockland County

1980	1,251
1970	1,030

TOTAL

1980	2,421
1970	1,792

POMPEY, Town (Est. 1789)
Onondaga County

1980	4,492
1970	4,536
1960	3,469
1950	2,531
1940	2,099
1930	1,996
1920	1,882
1910	2,093
1900	2,546
1890	2,859
1880	3,240
1870	3,314
1860	3,931
1850	4,006
1840	4,371
1830	4,812
1820	6,701
1810	NA
1800	*2,332

PONQUOGUE(a)
Southampton Town
Suffolk County

1970	1,474(b)
1960	934(b)

(a)Included in HAMPTON BAYS, CDP in 1980.
(b)Derived by LIRPB from U.S. Census Data.

PONTIAC, CDP
Evans Town
Erie County

1870	100

POOLVILLE, CDP
Hamilton Town
Madison County

1880	172
1870	163

POOSPATUCK, CDP
Brookhaven Town
Suffolk County

1880	24

POOSPATUCK INDIAN RESERVATION
Suffolk County

1980	203(a)
1970	160 Rev.(b)
1940-1960	NA
1930	34(c)

(a)Boundary change; derived by LIRPB from U.S. Census Data.
(b)Derived by LIRPB from U.S. Census Data; population is comparable to 1980 boundaries.
(c)Derived by New York State. U.S. Census reported with SHINNECOCK INDIAN RESERVATION, population of 194.

POPE'S MILLS, CDP
Macomb Town
St. Lawrence County

1880	84
1870	76

POQUOTT, Village (Inc. 1931)
Brookhaven Town
Suffolk County

1980	588
1970	427
1960	295
1950	136
1940	73

PORTAGE, Town (Est. 1827)
Livingston County

1980	771
1970	731
1960	733
1950	737
1940	945
1930	793
1920	860
1910	1,273
1900	1,029
1890	1,130
1880	1,295

1870	1,338
1860	1,519
1850	2,478
1840	4,721(a)
1830	1,839(a)

(a)Reported in ALLEGANY County.

PORTAGEVILLE, CDP
  Genesee Falls Town
    Wyoming County

1870	491

PORT BAY, Town
  see HURON, Town
    Wayne County

PORT BYRON, Village (Inc. 1837)
  Mentz Town
    Cayuga County

1980	1,400
1970	1,330
1960	1,201
1950	1,013
1940	961
1930	890
1920	1,035
1910	1,085
1900	1,013
1890	1,105
1880	1,146
1870	1,089

PORT CHESTER, Village (Inc. 1868)
  Rye Town
    Westchester County

1980	23,565
1970	25,803
1960	24,960
1950	23,970
1940	23,073
1930	22,662
1920	16,573
1910	12,809
1900	7,440
1890	5,274
1880	3,254
1870	3,797

PORT CRANE, Town
  see FENTON, Town
    Broome County

PORT DICKINSON, Village (Inc. 1876)
  Dickinson Town
    Broome County

1980	1,974
1970	2,132
1960	2,295
1950	2,199
1940	2,436
1930	1,902
1920	883
1910	437
1900	379
1890	345(a)
1880	373(a)

(a)Reported in BINGHAMTON Town.

PORTER, Town (Est. 1812)
  Niagara County

1980	7,251
1970	7,429
1960	7,309
1950	4,276
1940	3,361
1930	2,954
1920	2,682
1910	2,655
1900	2,235
1890	2,210
1880	2,278
1870	2,042
1860	2,132
1850	2,455
1840	2,177
1830	1,490
1820	850

PORT EWEN, CDP
  Esopus Town
    Ulster County

1980	2,813
1970	2,882
1960	2,622
1950	1,885
1940	1,239
1900-1930	NA
1890	1,211
1880	1,580
1870	1,251

PORT GIBSON, CDP
  Manchester Town
    Ontario County

1880	299

PORT GLASGOW, CDP
  Huron Town
    Wayne County

1880	74

PORT HENRY, Village (Inc. 1869)
  Moriah Town
    Essex County

1980	1,450
1970	1,532
1960	1,767
1950	1,831
1940	1,935
1930	2,040
1920	2,183
1910	2,266
1900	1,751
1890	2,436
1880	2,494

PORT JACKSON, Village(a)
  Florida Town
    Montgomery County

1880	715
1870	446

(a)Incorporation date unavailable; merged
    into AMSTERDAM City in 1888.

PORT JEFFERSON, Village (Inc. 1963)
  Brookhaven Town
    Suffolk County
      1980   6,731(a)
      1970   5,515(b)
      1960   3,582 Rev.
      1950   3,296
      1940   2,196
      1900-1930   NA
      1890   2,026
      1880   1,724
(a)Boundary change.
(b)Population of 5,795 is comparable to
   1980 boundaries.

PORT JEFFERSON STATION, CDP
  Brookhaven Town
    Suffolk County
      1980   17,009(a)
      1970   7,403(b)
      1960   2,127 Rev.
      1950   NA
      1940   600
(a)Boundary change.
(b)Population of 14,808 is comparable
   to 1980 boundaries.

PORT JERVIS, City (Inc. 1907)(a)
  Orange County
      1980   8,699
      1970   8,852
      1960   9,268
      1950   9,372(b)
      1940   9,749
      1930   10,243
      1920   10,171
      1910   9,564
(a)PORT JERVIS Village incorporated as
   PORT JERVIS City and made independent of DEERPARK Town in 1907.
(b)Boundary change.

PORT JERVIS, Village (Inc. 1853)(a)
  Deerpark Town
    Orange County
      1900   9,385
      1890   9,327
      1880   8,678
      1870   6,377
(a)PORT JERVIS Village incorporated as
   PORT JERVIS City and made independent of DEERPARK Town in 1907.

PORT KENT, CDP
  Chesterfield Town
    Essex County
      1880   139

PORTLAND, Town (Est. 1813)
  Chautauqua County
      1980   4,433
      1970   3,802
      1960   3,605
      1950   3,339
      1940   2,965
      1930   3,001
      1920   3,140
      1910   3,058
      1900   2,690

      1890   2,423
      1880   2,014
      1870   1,887
      1860   1,984
      1850   1,905
      1840   2,136
      1830   1,771
      1820   1,162

PORT LEYDEN, Village (Inc. 1871)
  Leyden Town, part in
    Lewis County
      1980   539
      1970   625
      1960   671
      1950   660
      1940   624
      1930   571
      1920   592
      1910   603
      1900   578
      1890   462
      1880   NA
      1870   723
  Lyonsdale Town, part in
    Lewis County
      1980   201
      1970   237
      1960   227
      1950   181
      1940   170
      1930   146
      1920   143
      1910   161
      1900   168
  TOTAL
      1980   740
      1970   862
      1960   898
      1950   841
      1940   794
      1930   717
      1920   735
      1910   764
      1900   746
      1890   (a)
      1880   NA
      1870   977(b)
(a)Reported in LEYDEN Town only.
(b)Part in GREIG Town 254; part in
   LEYDEN Town, 723.

PORT RICHMOND, Village (Inc. 1866)(a)
  Northfield Town
    Richmond County
      1890   6,290
      1880   3,561
      1870   3,028
(a)Merged into STATEN ISLAND Borough in
   NEW YORK City in 1898.

PORTVILLE, Town (Est. 1837)
  Cattaraugus County
      1980   4,486
      1970   4,252
      1960   3,321
      1950   3,029
      1940   2,593
      1930   2,407

1920	2,164
1910	2,371
1900	2,319
1890	2,339
1880	2,400
1870	1,814
1860	1,625
1850	747
1840	462

PORTVILLE, Village (Inc. 1895)
Portville Town
St. Cattaraugus County

1980	1,136
1970	1,304
1960	1,336
1950	1,151
1940	1,018
1930	969
1920	606
1910	758
1900	748
1890	NA
1880	683
1870	450

PORT WASHINGTON, CDP
North Hempstead Town
Nassau County

1980	14,521
1970	15,923
1960	15,657
1950	NA
1940	10,509
1890-1930	NA
1880	1,038(a)
1870	804(a)

(a)Reported in QUEENS County.

PORT WASHINGTON NORTH, Village (Inc. 1932)
North Hempstead Town
Nassau County

1980	3,147
1970	2,883 Rev.
1960	722(a)
1950	650
1940	628

(a)Boundary change.

PORT WASHINGTON NORTHEAST & NORTHWEST
North Hempstead Town
Nassau County

1980	1,701(a)
1970	1,734(a)
1960	1,484(a)

(a)Derived by LIRPB from U.S. Census Data.

POTSDAM, Town (Est. 1806)
St. Lawrence County

1980	17,411
1970	16,700 Rev.
1960	14,045
1950	12,437
1940	9,609
1930	8,880
1920	8,794
1910	8,725

1900	9,054
1890	8,939
1880	7,610
1870	7,774
1860	6,737
1850	5,349
1840	4,473(a)
1830	3,650
1820	1,911

(a)Reported as Pottsdam.

POTSDAM, Village (Inc. 1831)
Potsdam Town
St. Lawrence County

1980	10,635(a)
1970	10,303 Rev.
1960	7,765
1950	7,491
1940	4,821
1930	4,136
1920	4,039
1910	4,036
1900	3,843
1890	3,961
1880	2,762
1870	2,891

(a)Boundary change.

POTSDAM JUNCTION, CDP
Potsdam Town
St. Lawrence County

1870	966

POTTER, Town (Est. 1832)
Yates County

1980	1,436
1970	1,082
1960	1,106
1950	1,157
1940	1,109
1930	1,190
1920	1,200
1910	1,495
1900	1,520
1890	1,680
1880	1,940
1870	1,970
1860	2,151
1850	2,194
1840	2,245

POTTER HOLLOW, CDP
Rensselaerville Town
Albany County

1880	91(a)
1870	138(a)

(a)Reported as Potter's Hollow.

POTTERSVILLE, CDP
Chester Town
Warren County

1880	168

POTTSDAM, Town
see POTSDAM, Town
St. Lawrence County

POUGHKEEPSIE, City (Inc. 1854)(a)
    Dutchess County
        1980   29,757
        1970   32,029
        1960   38,330
        1950   41,023
        1940   40,478
        1930   40,288(b)
        1920   35,000
        1910   27,936
        1900   24,029
        1890   22,206
        1880   20,207
        1870   20,080
        1860   14,726
        1850   11,511(c)
(a)Poughkeepsie Village (Inc. 1801) in-
    corporated as POUGHKEEPSIE City and
    made independent of POUGHKEEPSIE Town
    in 1854.
(b)Boundary change.
(c)Estimated.

POUGHKEEPSIE, Town (Est. 1788)
    Dutchess County
        1980   39,549
        1970   41,087 Rev.
        1960   32,164
        1950   19,984
        1940   14,495
        1930   12,707(a)
        1920   10,519
        1910   8,626
        1900   6,820
        1890   4,782
        1880   4,628
        1870   4,009
        1860   NA
        1850   13,944
        1840   10,006
        1830   7,222
        1820   5,726
        1810   NA
        1800   *3,246
        1790   2,529
(a)Boundary change.

POUGHKEEPSIE, Village
    see POUGHKEEPSIE, City
        Dutchess County

POULTNEY, Town
    see PULTENEY, Town
        Steuben County

POUNDRIDGE, CDP
    Pound Ridge Town
    Westchester County
        1880   92

POUND RIDGE, Town (Est. 1788)
    Westchester County
        1980   4,009
        1970   3,792
        1960   2,573
        1950   1,234
        1940   806(a)
        1930   602(a)
        1920   515(a)

        1910   725(a)
        1900   823(a)
        1890   830
        1880   1,034
        1870   1,194
        1860   1,471(a)
        1850   1,486(a)
        1840   1,407(a)
        1830   1,437
        1820   1,357
        1810   NA
        1800   *1,266(a)
        1790   1,062(a)
(a)Reported as Poundridge.

PRATTSBURG, Town (Est. 1813)
    Steuben County
        1980   1,657
        1970   1,523
        1960   1,448
        1950   1,353
        1940   1,364
        1930   1,421
        1920   1,663
        1910   1,834
        1900   2,197
        1890   2,170
        1880   2,349
        1870   2,479
        1860   2,790
        1850   2,786(a)
        1840   2,455
        1830   2,402(a)
        1820   1,377(a)
(a)Reported as Prattsburgh.

PRATTSBURG, Village (Inc. 1877)(a)
    Prattsburg Town
    Steuben County
        1970   765
        1960   690
        1950   653
        1940   635
        1930   584
        1920   654
        1910   684
        1900   713
        1890   607
        1880   661
        1870   639
(a)Dissolved in 1972.

PRATTSBURGH, Town
    see PRATTSBURG, Town
        Steuben County

PRATTS HOLLOW, CDP
    Eaton Town
    Madison County
        1880   102(a)
(a)Reported as Pratt's Hollow.

PRATTSVILLE, Town (Est. 1833)
    Greene County
        1980   666
        1970   721
        1960   790
        1950   825
        1940   848

1930	706
1920	830
1910	781
1900	775
1890	876
1880	1,118
1870	1,240
1860	1,511
1850	1,989
1840	1,613

PRATTSVILLE, Village (Inc. 1883)(a)
Prattsville Town
  Greene County

1890	384
1880	398(b)
1870	489

(a)Dissolved in 1899.
(b)Reported as Prattville.

PREBLE, CDP
Preble Town
  Cortland County

1880	200
1870	195

PREBLE, Town (Est. 1808)
Cortland County

1980	1,637
1970	1,601
1960	991
1950	808
1940	729
1930	642
1920	678
1910	757
1900	857
1890	885
1880	1,138
1870	1,150
1860	1,277
1850	1,312
1840	1,247
1830	1,435
1820	1,257

PRESTON, Town (Est. 1806)
Chenango County

1980	941
1970	714
1960	753
1950	676
1940	672
1930	579
1920	618
1910	649
1900	662
1890	762
1880	909
1870	957
1860	1,013
1850	1,082
1840	1,117
1830	1,213
1820	1,092

PRESTON CORNERS, CDP
Preston Town
  Chenango County

1870	102

PRESTON HOLLOW, CDP
Rensselaerville Town
  Albany County

1880	212
1870	284

PRINCETOWN, Town (Est. 1798)
Schenectady County

1980	1,804
1970	1,405
1960	912
1950	774
1940	553
1930	472
1920	487
1910	684
1900	694
1890	732
1880	826
1870	846
1860	996
1850	1,031
1840	1,201(a)
1830	812
1820	1,073
1810	NA
1800	*812(b)

(a)Reported as Princeton.
(b)Reported in ALBANY County.

PROMISED LAND, CDP
East Hampton Town
  Suffolk County

1880	71

PROSPECT, Village (Inc. 1890)
Trenton Town
  Oneida County

1980	368
1970	392
1960	348
1950	318
1940	285
1930	277
1920	282
1910	278
1900	333
1890	NA
1880	326
1870	312

PROSPECT HILL, CDP
Pembroke Town
  Genesee County

1880	59

PROTECTION, CDP
Holland Town
  Erie County

1880	50

PROVIDENCE, Town (Est. 1796)
Saratoga County

1980	1,210

1970	803 Rev.
1960	556
1950	369
1940	409
1930	470
1920	462
1910	520
1900	607
1890	874
1880	994
1870	1,155
1860	1,443
1850	1,458
1840	1,507
1830	1,579
1820	1,515
1810	NA
1800	*1,888

PULASKI, Village (Inc. 1832)
  Richland Town
    Oswego County

1980	2,415
1970	2,480
1960	2,256
1950	2,033
1940	1,895
1930	2,046
1920	1,895
1910	1,788
1900	1,493
1890	1,517
1880	1,501

PULTENEY, CDP
  Pulteney Town
    Steuben County

1880	202

PULTENEY, Town (Est. 1808)
  Steuben County

1980	1,274
1970	1,167
1960	1,106
1950	1,138
1940	957
1930	983
1920	1,062
1910	1,316
1900	1,590
1890	1,769
1880	1,660
1870	1,393
1860	1,470
1850	1,815(a)
1840	1,784(b)
1830	1,724(a)
1820	1,162

(a)Reported as Pultney.
(b)Reported as Poultney.

PULTNEYVILLE, CDP
  Williamson Town
    Wayne County

1880	247

PURDYS, CDP
  North Salem Town
    Westchester County

1880	228(a)

(a)Reported as Purdy's.

PUTNAM, CDP
  Putnam Town
    Washington County

1880	30

PUTNAM, County (Est. 1812)

1980	77,193
1970	56,696
1960	31,722
1950	20,307
1940	16,555
1930	13,744
1920	10,802
1910	14,665
1900	13,787
1890	14,849
1880	15,181
1870	15,420
1860	14,002
1850	14,138
1840	12,825
1830	12,628
1820	11,268

PUTNAM, Town (Est. 1806)
  Washington County

1980	506
1970	579
1960	490
1950	534
1940	534
1930	479
1920	528
1910	504
1900	505
1890	568
1880	611
1870	603
1860	754
1850	753
1840	784
1830	718
1820	892

PUTNAM LAKE, CDP
  Patterson Town
    Putnam County

1970	1,425

PUTNAM VALLEY, Town (Est. 1839)(a)
  Putnam County

1980	8,994
1970	5,209
1960	3,070
1950	1,908
1940	1,187
1930	859
1920	704
1910	924
1900	1,034
1890	1,193
1880	1,555
1870	1,566

1860	1,583
1850	1,626
1840	1,659(b)

(a)Established as Quincy in 1839; name
   changed in 1840.
(b)Reported as Quincy--Putnam Valley.

Q

QUAKER SPRINGS, CDP
   Saratoga Town
      Saratoga County

1880	150

QUAKER STREET, CDP
   Duanesburg Town
      Schenectady County

1880	250

QUAKER STREET DEPOT, CDP
   Duanesburg Town
      Schenectady County

1880	163

QUALITY HILL, CDP
   Lenox Town
      Madison County

1880	84

QUEECHY, CDP
   Canaan Town
      Columbia County

1880	64(a)

(a)Reported as Queechey.

QUEENS, Borough
   see NEW YORK City, QUEENS Borough

QUEENS, CDP
   Hempstead & Jamaica Towns
      Queens County

1880	347

QUEENS, County (Est. 1683)(a)

1980	1,891,325
1970	1,987,174 Rev.
1960	1,809,578
1950	1,550,849(b)
1940	1,297,634(b)
1930	1,079,129(b)
1920	469,042(b)
1910	284,041
1900	152,999(c)
1890	128,059
1880	90,574
1870	73,803
1860	57,391
1850	36,833
1840	30,324
1830	22,460

1820	21,519
1810	19,336
1800	16,916
1790	16,014

(a)In 1898 the Borough of QUEENS in NEW
   YORK City was established with the
   same boundaries as QUEENS County.
(b)Boundary change.
(c)Boundary change; NASSAU County formed
   from QUEENS in 1899.

QUEENSBURY, Town (Est. 1786)
   Warren County

1980	18,978
1970	14,506
1960	10,004
1950	5,907
1940	4,199
1930	3,169
1920	2,584
1910	2,667(a)
1900	14,990
1890	11,849
1880	9,805
1870	8,387
1860	7,146
1850	2,597
1840	3,789
1830	3,080
1820	2,433
1810	NA
1800	*1,435(b)
1790	1,080(c)

(a)Boundary change.
(b)Reported in WASHINGTON County.
(c)Reported as Queensberry in WASHING-
   TON County.

QUINCY, CDP
   Ripley Town
      Chautauqua County

1870	350

QUINCY, Town
   see PUTNAM VALLEY, Town
      Putnam County

QUINCY--PUTNAM VALLEY, Town
   see PUTNAM, Town
      Putnam County

QUIOGUE
   Southampton Town
      Suffolk County

1980	609(a)
1970	649(a)
1960	413(a)

(a)Derived by LIRPB from U.S. Census
   Data.

QUOGUE, Village (Inc. 1928)
   Southampton Town
      Suffolk County

1980	966
1970	865
1960	692
1950	625
1940	633
1930	758

1890-1920	NA
1880	194
1870	137

R

RAMAPO, Town (Est. 1791)(a)
Rockland County

1980	89,060
1970	76,702
1960	35,064
1950	20,584(b)
1940	18,007
1930	16,321
1920	11,709
1910	11,537
1900	7,502
1890	5,910
1880	4,954
1870	4,649
1860	3,435
1850	3,197
1840	3,222
1830	2,837
1820	2,072
1810	NA
1800	*1,981(c)

(a)Established as New Hampstead in 1791;
   name changed to Hampstead in 1797,
   and to RAMAPO in 1828.
(b)Boundary change.
(c)Reported as Hemstead.

RAMPASTURE--TIANA(a)
Southampton Town
   Suffolk County

1970	682(b)
1960	432(b)

(a)Included in HAMPTON BAYS, CDP in
   1980.
(b)Derived by LIRPB from U.S. Census
   Data.

RANDALL'S ISLAND, CDP
New York County

1860	1,953

RANDOLPH, Town (Est. 1826)
Cattaraugus County

1980	2,593
1970	2,621
1960	2,513
1950	2,535
1940	2,206
1930	2,255
1920	2,171
1910	2,486
1900	2,605
1890	2,448
1880	2,459

1870	2,167
1860	1,954
1850	1,606
1840	1,283
1830	776

RANDOLPH, Village (Inc. 1867)
Randolph Town
   Cattaraugus County

1980	1,398
1970	1,498
1960	1,414
1950	1,455
1940	1,321
1930	1,308
1920	1,310
1910	1,298
1900	1,209
1890	1,201
1880	1,111

RANSOMVILLE, CDP
Porter & Wheatfield Towns
   Niagara County

1980	1,401
1970	1,034
1950-1960	NA
1940	573
1890-1930	NA
1880	275(a)

(a)Reported in PORTER Town only.

RATHBONE, Town (Est. 1856)
Steuben County

1980	913
1970	873
1960	726
1950	741
1940	699
1930	695
1920	761
1910	917
1900	1,059
1890	1,269
1880	1,371
1870	1,357
1860	1,381

RATHBONEVILLE, CDP
Rathbone Town
   Steuben County

1880	131

RAVENA, Village (Inc. 1914)
Coeymans Town
   Albany County

1980	3,091
1970	2,797
1960	2,410(a)
1950	2,006
1940	1,810
1930	1,963
1920	2,093

(a)Boundary change.

RAVENSWOOD, CDP
    Newtown Town
        Queens County
        1870   1,536

RAYMONDVILLE, CDP
    Norfolk Town
        St. Lawrence County
        1880   134

RAYNBECK, Town
    see RHINEBECK, Town
        Dutchess County

RAYVILLE, CDP
    Chatham Town
        Columbia County
        1880   31

READFIELD, Town
    see REDFIELD, Town
        Oswego County

READING, Town (Est. 1806)
    Schuyler County
        1980   1,813
        1970   1,768
        1960   1,410
        1950   1,373
        1940   1,205
        1930   1,257
        1920   1,166
        1910   1,318
        1900   1,335
        1890   1,386
        1880   1,581
        1870   1,751
        1860   1,453
        1850   1,434
        1840   1,541(a)
        1830   1,568(a)
        1820   3,009(a)
(a)Reported in STEUBEN County.

READING CENTER, CDP
    Reading Town
        Schuyler County
        1880   128

RED CREEK, CDP
    Southampton Town
        Suffolk County
        1870   46

RED CREEK, Village (Inc. 1852)
    Wolcott Town
        Wayne County
        1980   645
        1970   626
        1960   689
        1950   617
        1940   539
        1930   560
        1920   499
        1910   457
        1900   480
        1890   492
        1880   525
        1870   529

        1860   429

RED FALLS, CDP
    Prattsville Town
        Greene County
        1880   79

REDFIELD, Town (Est. 1800)
    Oswego County
        1980   459
        1970   386
        1960   388
        1950   418
        1940   517
        1930   583
        1920   647
        1910   803
        1900   911
        1890   1,060
        1880   1,294
        1870   1,324
        1860   1,087
        1850   752
        1840   507(a)
        1830   341
        1820   336
        1810   NA
        1800   *107(b)
(a)Reported as Readfield.
(b)Reported in ONEIDA County.

REDFORD, CDP
    Saranac Town
        Clinton County
        1880   447

RED HOOK, Town (Est. 1812)
    Dutchess County
        1980   8,351
        1970   7,548
        1960   6,023
        1950   4,219
        1940   3,405
        1930   3,404
        1920   3,218
        1910   3,705
        1900   3,895
        1890   4,388
        1880   4,471
        1870   4,350
        1860   3,964(a)
        1850   3,264
        1840   2,829
        1830   2,983
        1820   2,714
(a)Reported as Redhook.

RED HOOK, Village (Inc. 1894)
    Red Hook Town
        Dutchess County
        1980   1,692
        1970   1,680
        1960   1,719
        1950   1,225
        1940   1,056
        1930   996
        1920   827
        1910   960
        1900   857

1890	935
1880	936
1870	861

RED HOUSE, Town (Est. 1869)
    Cattaraugus County

1980	110	
1970	158	
1960	235	
1950	234	
1940	299	
1930	313	
1920	434	
1910	613	Rev.(a)
1900	710	Rev.(a)
1890	1,156	
1880	487	
1870	407	

(a)In 1920 the Census Bureau revised the
    1910 figure of 781 and the 1900 figure
    of 973 to exclude the ALLEGANY INDIAN
    RESERVATION.

RED MILLS, CDP
    see CLAVERACK--RED MILLS, CDP
        Columbia County

RED OAKS MILL, CDP
    La Grange & Poughkeepsie Towns
        Dutchess County

1980	5,236
1970	3,919

RED ROCK, CDP
    Canaan Town
        Columbia County

1880	92

REDWOOD, CDP
    Alexandria Town
        Jefferson County

1880	541

REED'S CORNERS, CDP
    Gorham Town
        Ontario County

1880	76

REIDSVILLE, CDP
    Berne Town
        Albany County

1880	227

REMSEN, Town (Est. 1798)
    Oneida County

1980	1,614
1970	1,366
1960	1,128
1950	962
1940	798
1930	867
1920	969
1910	1,087
1900	1,208
1890	1,099
1880	1,195
1870	1,184
1860	2,670
1850	2,407

1840	1,638
1830	1,400
1820	912
1810	NA
1800	*254

REMSEN, Village (Inc. 1845)
    Remsen Town, part in
        Oneida County

1980	587
1970	574
1960	539
1950	454
1940	394
1930	407
1920	429
1910	395
1900	389
1890	358
1880	NA
1870	289

    Trenton Town, part in
        Oneida County

1980	34
1970	28
1960	28
1950	29
1940	28
1930	30
1920	19
1910	26

TOTAL

1980	621
1970	602
1960	567
1950	483
1940	422
1930	437
1920	448
1910	421
1870-1900	(a)

(a)Reported in REMSEN Town only.

REMSENBURG--SPEONK, CDP
    Southampton Town
        Suffolk County

1980	1,868
1970	1,512(b)
1960	1,163(b)

(a)Included, in part, in SPEONK, CDP in
    1870-1950.
(b)Derived by LIRPB from U.S. Census
    Data.

RENSSELAER, City (Inc. 1897)(a)
    Rensselaer County

1980	9,047
1970	10,136
1960	10,506
1950	10,856
1940	10,768
1930	11,223
1920	10,823
1910	10,711
1900	7,466

(a)GREENBUSH Village and GREENBUSH Town
    consolidated and incorporated as
    RENSSELAER City in 1897.

RENSSELAER, County (Est. 1791)
```
        1980        151,966
        1970        152,510
        1960        142,585
        1950        132,607
        1940        121,834
        1930        119,781
        1920        113,129
        1910        122,276
        1900        121,697
        1890        124,511
        1880        115,328
        1870         99,549
        1860         86,328
        1850         73,363
        1840         60,259
        1830         49,424
        1820         40,114 Rev.
        1810         36,309
        1800         30,351 Rev.
```

RENSSELAER FALLS, Village (Inc. 1912)
  Canton Town
    St. Lawrence County
```
        1980        360
        1970        332
        1960        375
        1950        323
        1940        265
        1930        285
        1920        328
        1890-1910   NA
        1880        409(a)
        1870        395
```
(a)Reported in CLINTON Town.

RENSSELAERVILLE, CDP
  Rensselaerville Town
    Albany County
```
        1880        393
        1870        526
```

RENSSELAERVILLE, Town (Est. 1790)
  Albany County
```
        1980        1,780
        1970        1,531
        1960        1,232
        1950        1,310
        1940        1,285
        1930        1,203
        1920        1,345
        1910        1,609
        1900        1,795
        1890        2,112
        1880        2,488
        1870        2,492
        1860        3,008
        1850        3,629
        1840        3,705
        1830        3,685
        1820        3,435
        1810        NA
        1800       *4,560
        1790        2,771(a)
```
(a)Reported as Ransselaer-Ville.

RENSSELAERWICK, Town
  Albany County
  see TROY, Town
        Rensselaer County

REXFORD'S FLATS, CDP
  Clifton Park Town
    Saratoga County
```
        1880        163
```

RHINEBECK, Town (Est. 1788)
  Dutchess County
```
        1980        7,062
        1970        5,658
        1960        4,612
        1950        3,746
        1940        3,264
        1930        2,968
        1920        2,770
        1910        3,532
        1900        3,472
        1890        3,367
        1880        3,902
        1870        3,719
        1860        3,289
        1850        2,816
        1840        2,659(a)
        1830        2,938
        1820        2,729
        1810        NA
        1800       *4,022(b)
        1790        3,662(c)
```
(a)Reported as Rinebeck.
(b)Reported as Raynbeck.
(c)Reported as Rhynebeck.

RHINEBECK, Village (Inc. 1834)
  Rhinebeck Town
    Dutchess County
```
        1980        2,542
        1970        2,336
        1960        2,093
        1950        1,923
        1940        1,697
        1930        1,569
        1920        1,397
        1910        1,548
        1900        1,494
        1890        1,649
        1880        1,569
        1870        1,322
```

RHINECLIFF, CDP
  Rhinebeck Town
    Dutchess County
```
        1880        585
```

RHYNEBECK, Town
  see RHINEBECK, Town
        Dutchess County

RICE, Town
  see ISCHUA, Town
        Cattaraugus County

RICHBURG, Village (Inc. 1881)
  Bolivar Town, part in
    Allegany County
```
        1980        139
```

1970	79
1960	78
1950	93
1940	111
1930	118
1920	61

Wirt Town, part in
Allegany County

1980	355
1970	403
1960	415
1950	421
1940	453
1930	462
1920	290
1910	451
1900	343
1890	374

TOTAL

1980	494
1970	482
1960	493
1950	514
1940	564
1930	580
1920	351
1890-1910	(a)

(a)Reported in WIRT Town only.

RICHFIELD, CDP
  Richfield Town
  Otsego County

1880	84

RICHFIELD, Town (Est. 1792)
  Otsego County

1980	2,608
1970	2,602
1960	2,662
1950	2,339
1940	1,970
1930	2,099
1920	2,133
1910	2,212
1900	2,526
1890	2,699
1880	2,515
1870	1,831
1860	1,648
1850	1,502
1840	1,680
1830	1,752
1820	1,772
1810	NA
1800	*1,405

RICHFIELD JUNCTION, CDP
  Paris Town
  Oneida County

1940	510

RICHFIELD SPRINGS, Village (Inc. 1861)
  Richfield Town
  Otsego County

1980	1,561(a)
1970	1,540
1960	1,630
1950	1,534
1940	1,209

1930	1,333
1920	1,388
1910	1,503
1900	1,537
1890	1,623
1880	1,307
1870	696

(a)Boundary change.

RICHFORD, CDP
  Richford Town
  Tioga County

1880	317

RICHFORD, Town (Est. 1831)(a)
  Tioga County

1980	906
1970	916
1960	804
1950	787
1940	794
1930	805
1920	831
1910	925
1900	1,142
1890	1,267
1880	1,477
1870	1,434
1860	1,404
1850	1,208
1840	939

(a)Established as Arlington in 1831;
  name changed in 1832.

RICHLAND, Town (Est. 1807)
  Oswego County

1980	5,594
1970	5,324
1960	4,554
1950	4,067
1940	3,848
1930	3,816
1920	3,738
1910	3,791
1900	3,535
1890	3,771
1880	3,991
1870	3,975
1860	4,128
1850	4,079
1840	4,050
1830	2,733
1820	2,728

RICHMOND, Borough
  see NEW YORK City, STATEN ISLAND
  Borough

RICHMOND, CDP
  Northfield Town
  Richmond County

1880	88

RICHMOND, County (Est. 1683)(a)

1980	352,029 Rev.
1970	295,443
1960	221,991
1950	191,555
1940	174,441

1930	158,346
1920	116,531
1910	85,969
1900	67,021(b)
1890	51,693
1880	38,991
1870	33,029
1860	25,492
1850	15,061
1840	10,965
1830	7,082
1820	6,135
1810	5,347
1800	4,564 Rev.
1790	3,835

(a)In 1898, the Borough of Richmond in NEW YORK City was established with the same boundaries as RICHMOND County. The name of the Borough was changed to STATEN ISLAND in 1975.
(b)Boundary change.

RICHMOND, Town (Est. 1796)(a)
Ontario County

1980	2,703
1970	1,925
1960	1,384
1950	959
1940	897
1930	883
1920	1,071
1910	1,277
1900	1,381
1890	1,511
1880	1,772
1870	1,622
1860	1,650
1850	1,852
1840	1,937
1830	1,876
1820	2,765
1810	NA
1800	*635

(a)Established as Pittstown in 1796; name changed to Honeoye in 1808, and to RICHMOND in 1815.

RICHMOND HILL, CDP
Jamaica Town
Queens County

1890	626

RICHMONDVILLE, Town (Est. 1845)
Schoharie County

1980	2,186
1970	1,903
1960	1,746
1950	1,728
1940	1,503
1930	1,463
1920	1,378
1910	1,430
1900	1,719
1890	1,917
1880	2,082
1870	2,307
1860	2,023
1850	1,666

RICHMONDVILLE, Village (Inc. 1881)
Richmondville Town
Schoharie County

1980	792
1970	826
1960	743
1950	709
1940	598
1930	618
1920	581
1910	599
1900	651
1890	663
1880	653
1870	630

RICHVILLE, Village (Inc. 1884)
De Kalb Town
St. Lawrence County

1980	336
1970	334
1960	292
1950	254
1940	274
1930	302
1920	302
1910	307
1900	331
1890	336
1880	339

RIDER'S MILLS, CDP
Chatham Town
Columbia County

1880	53

RIDGE, CDP(a)
Brookhaven Town
Suffolk County

1980	8,977(a)
1970	2,335(b)

(a)Reported, in part, in MIDDLE ISLAND-- RIDGE, CDP in 1960.
(b)Derived by LIRPB from U.S. Census Data.

RIDGEWAY, CDP
Ridgeway Town
Orleans County

1880	119
1870	118

RIDGEWAY, Town (Est. 1812)
Orleans County

1980	7,278
1970	7,209
1960	6,911
1950	6,217
1940	5,826
1930	6,068
1920	5,969
1910	6,538
1900	5,898
1890	5,790
1880	5,495
1870	5,096
1860	4,706
1850	4,591
1840	3,554

1830	1,972
1820	1,496(a)

(a)Reported in GENESEE County.

RIFTON, Village (Inc. 1901)(a)
  Esopus Town
    Ulster County

1920	349
1910	745

(a)Dissolved in 1919.

RIGA, Town (Est. 1808)
  Monroe County

1980	4,309
1970	3,746
1960	2,800
1950	1,906
1940	1,669
1930	1,718
1920	1,649
1910	1,853
1900	1,864
1890	2,031
1880	2,221
1870	2,171
1860	2,177
1850	2,159
1840	1,984
1830	1,907
1820	3,139(a)

(a)Reported in GENESEE County.

RINEBECK, Town
  see RHINEBECK, Town
          Dutchess County

RIPLEY, CDP
  Ripley Town
    Chautauqua County

1980	1,205
1970	1,173
1960	1,247
1950	1,229
1940	1,033

RIPLEY, Town (Est. 1817)
  Chautauqua County

1980	3,181 Rev.
1970	2,934
1960	2,848
1950	2,694
1940	2,250
1930	2,254
1920	2,116
1910	2,239
1900	2,256
1890	2,020
1880	1,990
1870	1,946
1860	2,013
1850	1,732
1840	2,197
1830	1,647
1820	1,111

RISINGVILLE, CDP
  Thurston Town
    Steuben County

1880	34

RIVERHEAD, CDP
  Riverhead Town
    Suffolk County

1980	6,339(a)
1970	7,585(b)
1960	5,830
1950	4,892
1940	5,622
1890-1930	NA
1880	1,757
1870	1,296(c)

(a)Boundary change.
(b)Population of 7,632 is comparable to
   1980 boundaries.
(c)Part in RIVERHEAD Town, 1,144; part
   in SOUTHAMPTON Town, 152.

RIVERHEAD, Town (Est. 1792)
  Suffolk County

1980	20,243
1970	18,909
1960	14,519
1950	9,973
1940	8,922
1930	7,956
1920	5,753
1910	5,345
1900	4,503
1890	4,010
1880	3,939
1870	3,461
1860	3,044
1850	2,540
1840	2,449
1830	2,016
1820	1,857
1810	1,711
1800	*1,498(a)

(a)Reported as River Head.

RIVERSIDE, CDP(a)
  Southampton Town
    Suffolk County

1960	1,277

(a)Reported, in part, in RIVERSIDE--
   FLANDERS, CDP in 1970-1980

RIVERSIDE, Village (Inc. 1922)
  Corning Town
    Steuben County

1980	684
1970	911
1960	1,030
1950	818
1940	643
1930	671

RIVERSIDE--FLANDERS, CDP(a)
  Southampton Town
    Suffolk County

1980	5,400(b)
1970	1,698(c)

(a)U.S. Census reported, in part, in
   FLANDERS, CDP in 1870-1970.
(b)Boundary change.
(c)Derived by LIRPB from U.S. Census
   Data; population of 4,654 is
   comparable to 1980 boundaries.

ROANOKE(a)
   Riverhead Town
      Suffolk County
         1970   1,529(b)
         1960   1,073(b)
(a)Included in CALVERTON--ROANOKE, CDP
   in 1980.
(b)Derived by LIRPB from U.S. Census
   Data.

ROBERT MOSES PARK
   Babylon Town
      Suffolk County
         1980   7(a)
(a)Derived by LIRPB from U.S. Census
   Data.

ROBIN'S ISLAND, CDP
   Clayton Town
      Jefferson County
         1870   5

ROBINS ISLAND
   Southold Town
      Suffolk County
         1980   0(a)
         1970   5(a)
(a)Derived by LIRPB from U.S. Census
   Data.

ROCHDALE, CDP
   Poughkeepsie Town
      Dutchess County
         1980   1,825
         1970   1,849
         1960   1,800
         1950   1,219
         1890-1940   NA
         1880   129
         1870   75(a)
(a)Reported as Rockdale.

ROCHESTER, City (Inc. 1834)(a)
   Monroe County
         1980   241,741(b)
         1970   295,011 Rev.
         1960   318,611(b)
         1950   332,488(b)
         1940   324,975(b)
         1930   328,132(b)
         1920   295,750(b)
         1910   218,149
         1900   162,608(b)
         1890   133,896
         1880   89,366
         1870   62,386
         1860   48,204
         1850   36,403
         1840   20,191
         1830   9,207
(a)ROCHESTER Village (Inc. 1817) incorporated as ROCHESTER City and made
   independent of ROCHESTER Town in 1834.
(b)Boundary change.

ROCHESTER, Town (Est. 1788)
   Ulster County
         1980   5,344
         1970   3,940

         1960   3,012
         1950   2,532
         1940   2,454
         1930   2,051
         1920   2,188
         1910   2,760
         1900   2,874
         1890   3,557
         1880   4,109
         1870   4,088
         1860   4,539
         1850   3,174
         1840   2,674(a)
         1830   2,420
         1820   2,063
         1810   NA
         1800   *2,423
         1790   1,628
(a)Boundary change.

ROCHESTER, Town
   Warren County
   see HAGUE, Town
      Warren County

ROCKAWAY BEACH, Village (Inc. 1897)(a)
   Hempstead Town
      Nassau County
         1890   1,502
(a)Merged into QUEENS Borough in NEW
   YORK City in 1898.

ROCK CITY, CDP
   Milan Town
      Dutchess County
         1880   56

ROCK CITY FALLS, CDP
   Milton Town
      Saratoga County
         1880   303

ROCKDALE, CDP
   see ROCHDALE, CDP
      Dutchess County

ROCKLAND, County (Est. 1798)
         1980   259,530
         1970   229,903
         1960   136,803
         1950   89,276
         1940   74,261
         1930   59,599
         1920   45,548
         1910   46,873
         1900   38,298
         1890   35,162
         1880   27,690
         1870   25,213
         1860   22,492
         1850   16,962
         1840   11,975
         1830   9,388
         1820   8,837
         1810   7,758
         1800   6,353

ROCKLAND, Town (Est. 1809)
    Sullivan County
        1980   4,207
        1970   3,919
        1960   4,216
        1950   3,502
        1940   3,375
        1930   3,286
        1920   3,247
        1910   3,455
        1900   3,426
        1890   2,868
        1880   2,481
        1870   1,946
        1860   1,616
        1850   1,175
        1840   826
        1830   547
        1820   405

ROCKLAND LAKE, CDP
    Clarkstown Town
        Rockland County
        1880   441
        1870   510

ROCKTON, Village
    Herkimer County
    see LITTLE FALLS, Village
        Herkimer County

ROCKTON, Village (Inc. 1892)(a)
    Amsterdam Town
        Montgomery County
        1900   1,052
(a)Merged into AMSTERDAM City in 1901.

ROCKVILLE CENTRE, Village (Inc. 1893)
    Hempstead Town
        Nassau County
        1980   25,412 Rev.
        1970   27,444
        1960   26,355(a)
        1950   22,362(a)
        1940   18,613(a)
        1930   13,718(a)
        1920   6,262
        1910   3,667
        1900   1,884
        1890   NA
        1880   1,882(b)
(a)Boundary change.
(b)Reported in QUEENS County.

ROCKWOOD, CDP
    Ephratah Town
        Fulton County
        1880   254

ROCKY POINT, CDP
    Broookhaven Town
        Suffolk County
        1980   7,012(a)
        1970   3,460(b)
        1960   2,004 Rev.
        1950   NA
        1940   538
        1890-1930   NA
        1880   200

(a)Boundary change.
(b)Derived by LIRPB from U.S. Census
    Data; population of 3,734 is
    comparable to 1980 boundaries.

RODMAN, CDP
    Rodman Town
        Jefferson County
        1880   228

RODMAN, Town (Est. 1804)(a)
    Jefferson County
        1980   836
        1970   772
        1960   765
        1950   816
        1940   856
        1930   935
        1920   1,027
        1910   1,123
        1900   1,212
        1890   1,287
        1880   1,517
        1870   1,604
        1860   1,808
        1850   1,784
        1840   1,702
        1830   1,901
        1820   1,735
(a)Established as Harrison in 1804;
    name changed in 1808.

ROESSLEVILLE, CDP
    Colonie & Guilderland Towns
        Albany County
        1980   11,685
        1970   5,351

ROGERSVILLE, CDP
    Dansville Town
        Steuben County
        1880   175

ROLLING ACRES, CDP
    Ogden Town
        Monroe County
        1970   1,152

ROME, City (Inc. 1870)(a)
    Oneida County
        1980   43,826
        1970   50,148
        1960   51,646
        1950   41,682
        1940   34,214
        1930   32,338
        1920   26,341
        1910   20,497
        1900   15,343
        1890   14,991
        1880   12,194
        1870   11,000
        1860   3,584
(a)ROME Town and Rome Village (Inc. 1819)
    consolidated and incorporated as ROME
    City in 1870.

ROME, Town (Est. 1796)(a)
    Oneida County
        1860   6,246
        1850   7,918
        1840   5,680
        1830   4,360
        1820   3,569
        1810   NA
        1800   *1,479
(a)ROME Town and Rome Village (Inc. 1819)
   consolidated and incorporated as ROME
   City in 1870.

ROME, Village
  see ROME, City
        Oneida County

ROMULUS, CDP
  Romulus & Varick Towns
    Seneca County
        1880   178

ROMULUS, Town (Est. 1794)
    Seneca County
        1980   2,464
        1970   4,284
        1960   3,509
        1950   4,263
        1940   2,865
        1930   2,856
        1920   2,754
        1910   2,803
        1900   2,895
        1890   2,852
        1880   2,765
        1870   2,223
        1860   2,170
        1850   2,050
        1840   2,235
        1830   2,089
        1820   3,698
        1810   NA
        1800   *1,025(a)
(a)Reported in CAYUGA County.

RONKONKOMA, CDP(a)
  Brookhaven Town
    Suffolk County
        1970   7,284
        1960   4,220
        1950   1,334(b)
        1940   646
      1890-1930   NA
        1880   96(c)
(a)Included in LAKE RONKONKOMA, CDP in
  1980.
(b)Part in BROOKHAVEN Town, 706; part in
  ISLIP Town, 628.
(c)Reported in ISLIP Town.

RONKONKOMA WEST, CDP
  Brookhaven Town
    Suffolk County
        1960   1,446

ROOSEVELT, CDP
  Hempstead Town
    Nassau County
        1980   14,109

        1970   15,008
        1960   12,883
        1950   NA
        1940   8,248

ROOT, Town (Est. 1823)
    Montgomery County
        1980   1,801
        1970   1,513
        1960   1,243
        1950   1,214
        1940   1,106
        1930   1,021
        1920   1,198
        1910   1,512
        1900   1,653
        1890   2,041
        1880   2,275
        1870   2,492
        1860   2,622
        1850   2,736
        1840   2,979
        1830   2,750

ROSCOE, CDP
  Rockland Town
    Sullivan County
        1940   739

ROSE, Town (Est. 1826)
    Wayne County
        1980   2,684
        1970   2,356
        1960   2,122
        1950   2,013
        1940   1,882
        1930   1,921
        1920   1,928
        1910   1,883
        1900   2,055
        1890   2,107
        1880   2,244
        1870   2,056
        1860   2,119
        1850   2,264
        1840   2,038
        1830   1,641

ROSEBOOM, CDP
  Roseboom Town
    Otsego County
        1880   168

ROSEBOOM, Town (Est. 1854)
    Otsego County
        1980   630
        1970   483
        1960   518
        1950   570
        1940   534
        1930   633
        1920   773
        1910   885
        1900   1,031
        1890   1,190
        1880   1,515
        1870   1,589
        1860   1,870

ROSENDALE, Town (Est. 1844)
Ulster County

1980	5,933
1970	5,422
1960	4,228
1950	2,950
1940	2,548
1930	2,192
1920	1,959
1910	3,717
1900	6,278
1890	6,063
1880	4,724
1870	3,625
1860	2,826
1850	2,418

ROSENDALE VILLAGE, CDP(a)
Rosendale Town
Ulster County

1980	1,134
1970	1,220(b)
1960	1,033
1950	883(b)
1940	671
1930	539
1920	555
1910	1,125
1900	1,840
1890	1,706

(a)Incorporated as a Village in 1890;
  Village dissolved in 1977.
(b)Reported as Rosendale.

ROSETON, CDP
Newburgh Town
Orange County

1940	561

ROSE VALLEY, CDP
Rose Town
Wayne County

1880	502

ROSLYN, Village (Inc. 1932)
North Hempstead Town
Nassau County

1980	2,134
1970	2,607 Rev.
1960	2,681
1950	1,612
1940	972
1900-1930	NA
1890	1,251(a)
1880	1,101(a)
1870	655(a)

(a)Reported in QUEENS County.

ROSLYN ESTATES, Village (Inc. 1931)
North Hempstead Town
Nassau County

1980	1,292
1970	1,420
1960	1,289
1950	612
1940	464

ROSLYN HARBOR, Village (Inc. 1931)
North Hempstead Town, part in
Nassau County

1980	785
1970	830 Rev.
1960	804
1950	316
1940	233

Oyster Bay Town, part in
Nassau County

1980	344
1970	295 Rev.
1960	121
1950	86
1940	70

TOTAL

1980	1,129
1970	1,125 Rev.
1960	925
1950	402
1940	303

ROSLYN HEIGHTS, CDP
North Hempstead Town
Nassau County

1980	6,546
1970	7,242
1960	7,473(a)

(a)Derived by LIRPB from U.S. Census
Data.

ROSSIE, CDP
Rossie Town
St. Lawrence County

1880	135
1870	149

ROSSIE, Town (Est. 1813)
St. Lawrence County

1980	842
1970	643
1960	649
1950	611
1940	706
1930	720
1920	866
1910	981
1900	1,136
1890	1,493
1880	1,709
1870	1,661
1860	1,609
1850	1,471
1840	1,553
1830	641
1820	869

ROSSMAN'S MILLS, CDP
Stockport Town
Columbia County

1880	88

ROSSVILLE, CDP
Westfield Town
Richmond County

1880	577

ROTTERDAM, CDP
    Rotterdam Town
        Schenectady County
            1980   22,933
            1970   25,214 Rev.
            1960   16,871

ROTTERDAM, Town (Est. 1820)
    Schenectady County
            1980   29,451
            1970   21,067
            1960   27,493
            1950   19,762
            1940   12,560
            1930   9,920(a)
            1920   7,853(a)
            1910   5,406
            1900   7,711
            1890   3,098
            1880   2,326
            1870   2,355
            1860   2,224
            1850   2,446
            1840   2,284
            1830   1,481
            1820   1,529
(a)Boundary change.

ROTTERDAM JUNCTION, CDP
    Rotterdam Town
        Schenectady County
            1980   1,010
            1950-1970   NA
            1940   756

ROUND LAKE, Village (Inc. 1969)
    Malta Town
        Saratoga County
            1980   791
            1970   886

ROUSES POINT, Village (Inc. 1877)
    Champlain Town
        Clinton County
            1980   2,266
            1970   2,250(a)
            1960   2,160
            1950   2,001
            1940   1,846
            1930   1,920
            1920   1,700
            1910   1,638
            1900   1,675
            1890   1,856
            1880   1,485(b)
            1870   1,266
(a)Boundary change.
(b)Estimated.

ROXBURY, Town (Est. 1799)
    Delaware County
            1980   2,291
            1970   2,252
            1960   2,238
            1950   2,227
            1940   2,277
            1930   2,267
            1920   2,258
            1910   2,164

            1900   2,134
            1890   2,272
            1880   2,344
            1870   2,188
            1860   2,558
            1850   2,853
            1840   3,013
            1830   3,234
            1820   2,488
            1810   NA
            1800   *936

ROXBURY, Village (Inc. 1888)(a)
    Roxbury Town
        Delaware County
            1900   418
            1890   NA
            1880   335
(a)Dissolved in 1899.

ROYALTON, Town (Est. 1817)
    Niagara County
            1980   7,765
            1970   7,375
            1960   6,585
            1950   5,297
            1940   4,617
            1930   4,660
            1920   4,485
            1910   4,956
            1900   4,797
            1890   4,632
            1880   4,888
            1870   4,726
            1860   4,793
            1850   4,024
            1840   3,549
            1830   3,138
            1820   1,849

RUBY, CDP
    Ulster Town
        Ulster County
            1980   1,059

RUFFLE BAR ISLAND, CDP
    Flatlands Town
        Kings County
            1880   14

RURAL GROVE, CDP
    Root Town
        Montgomery County
            1880   117

RUSH, CDP
    Rush Town
        Monroe County
            1880   216

RUSH, Town (Est. 1818)
    Monroe County
            1980   3,001
            1970   3,287
            1960   2,555
            1950   2,052
            1940   1,791
            1930   1,901
            1920   2,091

1910	2,150
1900	1,491
1890	1,695
1880	1,741
1870	1,654
1860	1,613
1850	2,015
1840	1,929
1830	2,098
1820	1,701

RUSHFORD, CDP
  Rushford Town
    Allegany County

1880	439
1870	543

RUSHFORD, Town (Est. 1816)
    Allegany County

1980	1,125
1970	1,021
1960	995
1950	935
1940	967
1930	936
1920	1,118
1910	1,260
1900	1,300
1890	1,355
1880	1,453
1870	1,636
1860	1,839
1850	1,816
1840	1,512
1830	1,115
1820	609

RUSHVILLE, Village
  Gorham Town, part in (Inc. 1860)
    Ontario County, part in

1980	148
1970	194
1960	159
1950	141
1940	121
1930	137
1920	130
1910	124
1900	130
1890	128
1880	160

  Potter Town, part in (Inc. 1927)
    Yates County, part in

1980	400
1970	374(a)
1960	306
1950	324
1940	307
1930	315
1920	411
1910	339
1900	286
1890	322
1880	343

  TOTAL

1980	548
1970	568(a)
1960	465
1950	465

1940	428
1930	452
1920	541
1910	463
1900	416
1890	450
1880	503

(a)Boundary change.

RUSSEL, Town
  see RUSSELL, Town
        St. Lawrence County

RUSSELL, CDP
  Russell Town
    St. Lawrence County

1870	335

RUSSELL, Town (Est. 1807)
    St. Lawrence County

1980	1,638
1970	1,586
1960	1,588
1950	1,472
1940	1,529
1930	1,585
1920	1,757
1910	1,842
1900	2,067
1890	2,132
1880	2,403
1870	2,688
1860	2,380(a)
1850	1,808
1840	1,373
1830	541
1820	486

(a)Reported as Russel.

RUSSELL GARDENS, Village (Inc. 1931)
  North Hempstead Town
    Nassau County

1980	1,263
1970	1,207 Rev.
1960	1,156
1950	912
1940	556

RUSSIA, Town (Est. 1806)(a)
    Herkimer County

1980	2,405
1970	2,160
1960	1,761
1950	1,420
1940	1,281
1930	1,347
1920	1,433
1910	1,772
1900	2,025
1890	2,145
1880	2,177
1870	2,220
1860	2,389
1850	2,349
1840	2,298
1830	2,458
1820	1,685

(a)Established as Union in 1806; name
  changed in 1808.

RUSSIA CORNERS, CDP
  Russia Town
    Herkimer County
       1870   58

RUTLAND, Town (Est. 1802)
    Jefferson County
       1980   2,685
       1970   2,448
       1960   2,229
       1950   1,925
       1940   1,622
       1930   1,734
       1920   1,810
       1910   1,862
       1900   1,885
       1890   1,798
       1880   1,796
       1870   1,903
       1860   2,097
       1850   2,265
       1840   2,090
       1830   2,339
       1820   1,946

RYE, City (Inc. 1942)(a)
    Westchester County
       1980   15,083
       1970   15,869
       1960   14,225
       1950   11,721
(a)RYE Village incorporated as RYE City
   and made independent of RYE Town in
   1942.

RYE, Town (Est. 1788)
    Westchester County
       1980   38,896
       1970   43,234
       1960   38,147
       1950   32,796(a)
       1940   40,135(a)
       1930   37,495
       1920   25,819
       1910   19,652
       1900   12,861
       1890   9,477
       1880   6,576
       1870   7,150
       1860   4,447
       1850   2,584
       1840   1,803
       1830   1,602
       1820   1,342
       1810   NA
       1800   *1,074
       1790   986
(a)Boundary change.

RYE, Village (Inc. 1904)(a)
  Rye Town
    Westchester County
       1940   9,865
       1930   8,712(b)
       1920   5,308
       1910   3,964
(a)RYE Village incorporated as RYE City
   and made independent of RYE Town in
   1942.

(b)Boundary change.

RYE BROOK, Village (Inc. 1982)(a)
  Rye Town
    Westchester County
(a)Population of 7,996 at incorporation.

S

SACKETS HARBOR, Village (Inc. 1814)
  Hounsfield Town
    Jefferson County
       1980   1,017
       1970   1,202
       1960   1,279
       1950   1,247
       1940   1,962
       1930   1,680 Rev.
       1920   1,094 Rev.
       1910   868
       1900   1,266
       1890   787
       1880   885
       1870   713

SADDLE ROCK, Village (Inc. 1911)
  North Hempstead Town
    Nassau County
       1980   921
       1970   895
       1960   1,109
       1950   33
       1940   69
       1930   74
       1920   71

SAGAPONACK
  Southampton Town
    Suffolk County
       1980   245(a)
       1970   1,041(b)
       1960   466(c)
(a)Boundary change; derived by LIRPB
   from U.S. Census Data.
(b)Derived by LIRPB from U.S. Census
   Data; population of 361 is comparable
   to 1980 boundaries.
(c)Derived by LIRPB from U.S. Census
   Data.

SAG HARBOR, Village (Inc. 1846)
  East Hampton Town, part in
    Suffolk County
       1980   895
       1970   835
       1960   874
       1950   915
       1940   952
       1930   989
       1920   NA

1910	1,168
1900	1,022
1890	714
1880	532

Southampton Town, part in
Suffolk County

1980	1,686
1970	1,528
1960	1,472
1950	1,458
1940	1,565
1930	1,784
1920	NA
1910	2,240
1900	947
1890	NA
1880	1,464
1870	1,723

TOTAL

1980	2,581
1970	2,363
1960	2,346
1950	2,373
1940	2,517
1930	2,773
1920	2,993
1910	3,408
1900	1,969
1890	714
1880	1,996
1870	(a)

(a)Reported in SOUTHAMPTON Town only.

ST. ARMAND, Town (Est. 1844)
Essex County

1980	1,064
1970	903
1960	868
1950	1,142
1940	1,233
1930	1,190
1920	727
1910	746
1900	769
1890	633
1880	452
1870	335
1860	331
1850	210

ST. BONAVENTURE, CDP
Allegany Town
Cattaraugus County

1980	2,587

ST. JAMES, CDP
Smithtown Town
Suffolk County

1980	12,122(a)
1970	10,500 Rev.(b)
1960	4,744 Rev.
1950	1,390
1940	1,241

(a)Boundary change.
(b)Population of 11,727 is comparable
   to 1980 boundaries.

ST. JOHNLAND, CDP
Smithtown Town
Suffolk County

1880	216

ST. JOHNSVILLE, Town (Est. 1838)
Montgomery County

1980	3,064
1970	2,915
1960	2,958
1950	2,934
1940	2,974
1930	3,000
1920	3,123
1910	3,369
1900	2,674
1890	2,081
1880	2,002
1870	2,189
1860	1,688
1850	1,627
1840	1,923

ST. JOHNSVILLE, Village (Inc. 1868)
St. Johnsville Town
Montgomery County

1980	1,974
1970	2,089(a)
1960	2,196
1950	2,210
1940	2,283
1930	2,273
1920	2,469
1910	2,536
1900	1,873
1890	1,263
1880	1,072
1870	1,376

(a)Boundary change.

ST. LAWRENCE, County (Est. 1802)

1980	114,254
1970	112,309 Rev.
1960	111,239
1950	98,897
1940	91,098
1930	90,960
1920	88,121
1910	89,005
1900	89,083
1890	85,048
1880	85,997
1870	84,826(a)
1860	83,689
1850	68,617
1840	56,706
1830	36,354
1820	16,037
1810	7,885

(a)Boundary change.

ST. REGIS FALLS, CDP
Waverly Town
Franklin County

1940	1,005
1910-1930	NA
1900	879
1890	1,210

ST. REGIS INDIAN RESERVATION
Franklin County

1980	1,802
1970	1,536
1960	1,774
1950	1,409
1940	1,262
1930	945
1920	1,016
1910	1,249
1900	1,253

SALAMANCA, City (Inc. 1913)(a)
Cattaraugus County

1980	6,890
1970	7,877
1960	8,480
1950	8,861
1940	9,011
1930	9,577
1920	9,276

(a)SALAMANCA and WEST SALAMANCA Villages
consolidated and incorporated as
SALAMANCA City and made independent
of SALAMANCA Town in 1913.

SALAMANCA, Town (Est. 1854)(a)
Cattaraugus County

1980	608
1970	571
1960	432
1950	355
1940	313
1930	330
1920	361(b)
1910	6,638 Rev.(c)
1900	5,074 Rev.(c)
1890	4,572
1880	3,498
1870	1,881
1860	900

(a)Established as Bucktooth in 1854;
name changed in 1862.
(b)Boundary change.
(c)In 1920 the Census Bureau revised the
1910 figure of 6,760 and the 1900
figure of 5,174 to exclude the
ALLEGANY INDIAN RESERVATION.

SALAMANCA, Village (Inc. 1879)(a)
Salamanca Town
Cattaraugus County

1910	5,792
1900	4,251
1890	3,692
1880	2,531

(a)SALAMANCA and WEST SALAMANCA Villages
consolidated and incorporated as
SALAMANCA City and made independent
of SALAMANCA Town in 1913.

SALEM, Town (Est. 1786)
Washington County

1980	2,377
1970	2,346
1960	2,258
1950	2,171
1940	2,127
1930	2,145
1920	2,235
1910	2,780
1900	2,978
1890	3,127
1880	3,498
1870	3,556
1860	3,181
1850	2,904
1840	2,855
1830	2,972
1820	2,985
1810	NA
1800	*2,861
1790	2,186

SALEM, Town
Westchester County
see LEWISBORO, Town
Westchester County

SALEM, Village (Inc. 1803)
Salem Town
Washington County

1980	959
1970	1,025
1960	1,076
1950	1,067
1940	1,034
1930	1,081
1920	1,083
1910	1,250
1900	1,391
1890	NA
1880	1,410
1870	1,239

SALINA, Town (Est. 1809)
Onondaga County

1980	37,400
1970	38,281
1960	33,076
1950	19,125
1940	11,168
1930	10,117(a)
1920	4,257(a)
1910	3,208
1900	3,745
1890	3,490
1880	2,888
1870	2,688
1860	2,400
1850	2,142(a)
1840	11,014 Rev.
1830	6,929
1820	1,814

(a)Boundary change.

SALINA, Village
see SYRACUSE, City
Onondaga County

SALISBURY, Town (Est. 1797)
Herkimer County

1980	1,946
1970	1,741
1960	1,551
1950	1,469
1940	1,319
1930	1,244

1920	1,418
1910	1,468
1900	1,426
1890	1,800
1880	1,884
1870	1,933
1860	2,325
1850	2,035
1840	1,859
1830	1,999
1820	1,438
1810	NA
1800	*716(a)

(a)Reported as Salsbury in MONTGOMERY County.

SALISBURY CENTRE, CDP
   Salisbury Town
      Herkimer County

1880	341

SALISBURY CORNERS, CDP
   Salisbury Town
      Herkimer County

1880	124

SALSBURY, Town
      Montgomery County
   see SALISBURY, Town
         Herkimer County

SALTAIRE, Village (Inc. 1917)
   Islip Town
      Suffolk County

1980	35
1970	37
1960	28
1950	21
1940	22
1930	64
1920	12

SAMMONSVILLE, CDP
   Johnstown Town
      Fulton County

1880	138

SANBORN, CDP
   Lewiston Town
      Niagara County

1880	177

SAND BANK, Village
   see ALTMAR, Village
         Oswego County

SAND LAKE, CDP
   Sand Lake Town
      Rensselaer County

1880	777
1870	503

SAND LAKE, Town (Est. 1812)
   Rensselaer County

1980	7,022
1970	5,843
1960	4,629
1950	3,254
1940	2,488(a)

1930	2,022(a)
1920	1,916(a)
1910	2,128(a)
1900	2,299(a)
1890	2,555
1880	2,550
1870	2,633
1860	2,502
1850	2,559
1840	4,303
1830	3,650
1820	3,302(a)

(a)Reported as Sandlake.

SAND RIDGE, CDP
   Schroeppel Town
      Oswego County

1980	1,293
1970	1,109

SANDS POINT, Village (Inc. 1910)
   North Hempstead Town
      Nassau County

1980	2,742
1970	2,916
1960	2,161
1950	860
1940	628(a)
1930	438
1920	284

(a)Boundary change.

SAND SPRINGS, CDP
   Van Buren Town
      Onondaga County

1880	68

SANDUSKY, CDP
   Freedom Town
      Cattaraugus County

1880	299

SANDY BEACH, CDP
   Grand Island Town
      Erie County

1970	1,691

SANDY CREEK, Town (Est. 1825)
   Oswego County

1980	3,256
1970	2,644
1960	2,506
1950	2,354
1940	1,821
1930	2,156
1920	2,018
1910	2,106(a)
1900	2,232
1890	2,279
1880	2,878
1870	2,629
1860	2,431
1850	2,456
1840	2,420
1830	1,839

(a)Boundary change.

SANDY CREEK, Village (Inc. 1878)
  Sandy Creek Town
    Oswego County
      1980   765
      1970   731
      1960   697
      1950   708
      1940   646
      1930   648
      1920   566
      1910   617
      1900   692
      1890   723
      1880   951
      1870   986

SANDY HILL, Village
  see HUDSON FALLS, Village
    Washington County

SANFORD, Town (Est. 1821)
  Broome County
    1980   2,635
    1970   2,528
    1960   2,489
    1950   2,416
    1940   2,502
    1930   2,538
    1920   2,681
    1910   2,980
    1900   3,514
    1890   3,265
    1880   3,495
    1870   3,249
    1860   3,061
    1850   2,508
    1840   1,173
    1830   931

SANGERFIELD, Town (Est. 1795)
  Oneida County
    1980   2,397
    1970   2,475
    1960   2,482
    1950   2,143
    1940   1,961
    1930   1,862
    1920   1,795
    1910   2,086
    1900   2,440
    1890   3,017
    1880   3,171
    1870   2,513
    1860   2,343
    1850   2,371
    1840   2,251
    1830   2,272(a)
    1820   2,011(a)
    1810   NA
    1800   *1,144(b)
(a)Reported as Sangersfield.
(b)Reported as Sangersfield in CHENANGO
  County.

SAN REMO, CDP(a)
  Smithtown Town
    Suffolk County
      1970   8,302
      1960   2,161 Rev.

(a)Included in KINGS PARK and SMITHTOWN,
  CDPs in 1980.

SANTA CLARA, Town (Est. 1888)
  Franklin County
    1980   310
    1970   168
    1960   158
    1950   251
    1940   258
    1930   528
    1920   541
    1910   675
    1900   580
    1890   1,690

SARANAC, Town (Est. 1824)
  Clinton County
    1980   3,389
    1970   3,127
    1960   2,881 Rev.
    1950   2,399
    1940   2,820
    1930   2,367
    1920   2,684
    1910   3,000
    1900   3,463
    1890   3,496
    1880   4,552
    1870   3,802
    1860   3,644
    1850   2,582
    1840   1,462
    1830   316

SARANAC LAKE, Village (Inc. 1892)
  North Elba Town, part in
    Essex County, part in
      1980   1,462(a)
      1970   1,665
      1960   1,780 Rev.
      1950   1,654
      1940   1,643
      1930   1,803
      1920   1,010
      1910   1,019
      1900   316
  St. Armand Town, part in
    Essex County, part in
      1980   174
      1970   169
      1960   223(a)
      1950   202(a)
      1940   223
      1930   258
      1920   109
      1910   67
      1900   30
  Harrietstown Town, part in
    Franklin County, part in
      1980   4,116
      1970   4,421
      1960   4,641
      1950   5,057
      1940   5,272
      1930   5,959
      1920   4,055
      1910   3,897
      1900   2,248

1890	768
1880	191
TOTAL	
1980	5,578
1970	6,086
1960	6,421(a)
1950	6,913(a)
1940	7,138
1930	8,020
1920	5,174
1910	4,983
1900	2,594
1880-1890	(b)

(a)Boundary change.
(b)Reported in FRANKLIN County only.

SARATOGA, County (Est. 1791)

1980	153,759
1970	121,764 Rev.
1960	89,096
1950	74,869
1940	65,606
1930	63,314
1920	60,029
1910	61,917
1900	61,089
1890	57,663
1880	55,156
1870	51,529
1860	51,729
1850	45,646
1840	40,553
1830	38,679
1820	36,052
1810	33,147
1800	24,564 Rev.

SARATOGA, Town (Est. 1788)
  Saratoga County

1980	4,595
1970	4,206
1960	3,515
1950	3,255
1940	3,212
1930	3,027
1920	3,680
1910	3,942
1900	3,999
1890	3,855
1880	4,539
1870	4,052
1860	NA
1850	3,492
1840	2,624
1830	2,461
1820	2,233
1810	NA
1800	*2,491
1790	3,071(a)

(a)Reported in ALBANY County.

SARATOGA SPRINGS, City (Inc. 1915)(a)
  Saratoga County

1980	23,906(b)
1970	18,845
1960	16,630
1950	15,473
1940	13,705
1930	13,169

1920	13,181

(a)SARATOGA SPRINGS Village and SARA-
TOGA SPRINGS Town consolidated and
incorporated as SARATOGA SPRINGS
City in 1915.
(b)Boundary change.

SARATOGA SPRINGS, Town (Est. 1819)(a)
  Saratoga County

1910	13,710
1900	13,534
1890	13,171
1880	10,820
1870	8,537
1860	7,496
1850	4,650
1840	3,384
1830	2,204
1820	1,909

(a)SARATOGA SPRINGS Village and SARA-
TOGA SPRINGS Town consolidated and
incorporated as SARATOGA SPRINGS
City in 1915.

SARATOGA SPRINGS, Village (Inc. 1866)(a)
  Saratoga Springs Town
    Saratoga County

1910	12,693
1900	12,409
1890	11,975
1880	8,421
1870	7,516

(a)SARATOGA SPRINGS Village and SARA-
TOGA SPRINGS Town consolidated and
incorporated as SARATOGA SPRINGS
City in 1915.

SARDINIA, CDP
  Sardinia Town
    Erie County

1880	272

SARDINIA, Town (Est. 1821)
  Erie County

1980	2,792
1970	2,505
1960	2,145
1950	1,778
1940	1,700
1930	1,518
1920	1,518
1910	1,644
1900	1,548
1890	1,728
1880	1,767
1870	1,704
1860	1,942
1850	1,761
1840	1,743
1830	1,453

SAUGERTIES, Town (Est. 1811)
  Ulster County

1980	17,975
1970	16,961
1960	13,608
1950	9,232
1940	8,960
1930	8,752

1920	8,245
1910	9,632
1900	9,754
1890	10,436
1880	10,375
1870	10,455
1860	9,537
1850	8,041
1840	6,216
1830	3,747
1820	2,699

SAUGERTIES, Village (Inc. 1831)
  Saugerties Town
    Ulster County

1980	3,882(a)
1970	4,190
1960	4,286
1950	3,907
1940	3,916
1930	4,060(a)
1920	4,013
1910	3,929
1900	3,697
1890	4,237
1880	3,923
1870	3,731

(a)Boundary change.

SAUGERTIES SOUTH, CDP
  Saugerties Town
    Ulster County

1980	2,919
1970	3,159

SAUQUOIT, CDP
  Paris Town
    Oneida County

1960	1,715
1950	1,227
1940	1,077
1900-1930	NA
1890	504
1880	NA
1870	459

SAVANNAH, Town (Est. 1824)
  Wayne County

1980	1,905
1970	1,676
1960	1,667
1950	1,494
1940	1,456
1930	1,485
1920	1,524
1910	1,586
1900	1,733
1890	1,788
1880	1,867
1870	1,933
1860	1,910
1850	1,700
1840	1,718
1830	886

SAVANNAH, Village (Inc. 1867)(a)
  Savannah Town
    Wayne County

1970	636

1960	602
1950	582
1940	601
1930	600
1920	516
1910	521
1900	573
1890	505
1880	418

(a)Dissolved in 1979.

SAVONA, Town (Est. 1859)(a)
  Steuben County

1860	1,394

(a)Merged into BATH Town in 1862.

SAVONA, Village (Inc. 1883)
  Bath Town
    Steuben County

1980	932
1970	933
1960	904
1950	869
1940	653
1930	545
1920	554
1910	587
1900	611
1890	569
1880	447

SAYVILLE, CDP
  Islip Town
    Suffolk County

1980	12,013
1970	11,680
1960	6,480(a)
1950	4,251
1940	4,183
1890-1930	NA
1880	1,589
1870	1,200

(a)Derived by LIRPB from U.S. Census
   Data.

SCARSDALE, Town (Est. 1788)(a)
  Westchester County

1980	17,650
1970	19,229
1960	17,968
1950	13,156
1940	12,966
1930	9,690
1920	3,506
1910	1,300
1900	885
1890	633
1880	614
1870	517
1860	548
1850	342
1840	255(b)
1830	317
1820	329
1810	NA
1800	*258
1790	281

(a)Established town and village of
   SCARSDALE, with identical boundaries,

in 1915.
(b)Reported as Searsdale.

SCARSDALE, Village
    see SCARSDALE, Town
            Westchester County

SCHAGHTICOKE, Town (Est. 1788)
    Rensselaer County
            1980   7,094
            1970   6,220
            1960   5,269
            1950   4,019
            1940   3,246
            1930   3,006
            1920   2,177
            1910   2,780(a)
            1900   2,631
            1890   3,059
            1880   3,591
            1870   3,125
            1860   2,929
            1850   3,290
            1840   3,389(b)
            1830   3,002
            1820   2,522
            1810   NA
            1800   *2,352(c)
            1790   1,833(d)
(a)Boundary change.
(b)Reported as Schatecoke.
(c)Reported as Schaghtikote.
(d)Reported as Schachticoke in ALBANY
    County.

SCHAGHTICOKE, Village (Inc. 1867)
    Schaghticoke Town
        Rensselaer County
            1980   677
            1970   860
            1960   720
            1950   687
            1940   603
            1930   555
            1920   568
            1910   765
            1900   1,061
            1890   1,258

SCHAGHTIKOTE, Town
    see SCHAGHTICOKE, Town
            Rensselaer County

SCHATECOKE, Town
    see SCHAGHTICOKE, Town
            Rensselaer County

SCHENECTADY, City (Inc. 1798)(a)
    Schenectady County
            1980   67,972
            1970   77,958 Rev.
            1960   81,682
            1950   91,785(b)
            1940   87,549(b)
            1930   95,692(b)
            1920   88,723(b)
            1910   72,826
            1900   31,682
            1890   19,902

            1880   13,655
            1870   11,026
            1860   9,579
            1850   8,921
            1840   6,784
            1830   4,268
            1820   3,939
            1810   5,903
            1800   *5,289(c)
(a)SCHENECTADY Town incorporated as
    SCHENECTADY City in 1798.
(b)Boundary change.
(c)Reported in ALBANY County.

SCHENECTADY, County (Est. 1809)
            1980   149,946
            1970   161,078 Rev.
            1960   152,896
            1950   142,497
            1940   122,494
            1930   125,021
            1920   109,363
            1910   88,235
            1900   46,852
            1890   29,797
            1880   23,538
            1870   21,347
            1860   20,002
            1850   20,054
            1840   17,387
            1830   12,347
            1820   12,876 Rev.
            1810   10,201

SCHENECTADY, Town (Est. 1788)(a)
    Albany County
            1790   756
(a)SCHENECTADY Town incorporated as
    SCHENECTADY City in 1798.

SCHENECTADY SOUTH OF THE MOHAWK
    Albany County
            1790   3,472

SCHENEVUS, Village (Inc. 1870)
    Maryland Town
        Otsego County
            1980   625
            1970   540
            1960   493
            1950   568
            1940   472
            1930   562
            1920   526
            1910   576
            1900   613
            1890   665
            1880   NA
            1870   549

SCHLOSSER, Town
    see NIAGARA, Town
            Niagara County

SCHODACK, Town (Est. 1795)
    Rensselaer County
            1980   11,345
            1970   11,196
            1960   8,052

1950	6,164
1940	5,081
1930	4,639
1920	3,992
1910	4,780
1900	4,334
1890	4,388
1880	4,319
1870	4,442
1860	3,993
1850	3,509
1840	4,125
1830	3,794
1820	3,493(a)
1810	NA
1800	*3,688

(a)Reported as Schodac.

SCHODACK LANDING, CDP
  Schodack Town
    Rensselaer County

1880	401

SCHOHARIE, County (Est. 1795)

1980	29,710
1970	24,750
1960	22,616
1950	22,703
1940	20,812
1930	19,667
1920	21,303
1910	23,855
1900	26,854
1890	29,164
1880	32,910
1870	33,340
1860	34,469
1850	33,548
1840	32,358
1830	27,902
1820	23,147 Rev.
1810	18,945
1800	9,808(a)

(a)Reported as Schohary.

SCHOHARIE, Town (Est. 1788)
  Schoharie County

1980	3,107
1970	3,088
1960	3,063
1950	2,777
1940	2,417
1930	2,193
1920	2,132
1910	2,526
1900	2,700
1890	2,944
1880	3,350
1870	3,207
1860	3,090
1850	2,588
1840	5,534
1830	5,157
1820	3,820
1810	NA
1800	*1,696(a)
1790	2,073(b)

(a)Reported as Schohary.
(b)Reported as Schohary in ALBANY

County.

SCHOHARIE, Village (Inc. 1867)
  Schoharie Town
    Schoharie County

1980	1,016
1970	1,125
1960	1,168
1950	1,059
1940	941
1930	827
1920	851
1910	996
1900	1,006
1890	1,028
1880	1,188
1870	1,200

SCHOHARY, County & Town
  see SCHOHARIE, County & Town

SCHROEPPEL, Town (Est. 1832)
  Oswego County

1980	8,016
1970	7,153
1960	5,554
1950	4,037
1940	3,219
1930	3,010
1920	2,617
1910	2,707
1900	3,012
1890	3,026
1880	3,381
1870	3,987
1860	4,011
1850	2,386
1840	2,098(a)

(a)Reported as Schroepel.

SCHROON, CDP
  Schroon Town
    Essex County

1870	300

SCHROON, Town (Est. 1804)
  Essex County

1980	1,606
1970	1,403
1960	1,220
1950	1,176
1940	1,044
1930	932
1920	852
1910	1,013
1900	1,272
1890	1,474
1880	1,731
1870	1,899
1860	2,550
1850	2,031
1840	1,660
1830	1,614
1820	888

SCHROON LAKE, CDP
  Schroon Town
    Essex County

1940	575

1890-1930	NA
1880	324

SCHUYLER, County (Est. 1854)

1980	17,686
1970	16,737
1960	15,044
1950	14,182
1940	12,979
1930	12,909
1920	13,098
1910	14,004
1900	15,811
1890	16,711
1880	18,842
1870	18,989
1860	18,840

SCHUYLER, Town (Est. 1792)
Herkimer County

1980	2,886
1970	2,808 Rev.
1960	1,893
1950	1,169
1940	1,176
1930	1,146
1920	1,007
1910	1,227
1900	1,365
1890	1,259
1880	1,452
1870	1,558
1860	1,715
1850	1,696
1840	1,798
1830	2,074
1820	1,837
1810	NA
1800	*963

SCHUYLER FALLS, Town (Est. 1848)
Clinton County

1980	4,184
1970	2,884
1960	2,419 Rev.
1950	1,585
1940	1,480
1930	1,350
1920	1,400
1910	1,588
1900	1,665
1890	1,456
1880	1,640
1870	1,684
1860	1,976(a)
1850	2,110(a)

(a)Reported as Schuyler's Falls.

SCHUYLER'S LAKE, CDP
Exeter Town
Otsego County

1880	265

SCHUYLERVILLE, Village (Inc. 1831)
Saratoga Town
Saratoga County

1980	1,256
1970	1,402
1960	1,361

1950	1,314
1940	1,447
1930	1,411
1920	1,625
1910	1,614
1900	1,601
1890	1,387
1880	1,617
1870	1,367
1860	1,348

SCIO, CDP
Scio Town
Allegany County

1940	532
1890-1930	NA
1880	419

SCIO, Town (Est. 1823)
Allegany County

1980	1,971
1970	1,674
1960	1,513
1950	1,511
1940	1,353
1930	1,205
1920	1,062
1910	1,196
1900	1,281
1890	1,391
1880	1,555
1870	1,652
1860	1,631
1850	1,922
1840	1,156
1830	602

SCIOTA, CDP
Chazy Town
Clinton County

1880	228

SCIPIO, CDP
Scipio Town
Cayuga County

1880	141

SCIPIO, Town (Est. 1794)
Cayuga County

1980	1,471
1970	1,290
1960	1,143
1950	1,202
1940	1,104
1930	991
1920	1,218
1910	1,470
1900	1,657
1890	1,836
1880	2,093
1870	2,070
1860	2,066
1850	2,135
1840	2,255
1830	2,691
1820	8,105
1810	NA
1800	*3,147

SCIPIOVILLE, CDP
  Scipio Town
    Cayuga County
      1880   128

SCOTCH BUSH, CDP
  Florida Town
    Montgomery County
      1880   95
      1870   120

SCOTCHTOWN, CDP
  Wallkill Town
    Orange County
      1980   7,352
      1970   2,119

SCOTIA, Village (Inc. 1904)
  Glenville Town
    Schenectady County
      1980   7,280
      1970   7,370 Rev.(a)
      1960   7,625
      1950   7,812
      1940   7,960(a)
      1930   7,437(a)
      1920   4,358
      1910   2,957
      1890-1900   NA
      1880   222
(a)Boundary change.

SCOTT, CDP
  Scott Town
    Cortland County
      1880   117

SCOTT, Town (Est. 1815)
  Cortland County
      1980   1,193
      1970   805
      1960   600
      1950   527
      1940   535
      1930   544
      1920   625
      1910   718
      1900   852
      1890   987
      1880   980
      1870   1,083
      1860   1,208
      1850   1,290
      1840   1,332
      1830   1,452
      1820   775

SCOTTSVILLE, Village (Inc. 1914)
  Wheatland Town
    Monroe County
      1980   1,789
      1970   1,967
      1960   1,863(a)
      1950   1,025
      1940   925
      1930   936
      1920   784
      1890-1910   NA
      1880   784

(a)Boundary change.

SCRANTON, CDP
  Hamburg Town
    Erie County
      1960   1,078

SCRIBA, Town (Est. 1811)
  Oswego County
      1980   5,455
      1970   3,619
      1960   2,489
      1950   2,248
      1940   2,184
      1930   1,973
      1920   1,817
      1910   2,199
      1900   2,480
      1890   2,480
      1880   2,971
      1870   3,065
      1860   3,282
      1850   2,738
      1840   4,051
      1830   2,073
      1820   741

SEA CLIFF, Village (Inc. 1883)
  Oyster Bay Town
    Nassau County
      1980   5,364
      1970   5,890
      1960   5,669
      1950   4,868
      1940   4,416(a)
      1930   3,456
      1920   2,108
      1910   1,694
      1900   1,558
      1890   NA
      1880   554(b)
(a)Boundary change.
(b)Reported in QUEENS County.

SEAFORD, CDP
  Hempstead Town
    Nassau County
      1980   16,117
      1970   17,379
      1960   14,718
      1950   NA
      1940   2,216
      1900-1930   NA
      1890   503(a)
(a)Reported in QUEENS County.

SEARINGTOWN
  North Hempstead Town
    Nassau County
      1980   4,900(a)
      1970   4,595(a)
      1960   3,424(a)
(a)Derived by LIRPB from U.S. Census
   Data.

SEARSBURGH, CDP
  Hector Town
    Schuyler County
      1880   70

SEARSDALE, Town
  see SCARSDALE, Town
        Westchester County

SEAVIEW, CDP
  see FIRE ISLAND
        Islip Town
          Suffolk County

SELDEN, CDP
  Brookhaven Town
    Suffolk County
        1980   17,259(a)
        1970   11,613(b)
        1960   4,387 Rev.
        1950   1,743
        1940   849
        1890-1930   NA
        1880   88
(a)Boundary change.
(b)Population of 14,028 is comparable
   to 1980 boundaries.

SEMPRONIUS, CDP
  Sempronius Town
    Cayuga County
        1880   62

SEMPRONIUS, Town (Est. 1799)
  Cayuga County
        1980   733
        1970   649
        1960   548
        1950   572
        1940   526
        1930   543
        1920   575
        1910   756
        1900   896
        1890   981
        1880   1,138
        1870   1,165
        1860   1,262
        1850   1,266
        1840   1,304
        1830   5,705
        1820   5,033
        1810   NA
        1800   *875

SENECA, County (Est. 1804)
        1980   33,733
        1970   35,083
        1960   31,984
        1950   29,253
        1940   25,732
        1930   24,983
        1920   24,735
        1910   26,972
        1900   28,114
        1890   28,227
        1880   29,278
        1870   27,823
        1860   28,138
        1850   25,441
        1840   24,874
        1830   21,041
        1820   23,619
        1810   16,609

SENECA, Town
  Erie County
    see WEST SENECA, Town
        Erie County

SENECA, Town (Est. 1793)
  Ontario County
        1980   2,749
        1970   2,808
        1960   2,698
        1950   2,535
        1940   2,570
        1930   2,635
        1920   2,638
        1910   2,669
        1900   2,654
        1890   2,690
        1880   2,877
        1870   9,188
        1860   8,448
        1850   8,505
        1840   7,073
        1830   6,207
        1820   4,802
        1810   NA
        1800   *1,522

SENECA CASTLE, CDP
  Seneca Town
    Ontario County
        1880   149

SENECA FALLS, Town (Est. 1829)
  Seneca County
        1980   9,886
        1970   9,900
        1960   9,264
        1950   7,845
        1940   7,352
        1930   7,166
        1920   7,179
        1910   7,407
        1900   7,305
        1890   6,961
        1880   6,853
        1870   6,860
        1860   5,960
        1850   4,296
        1840   4,281
        1830   2,603

SENECA FALLS, Village (Inc. 1831)
  Seneca Falls Town
    Seneca County
        1980   7,466(a)
        1970   7,794(a)
        1960   7,439
        1950   6,634
        1940   6,452
        1930   6,443
        1920   6,389
        1910   6,588
        1900   6,519
        1890   6,116
        1880   5,880
        1870   5,890
(a)Boundary change.

SENECA HILL, CDP
  Volney Town
    Oswego County
      1880   107

SENNETT, Town (Est. 1827)
  Cayuga County
    1980   2,561
    1970   2,553
    1960   2,283
    1950   1,730
    1940   1,664
    1930   1,528
    1920   1,358
    1910   1,423
    1900   1,440
    1890   1,498
    1880   1,644
    1870   1,748
    1860   1,923
    1850   2,347
    1840   2,060
    1830   2,297

SETAUKET, CDP(a)
  Brookhaven Town
    Suffolk County
      1960   1,207
(a)Included in SETAUKET--SOUTH SETAUKET,
   CDP in 1970; in SETAUKET--EAST
   SETAUKET, CDP in 1980.

SETAUKET--EAST SETAUKET, CDP
  Brookhaven Town
    Suffolk County
      1980   10,176(a)
      1970   8,246(b)
      1890-1960   NA
      1880   492
(a)Boundary change.
(b)Derived by LIRPB from U.S. Census
   Data; population is comparable to
   1980 boundaries.

SETAUKET--SOUTH SETAUKET, CDP(a)
  Brookhaven Town
    Suffolk County
      1970   6,857(b)
      1960   1,395(c)
(a)Included in SETAUKET--EAST SETAUKET,
   CDP in 1980.
(b)Boundary change.
(c)Derived by LIRPB from U.S. Census
   Data.

SEWARD, Town (Est. 1840)
  Schoharie County
    1980   1,587
    1970   1,271
    1960   1,210
    1950   1,224
    1940   1,146
    1930   1,128
    1920   1,193
    1910   1,419
    1900   1,404
    1890   1,626
    1880   1,734
    1870   1,765

    1860   1,948
    1850   2,203
    1840   2,088

SEWARD VALLEY, CDP
  Seward Town
    Schoharie County
      1880   141

SHAKER, CDP
  Watervliet Town
    Albany County
      1880   139

SHAKER, CDP
  Canaan Town
    Columbia County
      1880   59

SHANDAKEN, Town (Est. 1804)
  Ulster County
    1980   2,912
    1970   2,593
    1960   2,078
    1950   1,887
    1940   1,875
    1930   2,066
    1920   2,372
    1910   2,657
    1900   3,053
    1890   3,170
    1880   2,829
    1870   2,751
    1860   2,430
    1850   2,307
    1840   1,455
    1830   966(a)
    1820   1,043
(a)Reported as Shandakan.

SHARON, Town (Est. 1792)(a)
  Schoharie County
    1980   1,915
    1970   1,566
    1960   1,405
    1950   1,463
    1940   1,476
    1930   1,319
    1920   1,494
    1910   1,825
    1900   2,058
    1890   2,202
    1880   2,591
    1870   2,648
    1860   2,754
    1850   2,632
    1840   2,520
    1830   4,247
    1820   3,982
    1810   NA
    1800   *2,650
(a)Established as Dorlach in 1792; name
   changed in 1797.

SHARON SPRINGS, Village (Inc. 1871)
  Sharon Town
    Schoharie County
      1980   514
      1970   421

1960	351
1950	361
1940	433
1930	364
1920	400
1910	459
1900	567
1890	622
1880	627
1870	520

SHAWANGUNK, Town (Est. 1788)
Ulster County

1980	8,186
1970	5,749
1960	4,604
1950	3,561
1940	3,117
1930	2,127
1920	2,087
1910	2,548
1900	2,406
1890	2,456
1880	2,910
1870	2,823
1860	2,870
1850	4,036
1840	3,886
1830	3,681
1820	3,372
1810	NA
1800	*2,809
1790	2,128

SHELBY, Town (Est. 1818)
Orleans County

1980	5,361
1970	5,366
1960	5,051
1950	4,482
1940	3,961
1930	3,946
1920	3,937
1910	3,945
1900	3,679
1890	3,702
1880	3,824
1870	3,366
1860	3,326
1850	3,082
1840	2,643
1830	1,879
1820	1,158(a)

(a)Reported in GENESEE County.

SHELBY CENTER, CDP
Shelby Town
Orleans County

1880	162

SHELDON, Town (Est. 1808)
Wyoming County

1980	2,644
1970	2,296
1960	1,898
1950	1,618
1940	1,578
1930	1,545
1920	1,593

1910	1,713
1900	1,801
1890	2,059
1880	2,257
1870	2,258
1860	2,794
1850	2,527
1840	2,353(a)
1830	1,731(a)
1820	887(a)

(a)Reported in GENESEE County.

SHELTER ISLAND, CDP
Shelter Island Town
Suffolk County

1980	1,115(a)
1970	1,052(b)
1960	743(c)
1950	NA
1940	928

(a)Boundary change.
(b)Derived by LIRPB from U.S. Census
   Data; population of 913 is comparable to 1980 boundaries.
(c)Derived by LIRPB from U.S. Census
   Data.

SHELTER ISLAND, Town (Est. 1788)
Suffolk County

1980	2,071
1970	1,644
1960	1,312
1950	1,144
1940	1,073
1930	1,113
1920	890
1910	1,064
1900	1,066
1890	921
1880	732
1870	645
1860	506
1850	386
1840	379
1830	330
1820	389
1810	329
1800	*260
1790	201

SHELTER ISLAND HEIGHTS
Shelter Island Town
Suffolk County

1980	940(a)
1970	568(b)
1960	550(c)

(a)Boundary change; derived by LIRPB
   from U.S. Census Data.
(b)Derived by LIRPB from U.S. Census
   Data; population of 707 is comparable
   to 1980 boundaries.
(c)Derived by LIRPB from U.S. Census
   Data.

SHERBURNE, Town (Est. 1795)
Chenango County

1980	3,657
1970	3,578
1960	3,338

1950	3,046
1940	2,928
1930	2,619
1920	2,820
1910	2,683
1900	2,614
1890	2,847
1880	3,128
1870	2,927
1860	2,701
1850	2,625
1840	2,791
1830	2,601
1820	2,590
1810	NA
1800	*1,282(a)

(a)Reported as Sherburn.

SHERBURNE, Village (Inc. 1830)
  Sherburne Town
    Chenango County

1980	1,561(a)
1970	1,613
1960	1,647
1950	1,604(a)
1940	1,192
1930	1,077
1920	1,104
1910	960
1900	899
1890	960
1880	944

(a)Boundary change.

SHERBURNE QUARTER, CDP
  Sherburne Town
    Chenango County

1880	337

SHERIDAN, Town (Est. 1827)
  Chautauqua County

1980	2,659
1970	2,527
1960	2,539
1950	2,037
1940	1,826
1930	2,035
1920	1,887
1910	1,888
1900	1,633
1890	1,511
1880	1,551
1870	1,686
1860	1,716
1850	2,173
1840	1,883
1830	1,666

SHERMAN, Town (Est. 1832)
  Chautauqua County

1980	1,490
1970	1,428
1960	1,511
1950	1,611
1940	1,101
1930	1,350
1920	1,467
1910	1,568
1900	1,560

1890	1,531
1880	1,558
1870	1,470
1860	1,394
1850	1,292
1840	1,099

SHERMAN, Village (Inc. 1890)
  Sherman Town
    Chautauqua County

1980	775
1970	769
1960	873
1950	861
1940	675
1930	769
1920	847
1910	836
1900	760
1890	785
1880	731
1870	610

SHERRILL, City (Inc. 1916)(a)
  Vernon Town
    Oneida County

1980	2,830
1970	2,986
1960	2,922(b)
1950	2,236(b)
1940	2,184
1930	2,150(b)
1920	1,761

(a)Incorporated as a city, but remains
   a part of VERNON Town.
(b)Boundary change.

SHERWOOD, CDP
  Scipio Town
    Cayuga County

1880	169

SHINNECOCK HILLS, CDP
  Southampton Town
    Suffolk County

1980	2,344(a)
1970	1,822(b)
1960	578(c)

(a)Boundary change.
(b)Derived by LIRPB from U.S. Census
   Data; population of 1,894 is
   comparable to 1980 boundaries.
(c)Derived by LIRPB from U.S. Census
   Data.

SHINNECOCK INDIAN RESERVATION
  Suffolk County

1980	297
1970	174
1960	234
1950	183
1940	156
1930	160(a)
1920	112
1910	171
1880-1900	NA
1870	97

(a)Derived by New York State. U.S.
   Census reported with POOSPATUCK

INDIAN RESERVATION, population of
194.

SHIRLEY, CDP
  Brookhaven Town
    Suffolk County
      1980   18,072(a)
      1970   6,280 Rev.(b)
      1960   2,986(c)
(a)Boundary change.
(b)Population of 6,678 is comparable
   to 1980 boundaries.
(c)Derived by LIRPB from U.S. Census
   Data; U.S. Census reported as MASTIC--
   SHIRLEY, CDP with total population
   of 3,397.

SHIRLEY, Town
  see NORTH COLLINS, Town
        Erie County

SHONGO, CDP
  Willing Town
    Allegany County
      1880   62

SHOREHAM, Village (Inc. 1913)
  Brookhaven Town
    Suffolk County
      1980   555
      1970   524(a)
      1960   164(a)
      1950   90
      1940   25
      1930   135
      1920   11
(a)Boundary change.

SHORTSVILLE, Village (Inc. 1889)
  Manchester Town
    Ontario County
      1980   1,669(a)
      1970   1,516
      1960   1,382
      1950   1,314
      1940   1,316
      1930   1,332
      1920   1,300
      1910   1,112
      1900   922
      1890   NA
      1880   620(b)
(a)Boundary change.
(b)Reported as Shortville.

SHRUB OAK, CDP
  Yorktown Town
    Westchester County
      1960   1,874
      1950   NA
      1940   640

SHULL TOWN, CDP
  German Town
    Herkimer County
      1880   144

SHUSHAN, CDP
  Salem Town
    Washington County
      1880   328

SIDNEY, Town (Est. 1801)
  Delaware County
      1980   6,856
      1970   6,984
      1960   7,110
      1950   6,669
      1940   4,509
      1930   3,854
      1920   4,133
      1910   4,148
      1900   4,023
      1890   3,122
      1880   2,461
      1870   2,597
      1860   1,916
      1850   1,807
      1840   1,732
      1830   1,410
      1820   1,107

SIDNEY, Village (Inc. 1888)
  Sidney Town
    Delaware County
      1980   4,861(a)
      1970   4,789(a)
      1960   5,157(a)
      1950   4,815(a)
      1940   3,012
      1930   2,444
      1920   2,670
      1910   2,507
      1900   2,331
      1890   1,358
(a)Boundary change.

SIDNEY CENTER, CDP
  Sidney Town
    Delaware County
      1880   141(a)
(a)Reported as Sidney Centre.

SIDNEY PLAINS, CDP
  Sidney Town
    Delaware County
      1870   405

SILVER CREEK, Village (Inc. 1848)
  Hanover Town
    Chautauqua County
      1980   3,088
      1970   3,182
      1960   3,310
      1950   3,068
      1940   3,067
      1930   3,160
      1920   3,260
      1910   2,512
      1900   1,944
      1890   1,678
      1880   1,036
      1870   666
      1860   661

SILVER LAKE, CDP
  Black Brook Town
    Clinton County
      1880   11

SILVER SPRINGS, Village (Inc. 1895)
  Gainesville Town
    Wyoming County
      1980   801
      1970   823
      1960   726
      1950   830
      1940   766
      1930   879
      1920   1,155
      1910   974
      1900   667

SINCLAIRVILLE, Village (Inc. 1887)
  Charlotte Town, part in
    Chautauqua County
      1980   596
      1970   629
      1960   629
      1950   562
      1940   499
      1930   508
      1920   442
      1910   475
      1900   489
      1890   510
      1880   540
  Gerry Town, part in
    Chautauqua County
      1980   176
      1970   143
      1960   97
      1950   110
      1940   86
      1930   81
      1920   72
      1910   67
      1900   88
  TOTAL
      1980   772
      1970   772
      1960   726
      1950   672
      1940   585
      1930   589
      1920   514
      1910   542
      1900   577
      1890   510
      1880-1890   (a)
(a)Reported in CHARLOTTE Town only.

SING SING, Village
  see OSSINING, Village
         Westchester County

SKANEATELES, Town (Est. 1830)
  Onondaga County
      1980   7,795
      1970   7,825
      1960   6,603
      1950   5,193
      1940   4,639
      1930   4,795

      1920   4,247
      1910   4,274
      1900   4,205
      1890   4,662
      1880   4,866
      1870   4,524
      1860   4,335
      1850   4,081
      1840   3,981
      1830   3,812

SKANEATELES, Village (Inc. 1833)
  Skaneateles Town
    Onondaga County
      1980   2,789(a)
      1970   3,055
      1960   2,921
      1950   2,331
      1940   1,949
      1930   1,882
      1920   1,635
      1910   1,615
      1900   1,495
      1890   1,559
      1880   1,669
      1870   1,409
(a)Boundary change.

SKANEATELES FALLS, CDP
  Skaneateles Town
    Onondaga County
      1940   524

SKENESBOROUGH, Town
  see WHITEHALL, Town
         Washington County

SKINNERSVILLE, CDP
  Stockholm Town
    St. Lawrence County
      1880   78

SLABTOWN, CDP
  Horseheads Town
    Chemung County
      1970   2,753

SLEIGHTBURGH, CDP
  Esopus Town
    Ulster County
      1880   282
      1870   203(a)
(a)Reported as Sleightsburgh.

SLOAN, Village (Inc. 1896)
  Cheektowaga Town
    Erie County
      1980   4,529
      1970   5,216
      1960   5,803
      1950   4,698
      1940   3,836
      1930   3,482
      1920   1,791
      1910   1,259
      1900   873

SLOANSVILLE, CDP
  Esperance Town
    Schoharie County
      1880   200

SLOATSBURG, Village (Inc. 1929)
  Ramapo Town
    Rockland County
      1980   3,154
      1970   3,134
      1960   2,565
      1950   2,018
      1940   1,771
      1930   1,623

SMALLWOOD, Town
    see BRIGHTON & PITTSFORD Towns
      Monroe County

SMITHBORO, CDP
  Tioga Town
    Tioga County
      1880   294
      1870   304(a)
(a)Reported as Smithborough.

SMITHFIELD, Town (Est. 1807)
    Madison County
      1980   1,001
      1970   864
      1960   804
      1950   758
      1940   630
      1930   653
      1920   767
      1910   880
      1900   989
      1890   1,043
      1880   1,226
      1870   1,227
      1860   1,509
      1850   1,669
      1840   1,699
      1830   2,636
      1820   3,338

SMITH MILLS, CDP
  Hanover Town
    Chautauqua County
      1880   148
      1870   128(a)
      1860   159(a)
(a)Reported as Smith's Mills.

SMITHTOWN, CDP
  Smithtown Town
    Suffolk County
      1980   30,906(a)
      1970   3,340(b)
      1960   2,386(c)
(a)Boundary change.
(b)Derived by LIRPB from U.S. Census
   Data; population of 29,735 is
   comparable to 1980 boundaries.
(c)Derived by LIRPB from U.S. Census
   Data.

SMITHTOWN, Town (Est. 1788)
    Suffolk County
      1980   116,663
      1970   114,657 Rev.
      1960   50,347
      1950   20,993
      1940   13,970
      1930   11,855
      1920   9,114
      1910   7,073
      1900   5,863
      1890   3,357
      1880   2,249
      1870   2,136
      1860   2,130
      1850   1,972
      1840   1,932
      1830   1,686
      1820   1,874
      1810   1,592
      1800   *1,413(a)
      1790   1,022
(a)Reported as Smith-Town.

SMITHTOWN BRANCH, CDP
  Smithtown Town
    Suffolk County
      1960   1,986
      1950   1,424
      1940   1,298

SMITHVILLE, CDP
  Smithville Town
    Chenango County
      1880   275

SMITHVILLE, CDP
  Henderson Town
    Jefferson County
      1880   79

SMITHVILLE, Town (Est. 1808)
    Chenango County
      1980   1,174
      1970   956
      1960   891
      1950   845
      1940   805
      1930   831
      1920   843
      1910   949
      1900   1,105
      1890   1,318
      1880   1,492
      1870   1,405
      1860   1,661
      1850   1,771
      1840   1,762
      1830   1,839
      1820   1,553

SMOKETOWN, CDP
  North Hempstead Town
    Nassau County
      1880   179(a)
(a)Reported in QUEENS County.

SMYRNA, Town (Est. 1808)(a)
    Chenango County
        1980   1,142
        1970   1,106
        1960   1,055
        1950   996
        1940   971
        1930   1,020
        1920   1,058
        1910   1,205
        1900   1,290
        1890   1,396
        1880   1,651
        1870   1,668
        1860   1,822
        1850   1,940
        1840   2,246
        1830   1,859
        1820   1,390
(a)Established as Stafford in Mar., 1808;
   name changed in Apr., 1808.

SMYRNA, Village (Inc. 1829)
    Smyrna Town
        Chenango County
            1980   225
            1970   247
            1960   286
            1950   269
            1940   256
            1930   226
            1920   261
            1910   257
            1900   300
            1890   NA
            1880   308

SNELL, Town
    see BENTON, Town
        Yates County

SNYDER, CDP
    Amherst Town
        Erie County
            1940   4,856

SODUS, Town (Est. 1789)
    Wayne County
        1980   9,485
        1970   8,754
        1960   6,587
        1950   5,706
        1940   5,162
        1930   5,003
        1920   4,408
        1910   4,857
        1900   5,118
        1890   5,157
        1880   5,285
        1870   4,631
        1860   4,745
        1850   4,598
        1840   4,472
        1830   3,528
        1820   2,013(a)
        1810   NA
        1800   *416(a)
(a)Reported in ONTARIO County.

SODUS, Village (Inc. 1918)
    Sodus Town
        Wayne County
            1980   1,790(a)
            1970   1,813(a)
            1960   1,645(a)
            1950   1,588
            1940   1,513
            1930   1,444
            1920   1,329
            1900-1910   NA
            1890   1,028
            1880   842
            1870   516
(a)Boundary change.

SODUS POINT, Village (Inc. 1957)
    Sodus Town
        Wayne County
            1980   1,334
            1970   1,172
            1960   868

SOLON, CDP
    Solon Town
        Cortland County
            1880   87

SOLON, Town (Est. 1798)
    Cortland County
        1980   865
        1970   687
        1960   549
        1950   522
        1940   486
        1930   483
        1920   498
        1910   518
        1900   622
        1890   687
        1880   842
        1870   872
        1860   1,148
        1850   1,150
        1840   2,311
        1830   2,033
        1820   1,262
        1810   NA
        1800   *370(a)
(a)Reported in ONONDAGA County.

SOLVAY, Village (Inc. 1894)
    Geddes Town
        Onondaga County
            1980   7,140
            1970   8,280
            1960   8,732
            1950   7,868
            1940   8,201
            1930   7,986
            1920   7,352
            1910   5,139
            1900   3,493
            1890   563

SOMERS, Town (Est. 1788)(a)
    Westchester County
        1980   13,133
        1970   9,402

1960	5,468
1950	3,159
1940	2,406
1930	1,514
1920	1,117
1910	1,228
1900	1,338
1890	1,897
1880	1,630
1870	1,721
1860	2,012
1850	1,722
1840	2,082
1830	1,997
1820	1,841
1810	NA
1800	*1,578(b)
1790	1,297

(a)Established as Stephentown in 1788;
name changed in 1808.
(b)Reported as Stephen Town.

SOMERSET, Town (Est. 1823)
    Niagara County

1980	2,701
1970	2,677
1960	2,489
1950	2,227
1940	2,041
1930	1,892
1920	2,003
1910	2,260
1900	1,923
1890	1,962
1880	2,015
1870	1,862
1860	2,132
1850	2,154
1840	1,742
1830	871

SOMERVILLE, CDP
    Rossie Town
        St. Lawrence County

1870	113

SOUND AVENUE, Village
    see NORTHVILLE, CDP
        Suffolk County

SOUND BEACH, CDP
    Brookhaven Town
        Suffolk County

1980	8,071
1970	4,878(a)
1960	1,625

(a)Derived by LIRPB from U.S. Census
Data.

SOUTH ALABAMA, CDP
    Alabama Town
        Genesee County

1880	113

SOUTH AMENIA, CDP
    Amenia Town
        Dutchess County

1880	82

SOUTHAMPTON, Town
    Livingston County
    see CALEDONIA, Town
        Livingston County

SOUTHAMPTON, Town (Est. 1788)
    Suffolk County

1980	42,849
1970	36,154 Rev.
1960	27,095 Rev.
1950	16,830
1940	15,295
1930	15,341
1920	11,614
1910	11,069 Rev.(a)
1900	10,371
1890	8,200
1880	6,352
1870	6,135
1860	6,803(b)
1850	6,501
1840	6,205
1830	4,850
1820	4,229(b)
1810	3,899
1800	*3,670(b)
1790	3,408(b)

(a)In 1920 the Census Bureau revised the
1910 figure of 11,240 to exclude the
SHINNECOCK INDIAN RESERVATION.
(b)Reported as South Hampton.

SOUTHAMPTON, Village (Inc. 1894)
    Southampton Town
        Suffolk County

1980	4,000
1970	4,904
1960	4,582
1950	4,042
1940	3,818
1930	3,738(a)
1920	2,891
1910	2,509
1900	2,289
1890	NA
1880	949
1870	943

(a)Boundary change.

SOUTH ARGYLE, CDP
    Argyle Town
        Washington County

1880	50

SOUTH BALLSTON, CDP(a)
    Ballston Town
        Saratoga County

1880	80

(a)Also called BRANCH.

SOUTH BAY, CDP
    Fort Ann Town
        Washington County

1880	483

SOUTH BAY, Town
    see DRESDEN, Town
        Washington County

SOUTH BERNE, CDP
   Berne Town
      Albany County
         1870   50

SOUTH BETHLEHEM, CDP
   Bethlehem Town
      Albany County
         1880   89

SOUTH BRADFORD, CDP
   Bradford Town
      Steuben County
         1880   70

SOUTH BRISTOL, Town (Est. 1838)
   Ontario County
         1980   1,205
         1970   794
         1960   617
         1950   542
         1940   581
         1930   654
         1920   696
         1910   965
         1900   1,104
         1890   1,225
         1880   1,327
         1870   1,218
         1860   1,216
         1850   1,129
         1840   1,375

SOUTH BROOKFIELD, CDP
   Brookfield Town
      Madison County
         1880   76

SOUTH BUTLER, CDP
   Butler & Savannah Towns
      Wayne County
         1880   343(a)
(a)Part in BUTLER Town, 290; part in
   SAVANNAH Town, 53.

SOUTH BYRON, CDP
   Byron Town
      Genesee County
         1880   251

SOUTH CENTEREACH(a)
   Brookhaven Town
      Suffolk County
         1970   6,285(b)
         1960   2,757(b)
(a)Included in CENTEREACH, CDP in 1980.
(b)Derived by LIRPB from U.S. Census
   Data.

SOUTH COLTON, CDP
   Colton Town
      St. Lawrence County
         1880   132

SOUTH COLUMBIA, CDP
   Columbia Town
      Herkimer County
         1880   126

SOUTH CORNING, Village (Inc. 1920)
   Corning Town
      Steuben County
         1980   1,195
         1970   1,414
         1960   1,448(a)
         1950   880
         1940   681
         1930   714
(a)Boundary change.

SOUTH CORTLAND, CDP
   Cortlandville Town
      Cortland County
         1870   54

SOUTH DAYTON, Village (Inc. 1915)
   Dayton Town
      Cattaraugus County
         1980   661
         1970   688
         1960   696
         1950   727
         1940   643
         1930   570
         1920   655
         1890-1910   NA
         1880   318

SOUTHEAST, Town (Est. 1788)
   Putnam County
         1980   11,416
         1970   9,901
         1960   6,844
         1950   4,388
         1940   4,053
         1930   3,503
         1920   2,600
         1910   3,282
         1900   2,843
         1890   4,082
         1880   3,500
         1870   2,975
         1860   2,350
         1850   2,079
         1840   1,910
         1830   2,036
         1820   2,247(a)
         1810   NA
         1800   *1,956(a)
         1790   921(b)
(a)Reported as South East.
(b)Reported in DUTCHESS County.

SOUTH EDMESTON, CDP
   Edmeston Town
      Otsego County
         1880   163

SOUTH FALLSBURG, CDP
   Fallsburg Town
      Sullivan County
         1980   2,196
         1970   1,590
         1960   1,290
         1950   1,147
         1940   754

SOUTH FARMINGDALE, CDP
    Oyster Bay Town
        Nassau County
            1980   16,439
            1970   20,464
            1960   16,318
            1950   NA
            1940   1,000

SOUTHFIELD, Town
        Orange County
    see MONROE, Town
            Orange County

SOUTHFIELD, Town (Est. 1788)(a)
    Richmond County
            1890   6,644
            1880   4,980
            1870   5,082
            1860   3,645
            1850   2,709
            1840   1,619
            1830   971
            1820   1,012
            1810   NA
            1800   *932
            1790   855
(a)Merged into STATEN ISLAND Borough
in NEW YORK CITY in 1898.

SOUTH FLANDERS(a)
    Southampton Town
        Suffolk County
            1970   1,527(b)
            1960   945(b)
(a)Included in HAMPTON BAYS, RIVERSIDE--
    FLANDERS, and WESTHAMPTON, CDPs in
    1980.
(b)Derived by LIRPB from U.S. Census
    Data.

SOUTH FLORAL PARK, Village (Inc. 1925)(a)
    Hempstead Town
        Nassau County
            1980   1,490
            1970   1,032
            1960   1,090
            1950   572
            1940   510
            1930   460
(a)Incorporated as Jamaica Square in
    1925; name changed in 1931.

SOUTH GILBOA, CDP
    Gilboa Town
        Schoharie County
            1880   50

SOUTH GLEN COVE, CDP
    Oyster Bay Town
        Nassau County
            1880   2,244(a)
(a)Reported in QUEENS County.

SOUTH GLENS FALLS, Village (Inc. 1895)
    Moreau Town
        Saratoga County
            1980   3,714
            1970   4,013(a)

            1960   4,129(a)
            1950   3,645
            1940   3,081
            1930   2,689
            1920   2,158
            1910   2,247
            1900   2,025
            1890   1,606
            1880   1,083
            1870   1,047
(a)Boundary change.

SOUTH HAMPSTEAD, Town
    see HEMPSTEAD, Town
            Nassau County

SOUTH HAMPTON, Town
    see SOUTHAMPTON, Town
            Suffolk County

SOUTH HANNIBAL, CDP
    Hannibal Town
        Oswego County
            1880   50

SOUTH HAUPPAUGE(a)
    Islip Town
        Suffolk County
            1970   5,381(b)
            1960   894(b)
(a)Included in CENTRAL ISLIP and
    HAUPPAUGE, CDPs in 1980.
(b)Derived by LIRPB from U.S. Census
    Data.

SOUTH HAVEN, CDP
    Brookhaven Town
        Suffolk County
            1880   51

SOUTH HEMPSTEAD, Town
    Queens County
    see HEMPSTEAD, Town
            Nassau County

SOUTH HEMPSTEAD, Unincorporated
    Hempstead Town
        Nassau County
            1980   3,217(a)
            1970   3,274(a)
            1960   3,685(a)
(a)Derived by LIRPB from U.S. Census
    Data.

SOUTH HILL, CDP
    Ithaca Town
        Tompkins County
            1980   5,276

SOUTH HOLBROOK, CDP(a)
    Islip Town
        Suffolk County
            1970   6,700
            1960   1,149(b)
(a)Included in HOLBROOK, CDP in 1980.
(b)Derived by LIRPB from U.S. Census
    Data.

SOUTH HOLD, Town
    see SOUTHOLD, Town
        Suffolk County

SOUTH HUDSON FALLS, CDP
    Fort Edward Town
      Washington County

1980	1,955
1970	2,097

SOUTH HUNTINGTON, CDP
    Huntington Town
      Suffolk County

1980	14,854(a)
1970	9,115(b)
1960	7,084
1950	1,274
1940	1,083

(a)Boundary change.
(b)Population of 15,239 is comparable
   to 1980 boundaries.

SOUTH ILION, CDP
    German Flatts Town
      Herkimer County

1880	104

SOUTH LIMA, CDP
    Lima Town
      Livingston County

1880	52

SOUTH LIVONIA, CDP
    Livonia Town
      Livingston County

1880	130

SOUTH LOCKPORT, CDP
    Lockport Town
      Niagara County

1980	3,366
1970	1,341

SOUTH MEDFORD(a)
    Brookhaven Town
      Suffolk County

1970	4,178(b)
1960	1,497(b)

(a)Included in MEDFORD and EAST
   PATCHOGUE, CDPs in 1980.
(b)Derived by LIRPB from U.S. Census
   Data.

SOUTH NEW BERLIN, CDP
    New Berlin Town
      Chenango County

1880	217

SOUTH NYACK, Village (Inc. 1878)
    Orangetown Town
      Rockland County

1980	3,602
1970	3,435
1960	3,113
1950	3,102
1940	2,093
1930	2,212
1920	1,799
1910	2,068

1900	1,601
1890	1,496

SOUTHOLD, CDP
    Southold Town
      Suffolk County

1980	4,770(a)
1970	2,030(b)
1960	1,285(c)
1950	1,027
1940	1,368
1890-1930	NA
1880	1,221

(a)Boundary change.
(b)Population of 3,749 is comparable
   to 1980 boundaries.
(c)Derived by LIRPB from U.S. Census
   Data.

SOUTHOLD, Town (Est. 1788)
    Suffolk County

1980	19,172
1970	16,804
1960	13,295
1950	11,632
1940	12,046
1930	11,669
1920	10,147
1910	10,577
1900	8,301
1890	7,705
1880	7,267
1870	6,715
1860	5,833
1850	4,723
1840	3,907
1830	2,900
1820	2,968
1810	2,613
1800	*2,200(a)
1790	3,219(b)

(a)Reported as South Hold.
(b)Reported as Southhold.

SOUTH ONONDAGA, CDP
    Onondaga Town
      Onondaga County

1870	242

SOUTH OTSELIC, CDP
    Otselic Town
      Chenango County

1880	230

SOUTHPORT, CDP
    Southport Town
      Chemung County

1980	8,329
1970	8,685
1960	6,698

SOUTHPORT, Town (Est. 1822)
    Chemung County

1980	11,586
1970	11,976
1960	11,433
1950	9,164
1940	5,774
1930	5,421

1920	3,084
1910	2,034
1900	2,201
1890	2,044(a)
1880	3,619
1870	2,185
1860	4,733
1850	3,184
1840	2,101
1830	1,454(b)

(a)Boundary change.
(b)Reported in TIOGA County.

SOUTH RONDOUT, CDP
Esopus Town
Ulster County

1880	493
1870	405

SOUTH SALEM, CDP
Lewisboro Town
Westchester County

1940	547

SOUTH SALEM, Town
see LEWISBORO, Town
Westchester County

SOUTH SCHENECTADY, CDP
Rotterdam Town
Schenectady County

1940	547

SOUTH SCHODACK, CDP
Schodack Town
Rensselaer County

1880	91

SOUTH SETAUKET
see SETAUKET--SOUTH SETAUKET, CDP
Suffolk County

SOUTH STONY BROOK, CDP(a)
Brookhaven Town
Suffolk County

1970	15,329
1960	626(b)

(a)Included in STONY BROOK, CDP and
S.U.N.Y. at STONY BROOK in 1980.
(b)Derived by LIRPB from U.S. Census
Data.

SOUTH TRENTON, CDP
Trenton Town
Oneida County

1880	134
1870	206

SOUTH VALLEY, CDP
Roseboom Town
Otsego County

1880	122

SOUTH VALLEY, Town (Est. 1847)
Cattaraugus County

1980	212
1970	164
1960	205
1950	238

1940	240
1930	310
1920	356
1910	487 Rev.(a)
1900	540 Rev.(b)
1890	1,249
1880	995
1870	743
1860	718
1850	561

(a)In 1920 the Census Bureau revised the
1910 figure of 584 to exclude the
ALLEGANY INDIAN RESERVATION.
(b)Boundary change. In 1920 the Census
Bureau revised the 1900 figure of 713
to exclude the ALLEGANY INDIAN
RESERVATION.

SOUTH VALLEY STREAM, CDP
Hempstead Town
Nassau County

1980	5,462
1970	6,595
1960	6,222(a)

(a)Derived by LIRPB from U.S. Census
Data.

SOUTH WESTBURY, CDP
Hempstead Town
Nassau County

1980	9,732
1970	10,978
1960	11,977

SOUTH WESTERLO, CDP
Westerlo Town
Albany County

1870	147

SOUTH WORCESTER, CDP
Worcester Town
Otsego County

1880	131

SOUTH YAPHANK(a)
Brookhaven Town
Suffolk County

1970	506(b)
1960	831(b)

(a)Included in MEDFORD and YAPHANK,
CDPs in 1980.
(b)Derived by LIRPB from U.S. Census
Data.

SPACKENKILL, CDP
Poughkeepsie Town
Dutchess County

1980	4,848
1970	2,725

SPAFFORD, Town (Est. 1811)
Onondaga County

1980	1,596
1970	1,148
1960	974
1950	829
1940	742
1930	767
1920	875

1910	1,064
1900	1,159
1890	1,227
1880	1,450
1870	1,595
1860	1,814
1850	1,903
1840	1,873
1830	2,647
1820	1,294

SPARKILL, CDP
  Orangetown Town
    Rockland County

1940	584
1900-1930	NA
1890	816

SPARROW BUSH, CDP
  Deerpark Town
    Orange County

1980	1,049
1950-1970	NA
1940	617

SPARTA, Town (Est. 1789)
  Livingston County

1980	1,458
1970	1,157
1960	1,019
1950	971
1940	887
1930	974
1920	833
1910	985
1900	1,189
1890	1,136
1880	1,201
1870	1,182
1860	1,248
1850	1,372
1840	5,841
1830	3,777
1820	1,475(a)
1810	NA
1800	*503(a)

(a)Reported in ONTARIO County.

SPECULATOR, Village (Inc. 1925)
  Lake Pleasant Town
    Hamilton County

1980	408
1970	390
1960	372
1950	370
1940	278
1930	261

SPEEDSVILLE, CDP
  Caroline Town
    Tompkins County

1880	96
1870	153

SPENCER, Town (Est. 1806)
  Tioga County

1980	2,633
1970	2,232
1960	1,790

1950	1,561
1940	1,462
1930	1,480
1920	1,526
1910	1,529
1900	1,868
1890	2,211
1880	2,382
1870	1,863
1860	1,881
1850	1,782
1840	1,532
1830	1,278
1820	1,252

SPENCER, Village (Inc. 1886)
  Spencer Town
    Tioga County

1980	863
1970	854
1960	767
1950	694
1940	615
1930	628
1920	661
1910	569
1900	707
1890	810
1880	700

SPENCERPORT, Village (Inc. 1867)
  Ogden Town
    Monroe County

1980	3,424
1970	2,929
1960	2,461(a)
1950	1,595
1940	1,340
1930	1,249
1920	926
1910	1,000
1900	715
1890	695
1880	670
1870	591

(a)Boundary change.

SPEONK, CDP(a)
  Southampton & Brookhaven Towns
    Suffolk County

1880	196
1870	174

(a)Included, in part, in REMSENBERG--
  SPEONK, CDP in 1960-1980, and in
  EASTPORT--SPEONK, CDP in 1950.

SPRAKER'S BASIN, CDP
  Root Town
    Montgomery County

1880	219

SPRING BROOK, CDP
  Elma Town
    Erie County

1880	156

SPRINGFIELD, CDP
  Springfield Town
    Otsego County
      1880   74

SPRINGFIELD, CDP
  Jamaica Town
    Queens County
      1880   197

SPRINGFIELD, Town (Est. 1797)
  Otsego County
      1980   1,239
      1970   1,136
      1960   1,121
      1950   1,184
      1940   1,135
      1930   1,305
      1920   1,287
      1910   1,468
      1900   1,762
      1890   1,726
      1880   2,016
      1870   2,022
      1860   2,390
      1850   2,322
      1840   2,382
      1830   2,816
      1820   2,065
      1810   NA
      1800   *1,586

SPRING LAKE, CDP
  Conquest Town
    Cayuga County
      1880   96

SPRING MILL, CDP
  Independence Town
    Allegany County
      1880   85

SPRINGPORT, Town (Est. 1823)
  Cayuga County
      1980   2,210
      1970   1,911
      1960   1,700
      1950   1,534
      1940   1,418
      1930   1,316
      1920   1,146
      1910   1,447
      1900   1,770
      1890   1,991
      1880   2,125
      1870   2,175
      1860   2,129
      1850   2,041
      1840   1,890
      1830   1,528

SPRINGS, CDP
  East Hampton Town
    Suffolk County
      1980   3,197(a)
      1970   1,027(b)
      1960   729(c)
      1890-1950   NA
      1880   339

(a)Boundary change.
(b)Derived by LIRPB from U.S. Census
   Data; population of 2,106 is
   comparable to 1980 boundaries.
(c)Derived by LIRPB from U.S. Census
   Data.

SPRINGTOWN, CDP
  New Paltz Town
    Ulster County
      1880   35

SPRING VALLEY, Village (Inc. 1902)
  Clarkstown Town, part in
    Rockland County
      1980   1,970
      1970   1,772(a)
      1960   657(a)
  Ramapo Town, part in
    Rockland County
      1980   18,567
      1970   16,340(a)
      1960   5,881(a)
      1950   4,500
      1940   4,308
      1930   3,948(a)
      1920   3,818
      1910   2,353
      1900   NA
      1890   1,028
      1880   810
    TOTAL
      1980   20,537
      1970   18,112(a)
      1960   6,538(a)
      1880-1950   (b)
(a)Boundary change.
(b)Reported in RAMAPO Town only.

SPRINGVILLE, Village (Inc. 1834)
  Concord Town
    Erie County
      1980   4,285
      1970   4,350(a)
      1960   3,852
      1950   3,322
      1940   2,849(a)
      1930   2,540
      1920   2,331
      1910   2,246
      1900   1,992
      1890   1,883
      1880   1,227
      1870   1,006
(a)Boundary change.

SPRINGWATER, CDP
  Springwater Town
    Livingston County
      1880   339

SPRINGWATER, Town (Est. 1816)
  Livingston County
      1980   2,143
      1970   1,678
      1960   1,293
      1950   1,318
      1940   1,274
      1930   1,381

1920	1,416
1910	1,808
1900	2,016
1890	2,085
1880	2,279
1870	2,174
1860	2,399(a)
1850	2,670
1840	2,832
1830	2,253
1820	1,154(b)

(a)Reported as Spring Water.
(b)Reported in ONTARIO County.

SPROUT BROOK, CDP
  Canajoharie Town
    Montgomery County

1880	72

SPROUTVILLE, CDP
  East Fishkill Town
    Dutchess County

1980	2,303
1970	1,871

SQUIRETOWN(a)
  Southampton Town
    Suffolk County

1970	787(b)
1960	300(b)

(a)Included in HAMPTON BAYS, CDP in
  1980.
(b)Derived by LIRPB from U.S. Census
  Data.

STAFFORD, CDP
  Stafford Town
    Genesee County

1880	212

STAFFORD, Town
  Chenango County
  see SMYRNA, Town
    Chenango County

STAFFORD, Town (Est. 1820)
  Genesee County

1980	2,508
1970	2,461
1960	2,005
1950	1,355
1940	1,246
1930	1,231
1920	1,057
1910	1,288
1900	1,338
1890	1,625
1880	1,808
1870	1,847
1860	2,077
1850	1,974
1840	2,561
1830	2,368
1820	2,069

STAMFORD, Town (Est. 1792)
  Delaware County

1980	2,038 Rev.
1970	2,072

1960	2,103
1950	2,121
1940	1,993
1930	2,141
1920	2,104
1910	2,113
1900	1,997
1890	1,940
1880	1,638
1870	1,658
1860	1,661
1850	1,708
1840	1,681
1830	1,597
1820	1,495
1810	NA
1800	*924

STAMFORD, Town
  Dutchess County
  see STANFORD, Town
    Dutchess County

STAMFORD, Village (Inc. 1870)
  Harpersfield Town, part in
    Delaware County

1980	499
1970	521(a)
1960	428
1950	389
1940	358
1930	372
1920	291
1910	289
1900	248
1890	267

  Stamford Town, part in
    Delaware County

1980	741
1970	765(a)
1960	738
1950	773
1940	730
1930	731
1920	656
1910	684
1900	653
1890	552

  TOTAL

1980	1,240
1970	1,286(a)
1960	1,166
1950	1,162
1940	1,088
1930	1,103
1920	947
1910	973
1900	901
1890	819
1880	522

(a)Boundary change.

STANFORD, Town (Est. 1793)
  Dutchess County

1980	3,319
1970	2,479
1960	1,614
1950	1,473
1940	1,386

1930	1,269
1920	1,368
1910	1,520
1900	1,624
1890	1,859
1880	2,092
1870	2,116
1860	2,323(a)
1850	2,158
1840	2,278
1830	2,521
1820	2,518
1810	NA
1800	*2,344

(a)Reported as Stamford.

STANFORDVILLE, CDP
Stanford Town
Dutchess County

1880	340

STANLEY, CDP
Seneca Town
Ontario County

1940	659
1890-1930	NA
1880	242(a)

(a)Reported as Stanley Corners.

STANNARDS, CDP
Wellsville Town
Allegany County

1980	1,026

STANWIX, CDP
Rome Town
Oneida County

1880	96

STARK, Town (Est. 1828)
Herkimer County

1980	824
1970	739
1960	783
1950	793
1940	858
1930	844
1920	811
1910	897
1900	1,030
1890	1,248
1880	1,476
1870	1,541
1860	1,543
1850	1,576
1840	1,766
1830	1,781

STARKEY, Town (Est. 1824)
Yates County

1980	2,868
1970	2,783
1960	2,597
1950	2,345
1940	2,205
1930	2,237
1920	2,382
1910	2,538
1900	2,836

1890	2,862
1880	2,729
1870	2,370
1860	1,809
1850	2,675
1840	2,426
1830	2,285

STARKVILLE, CDP
Stark Town
Herkimer County

1870	174

STAR LAKE, CDP
Clifton & Fine Towns
St. Lawrence County

1980	1,239

STATEN ISLAND, Borough
see NEW YORK City, STATEN ISLAND
Borough

STEAMBURG, CDP
Cold Spring Town
Cattaraugus County

1880	242

STELLA, CDP
Dickinson Town
Broome County

1940	1,409

STEPHENTOWN, Town (Est. 1784)
Rensselaer County

1980	2,031
1970	1,731
1960	1,361
1950	1,295
1940	1,181
1930	1,093
1920	1,109
1910	1,289
1900	1,545
1890	1,764
1880	1,986
1870	2,133
1860	2,311
1850	2,622
1840	2,753
1830	2,716
1820	2,592
1810	NA
1800	*4,968(a)
1790	6,795(b)

(a)Reported as Stephen Town.
(b)Reported as Stephen-Town in ALBANY
County.

STEPHENTOWN, Town
Westchester County
see SOMERS, Town
Westchester County

STERLING, CDP
Sterling Town
Cayuga County

1870	237

STERLING, Town (Est. 1812)
  Cayuga County

1980	3,301
1970	2,589
1960	2,495
1950	2,050
1940	1,943
1930	1,966
1920	2,039
1910	2,359
1900	2,516
1890	2,959
1880	3,034
1870	2,840
1860	3,008
1850	2,808
1840	2,533
1830	1,436
1820	792

STERLINGBUSH, CDP
  Diana Town
    Lewis County

1880	108

STERLING CENTER, CDP
  Sterling Town
    Cayuga County

1880	167

STERLING VALLEY, CDP
  Sterling Town
    Cayuga County

1880	111
1870	172

STEUBEN, County (Est. 1796)

1980	99,217 Rev.
1970	99,546
1960	97,691
1950	91,439
1940	84,927
1930	82,671
1920	80,627
1910	83,362
1900	82,822
1890	81,473
1880	77,586
1870	67,717
1860	66,690(a)
1850	63,771
1840	46,138
1830	33,851
1820	21,989
1810	7,246
1800	1,788

(a)Boundary change.

STEUBEN, Town (Est. 1792)
  Oneida County

1980	897
1970	735
1960	586
1950	540
1940	581
1930	690
1920	786
1910	785
1900	902

1890	1,005
1880	1,223
1870	1,261
1860	1,541
1850	1,744
1840	1,993
1830	2,094
1820	1,461
1810	NA
1800	*552

STEVENSBURGH, CDP
  Allegany Town
    Cattaraugus County

1880	91

STEWART, CDP
  Newburgh & New Windsor Towns
    Orange County

1980	2,797
1970	1,230

STEWART MANOR, Village (Inc. 1927)
  Hempstead Town
    Nassau County

1980	2,373
1970	2,183
1960	2,422(a)
1950	1,879
1940	1,625
1930	1,291

(a)Boundary change.

STILLVILLE, CDP
  Trenton Town
    Oneida County

1880	184

STILLWATER, Town (Est. 1788)
  Saratoga County

1980	6,316
1970	5,023
1960	4,416
1950	4,055
1940	3,709
1930	3,942
1920	3,882(a)
1910	5,955
1900	4,989
1890	3,868
1880	3,412
1870	3,401
1860	3,238
1850	2,967
1840	2,733
1830	2,601
1820	2,821
1810	NA
1800	*2,872
1790	3,071(b)

(a)Boundary change.
(b)Reported as Still-Water in ALBANY
   County.

STILLWATER, Village (Inc. 1816)
  Stillwater Town
    Saratoga County

1980	1,572
1970	1,428

1960	1,398
1950	1,276(a)
1940	971
1930	1,051
1920	982
1910	1,004
1900	1,007
1890	747
1880	877
1870	737

(a)Boundary change.

STITTVILLE, CDP
  Marcy & Trenton Towns
    Oneida County

1870	243(a)

(a)Part in MARCY Town, 28; part in
  TRENTON Town, 215.

STOCKBRIDGE, CDP
  Stockbridge Town
    Madison County

1880	217

STOCKBRIDGE, Town (Est. 1836)
  Madison County

1980	1,947
1970	1,711
1960	1,574
1950	1,537
1940	1,258
1930	1,369
1920	1,413
1910	1,485
1900	1,622
1890	1,845
1880	2,023
1870	1,847
1860	2,068
1850	2,081
1840	2,320

STOCKHOLM, Town (Est. 1806)(a)
  St. Lawrence County

1980	3,676
1970	3,597(b)
1960	3,465
1950	2,558
1940	2,406
1930	2,253
1920	2,437
1910	2,614
1900	2,826
1890	2,999
1880	3,441
1870	3,819
1860	4,074
1850	3,661
1840	2,995
1830	1,944
1820	822

(a)In 1800 the Census Bureau reported a
  Stockholm Town in ONEIDA County,
  population 8.
(b)Erroneously includes part of NORWOOD
  Village.

STOCKHOLM CENTRE, CDP
  Stockholm Town
    St. Lawrence County

1880	50

STOCKHOLM DEPOT, CDP
  Stockholm Town
    St. Lawrence County

1880	146

STOCKPORT, CDP
  Stockport Town
    Columbia County

1880	302

STOCKPORT, Town (Est. 1833)
  Columbia County

1980	2,847
1970	2,324
1960	2,025
1950	2,054
1940	2,229
1930	2,422
1920	1,909
1910	2,506
1900	2,719
1890	2,345
1880	1,980
1870	1,438
1860	1,445
1850	1,655
1840	1,815

STOCKTON, Town (Est. 1821)
  Chautauqua County

1980	2,331
1970	2,213
1960	2,156
1950	1,889
1940	1,651
1930	1,574
1920	1,674
1910	1,781
1900	1,852
1890	1,730
1880	1,868
1870	1,639
1860	1,887
1850	1,640
1840	2,078
1830	1,605

STONE CHURCH, CDP
  Bergen Town
    Genesee County

1880	66

STONINGTON, Town
  see PHARSALIA, Town
    Chenango County

STONY BROOK, CDP
  Brookhaven Town
    Suffolk County

1980	16,155(a)
1970	6,391(b)
1960	3,548
1950	NA
1940	768

1900-1930	NA
1890	506
1880	549

(a)Boundary change.
(b)Population of 16,881 is comparable
to 1980 boundaries.

STONY CREEK, Town (Est. 1852)
Warren County

1980	528
1970	560
1960	459
1950	479
1940	457
1930	464
1920	651
1910	858
1900	1,019
1890	1,342
1880	1,253
1870	1,127
1860	960

STONY POINT, CDP
Stony Point Town
Rockland County

1980	8,686
1970	8,270
1960	3,330
1950	1,438
1940	2,001
1900-1930	NA
1890	514

STONY POINT, Town (Est. 1865)
Rockland County

1980	12,838
1970	12,704
1960	8,739
1950	5,485
1940	4,898
1930	3,458
1920	3,211
1910	3,651
1900	4,161
1890	4,614
1880	3,308
1870	3,205

STOTTVILLE, CDP
Greenport & Stockport Towns
Columbia County

1980	1,387
1970	1,106
1960	1,040
1950	1,020
1940	1,075
1890-1930	NA
1880	720(a)

(a)Reported in STOCKPORT Town only.

STRATFORD, CDP
Stratford Town
Fulton County

1880	114

STRATFORD, Town (Est. 1805)
Fulton County

1980	625

1970	495
1960	421
1950	464
1940	401
1930	384
1920	453
1910	607
1900	830
1890	997
1880	1,066
1870	1,163
1860	1,172
1850	801
1840	500
1830	551
1820	407(a)

(a)Reported in MONTGOMERY County.

STUYVESANT, CDP
Stuyvesant Town
Columbia County

1940	660
1890-1930	NA
1880	925

STUYVESANT, Town (Est. 1823)
Columbia County

1980	2,216
1970	1,665
1960	1,496
1950	1,394
1940	1,433
1930	1,440
1920	1,541
1910	1,980
1900	2,125
1890	1,953
1880	2,097
1870	2,263
1860	2,366
1850	1,766
1840	1,779
1830	2,331

STUYVESANT FALLS, CDP
Stuyvesant Town
Columbia County

1940	611

SUCCESS, Village
see LAKE SUCCESS, Village
Nassau County

SUFFERN, Village (Inc. 1896)
Ramapo Town
Rockland County

1980	10,794
1970	8,273(a)
1960	5,094(a)
1950	4,010
1940	3,768
1930	3,757
1920	3,154
1910	2,663
1900	1,619

(a)Boundary change.

SUFFOLK, County (Est. 1683)(a)

1980	1,284,231
1970	1,127,030 Rev.
1960	666,784
1950	276,129
1940	197,355
1930	161,055
1920	110,246
1910	96,138
1900	77,582
1890	62,491
1880	53,888
1870	46,924
1860	43,275
1850	36,922
1840	32,469
1830	26,780
1820	23,930 Rev.
1810	21,113
1800	19,735 Rev.
1790	16,440

SUFFOLK AIRFORCE BASE(a)
    Southampton Town
        Suffolk County

1970	345(b)
1960	1,458(b)

(a)Included in WESTHAMPTON, CDP in
   1980.
(b)Derived by LIRPB from U.S. Census
   Data.

SUFFOLK DEVELOPMENTAL CENTER
    Huntington Town
        Suffolk County

1980	2,241(a)
1970	2,085(b)

(a)Boundary change; derived by LIRPB
   from U.S. Census Data.
(b)Derived by LIRPB from U.S. Census
   Data; population is comparable to
   1980 boundaries.

SUFFRAGE, Town
    see MILFORD, Town
            Otsego County

SULLIVAN, County (Est. 1809)

1980	65,155
1970	52,580
1960	45,272
1950	40,731
1940	37,901
1930	35,272
1920	33,163
1910	33,808
1900	32,306
1890	31,031
1880	32,491
1870	34,550
1860	32,385
1850	25,088
1840	15,629
1830	12,364
1820	8,900
1810	6,108

SULLIVAN, Town (Est. 1803)
    Madison County

1980	13,371
1970	11,969
1960	9,369
1950	4,905
1940	3,775
1930	3,383
1920	3,002
1910	3,367
1900	3,778
1890	4,046
1880	4,803
1870	4,921
1860	5,233
1850	4,764
1840	4,390
1830	4,077
1820	2,932

SULLIVANVILLE, CDP
    Veteran Town
        Chemung County

1870	157

SUMMERFIELD, CDP
    Northfield Town
        Richmond County

1880	179

SUMMERHILL, Town (Est. 1831)(a)
    Cayuga County

1980	850
1970	670
1960	667
1950	542
1940	505
1930	448
1920	539
1910	613
1900	779
1890	864(b)
1880	1,028(b)
1870	1,036(b)
1860	1,194
1850	1,251
1840	1,446

(a)Established as Plato in 1831; name
   changed in 1832.
(b)Reported as Summer Hill.

SUMMIT, CDP
    Summit Town
        Schoharie County

1880	121

SUMMIT, Town (Est. 1819)
    Schoharie County

1980	903
1970	690
1960	704
1950	850
1940	790
1930	705
1920	871
1910	1,105
1900	1,217
1890	1,399
1880	1,405

1870	1,631
1860	1,924
1850	1,800
1840	2,010
1830	1,733
1820	1,468

SUMMITVILLE, CDP
    Mamakating Town
        Sullivan County

1880	223

S.U.N.Y. AT STONY BROOK
    Brookhaven Town
        Suffolk County

1980	6,238(a)
1970	4,839(b)

(a)Boundary change; derived by LIRPB
    from U.S. Census Data.
(b)Derived by LIRPB from U.S. Census
    Data; population is comparable to
    1980 boundaries.

SURREY MEADOWS, CDP
    Chester Town
        Orange County

1980	1,203

SUSPENSION BRIDGE, Village (Inc.1854)(a)
    Niagara Town
        Niagara County

1890	4,405
1880	2,476
1870	2,276

(a)Incorporated as Niagara City, Village
    in 1854; name changed in 1874.
    NIAGARA FALLS and SUSPENSION BRIDGE
    Villages consolidated and incorporated
    as NIAGARA FALLS City and made inde-
    pendent of NIAGARA Town in 1892.

SWAIN, CDP
    Grove Town
        Allegany County

1880	183(a)

(a)Reported as Swainville.

SWEDEN, Town (Est. 1813)
    Monroe County

1980	14,859
1970	11,461
1960	7,224
1950	5,982
1940	4,698
1930	4,613
1920	3,984
1910	4,885
1900	4,743
1890	5,201
1880	5,734
1870	4,558
1860	4,045
1850	3,623
1840	1,884
1830	2,146
1820	2,761(a)

(a)Reported in GENESEE County.

SYLVAN BEACH, Village (Inc. 1971)(a)
    Vienna Town
        Oneida County

1980	1,243
1970	799
1930-1960	NA
1920	105
1910	169

(a)First incorporated in 1896; Village
    dissolved in 1911 and re-incorporated
    in 1971.

SYOSSET, CDP
    Oyster Bay Town
        Nassau County

1980	9,818
1970	10,084
1960	8,560(a)
1950	1,133
1940	1,336

(a)Derived by LIRPB from U.S. Census
    Data.

SYRACUSE, City (Inc. 1847)(a)
    Onondaga County

1980	170,105(b)
1970	197,297 Rev.(b)
1960	216,038(b)
1950	220,583
1940	205,967(b)
1930	209,326(b)
1920	171,717(b)
1910	137,249
1900	108,374(b)
1890	88,143(b)
1880	51,792
1870	43,051
1860	28,119
1850	22,271

(a)Salina (Inc. 1824) and Syracuse
    (Inc. 1825) Villages consolidated
    and incorporated as SYRACUSE City
    and made independent of SALINA
    Town in 1847.
(b)Boundary change.

SYRACUSE, Village
    see SYRACUSE, City
        Onondaga County

T

TABERG, CDP
    Annsville Town
        Oneida County

1890	331
1880	558
1870	400

TAGHKANIC, Town (Est. 1803)
    Columbia County
        1980   1,101
        1970   804
        1960   727
        1950   575
        1940   604
        1930   683
        1920   666
        1910   771
        1900   894
        1890   1,062
        1880   1,308
        1870   1,485
        1860   1,717
        1850   1,539
        1840   1,674
        1830   1,654
        1820   3,600(b)
(a)Established as Granger in 1803; name
   changed in 1814.
(b)Reported as Taughkanick.

TAGHKANICK, CDP
    Taghkanic Town
        Columbia County
            1880   72

TALLCOTTVILLE, CDP
    Leyden Town
        Lewis County
            1880   129

TALLMAN, CDP
    Ramapo Town
        Rockland County
            1940   519

TANNERSVILLE, Village (Inc. 1895)
    Hunter Town
        Greene County
            1980   685(a)
            1970   650
            1960   580
            1950   639
            1940   640
            1930   656
            1920   597
            1910   660
            1900   593
(a)Boundary change.

TAPPAN, CDP
    Orangetown Town
        Rockland County
            1980   8,267
            1970   7,424
            1950-1960   NA
            1940   1,249

TARRYTOWN, Village (Inc. 1870)
    Greenburgh Town
        Westchester County
            1980   10,648
            1970   11,115
            1960   11,109
            1950   8,851(a)
            1940   6,874
            1930   6,841

        1920   5,807
        1910   5,600
        1900   4,770
        1890   3,562
        1880   3,025
(a)Boundary change.

TAUGHKANICK, Town
    see TAGHKANIC, Town
        Columbia County

TAYLOR, Town (Est. 1849)
    Cortland County
        1980   481
        1970   493
        1960   474
        1950   496
        1940   531
        1930   504
        1920   647
        1910   711
        1900   762
        1890   815
        1880   993
        1870   1,016
        1860   1,265
        1850   1,232

TERRYVILLE(a)
    Brookhaven Town
        Suffolk County
            1970   5,474(b)
            1960   2,069(b)
(a)Included in PORT JEFFERSON STATION,
   CDP in 1980.
(b)Derived by LIRPB from U.S. Census
   Data.

TEXAS, CDP
    Mexico Town
        Oswego County
            1870   150

THE BRANCH, Village
    see VILLAGE OF THE BRANCH, Village
        Suffolk County

THE HOOK, CDP
    Argyle Town
        Washington County
            1880   41

THE LANDING, Village
    see VILLAGE OF THE LANDING, Village
        Suffolk County

THERESA, Town (Est. 1841)
    Jefferson County
        1980   1,853
        1970   1,754
        1960   1,635
        1950   1,660
        1940   1,675
        1930   1,715
        1920   1,762
        1910   2,036
        1900   2,130
        1890   2,391
        1880   2,389

THREE MILE HARBOR(a)
  East Hampton Town
    Suffolk County
      1970   884(b)
      1960   382(b)
(a)Included in SPRINGS, CDP in 1980.
(b)Derived by LIRPB from U.S. Census
  Data.

THREE RIVER POINT, CDP
  Clay Town
    Onondaga County
      1870   43

THROOP, Town (Est. 1859)
  Cayuga County
      1980   1,797
      1970   1,757
      1960   1,559
      1950   1,251
      1940   1,083
      1930   990
      1920   958
      1910   960
      1900   1,038
      1890   1,056
      1880   1,188
      1870   1,302
      1860   1,348

THROOPVILLE, CDP
  Throop Town
    Cayuga County
      1880   110
      1870   126(a)
(a)Reported as Throopsville.

THURMAN, Town (Est. 1852)
  Warren County
      1980   852
      1970   708
      1960   548
      1950   529
      1940   535
      1930   521
      1920   680
      1910   805
      1900   809
      1890   1,106
      1880   1,174
      1870   1,084
      1860   1,084

THURMAN, Town (Est. 1792)(a)
  Washington County
      1800   *1,332
(a)Divided into ATHOL and WARRENSBURG
  Towns in 1813.

THURSTON, Town (Est. 1844)
  Steuben County
      1980   986
      1970   810
      1960   619
      1950   719
      1940   607
      1930   646
      1920   674
      1910   840

      1870   2,364
      1860   2,628
      1850   2,342

THERESA, Village (Inc. 1871)
  Theresa Town
    Jefferson County
      1980   827
      1970   985
      1960   956
      1950   925
      1940   908
      1930   873
      1920   857
      1910   932
      1900   917
      1890   1,028
      1880   882
      1870   798

THIELLS, CDP
  Haverstraw Town
    Rockland County
      1940   631

THOMASTON, Village (Inc. 1931)
  North Hempstead Town
    Nassau County
      1980   2,684
      1970   2,811 Rev.
      1960   2,767(a)
      1950   2,045
      1940   1,159
(a)Boundary change.

THOMPSON, Town (Est. 1803)
  Sullivan County
      1980   13,550
      1970   11,418
      1960   8,792
      1950   6,912
      1940   6,054
      1930   5,950
      1920   4,597
      1910   4,196
      1900   3,739
      1890   3,462
      1880   3,763
      1870   3,514
      1860   3,834
      1850   3,198
      1840   2,610
      1830   2,457
      1820   1,897

THORNWOOD, CDP
  Mount Pleasant Town
    Westchester County
      1980   7,197
      1970   6,874
      1950-1960   NA
      1940   1,347

THREE MILE BAY, CDP
  Lyme Town
    Jefferson County
      1880   1,041(a)
      1870   417(a)
(a)Reported as Three-Mile Bay.

1900	1,017
1890	1,113
1880	1,366
1870	1,215
1860	1,100
1850	726

TIANA
see RAMPASTURE--TIANA
Suffolk County

TICONDEROGA, Town (Est. 1804)
Essex County

1980	5,436
1970	5,839
1960	5,617
1950	5,204
1940	4,859
1930	5,105
1920	5,267
1910	4,940
1900	5,048
1890	3,980
1880	3,304
1870	2,590
1860	2,271
1850	2,669
1840	2,169
1830	1,996
1820	1,493

TICONDEROGA, Village (Inc. 1889)(a)
Ticonderoga Town
Essex County

1980	2,938(b)
1970	3,268(b)
1960	3,568
1950	3,517
1940	3,402
1930	3,680(b)
1920	2,102
1910	2,475
1900	1,911
1890	2,267
1880	1,795(c)

(a)Ticonderoga Lower Falls and Ticonderoga Upper Falls, CDPs consolidated and incorporated as TICONDEROGA Village in 1889.
(b)Boundary change.
(c)Part in Ticonderoga Lower Falls, 1,198; part in Ticonderoga Upper Falls, 597.

TILLSON, CDP
Rosendale Town
Ulster County

1980	1,529
1970	1,256

TIOGA, County (Est. 1791)

1980	49,812
1970	46,513
1960	37,802
1950	30,166
1940	27,072
1930	25,480
1920	24,212
1910	25,624
1900	27,951
1890	29,935
1880	32,673
1870	30,572
1860	28,748
1850	24,880
1840	20,527
1830	27,690
1820	16,971
1810	7,899
1800	7,109 Rev.

TIOGA, Town (Est. 1800)
Tioga County

1980	4,432
1970	3,621
1960	2,814
1950	2,000
1940	1,782
1930	1,587
1920	1,677
1910	1,940
1900	2,113
1890	2,455
1880	3,192
1870	3,272
1860	3,202
1850	2,839
1840	2,464
1830	1,411
1820	1,816
1810	NA
1800	*751

TIOGA CENTER, CDP
Tioga Town
Tioga County

1870	304(a)

(a)Reported as Tioga Centre.

TITUSVILLE, CDP
La Grange Town
Dutchess County

1880	79

TIVOLI, Village (Inc. 1872)
Red Hook Town
Dutchess County

1980	711
1970	739
1960	732
1950	753
1940	761
1930	713
1920	876
1910	1,034
1900	1,153
1890	1,350
1880	1,254
1870	452

TOMKINS COVE, CDP
Stony Point Town
Rockland County

1940	684

TOMPKINS, County (Est. 1817)

1980	87,085
1970	77,064 Rev.

1960	66,164
1950	59,122
1940	42,340
1930	41,490
1920	35,285
1910	33,647
1900	33,830
1890	32,923
1880	34,445
1870	33,178
1860	31,409(a)
1850	38,746
1840	37,948
1830	36,545
1820	20,681

(a)Boundary change.

TOMPKINS, Town (Est. 1806)(a)
    Delaware County

1980	968
1970	905
1960	1,463
1950	1,680
1940	1,642
1930	1,665
1920	1,737
1910	2,127
1900	2,482
1890	2,626
1880	2,534
1870	4,046
1860	3,589
1850	3,022
1840	2,035
1830	1,774
1820	1,206

(a)Established as Pinefield in 1806;
name changed in 1808.

TONAWANDA, CDP
  Tonawanda Town
    Erie County

1980	72,795
1970	NA
1960	83,771

TONAWANDA, City (Inc. 1903)(a)
    Erie County

1980	18,693
1970	21,898
1960	21,561
1950	14,617
1940	13,008
1930	12,681
1920	10,068
1910	8,290

(a)TONAWANDA Village incorporated as
TONAWANDA City and made independent
of TONAWANDA Town in 1903.

TONAWANDA, Town (Est. 1836)
    Erie County

1980	91,269
1970	107,282
1960	105,032
1950	55,270
1940	32,155
1930	25,006
1920	5,505

1910	2,175(a)
1900	8,626
1890	7,666
1880	4,909
1870	3,039
1860	2,489
1850	2,072(b)
1840	1,261(c)

(a)Boundary change.
(b)Reported as Tonewanda.
(c)Reported as Tonnewanta.

TONAWANDA, Village (Inc. 1853)(a)
  Tonawanda Town
    Erie County

1900	7,421
1890	7,145
1880	3,864
1870	2,812(b)

(a)TONAWANDA Village incorporated as
TONAWANDA City and made independent
of TONAWANDA Town in 1903.
(b)Part in TONAWANDA Town, ERIE County,
2,125; part in WHEATFIELD Town,
NIAGARA County, 687.

TONAWANDA INDIAN RESERVATION
  Erie County, part in

1980	12
1970	16
1960	30
1950	58
1940	43
1930	56
1920	55
1910	63
1900	142

  Genesee County, part in

1980	455
1970	488
1960	426
1950	410
1940	496
1930	387
1920	345
1910	434
1900	346

  Niagara County, part in

1930-1980	0

  TOTAL

1980	467
1970	504
1960	456
1950	468
1940	539
1930	443
1920	400
1910	497
1900	488

TONEWANDA, Town
  see TONAWANDA, Town
      Erie County

TONNEWANTA, Town
  see TONAWANDA, Town
      Erie County

TORREY, Town (Est. 1851)
    Yates County
        1980   1,363
        1970   1,186
        1960   1,007
        1950   948
        1940   765
        1930   804
        1920   916
        1910   1,018
        1900   1,065
        1890   1,197
        1880   1,245
        1870   1,281
        1860   1,364

TOTTENVILLE, Village (Inc. 1869)(a)
    Westfield Town
        Richmond County
        1880   1,147
        1870   1,571
(a)Merged into STATEN ISLAND Borough in
    NEW YORK City in 1898.

TOWNER HILL, CDP
    Crown Point Town
        Essex County
        1880   70

TOWNERS, CDP
    Patterson Town
        Putnam County
        1880   113

TOWN LINE, CDP
    Alden & Lancaster Towns
        Erie County
        1980   2,917
        1970   2,434

TRAVISVILLE, CDP
    Northfield Town
        Richmond County
        1880   304

TREMONT, CDP
    West Farms Town
        Westchester County
        1870   2,025

TRENTON, Town (Est. 1797)
    Oneida County
        1980   4,449
        1970   4,429
        1960   3,417
        1950   2,522
        1940   2,295
        1930   2,262
        1920   2,389
        1910   2,402
        1900   2,628
        1890   2,709
        1880   3,097
        1870   3,156
        1860   3,504
        1850   3,540
        1840   3,178
        1830   3,221
        1820   2,617

        1810   NA
        1800   *624

TRENTON, Village
    see BARNEVELD, Village
        Oneida County

TRENTON FALLS, CDP
    Trenton Town
        Oneida County
        1880   138
        1870   128

TRIANGLE, CDP
    Triangle Town
        Broome County
        1880   167
        1870   273

TRIANGLE, Town (Est. 1831)
    Broome County
        1980   2,618
        1970   2,285
        1960   2,019
        1950   1,733
        1940   1,575
        1930   1,452
        1920   1,458
        1910   1,600
        1900   1,727
        1890   1,879
        1880   2,073
        1870   1,944
        1860   1,693
        1850   1,728
        1840   1,692

TRIBES HILL, CDP
    Amsterdam & Mohawk Towns
        Montgomery County
        1980   1,202
        1970   1,184
        1950-1960   NA
        1940   647
        1880-1930   NA
        1870   365(a)
(a)Part in AMSTERDAM Town, 150; part in
    MOHAWK Town, 215.

TROUPSBURG, CDP
    Troupsburg Town
        Steuben County
        1880   196(a)
        1870   100(b)
(a)Reported as Troupsburgh.
(b)Reported as Troupsburgh Centre.

TROUPSBURG, Town (Est. 1808)
    Steuben County
        1980   1,005
        1970   1,004
        1960   1,074
        1950   1,092
        1940   1,131
        1930   1,124
        1920   1,406
        1910   1,712
        1900   2,015
        1890   2,174

1880	2,494(a)
1870	2,281(a)
1860	2,096
1850	1,754(a)
1840	1,171
1830	666(a)
1820	650(a)

(a)Reported as Troupsburgh.

TROUT CREEK, CDP
  Tompkins Town
    Delaware County

1880	90

TROY, City (Inc. 1816)(a)
    Rensselaer County

1980	56,638
1970	62,918
1960	67,492
1950	72,311
1940	70,304
1930	72,763
1920	71,996 Rev.
1910	76,813(b)
1900	60,651
1890	60,956
1880	56,747
1870	46,465
1860	39,235
1850	28,785
1840	19,334
1830	11,556
1820	5,264

(a)TROY Town incorporated as Troy Village
   in 1801, and as TROY City in 1816.
(b)Boundary change.

TROY, Town (Est. 1790)(a)
    Rensselaer County

1800	*4,926
1790	8,318(b)

(a)Established as Rensselaerwick in
   ALBANY County in 1790; name changed
   to Troy in 1791. TROY Town incorporated as TROY Village in 1801, and
   as TROY City in 1816.
(b)Reported in ALBANY County.

TROY, Village
  see TROY, City
    Rensselaer County

TRUMANSBURG, Village (Inc. 1872)
  Ulysses Town
    Tompkins County

1980	1,722(a)
1970	1,803 Rev.
1960	1,768
1950	1,479
1940	1,130
1930	1,077
1920	1,011
1910	1,188
1900	1,225
1890	1,211
1880	1,376
1870	1,246

(a)Boundary change.

TRUMBULL'S CORNERS, CDP
  Newfield Town
    Tompkins County

1880	84

TRUXTON, CDP
  Truxton Town
    Cortland County

1880	276
1870	314

TRUXTON, Town (Est. 1808)
    Cortland County

1980	988
1970	955
1960	907
1950	922
1940	1,008
1930	997
1920	920
1910	1,132
1900	1,217
1890	1,328
1880	1,550
1870	1,618
1860	1,914
1850	3,623
1840	3,658
1830	3,885
1820	2,956

TRYON, County
  see MONTGOMERY, County

TUCKAHOE
  Southampton Town
    Suffolk County

1980	953(a)
1970	1,010(b)
1960	853(c)

(a)Boundary change; derived by LIRPB
   from U.S. Census Data.
(b)Derived by LIRPB from U.S. Census
   Data; population of 938 is comparable
   to 1980 boundaries.
(c)Derived by LIRPB from U.S. Census
   Data.

TUCKAHOE, Village (Inc. 1903)
  Eastchester Town
    Westchester County

1980	6,076
1970	6,236
1960	6,423
1950	5,991
1940	6,563
1930	6,138
1920	3,509
1910	2,722

TULLY, Town (Est. 1803)
    Onondaga County

1980	2,409
1970	1,901
1960	1,633
1950	1,554
1940	1,430
1930	1,461
1920	1,358

1910	1,386
1900	1,465
1890	1,380
1880	1,476
1870	1,569
1860	1,690
1850	1,559
1840	1,663
1830	1,640
1820	1,194

TULLY, Village (Inc. 1876)
  Tully Town
    Onondaga County

1980	1,049
1970	899
1960	803
1950	744
1940	719
1930	680
1920	477
1910	551
1900	574
1890	498
1880	434

TUPPER LAKE, Village (Inc. 1902)
  Altamont Town
    Franklin County

1980	4,478(a)
1970	4,854
1960	5,200
1950	5,441
1940	5,451
1930	5,271(a)
1920	2,508
1910	3,067

(a)Boundary change.

TURIN, Town (Est. 1800)
  Lewis County

1980	824
1970	805
1960	878
1950	856
1940	859
1930	897
1920	1,016
1910	1,030
1900	1,157
1890	1,277
1880	1,386
1870	1,493
1860	1,849
1850	1,826
1840	1,704
1830	1,661
1820	1,812
1810	NA
1800	*440(a)

(a)Reported in ONEIDA County.

TURIN, Village (Inc. 1873)
  Turin Town
    Lewis County

1980	284
1970	293
1960	323
1950	273

1940	247
1930	260
1920	327
1910	349
1900	363
1890	359
1880	419
1870	552

TUSCARORA, CDP
  Mount Morris Town
    Livingston County

1880	124

TUSCARORA, Town (Est. 1859)
  Steuben County

1980	1,338
1970	1,071
1960	1,043
1950	989
1940	859
1930	839
1920	854
1910	1,006
1900	1,301
1890	1,438
1880	1,544
1870	1,528
1860	1,566

TUSCARORA INDIAN RESERVATION
  Niagara County

1980	921 Rev.
1970	1,134
1960	1,934
1950	634
1940	462
1930	402
1920	319
1910	417
1900	337

TUSTEN, Town (Est. 1853)
  Sullivan County

1980	1,424
1970	1,224
1960	1,087
1950	1,042
1940	950
1930	914
1920	881
1910	878
1900	890
1890	1,004
1880	1,050
1870	1,028
1860	871

TUTHILL, CDP
  Gardiner Town
    Ulster County

1880	83

TUXEDO, Town (Est. 1889)
  Orange County

1980	3,069
1970	2,967
1960	2,227
1950	2,281

1940	2,314
1930	2,606
1920	2,355
1910	2,858
1900	2,277
1890	1,678

TUXEDO PARK, Village (Inc. 1952)
Tuxedo Town
Orange County

1980	809(a)
1970	861
1960	723
1950	NA
1940	1,651

(a)Boundary change.

TWIN ORCHARDS, CDP
see VESTAL--TWIN ORCHARDS, CDP
Broome County

TYRE, CDP
Tyre Town
Seneca County

1880	77

TYRE, Town (Est. 1829)
Seneca County

1980	887
1970	837
1960	815
1950	729
1940	724
1930	743
1920	798
1910	900
1900	954
1890	991
1880	1,168
1870	1,280
1860	1,437
1850	1,356
1840	1,506
1830	1,482

TYRONE, CDP
Tyrone Town
Schuyler County

1880	227

TYRONE, Town (Est. 1822)
Schuyler County

1980	1,479
1970	1,254
1960	1,137
1950	1,076
1940	1,024
1930	1,050
1920	1,100
1910	1,285
1900	1,586
1890	1,680
1880	2,059
1870	1,993
1860	2,096
1850	1,894(a)
1840	2,122(a)
1830	1,880(a)

(a)Reported in STEUBEN County.

U

ULSTER, County (Est. 1683)

1980	158,158
1970	141,241
1960	118,804
1950	92,621
1940	87,017
1930	80,155
1920	74,979
1910	91,769
1900	88,422
1890	87,062
1880	85,838
1870	84,075
1860	76,381
1850	59,384
1840	45,822
1830	36,550
1820	30,934
1810	26,576
1800	24,855
1790	29,397

ULSTER, Town (Est. 1879)
Ulster County

1980	12,319 Rev.
1970	11,711
1960	8,448
1950	4,411
1940	3,993
1930	3,597
1920	2,622
1910	3,554
1900	3,582
1890	3,222
1880	2,806

ULYSSES, Town (Est. 1799)
Tompkins County

1980	4,666
1970	4,500 Rev.
1960	4,307
1950	3,474
1940	2,584
1930	2,382
1920	2,105
1910	2,612
1900	2,776
1890	2,954
1880	3,458
1870	3,271
1860	3,329
1850	3,122
1840	2,976
1830	1,130
1820	6,345
1810	NA
1800	*927(a)

(a)Reported in CAYUGA County.

UNADILLA, Town (Est. 1792)
Otsego County

1980	4,020
1970	3,863

1960	3,649
1950	2,689
1940	2,277
1930	2,276
1920	2,395
1910	2,376
1900	2,601
1890	2,723
1880	2,523
1870	2,555
1860	2,702
1850	2,463
1840	2,272
1830	2,313
1820	2,194
1810	NA
1800	*828

UNADILLA, Village (Inc. 1827)
  Unadilla Town
    Otsego County

1980	1,367
1970	1,489
1960	1,586
1950	1,317
1940	1,079
1930	1,063
1920	1,157
1910	1,009
1900	1,172
1890	1,157
1880	922
1870	875

UNADILLA FORKS, CDP
  Plainfield Town
    Otsego County

1880	210

UNION, Town (Est. 1791)
  Broome County

1980	61,179
1970	64,490(a)
1960	64,423
1950	55,676
1940	50,195
1930	42,579
1920	25,651
1910	9,486
1900	5,707
1890	2,711
1880	2,596
1870	2,538
1860	2,092
1850	2,143
1840	3,165
1830	2,121
1820	2,037
1810	NA
1800	*921(b)

(a)Boundary change.
(b)Reported in TIOGA County.

UNION, Town
  Herkimer County
  see RUSSIA, Town
    Herkimer County

UNION, Town
  Monroe County
  see HAMLIN, Town
    Monroe County

UNION, Village (Inc. 1871)(a)
  Union Town
    Broome County

1920	3,303
1910	1,544
1900	982
1890	821
1880	737

(a)Merged into ENDICOTT Village in 1921.

UNION CENTER, CDP
  Union Town
    Broome County

1880	116

UNION CORNERS, CDP
  Mansfield Town
    Cattaraugus County

1880	50

UNIONDALE, CDP
  Hempstead Town
    Nassau County

1980	20,016
1970	22,077
1960	20,041
1950	NA
1940	1,104

UNION FALLS, CDP
  Black Brook Town
    Clinton County

1880	53

UNION GROVE, CDP
  Andes Town
    Delaware County

1880	153

UNION MILLS, CDP
  Broadalbin Town
    Fulton County

1880	74

UNION SPRINGS, Village (Inc. 1837)
  Springport Town
    Cayuga County

1980	1,201
1970	1,183
1960	1,066
1950	957
1940	905
1930	794
1920	642
1910	798
1900	994
1890	1,066
1880	1,210
1870	1,150

UNION VALE, Town (Est. 1827)
  Dutchess County

1980	2,658
1970	1,702

1960	1,138
1950	970
1940	1,056
1930	1,025
1920	987
1910	1,097
1900	945
1890	1,033
1880	1,407
1870	1,434
1860	1,502
1850	1,552
1840	1,498
1830	1,833

UNIONVILLE, Village (Inc. 1871)
  Minisink Town
    Orange County

1980	574
1970	576(a)
1960	511
1950	454
1940	387
1930	438
1920	402
1910	351
1900	454
1890	316
1880	316

(a)Boundary change.

UPPER BROOKVILLE, Village (Inc. 1932)
  Oyster Bay Town
    Nassau County

1980	1,245
1970	1,182
1960	1,045
1950	469
1940	456

UPPER JAY, CDP
  Jay Town
    Essex County

1880	146

UPPER LISLE, CDP
  Triangle Town
    Broome County

1880	150
1870	247

UPPER NYACK, Village (Inc. 1872)
  Clarkstown Town
    Rockland County

1980	1,906
1970	2,096
1960	1,833(a)
1950	1,195
1940	924
1930	842
1920	538
1910	591
1900	516
1890	668
1880	412

(a)Boundary change.

UPPER RED HOOK, CDP
  Red Hook Town
    Dutchess County

1880	184
1870	206

UPPER ST. JOHNSVILLE, CDP
  St. Johnsville Town
    Montgomery County

1880	149

URBANA, Town (Est. 1822)
  Steuben County

1980	2,982
1970	2,694
1960	2,592
1950	2,450
1940	2,322
1930	2,108
1920	2,300
1910	2,659
1900	2,692
1890	2,590
1880	2,318
1870	2,082
1860	1,983
1850	2,079
1840	1,884
1830	1,288

UTICA, City (Inc. 1832)(a)
  Oneida County

1980	75,632
1970	91,373 Rev.(b)
1960	100,410(b)
1950	101,531
1940	100,518
1930	101,740
1920	94,156(b)
1910	74,419
1900	56,383
1890	44,007
1880	33,914
1870	28,804
1860	22,529
1850	17,565
1840	12,782

(a)UTICA Town and Utica Village
  (Inc. 1798) consolidated and incorporated as UTICA City in 1832.
(b)Boundary change.

UTICA, Town (Est. 1817)(a)
  Oneida County

1830	8,323
1820	2,972

(a)UTICA Town and Utica Village
  (Inc. 1798) consolidated and incorporated as UTICA City in 1832.

UTICA, Village
  see UTICA, City
    Oneida County

V

VAILS GATE, CDP
  New Windsor Town
  Orange County
  1980   3,156

VALATIE, Village (Inc. 1856)
  Kinderhook Town
  Columbia County
  1980   1,492
  1970   1,288
  1960   1,237
  1950   1,225
  1940   1,208
  1930   1,246
  1920   1,301
  1910   1,219
  1900   1,300
  1890   1,437
  1880   1,775

VALHALLA, CDP
  Mount Pleasant Town
  Westchester County
  1940   2,139

VALLEY COTTAGE, CDP
  Clarkstown Town
  Rockland County
  1980   8,214
  1970   6,007
  1950-1960   NA
  1940   942

VALLEY FALLS, Village (Inc. 1904)
  Pittstown Town, part in
  Rensselaer County
  1980   453
  1970   606
  1960   490
  1950   473
  1940   489
  1930   483
  1920   523
  1910   700
  1880-1900   NA
  1870   400
  Schaghticoke Town, part in
  Rensselaer County
  1980   101
  1970   75
  1960   99
  1950   82
  1940   75
  1930   94
  1920   110
  1910   135
  1880-1900   NA
  1870   200
  TOTAL
  1980   554
  1970   681
  1960   589
  1950   555

  1940   564
  1930   577
  1920   633
  1910   835
  1890-1900   NA
  1880   782
  1870   600

VALLEY STREAM, Village (Inc. 1925)
  Hempstead Town
  Nassau County
  1980   35,769
  1970   40,413
  1960   38,629
  1950   26,854
  1940   16,679
  1930   11,790
  1890-1920   NA
  1880   605(a)
(a)Reported in QUEENS County.

VAN BUREN, Town (Est. 1829)
  Onondaga County
  1980   12,585
  1970   11,859
  1960   8,754
  1950   4,900
  1940   3,691
  1930   3,814
  1920   3,425
  1910   3,200
  1900   3,297
  1890   3,444
  1880   3,091
  1870   3,038
  1860   3,037
  1850   3,873
  1840   3,021
  1830   2,890

VAN ETTEN, Town (Est. 1854)
  Chemung County
  1980   1,519
  1970   1,375
  1960   1,285
  1950   1,249
  1940   1,055
  1930   1,004
  1920   1,028
  1910   1,134
  1900   1,406
  1890   1,658
  1880   1,991
  1870   1,533
  1860   1,508

VAN ETTEN, Village (Inc. 1876)
  Van Etten Town
  Chemung County
  1980   559
  1970   522
  1960   507
  1950   504
  1940   440
  1930   370
  1920   350
  1910   476
  1900   474
  1890   567(a)

```
        1880         553
(a)Reported as Van Ettenville.

VAN HORNESVILLE, CDP
  Stark Town
    Herkimer County
        1880         199
        1870         169

VAN KEURENS, CDP
  Poughkeepsie Town
    Dutchess County
        1970       3,292

VARICK, Town (Est. 1830)
  Seneca County
        1980       1,868
        1970       1,700
        1960       1,480
        1950       1,086
        1940       1,056
        1930       1,013
        1920       1,020
        1910       1,173
        1900       1,270
        1890       1,388
        1880       1,739
        1870       1,741
        1860       1,904
        1850       1,872
        1840       1,971
        1830       1,890

VAROGA, Town
  see CAROGA, Town
        Fulton County

VARYSBURG, CDP
  Orangeville Town
    Wyoming County
        1880         83(a)
(a)Reported as Varysburgh.

VENICE, Town (Est. 1823)
  Cayuga County
        1980       1,268
        1970       1,261
        1960       1,203
        1950       1,026
        1940       1,125
        1930       1,050
        1920       1,215
        1910       1,343
        1900       1,448
        1890       1,672
        1880       1,889
        1870       1,880
        1860       2,012
        1850       2,028
        1840       2,105
        1830       2,445

VERBANK, CDP
  Union Vale Town
    Dutchess County
        1880         144
```

```
VERNON, Town (Est. 1802)(a)
  Oneida County
        1980       8,184 Rev.
        1970       7,857
        1960       7,146(b)
        1950       5,397(b)
        1940       5,124
        1930       4,854
        1920       4,522
        1910       3,197
        1900       2,784
        1890       3,016
        1880       3,056
        1870       2,840
        1860       2,908
        1850       3,093
        1840       3,043
        1830       3,045
        1820       2,707
(a)Includes SHERRILL City.
(b)Boundary change.

VERNON, Town
  Yates County
  see BENTON, Town
        Yates County

VERNON, Village (Inc. 1827)
  Vernon Town
    Oneida County
        1980       1,373
        1970       1,108(a)
        1960         913(a)
        1950         754
        1940         587
        1930         602
        1920         541
        1910         451
        1900         380
        1890         377
        1880         345
        1870         391
(a)Boundary change.

VERNON CENTER, CDP
  Vernon Town
    Oneida County
        1880         190

VERNON VALLEY, CDP(a)
  Huntington Town
    Suffolk County
        1970       7,925
        1960       5,998
(a)Included in EAST NORTHPORT, CDP in
   1980.

VERONA, CDP
  Vernon Town
    Oneida County
        1980       1,057
        1880-1970    NA
        1870         229

VERONA, Town (Est. 1802)
  Oneida County
        1980       6,681
        1970       6,290
        1960       5,305
```

1950	4,017
1940	3,636
1930	3,192
1920	3,136
1910	3,456
1900	3,875
1890	4,535
1880	5,287
1870	5,757
1860	5,567
1850	5,570
1840	4,504
1830	3,739
1820	2,447

VERPLANCK, CDP
  Cortlandt Town
    Westchester County

1940	1,127
1900-1930	NA
1890	1,515
1880	1,337(a)
1870	1,500

(a)Reported as Verplanck's Point.

VESPER, CDP
  Tully Town
    Onondaga County

1880	137

VESTAL, Town (Est. 1823)
  Broome County

1980	27,238
1970	26,909
1960	16,806
1950	8,902
1940	5,710
1930	2,848
1920	1,910
1910	1,618
1900	1,850
1890	2,076
1880	2,184
1870	2,221
1860	2,211
1850	2,054
1840	1,253
1830	946

VESTAL--TWIN ORCHARDS, CDP
  Vestal Town
    Broome County

1970	8,303

VETERAN, Town (Est. 1823)
  Chemung County

1980	3,651
1970	3,543
1960	2,729
1950	1,856
1940	1,582
1930	1,515
1920	1,471
1910	1,470
1900	1,652
1890	1,816
1880	2,263
1870	2,479
1860	2,171

1850	2,698
1840	2,279
1830	1,616(a)

(a)Reported in TIOGA County.

VICTOR, Town (Est. 1812)
  Ontario County

1980	5,784
1970	5,071
1960	3,295
1950	2,640
1940	2,437
1930	2,424
1920	2,319
1910	2,393
1900	2,249
1890	2,620
1880	2,804
1870	2,437
1860	2,404
1850	2,230
1840	2,393
1830	2,270
1820	2,084

VICTOR, Village (Inc. 1879)
  Victor Town
    Ontario County

1980	2,370
1970	2,187(a)
1960	1,180
1950	1,066
1940	1,111
1930	1,042
1920	945
1910	881
1900	649
1890	778
1880	704
1870	506

(a)Boundary change.

VICTORY, CDP
  Victory Town
    Cayuga County

1880	192

VICTORY, Town (Est. 1821)
  Cayuga County

1980	1,519
1970	1,251
1960	1,159
1950	1,154
1940	1,152
1930	1,037
1920	1,078
1910	1,208
1900	1,398
1890	1,706
1880	1,952
1870	1,898
1860	2,077
1850	2,298
1840	2,371
1830	1,819

VICTORY, Village (Inc. 1848)
  Saratoga Town
    Saratoga County
      1980   571
      1970   718
      1960   497
      1950   488
      1940   520
      1930   473
      1920   725(a)
      1910   748(a)
      1900   795(a)
      1890   822(a)
      1880   1,120
      1870   870
      1860   636
(a)Reported as Victory Mills.

VICTORY HEIGHTS, CDP
  Horseheads Town
    Chemung County
      1960   2,528
      1950   1,857

VICTORY MILLS, Village
  see VICTORY, Village
        Saratoga County

VIENNA, CDP
  Vienna Town
    Oneida County
      1870   156

VIENNA, Town (Est. 1807)(a)
  Oneida County
      1980   5,197
      1970   3,979
      1960   2,896
      1950   2,196
      1940   1,645
      1930   1,554
      1920   1,544
      1910   1,904
      1900   2,218
      1890   2,220
      1880   2,834
      1870   3,189
      1860   3,460
      1850   3,393
      1840   2,530
      1830   1,766
      1820   1,307
(a)Established as Orange in 1807; name
   changed to Bengal in 1808, and to
   VIENNA in 1816.

VILLAGE OF THE BRANCH, Village
(Inc. 1927)
  Smithtown Town
    Suffolk County
      1980   1,707
      1970   1,675
      1960   886
      1950   163
      1940   185
      1930   114

VILLAGE OF THE LANDING, Village
(Inc. 1927)(a)
  Smithtown Town
    Suffolk County
      1930   144
(a)Dissolved in 1939.

VILLENOVA, Town (Est. 1823)
  Chautauqua County
      1980   1,061
      1970   970
      1960   969
      1950   888
      1940   877
      1930   917
      1920   961
      1910   1,140
      1900   1,206
      1890   1,242
      1880   1,446
      1870   1,401
      1860   1,274(a)
      1850   1,536(b)
      1840   1,655(a)
      1830   1,126
(a)Reported as Villanovia.
(b)Reported as Villanova.

VIOLA, CDP
  Ramapo Town
    Rockland County
      1980   5,340
      1970   5,136

VIRGIL, CDP
  Virgil Town
    Cortland County
      1880   175

VIRGIL, Town (Est. 1804)
  Cortland County
      1980   2,053
      1970   1,692
      1960   1,420
      1950   1,257
      1940   1,257
      1930   1,137
      1920   1,069
      1910   1,136
      1900   1,326
      1890   1,518
      1880   1,854
      1870   1,889
      1860   2,223
      1850   2,410
      1840   4,502
      1830   3,912
      1820   2,411

VISCHER'S FERRY, CDP
  Clifton Park Town
    Saratoga County
      1880   206

VOLNEY, Town (Est. 1806)(a)
  Oswego County
      1980   5,358
      1970   4,520
      1960   3,785

1950	3,106
1940	2,659
1930	2,347
1920	1,995
1910	2,407(b)
1900	7,674
1890	6,527
1880	6,588
1870	6,565
1860	8,045
1850	2,966
1840	3,155
1830	3,618
1820	1,691

(a)Established as Fredericksburgh in
   1806; name changed in 1811.
(b)Boundary change.

VOORHEESVILLE, Village (Inc. 1899)
   New Scotland Town
      Albany County

1980	3,320
1970	2,826
1960	1,228(a)
1950	895
1940	717
1930	644
1920	614
1910	533
1900	554

(a)Boundary change.

W

WADDINGTON, Town (Est. 1859)
   St. Lawrence County

1980	2,116
1970	2,054
1960	1,972
1950	1,745
1940	1,645
1930	1,709
1920	1,742
1910	1,888
1900	2,001
1890	2,209
1880	2,608
1870	2,599
1860	2,768

WADDINGTON, Village (Inc. 1839)
   Waddington Town
      St. Lawrence County

1980	980
1970	955
1960	921
1950	819
1940	671
1930	679
1920	702

1910	731
1900	757
1890	900
1880	977
1870	710

WADHAM'S MILLS, CDP
   Westport Town
      Essex County

1880	165

WADING RIVER, CDP
   Riverhead Town
      Suffolk County

1980	4,405(a)
1970	2,768(a)
1960	1,234(a)
1890-1950	NA
1880	397(b)

(a)Derived by LIRPB from U.S. Census
   Data.
(b)Reported in BROOKHAVEN and RIVERHEAD
   Towns.

WAINSCOTT, CDP
   East Hampton Town
      Suffolk County

1980	421(a)
1970	311(a)
1960	234(a)
1890-1950	NA
1880	100

(a)Derived by LIRPB from U.S. Census
   Data.

WAKEFIELD, CDP
   Westchester Town
      Westchester County

1880	478

WALCOTT, Town
   see WOLCOTT, Town
      Wayne County

WALDEN, Village (Inc. 1855)
   Montgomery Town
      Orange County

1980	5,659(a)
1970	5,277
1960	4,851
1950	4,559
1940	4,262
1930	4,283
1920	5,493
1910	4,004
1900	3,147
1890	2,132
1880	1,804
1870	1,254

(a)Boundary change.

WALES, CDP
   Wales Town
      Erie County

1880	63

WALES, Town (Est. 1818)
   Erie County

1980	2,844

1970	2,617
1960	1,910
1950	1,370
1940	1,198
1930	1,086
1920	985
1910	1,203
1900	1,220
1890	1,200
1880	1,392
1870	1,416
1860	1,710
1850	2,124
1840	1,987
1830	1,470
1820	903(a)

(a)Reported in NIAGARA County.

WALES CENTER, CDP
  Wales Town
    Erie County

1880	134

WALESVILLE, CDP
  Whitestown Town
    Oneida County

1870	115

WALKILL, Town
  see WALLKILL, Town
        Orange County

WALLACE, CDP
  Avoca Town
    Steuben County

1880	170

WALLKILL, CDP
  Shawangunk Town
    Ulster County

1980	2,064
1970	1,849
1960	1,215
1950	1,145
1940	856

WALLKILL, Town (Est. 1788)
  Orange County

1980	20,481(a)
1970	11,518
1960	8,176(a)
1950	5,947(a)
1940	4,753(a)
1930	3,835
1920	2,598
1910	2,578
1900	2,725
1890	2,755(a)
1880	11,486
1870	9,477
1860	6,603(b)
1850	4,942(b)
1840	4,268(b)
1830	4,056(b)
1820	4,887(b)
1810	NA
1800	*3,592
1790	2,571(c)

(a)Boundary change.

(b)Reported as Walkill.
(c)Reported in ULSTER County.

WALTON, Town (Est. 1797)
  Delaware County

1980	5,839
1970	5,882
1960	5,753(a)
1950	5,724
1940	5,220
1930	5,111
1920	5,425
1910	5,088
1900	4,869
1890	4,543
1880	3,544
1870	3,216
1860	2,740
1850	2,271
1840	1,846
1830	1,663
1820	1,432
1810	NA
1800	*1,154

(a)Boundary change.

WALTON, Village (Inc. 1851)
  Walton Town
    Delaware County

1980	3,329
1970	3,744
1960	3,855
1950	3,947
1940	3,697
1930	3,496
1920	3,598
1910	3,103
1900	2,811
1890	2,299
1880	1,389
1870	866

WALTON PARK, CDP
  Chester & Monroe Towns
    Orange County

1980	1,475

WALWORTH, CDP
  Walworth Town
    Wayne County

1870	362

WALWORTH, Town (Est. 1829)
  Wayne County

1980	5,281
1970	4,584
1960	2,782
1950	2,336
1940	1,956
1930	2,047
1920	1,997
1910	2,187
1900	2,137
1890	2,195
1880	2,338
1870	2,236
1860	2,096
1850	1,981
1840	1,734

1830	1,753

WAMPSVILLE, Village (Inc. 1907)
  Lenox Town
    Madison County

1980	569
1970	586
1960	564
1950	379
1940	282
1930	280
1920	276
1910	212

WANTAGH, CDP
  Hempstead Town
    Nassau County

1980	19,817
1970	21,873(a)
1960	18,894(b)
1950	NA
1940	2,780

(a)Boundary change.
(b)Derived by LIRPB from U.S. Census
    Data. U.S. Census figure of 34,172
    included NORTH WANTAGH, CDP which was
    separated from WANTAGH in 1970.

WAPPINGER, Town (Est. 1875)
  Dutchess County

1980	26,776
1970	22,040
1960	9,577
1950	5,090
1940	4,345
1930	4,083
1920	3,467
1910	3,813
1900	4,319
1890	4,575
1880	4,961

WAPPINGERS FALLS, Village (Inc. 1871)
  Poughkeepsie Town, part in
    Dutchess County

1980	955
1970	1,126(a)
1960	1,035
1950	1,015
1940	1,079
1930	872
1920	1,017
1910	924
1900	877
1890	976
1880	NA
1870	651

  Wappinger Town, part in
    Dutchess County

1980	4,155
1970	4,481(a)
1960	3,412(a)
1950	2,475
1940	2,348
1930	2,464
1920	2,218
1910	2,271
1900	2,627
1890	2,742

1880	NA
1870	1,612(b)

  TOTAL

1980	5,110
1970	5,607(a)
1960	4,447(a)
1950	3,490
1940	3,427
1930	3,336
1920	3,235
1910	3,195
1900	3,504
1890	3,718
1880	NA
1870	2,263

(a)Boundary change.
(b)Reported in FISHKILL Town.

WAPPINGERS FALLS EAST, CDP
  Wappinger Town
    Dutchess County

1980	1,818
1970	2,017

WAPPINGERS FALLS NORTH, CDP
  Poughkeepsie Town
    Dutchess County

1980	1,799

WAPPINGERS LAKE, CDP
  Poughkeepsie Town
    Dutchess County

1970	1,958

WARD, Town (Est. 1856)
  Allegany County

1980	362
1970	271
1960	234
1950	239
1940	250
1930	299
1920	400
1910	496
1900	547
1890	567
1880	620
1870	745
1860	877

WARD'S ISLAND, CDP
  New York County

1860	772

WARDVILLE, CDP
  Bergen Town
    Genesee County

1870	788

WARNERS, CDP
  Camillus & Van Buren Towns
    Onondaga County

1940	546

WARNERVILLE, CDP
  Richmondville Town
    Schoharie County

1880	263(a)

(a)Reported as Warnersville.

WARREN, County (Est. 1813)
```
        1980        54,854
        1970        49,402
        1960        44,002
        1950        39,205
        1940        36,035
        1930        34,174
        1920        31,673
        1910        32,223
        1900        29,943
        1890        27,866
        1880        25,179
        1870        22,592
        1860        21,434
        1850        17,199
        1840        13,422
        1830        11,796
        1820         9,453
```

WARREN, Town (Est. 1796)
Herkimer County
```
        1980         1,065
        1970           978
        1960           918
        1950           956
        1940           873
        1930           974
        1920           959
        1910         1,071
        1900         1,240
        1890         1,339
        1880         1,430
        1870         1,503
        1860         1,812
        1850         1,756
        1840         2,003
        1830         2,084
        1820         2,013
        1810            NA
        1800        *2,445
```

WARREN, Village
see HAVERSTRAW, Village
Rockland County

WARRENSBURG, CDP
Warrensburg Town
Warren County
```
        1980         2,834
        1970         2,743(a)
        1960         2,240
        1950         2,358
        1940         2,043
        1900-1930       NA
        1890           893
        1880           748
        1870           715(b)
```
(a)Reported as Warrensburg Center.
(b)Reported as Warrensburgh.

WARRENSBURG, Town (Est. 1813)
Warren County
```
        1980         3,810
        1970         3,330
        1960         2,907
        1950         2,894
        1940         2,566
        1930         2,263
        1920         2,025
```

```
        1910         2,385
        1900         2,352
        1890         1,795
        1880         1,725(a)
        1870         1,579(a)
        1860         1,704
        1850         1,874(a)
        1840         1,468
        1830         1,191(a)
        1820           956(a)
```
(a)Reported as Warrensburgh.

WARRENSBURG CENTER, CDP
see WARRENSBURG, CDP
Warren County

WARRENSBURGH, CDP & Town
see WARRENSBURG, CDP & Town
Warren County

WARSAW, Town (Est. 1808)
Wyoming County
```
        1980         5,074
        1970         4,721
        1960         4,803
        1950         4,585
        1940         4,452
        1930         4,361
        1920         4,396
        1910         4,308
        1900         4,341
        1890         4,468
        1880         3,227
        1870         3,143
        1860         2,958
        1850         2,624
        1840         2,841(a)
        1830         2,474(a)
        1820         1,658(a)
```
(a)Reported in GENESEE County.

WARSAW, Village (Inc. 1843)
Warsaw Town
Wyoming County
```
        1980         3,619
        1970         3,619
        1960         3,653
        1950         3,713
        1940         3,554
        1930         3,477
        1920         3,622
        1910         3,206
        1900         3,048
        1890         3,120
        1880         1,910
        1870         1,631
```

WARWASINK, Town
see WAWARSING, Town
Ulster County

WARWICK, Town (Est. 1788)
Orange County
```
        1980        20,976
        1970        16,956
        1960        12,551
        1950         9,828
        1940         9,369
        1930         8,017
```

1920	7,462
1910	7,141
1900	6,403
1890	6,000
1880	5,699
1870	5,736
1860	4,628
1850	4,902
1840	5,113
1830	5,009
1820	4,506
1810	NA
1800	*3,816
1790	3,603

WARWICK, Village (Inc. 1867)
  Warwick Town
    Orange County

1980	4,320(a)
1970	3,604(a)
1960	3,218(a)
1950	2,674(a)
1940	2,534
1930	2,443
1920	2,420
1910	2,318
1900	1,735
1890	1,537
1880	1,043
1870	938

(a)Boundary change.

WASHINGTON, County (Est. 1772)(a)

1980	54,795
1970	52,725
1960	48,476
1950	47,144
1940	46,726
1930	46,482
1920	44,888
1910	47,778
1900	45,624
1890	45,690
1880	47,871
1870	49,568
1860	45,904
1850	44,750
1840	41,080
1830	42,635
1820	38,831
1810	44,289
1800	35,792
1790	14,042

(a)Established as Charlotte in 1772;
  name changed in 1784.

WASHINGTON, Town (Est. 1788)
  Dutchess County

1980	4,382
1970	4,407
1960	3,695
1950	3,427
1940	3,080
1930	3,042
1920	2,795
1910	3,027
1900	3,032
1890	2,766
1880	2,797

1870	2,792
1860	2,685
1850	2,805
1840	2,833
1830	3,036
1820	2,882
1810	NA
1800	*2,666
1790	5,189

WASHINGTON, Town
  Seneca County
  see FAYETTE, Town
    Seneca County

WASHINGTON, Village
  see WASHINGTONVILLE, Village
    Orange County

WASHINGTON HEIGHTS, CDP
  Wallkill Town
    Orange County

1980	1,233
1970	1,204
1960	1,231

WASHINGTON ISLAND, CDP
  Clayton Town
    Jefferson County

1870	4

WASHINGTON MILLS, CDP
  New Hartford Town
    Oneida County

1890	1,195

WASHINGTON SQUARE, CDP
  Hempstead Town
    Nassau County

1880	128(a)

(a)Reported in QUEENS County.

WASHINGTONVILLE, CDP
  Eastchester Town
    Westchester County

1880	206

WASHINGTONVILLE, Village (Inc. 1895)
  Blooming Grove Town
    Orange County

1980	2,380
1970	1,887(a)
1960	1,178(a)
1950	823
1940	801
1930	663
1920	631
1910	631
1900	667
1890	691(b)

(a)Boundary change.
(b)Reported as Washington.

WASSAIC, CDP
  Amenia Town
    Dutchess County

1880	228

WATERFORD, Town (Est. 1816)
   Saratoga County

1980	7,194
1970	7,644 Rev.
1960	7,231
1950	6,052
1940	5,709
1930	5,667
1920	4,552
1910	6,128
1900	6,157
1890	5,286
1880	4,328
1870	3,631
1860	3,260
1850	2,683
1840	1,824
1830	1,473
1820	1,184

WATERFORD, Village (Inc. 1794)
   Waterford Town
    Saratoga County

1980	2,405
1970	2,879
1960	2,915
1950	2,968
1940	2,903
1930	2,921
1920	2,637
1910	3,245
1900	3,146
1890	NA
1880	1,822
1870	3,071

WATERLOO, Town (Est. 1829)
   Seneca County

1980	7,811
1970	7,763
1960	6,891
1950	5,524
1940	4,730
1930	4,569
1920	4,287
1910	4,429
1900	4,659
1890	4,681
1880	4,399
1870	4,469
1860	4,594
1850	3,795
1840	3,036
1830	1,847

WATERLOO, Village (Inc. 1824)
   Fayette Town, part in
    Seneca County

1980	732
1970	645
1960	703
1950	678
1940	620
1930	587
1920	517
1910	563
1900	655
1890	644
1880	584

1870	646

Waterloo Town, part in
   Seneca County

1980	4,571
1970	4,773
1960	4,395
1950	3,760
1940	3,390
1930	3,460
1920	3,292
1910	3,368
1900	3,601
1890	3,706
1880	3,309
1870	3,440

TOTAL

1980	5,303
1970	5,418
1960	5,098
1950	4,438
1940	4,010
1930	4,047
1920	3,809
1910	3,931
1900	4,256
1890	4,350
1880	3,893
1870	4,086

WATERMILL, CDP
   Southampton Town
    Suffolk County

1980	722(a)
1970	732(b)
1960	715(c)
1890-1950	NA
1880	173(d)

(a)Boundary change; derived by LIRPB
   from U.S. Census Data.
(b)Derived by LIRPB from U.S. Census
   Data; population of 368 is comparable
   to 1980 boundaries.
(c)Derived by LIRPB from U.S. Census
   Data.
(d)Reported as Water Mills.

WATERTOWN, City (Inc. 1869)(a)
   Jefferson County

1980	27,861
1970	30,787
1960	33,306(b)
1950	34,350
1940	33,385
1930	32,205
1920	31,285
1910	26,730
1900	21,696
1890	14,725
1880	10,697
1870	9,336

(a)Watertown Village (Inc. 1816) incorporated as WATERTOWN City and made
   independent of WATERTOWN Town in 1869.
(b)Boundary change.

WATERTOWN, Town (Est. 1800)
   Jefferson County

1980	3,098
1970	3,026

1960	2,492(a)
1950	1,752
1940	1,399
1930	1,270
1920	1,116
1910	1,097
1900	1,159
1890	1,215
1880	1,264
1870	1,373(a)
1860	7,572
1850	7,201
1840	5,027
1830	4,768
1820	2,766
1810	NA
1800	*119(b)

(a)Boundary change.
(b)Reported in ONEIDA County.

WATERTOWN, Village
  see WATERTOWN, City
        Jefferson County

WATERVILLE, Village (Inc. 1871)
  Marshall Town, part in
    Oneida County

1980	306
1970	295
1960	288
1950	270
1940	243
1930	216
1920	172
1910	242
1900	238
1890	290
1880	NA
1870	152

  Sangerfield Town, part in
    Oneida County

1980	1,366
1970	1,513
1960	1,613
1950	1,364
1940	1,246
1930	1,082
1920	1,083
1910	1,168
1900	1,333
1890	1,734
1880	NA
1870	1,030

  TOTAL

1980	1,672
1970	1,808
1960	1,901
1950	1,634
1940	1,489
1930	1,298
1920	1,255
1910	1,410
1900	1,571
1890	2,024
1880	NA
1870	1,182

WATERVLIET, City (Inc. 1896)(a)
  Albany County

1980	11,354
1970	12,404
1960	13,917
1950	15,197
1940	16,114
1930	16,083
1920	16,073
1910	15,074
1900	14,321

(a)WEST TROY Village incorporated as
WATERVLIET City and made independent
of WATERVLIET Town in 1896.

WATERVLIET, Town (Est. 1788)(a)
  Albany County

1890	24,709
1880	22,220
1870	22,609(b)
1860	6,229
1850	4,882
1840	10,141
1830	4,952
1820	2,806
1810	NA
1800	*4,992
1790	7,419(c)

(a)Dissolved in 1896.
(b)Boundary change.
(c)Reported as Water-Vliet.

WATERVLIET, Village
  see COLONIE, Village
        Albany County

WATKINS GLEN, Village (Inc. 1842)(a)
  Dix Town, part in
    Schuyler County

1980	2,008
1970	2,265(b)
1960	2,438
1950	2,682
1940	2,644
1930	2,597
1920	2,517
1910	2,458
1900	2,635
1890	2,321
1880	2,378

  Reading Town, part in
    Schuyler County

1980	432
1970	451
1960	375
1950	370
1940	269
1930	359
1920	268
1910	359
1900	308
1890	283
1880	338

  TOTAL

1980	2,440
1970	2,716(b)
1960	2,813
1950	3,052
1940	2,913

1930	2,956
1920	2,785
1910	2,817
1900	2,943
1890	2,604
1880	2,716
1870	2,639

(a)Incorporated as Jefferson in 1842;
    name changed to Watkins in 1852, and
    to WATKINS GLEN in 1926.
(b)Boundary change.

WATSON, Town (Est. 1821)
    Lewis County

1980	1,272
1970	1,072
1960	781
1950	586
1940	536
1930	528
1920	707
1910	757
1900	981
1890	1,299
1880	1,470
1870	1,146
1860	1,028
1850	1,138
1840	1,707
1830	909

WATTS FLATS, CDP
    Harmony Town
    Chautauqua County

1880	243

WAVERLY, CDP
    Otto Town
    Cattaraugus County

1880	366

WAVERLY, Town (Est. 1880)
    Franklin County

1980	1,110
1970	1,022
1960	1,050
1950	979
1940	1,017
1930	1,337
1920	1,695
1910	2,170
1900	1,615(a)
1890	2,270

(a)Boundary change.

WAVERLY, Village (Inc. 1853)
    Barton Town
    Tioga County

1980	4,738(a)
1970	5,261
1960	5,950
1950	6,037
1940	5,450
1930	5,662
1920	5,270
1910	4,855
1900	4,465
1890	4,123
1880	2,767

1870	2,239

(a)Boundary change.

WAWARSING, Town (Est. 1806)
    Ulster County

1980	12,956
1970	11,690
1960	11,245
1950	9,912
1940	9,260
1930	7,437
1920	6,910
1910	7,787
1900	7,225
1890	7,758
1880	8,547
1870	8,151
1860	8,311
1850	6,459
1840	4,044
1830	2,738
1820	1,811(a)

(a)Reported as Warwasink.

WAWAYANDA, Town (Est. 1849)
    Orange County

1980	4,298(a)
1970	3,408
1960	3,229
1950	2,435
1940	2,218(a)
1930	1,946
1920	1,689
1910	1,603
1900	1,539
1890	1,625
1880	1,879
1870	1,900
1860	2,085

(a)Boundary change.

WAYFIELD, Town
    see MAYFIELD, Town
        Fulton County

WAYLAND, Town (Est. 1848)
    Steuben County

1980	3,881
1970	3,546
1960	3,385
1950	3,178
1940	3,078
1930	3,071
1920	3,004
1910	2,836
1900	2,984
1890	2,334
1880	2,591
1870	2,553
1860	2,809
1850	2,067

WAYLAND, Village (Inc. 1877)
    Wayland Town
    Steuben County

1980	1,846
1970	2,022
1960	2,003
1950	1,834

1940	1,795
1930	1,814
1920	1,790
1910	1,392
1900	1,307
1890	679
1880	605

WAYNE, CDP
  Tyrone Town
    Schuyler County

1880	182

WAYNE, CDP
  Wayne Town
    Steuben County

1880	78

WAYNE, County (Est. 1823)

1980	84,581 Rev.
1970	79,404
1960	67,989
1950	57,323
1940	52,747
1930	49,995
1920	48,827
1910	50,179
1900	48,660
1890	49,729
1880	51,700
1870	47,710
1860	47,762
1850	44,953
1840	42,057
1830	33,643

WAYNE, Town (Est. 1796)(a)
  Steuben County

1980	1,066
1970	902
1960	715
1950	581
1940	577
1930	516
1920	516
1910	643
1900	838
1890	889
1880	827
1870	891
1860	944
1850	1,347
1840	1,377
1830	1,172
1820	3,607
1810	NA
1800	*258(b)

(a)Established as Frederickstown in 1796;
   name changed in 1808.
(b)Reported as Frederick-Town.

WEAVERTOWN, CDP
  Johnsburg Town
    Warren County

1880	176

WEBB, Town (Est. 1896)
  Herkimer County

1980	1,701

1970	1,616
1960	1,562
1950	1,308
1940	1,373
1930	1,785
1920	1,357(a)
1910	1,250
1900	920

(a)Boundary change.

WEBSTER, Town (Est. 1840)
  Monroe County

1980	28,925
1970	24,739
1960	16,434
1950	7,174
1940	5,520
1930	4,778
1920	3,976
1910	3,755
1900	3,299
1890	3,139
1880	2,950
1870	2,749
1860	2,650
1850	2,446
1840	2,235

WEBSTER, Village (Inc. 1905)
  Webster Town
    Monroe County

1980	5,499
1970	5,037(a)
1960	3,060(a)
1950	1,773
1940	1,680
1930	1,552
1920	1,247
1910	1,032
1900	NA
1890	634
1880	381
1870	291

(a)Boundary change.

WEEDSPORT, Village (Inc. 1831)
  Brutus Town
    Cayuga County

1980	1,952
1970	1,900(a)
1960	1,731
1950	1,588
1940	1,341
1930	1,325
1920	1,379
1910	1,344
1900	1,525
1890	1,580
1880	1,411
1870	1,348

(a)Boundary change.

WEGATCHIE, CDP
  Rossie Town
    St. Lawrence County

1870	201

WELLS, CDP
    Wells Town
        Hamilton County
            1880   227

WELLS, Town (Est. 1805)
    Hamilton County
            1980   627
            1970   604
            1960   539
            1950   507
            1940   567
            1930   527
            1920   652
            1910   742
            1900   908
            1890   1,298
            1880   1,113
            1870   817
            1860   738
            1850   486
            1840   365
            1830   340
            1820   331

WELLSBURG, Village (Inc. 1872)
    Ashland Town
        Chemung County
            1980   647
            1970   779
            1960   643
            1950   638
            1940   560
            1930   581
            1920   465
            1910   432
            1900   536
            1890   NA
            1880   634
            1870   542(a)
(a)Reported as Wellsburgh.

WELLSBURGH, Town
        Clinton County
    see WILLSBORO, Town
            Essex County

WELLSVILLE, Town (Est. 1855)
    Allegany County
            1980   8,658
            1970   8,368
            1960   8,278
            1950   8,555
            1940   7,641
            1930   6,909
            1920   6,171
            1910   5,663
            1900   4,981
            1890   4,765
            1880   4,259
            1870   3,781
            1860   2,432(a)
(a)Reported as Willsville.

WELLSVILLE, Village (Inc. 1857)(a)
    Wellsville Town
        Allegany County
            1980   5,769(b)
            1970   5,815

            1960   5,967(b)
            1950   6,402(b)
            1940   5,942(b)
            1930   5,674
            1920   4,996
            1910   4,382
            1900   3,556
            1890   3,435
            1880   2,049
            1870   2,034
(a)Name changed to Genesee in 1871;
    original name restored in 1873.
(b)Boundary change.

WESLEY HILLS, Village (Inc. 1982)(a)
    Ramapo Town
        Rockland County
(a)Population of 5,500 at incorporation.

WEST ALBANY, CDP
    Colonie Town
        Albany County
            1940   3,786
            1890-1930   NA
            1880   367(a)
(a)Reported in WATERVLIET Town.

WEST ALDEN, CDP
    Alden Town
        Erie County
            1880   52

WEST ALMOND, Town (Est. 1833)
    Allegany County
            1980   357
            1970   213
            1960   293
            1950   320
            1940   390
            1930   391
            1920   416
            1910   458
            1900   601
            1890   649
            1880   803
            1870   799
            1860   935
            1850   976
            1840   808

WEST ALMOND CENTER, CDP
    West Almond Town
        Allegany County
            1880   53

WEST AMAGANSETT(a)
    East Hampton Town
        Suffolk County
            1970   676(b)
            1960   511(b)
(a)Included in AMAGANSETT, CDP in 1980.
(b)Derived by LIRPB from U.S. Census
    Data.

WEST AMBOY, CDP
    Amboy Town
        Oswego County
            1880   100

WEST AMITYVILLE, CDP
  Oyster Bay Town
    Nassau County
        1980   6,623
        1970   6,424
        1960   4,829(a)
        1950   NA
        1940   548(b)
(a)Derived by LIRPB from U.S. Census
   Data.
(b)Reported in OYSTER BAY and BABYLON
   Towns.

WEST BABYLON, CDP
  Babylon Town
    Suffolk County
        1980   41,699(a)
        1970   12,893(b)
        1960   8,501(c)
(a)Boundary change.
(b)Population of 39,353 is comparable
   to 1980 boundaries.
(c)Derived by LIRPB from U.S. Census
   Data.

WEST BANGOR, CDP
  Bangor Town
    Franklin County
        1880   113

WEST BAY SHORE, CDP
  Islip Town
    Suffolk County
        1980   5,118(a)
        1970   8,747(b)
        1960   6,517(c)
(a)Boundary change.
(b)Derived by LIRPB from U.S. Census
   Data; population of 4,939 is
   comparable to 1980 boundaries.
(c)Derived by LIRPB from U.S. Census
   Data.

WEST BELLPORT(a)
  Brookhaven Town
    Suffolk County
        1970   4,138(b)
        1960   1,913(b)
(a)Included in EAST PATCHOGUE, CDP in
   1980.
(b)Derived by LIRPB from U.S. Census
   Data.

WEST BERNE, CDP
  Berne Town
    Albany County
        1870   100

WEST BLOOMFIELD, CDP
  West Bloomfield Town
    Ontario County
        1880   317

WEST BLOOMFIELD, Town (Est. 1833)
  Ontario County
        1980   2,281
        1970   1,990
        1960   1,444
        1950   1,155

        1940   1,068
        1930   1,040(a)
        1920   1,113
        1910   1,181
        1900   1,306
        1890   1,481
        1880   1,713
        1870   1,651
        1860   1,646
        1850   1,698
        1840   2,094
(a)Boundary change.

WEST BRANCH, CDP
  Lee Town
    Oneida County
        1870   97

WEST BRENTWOOD(a)
  Islip Town
    Suffolk County
        1970   7,072(b)
        1960   5,658(b)
(a)Included in NORTH BAY SHORE, CDP in
   1980.
(b)Derived by LIRPB from U.S. Census
   Data.

WEST BRUNSWICK, Town
  see OHIO, Town
          Herkimer County

WEST BURLINGTON, CDP
  Burlington Town
    Otsego County
        1880   107

WESTBURY, CDP
  Victory Town
    Cayuga County
        1880   137
        1870   152

WESTBURY, Village (Inc. 1932)
  North Hempstead Town
    Nassau County
        1980   13,871
        1970   15,362
        1960   14,757
        1950   7,112
        1940   4,524

WEST CAMP, CDP
  Saugerties Town
    Ulster County
        1940   540

WEST CARTHAGE, Village (Inc. 1888)
  Champion Town
    Jefferson County
        1980   1,824
        1970   2,047
        1960   2,167
        1950   2,000
        1940   1,767
        1930   1,722
        1920   1,666
        1910   1,393
        1900   1,135

1890	932
1880	807

WEST CASSADAGA, CDP
Stockton Town
Chautauqua County

1880	94

WEST CHAZY, CDP
Chazy Town
Clinton County

1880	407

WESTCHESTER, County (Est. 1683)

1980	866,599
1970	894,406 Rev.
1960	808,891
1950	625,816
1940	573,558
1930	520,947
1920	344,436
1910	283,055
1900	184,257(a)
1890	146,772
1880	108,988(a)
1870	131,348
1860	99,497
1850	58,263
1840	48,686(b)
1830	36,456(b)
1820	32,638
1810	30,272
1800	27,373 Rev.
1790	24,003

(a)Boundary change.
(b)Reported as West Chester.

WESTCHESTER, Town (Est. 1788)(a)
Westchester County

1890	10,029
1880	6,789
1870	6,015
1860	4,250(b)
1850	2,492(b)
1840	4,154(b)
1830	2,362(b)
1820	2,162
1810	NA
1800	*997(b)
1790	1,203(b)

(a)Merged into BRONX Borough in NEW YORK
City in 1895.
(b)Reported as West Chester.

WEST DANBY, CDP
Danby Town
Tompkins County

1880	157

WEST DAY, CDP
Day Town
Saratoga County

1880	93

WEST EDMESTON, CDP
Edmeston Town
Otsego County

1880	116

WEST ELMIRA, CDP
Elmira Town
Chemung County

1980	5,485
1970	5,901
1960	5,763
1950	3,833
1940	3,223

WEST END, CDP
Oneonta Town
Otsego County

1980	1,715
1970	1,692
1960	1,436
1950	1,285

WESTERLO, Town (Est. 1815)
Albany County

1980	2,929
1970	2,242
1960	1,681
1950	1,536
1940	1,338
1930	1,220
1920	1,240
1910	1,307
1900	1,632
1890	1,949
1880	2,324
1870	2,384
1860	2,692
1850	2,860
1840	3,096(a)
1830	3,321
1820	3,458

(a)Reported as Westerloo.

WESTERN, Town (Est. 1797)
Oneida County

1980	1,954
1970	2,072
1960	1,811
1950	1,352
1940	1,103
1930	1,139
1920	1,061
1910	1,355
1900	1,621
1890	1,817
1880	2,264
1870	2,423
1860	2,497
1850	2,516
1840	3,488
1830	2,419
1820	2,237
1810	NA
1800	*1,453(a)

(a)Reported as Wistern.

WESTERNVILLE, CDP
Western Town
Oneida County

1880	206
1870	235

WEST EXETER, CDP
Exeter Town
Otsego County
1880   111

WEST FARMS, CDP
West Farms Town
Westchester County
1870   1,761

WEST FARMS, Town (Est. 1846)(a)
Westchester County
1870   9,372
1860   7,098
1850   4,436
(a)Merged into BRONX Borough in NEW YORK
City in 1873.

WESTFIELD, Town (Est. 1829)
Chautauqua County
1980   5,102 Rev.
1970   5,200
1960   5,498
1950   5,001
1940   4,638
1930   4,785
1920   4,390
1910   4,481
1900   3,882
1890   3,401
1880   3,323
1870   3,645
1860   3,640
1850   3,100
1840   3,199
1830   2,477

WESTFIELD, Town (Est. 1788)(a)
Richmond County
1890   8,258
1880   5,289
1870   4,905
1860   3,985
1850   2,943
1840   2,326
1830   1,733
1820   1,616
1810   NA
1800   *1,198
1790   1,151
(a)Merged into STATEN ISLAND Borough
in NEW YORK City in 1898.

WESTFIELD, Town
Washington County
see FORT ANN, Town
Washington County

WESTFIELD, Village (Inc. 1833)
Westfield Town
Chautauqua County
1980   3,446
1970   3,651
1960   3,878
1950   3,663
1940   3,434
1930   3,466
1920   3,413
1910   2,985

1900   2,430
1890   1,983
1880   1,924
1870   3,000

WESTFORD, CDP
Westford Town
Otsego County
1880   139

WESTFORD, Town (Est. 1808)
Otsego County
1980   652
1970   435
1960   526
1950   602
1940   685
1930   652
1920   735
1910   803
1900   910
1890   1,023
1880   1,271
1870   1,300
1860   1,382
1850   1,423
1840   1,478
1830   1,645
1820   1,526

WEST FORT SALONGA
Huntington Town
Suffolk County
1970   4,258(a)
1960   2,295(a)
(a)Derived by LIRPB from U.S. Census
Data.

WEST GLENS FALLS, CDP
Queensbury Town
Warren County
1980   5,331
1970   3,363
1960   2,725
1950   1,665

WEST GRANVILLE CORNERS, CDP
Granville Town
Washington County
1880   67

WEST GROVE, Town
see GRANGER, Town
Allegany County

WESTHAMPTON, CDP
Southampton Town
Suffolk County
1980   2,774(a)
1970   1,156(b)
1960   1,022(c)
1950   NA
1940   736(d)
1890-1930   NA
1880   437
1870   439
(a)Boundary change.
(b)Population of 1,886 is comparable to
1980 boundaries.

(c)Derived by LIRPB from U.S. Census
   Data.
(d)Reported in SOUTHOLD Town.

WESTHAMPTON BEACH, Unincorporated(a)
   Southampton Town
      Suffolk County
         1980   39(b)
(a)Included in REMSENBERG--SPEONK in
   1970.
(b)Derived by LIRPB from U.S. Census
   Data.

WESTHAMPTON BEACH, Village (Inc. 1928)
   Southampton Town
      Suffolk County
         1980   1,629
         1970   1,926
         1960   1,460
         1950   1,087
         1940   969
         1930   994

WEST HAVERSTRAW, Village (Inc. 1883)
   Haverstraw Town
      Rockland County
         1980   9,181
         1970   8,558(a)
         1960   5,020(a)
         1950   3,099
         1940   2,533
         1930   2,834
         1920   2,018
         1910   2,369
         1900   2,079
         1890   180
(a)Boundary change.

WEST HEBRON, CDP
   Hebron Town
      Washington County
         1880   205

WEST HEMPSTEAD, CDP
   Hempstead Town
      Nassau County
         1980   18,536
         1970   20,375
         1960   19,954(a)
         1950   NA
         1940   3,384(b)
(a)Derived by LIRPB from U.S. Census
   Data. U.S. Census reported as WEST
   HEMPSTEAD--LAKEVIEW, CDP; total population of 24,783.
(b)Excludes HEMPSTEAD GARDENS, CDP.

WEST HEMPSTEAD--LAKEVIEW, CDP(a)
   Hempstead Town
      Nassau County
         1960   24,783
(a)Included in WEST HEMPSTEAD and LAKE-
   VIEW, CDPs in 1970-1980.

WEST HENRIETTA, CDP
   Henrietta Town
      Monroe County
         1880   130

WEST HILLS, CDP
   Huntington Town
      Suffolk County
         1980   6,071
         1970   6,112(a)
         1960   4,773(a)
(a)Derived by LIRPB and reported as
   West Huntington.

WEST HUNTINGTON, CDP
   see WEST HILLS, CDP
      Suffolk County

WEST HURLEY, CDP
   Hurley & Woodstock Towns
      Ulster County
         1980   2,382
         1950-1970   NA
         1940   606

WEST ISLIP, CDP
   Islip Town
      Suffolk County
         1980   29,533(a)
         1970   17,374(b)
         1960   13,924(c)
         1950   NA
         1940   1,651
         1890-1930   NA
         1880   398
(a)Boundary change.
(b)Population of 31,412 is comparable to
   1980 boundaries.
(c)Derived by LIRPB from U.S. Census
   Data.

WEST LEYDEN, CDP
   Lewis Town
      Lewis County
         1880   181

WEST MELVILLE(a)
   Huntington Town
      Suffolk County
         1970   1,614(b)
         1960   539(b)
(a)Included in MELVILLE, CDP in 1980.
(b)Derived by LIRPB from U.S. Census
   Data.

WESTMERE, CDP
   Guilderland Town
      Albany County
         1980   6,881
         1970   6,364

WEST MILTON, CDP
   Milton Town
      Saratoga County
         1880   241

WEST MONROE, Town (Est. 1839)
   Oswego County
         1980   3,482
         1970   2,535
         1960   1,417
         1950   1,002
         1940   731
         1930   666

1920	782
1910	915
1900	936
1890	1,100
1880	1,314
1870	1,304
1860	1,416
1850	1,197
1840	918

WESTMORELAND, CDP
  Westmoreland Town
    Oneida County

1880	403

WESTMORELAND, Town (Est. 1792)
  Oneida County

1980	5,458
1970	5,093
1960	4,084
1950	2,811
1940	2,235
1930	2,170
1920	1,984
1910	1,995
1900	2,192
1890	2,313
1880	2,744
1870	2,952
1860	3,166
1850	3,291
1840	3,105
1830	3,303
1820	2,791
1810	NA
1800	*1,542

WEST MOUNT VERNON, Village (Inc. 1869)(a)
  Eastchester Town
    Westchester County

1870	1,200

(a)CENTRAL MOUNT VERNON, CDP and West
  Mount Vernon incorporated as WEST
  MOUNT VERNON Village in 1869; merged
  into MOUNT VERNON Village in 1878.

WEST NEW BRIGHTON, CDP
  Castleton Town
    Richmond County

1880	2,276

WEST NYACK, CDP
  Clarkstown Town
    Rockland County

1980	8,553
1970	5,510
1950-1960	NA
1940	775

WESTON, CDP
  Tyrone Town
    Schuyler County

1880	167

WEST ONEONTA, CDP
  Oneonta Town
    Otsego County

1880	165

WESTON MILLS, CDP
  Otto & Randolph Towns
    Cattaraugus County

1980	1,837

WESTOVER, CDP
  Union Town
    Broome County

1940	1,172

WEST PHOENIX, CDP
  Lysander Town
    Onondaga County

1880	68

WEST POINT, CDP
  Highlands Town
    Orange County

1980	8,105
1890-1970	NA
1880	1,131
1870	942(a)

(a)Reported in CORNWALL Town.

WESTPORT, Town (Est. 1815)
  Essex County

1980	1,439
1970	1,453
1960	1,565
1950	1,597
1940	1,657
1930	1,534
1920	1,492
1910	1,867
1900	1,727
1890	1,864
1880	1,737
1870	1,577
1860	1,981
1850	2,352
1840	1,932
1830	1,513
1820	1,095

WESTPORT, Village (Inc. 1907)
  Westport Town
    Essex County

1980	613
1970	673
1960	723
1950	733
1940	654
1930	790
1920	669
1910	692
1900	NA
1890	563
1880	364

WEST RONKONKOMA(a)
  Islip Town
    Suffolk County

1970	4,820(b)
1960	1,720(b)

(a)Included in LAKE RONKONKOMA, CDP in
  1980.
(b)Derived by LIRPB from U.S. Census
  Data.

WEST SAINT JAMES(a)
Smithtown Town
Suffolk County
1970   618(b)
(a)Included in SMITHTOWN, CDP in 1980.
(b)Derived by LIRPB from U.S. Census
Data.

WEST SALAMANCA, Village (Inc. 1884)(a)
Salamanca Town
Cattaraugus County
1910   530
1900   483
1890   495
1880   469
(a)SALAMANCA and WEST SALAMANCA Villages
consolidated and incorporated as SALA-
MANCA City and made independent of
SALAMANCA Town in 1913.

WEST SAND LAKE, CDP
Sand Lake Town
Rensselaer County
1980   2,153
1970   1,875
1950-1960   NA
1940   630(a)
1890-1930   NA
1880   185(a)
1870   315
(a)Reported as West Sandlake.

WEST SAYVILLE, CDP
Islip Town
Suffolk County
1980   8,185
1970   7,386
1960   5,849(a)
1950   1,370
1940   740
(a)Derived by LIRPB from U.S. Census
Data.

WEST SENECA, CDP
West Seneca Town
Erie County
1980   51,210
1970   NA
1960   23,138

WEST SENECA, Town (Est. 1851)(a)
Erie County
1980   51,210
1970   48,404
1960   33,644
1950   17,417(b)
1940   12,694(b)
1930   10,401
1920   7,062
1910   4,605
1900   5,363
1890   3,485
1880   3,463
1870   3,196
1860   2,784
(a)Established as Seneca in 1851; name
changed in 1852.
(b)Boundary change.

WEST SMITHTOWN(a)
Smithtown Town
Suffolk County
1970   12,718(b)
1960   3,153(b)
(a)Included in COMMACK, KINGS PARK, and
SMITHTOWN, CDPs in 1980.
(b)Derived by LIRPB from U.S. Census
Data.

WEST SPARTA, Town (Est. 1846)
Livingston County
1980   1,100
1970   935
1960   817
1950   724
1940   688
1930   667
1920   695
1910   772
1900   906
1890   1,008
1880   1,157
1870   1,244
1860   1,501
1850   1,619

WEST TIANA
see PINE NECK--WEST TIANA, CDP
Suffolk County

WEST TOWN, CDP
Minisink Town
Orange County
1880   175

WEST TROY, Village (Inc. 1836)(a)
Watervliet Town
Albany County
1890   12,967
1880   8,820
1870   10,693
1860   8,820
1850   7,564
(a)WEST TROY Village incorporated as
WATERVLIET City and made independent
of WATERVLIET Town in 1896.

WEST TURIN, Town (Est. 1830)
Lewis County
1980   1,867(a)
1970   1,713
1960   1,905
1950   1,781
1940   1,806
1930   1,886
1920   1,929
1910   1,941
1900   1,779
1890   1,803
1880   2,006
1870   2,111
1860   2,410
1850   3,793
1840   2,042
1830   1,635
(a)Boundary change.

WEST UNION, Town (Est. 1845)
　　Steuben County

1980	431
1970	426
1960	430
1950	504
1940	630
1930	715
1920	781
1910	985
1900	1,025
1890	1,167
1880	1,271
1870	1,264
1860	1,392
1850	950

WESTVALE, CDP
　　Geddes Town
　　　Onondaga County

1980	6,169
1970	7,253

WEST VIENNA, CDP
　　Vienna Town
　　　Oneida County

1880	138
1870	113

WESTVILLE, CDP
　　Westford Town
　　　Otsego County

1880	69

WESTVILLE, Town (Est. 1829)
　　Franklin County

1980	1,491
1970	1,299
1960	1,287
1950	877
1940	831
1930	880
1920	1,028
1910	1,121
1900	1,237
1890	1,376
1880	1,687
1870	1,658
1860	1,635
1850	1,301
1840	1,028
1830	619

WESTVILLE, Town
　　Tioga County
　　see NEWARK VALLEY, Town
　　　Tioga County

WEST WATERFORD, CDP
　　Waterford Town
　　　Saratoga County

1880	441

WEST WEBSTER, CDP
　　Webster Town
　　　Monroe County

1940	645

WEST WINFIELD, Village (Inc. 1898)
　　Winfield Town
　　　Herkimer County

1980	979
1970	1,018
1960	960
1950	832
1940	754
1930	779
1920	725
1910	726
1900	771
1890	741
1880	594

WETHERSFIELD, CDP
　　Wethersfield Town
　　　Wyoming County

1870	170

WETHERSFIELD, Town (Est. 1823)
　　Wyoming County

1980	674
1970	674
1960	650
1950	616
1940	616
1930	641
1920	744
1910	928
1900	927
1890	1,032
1880	1,311
1870	1,219
1860	1,583
1850	1,489
1840	1,728(a)
1830	1,179(a)

(a)Reported in GENESEE County.

WHEATFIELD, Town (Est. 1836)
　　Niagara County

1980	9,609
1970	9,722
1960	8,008
1950	4,720
1940	3,077
1930	2,212
1920	1,884
1910	1,792
1900	1,926(a)
1890	8,808
1880	4,390
1870	3,406
1860	3,484
1850	2,659
1840	1,057

(a)Boundary change.

WHEATLAND, Town (Est. 1821)(a)
　　Monroe County

1980	4,897
1970	4,265
1960	3,711
1950	2,502
1940	2,323
1930	2,364
1920	2,076
1910	2,453

1900	2,071
1890	2,400
1880	2,599
1870	2,565
1860	2,560
1850	2,916
1840	2,871
1830	2,240

(a)Established as Inverness in Feb., 1821; name changed in Apr., 1821.

WHEATVILLE, CDP
Alabama Town
  Genesee County

1880	96

WHEELER, Town (Est. 1820)
Steuben County

1980	1,014
1970	858
1960	766
1950	653
1940	690
1930	677
1920	808
1910	959
1900	1,188
1890	1,285
1880	1,424
1870	1,330
1860	1,376
1850	1,471
1840	1,294
1830	1,389
1820	798

WHISPERING WOODS(a)
East Hampton Town
  Suffolk County

1970	420(b)
1960	129(b)

(a)Included in SPRINGS, CDP in 1980.
(b)Derived by LIRPB from U.S. Census Data.

WHITE CREEK, CDP
White Creek Town
  Washington County

1880	189

WHITE CREEK, Town (Est. 1815)
Washington County

1980	2,988
1970	2,644
1960	2,365
1950	2,120
1940	2,103
1930	2,180
1920	2,170
1910	2,342
1900	2,496
1890	2,690
1880	2,742
1870	2,881
1860	2,802
1850	2,994
1840	2,195
1830	2,446
1820	2,377(a)

(a)Reported as White-creek.

WHITEHALL, Town (Est. 1786)(a)
Washington County

1980	4,427
1970	4,794
1960	4,757
1950	5,256
1940	5,670
1930	5,975
1920	6,008
1910	5,869
1900	5,295
1890	5,402
1880	5,347
1870	5,564
1860	4,862
1850	4,726
1840	3,813
1830	2,889
1820	2,341
1810	NA
1800	*1,604
1790	806

(a)Established as Skenesborough in 1763; name changed in 1786.

WHITEHALL, Village (Inc. 1806)(a)
Whitehall Town
  Washington County

1980	3,241
1970	3,764
1960	4,016
1950	4,457
1940	4,851
1930	5,191
1920	5,258
1910	4,917
1900	4,377
1890	4,434
1880	4,270
1870	4,322

(a)Incorporated as Whitehall Landing in 1806; name changed in 1820.

WHITE PLAINS, City (Inc. 1916)(a)
Westchester County

1980	46,999
1970	50,346 Rev.
1960	50,485
1950	43,466
1940	40,327
1930	35,830
1920	21,031

(a)WHITE PLAINS Village and WHITE PLAINS Town consolidated and incorporated as WHITE PLAINS City in 1916.

WHITE PLAINS, Town (Est. 1788)(a)
Westchester County

1910	15,045
1900	7,869
1890	4,508
1880	4,094
1870	2,630
1860	1,846
1850	1,414
1840	1,087
1830	759

1820	675
1810	NA
1800	*571(b)
1790	505

(a)WHITE PLAINS Village and WHITE
   PLAINS Town consolidated and incorporated as WHITE PLAINS City in 1916.
(b)Reported as Whiteplains.

WHITE PLAINS, Village (Inc. 1866)(a)
  Greenburgh Town, part in
    Westchester County

1910	2,045
1900	670
1890	223

    White Plains Town, part in
    Westchester County

1910	13,904
1900	7,229
1890	3,819
1880	2,381

  TOTAL

1910	15,949
1900	7,899
1890	4,042
1880	(b)

(a)WHITE PLAINS Village and WHITE
   PLAINS Town consolidated and incorporated as WHITE PLAINS City in 1916.
(b)Reported in WHITE PLAINS Town only.

WHITEPORT, CDP
  Rosendale Town
    Ulster County

1880	198

WHITESBORO, Village (Inc. 1813)
  Whitestown Town
    Oneida County

1980	4,460
1970	4,805(a)
1960	4,784
1950	3,902
1940	3,532
1930	3,375
1920	3,038
1910	2,375
1900	1,958
1890	1,663
1880	1,370
1870	964

(a)Boundary change.

WHITESTONE, Village (Inc. 1868)(a)
  Flushing Town
    Queens County

1890	2,808
1880	2,520
1870	1,907

(a)Merged into QUEENS Borough in NEW
   YORK City in 1898.

WHITESTOWN, Town (Est. 1788)
  Oneida County

1980	20,150
1970	21,382
1960	19,185
1950	12,686
1940	11,580

1930	11,818
1920	10,183
1910	7,798
1900	6,235
1890	5,155
1880	4,498
1870	4,339
1860	4,367
1850	6,810
1840	5,156
1830	4,410
1820	5,219
1810	NA
1800	*4,212(a)
1790	1,891(b)

(a)Reported as Whites Town.
(b)Reported as Whites-Town in MONTGOMERY
   County.

WHITESVILLE, CDP
  Independence Town
    Allegany County

1880	297

WHITNEY POINT, Village (Inc. 1871)
  Triangle Town
    Broome County

1980	1,093
1970	1,058
1960	1,049
1950	883
1940	733
1930	639
1920	665
1910	744
1900	807
1890	842
1880	818(a)
1870	480(a)

(a)Reported as Whitney's Point.

WILLARD, CDP
  Lodi & Ovid Towns
    Seneca County

1980	1,339
1950-1970	NA
1940	602(a)
1890-1930	NA
1880	195(a)

(a)Reported in ROMULUS Town.

WILLARD ASYLUM, CDP
  Ovid & Romulus Towns
    Seneca County

1880	1,826

WILLET, CDP
  Willet Town
    Cortland County

1880	147

WILLET, Town (Est. 1818)
  Cortland County

1980	747
1970	621
1960	535
1950	553
1940	571
1930	512

1920	592(a)
1910	643
1900	687
1890	800
1880	853
1870	899
1860	983
1850	923
1840	872(a)
1830	840(a)
1820	437(a)

(a)Reported as Willett.

WILLIAMSBRIDGE, Village (Inc. 1888)(a)
   Westchester Town
      Westchester County

1890	1,685
1880	NA
1870	144(b)

(a)Merged into BRONX Borough in NEW YORK
   City in 1895.
(b)Reported as William's Bridge.

WILLIAMSBURG, CDP(a)
   Rensselaerville Town
      Albany County

1880	22

(a)Also called CONNERSVILLE.

WILLIAMSBURGH, CDP
   Black Brook Town
      Clinton County

1880	256

WILLIAMSBURGH, City
   see WILLIAMSBURGH, Town
            Kings County

WILLIAMSBURGH, Town (Est. 1840)(a)
   Kings County

1850	30,780
1840	5,094
1830	1,620(b)

(a)WILLIAMSBURGH Town and Williamsburgh
   Village (Inc. 1827) consolidated and
   incorporated as Williamsburgh City in
   1851; the City merged into BROOKLYN
   City in 1854.
(b)Reported with BUSHWICK Town.

WILLIAMSBURGH, Village
   see WILLIAMSBURGH, Town
            Kings County

WILLIAMSON, CDP
   Williamson Town
      Wayne County

1980	1,768
1970	1,991
1960	1,690
1950	1,520
1940	1,131
1890-1930	NA
1880	335(a)

(a)Reported as Williamson Center.

WILLIAMSON, Town (Est. 1802)
   Wayne County

1980	6,319

1970	6,356
1960	5,294
1950	4,226
1940	3,700
1930	3,504
1920	3,293
1910	3,060
1900	2,670
1890	2,670
1880	2,745
1870	2,430
1860	2,682
1850	2,380
1840	2,147
1830	1,801
1820	2,521(a)

(a)Reported in ONTARIO County.

WILLIAMSON CENTER, CDP
   see WILLIAMSON, CDP
         Wayne County

WILLIAMSTOWN, Town (Est. 1804)
   Oswego County

1980	1,008
1970	883
1960	739
1950	707
1940	710
1930	706
1920	767
1910	896
1900	1,028
1890	1,215
1880	1,820
1870	1,833
1860	1,144
1850	1,121
1840	842
1830	606
1820	652

WILLIAMSVILLE, Village (Inc. 1869)
   Amherst Town
      Erie County

1980	6,017(a)
1970	6,878 Rev.
1960	6,316(a)
1950	4,649(a)
1940	3,614
1930	3,119(a)
1920	1,667 Rev.
1910	1,105
1900	905
1890	NA
1880	880
1870	912

(a)Boundary change.

WILLING, Town (Est. 1851)
   Allegany County

1980	1,451
1970	1,296
1960	1,208
1950	1,089
1940	836
1930	820
1920	755
1910	993

1900	1,246
1890	1,206
1880	1,267
1870	1,199
1860	1,238

WILLINK, Town
see AURORA, Town
Erie County

WILLINGSBUROUGH, Town
see WILLSBORO, Town
Essex County

WILLISTON PARK, Village (Inc. 1926)
North Hempstead Town
Nassau County

1980	8,216(a)
1970	9,154
1960	8,255
1950	7,505
1940	5,750
1930	4,427

(a)Boundary change.

WILLOWVALE, CDP
New Hartford Town
Oneida County

1940	543

WILLSBORO, CDP
Willsboro Town
Essex County

1940	946
1890-1930	NA
1880	250(a)

(a)Reported as Willsborough.

WILLSBORO, Town (Est. 1788)
Essex County

1980	1,759
1970	1,688
1960	1,716
1950	1,646
1940	1,780
1930	1,612
1920	1,684
1910	1,580
1900	1,522
1890	1,568
1880	1,450(a)
1870	1,719(a)
1860	1,519(a)
1850	1,932(a)
1840	1,658(a)
1830	1,316(a)
1820	888(a)
1810	NA
1800	*1,716(b)
1790	375(c)

(a)Reported as Willsborough.
(b)Reported as Willingsburough.
(c)Reported as Wellsburgh in CLINTON
County.

WILLSBOROUGH, CDP & Town
see WILLSBORO, CDP & Town
Essex County

WILLSEYVILLE, CDP
Candor Town
Tioga County

1880	588

WILLSVILLE, Town
see WELLSVILLE, TOWN
Allegany County

WILMINGTON, Town (Est. 1821)(a)
Essex County

1980	1,051
1970	777
1960	683
1950	574
1940	737
1930	567
1920	545
1910	573
1900	634
1890	678
1880	899
1870	794
1860	861
1850	1,218
1840	928
1830	695

(a)Established as Dansville in 1821;
name changed in 1822.

WILMURT, Town (Est. 1836)(a)
Herkimer County

1910	178
1900	353(b)
1890	373
1880	271
1870	191
1860	260
1850	112(c)
1840	60

(a)Merged into OHIO and WEBB Towns in
1919.
(b)Boundary change.
(c)Reported as Wilmut.

WILNA, Town (Est. 1813)
Jefferson County

1980	6,227
1970	6,538
1960	6,809
1950	6,969
1940	7,029
1930	7,322
1920	7,014
1910	6,218
1900	5,172
1890	4,522
1880	4,393
1870	4,060
1860	3,662
1850	2,993
1840	2,591
1830	1,602
1820	648

WILSON, Town (Est. 1818)
Niagara County

1980	5,792
1970	5,316

1960	5,319
1950	3,696
1940	3,061
1930	2,801
1920	2,753
1910	2,979
1900	2,881
1890	2,978
1880	3,234
1870	2,912
1860	3,372(a)
1850	2,955(a)
1840	1,753
1830	913
1820	688

(a)Reported as Wilson's.

WILSON, Village (Inc. 1858)
Wilson Town
Niagara County

1980	1,259
1970	1,284
1960	1,320(a)
1950	962
1940	849
1930	660
1920	631
1910	655
1900	612
1890	683
1880	662
1870	661

(a)Boundary change.

WILTON, Town (Est. 1818)
Saratoga County

1980	7,221
1970	2,984 Rev.
1960	1,902
1950	1,407
1940	1,231
1930	997
1920	826
1910	908
1900	989
1890	1,116
1880	1,118
1870	1,204
1860	1,499
1850	1,458
1840	1,438
1830	1,373
1820	1,293

WILTONVILLE, CDP
Wilton Town
Saratoga County

1880	81

WINANT'S KILL, CDP
see WYNANTSKILL, CDP
Rensselaer County

WINCHESTER, CDP
West Seneca Town
Erie County

1940	1,165

WINCHESTER, Town
see MARION, Town
Wayne County

WINDHAM, CDP
Windham Town
Greene County

1880	344

WINDHAM, Town (Est. 1798)
Greene County

1980	1,663
1970	1,190
1960	1,289
1950	1,360
1940	1,269
1930	1,269
1920	1,246
1910	1,438
1900	1,387
1890	1,503
1880	1,461
1870	1,485
1860	1,659
1850	2,048
1840	2,417
1830	3,471
1820	2,536
1810	NA
1800	*1,688

WINDSOR, Town (Est. 1807)
Broome County

1980	5,911
1970	5,646
1960	4,373
1950	2,974
1940	2,625
1930	2,183
1920	2,137
1910	2,495
1900	2,967
1890	3,035
1880	3,286
1870	2,958
1860	2,672
1850	2,645
1840	2,368
1830	2,180
1820	3,354

WINDSOR, Village (Inc. 1897)
Windsor Town
Broome County

1980	1,155
1970	1,098
1960	1,026
1950	822
1940	766
1930	661
1920	598
1910	637
1900	739
1890	524
1880	NA
1870	325

WINDSOR TERRACE, CDP
  Flatbush Town
    Kings County
      1890   1,645

WINFIELD, CDP
  Newtown Town
    Queens County
      1890   819

WINFIELD, Town (Est. 1816)
  Herkimer County
      1980   2,053
      1970   2,013
      1960   1,750
      1950   1,462
      1940   1,333
      1930   1,449
      1920   1,312
      1910   1,386
      1900   1,475
      1890   1,625
      1880   1,597
      1870   1,561
      1860   1,480
      1850   1,481
      1840   1,652
      1830   1,778
      1820   1,752

WINONA LAKES, CDP
  Newburgh Town
    Orange County
      1960   1,655

WINTHROP
  see BRASHER FALLS--WINTHROP, CDP
    St. Lawrence County

WIRT, Town (Est. 1838)
  Allegany County
      1980   1,137
      1970   1,094
      1960   1,117
      1950   1,243
      1940   1,348
      1930   1,269
      1920   974
      1910   1,209
      1900   1,163
      1890   1,219
      1880   1,225
      1870   1,204
      1860   1,390
      1850   1,544
      1840   1,207

WISCOY, CDP
  Hume Town
    Allegany County
      1870   193

WISTERN, Town
  see WESTERN, Town
      Oneida County

WITHERBEE, CDP(a)
  Moriah Town
    Essex County
      1940   1,288
(a)Included, in part, in MINEVILLE--
    WITHERBEE, CDP in 1950 and 1980.

WITHERBEE--MINEVILLE, CDP
  see MINEVILLE--WITHERBEE, CDP
    Essex County

WOLCOTT, Town (Est. 1807)
  Wayne County
      1980   4,021
      1970   3,764
      1960   3,498
      1950   3,276
      1940   3,021
      1930   2,876
      1920   2,792
      1910   2,952
      1900   3,207
      1890   3,216
      1880   3,731
      1870   3,223
      1860   2,634
      1850   2,751(a)
      1840   2,481
      1830   1,085
      1820   2,867(b)
(a)Reported as Walcott.
(b)Reported in SENECA County.

WOLCOTT, Village (Inc. 1873)
  Butler Town, part in
    Wayne County
      1980   246
      1970   314
      1960   273
      1950   232
      1940   170
      1930   188
      1920   156
      1910   160
      1900   139
  Wolcott Town, part in
    Wayne County
      1980   1,250
      1970   1,303
      1960   1,368
      1950   1,284
      1940   1,156
      1930   1,072
      1920   1,030
      1910   1,056
      1900   1,140
      1890   902
      1880   NA
      1870   658
  TOTAL
      1980   1,496
      1970   1,617
      1960   1,641
      1950   1,516
      1940   1,326
      1930   1,260
      1920   1,186
      1910   1,216
      1900   1,279

```
            1870-1890             (a)
(a)Reported in WOLCOTT Town only.


WOLCOTTSVILLE, CDP
   Royalton Town
      Niagara County
         1870               756


WOODBOURNE, CDP
   Fallsburg Town
      Sullivan County
         1970             1,155


WOODBURY, CDP
   Oyster Bay Town
      Nassau County
         1980             7,043
         1970             4,609(a)
         1960             1,904(a)
(a)Derived by LIRPB from U.S. Census
   Data.


WOODBURY, Town (Est. 1899)
   Orange County
         1980             6,494
         1970             4,660
         1960             2,887
         1950             2,138
         1940             1,960
         1930             1,923
         1920             1,885
         1910             2,216
         1900             1,666
         1890             1,528


WOODHULL, Town (Est. 1828)
   Steuben County
         1980             1,460
         1970             1,270
         1960             1,224
         1950             1,255
         1940             1,292
         1930             1,151
         1920             1,343
         1910             1,455
         1900             1,787
         1890             2,006
         1880             1,963
         1870             1,997
         1860             2,207
         1850             1,769
         1840               827
         1830               501


WOODHULL, Village (Inc. 1899)
   Woodhull Town
      Steuben County
         1980               315
         1970               313
         1960               321
         1950               332
         1940               339
         1930               290
         1920               300
         1910               316
         1900               343
         1890                NA
         1880               317
         1870               392
```

```
WOODLAWN, CDP
   Hamburg Town
      Erie County
         1940             1,535


WOODMERE, CDP
   Hempstead Town
      Nassau County
         1980            17,205
         1970            19,831
         1960            14,011
         1950                NA
         1940             6,359


WOODRIDGE, Village (Inc. 1911)(a)
   Fallsburg Town
      Sullivan County
         1980               809(b)
         1970             1,071
         1960             1,034
         1950               951
         1940               854
         1930               774
         1920               944
(a)Incorporated as Centerville Station
   in 1911; name changed in 1917.
(b)Boundary change.


WOODROW, CDP
   Westfield Town
      Richmond County
         1880               389


WOODSBURGH, Village (Inc. 1912)
   Hempstead Town
      Nassau County
         1980               847
         1970               817
         1960               907
         1950               745
         1940               702
         1930               376
         1920               220


WOOD'S FALLS, CDP
   Mooers Town
      Clinton County
         1880               175


WOODSIDE, CDP
   Newtown Town
      Queens County
         1890               710
         1880               500


WOODSTOCK, CDP
   West Farms Town
      Westchester County
         1870               307


WOODSTOCK, CDP
   Woodstock Town
      Ulster County
         1980             2,280
         1970             1,073
         1950-1960           NA
         1940             1,067
         1890-1930           NA
         1880               170
```

WOODSTOCK, Town (Est. 1787)
    Ulster County

1980	6,823 Rev.
1970	5,714
1960	3,836
1950	2,271
1940	1,983
1930	1,652
1920	1,488
1910	1,647
1900	1,675
1890	1,628
1880	1,968
1870	2,022
1860	1,858
1850	1,650
1840	1,691
1830	1,376
1820	1,317
1810	NA
1800	*1,244
1790	1,025

WOODVILLE, CDP
    Ellisburg Town
      Jefferson County

1880	179

WORCESTER, CDP
    Worcester Town
      Otsego County

1940	980
1890-1930	NA
1880	682

WORCESTER, Town (Est. 1797)
    Otsego County

1980	1,993
1970	1,925
1960	1,946
1950	2,098
1940	2,038
1930	1,946
1920	2,136
1910	2,185
1900	2,409
1890	2,741
1880	2,513
1870	2,327
1860	2,154
1850	2,047
1840	2,390
1830	2,093
1820	1,938
1810	NA
1800	*2,235

WORMLY, Town
    see CATON, Town
      Steuben County

WORTH, Town (Est. 1848)
    Jefferson County

1980	153
1970	185
1960	193
1950	253
1940	318
1930	415

1920	545
1910	597
1900	875
1890	905
1880	951
1870	727
1860	634
1850	326

WORTHVILLE, CDP
    Worth Town
      Jefferson County

1880	78

WRIGHT, Town (Est. 1846)
    Schoharie County

1980	1,302
1970	1,068
1960	910
1950	903
1940	786
1930	755
1920	833
1910	963
1900	1,155
1890	1,295
1880	1,591
1870	1,525
1860	1,717
1850	1,716

WURTSBORO, Village (Inc. 1866)
    Mamakating Town
      Sullivan County

1980	1,128
1970	732
1960	655
1950	628
1940	487
1930	423
1920	362
1910	478
1900	450
1890	490
1880	538
1870	797

WYANDANCH, CDP
    Babylon Town
      Suffolk County

1980	13,215(a)
1970	15,716(b)
1960	6,930(c)
1950	NA
1940	647

(a)Boundary change.
(b)Population of 12,875 is comparable
    to 1980 boundaries.
(c)Derived by LIRPB from U.S. Census
    Data.

WYNANTSKILL, CDP
    North Greenbush Town
      Rensselaer County

1940	1,428
1890-1930	NA
1880	176
1870	140(a)

(a)Reported as Winant's Kill.

WYOMING, County (Est. 1841)
```
       1980        39,895
       1970        37,688
       1960        34,793
       1950        32,822
       1940        31,394
       1930        28,764
       1920        30,314
       1910        31,880
       1900        30,413
       1890        31,193
       1880        30,907
       1870        29,164
       1860        31,968
       1850        31,981
```

WYOMING, Village (Inc. 1916)
  Middlebury Town
    Wyoming County
```
       1980          507
       1970          514
       1960          526
       1950          508
       1940          430
       1930          376
       1920          386
       1900-1910      NA
       1890          525
       1880          387
       1870          338
```

Y

YAPHANK, CDP
  Brookhaven Town
    Suffolk County
```
       1980        2,812(a)
       1970        8,793 Rev.(b)
       1960        2,852(c)
       1900-1950      NA
       1890          517
       1880          424
```
(a)Boundary change; derived by LIRPB
   from U.S. Census Data.
(b)Population of 1,956 is comparable to
   1980 boundaries.
(c)Derived by LIRPB from U.S. Census
   Data.

YATES, County (Est. 1823)
```
       1980        21,459
       1970        19,831
       1960        18,614
       1950        17,615
       1940        16,381
       1930        16,848
       1920        16,641
       1910        18,642
       1900        20,318
       1890        21,001
```
```
       1880        21,087
       1870        19,595
       1860        20,290
       1850        20,590
       1840        20,444
       1830        19,009
```

YATES, Town (Est. 1822)(a)
  Orleans County
```
       1980        2,447
       1970        2,303
       1960        2,063
       1950        2,086
       1940        1,975
       1930        1,914
       1920        1,940
       1910        2,156
       1900        1,884
       1890        1,969
       1880        2,020
       1870        2,014
       1860        2,105
       1850        2,242
       1840        2,230
       1830        1,375
```
(a)Established as Northton in 1822;
   name changed in 1823.

YATES CENTER, CDP
  Yates Town
    Orleans County
```
       1880          190
```

YONKERS, City (Inc. 1872)(a)
  Westchester County
```
       1980       195,351
       1970       204,297
       1960       190,634
       1950       152,798
       1940       142,598
       1930       134,646
       1920       100,176
       1910        79,803
       1900        47,931
       1890        32,033
       1880        18,892
```
(a)YONKERS Town and YONKERS Village
   consolidated and incorporated as
   YONKERS City in 1872.

YONKERS, Town (Est. 1788)(a)
  Westchester County
```
       1870        18,357
       1860        11,848
       1850         4,160
       1840         2,968
       1830         1,761
       1820         1,586
       1810           NA
       1800         1,176*
       1790         1,125
```
(a)YONKERS Town and YONKERS Village
   consolidated and incorporated as
   YONKERS City in 1872.

YONKERS, Village (Inc. 1853)(a)
  Yonkers Town
    Westchester County
```
       1870        12,733
```

```
            1860              8,218(b)
(a)YONKERS Town and YONKERS Village
   consolidated and incorporated as
   YONKERS City in 1872.

YORK, Town (Est. 1819)
     Livingston County
            1980              3,212
            1970              3,166
            1960              2,695
            1950              2,329
            1940              2,287
            1930              2,349
            1920              2,640
            1910              2,562
            1900              2,730
            1890              2,868
            1880              2,482
            1870              2,564
            1860              2,743
            1850              2,785
            1840              3,049
            1830              2,636
            1820              1,729(a)
(a)Reported in GENESEE County.


YORK, Town
     Westchester County
  see YORKTOWN, Town
          Westchester County

YORK CENTER, CDP
     York Town
        Livingston County
            1880                277

YORKSHIRE, CDP
     Yorkshire Town
        Cattaraugus County
            1980              1,236
            1890-1970           NA
            1880                257

YORKSHIRE, Town (Est. 1820)
     Cattaraugus County
            1980              3,620
            1970              2,627
            1960              2,012
            1950              1,633
            1940              1,410
            1930              1,512
            1920              1,524
            1910              1,563
            1900              1,738
            1890              1,723
            1880              1,784
            1870              1,575
            1860              1,844
            1850              2,010
            1840              1,292
            1830                823

YORKSHIRE CENTER, CDP
  see DELEVAN, Village
          Cattaraugus County
```

```
YORKTOWN, CDP(a)
     Yorktown Town
        Westchester County
            1960              3,576
(a)Reported in part in JEFFERSON VALLEY--
   YORKTOWN, CDP in 1970-1980.

YORKTOWN, Town (Est. 1788)
     Westchester County
            1980             31,988
            1970             28,064
            1960             16,453
            1950              4,731
            1940              3,642
            1930              2,724
            1920              1,441
            1910              3,020
            1900              2,421
            1890              2,378
            1880              2,481
            1870              2,625
            1860              2,231
            1850              2,273
            1840              2,819
            1830              2,141
            1820              1,992(a)
            1810                NA
            1800             *1,806(a)
            1790              1,609(b)
(a)Reported as York Town.
(b)Reported as York.

YORKTOWN HEIGHTS, CDP
     Yorktown Town
        Westchester County
            1980              7,696
            1970              6,805
            1960              2,478
            1950                NA
            1940              1,076

YORKVILLE, Village (Inc. 1902)
     Whitestown Town
        Oneida County
            1980              3,115
            1970              3,425
            1960              3,749
            1950              3,528
            1940              3,311
            1930              3,406
            1920              1,512
            1910                691
            1890-1900           NA
            1880                295
            1870                213

YOUNGSPORT, CDP
     Islip Town
        Suffolk County
            1880                299

YOUNGSTOWN, Village (Inc. 1854)
     Porter Town
        Niagara County
            1980              2,191(a)
            1970              2,169
            1960              1,848(a)
            1950                932
            1940                799
```

```
          1930            639
          1920            539
          1910            556
          1900            547
          1890            490
          1880            500
          1870            476
(a)Boundary change.
```

YOUNGSVILLE, CDP
   Callicoon Town
      Sullivan County

```
          1880            113
```

Z

ZENA, CDP
   Woodstock Town
      Ulster County

```
          1980          1,435
```